2002

Machiavelli's Romans

Machiavelli's Romans

Liberty and Greatness in the Discourses on Livy

J. Patrick Coby

LEXINGTON BOOKS
Lanham • Boulder • New York • Oxford

LEXINGTON BOOKS

Published in the United States of America
by Lexington Books
4720 Boston Way, Lanham, Maryland 20706

12 Hid's Copse Road
Cumnor Hill, Oxford OX2 9JJ, England

British Library Cataloguing in Publication Information Available

Library of Congress Cataloging-in-Publication Data

Coby, Patrick, 1948–
    Machiavelli's Romans : liberty and greatness in the discourses on
Livy / J. Patrick Coby
        p.   cm. — (Applications of political theory)
    Includes bibliographical references.
    ISBN0-7391-0069-6 (alk. paper). — ISBN 0-7391-0070-X (pbk. :
alk. paper)
    1. Machiavelli, Niccolò, 1469–1527 Discorsi sopra la prima deca
di Tito Livio.   2. Rome—Politics and government.   I. Title.
II. Series.
JC143.M167C62   1999
320.1'01—dc21   99-19460
                                                           CIP

Printed in the United States of America

⊖™ The paper used in this publication meets the minimum requirements of American
National Standard for Information Sciences—Permanence of Paper for Printed Library
Materials, ANSI/NISO Z39.48–1992.

To my parents

Contents

Chapter One

Introduction: Reading the *Discourses*

It is a puzzling fact that in the *Discourses on Livy* Machiavelli proposes a return to Roman modes and orders while simultaneously proclaiming the radical novelty of his own ideas. There is an old Machiavelli who breathes the air of republican Rome and a new Machiavelli who walks a path untrodden by others. In many treatments of the *Discourses*, the Roman antecedent is hurriedly gotten past in order that Machiavelli's declared innovation might be investigated at leisure.[1] But then in many treatments of Machiavelli, the *Discourses* is not considered extensively and alone, but is confined to an obligatory single chapter in what aspire to be comprehensive studies of the Machiavelli corpus.[2] Just as often, the topic is the Italian Renaissance and Machiavelli's role therein—his personal relationship to Florentine politics and to the Medici princes. Secure in the belief that the life and times of Machiavelli explain the content of his writings, researchers compile detailed histories of the Quattrocento and early Cinquecento periods.[3] Finally, there are the biographies, which deal with the works as a stage in the life.[4] Admid all this scholarly bustle, the plain subject of the *Discourses*, the modes and orders of the Roman republic, goes largely unremarked. Compared with *The Prince*, the *Discourses* is a neglected work; and compared with the scholarship on the *Discourses*, Roman modes and orders are a neglected topic. Hence the purpose of this present study, of its first part at least, is to discover what Machiavelli was doing in those evening hours he spent conversing with the ancients. What did Machiavelli learn from the ancient authors he read, and what ambitions, practices, and institutions did he wish his contemporaries to adopt through conscious imitation of Roman ways?

Machiavelli can be maddeningly vague about what it is he wants. He says he wants a rebirth of republican Rome; but why he wants it and for whom are uncertain, as is the time when he expects it to happen and whether a rebirth encompasses the whole of his intention. For he does speak of having an intention, in the preface to the first book; and in the second preface he once again alludes to plans he would have implemented in the future. It seems there exists then, in

1

these two prefaces, some textual warrant for considering Machiavelli's relation to the future (as in the dedication there is some warrant for considering his relation to the present and the near-past).[5] If one is going to look beyond the Roman substance of the *Discourses*, perhaps the better reason is to look at Machiavelli's novel intent.[6] However, better yet is it to look at Machiavelli's Romans.

Because I turn first to the Roman model and so delay asking the question, what's new about Machiavelli, I give support to the proposition that there is much of consequence that is old about Machiavelli. This assumption puts me partly at odds with Leo Strauss, who, in tracing to Machiavelli and not to Thomas Hobbes the beginnings of modernity,[7] holds to the view that Machiavelli is an original. The second part of this study will address the question of originality, of whether Machiavelli articulates new modes and orders and whether owing to them he is properly called a modern. There I will argue that claims of novelty are oversold and that Machiavelli is more at home with the heroic ethos of antiquity than with the scientific liberalism of the Enlightenment. (Machiavelli's highest accolades go to those who work inside, not outside, of ancient orders.) But that argument is for later; at the moment I wish to state my differences with Strauss, since in many respects I agree with his analysis, and since I utilize his seminal study, *Thoughts on Machiavelli*, at numerous points along the way.

It seems fair to say that Strauss's Machiavelli is a political theorist first and a practitioner of politics second. The impression is pervasive that practice is subordinate and ministerial to theory. Describing *The Prince* as both a tract for the times and a theoretical treatise, Strauss argues, for example, that the book's tract-like exterior is used to conceal its treatise within;[8] he contends additionally that the substance of the treatise is "wholly new," whereas the actions prescribed by the tract are imitative of the past.[9] Foremost among these actions is the liberation of the Italian fatherland—a patriotic end surreptitiously introduced to provide cover, Strauss suggests, for the immoralism of the wholly new teaching.[10] But Machiavelli indicates in his private correspondence that he loves his fatherland more than his soul.[11] One would think, therefore, that Machiavelli takes seriously his citizenship as a Florentine and Italian. Strauss is willing to concede that he does, though Strauss understands the true "fatherland" of Machiavelli's affections to be a "comprehensive reflection" on God, man, and country, and to be a state not of this world.[12] So what sound like the sentiments of a patriot (whether of city or province) are judged instead to be the ruminations of a philosopher. In the same vein, Machiavelli's evident interest in political and military affairs is expanded to incorporate other branches of inquiry. Machiavelli is thought to be a student of natural science and cosmology on the strength of a remark in the dedication that the *Discourses* contains all that he knows about "the things of the world."[13] Strauss goes further: Machiavelli is an Averroist, one of the worldly wise who trust in reason and not in revelation.[14]

But then it falls to Strauss to supply the details and fill in the gaps since Machiavelli is himself reticent and offers intimations only of his philosophical convictions.[15] (He intimates, for example, an attraction to the thought of Aristippus and Diogenes by the sayings he has Castruccio Castracani utter and hear.)[16] He is similarly reluctant to speak about theological topics, though reflecting on them all the same; for it is allowed that when Machiavelli refers to princes, he sometimes is referring to superhuman beings and so is referring to ordinary mortals when he seems to be referring to the people or the plebs.[17] The same holds true when the subject is the captain who is a knower of sites (III.39)—for here Machiavelli's captain is a student, and his sites are passages in Livy and the Bible rather than forests and rivers and undulations in terrain.[18] The man of action—out-of-doors, under the stars, riding, hunting, fighting—becomes the man of thought—in his study, huddled over books, reading by candlelight.[19]

The man of action has indeed a nighttime calling, namely amorous dalliance; it is what prompts Machiavelli to divide human affairs into the grave and the light. Strauss though gives this Machiavellian theme a Platonic twist, assigning to gravity the knowledge of truth and to levity the communication of truth.[20] Machiavelli is classed with the philosophers; he rates knowing higher than doing, and speaking he equates with acting. It follows then that he would place first in rank those who discover nature's modes and orders (knowers),[21] that second-rank status he would accord to artists and writers (speakers),[22] and that founders, reformers, and captains (doers) he would rank third. Machiavelli's own artistry, Strauss implies, is devoted to the making of a perfect book, one which obeys "merciless laws" of "logographic necessity." The perfect book or speech, says Strauss,

> contains nothing slipshod; in it there are no loose threads; it contains no word that has been picked up at random; it is not marred by errors due to faulty memory or to any other kind of carelessness; strong passions and a powerful and fertile imagination are guided with ease by a reason which knows how to use the unexpected gift, which knows how to persuade and which knows how to forbid; it allows no adornment which is not imposed by the gravity and the aloofness of the subject matter.[23]

Not just any artist is Machiavelli, but one involved in writing a masterpiece.

There is, to be sure, considerable evidence that Machiavelli reflects on his own status as a student of politics and as a writer: he is the observer, the adviser, the man behind the scenes. There also is some evidence that he appreciates the written word as an instrument of propaganda and that he regards the historian-theorist as an alternative founder of modes and orders. Strauss notes, for example, that Cyrus, king of the Persians, who in *Prince* 6 is celebrated as an exemplary new prince and a model for imitation, is in *Prince* 14 known to posterity because of Xenophon's history of him and is in *Discourses* II.13.1 largely a creature of Xenophon's literary imagination, a character whom Xenophon

"makes" seize a kingdom and "makes" deceive an enemy.[24] The clear implication is that the writer is positioned to shape the present's perception of the past
and to affect the present's agenda for the future. The writer is powerful, perhaps
even a new prince in his own right.

But from these reflections and appreciations one ought not conclude that
Machiavelli admires writers ahead of warriors, the leisured life of contemplation
ahead of the active life of virtue. After all, in his own ranking of glorious characters, Machiavelli places literary men behind captains and behind founders of
political and religious orders (all of whom a revised assessment places behind
reformers [I.10.1, 6]). Likewise, one ought not suppose that Machiavelli's love
of learning overshadows his passion for politics. Strauss cites the famous letter
to Francesco Vettori in which Machiavelli boasts of his kinship with the ancients and of his special aptitude for engaging them in instructive dialogue ("I
feed on that food which only is mine and which I was born for").[25] But Strauss
does not mention (at least not on the occasion) that Machiavelli ends the letter
confessing to a desperate desire for employment with the Medicis, or that he
describes his "little work *On Princedoms*" as a job application (having earlier
described it as a mnemonic device). It is hard to fathom why someone, ostensibly busy composing the perfect book, would wish to cut short his creative labors, leaving the work forever unfinished, in order to take "entry-level" employment with the new power in town (he will start out rolling a stone, if that's
what the Medicis require).[26] If Machiavelli so clearly affirms the superiority of
knowing over doing and if the contemplative life is so agreeable to him, why
does he begrudge the time spent in seclusion away from the intrigues of court or
Signoria? If he rates writers higher than heroes and understands that glory goes
to the person who chronicles events and has the last say, why does he not realize
that his own power is as an author and that his own fame is hitched to the success of his books? Machiavelli's biography simply does not sort well with this
portrait of the philosopher in his study. Besides, there is another letter to Vettori,
perhaps not so famous, in which Machiavelli admits to an obsession with affairs
of state, complaining—in light of his forced retirement—that if he cannot reason
about government, nothing remains for him but to take a vow of silence.[27]

Machiavelli is both thinker and doer, and as a thinker he is mostly a theoretician of action.[28] So it is important that Machiavelli's philosophic side not
overwhelm the practical—because there are interpretive consequences when it
does. Seen as a philosopher, Machiavelli is expected to address large and enduring questions, to travel in the ethereal regions of metaphysical thought. He is
not expected to take serious interest in soldiers, weapons, and battlefield tactics,
in the ways and means of disciplining troops on campaign. The war of ideas
might engage his attention, but not the clash of arms. Thus when Machiavelli
speaks of military affairs, there is the temptation to find in his remarks allusions
to weightier matters. From viewing Machiavelli as a theoretician, one moves all
too easily to reading the *Discourses* metaphorically and to treating the literal

surface of the book as a starting point and launching pad for profound but highly speculative interpretations. Strauss implies that attention to the surface, to the modes and orders of republican Rome, yields a "vulgar understanding" of Machiavelli.[29] Maybe so. But I think it better to begin there and not to suppose from the outset that Machiavelli is unbeholden to the Roman paradigm.

On two issues in particular does Strauss have recourse to metaphorical explanations: Machiavelli's actions as founder and captain; and Machiavelli's spiritual war against Christianity. Concerning the first, I mentioned already that Machiavelli has plans and ambitions which he means to achieve through the writing of books. He twice refers to the fact that he needs and is recruiting disciples to carry forward his enterprise, followers who may exceed him in virtue, discourse, and judgment and who, being younger, more spirited, and more beloved of heaven, can "work" the good which malignant fortune has prevented him from accomplishing (I.Pr.1, II. Pr.3). Twice, too, he issues calls for prudent men and lovers of antiquity to deliver their contemporaries from the infirmities of the day by building republics and mastering fortune (I.55.4, II.30.5). And once he tells of the inspirational effect and instructional aid provided by the written word (of Cleomenes assisted by the writings of Agis); and so possibly he refers to himself as a writer whose books will motivate and direct the actions of others (I.9.4).[30] But Strauss finds many more references to Machiavelli's captaincy than just these four or five. For example, Machiavelli is seen to be a captain recruiting troops when in III.37.4 he relates a decision by the consul Marius to position his army in a secure place advantageous for viewing the enemy as it passed by. Behind the safety of a stockade, Roman sentries, frequently rotated, observed the disorderly character of the Cimbri until familiarity with the enemy's way dispelled the Romans' fear. Strauss then applies what is said of the Cimbri to the classical-Christian tradition, claiming that "this is the way in which the established order . . . presented itself to him [Machiavelli]: as oblivious of the fundamental issue and therefore rent into many warring schools or factions, as encumbered with innumerable texts, treatises and discourses, and as boasting of many proofs which were no proofs."[31] But the tradition is never actually mentioned, nor is it clearly alluded to; and even if the Marius episode is meant as a metaphor, reference to it does not advance the analysis beyond identifying "the tradition" as the enemy to be overcome. If Machiavelli is enlisting compatriots in the fatherland of nature's true modes and orders (and Machiavelli's own), he fails to explain what it is he would have his troops do.

One drawback of esoteric prose, especially disabling when the prose is expected to affect action, is that too few people understand its significance and meaning. So it is a real question as to how a book as esoteric as Strauss thinks the *Discourses* to be can serve as a vehicle for the recruitment of disciples. Has anyone prior to Strauss deciphered the *Discourses*, since even readers the caliber of Spinoza and Rousseau have, in Strauss's opinion, misconstrued its teaching?[32] Machiavelli once faults Friar Savonarola, the unarmed prophet, for

complaining that because of Christianity no ecumenical empire has emerged since the fall of Rome. But this imperialist complaint is the "outer layer" of Machiavelli's indictment, says Strauss;[47] the inner layer and more serious charge, one thus infers, reflects the beliefs and sentiments of the "political left."

The bill of particulars is as follows. First, Christianity is cruel—piously cruel. The expression, "pious cruelty," is used to describe Ferdinand's expulsion of the Marranos from Spain in the early sixteenth century (*Prince*, 21). Unlike cruelty well-used, which is a Machiavellian virtue (*Prince*, 8), pious cruelty is a Machiavellian vice. Pious cruelty is excessive and imprudent cruelty, and Judaeo-Christianity, in particular, is admonished for its use. Machiavelli indicates his disapproval by depicting a Roman hero in terms reminiscent of a biblical archetype. Strauss sees the similarity and completes the parallel, comparing Manlius Torquatus with David, the youth. Each killed in combat a giant of a man, but whereas Manlius celebrated by taking his opponent's collar, or torque (III.34.2), David celebrated by severing Goliath's head.[48] Likewise, David the elder, when giving laws to his people, was inhumanly cruel (I.26.1), whereas Romulus, the Roman lawgiver, confined the killing to his brother and one colleague (I.9.1).[49] And Christianity is no better, for as Rome's successor, this religion of love tried destroying all remnants of pagan faith (II.5.1).[50] Christianity is cruel not despite the primacy of love, but because of it, since Christianity makes demands which sinful men are unable to meet.[51]

Tyranny is the political form which pious cruelty assumes. The God of Judeo-Christianity is a tyrant. Strauss infers as much from the fact that a New Testament passage describing the justice of God is wantonly misused to describe the tyranny of King David.[52] The reason given for Machiavelli's uncompromising judgment is that politicized Christianity is theocratic—the rule of God mediated through the rule of priests—and that theocracy is logically and ineluctably tyrannical; for in a theocracy ordinary lawgiving carries the imprimatur of divine command. Citizens cannot resist their rulers whose decisions are the dictates of God; and rulers need not bother themselves with the responsibilities of governance or with securing their own fitness for high office. An ecclesiastical principality, observes Strauss, is supremely powerful because it is completely secure.[53]

In addition to being cruel and oppressive, Christianity is dishonest, for it makes hypocrites of its practitioners. Christian modes and orders are *un*natural, since in origin and content they are *super*natural. Christians are to follow in the ways of Christ. But how does one live on this earth while obeying the laws of a kingdom that is not of this world? By hypocrisy and casuistic evasion—that's how. Machiavelli directs a "hidden argument" against his opponents whose principles "lead to unctuous hypocrisy because those principles are at variance with the nature of things."[54] Nature is necessity and necessity is evil. But a religion which preaches non-resistance to evil leaves its flock unarmed against predators or obliges it to lie about the prudent measures it has taken for its defense.[55] Nature also is character, which is inflexible. It is unreasonable to condemn as sin conduct that is predetermined by character;[56] and it is disingenuous to present as love or piety "acts of savagery or of astuteness prompted by necessity or even by the desire for honor or glory."[57] Dishonest about the motives of men, Christianity is destructive of nobility and integrity.

Finally, Christianity is authoritative and doctrinaire, not free and rational. As a revealed religion, Christianity rests on faith in the unevident and the unseen. Such belief is exceptionally wayward, since experience belies its content and argument is not available to keep it firm. Force then is utilized against those who stray—not the prodding and correcting force of an exacting instructor but the intolerant persecution of a vindictive inquisitor. It is a rule, says Machiavelli, that when commands are issued, they must be enforced by a harshness proportionate to the difficulty of carrying them out (III.22.2).[58] Christianity's commands are difficult to obey, since they require inward conviction along with outward compliance. Belief in the truth of miracles is what Christianity commands, and its punishments in consequence are stern and unending, with hell and its devils awaiting those who disbelieve orthodoxy. Eternal damnation is a particularly horrific punishment, the ultimate in pious cruelty, and its imposition is the work of a tyranny. Thus it seems that all of the charges are interconnected or fold into one: that the Christian religion, intolerant of dissent, obliges doubters to be hypocrites and enforces its commands with a degree of cruelty characteristic of tyrannical regimes.

Machiavelli is generally associated with the dark and dirty underside of political life, with raw power in the service of private interest; and so it is a little surprising to hear that Machiavelli is offended by Christianity's severity or to have it suggested that the values most prized by Machiavelli are rationality, honesty, personal integrity, justice, freedom, and gentleness toward others. But in fact these conclusions fit well with Strauss's other main thesis that Machiavelli initiates the Enlightenment.[59] If Machiavelli is the forebear and soulmate of Montaigne, Bacon, Harrington, Hobbes, Descartes, Spinoza, Locke, Montesquieu, Rousseau, etc.,[60] it stands to reason that his political thought, however hard on the outside, would on the inside contain a soft and humane core; or that Machiavelli, like the liberal philosophers who succeed him, would in truth be a philanthropist dedicated to ameliorating the human condition. After all, Machiavelli once does describe himself as possessed of a "natural desire" to "bring common benefit to everyone" (I.Pr.1).

No doubt, Machiavelli would have cause to conceal himself if he were preparing the ground for a secular paradise to rival the heavenly paradise of Christianity; but the question is whether Machiavelli really does harbor these "leftist" sympathies and ambitions. As far as I know, only once does Machiavelli use the expression "pious cruelty"—to describe, as noted, the expulsion of the Marranos by Ferdinand. Machiavelli judges this action "wretched," but he also calls it rare: "nor could there be an example more wretched [*più miserabile*] or rarer [*più raro*] than this" (*Prince*, 21). He calls it rare in a chapter which recommends the performance of rare deeds and in a paragraph which is consistently laudatory of the actions of Ferdinand, denominated a "new prince" because of his rapid ascent from a "weak king" to the "first king among the Christians." So is Machiavelli blaming Ferdinand for the wretchedness of his conduct or praising him for the rarity of his deeds? Does "wretched" trump "rare" or "rare" trump "wretched" in the Machiavellian hierarchy of qualities? Probably the latter, as Machiavelli would think it preferable to be remembered for cruelty than to be decent and obscure.[61] For that matter, it is not even certain that "wretched" is a term of reproach for Machiavelli, an author who sports some rather peculiar notions about virtue.[62] Nor is it certain that Machiavelli would demur from threatening miscreants with the fires of hell; for if as an Averroist he "knows" that there is no hell, he knows as well that no one actually goes to hell to suffer there eternal perdition. On the other hand, he might regard the doctrine of damnation as a useful fiction for controlling the actions of the faithful. And while he surely would object to the exercise of this power by the clergy, the power itself has interesting possibilities.

As for the other charges which Machiavelli purportedly levels against Christianity—that its rule is tyrannical, that its subjects are hypocrites, and that its stress is on obedience at the expense of free thought—regarding these the following observations can be made. First, though Machiavelli may favor republics over principalities, he is no consistent critic of princely government, even when calling it a tyranny; and Strauss himself admits that the case against tyranny is incomplete.[63] Thus it is wrong to think that Machiavelli would oppose Christianity simply because he regards its rule as tyrannical. Second, while Machiavelli appreciates the integrity of "knower[s] of the world" (III.31.3) who are honest about their own base motives no less than the base motives of others,[64] it must not be forgotten that his highly touted new prince is a "fox" who rises by fraud. Self-knowledge cannot be that attractive nor hypocrisy that repellent to someone who condones—nay celebrates—deceit at every turn.[65] At least it is hard to imagine that Machiavelli would hold it against Christianity that under its imperium professions of belief are sometimes insincere. It's not as if pagan princes actually believed that animal entrails were a predictor of the future, though they acted as if they did. Lastly, while it is true that Christianity, being more autocratic than liberal, views obedience to authority as a virtue, all regimes require obedience of their subjects, and republican regimes, Machiavelli insists, are more demanding than principalities (III.22.4). In sum, I am doubtful that Machiavelli's war with Christianity is covert or that he launches his attack on behalf of an emerging new humanism later to be called modernity. One difficulty with Strauss's interpretation is that it considers Machiavelli to be both a master of esoteric prose and a propagandist who goes public with hitherto secret teachings.[66] The former position presupposes that the few and the many are distinguished by nature; the latter position, as Strauss asserts time and again,[67] presupposes that all such distinctions are conventional and tractable.

My purpose is not so much to disprove the Straussian reading as to make the case for looking closely at Rome. Whatever the truth about Machiavelli's new modes and orders, Rome's old modes and orders deserve a fuller accounting. I realize, of course, that the two purposes are interconnected and beggar perfect compatibility—that if Strauss is right, Rome is not so important, except as a feint; and that if Strauss is wrong, Rome rises in importance, and Machiavelli is not so original. Machiavelli states in each of his political works that his thought is brand new and that his thought is borrowed from others.[68] Strauss fastens upon what is new in Machiavelli, explaining the old as a rhetorical subterfuge. The premise of the present study is that the old is predominate, that Machiavelli is more Roman than modern, and that impressions of newness derive from the fact that liberty and greatness, Machiavelli's twin objectives, occasionally appear in modern guise, as enlightened and unenlightened acquisitiveness respectively; also that the new in Machiavelli is evidence of an uncertain mind, or evidence that Machiavelli is tempted by modern, "fox-like," modes of acquisition which mainly he rejects or regards as preliminary. There is newness, to be sure, in Machiavelli's ethical thought, but the novelty there is less than is generally assumed.

The book's subtheme is the relationship of liberty to greatness. The presence of this subtheme is not everywhere apparent, and explicit discussion occurs only in the book's last chapter. The reason for the delayed treatment is Machiavelli's initial choice of Rome over Sparta. By emphasizing the incongruity of greatness and tranquility (the fact that Rome could not achieve world empire without sacrificing domestic harmony), Machiavelli obscures for a time the tense and conflictual relationship between greatness and liberty. He invites the reader to think that Rome's two principles were complementary, or that they combined to provide Rome with a single desideratum. But that is not quite so, as will be seen.

The book reflects the opinion that Machiavelli is an ambivalent writer who moves in contrary directions because his loyalties are divided and his temperament mixed. It argues that liberty and greatness are at the center of these divisions or antinomies. As a lover of liberty Machiavelli is cautious, a denizen of the "middle way." He builds the balanced institutions of a republican regime, institutions which mature slowly, evolve over time, and which by their conservation and renewal extend the life of the state. But as an admirer of greatness he is impetuous, an extremist who wrestles with Fortune on the hope that she will yield her favors to the ardor of youth. Selfish ambition he condones, even though recognizing that it destroys the common good it once helped to construct. Like a careful householder, he saves for a rainy day; but then like a reckless gambler he risks his savings on a roll of the dice.

Is there any reconciling of these commitments and dispositions? Liberty and greatness align respectively with republics and principalities (the Roman republic became a world power when it was no longer healthy, and its borders reached their ultimate extension under the caesars). Machiavelli does not defend one against the other or see liberty and greatness as opposites exactly. They intermingle and temporarily cooperate within a single regime. Eventually they break apart. But whether together or apart, liberty and greatness represent the two faces of ancient virtue: virtue in the many, dispersed and disciplined, and virtue in the one, concentrated and immoderate. So long as virtue survives, Machiavelli is indifferent as to where virtue locates or what form virtue takes. Rome can change the face of its virtue or even lose its virtue altogether, and Machiavelli is undisturbed, provided that successor states step forward to take a fallen Rome's place.

⚜

Next in order is a description of the structure of the book and of the analysis as it unfolds. Three chapters deal with book 1 of the *Discourses*, the first of these with Machiavelli's selection of Rome and rejection of Sparta. Machiavelli prefers mixed regimes to simple regimes, and among mixed regimes his focus is on those which build up their institutions over time and by accident as opposed to those which are created all at once in accordance with the vision and specifications of a single founder. He wants to know how a city can arrive at a mixed regime if it is not founded as a mixed regime in the beginning. Three answers are discovered: (1) it must follow the proper sequence of regimes so that the few who are prudent make concessions to the multitude which is good; (2) it must institutionalize the power of the great; and (3) it must expand its borders so as to be in need of and in debt to the people. Machiavelli also wants to know how accidents can cause a regime to improve the quality of its mixture. The answer is that classes, called humors, must be moderate in their goals, free of the demand for ideological correctness. This moderation is achieved, surprisingly, not by an education which trains each party to respect the virtues of its adversary, but by the routinizing of class conflict which causes each party to realize the selfishness of its demands and therewith to accept that its class opponent has, and is entitled to have, selfish interests of its own. Contact with the seamy side of human motivation renders the body politic resistant to the attractions of imaginary republics and disposed to accept what is practically good but theoretically not best. And the practically good regime recommended by Machiavelli is a democratic mixed regime modeled after Rome's. It is a regime well-suited to endure the vagaries of foreign affairs and honorable because of its strength. Nevertheless, Machiavelli's decision for Rome pays homage to Sparta in that elements of the past are preserved along with new possessions added on. Expansion requires both conservation and acquisition, and any ambition which tries obliterating the past is the enemy of collective greatness. Reform, therefore, is to be carried on inside, not outside, of ancient orders. Caesar is condemned for discarding the centuries-old republic in order to create a regime altogether new; he also is condemned for failing to understand that the greatest glory goes to the reformer of corrupt regimes and thus for failing to understand his own self-interest.

The second of these opening chapters examines the domestic institutions of Rome. Notice is taken of Machiavelli's special regard for executive power: lawmaking is slighted unless it is the exceptional, executive-like lawmaking of founders and reformers; ordinary adjudication is upgraded to extraordinary "execution"; and consuls, two in number, are superseded by the single, more effective, dictator. Machiavelli's fascination with the executive side of affairs is an early indication that administration is more important than law.

Rome was a class society; its population divided between patricians and plebs. Machiavelli approves of the division—of including the plebs and retaining the patricians—and examines how the classes related so as to accomplish the ends of guarding liberty and expanding the state. Class relations were tense but meliorated by various measures, of which civil religion was one and seemingly the most important. Civil religion served the double purpose of building intra-class solidarity (i.e., a single community protected by its gods), while allowing the patricians surreptitiously to rule. The final word on civil religion is ambiguous, however: it was vulnerable to corruption—both belief in by the people and use of by the great—and other means availed for achieving the same ends.

Class relations were also dynamic, for the balance of power was continually shifting, and usually from the patricians to the plebs. Which party then in the so-called "conflict of the orders" does Machiavelli support? The answer is nuanced but not inconsistent: Machiavelli sides with the nobles because of their ambitiousness; he also sides with the plebs because its inclusion was needed for expansion and because its empowerment was required by distributive justice. But of greater importance than distributive justice was the fact that inclusion of the plebs opened the door to inclusion of the young, who, being energetic beginners, were spirited and ambitious like the nobles, some of whom, being old men of the senate, were conservative and satisfied like the plebs.

Recognition that Rome was a class-divided city raises the question of just how different or how alike these classes in fact were. The argument of chapter 4, the last of the chapters dealing with book 1, is that the classes in Rome were situated on a continuum, their positions determined partly by accident and partly by nature. It was by accident that particular persons had the material resources and the family connections to develop their talents and rise in the city's hierarchy; it was by nature that particular persons had the ambition. The plebeians of Rome were ambitious, but their ambition was reactive and sporadic. For the nobles, on the other hand—or those worthy of the name—ambition was sui generis, and ambition never let them rest. On this score the humors were unlike, as they were unlike in their respective views about necessity—whether true character is revealed or distorted by fear. Nevertheless, by certain laws, such as the institution of the tribunate, the people came to resemble the nobles; and an ennobled people, eager for combat and adventure, proved an invaluable asset to Rome. But the ennoblement of the plebs had its limits, and there was always the danger that amalgamating the humors would cost the great their identity.

The people's virtue, called civic virtue, was a mixture of obedience and independence; it was produced by a mixture of necessity and choice. Was civic virtue important to Rome? The initial answer is that it was vitally important, for it enabled the people to receive liberty and to resist the urge to collaborate with kings. But civic virtue in Rome had a corruption problem, and in modern regimes the corruption problem continues on. So the next question is whether freedom and corruption can coexist. They can if law substitutes for virtue and if law changes to keep pace with moral decline. The smaller the community to which citizens are loyal (their city, their class, their party, their family), the more corrupt is their virtue or goodness. The people's goodness is not a unified disposition but consists of pairs of contrasting qualities (trust-distrust, gratitude-ingratitude, submissiveness-rebelliousness, etc.), one set for use with friends and supporters the other for use with adversaries and enemies. As the community contracts and more opponents than comrades are encountered, the law must adjust to reflect the suspicious and assertive side of the people's goodness. Even so, the number of adjustments is finite, since eventually community dissolves and only jealous individuals remain. The other problem is that piecemeal reform aimed at keeping customs in balance with laws and constitutional orders requires a level of perspicacity beyond the people's power. Freedom, guarded by law, cannot then coexist with corruption unless there is a prince who reforms not slowly and by legal means but all at once and tyrannically. In that case, however, corruption and freedom are not coexisting so much as virtue is being restored. As for Rome, it can hardly be said that its chief objective was the preservation of civic virtue. Rome traded its goodness for the bigger prize of glory. Rome was not Sparta.

One part of civic virtue Rome tenaciously guarded, namely the discipline and prowess of its citizen armies. Book 2 of the *Discourses*—and chapter 5 of this study—are about Rome's imperial policies. Rome conquered the world, and so Rome is Machiavelli's model of the acquisitive state. But strangely Rome's accomplishment depended on tactics both primitive and austere. The backbone of the Roman army was the infantry; and Machiavelli, enamored of Rome, tries persuading his contemporaries that the infantry is indispensable and that its revival in the modern world is a matter of first importance. The exhortation, however, borders on the hyperbolic and might properly be called a "noble lie." There is a refrain sounded in many of the second book's chapters that easy alternatives to martial virtue (wealth, cavalry, fortresses, auxiliaries, tribute, etc.) are traps and illusions unless accompanied by the virtue they are meant to replace. The strong can use easy, indirect means of conquest and defense but not the weak, whose only recourse is to become strong themselves. It happens though that this argument, a discouragement to any hope of combining liberty with corruption, is unsubstantiated by the historical record referenced by Machiavelli. The argument thus serves as an example of Machiavelli's emancipation from the authority of Rome and is taken as a first clue of Machiavelli's true understanding and intent—that *virtù* be valued as an end and not simply as a means.

As stated, the strong acquire by direct and indirect means alike. Machiavelli emphasizes Rome's indirection in the conquest and governance of subject states. The distinction between conquest and governance helps to explain some of the textual ambiguities as does the fact that Rome increased its size, or added to its "trunk," by a corruption strategy which unfolded in stages. Good government, paradoxically, was the culminating stage.

Chapter 6—about book 3—looks at the role of the individual in Rome. Two types, locked in combat though motivated by similar passions, provide the template for organizing the chapters of this very diffuse book. They are the patriot and the conspirator. Various plans and procedures are identified for exposing and blocking the conspiratorial individual, but together these modes do not add up to an effective strategy. Conspiracy, therefore, is a fact of life which principalities and republics must each address. But whereas conspiracies are the bane of princely governments, republican governments are restored to health by the dangers which conspiracies pose. Republics are benefited, but only on condition that a patriot-savior meets up with and stops the conspirator. Extrapolating from the Roman experience, one sees that politics, Machiavelli-style, depends heavily on heroic individuals, princes, who arguably are more important to its success than the well-crafted institutions of a mixed regime.

There is more to the study of princely types than the contrast between patriots and conspirators; also there is a problem at the core of Machiavelli's analysis. The problem is that the prince is described as an impersonator, able to be all things to all people; but then the prince is described as possessing an unalterable character, fixed in its habits by nature, experience, and education. How can the same person be so flexible as to have no character and so rigid as to act always according to type? The solution turns on the distinction between accumulating power and exercising power: in the matter of ruling citizens so as to earn their praise and secure their cooperation, the prince should show qualities disconnected from character traits (some princes can do this, though many cannot); but in the matter of choosing enterprises and executing policy, the prince is a prisoner of his nature and succeeds or fails depending on the chance conformity of his nature to the times. No prince can achieve a perfect liberation from character, meaning that virtue is constrained by fortune; but then little good would come from such extravagant freedom if character is required to supply the confidence and charisma needed for leadership. Combating fortune is in any event better done by republics switching captains than by individuals transfixed by character.

Captains are one type of prince; reform-minded lawgivers are another. Captains act on character and are useful to their states if their characters match the times. Here the times refer to emergencies and dangers which are best handled cautiously or impetuously, by going slow or by charging ahead. In the case of lawgivers, however, the times refer to something quite different, to the moral health of the state. Lawgivers build "dikes" and "dams" in quiet times because in quiet times the people's virtue wanes. These princes are in sync with the times by being out of sync with the character of the people. Their job is to return the state to its moral beginnings, a duty they usually discharge through acts of violence and cruelty. In a five-chapter subsection, Machiavelli explains the why-and-the-when of ruling by fear. Likewise, he ends the book by praising decimation and other spectacular punishments. Again, the personal takes precedence over the institutional, the execution of law over the rule of law.

Chapter 7 begins the second part of the book. Machiavelli is now the focal point, his originality and his intention being the subjects canvassed. Since Machiavelli has no obvious modes and orders of his own, one way to assess his originality is to examine the criticisms he lays against the modes and orders of Rome. What is discovered is that as a constitutional thinker Machiavelli stands for tighter checks and balances during ordinary times and looser restraints upon the executive during extraordinary times. He leaves it to the parties to decide the nature of the times, and he exposes the executive to the people's ingratitude should the executive prevail and the people dispute the victory or be disappointed with the results. An alternate way of judging Machiavelli's novelty is to note what Roman practices are praised by him but criticized by others—in which case Machiavelli is new for endorsing imperfect beginnings, faction between the humors, and the people's capacity for self-rule. Taken together, the picture created is of a republicanism rancorous, muscular, and dramatic. Accordingly, Machiavelli is miscast for the role of forefather of liberalism, if by liberalism one means a politics in which elites compete for public support and the goal of government is civil peace and prosperity. No better is the effort to ascribe to Machiavelli a scientific statecraft. Machiavelli desires to teach his readers the art of prudence but not statecraft as a science. On the other hand, it is a fair statement that Machiavelli separates politics from ethics; but then his new modes and orders refer not to constitutional forms and political practices but to first principles and ethical theory. It is agreed that Machiavelli preaches an amoral politics; what is examined—because the point is contested by scholars— is the audience to whom he preaches it. Is Machiavelli concerned to enlighten the public, and what sort of enlightenment is it?

In chapter 8 Machiavelli's ethical teaching in further scrutinized. Its novelty lies in its extremism, or in its brazen rejection of the middle way. The middle way is variously conceived: as moral perfection, exact justice, unwanted compromise, cowardly indecision; once it is portrayed positively as maximized acquisition. In all cases though, whether useless or useful, bad or good, the middle way is declared beyond man's competence to navigate—hence the famous Machiavellian counsel to avoid the middle. But a second look at the *Discourses* reveals that the work is suffused with middle ways, that Machiavelli is moderate in his advice, espousing an ethic anticipatory of modern utilitarianism, and that on one reading the goal of his politics is a world order resting on a balance of power among states modeled after the balance of power between classes. In other words, limitless acquisition is classified a false hope and is dismissed. But sustaining this argument proves difficult, since Machiavelli's protagonist is republican Rome whose ambition for ecumenical empire made it the enemy of every state both near and far. Machiavelli cannot endorse Rome's imperial designs and at the same time think it commendable that political adversaries check and balance each others' ambitions. What Machiavelli ultimately wants then is a mystery, and so investigating this mystery is the object of the book's final chapter.

Chapter 9 begins with a review of past attempts to answer the question of Machiavelli's identity and ambition: that Machiavelli is an evil man, is a value-neutral political scientist, is a monarchist in one book and a republican in another, is only a republican. This review sets up the analysis of liberty and greatness, judged to lie at the core of Machiavelli's thought and intention. Machiavelli is a republican who puts liberty first—except that textual exegesis shows Machiavelli to be putting liberty second, as a means to greatness, the end. Thus Machiavelli is an imperialist, perhaps even a monarchist. Further examination suggests, however, that the relationship is more complicated than means-ends; liberty and greatness also relate as stages in a cycle, and the ambivalence detectable in Machiavelli's thought is owing to the fact that he is equally committed to them both. (Since Christianity is held responsible for interrupting the cycle, the opportunity is taken for considering Machiavelli's criticisms of the Christian religion. His indictment consists of three charges, but his plans for dealing with the modes and orders of Christianity are deemed to be inconclusive.) Liberty and greatness are manifestations of the spirited part of the soul. Machiavelli regards spiritedness as higher than reason, which is its auxiliary, and higher than appetite, which is its rival. Spiritedness ranks highest because it supplies the passion behind heroic exertion, and because heroic exertion supplies the materials of historiography, tableaux of aesthetic delight. But worry that glory and greatness are imaginary goods sets Machiavelli at odds with himself. He is an idealist in wanting Christian Rome to be as glorious as its pagan namesake; and he is a realist in recognizing the pull of private ambition and the downward trajectory it eventually does take. Acquisitiveness can be ennobled, but chances are that the low will supplant the high. Machiavelli is more ancient than modern in his thoughts about the human good, but in truth he is some of each.

✤

In calling Machiavelli an ancient, I do not mean to suggest that he bears a close resemblance to Plato or Aristotle. On the contrary, Machiavelli is akin to a pre-philosophic ancient or akin to a republican Roman.[69] Strauss maintains the opposite, that Machiavelli is a modern for the reason that he paves the way for the modern project. What that project is can perhaps be inferred from Strauss's *Thoughts on Machiavelli*; but then Strauss, in another of his writings, provides a handy and succinct account: it is a lowering of moral standards for the purpose of conquering chance.[70] Machiavelli's central insight, Strauss avers, is that steady focus on the "effectual truth of the thing" (*verità effetuale della cosa* [*Prince*, 15]), the "is" as opposed to the "ought to be," improves the earthly existence of humankind. Shadia Drury, in her study of Strauss, elaborates on the meaning of the modern project. It is a three-pronged assault on antiquity, consisting of: (1) a preference for action over contemplation; (2) a judgment favoring the democratic multitude over the aristocratic few; and (3) a change in the style of philosophic communication—and hence in philosophy itself—from esoteric writing to propaganda for the state.[71]

I contend, contrarily (and in defense of the thesis that Machiavelli is a Roman avatar), that Machiavelli's hopes for victory over chance are faint at best, that his methods are far different from those employed by the moderns (war in place of science), and that his moral standards, taken from an antique heroic code, are for the virtue they support more than for the acquisitions they supply.[72] I further contend—against Strauss as expounded by Drury—that the conviction is stronger among Romans than among moderns that action takes precedence over contemplation, or that the political portion of the *vita activa* constitutes the optimal life for man;[73] also, that the portrayal of Machiavelli as a populist partisan is incorrect (once allowances are made for the aristocrat's change of occupation, from gentleman farmer to warrior prince); and finally, that Machiavelli's propagandizing is confined to enlightening the public about a lost ancient wisdom and is for the sake of providing his princes with greater freedom of action.

On the other hand, when the modern project looks forward to the future and not backward at its enemies in the rear, the object of its attention, Strauss rightly observes, is the satisfaction of desire; and there one finds Machiavelli giving his blessing to acquisition—"a very natural and ordinary thing" (*Prince*, 3). So knowing who Machiavelli is and what he wants is a business beset with difficulties. Machiavelli defies easy representation, and troubles await any attempt to draw a wholly consistent picture.

PART ONE

ROME

Chapter Two

Why Rome ?

The trouble begins in the preface to the first book. Machiavelli associates himself with discoverers of new modes and orders and declares himself a benefactor of mankind. But he does not quite say that he too is a discoverer or that it is by discovery that he contributes to the common benefit of everyone. He announces that he will travel a heretofore untrodden path; but he does not further explain the novelty of his endeavor or whether the path he enters upon is the same as or different from the modes and orders he has (or has not) discovered. Finally, and more to the present purpose, he reveals that he has an "end" (*il fine*), an "intention" (*mia intenzione*), and a "destined place" (*loco destinato*); but he holds back from saying what exactly they are, or it is. Rather, he complains generally about the weakness and evil of the modern world and about people who try rectifying the current malaise by imitating the accomplishments of the past. Not that Machiavelli abjures imitation or dissents from the renaissance of his times. He just is amazed and aggrieved that the love shown by his contemporaries for ancient art, law, and medicine does not extend to ancient politics as well. In these other endeavors, the ancient model is faithfully imitated. But in politics, by which he means "ordering republics, maintaining states, governing kingdoms, ordering the military and administering war, judging subjects, [and] increasing empire" (I.Pr.2)—in politics imitation is not attempted. The ancient histories are much read and much admired, but strangely the thought seems not to occur that the deeds recounted therein might themselves be imitated. The reason for this lapse is traced to Christian influences, but mainly it stems from "not having a true knowledge of histories." Such knowledge is missing, Machiavelli judges, whenever the reader fails to get the "sense" (*senso*), taste the "flavor" (*sapore*), and understand the "utility" (*utilità*) of these histories. While the precise meaning of this historical knowledge is not immediately clear (and more will be said about it later), for now it appears evident that the "end," the "intention," and the "destined place" of Machiavelli is the restoration of ancient politi-

21

cal and military practices, or, as Machiavelli more concisely puts it, the reclamation of ancient virtue (*antiqua virtù*).

Ancient virtue is not Roman virtue, per se. It could be Persian, Egyptian, Athenian, or Spartan. Machiavelli's attention is drawn to Rome because his source and authority is Titus Livy whose *First Decade* tells the story of the early Roman republic. But Machiavelli does not fully explain his choice of Livy. Sallust, Plutarch, Tacitus, Polybius—to say nothing of Thucydides or Xenophon—are available alternatives.[1] Perhaps then Livy is chosen because early Rome is Machiavelli's source and authority and Livy's history is practically the only account of the period extant in Machiavelli's time.[2] It may be difficult to demonstrate which of these comes first,[3] but one reason for thinking it Rome is that Machiavelli does not just assert a preference for Rome (as he does for Livy) but fights to establish it. That Rome among the ancient cities is the true model for imitation is a proposition which Machiavelli defends against all comers.

The Right Way to Perfection

The defense begins in the book's first chapter. Rome is twice praised for the good order of its beginning (I.1.1, 5). Founded on a fertile site by an authoritative figure (either Romulus or Aeneas) leading a free and independent people, who were either natives (Albans) or foreigners (Trojans), Rome possessed abundant virtue of long duration and in time attained to empire. For Rome's laws, doing the work of necessity, so constrained the city "that the fertility of the site, the advantages of the sea, the frequent victories, and the greatness of its empire could not corrupt it for many centuries." Accordingly, Rome maintained "as much virtue as has ever adorned any other city or republic" (§5). But while Rome's founding is highly praised, it is not compared with the founding of any competitor city but with "what have universally been the beginnings of any city whatever" (title);[4] and while highly praised, Rome's founding is not said to be the very best. In point of fact, this honor Machiavelli soon confers on Sparta.

Machiavelli examines three regimes in chapter 2: Spartan, Roman, and Athenian. He ranks them respectively as best, second-best, and third-best. Sparta is best both with respect to what it was and how it came into being. It was a mixed regime, and it came into being "at a stroke" (*ad un tratto*) and by the labors of "one prudent orderer" (§1). Founded by Lycurgus, Sparta was the happiest (*felice*) of cities, enjoying its liberty for over 800 years under laws it maintained without corruption and without dangerous tumult. Rome, on the other hand, suffered a degree of unhappiness in that it was forever forced to reorder itself, enduring tumults and numerous accidents which threatened its existence. Athens, presumably, was the unhappiest of the three, for while it had a single orderer in Solon, he made the mistake of giving Athens a simple rather than a mixed regime. This was a mistake from which Athens never recovered.

In order to explain the special virtue of the mixed regime, Machiavelli discusses the "cycle of regimes," a concept he borrows, without attribution, from the historian Polybius (who borrowed it, with attribution and much alteration, from Plato).[5] Sparta did not pass through this cycle because it was made perfect early in its history. Rome did but in a marvelous way that allowed for Rome's temporary escape.

The argument, in brief, is this: *Monarchy* is naturally the first regime (although Machiavelli says "by chance" where Polybius says "by nature"),[6] and the first monarch is naturally a warrior outstanding for his strength and courage. His successors, ruling more by wisdom and justice than by might and valor, bring monarchy to its perfection as kingship. But kings lose their goodness when heredity determines the succession; over time, therefore, the kingship becomes a *tyranny*.[7] Tyranny provokes a revolution led by the more noble and spirited elements of society who upon seizing power institute an *aristocracy*. But hereditary succession has the same corrupting effect on aristocrats as it has on kings; thus aristocrats decline into money-lovers, and the regime changes to *oligarchy*. The injustice of oligarchs incites a popular uprising followed then by creation of the first *democracy*. But democratic freedom degenerates into licentiousness, and a strongman returns the regime to monarchical rule. Thus we have a cycle from the rule of *one* to the rule of a *few* to the rule of the *many* back to the rule of *one*.

The relative merits of simple and mixed regimes is a matter much disputed in the classical tradition, and Machiavelli undertakes to join the debate. He notes a disagreement over the types of regimes, whether they are three in number or six. Those who argue for three (clumsily named by Machiavelli "principality," "aristocrats," and "popular government" [§5]) apparently have in mind that any of these simple regimes (and the best among them seems not to be at issue) can be made permanent. On the other hand, those who argue for six, contending that a corrupt companion attaches to each of the original three, think not that they are bringing morality into politics (e.g., good and bad forms of monarchical rule) but rather are discovering in politics the necessity of change. It is a question of form being supplanted by process. No form endures because all forms are inherently corruptible. Virtue is intermixed with vice; every good form is shadowed by an evil twin. Thus the six-regime proponents are actually diminishing the role of morality in politics. They see gray and black, whereas the three-regimers see only white.

Machiavelli hesitates endorsing either group, but he plainly favors the six-regime typology: those defending it are said to be "wiser according to the opinion of many" (§2); it is their argument which Machiavelli repeats; and when finished he allows that prudent lawgivers treat simple regimes as pestiferous or malign (§5). A simple regime places all power in the hands of a king, or a class of aristocrats, or the people. But the corruption of each is inevitable since "no remedy can be applied there to prevent it from slipping into its contrary" (§2). The six regimes therefore become three, since good and bad forms are kindred types; and the three regimes become one, since rotation through the cycle is predetermined. If six regimes are identified at the beginning, at the end they combine into a single, cyclic mass.

The alternative to the simple regime, which affords no remedy, is the mixed regime, which needs no remedy, or which is remedy personified. The mixed regime is an alliance of princely, aristocratic, and popular elements which, because each element "watches" the others, forestalls the decline to which simple regimes are prone. Total power corrupts, Machiavelli concedes, at least over time and when removed from the memory of its origins; and particularly invidious is the hereditary transmission of power. Shared power, on the other hand, either prevents corruption or protects against the effects of corruption.

It was noted above that Machiavelli's discussion of regimes, dependent on Polybius, is silent about the relative merits of kingship, aristocracy, and democracy. Accordingly, movement through the cycle cannot truly be portrayed as decline. There is decline from kingship to tyranny (from good to evil twin), but not from kingship to aristocracy. (The movement is more like the ups and downs of a roller coaster proceeding along a circular track.)[8] And since the triumph of aristocracy brings generous, high-spirited revolutionaries to office, replacing the vicious and degenerate tyrant, one might conclude that the cycle of regimes is a healthy process whereby new virtue replaces old vice. Why then treat the cycle as a process from which the city must escape? Machiavelli's answer is straightforward and well-known, that domestic instability invites a takeover from without. A state weakened by internal disorder will likely be conquered by its more orderly neighbors. There thus is little prospect of traveling the cycle endlessly, with bad regimes once good replaced by good regimes that are new and vigorous. Preservation requires stopping the cycle[9]—or prolonging it at least—a feat which no simple regime can accomplish, but which a mixed regime can, either "at a stroke" or, as Machiavelli says of Rome, by traveling the "right way" to perfection.

Sparta was founded "at a stroke" as a mixed regime. Athens and Rome traveled the cycle, but only Rome along the "right road" (*diritto cammino*) and "right way" (*diritta via*). Rome and Athens are examples of cities whose foundings, to repeat, were second-best and third-best respectively. To be second-best like Rome is to have a beginning, not perfect, but good enough so as to profit by accidents. A city profits when revolution brings a mixing, not an alternation, of regime types, and when the main source of accidents is the competition between the senate and the plebs. It seems then that two attributes must be present if a city is to arrive at a mixed regime: a capacity for preservation, its cause unstated as yet, and a capacity for change, its cause located in the rivalry between classes. Rome possessed these attributes; Athens did not.

What Machiavelli tells us of Romulus and Solon as lawgivers is that the former created a kingship and the latter created a democracy; that Romulus's kingship evolved into a mixed regime and Solon's democracy dissolved into a tyranny. Why? Did it matter that Rome started out where the cycle prescribes, with strongman-kingly rule; whereas Athens started out near the cycle's end, with democracy, and that when the democracy changed into a tyranny—as expected—Athens again disturbed the cycle's natural rhythms by reverting to democracy after 40 years of Pisistratid rule? Perhaps Athens was unable to benefit from accidents because it never did experience the proper sequence of kingly, aristocratic, and popular rule. Why though is the movement from one, to few, to many the proper sequence? It is not that the people learns the true merits of kings and aristocrats by experiencing the governments of each, since when the Athenian demos experienced Pisistratus's usurpation of power, it came to suspect all the great of its society (I.28). In fact the Athenian case is an argument for mixed regimes founded "at a stroke," before experience can teach the demos the folly of trusting the great. Still, Rome's second-best way might work the same result of building all elements into the regime if the rulers are prudent and the ruled are good. Machiavelli contends in I.17.2 that Rome benefited by tumult because corruption had not spread from the head to the body, from the government to the citizens. The people was not so ambitious, or so jaded, as to desire total victory over its rulers and class opponents. At the same time the patricians were not so shortsighted as to demand retention of all of their powers. Prudence is normally an attribute of the few and goodness an attribute of the many. Perhaps it was helpful to Rome that it proceeded from few to many, because then the descending class could bring prudence to the negotiations and the ascending class could bring goodness. Athens, on the other hand, began as a democracy and could never convince itself, despite decades of constitutional tinkering, to mix democracy with princely and aristocratic forms. Rome began as a kingship and found the mixing to be quite easy.[10]

Rome, the argument goes, combined the goodness of a rising populace with the shrewdness of a declining nobility. If so, in what way did shrewd nobles manage the passions and aspirations of the plebs so as to place Rome on the *diritta via*? One way (and more will come later) was to telescope plebeian hostility onto a single patrician, whose prideful belligerence made him a handy scapegoat for the misdeeds of the entire patrician order. Coriolanus is an early case in point. He took the lead in a scheme to disestablish the tribunate (491 BC). His plan was to exploit a shortage of local grain, a shortage thought to have been caused by neglect of the land during the secession of the plebs (494 BC), by withholding from distribution imported supplies: either the plebs would surrender the tribunate (created in 494) or continue paying prices inflated by artificial scarcity. When word of the plan reached the people, Coriolanus was accosted in the street; and he would have been killed in a tumult had not the tribunes intervened, accusing him of wrongdoing and summoning him to trial. Machiavelli's stated lesson in I.7 is that accusation is a useful order worthy of imitation by others. His unstated lesson, found in Livy's narration of the incident, is that nobles know how to cut their losses and save themselves. At the time, accusation was an unprecedented power, claimed unilaterally by the tribunes and denounced as illegal by Coriolanus. But the senate acquiesced in this usurpation; and even though senators defended Coriolanus strenuously, they were perfectly willing to sacrifice one of their own in order to appease the populace (Livy, II.35). Harvey Mansfield contends that the Roman nobles (perhaps with some correcting by Machiavelli) knew how to deflect popular indignation from their class as a whole by focusing it on one individual alone, whose ambition, in many cases, was as much a long-term threat to them as it was a short-term threat to the people.[11]

It was said that Romulus created a kingship; but actually what he created was an imperfect mixed regime since he shared power with a senate and since he established a "free way of life" (*vivere libero*), presumably through the institution of a citizen army (I.2.7; I.9.2). Romulus gave official recognition to the great of Rome and gave them a senate in which to protect themselves. Of the three orders of society—the kingly, the aristocratic, and the democratic—the aristocratic is the most vulnerable. Its numbers are insufficient to stand against the many, and the deliberative function it performs is not peculiar to itself. The people also deliberates in assembly. Not so often, though, does the people execute policy. Thus there is a natural place in society for an executive officer, if not always for a king. (When Romans expelled their kings, they nonetheless retained the "kingly power" [I.2.7].) And of course the people, as the body politic, is indispensable. But a suspicion always attaches to the great because of the superiority they claim for themselves, the powers which they exercise, and the privileges they enjoy. Over these and other matters the great and the people fight, and it is the task of the constitution to prevent the conflict from threatening the rights of either party. In Athens, the constitution of Solon was frequently amended in order that "the insolence of the great and the license of the collectivity" might be repressed. "Nonetheless," reports Machiavelli, "because it did not mix them with the power of the principality and with that of the aristocrats, Athens lived a very short time in respect to Sparta" (I.2.6). By contrast, the contest in Rome was between "the plebs and the Senate" (§7), or between the people and the institutionalized power of the great. Perhaps it mattered then that the great were given the senate.

Another, and more salient, reason is suggested as to why Rome followed the *diritta via* and Athens went astray. Because Rome sought greatness and needed its people for expansion (I.4.1), the patricians had to heed the complaints of the plebs, making concessions and ceding power until the plebs had won for itself full partnership in the regime. The Athenian democrats were hardly less ambitious, for it was under the democracy that Athens became an empire. But the democrats were less in need of the willing cooperation of their class antagonists.[12] Being outnumbered, the aristocrats in Athens had not the option of withholding financial support as the plebs in Rome had the option of fleeing to the Sacred Mount and refusing to fight. In a test of strength, the many will prevail over the few. Thus the many in power is given to tests of strength.

Salutary Accidents

Founded as a kingship with a senate and a free way of life, second-best Rome was positioned to take advantage of regime-altering accidents. Machiavelli discusses one of these accidents (*accidenti*) in chapter 3. It was the early exposure of the malignities of the senate and the consequent creation of the tribunate. After the expulsion of the Tarquins in 509, the new Roman republic was ruled principally by the senate. The people's role was not appreciably augmented because "the nobles had put away that pride of theirs, had taken on a popular spirit, and were tolerable to anyone, however mean." But with the death of Tarquinius Superbus in 496, the nobles changed their ways, reverted to form, and began again "to spit out that poison against the plebs that they had held in their breasts." Two years later, "after many confusions, noises, and dangers of scandals," the office of tribune was instituted as an intermediary between the plebs and the senate and as a bulwark against the insolence of the nobles (§2).

Rome was fortunate because the malignities of the senate did not remain hidden for longer than 13 years. But hiding malignities is much the same as governing well. For 13 years, that is to say, Rome was governed by a senate serving not its selfish interests but the common good. Why then was Rome lucky to have this early period of good government come to a speedy end? Because Rome was effectively governed by an aristocracy, a simple regime; and because simple regimes are based on the premise—the false premise in Machiavelli's view—that people are good. The cycle implies as much, that people are naturally, if not permanently, good; for while the powerful invariably succumb to vice, invariably they are replaced by a rising class that is good by nature. Were goodness natural, simple regimes would be good. And that regime would be best that gave power to the best. But Machiavelli's desideratum is the mixed regime because goodness, he tells us, is not natural. By goodness is meant the willingness to sacrifice personal gain for the commonweal. People, naturally, prefer themselves and ignore the well-being of others. Thus Machiavelli's advice "to whoever disposes a republic, and orders laws in it," is "to presuppose that all men are bad" (§1); for what goodness they exhibit comes not from their nature but from the laws under which they live.[13] He further advises that demonstrations of unforced goodness be carefully examined for the hidden cause that produces them. In the case of Rome, the hidden cause of patrician goodness was the fear the nobles felt of a Tarquin restoration.

Machiavelli continues with his theme of hidden causes and hidden malignities in chapter 4. Rome has detractors who object to its domestic politics, to the factiousness that characterized its class relations. These detractors, presumably, are proponents of simple regimes, of classless societies, or of rulers dedicated to the common good. What they fail to understand is that faction was the hidden cause of Rome's liberty and its power.

Faction is a political good because all men are wicked or must be treated as if they are by lawgivers (I.3.1) and because every population divides into two humors, the nobles and the plebs, the "haves" and the "have-nots." Machiavelli argues from effect to cause: Rome had liberty and power, reputedly good things; therefore, the stated cause of these good things—the tumult between the patricians and the plebs—was also good,[14] contrary to the opinion of detractors. "All the laws that are made in favor of freedom arise from [the] disunion" of the humors, says Machiavelli (§1). The diversity of humors is the cause of disunion; disunion is the cause of tumults; tumults are the cause of laws; laws are the cause of education (military training); and education is the cause of virtue. Where detractors see fortune and accidents, Machiavelli sees causal connections. But once again these causes lead to a paradoxical conclusion, for it is as if liberty were endangered whenever patricians and plebs worked harmoniously together; whenever Rome seemed to be doing right and doing well, it was in fact doing badly, its liberty suffering corruption (I.46).[15]

The republic with its two humors is rather like a company divided into management and labor; and the argument is that bad labor relations are a desirable thing. It is good if the workers are unsatisfied, quarrelsome, and suspicious; it is good if they hurl insults at their bosses, have work slowdowns, and go on strike. It is even better if these discontents (tumults) result in the formation of a union (tribunate), for random, chaotic, and uncontrollable actions are thus regularized and made predictable. The benefits of institutionalizing (law) labor unrest are two: more certain safeguards against exploitation of the workers (liberty); and greater profits for the company (power), since a protected and well-compensated work force is a productive work force, too. If one is tempted to go a step further and say that a happy work force is more productive still, the Machiavellian reply is that happiness is an unattainable objective because it rests upon the delusion that management is benevolent and that the classes can live as friends.

So what is the proof that tumults in Rome supported liberty or caused virtue? Machiavelli promises to examine the early history of republican Rome, from the death of the Tarquins to the institution of the tribunate (496-494 BC). He does not. Instead he argues that tumults caused no irreparable damage to the social order. The paucity of banishments and the leniency of punishments are taken by Machiavelli as evidence that class conflict in Rome was manageable

(I.7, I.8, I.28). But manageable is not agreeable, and many people who do "no other than read" of tumults are frightened and offended by the unruliness of the people.[16] Machiavelli takes a democratic line: If the people is to be utilized for expansion, it must be given some share of power; accordingly, the patricians (or all citizens of an orderly bent) must learn to live with the noise and crudity of the people. But, says Machiavelli assuringly, the ambition of the people wants only safety and guarantees against oppression; its bark is worse than its bite (I.16.5). Moreover, should false opinion capture the mind of the people, it is easily undeceived by a good man, worthy of faith, who addresses it in assembly. Here Machiavelli refers to Cicero's *De Amicitia*.

It is passing strange that Machiavelli would now cite a book on friendship, for he has just claimed that the people and its rulers are not friends and that no patrician is worthy of faith; that liberty is protected by the empowerment of mutually hostile and suspicious classes; and that the mixed regime is best because it entertains no illusions about human nature. But as Machiavelli concludes the chapter, the people is unexpectedly portrayed as a harmless innocent and the nobles as caring fathers; and the association of the classes is seen to depend on the truth-telling speech of a good man. This man, who calms the riotous crowd, appears at several places in the *Discourses* (I.13.2, I.53.1, I.54.1, I.58.4, III.6.14, III.22.6). His harmonizing speech, here and elsewhere, seems important to the smooth functioning of the mixed regime. Indeed the events which led to the creation of the tribunate featured the rhetoric of one such man, Menenius Agrippa, who quieted the plebs by explaining the interdependence of the classes—that the noblility supports the people and is supported by the people in turn, just as the belly, fed by the hand, the mouth, and the teeth, sends nourishment back to all of the body's parts (Livy, II.32). Perhaps then Machiavelli has overstated the degree to which class antagonism is useful to society. He is responding to the detractors of Rome who judge the city ill-founded and merely lucky because of the competition between the plebs and the patricians. He argues to the contrary that competition is essential to liberty. But the competition cannot be so intense as to result in banishments and violent prosecutions; class division must stop short of civil war. And if the city is to be powerful as well as free, as the chapter's title indicates, the classes must be able to set aside their hostility and work together.

Let's see if we can't make sense of this. Machiavelli begins with the assumption that human beings are out for themselves or that all people are bad (I.3.1). He allows, however, that people can become good by subordinating their personal ambitions to the well-being of a group. Necessity is what makes them good, whereas choice, or the freedom to act on their malignant impulses, is what makes them bad (I.1.4). In its purest and surest form, necessity is external and physical—the deprivation caused by a sterile site or the danger posed by a foreign opponent. In the face of deprivation and danger, people band together, obey authority, and work hard. But relieved of these necessities, people fall to quarreling and soon destroy themselves. Human beings, it seems, cannot survive success, so it is sensible to keep success always beyond their reach—which is precisely why some founders choose sterile sites in out-of-the-way places.[17] But these external and physical necessities (or the necessities of nature) are beyond human control and are not always friendly to human interests. For instance, a city which is small because its soil is thin and its climate arid can do little to make itself grow should growth be necessary to its survival. Machiavelli's comment is that "this choice [of a sterile site] would without doubt be wiser and more useful if men were content to live off their own and did not wish to seek to command others" (I.1.4). The wisdom of the choice, unfortunately, depends on others' making it too. But not all will, and the opposite choice leads to power and wealth by means of which small states are attacked and defeated. So it is better, Machiavelli reasons, to replace necessity with law, over which people have control as its makers and maintainers. Law is a soft form of necessity, an internalization of outside restraint which incorporates enough choice for men to have power but not so much choice for men to lose virtue. As necessity's substitute then, law must make people good.[18] But since law is created by men, it is apt to reflect the wickedness of human nature. Thus only a certain kind of man-made law can succeed at making wicked men good. This law, or constitutional ordering, is mixed government which divides power between the two humors of rich and poor. Bad people with power do bad things, but when power is distributed between groups of bad men, each group prevents the other from doing harm—and protection from harm is liberty. The mixed regime is meant to prevent action when action is likely to be partisan, in easy times, and to allow action when action is likely to be patriotic, in hard times.[19] Easy times permit people to be selfish; thus it is important that in easy times sovereignty disperse across the social groups each with sufficient power to protect its interests. By contrast, hard times create common goods, the achievement of which (or the prevention of some common harm) requires that people act as one. It is then that sovereignty is assembled from agreement among the groups. (And should they persist in disagreeing, emergency institutions, such as the dictatorship, operate as fail-safe devices.) The natural state of a mixed regime is equipoise or rest because the natural state of man is wickedness. Liberty is secure to the degree that wickedness is inactive, and the many negative powers of a mixed regime (e.g., the tribune's veto) have the effect of minimizing action. At the same time, power is acquired when the factions work in concert. Not only is liberty a by-product of factious politics, but also strength. For the great, who want always to dominate, will content themselves with dominating the people if the people looks like easy prey unable to defend its interests. But a free, vigilant, combative people forces the great to go elsewhere for their conquests, enlarging their ambition beyond domestic oppression to imperial expansion. The state grows because ambition is projected outward, and liberty is safeguarded because it is the reward for the people's assistance.[20]

The common cause of defeating enemies helps to make friends of patricians and plebs. Perhaps also the confidence born of successfully defending liberty causes animosities between the humors to subside. An angry mob, for example, listens quietly to a dignified patrician, and domestic peace is restored. Some measure of good will is needed if the popular humor is to accept and preserve the humor of the great; for complete suspiciousness would lead to the demonization of the senate and the creation of a democracy in place of a mixed regime. In fact, Machiavelli announces in III.8.1 that the ability of the classes to work together (as in the prosecutions of Spurius Cassius and Manlius Capitolinus) "show[ed] the goodness of all the orders of that republic" more than anything else. On the other hand, if the people is too trusting of its rulers, the false belief takes hold that goodness is by nature, not by legal necessity, and the vigilance is relaxed that keeps the senate good. Thus Machiavelli can welcome the end of Rome's early experiment with aristocratic government, even if, or precisely because, that government was good. He can welcome the exposure of the hidden cause which kept the senate good, which was neither natural necessity (sterile site) nor law exactly, but custom, as he puts it in I.3.2. Machiavelli stresses the hidden character of the custom by which the nobles treated well the plebs—the nobles' fear that in a contest with the Tarquins the plebs would not take the nobles' side—and the "very great union between the plebs and the Senate" from which the people mistook the necessitated moderation of the nobles for genuine kindness (§2). Custom is perhaps the most dangerous of the sources of goodness for the reason that its cause is most hidden. By comparison, the goodness occasioned by hunger and poverty is less deceptive about its cause, for people who work hard all their lives never do forget the reason for their labors. And less deceptive still, less hidden, is law, which exists to prevent and punish expected misbehavior. The creation of the tribunate was preceded by street violence, and the law's ordinary functioning presupposed rivalry between the classes.

Machiavelli, then, welcomes the addition of the tribunate, arguing that the conflict between the humors placed Rome on the *diritta via* toward perfection, able to profit by the accidents which came its way. The one accident he has so far reported was the early death of the deposed Tarquin king. But several other accidents are cited connected with the development of Rome's mixed regime. Listed chronologically they are: (1) Rome's popular founding by Romulus in 753, which, when the regime went sour under the Tarquins, allowed for a bloodless revolution in 509 to replace it (III.7); (2) the brevity of kingly government, and particularly of its tyrannical phase, which enabled Rome to keep the liberty it accidentally received (I.16-17); and (3) the loyalty of its leading citizens early in its history, which saved Rome from excessive ingratitude and the alienation of the nobles (I.28).[21]

The first of these accidents, it should be noted, is examined by Machiavelli not with regards to the establishment of a mixed regime in Rome, but with regards to the level of violence which accompanies changes of regimes generally. Despite this shift in focus, bloodless revolutions might well be considered a necessary element in the creation of a mixed regime. Because Rome's government was not imposed on it against the "common consent of a collectivity," there were few who suffered injury from the government's installation and so few who demanded vengeance at the time of its demise. Only "the Tarquins were expelled, with no offense to anyone else." Rather like Tocqueville's America, Rome was spared the violence of a democratic revolution.[22]

The second accident was the quick collapse of the Tarquin tyranny which left the people still uncorrupted and able to make use of the liberty provided by chance. An uncorrupted populace is necessary to a mixed regime since then the "infinite tumults" caused by the struggle between the humors, or the conflict of the orders, helps rather than harms the republic. Tumult helps, declares Machiavelli, because in an uncorrupted city, "men [have] a good end" (I.17.2).[23]

The third and final accident was the inveterate republicanism of Rome's ruling class such that "from the expulsion of the kings until Sulla and Marius, freedom was never taken away by any of its citizens" (I.28.1). Unlike Athens, which had its liberty stolen by Pisistratus "under a deception of goodness" and which in consequence "became a very prompt avenger not only of the errors but of the shadow of errors in its citizens," Rome, since it never suffered the accident of betrayal, had no cause for suspecting its leading citizens or for "offending them inconsiderately." The people of Rome, therefore, was not averse to the presence of aristocratic elements in its constitution. By contrast, the Athenian demos, having been once deceived by Pisistratus, was thereafter distrustful of anyone in a position to do the same. A generalized suspicion that excellence is the enemy of equality was what caused Athenians to be ungrateful. Hence in defense of equality, Athenians became democrats rather than republicans.

Centuries of good behavior on the part of Rome's great was the product of two of the accidents heretofore considered, the early overthrow of the Tarquin tyranny (I.16-17) and the early death of the exiled Tarquinius Superbus (I.3). The first of these accidents meant that the Roman people was uncorrupted at the time it was set free; accordingly it was protective of its newfound liberty, and the patricians were obliged, lest they excite the people's jealousy, to conduct themselves with the utmost rectitude. Collatinus, who with Brutus led the republican revolt, was himself expelled for no better reason than that he bore the Tarquin name. And Publius Valerius drew suspicion upon himself and was also nearly exiled because he started construction of a home on the Caelian Hill (I.28). The second accident, while it released the nobles from the need to court the public's favor, replaced a hidden custom with a visible law (the tribunate), and so made patrician goodness all the more durable. Why then did Rome's rulers not conspire against the republic? Because they were constrained by popular virtue and well-conceived laws.

But of course they did conspire, at least once. Machiavelli exaggerates when he states that "from the expulsion of the kings until Sulla and Marius, freedom was never taken away by any of its citizens." Appius Claudius took Rome's freedom away in 451-450, less than 60 years after the republic was formed. Appius and his fellow decemvirs, Machiavelli confesses, "became tyrants of Rome and without any hesitation seized its liberty" (I.35.1). Perhaps though we should count the decemvirate an aberration for the way in which it concentrated power, since the Roman custom, as evidenced by the dictatorship (I.34), was to check and balance power. Also Rome protected itself ordinarily from the ambition of individuals by multiplying the commanders upon which it relied. This Rome did by being always at war, for continuous warfare meant that "so many virtuous men emerged in every age, decorated from various victories, that the people did not have cause to fear any one of them, since they were very many and guarded one another." It meant also that the commanders were upright and "hesitant to cast a shadow of any ambition or give cause to the people to offend them for being ambitious" (I.30.2). It was not then that the rulers, by some mysterious accident, were for centuries good. It was rather that the laws prevented them from being bad and that Roman laws were not often as foolish as that law that instituted the decemvirate. So while Machiavelli retracts the statement that Rome never was betrayed, he lets stand the statement that in Rome there was less ingratitude "than in Athens, and perhaps than in any other republic" (I.28). And if even this second statement falls also into doubt (e.g., the exile of Coriolanus in I.7), the praise of Rome might still be sustained on grounds that Rome more than Athens made a virtue of ingratitude (I.29).

Rome's capacity to benefit from the accidents of fortune did not then depend on the goodness of its rulers, which is just as the previous examination of Rome's second-best founding predicted—that the descending few would contribute prudence, not goodness, to negotiations producing a mixed regime. It is the people's job to supply the goodness, since the accident of receiving liberty requires goodness in the people in order to be of use (I.17). The people needs to be good in the sense of patriotic and trusting, otherwise it will not tolerate and defer to the senatorial element of the mixed regime. But it is also true that the people needs to be bad in the sense of self-interested and suspicious, otherwise it will cede too much authority and lose its liberty to power-hungry nobles.[24] We find ourselves positioned in a messy middle where opposites combine and co-exist, where the republican character is revealed to be simultaneously good and bad.

The place to look for clarification and a possible resolution of the problem is I.32. The subject of chapter 32 is benefiting in a timely fashion, and the example is Rome during the period when the Tarquins were attempting to effect their restoration, the period when, as Machiavelli notes in I.3.2, the nobles befriended the plebs to ensure its allegiance. The Tuscan king Porsenna supported the Tarquins and in 508 attacked Rome on their behalf. In response the senate removed the salt tax and other impositions from the people. The senate was worried that the people "would rather accept kings than sustain the war," and it argued that the people did enough for the commonweal by raising its children and by enduring the hardships of the siege. The senate was culpable in waiting so long to confer this benefit (the lesson of the chapter), but a past record of generous actions kept the people from drawing the conclusion that necessity forced the senate's hand and that the benefit would be withdrawn once the danger had passed. Thus the people stood firm, and Rome was saved.

What we notice is that the people, as described in I.32, was both bad and good, both selfish and naive; for it had to be bribed with tax relief in order to keep it true to the republic, and it had to be fooled with tax relief in order that it might look kindly upon a senate which it thought looked kindly upon it. Its goodness was a consequence of the fact that "the state was new and not yet solid," that past benefits, such as the right of appeal, made credible the appearance of goodness in the senate, and that its "memory of the kings, by whom [it] had been vilified and injured in many modes, was fresh." The people's goodness was Rome's good fortune, because it allowed the senate to escape the baneful consequences of deferring benefits until forced by necessity. For had the people already known of the hidden malignities driving patrician behavior (including the right of appeal), it would not have fallen for the tax relief ruse; instead, it would have thrown its support to the king, and the accident that provided Rome with its liberty (the rape of Lucretia [III.5.1]) would have been to no avail. The goodness of the people compensated for the foolishness of the senate making the reception of liberty an accident from which Rome could profit.

But then the people was imperfectly good; its patriotism was purchased by benefits. Its incomplete goodness, however, was perhaps what led the accident of Tarquin's death to advance the cause of liberty. When the king died and the necessity was removed which kept the patricians good, the Roman people was not so unsuspecting as to be blind to the malignities it saw exposed, nor so childlike as to be scandalized and outraged. Thus it could put to good use the timely unveiling of the badness of its rulers by instituting the tribunate for its own defense. Not to discover this badness in time; to expect goodness instead and then to be injured because of one's too-trusting nature, as were the good Athenians, is to risk having goodness turn into hatred, hatred into violence, violence into class warfare, and class warfare into the imposition of a simple regime representing the selfish interests of the victor. This course Rome did not travel because of the fortuitous combination of goodness and badness in the Roman people. Paradoxically, it was helpful to the making of Rome's mixed regime that the plebs was bad enough to consider an exchange of liberty for security and that the patricians were bad enough to attempt an exchange of liberty for power. Simple regimes, on the other hand, think they are replacing perfect badness with perfect goodness; they thus are closed to the idea of conserving elements of the old order.

The secret then to traveling the *diritta via* is tumult between the classes, but tumult conceived as regularized fighting, not as once-and-for-all revolution inspired by ideological certitude. When the classes routinely confront each other, locked in daily battles over the distribution of spoils, they come to see the basic selfishness of their demands and to accept that opponents are entitled to selfish interests of their own. Experience teaches that all political actors are imperfect, whereas innocence permits belief in the triumph of pure goodness. Moderation is thus the consequence of involvement in affairs. The alternate route to moderation is instruction regarding the qualities of the classes, the wisdom of the nobles and the patriotism of the plebs. Aristotle proceeds in this fashion, telling one class about the good points of the other.[25] Machiavelli proceeds by telling all classes of their own badness and of the badness of their rivals.

Mixed Regimes: Aristocratic and Democratic

The previous discussion of Rome's second-best founding which placed it on the *diritta via* toward perfection and of the accidents which it encountered along the way examined the regime in Rome from the point of view of process—that by which it was established (multiple founders and refounders) and that through which it changed (new orders added). What next needs to be done is to examine the Roman regime in terms of its form. The title of chapter 2 asks how many species of republics there are; and the answer which the chapter supplies—that republics are founded "at a stroke" or over time, and that republics are either simple or mixed regimes—makes the same distinction between process and form.

In chapter 5 Machiavelli introduces the concept of the "guardian of liberty." The chapter's question is which of the classes, the people or the great, better guards the liberty of the city. The question may come as a surprise since Machiavelli has contended that liberty is guarded by the conflict of the orders, or by the power of each humor to protect its interests. The defense of liberty, he implied, is the accidental by-product of the selfish grasping for power. But he also has contended that the classes must cooperate for the common good and keep tumults under control, that the plebs, however suspicious, must respect the dignity of august individuals. So it is conceivable that there be some party in the city capable of transcending narrow partisanship and designated the guardian of liberty for that reason.

But what exactly is a guardian of liberty? Machiavelli never really says. His contemporary and sometimes patron, Francesco Guicciardini, in his commentary on the *Discourses*, is no less puzzled by the chapter's question. He thinks the concept applicable only to simple regimes where one of the classes, nobles or plebeians, has sovereign power; but in a mixed regime, such as was

Rome's, guarding liberty would have to mean guarding the regime against the conspiratorial designs of ambitious individuals, something which noble and plebeian magistrates alike did by way of legal prosecutions.[26] While it often happened that liberty was defended in just this manner (Guicciardini cites the prosecutions of Spurius Maelius and Manlius Capitolinus), Machiavelli is plainly not referring to those times in Roman history when the classes united against an aspiring tyrant; for the danger arises from the classes themselves. Nor is Machiavelli referring—or referring mainly—to the tribunes' power of veto, that plebeian negative on patrician initiatives; for he says that "one should put on guard over a thing those who have less appetite for usurping it" (§2). The "thing" (*cosa*) and the "it" which is subject to usurpation (*usurparla*) is not the liberty of a class, which might be protected by veto, but the liberty of the city. Machiavelli is looking for someone to put in charge of the constitution, though only in the sense of being situated to defend the constitution or to betray it.[27] No one is quite sovereign in a mixed regime; and if one class is superior to the other, still the location of sovereignty is disguised and the issue of ruling finessed. A constitution orders the particular distribution of power—a senate for the nobles, a tribunate for the plebs. In a simple regime all power is concentrated; in a mixed regime power is divided between the classes. Because power is divided, it cannot so easily be abused; and protection from the abuse of power is the meaning of liberty. The difficulty, however, is that one of the parties to the mix—and not some impartial referee—bears principal responsibility for protecting the liberty of all. Who though can be entrusted with this much power? Who is to be appointed the city's guardian of liberty?

To answer this question Machiavelli consults both reason and experience. Reason's view is that the less acquisitive party makes the better guardian of liberty. To be moderate in one's desires, easily satisfied, sober and frugal is to qualify for this most responsible post. But do the nobles fit the bill, or does the plebs? Machiavelli invokes the Roman example and his previous description of the people's ambition to argue that the plebs should be entrusted to guard the city's liberty. The people wants not to be dominated; and were it to want more, it could hardly achieve its desire, presumably because it is too numerous to find advantage in the usurpation of power ("being less able to hope to usurp it" [§2]). But there is another argument which goes like this: The nobles, as society's well-to-do, are satisfied by the power they already possess. They make for a conservative ruling class because they have something valuable to protect. Also, the people is content to be without power, for at bottom it is apolitical (I.16.5). On the other hand, if the people is given a little power or awakened politically, it becomes insatiably acquisitive, as was also proven by the Roman example. For once the plebs was granted tribunes, it demanded plebeian consuls, censors, praetors, and took to following anti-nobility demagogues.[28]

Machiavelli confesses his uncertainty regarding these arguments of reason, but experience, or history, he concedes, is more conclusive in its results. Sparta and Venice, ancient and modern cities which took the side of the nobles, defended their liberty longer than did Rome. And what we have heard so far of Rome would seem to confirm the wisdom of favoring the nobility, for the danger to liberty in the early years of the Roman republic came chiefly from the populace, which expressed its dissatisfaction by threatening to restore the Tarquins to power.

Machiavelli is in trouble if he means to push for Rome. Reason is a toss-up, and history is against him. His reaction is to dispose of the historical evidence by distinguishing between states which expand and are imperial (Rome) and states which are stationary and isolationist, content to maintain themselves as they are (Sparta and Venice). The former should have the people as their guardians of liberty; the latter, if they wish, can give this responsibility to the nobles.

As for reason, Machiavelli tries again, though he changes the subject somewhat from guardians of liberty to disturbers of the peace (the second topic in the chapter title). Who does more harm in a republic, he asks, "those who desire to acquire or those who fear to lose what they have acquired" [§4]? It was previously the case that the plebeians were the acquirers and the nobles the possessors. But no longer is Machiavelli willing to accept the argument that possessing is less acquisitive than acquiring. For those who possess fear losing what they possess and assuage their fear by acquiring more. In addition, possessors are better situated to acquire something new and to "make an alteration." Finally, it is their acquiring which stimulates the desire to acquire in the hearts of those who possess little or nothing.

It is common moral reasoning which differentiates between fear and desire as motives of action. Fear is compulsory, and so actions caused by fear are excusable; desire is voluntary, and so actions caused by it are either praiseworthy or blameworthy. Machiavelli obliterates this distinction by making fear the cause of desire. Apply his reasoning to military matters, and offense is equivalent to defense. But in the very next sentence moral judgment is heard from again, since Machiavelli redeems the people's ambition by having it appear reactive. Yes, the people was vengeful and envious, but the nobles made it that way by their "incorrect and ambitious behavior." So Rome was right to empower the people as guardian of liberty because the people is less acquisitive than the nobles and less able to overstep the line.

But we remember that Machiavelli placed Sparta and Venice in a special category of cities that were satisfied to maintain themselves. The "maintainers" could be ruled by nobles, but the "acquirers" needed the people to be in charge. Now this distinction seems peculiar on several counts. Whoever are the guardians of liberty, they are assigned this role because of the moderate character of their desires. Machiavelli has taken us through an argument which at first seemed to favor the nobility, described as "possessors" or "maintainers," over the people described as "acquirers." But then we were told that possessing is the moral equivalent of acquiring and that successful, extravagant acquiring is better done by possessors. Next came the assertion that the people is excused its ambition, however extravagant it may prove to be (tribunes, censors, praetors—and dictators!), for its acquisitions are in reaction to the overreaching of the nobles. The people is righteous; the nobles are "incorrect." Why is it then that this good and moderate people is the preferred guardian in a city with imperial ambitions, whereas rapacious nobles are the guardians in a city that is holding still? Guarding liberty is itself a form of holding still, for it is to use one's dominant position to maintain the balance of power rather than to grasp for more. So how does guarding comport with acquiring?

We know one reason why the people is wanted in an expansionary city—to fill the armies sent off to battle. This service the people will provide if its liberty is secure; and securing liberty—at least in a large, wealthy, and imperial city—is something which the people must do for itself. But as the guardian of liberty the people occupies a quasi-governing position. It brings to this position appetites which are moderate unless aggravated by attacks from the nobility. Is it then the case that moderation governs domestically in order to restrain the city's collective desire for new conquests and acquisitions? Probably not, as will be seen later.[29] The people is designated the guardian of liberty because an expansionary state must be united domestically if it is to defeat its enemies abroad. The people "in charge" produces this unity, whereas the nobility in charge produces dissension, serious enough, as in the case of Rome, to send the plebs scurrying to the Sacred Mount. The people then is wanted for ballast, not just for propulsion. To think only in terms of propulsion (power, empire, taking) is to forget that ballast (liberty, balanced relations, holding) is a necessary part of the acquisitive enterprise. A light ship can move more quickly across the water, but a light ship more readily will capsize.

So the people is the guardian of liberty in an expansionary state. But there is one other point to consider before disposing of the subject. As noted, the title of chapter 5 identifies two subjects, guarding liberty and causing tumults. Presumably it is a good thing to guard liberty and a bad thing to cause tumults? Given this presumption, the chapter is overtly democratic: it enhances the status of the people by contending that the people was Rome's guardian of liberty, and it diminishes the status of the nobles by charging that they were to blame for faction in Rome. But with a little reflection we are reminded that causing tumults is itself a cause of liberty. Although the people appeared tumultuous when taking to the streets, the underlying cause of its unruliness was the misbehavior of the nobles. If the nobles then were the hidden cause of tumults in Rome, so too were they the hidden cause of liberty in Rome. (The people by its goodness was the visible cause of liberty—as in the case of a plebeian dictator who tried to prevent the nobles from corrupting the elections [Marcus Menenius in I.5.3].) The nobles were hidden and inadvertent guardians of liberty in that their grasping nature and abuse of power awakened the plebeians politically and excited in them their own acquisitive desires. Liberty requires that the people be good but also that it be proud, proud enough to defend its liberty. Proud plebeians begin to resemble nobles. By oppressing the plebeians, the nobles made the plebeians somewhat like themselves. Nor was the result altogether unwelcome, for a virile populace was needed in order for the city to expand through war. It also was needed if the liberty received was not at once to be given back (I.16). The nobles needed the plebeians to be lovers of liberty lest the plebeians decide that they rather would be ruled by kings (I.25.1, I.32.1, III.8.1).[30]

Whether it is the plebeians or the nobles who primarily are the guardians of liberty will determine whether the mixed regime is of the democratic or aristocratic variety.[31] In chapter 6 Machiavelli looks again and more closely at the Spartan and Venetian constitutions. His reason, as he explains at the outset, is that "controversies between the people and the Senate" caused finally "the ruin of a free way of life" at the time of the Gracchi (133-121 BC). It appears that Machiavelli is still defensive about the tumultuousness of Rome;[32] thus he entertains the objection that Rome could have been free and powerful without having suffered four centuries of domestic unrest.

Rome represents the democratic mixed regime, which according to Machiavelli is plagued by faction; Sparta and Venice represent the aristocratic mixed regime, which is not. We draw this inference because in Machiavelli's descriptions of the Spartan and Venetian constitutions, the democratic element is missing or concealed; and because, in the case of Sparta, the constitution is differently described than before. Machiavelli stated in I.2.6 that Lycurgus distributed power to "the kings, the aristocrats, and the people"; in I.6.1 he states that "Sparta made a king, with a small Senate, who governed it." In place of "kings"—and Sparta always had two kings—there is "a king," and no mention is made of the people's involvement.[33] Machiavelli enhances the aristocratic appearance of Sparta. Indeed, he makes Sparta appear like pre-republican Rome— a single king and a small senate.

What Machiavelli believes was distinct about Venice was the absence of titles and offices (no king, no senate). But Venice was not quite a democracy on this account. The population divided between first-comers and late-comers. The former, who eventually called themselves gentlemen, constituted the citizen body and had equal access to governing posts; the latter, called the populace, were excluded from government and were treated more like resident aliens than like fellow citizens. Venice maintained domestic peace for so long because its aristocracy was broad-based, because the excluded late-comers had no cause or opportunity to complain—since nothing was taken from or expected of them— and because the late-comers were never greater in number than the first-comers and their descendants. Also Venice was isolated in the sense of being located at the head of the Adriatic Sea ("since the sea had no exit" [I.1.2]), though as a commercial republic it had ample contact with the rest of the world. It was large and wealthy, and its wealth was shared unequally (I.55.6).

Sparta enjoyed a comparable tenure, but as an ancient republic it was organized quite differently. Sparta's strength depended on its unity; that was not said of Venice which looked like two societies separately existing. Sparta was small, for it chose not to add foreigners to its population, and it forbade contact with them. Also Sparta withheld political equality from its citizens, for the laws of Lycurgus instituted the offices of king and senate and excluded the plebs from participation in public affairs; to compensate, the laws imposed equal poverty, or social equality, on all. Only in the exclusion of plebs was Venice like Sparta, but even here the cities were different; for in Venice the exclusion was total—no office, no service, no real citizenship—whereas in Sparta military service was required of plebs. Sparta took three steps to mitigate and manage plebeian unrest: (1) by restricting public office to a tiny circle of citizens, it gave the plebs less reason to see its exclusion as a deprivation and injustice (Venice, by contrast, had a very large ruling class); (2) by pitting the king against the nobles in a constitutional tug-of-war, it made the king needy for supporters and so willing to extend his protection to the people; it thus spared the people the trouble of protecting itself; and (3) by removing the plebs as a rival for public office, it soothed the ambition and jealousy of the nobles, who, secure in their position and held in check by the king, treated the plebs more generously.[34] While it is competition between the humors which destroys domestic tranquility, competition between a king and the nobles is not nearly so tumultuous, perhaps because a king, as the royal power, is more a function than a class. In any event, removal of the people from this competitive arena was for Sparta the key to domestic harmony; and the use of the people as soldiers—thus their integration into the life of the community (equal poverty and equal education)—was the key to political union.

The one drawback of the aristocratic mixed regime is its unsuitability for expansion and power, this as a consequence of the limited number of soldiers it can put into battle. Sparta had a small population base, and Venice did not use its plebs for military service. Sparta could not become a large state and still be governed by so few citizens, and Venice could not employ it plebs and still deny them an equal share of power. Accordingly, it was imperative for each republic to control its growth. But the result of Sparta's victory in the Peloponnesian War (404 BC) was that it "subjected almost all of Greece to itself"; thus Sparta, ill-equipped to manage an empire, was "altogether ruined" by the rebellion begun at Thebes and by its subsequent defeat at the battle of Leuctra (371 BC).[35] Likewise Venice, "having seized a great part of Italy," in 1509 "lost everything in one day" at the battle of Agnadello, sometimes called Vailà (§4).[36]

Rome did just the opposite of Sparta and Venice; it grew in size, and it made soldiers of its people. Whereas Sparta and Venice combined liberty and tranquility, Rome combined liberty and greatness. Rome though was beleaguered by domestic tumult, while Sparta and Venice had their respective empires quickly taken from them. Thus Machiavelli wonders whether it would be possible to have it all, to have liberty and tranquility, plus greatness enough to fend off ruin. His speculations revolve around the Spartan and Venetian constitutions: "I would well believe," muses Machiavelli, "that to make a republic that would last a long time, the mode would be to order it within like Sparta or like Venice. . . ." A state can long endure, he contends, if it is positioned in a strong place and organized for defense: "For war is made on a republic for two causes: one, to become master of it; the other, for fear lest it seize you." State security is a matter then of not tempting neighbors with easy victory nor of frightening neighbors with likely defeat. A reputation for martial prowess coupled with a record of non-aggression and a constitution forbidding expansion should be enough to keep one's state secure, at least against any single power. What's more, a state so organized can enjoy "the true political way of life and the true quiet of a city" (*il vero vivere politico e la vera quiete d'una città*) (§4). Machiavelli does not elaborate on this imagined alternative, but we might read into his terse declaration Aristotle's defense of the aristocratic polis, an association of virtuous and like-minded citizens who deliberate about the just and the advantageous.[37] True politics, on this reading, would be deliberative rather than warlike; its deliberative temper would depend on quiet not tumult; and quiet would require that the people's participation in political affairs be held to a minimum.

Machiavelli's enthusiasm for this Spartan-Venetian regime of speech is expressed by a series of confident assertions: "takes away almost altogether," "rarely happen, or never," "will never occur." A well-armed and defensive republic "will never" be attacked by a single power (§4). But this he says just before withdrawing his support and discarding the Spartan-Venetian model. For it is tantamount to an imaginary republic, a theoretical "middle way" between the unpalatable choices of harmony and weakness on the one hand and faction and strength on the other. He describes it as a regime to which reason brings you, but not necessity. For the "true political way of life" is conditioned on maintaining a balance, and in a world of flux, balance cannot be maintained. Some necessity will arise forcing expansion on a city not organized for it; or, if spared this necessity, a city will become emasculated and divided by protracted ease. Thus the effectual truth of inter- and intra-state politics is that no perfect middle way exists between Spartan-Venetian weakness and Roman divisiveness. A choice must be made; and by Machiavelli's reckoning "the more honorable part" lies with Rome (§4).

Founders and Reformers

In the contest between Rome and Sparta as to which city is the more archetypal for modern imitators, one round went to Sparta, the round dealing with process (better to be founded at a stroke and by a single lawgiver). A second round, the round dealing with form, has now gone to Rome (better to be a democratic polity organized for expansion). In chapter 9 Machiavelli settles the issue in Rome's favor, but not without making an important concession to Sparta.

Machiavelli serves up a hypothetical objection, that nothing has been said about the orderers of Rome or about its religious and military orders. In response he volunteers the observation that criminal behavior by a political founder is justifiable if the power obtained is used to serve the common good. The problem is the bad example set by the lawlessness of the founder—will it not encourage usurpation on the part of others? Machiavelli's reply is "that when the deed accuses him, the effect excuses him" (§2)—in other words, the end justifies the means.

The bad examples in question are the killings by Romulus of Remus his brother and Titus Tatius, Romulus's Sabine royal colleague. But how can others ascertain that the lawlessness and usurpation of the founding serves the common good? The answer is that the founding prince establishes a "civil way of life" (*vivere civile*). A civil way of life is a republic, and a republic is any regime in which power is not absolute. "Republic" is a generic term; it includes republics proper as well as limited principalities that share power. Romulus's kingdom was a republic because the power of Romulus the king was limited: (1) no successor exercised the founder's power, and there was no hereditary succession (condemned in I.10.4); (2) the king shared power with a senate; (3) kingly power was confined to conducting war and convoking the senate; and (4) there was an easy conversion to full-fledged republican government when the Tarquins were overthrown. If the founder does not serve his own ambition, which is taken to be the absolutism of a tyrant, then he is the servant of the common good, and his violence is excusable. To be virtuous in the sense of non-ambitious is one measure of public service; the other offered by Machiavelli is to use violence to mend, not spoil.

The notions of mending and spoiling take us to the chapter's title: "That It Is Necessary to Be Alone If One Wants to Order a Republic Anew or to Reform It Altogether outside Its Ancient Orders." The founder who orders anew is perforce a spoiler of whatever preceded his ordering; so too is the reformer insofar as his reforms are "outside" (*fuor*) the ancient orders. It seems to be the purpose of the chapter, however, to keep reforms inside the ancient orders and thus to turn reforms from spoiling to mending. We say this because Machiavelli sets out to explain away the bad example of the founder's use of violence in order to discourage similarly destructive acts by others—or, as he states, lest "citizens might be able with the authority of their prince, through ambition and desire to command, to offend those who might be opposed to their authority" (§1). The explanation that the founder's violence serves the common good is meant to direct the violence of others toward mending, not spoiling, the founder's orders, for "he who is violent to mend" is also a servant of the common good (§2).

Establishing a civil way of life and mending rather than spoiling speak to the ends served by the founder. The means which the founder employs are those violent actions "necessary to be alone." The common good of a well-ordered republic requires that the ordering proceed from one mind alone, for the "many are not capable of ordering a thing because they do not know its good" (§2). If political ordering depends on one mind alone, then it would seem to follow that a founding accomplished all at once proceeds more from a single mind than one that is reformed over and over again. Accordingly, Lycurgus, who founded the Spartan constitution "at a stroke," would be superior to Romulus, whose founding of Rome was partial and imperfect and improved by many who came after (Machiavelli did judge the Lycurgean way more conducive to happiness and less the hostage of fortune). Initially at least, chapter 9 seems to support that judgment, the conclusion of the competition's first round. But another requirement of successful founding, besides being alone in power, is persuading future generations to live within the ancient orders bequeathed them. The founder, if he is prudent, needs to create defenders of his modes and orders, which he does by granting others a share of his power. These others are of two descriptions: those who, "when they have come to know it [the constitution], they do not agree to abandon it" (§2); and those who imagine themselves the equal of the founding prince and take his usurpation of authority as an invitation to found orders of their own. For the first defenders, it is enough that the founder create a republic wherein citizens share power with each other, ruling and being ruled in turn. These conservative maintainers are the many by whose labor the regime is preserved: ". . . if one individual is capable of ordering," says Machiavelli, "the thing is ordered to last long not if it remains on the shoulders of one individual but rather if it remains in the care of many and its maintenance stays with many" (§2). Lycurgus created such a republic which was defended over the centuries by an obedient, if not entirely self-governing, multitude. But by founding all at once, Lycurgus did not share his own power with future lawgivers. (Apparently he paid no price for monopolizing the office of founder in that no successor destroyed his orders—but see below.) Romulus, on the other hand, was a usurper (having killed his equals in authority), but his imperfect founding gave others a reason to work inside rather than outside his orders. Romulus compromised on being "one alone," *uno solo*, (both by founding imperfectly and by ruling in concert with others), and so he better supplied his orders with energetic supporters.

One problem with perfect foundings is that people grow lax in maintaining what another has wrought. To be founded all at once is to have a national character devoted to maintaining one's past. With a state made whole and complete from the start, all that subsequent generations can do is to conserve this perfect beginning, because any change from perfection is decline. Their job is to place flowers around a memorial.[38] But the habit of conserving a perfect beginning renders people less energetic than they might otherwise be and the state they conserve less powerful and important. Conserving and maintaining, even something as important as liberty, is inconsistent with the more urgent business of expanding power. Perhaps then it is better to be imperfect from the start and to enlist the energy of the generations in a movement of reform, the assumption being that striving for perfection is what makes nations grow and become strong.[39] If true, then there are two factors that contribute to a founder's glory, that he be alone in the beginning and that he create something that is large and long-lasting. And the lesson of the chapter is that in order to do the latter, the founder must compromise the former, that is, extend indefinitely the time of the beginning, giving to others a stake in the enterprise by sharing with them a portion of the glory.[40]

We have stumbled upon a solution to a problem as yet not identified. The violence of the founder is justified by the goodness of the founder, and the goodness of the founder is demonstrated by his creation of a republic. The founder, "prudent orderer of a republic," is someone "who has the intent to wish to help not himself but the common good." But why would anyone harbor such an intent if, as is also said, "men are more prone to evil than to good" (§2)? The answer is that goodness is in the interest of evil men who are also prudent.[41] Evil is tyranny, or absolute power. Goodness is power-sharing. The evil but prudent founder institutes a regime of shared power. If he is a ruler within that regime, as was Romulus, he imposes limits upon his rule. Most of all, he leaves the regime unfinished and open to future developments. Lycurgus did just the opposite, forcing his fellow Spartans to take an oath not to change his orders until he returned from consulting the oracle, and then arranging never to return by committing suicide away from home.[42]

Machiavelli takes us back to Sparta. Lycurgus's good orders lasted 800 years, but apparently they did not last that long in good health. By the third century BC the city was corrupt and out of steam. Since the fall of Sparta's empire in 371 (defeat at Leuctra and a Theban-led invasion of the Peloponnesus which cost Sparta its Messenian estates and subjects), the Greek mainland had witnessed the rise of Macedon under Philip and Alexander followed by the rise of the Aetolian and Achaean confederations. Throughout this period Spartan power was on the wane. Then along came two kings, Agis IV of the Eurypontid line and Cleomenes III of the Agiad line (Sparta's eponymous kings were Eurypon and Agis; they preceded Lycurgus by a century or more). The first of these, Agis, undertook "to return the Spartans to the limits within which the laws of Lycurgus had enclosed them." But his efforts were not appreciated, and perhaps they were not understood; for he was killed by the ephors who saw him as "a man who wanted to seize tyranny." When Cleomenes, a few years later, succeeded to the Agiad throne, he took up the same reformist cause, inspired by "the records and writings of Agis." But Cleomenes succeeded where Agis had failed, because Cleomenes, comprehending better the Machiavellian maxim that to benefit the fatherland one must be "alone in authority," killed off "all the ephors and anyone else who might be able to stand against him" (I.9.4).

Machiavelli wants to "excuse and not blame" Romulus for the murders of Remus and Titus Tatius (I.9.5). This exculpation Machiavelli accomplishes by exposing the violent beginnings of many other lawgivers. He concentrates on Agis and Cleomenes because their cases are not so well known. Three others he names—Moses, Lycurgus, and Solon—but because their cases are familiar, he does not recount how they came to be alone in authority. The implication though is that they too resorted to violent measures.[43] Thus the argument he uses to absolve Romulus of his crimes, that every founding is lawless, suggests the existence of a common political reality transcending and obscuring differences of regime types. Certain problems are enduring and universal, and it matters not whether one's republic is expansionary like Rome or isolationist like Sparta. Close contact with the necessities of founding and surviving leaves all regimes looking more or less alike. The only important difference is between regimes that succeed and regimes that fail. Both Rome and Sparta succeeded.

We need to compare Plutarch with Machiavelli in order to see more clearly the similarity of these two regimes. At the heart of the old Lycurgean constitution was a fixed division of estates whose owners constituted the Spartan citizenry and who were the soldiers that Sparta sent into battle (plus auxiliaries). But sometime after Sparta's victory over Athens, a law was passed allowing the free disposal of land. The result of this law was to exacerbate the already growing disparity between rich and poor and to reduce to 700 the number of Spartan families owning land and to 100 the number of families able to perform their duties as citizens.[44] Agis thought that by equalizing wealth he could restore Sparta's ancient virtue.[45] He also thought that he could reclaim Sparta's ancient glory.[46] Machiavelli observes, when describing Agis's plan, that the consequence of lost virtue was the loss of "strength and empire." But it was Machiavelli's judgment that Sparta was never organized for empire and that the possession of empire, which Agis wished to regain, was the cause of Sparta's undoing (I.6.4). Plutarch confirms that the original laws did not envision a Spartan empire, for one of the *rhetras* (divinely revealed constitutional ordinances) stipulated that Sparta was not to fight often with the same enemy lest by frequent contact the enemy come to learn Sparta's secrets of war (Agesilaus was blamed for the loss to Thebes since the effect of his many incursions into Boeotia was to make Thebans the equal of Spartans).[47] Plutarch concludes that it was not Lycurgus's intention for Sparta to have command over a great many cities.[48] Thus Agis's reform, insofar as empire was to follow from virtue, aimed at more than returning Spartans to the enclosure of Lycurgus's laws.

The point is even clearer in the case of Cleomenes. Cleomenes was the son of Leonidas, the Agiad king ruling at the time of Agis and a conspirator in Agis's death. It is said by Plutarch that Cleomenes desired that his native Sparta assume command over all of Greece.[49] Toward this end Cleomenes first undertook to return Sparta to its ancient ways. But the ephors stood in his path; and so he had them killed, and many of his enemies he expelled. He might also have been implicated in the death of the Eurypontid king, Archidamus (rather like Romulus was implicated in the death of Titus Tatius).[50] Next he attacked the Achaean League, the dominant power in the Peloponnesus. He bested Aratus, leader of the League, and from a position of strength he offered his enemies terms of alliance—constitutional reform throughout the Peloponnesus—with himself at the head.[51] Soon it was conceded by many of Cleomenes' critics that the restoration of ancient customs and ancient equality was what made Sparta strong again.[52] And one step in particular which Cleomenes took toward making Sparta strong was to increase the Spartan population by extending citizenship to the *perioci*, free country people living in Laconia and Messenia. Since Machiavelli believes that the chief deficiency of the Spartan state was its small population base (I.6.3-4, II.3), this Cleomenic reform had the effect of moving Sparta in the direction of Rome. Like Agis before him then, Cleomenes did a good deal more than reinvigorate the laws of Lycurgus.[53]

Despite their ambitions and alterations, neither Agis nor Cleomenes reformed altogether outside the ancient orders; rather they fit the pattern of the Roman reformer who stayed inside the ancient orders and shared glory with the original lawgiver. Machiavelli says of Cleomenes, "That decision was apt for making Sparta rise again and for giving to Cleomenes the reputation that Lycurgus had . . ." (I.9.4). This is an arresting remark, since it nullifies one of Machiavelli's main distinctions between Sparta and Rome—that Sparta was founded all at once by a single lawgiver and that Rome was founded piecemeal, over time by a multitude of founder-reformers. Only the bad luck of a battle fought two days too soon caused Cleomenes to fail.[54] Had he succeeded, he would have enjoyed a reputation equal to that of Lycurgus, and Sparta, like Rome, would have had multiple lawgivers.

Machiavelli's story of the two reformer kings includes references to the ephors, the overseers in the Spartan regime. As it happened, the ephorate was not the creation of Lycurgus but was added, according to Plutarch, 130 years later under the reign of Theopompus as a democratic counterweight to a constitution that was oligarchically biased.[55] The addition of the tribunes to the Roman constitution accomplished the same purpose and is Machiavelli's chief evidence that the Roman constitution was dynamic and perfected over time.[56] Should we not then draw the same conclusion about the Spartan constitution, that it was not delivered complete from the mind of Lycurgus but bore the imprint of many minds and was amended in response to discovered needs and changing circumstances?[57] We also heard it said that "Sparta made a king, with a small Senate" (I.6.1). The description is inaccurate of Sparta (always there were two kings) but not of Rome. Thus Sparta is wrongly described to look like Rome. Moreover, Rome is wrongly described to look like Sparta, for when Machiavelli claims, in testimony to Romulus, that following the expulsion of the Tarquins, "no ancient order was innovated by the Romans, except that in place of a perpetual king there were two annual consuls" (I.9.2), Machiavelli fails to mention the dictatorship, created only eight years later, the tribunate, created but 15 years later, and religious law, added by Numa. By this statement it is made to seem that Rome like Sparta was fashioned all at once and that Romulus like Lycurgus was a solitary lawgiver.

The question then that arises is why Machiavelli would hint at a union of these two regimes which heretofore he has treated as rivals in a competition for honors. Why make Sparta look like Rome and Rome look like Sparta? Perhaps the answer is that a romanized Sparta and a spartanized Rome would each be structured to maintain itself longer. Maintenance requires preservation, but of a substance understood to be always the same. It requires, in other words, the continuation of a constant identity. Fragile perfection cannot long endure, nor can innovating nimbleness hold on to the sense of a continuing self. For Sparta, romanization would mean providing a place within its ancient orders for the ambition of future founders; while for Rome, spartanization would mean respecting its first founder even though his orders had been replaced by others. When Rome was finished with royal government, Rome hated the name of king, however tolerant it remained of kingly power (I.2.7, I.58.3). And yet Machiavelli seems determined to defend the reputation of Romulus,[58] linking him to republican liberty even while admitting that the creation of the consuls marked "the beginning of their free way of life" (I.25.1). Machiavelli wants to project the image of a single, continuous history stretching from the kingship through the republic; for only if Rome was the same from Romulus to Caesar, free for 700-plus years, can Rome compete with Sparta, free for 800 years under the laws of Lycurgus. By the same token, Machiavelli intimates that Sparta under Agis and Cleomenes was reorganizing itself for expansion along Roman lines. The lesson is that in order to last, a regime must both change and conserve. Designed for change, Rome needed to remember the past; designed for conservation, Sparta needed to venture the future.

The Case of Julius Caesar

Was it necessary though for Rome's continuous history to terminate with the advent of the caesars, for one Rome to end and a second Rome to begin? Or could the interplay of conservation and innovation have kept republican Rome going? The reason for posing this question is Machiavelli's reflection on Julius Caesar in chapter 10.

Chapter 10, however, is not only about Caesar and his reputation as conveyed by historians. It also, and initially, is about princely types whom people praise and blame. So let's begin at the beginning, and before that let's review.

It is the argument of chapter 9: (1) that founding requires that princes be alone in authority; (2) that felonious violence is required to be alone; (3) that founders are not tyrants because violence is for the sake of the common good; (4) that the common good is tantamount to republican government and that republican government is tantamount to the sharing of power; and (5) that power-sharing is useful because it obviates reform outside the ancient orders. Chapter 10 now confirms the distinction between founders and tyrants and between republics and tyrannies, and it encourages the individual prince, confronted with a choice between goodness and badness, to live in imitation of the good on grounds that history proves the utility of virtue. The chapter tries to reestablish traditional morality because traditional morality, although a hindrance at the time of founding, is vital to the maintenance of regimes. The theme of chapter 10 is maintenance, and its hero is the good prince who wants to reign in peace.

Toward the goal of promoting goodness among princes, Machiavelli declares it certain that what is praiseworthy and blameworthy conduct is agreed to by all human beings. He supplies a list, a rank ordering of benefactors universally beloved and of despoilers universally reviled. All agree that founders of religions top the list of admirable men and that destroyers of religions top the list of detestable men—and so on down the lists of virtuous and villainous characters. Consensus is such that the whole of humanity is positioned in a great middle bounded by the extremes of wisdom and madness and of good and evil ("And no one will ever be so crazy or so wise, so wicked or so good. . ." [§1]). No human ever strays from the middle, into the "superhuman" or the "subhuman," so as to praise and blame differently.

What people praise, however, seems strangely not to govern what people do. People are almost as universal in their doing bad as they are in their praising good. The reason why is that people are "deceived by a false good and a false glory," the choice of which leads them into the ranks of those who "deserve more blame than praise" (§1). Machiavelli intends to set people straight, to prove the wisdom of doing good by means of examples taken from history (by means, almost, of statistical data: e.g., tyrants and bad emperors suffer a 91 percent chance of assassination, good emperors a 33 percent chance).

If the lessons of history are consistent, that goodness results in fame, glory, honor, security, quiet, and satisfaction of mind, and that badness results in infamy, shame, blame, danger, and disquiet, then those who do not perceive these advantages and disadvantages go "ignorantly" into bad conduct, and Machiavelli will try again to teach them what history has taught him. Some people, however, go "voluntarily" into bad conduct, and there are various possible explanations to account for their wrongdoing. If the loss of reputation is the principal disadvantage incurred, they might well conclude that words of praise are a false good when compared with the real good of material rewards. On the other hand, if the disadvantage is itself material, the forfeiture of power and authority, they might suppose that they are clever enough to deceive people about the selfish character of their actions. Finally, they might think that people, being selfish themselves, are irregular in their praise and blame (contrary to Machiavelli's original affirmation) and are willing, sometimes, to excuse the blameable behavior of others (e.g., the murder of Remus), in hopes of having their own blameable deeds excused, and to praise successful selfishness even when they do not themselves share in its profits. How else could there be "false glory" unless people sometimes confused the praiseworthy and the blameworthy? This confusion is exacerbated by the historians who cause their readers to love the good but who also celebrate the glory, the false glory, of Caesar.

Historians seem to be of three types. There are some who are mere worshippers of success (II.Pr.1). They are awed and corrupted by good fortune and the long duration of empire. They speak favorably of Caesar, applaud his achievements, and so part company from the universality of men who praise builders and blame destroyers. Accordingly, the consensus opinion noted above is something less than a consensus. A second type of historian speaks esoterically by praising a tyrant's enemies (Brutus) and attacking his less powerful predecessors (Catiline). This historian is not free to speak openly, and so his departure from the consensus is clear to some readers but not to others. And then there is a third type of historian who is privileged to live in "golden times" when the free expression of opinion is permitted. This perhaps is the historian who, influenced by the goodness of the times, freely declares that good ends come from good means; as such, this historian contributes to the consensus view that justice is advantageous.

We might ask what type of historian is Machiavelli. He cannot belong to the first type because he impugns the motives of those who do. And so far is he from celebrating Caesar's glory that he classifies Caesar a tyrant and an evildoer. Nor does Machiavelli belong to the second type since his attack upon Caesar is plain for all to see. Most likely then Machiavelli is an historian of the third type (if only by appearance and only for now). He fantasizes like a child about an ideal period in which to live; he tailors conduct to suit the age; and he blithely assumes that goodness will triumph in the end. Overall he seems determined to make the case that the world is morally uncomplicated because from good means come good ends (e.g., virtuous emperors rule in peace; criminal emperors die violent deaths). But of course the opposite is argued in I.9, and it is Machiavelli who says in *Prince* 15 that he who "makes a profession of good in all regards must come to ruin among so many who are not good." Although Machiavelli in chapter 10 sounds more upbeat about the benefits of justice than does Socrates in the *Republic*, we have to wonder whether Machiavelli is truly this confident and this hopeful. And although he does not employ esotericism to denounce Caesar, we might wonder whether he employs it to eulogize Caesar.

At the chapter's end, Machiavelli is critical of Caesar because he did not restore the republic when he had the chance. Caesar should have done for Rome what Agis and Cleomenes attempted for Sparta. But why? Immediately Machiavelli offers Caesar an excuse (as he offered Romulus an excuse in I.9.1): If re-storing the republic meant surrendering princely power, then Caesar is not to be faulted fully. (Romulus could maintain his kingship while sharing power with the senate.) Even so, to excuse Caesar is not to praise Caesar. Would it have been better—and better for Caesar, not just for Rome—if Caesar had reordered the republic? Says Machiavelli, "And truly, if a prince seeks the glory of the world, he ought to desire to possess a corrupt city—not to spoil it entirely as did Caesar but to reorder it as did Romulus. And truly the heavens cannot give to men a greater opportunity for glory, nor can men desire any greater" (§6). Hav-ing previously stated that anyone "born of man" would choose living in peaceful times, and having asserted that no human being would ever be "so crazy or so wise, so wicked or so good" to praise differently than all others (§1), Machia-velli now makes an exception for the glory-seeker. The glory-seeker is an ex-ceptional human being. He is not the peace-seeker, nor does he reason in concert with the generality. It seems then that the moral judgments previously issued, judgments which condemn Caesar, do not encompass the glory-seeker, a type which includes Caesar. So perhaps there is some ambiguity in Machiavelli's assessment.

We notice that Machiavelli calls Romulus a reorderer (§6)—a glory-seeker who took possession of a corrupt city to reorder it (*per riordinarla*). Strictly speaking, Romulus was an orderer, not a *re*orderer, for there was nothing pre-existing for Romulus to reorder. But the misnaming serves a purpose, for it eliminates the distinction between the one who comes first, the founder, and the many who follow in his path, reformers. The distinction implies that reformers are subordinate and derivative, maintainers of the modes and orders of another. In light of this distinction, Caesar's reordering of Romulus's Rome would have added to Romulus's glory. But reformers, jealous of their own glory, would rather order anew or reform altogether outside the ancient orders—which was precisely what Caesar did; he destroyed the orders of Romulus and ordered Rome anew. We have already examined the problem of continuity from the founder's perspective. The founder wants his orders to be preserved; the founder wants successors to reform inside, not outside, the ancient orders; the founder, Romulus, wants Caesar to reorder Rome, not wreck it. And the founder gets what he wants by sharing glory with the reformer, by, in this small case, dis-avowing the exalted, one-of-a-kind title of orderer and adopting the more equal and shareable title of reorderer. Of course it is Machiavelli who does the dis-avowing and adopting, for it is Machiavelli who is teaching founders and re-formers the interest they have in common.

But what interest had Caesar in continuing the republican orders of Rom-ulus? Romulus needed Caesar, but did Caesar need Romulus? Yes, Caesar did, because revolution is easier if made to look like restoration (I.25). Caesar was assassinated by the nobility because he threatened too overtly the institutions of

Rome's republican past—and assassination is one of the touchstones used in I.10 to differentiate good and bad emperors.

Caesar then failed to connect properly with the past. But Caesar was more successful in projecting himself into the future. The other touchstone of good and bad emperors is succession by adoption-election versus succession by heredity: "For all the emperors who succeeded to the empire by heredity, except Titus, were bad. Those who succeeded by adoption were all good" (§4). Caesar died before the empire was officially established (he rejected offers of a crown, and up to the moment of his death Roman citizens were punished for calling Caesar "rex"),[59] although Machiavelli names him the first of the emperors (§4), having previously styled him a private man in a republic (§2). Caesar's immediate successors were loosely related as members of the Julian family (I.17.1), but it would be incorrect to say that Caesar thereby instituted the practice of hereditary succession. For what rather is said about Caesar is that the empire ruled under his name and that a long line of successors, most of them not related, defended his name by prohibiting writers from speaking freely of him (§3).[60] This is an achievement comparable to the achievement of Romulus, who created a kingship that changed into a republic but still remembered Romulus as its founder. Caesar's name survived despite the fact that Caesar's heirs were not his sons, grandsons, and great-grandsons, despite the fact that what Caesar created (to the extent that he created anything) was an elective, not a dynastic, monarchy. The dynastic temptation is nearly irresistible, for kings try to control their reputations and make themselves immortal by instituting and legitimizing the succession of blood relations only, family members who, even if superior to the dynasty's founder, are never free to reorder anew, since their very existence implies the founder from whom they issued. As descendants, they cannot cut loose from their beginnings, and whatever they do in their own right is but an adding on to what was already there.[61] Caesar's name was defended because the name defined the regime ("caesarian Rome")[62] and conferred legitimacy on the holders of power. These strangers, ambitious glory-seekers themselves, required that historians celebrate the glory of Caesar. We do not know why the name of Caesar carried such magic; Machiavelli does not say. But an interesting conjecture is that Caesar's death, remembered as the sacrifice of a martyr and not as the execution of a bad emperor, was responsible for the conjuring power of Caesar's name (I.52).[63] If true, then the failure of Caesar to connect with Rome's past, made evident by Caesar's assassination, was the precondition of Caesar's creating Rome's future. If true, then Machiavelli's two lessons drawn from the history of the Roman empire are in disagreement: (1) that good emperors die natural deaths and bad emperors are assassinated; and (2) that good ordering requires succession by adoption-election and bad ordering permits succession by heredity. By dying in the manner of a "bad emperor," Caesar invested his name with such magic that adopted successors, called "caesar," had sufficient legitimacy to preside over the empire. And there was another way in which Caesar controlled the future—he wrote his own history!

Apparently then, Machiavelli's opinion of Caesar is more complicated than the sermonizing denunciation found on the surface. And even this denunciation has its dimensions. He concludes his extended philippic with the statement, "And he will then know very well how many obligations Rome, Italy, and the world owe to Caesar" (§5). How many indeed! Caesar has charged against him: war, sedition, regicide, the sacking of cities, the burning of Rome, the desolation of temples, the corruption of ceremonies, adultery among citizens, seas full of exiles and shores full of blood, innumerable cruelties, and virtue mistaken for sin. What Caesar founded was hell on earth, plain and simple. But just before this bill of particulars is an account of Rome's golden age, which existed during the empire, not during the republic, and which therefore is attributable to Caesar also. So credited to Caesar are: secure princes and secure citizens, peace and justice, the senate with authority and magistrates with honor, nobility and virtue exalted, riches enjoyed by the wealthy, free speech available to all, and the world triumphant. The obligation that Machiavelli says the world owes to Caesar is consequently an ambiguous one, no less ambiguous than the assurance Machiavelli provides that moral opinion is united because no one exists "who will not praise what is to be praised and blame what is to be blamed" when given the choice between two qualities of men (§1). Nor is it the case that the defense of Caesar's name always required intimidation and coercion, for there was a period, a golden age, during which historians were free to express their true opinions.

Caesar's legacy, therefore, was mixed. Caesar chose caesarism instead of the republic's restoration and so gave himself detractors as well as admirers.[64] Machiavelli appears to be both a detractor and an admirer. He says explicitly in I.37.2 that Caesar was a tyrant ("He was the first tyrant in Rome, such that never again was that city free."), and he says implicitly much the same thing in III.8.2 ("He [Manlius Capitolinus] would have had the same results and successes as Marius and Sulla and as others later who aspired to tyranny after them."). In Caesar's favor, Machiavelli admits that the republic had treated Caesar badly and that he took by force what ingratitude had denied him (I.29.3). On the other hand, it is Machiavelli's counsel to erring republics that having once offended a worthy man, they should never again trust him with high office, especially if he is vindictive (III.16.2, III.17).

More important, however, than any of these remarks is Machiavelli's consideration of whether the Roman republic was even salvageable in Caesar's day. This issue is raised in at least three places: In I.17.1 Machiavelli states that "after Caesar died, after Gaius Caligua died, after Nero died, when the whole line of Caesar was eliminated, not only could it never maintain but it could not even give a beginning to freedom." Similarly, in the *Florentine Histories*, Machiavelli states that "Rome, when its virtue was converted into arrogance, was reduced to such straits that it could not maintain itself without a prince" (III.1). Finally, in *Discourses* I.52.3, Machiavelli censures Cicero for having foolishly believed that Octavian, Caesar's nephew using Caesar's name, could be enlisted in the republican cause against the forces of Mark Antony. Says Machiavelli:

> Nor should that of which Tully persuaded himself have been believed, but that name that with so much glory had eliminated its enemies and acquired for itself the principate in Rome should have always been taken into account; nor should it have been believed that, either from his heirs or from his agents, anything could ever be had that would conform to the name of freedom.

From these three passages it seems reasonably clear that the republic was gone for good and that caesarism was the state's only salvation. But there is no hint of this view in I.10 where Machiavelli treats the republic as a regime forever revivable—as not dead but wantonly destroyed. Maybe then the cited passages are not so conclusive as they first appear. What they all suggest, in one way or another, is that Caesar was himself the turning point, not that he came after the point-of-no-return had passed. He was the head for a time of the Marian party which started corruption in Rome (I.17.1). After Caesar, and certainly after the death of the Julians, corruption was too advanced for virtue to be restored. But Caesar was more the cause of this corruption than he is excused by it. And the fact that Caesar's heirs and agents were unfriendly to liberty is no sure proof that Caesar, who made them what they were, needed to be that way too. The restoration of freedom in Rome would not have been easy and the work of wise legislation alone. But then Machiavelli welcomes reformations that are hazardous and that require princes to bring them about. Chapter 18 is where Machiavelli speaks most thoroughly about the reformer prince. He is a good man for wanting to reorder the city for a political way of life; but he is a bad man for becoming prince of a republic by violence and for using "an almost kingly power" to check the insolence of those who cannot be corrected by law (I.18.4-5). Caesar is not mentioned in chapter 18 where the problem is adjusting law, either little by little or all at once, to the changing state of corruption in a city. Still it was Caesar who all at once adjusted the Roman constitution to fit the state of Roman corruption. Caesar was not a good prince since his end was the institution of a tyranny instead of the restoration of Rome's republic. More importantly, however, he was not a wise prince, since the thought did not "occur to his mind to use well the authority that he [had] acquired badly" (I.18.4).[65] Caesar should have used his princely authority to restore the republic of Rome;[66] not for Rome's sake and because Caesar should have been good, but for Caesar's sake and because Caesar should have been wise. For the supreme glory or "the glory of the world," says Machiavelli in I.10.6, belongs not to orderers of religions (as he seems to say in I.10.1), but to reorderers of corrupt cities. Not ordering but reordering is accorded the highest place on the register of celebrated deeds.

What then is Machiavelli trying to accomplish with his case study of Julius Caesar? First, and most clearly, he wishes to create a place for maintainers who rule in good times. There are good times, from time to time, and good times allow for a different brand of politics. Not all princes are, or need be, criminal usurpers (such as was Caesar); for if they were, no orders would endure long enough to achieve greatness and fame. Second, and less clearly, Machiavelli is defending Caesar, whom he mostly denounces, because the perpetuation of political orders requires violent renewal to go with peaceful maintaining. Caesar reordered Rome. However, he reordered Rome outside, not inside, the ancient orders established by Romulus, and for this Caesar is faulted. Or better put, he is instructed—he and his glory-seeking kind. It has been suggested, and will be again, that the main purpose of the *Discourses* is to inform princes, potential princes, of the happy congruence of their duty and their interest (restorers of old orders receive the highest glory). Third, and least clearly, Machiavelli is honoring Caesar, whose assassination made lasting his caesarian orders, and whose long-lived orders made Caesar the equal of Romulus. Even if the republic were revivable in Caesar's day,[67] as a thing of this world it was fated to die; and devotion to particular mortal things is not absolute. Rather than labor to restore the republic, Caesar and his successors took what remained—a virtuous army—and made a mad dash for glory. As will be seen, Machiavelli's love of greatness and glory does not always lead him to demand the preservation of old and free orders.

Chapter Three

Rome's "Inside" Modes and Orders

At the close of chapter 1, Machiavelli offers the following description of the structure of the *Discourses*:

> Because the things worked by it, which are celebrated by Titus Livy, ensued either through public or through private counsel, and either inside or outside the city, I shall begin to discourse of things occurring inside and by public counsel that I shall judge worthy of greater notice, adding to them everything that might depend on them, to which discourses this first book, or in truth this first part, will be limited.[1]

Since it is Machiavelli's intention to have Roman modes and orders imitated by his contemporaries, it should prove useful to know in some detail what Rome's domestic modes and orders were. Their examination will also afford the opportunity to review the material of book 1 without, in commentary fashion, taking every chapter in its sequential context. Where needed for completeness, pertinent material from books 2 and 3 will be considered as well.

Constitutional Orders

Some of this ground we have been over before. For instance, Rome, founded as a kingship and/or aristocratic mixed regime, evolved into a democratic mixed regime or a polity with the addition of the tribunate. Several statements attest to the democratic leanings of Rome's mixed regime. It is said in I.2.7 that "fortune was so favorable to it that although it passed from the government of kings and of aristocrats to that of the people . . . nonetheless it never took away all authority from kingly qualities so as to give authority to the aristocrats, nor did it diminish the authority of the aristocrats altogether so as to give it to the people." This is Machiavelli's concluding statement as to how Rome came by its perfect mixed regime, and in it the popular element is vouchsafed the leading role. Similarly, in I.40.5, while referring to Appius Claudius's failure to build on the people, Machiavelli professes that "if one wishes to hold a thing with violence, whoever forces needs to be more powerful than whoever is forced." In terms then of raw political power, the people also was the dominant player. When discussing the people's appetite for bold initiatives, in I.53.5, Machiavelli cautions that "there is no easier way to make a republic where the people has authority come to ruin than to put it into mighty enterprises." This admonition Machiavelli deduces from Roman politics of the Second Punic War years, the period, arguably, when the senate's authority was at its peak (I.37.2). Nevertheless, Machiavelli describes the constitution as one in which "the people has authority." He also uses the Roman constitution when defending the wisdom and constancy of a governing multitude that is shackled by law (I.58). Rome's mixed regime is thus classified as a species of popular rule. A contrary opinion is offered in III.19.1, where Machiavelli states that "the Roman plebs had equal command in Rome with the nobility." But in context the assertion of equality asserts a great deal, for Machiavelli is arguing that a commander should treat considerately soldiers who are "ordinarily partners" in the regime. Even if the plebs was the dominant partner in civilian life, and not merely equal, when in the army and outside the city, it was more like a slave, since a consul's authority on campaign was absolute. And yet on campaign it was dealt with as an equal.

We recall that Machiavelli chose the people to be the guardian of liberty and that guarding liberty meant something more than protecting class interests (I.5). Machiavelli made this choice on behalf of all cities which like Rome committed themselves to growth and expansion. Expansionary cities must employ their populations in the war effort, and so the populations must be rewarded with political power. The reasoning is from Aristotle, even though Machiavelli does not credit him—it is the argument for distributive justice:[2] However a state defines its purpose (virtue, wealth, empire), all parties making a contribution must receive rewards proportionate to their deserts, and that party making the principal contribution must be granted supreme, if not complete, power. It was just, therefore, for Rome to be a polity (I.47.1); it also was prudent, since "whoever forces needs to be more powerful than whoever is forced" (above; also I.55.5 and III.22.2).

Machiavelli provides a brief definitional description of the Roman constitution in I.18.2. There he says that the constitution, or "the order of the state," divided sovereign authority among the people, the senate, the tribunes, and the consuls; that it created magistracies and modes of electing candidates thereto; and that it established procedures for the passage of laws. Little, if any, detail is offered respecting the various assemblies, or *comitia*, in which law was made.[3] Nor does Machiavelli's review of the kingship extend to Servius Tullius,[4] the king who effected Rome's most consequential legislative reform, the organization of the *comitia centuriata*. Ordinary lawmaking, as distinguished from modes and orders imposed by founders and reformers, is of marginal interest to Machiavelli.

But the election of magistrates engages his attention somewhat more. The consuls were Rome's chief executive officers.[5] Because these offices were elective rather than hereditary, and because the elections were open and free rather than deceitful and violent, Rome had no succession problems (I.20.1). The people though chose only patricians as consuls, in part because the consul's duties included the taking of auspices, and plebeians were deemed unworthy for so sacred a task (III.33.1). Unable to win admission to the city's highest office, the plebs replaced the consulate with a diluted substitute, the military tribune with consular powers. The law ordaining this change was the *Lex Canuleia* of 445. Formally it moved the Roman regime toward a representative democracy, but in practice no plebeian candidate was elected to the post for 45 years (I.47.1; also I.39.2).

A significant part of Rome's system of checks and balances was the dispersion of power through multiple offices of short duration. Always at war, Rome had many commanders who watched and supervised one another (I.30.2). There was the danger that personal rivalry would get out of hand; and in one instance, at the siege of Veii (402 BC), two Roman commanders, Sergius and Virginius, preferred to see the army defeated rather than ask for help from or give it to the other (I.31.2). Just as class vigilance sometimes degenerated into class warfare, so individual jealousy sometimes led to criminal malfeasance and betrayal of country. But Rome had a custom which ameliorated the problem. It was to honor subordinate service on the part of former commanders. Rome recycled its talent; and the picture which Machiavelli draws is of experienced officers serving as tutors of their younger colleagues, whose sudden superiority in rank was less a mark of imperium than a test of their competence—rather like star performers of one generation going on to become the coaches of the next. Former consuls, it would appear, taught, judged, and controlled their charges, "new men" who feared to err in the sight of their masters: "For one cannot reasonably believe in the latter [the citizen who rises from a lesser rank to govern in a greater] unless one sees men around him who are of so much reverence or so much virtue that his newness can be moderated with their counsel and authority" (I.36.1). Thus did Rome provide itself with capable leaders and protect against their ambition.

In ordinary times the consulate was Rome's chief magisterial office. But in emergency situations Rome had recourse to a more effective form of executive power—the dictatorship. The dictatorship invested a single individual with the power to decide without consultation and to execute decisions without appeal. But so powerful was this office, an office designed to defend Rome more effectively against it neighbors (I.33.1), that some thought it to be a threat to Rome itself; for anyone aspiring to tyranny might find in the dictatorship the perfect vehicle for attaining his goal. Machiavelli though is of the contrary opinion: The dictatorship, he affirms, "always did good to the city" (I.34.1); "no dictator ever did anything but good to the republic" (§1); the dictatorship "always helped" (§2).

Machiavelli is determined to beef up the executive power in a republic, because, as he observes, the division of offices impedes decision-making and prevents the timely application of remedies. Republican government is ill-equipped to deal with emergencies, and either the state is true to its orders and is ruined, or it violates its orders so as to be saved. Necessity is unkind to weakness, and the divided power of a republic renders that regime weak. Thus a republic must have the means of concentrating power when necessity threatens. Machiavelli implies that the dictatorship did for executive power what the tribunate did for judicial power, for both were vital improvements that contributed to "the greatness of so great an empire" (§3).

The question is how to arm republics for their own defense without exposing their liberty to attack by these same arms. And the answer is to employ ordinary modes. The virtue of the Roman dictatorship was that it protected against necessity by ordinary—which is to say legal—means. The dictatorship was kingly prerogative under the cover of law; and it was power freely given before it was taken. It thus was a safe and ordinary means of handling the extraordinary situations served up by necessity. If extraordinary measures are instead used, even to do good, a bad example is created, and "later, under that coloring, they [the orders] are broken for ill" (§3). Such was the problem of the founder-prince in I.9.1—his crimes were an inducement to criminal conduct by others. But a dictator regularizes and legitimizes the work of the founder. Hence Machiavelli argues in effect that the Roman dictatorship was not a slippery slope leading to caesarian tyranny.

Besides the ordinary mode of institution, other conditions were met which rendered the dictatorship a valuable addition to the Roman constitution. Roman citizens were virtuous in the sense that none were very rich or had very many adherents,[6] nor would the public have given its votes to an individual so formidable as to stand above the law. And the office itself was intelligently structured. For tenure and jurisdiction were strictly limited, the first to half a year and the second to resolving the problem at hand (although power within this jurisdiction was absolute—no consultation required and no appeal of the dictator's decisions). Also the orders of the state were left mostly undisturbed—the senate, the consuls, and the tribunes continuing to operate (I.35.1)—and no authority had the dictator to change the constitution. Finally, the mode of election ensured an orderly transferal of power, for the two consuls alone composed the electorate, the reasoning being that since need for a dictator reflected negatively on the performance of the consuls, power could be safely taken from them only if they took it from themselves.

Machiavelli turns next in chapter 35 to an episode in Roman history which contradicts, as he acknowledges, the main point of chapter 34 and which contradicts, as he does not acknowledge, the main point of chapter 28. The episode is the two-year reign of the decemvirs (451-450 BC), ten men who were elected by "public and free votes" (title) to rewrite the laws of Rome but who in time "became tyrants of Rome and without any hesitation seized its freedom" (§1). In I.34 it was the authority taken by individuals, not freely given, that did harm to republics; and in I.28 it was the loyalty of Rome's leaders that explained why Rome was the least ungrateful of ancient cities. Apparently, something more was needed besides popular consent to make executive power safely republican in Rome. And apparently something more was needed besides good luck to account for Roman gratitude. But in fact institutional explanations have been provided for both; and in fact Rome made a virtue of ingratitude (I.29.3).

Taken together, the dictatorship and the decemvirate represent a case study in the proper and improper management of executive power, showing "what causes kept the dictators good and what made the Ten wicked" (§1). Seven lessons in the art of constitution-making appear in this and the previous chapter: (1) free suffrage (power given, not taken); (2) social equality (no rich patrons with clients); (3) civic virtue (suspicion, jealousy, ingratitude toward the well-to-do); (4) limited jurisdiction (meeting a particular emergency); (5) full authority within that jurisdiction ("one alone," or number); (6) supervision (other institutions to check and balance—tribunes, consuls, senate); and (7) short term of office (no more than a year).

The dictatorship "always did good to the city" because it complied with all seven requirements. The decemvirate was harmful to liberty, indeed was a tyranny, because it violated several, and these the more important. The chief mistakes made in the appointment of the decemvirs concerned numbers 4, 6, and 7 above: jurisdiction, supervision, and term of office. The decemvirs had total power over the laws of Rome, supplanting even the authority of the Roman people. They replaced the consuls and the tribunes (though not the senate) and thus were free of effective supervision. And their one-year term of office was extended by a year. Other requirements were observed, or did operate, but they proved to be of little use in stopping the movement toward tyranny. For example, the decemvirs were freely elected; but popular election, without accompanying controls on jurisdiction and tenure, was not the palliative that it had shown itself to be for the dictatorship. Also, the society was equal and the people vigilant; but this civic virtue was quickly corrupted by autocratic power. In I.34.2 it was said that the usurper "needs to be very rich and to have very many adherents and partisans" and that in a non-corrupt republic he is unlikely to have either wealth or influence. But these social conditions, as constraints upon power, simply vanish in I.35: "Nor does it help, in this case, that the matter be incorrupt; for an absolute authority corrupts the matter in a very short time and makes friends and partisans for itself. Nor is it hurt either by being poor or by not having relatives; for riches and every other favor run after it at once . . ." (§1). The orders of the state appear more important than the virtue of the people.[7] Also important is the precise combination of orders. If tenure is indefinite—and Sparta and Venice are praised despite having permanent executives—then supervision by rival institutions is imperative. If jurisdiction is indefinite and power absolute, then it is imperative that the time in office be brief.

One of the drawbacks of divided authority is the possibility that authority will remain divided and incapacitated even in the face of grave danger. Rome, it happened, was spared the necessity of being frequently ungrateful, because the dispersion of authority over many commanders kept the ambition of each in check. But there was always the risk that rival officers would indulge their jealousies at the expense of the commonweal, that a Sergius or a Virginius would imperil the army merely to injure his co-commander. Likewise there was the chance that the election of dictators by consuls—thought to be so clever because constituting in effect an act of self-inflicted ingratitude and because, in Machiavelli's words, "wounds and every other ill that a man does to himself spontaneously and by choice hurt much less than those that are done to you by someone else" (I.34.4)—there was the chance that this mode of election would fail. And in fact it once did, for the consuls of 431, hopelessly deadlocked, "were in accord only in not wishing to create the dictator" which the senate requested (I.50.1). Divided power proved to be as much a problem as it was a solution. But a remedy presented itself, for the tribunes intervened, with the senate's blessing, and forced the consuls to name a dictator. Normally the role of the tribunate was to check "the ambition that the powerful used against the plebs" (§1), as well as, in less specified ways, to guard the liberty of the city. But this intervention into a dispute between nobles was an enlargement of the tribunes' authority, one which helped the mixed regime of Rome to function more smoothly.

When the tribunate was first created, in 494, its responsibility was to protect the plebs from the judicial might of patrician magistrates. But it was not long before the tribunes went on the offensive, taking for themselves the power of accusation. This accusatory power allowed the plebs to purge its wrath against individuals just as the establishment of the tribunate allowed it to purge its class ambition (I.4.1). The argument is this: Vengeance is better satisfied through public than private means, for public force (a system of criminal justice) has stopping points (verdicts and punishments) whereas private vendettas are unending. In the absence of courts and prosecutors, aggrieved people become vigilantes. But what looks like justice to the aggrieved looks like injustice to their opponents—who are offended, who fear for their lives and property, who look about for allies by which to protect themselves, who thus create partisans and divide the city into parties; the parties conspire, they fight, and the loser, rather than accept defeat, turns to outsiders for assistance (I.7). When recounting the cycle of regimes (I.2.3), Machiavelli supposed the process to be a short one, since a city weakened by internal division would soon be conquered by it neighbors. We see now the reason why.

Rome had internal divisions, the two humors of nobles and plebs, but Rome was not weakened by their differences because their differences were adjudicated by the ordinary modes of law. The Roman mixed regime was a government under law (I.58). Now one tenet of the rule of law is that no one is above the law or that the law applies to all citizens equally. All enjoy its protections and all suffer its penalties, regardless of status or of past merit. Rome began this practice under its kings, for it was during the reign of Tullus Hostilius (672-642 BC) that Horatius was prosecuted for the murder of his sister. Horatius was one of three brothers who fought a duel with the Alban Curiatii to determine which city, Alba or Rome, would dominate the other. As the lone survivor, Horatius was the cause of Rome's victory and thus a national hero. But on returning from the contest, he encountered and killed his sister because she dared to weep for one of the dead Curiatii who was her betrothed (I.22.1). Horatius was duly charged with homicide and brought to trial; for which reason some critics, who consider superficially, condemn the Romans for their ingratitude. But Machiavelli sees the matter differently: The Roman public is to be commended for having prosecuted Horatius, their savior, since "no well-ordered republic ever cancels the demerits with the merits of its citizens" (I.24.1). Nevertheless, the Roman public is to be censured for having absolved Horatius of any blame. It seems that the same result transpired when Quintus Fabius was prosecuted by the dictator Papirius Cursor, under whom Quintus served as master of horse (325 BC). Fabius was successful in battle against the Samnites, but by engaging the enemy he violated his commander's explicit instructions; and Papirius wanted him punished as a way of defending the good orders of the Roman military (III.36.2). At the trial Quintus's father maintained that the Roman people had never dealt so harshly with defeated captains as Papirius now wished to do with his victorious lieutenant (I.31.2). Indeed, it had not punished Horatius, several centuries earlier; and its general policy was to treat with leniency its failed commanders, punishing lightly those who erred due to malice (Sergius and Virginius) while punishing not at all those who erred due to ignorance. In the case of Varro, defeated by Hannibal at Cannae (216 BC), Rome in fact honored him for returning to Rome and not despairing of Roman things (I.31.2). Of course there is sense and justice to a policy which, when it forgives failure, does not then punish success; and the father of Quintus stressed the inconsistency that lay behind the dictator's determination to punish his master of horse. But Machiavelli is critical of Roman leniency carried this far. The rule of law requires that

> having ordered rewards for a good work and punishments for a bad one, and having rewarded one for having worked well, if that same one later works badly, it punishes him without any regard for his good works. . . . For if a citizen has done some outstanding work for the city, and on top of the reputation that this thing brings him, he has an audacity and confidence that he

can do some work that is not good without fearing punishment, in a short time he will become so insolent that any civility will be dissolved. (I.24.1)

It seems then that political considerations partly explain why the rule of law makes no exceptions and is stubbornly blind to outcomes. For victorious commanders, even if deserving of reward, represent a threat to republican freedom and need to be diminished in stature for the society's good; whereas defeated commanders, even if deserving of punishment, pose no threat to the regime and can be safely treated with kindness.[8]

The courts which heard the cases of Horatius and Quintus Fabius were popular tribunals. Horatius was judged by the Roman people, not by its king, who, in Livy, appointed special magistrates to render the guilty verdict and then invited the plaintiff to appeal the verdict to the people (Livy, I.26). The right of appeal, established in the early days of the republic by Publius Valerius Publicola (Livy, II.8), but seemingly previewed here during the reign of King Tullus, was what caused most cases to be tried by the people. Machiavelli observes that a second feature of a well-ordered judiciary, in addition to accusation as an ordinary mode, is a court composed of numerous judges able to stand up to "the ambition of powerful citizens," for "the few always behave in the mode of the few" (I.7.4) and are "always ministers of the few and of the most powerful" (I.49.3). Popular courts fulfill this function, while at the same time relieving the rulers of the odium which comes from sitting in judgment (II.21.2, III.22.3; *Prince*, 19). And while the courts in Rome were well-ordered because "one could appeal to the people ordinarily," they also were well-ordered because the judicial power could quickly revert to executive hands "if indeed an important thing did occur in which to defer the execution during the appeal was dangerous." At such moments Romans "had the refuge of the dictator, who executed immediately" (I.49.3).

Emergencies and political considerations are the reason why ordinary modes sometimes are not enough and why extraordinary, extra-legal, and even criminal punishments sometimes are needed. Punishment is a judicial act in relation to the individual, but it is a political or an executive act in relation to the society ("execute" having the double meaning of "to kill" and "to carry out").[9] For Machiavelli, the executive is invested with extraordinary judicial power because sensational punishments are one way in which the state is returned to its origins and made good again. Rome was witness to numerous such executions—political trials we might say—wherein the individual malefactor was punished less for his guilt than for the moral betterment of the public. The sons of Brutus conspired against the newly formed republic and were rightly punished for their treason. But it was for shock effect that their father sat on the tribunal and was present for their deaths (III.3.1). Likewise the beheading of Titus Manlius at his father's command had the effect of terrifying the troops into obedience and "was the cause of the victory that the Roman people had against the Latins"

(III.22.4; Livy, VIII.7-8). Machiavelli explains as follows the logic behind judicial violence:

> Because they [executions] were excessive and notable, such things made men draw back toward the mark whenever one of them arose; and when they began to be more rare, they also began to give more space to men to corrupt themselves and to behave with greater danger and more tumult. For one should not wish ten years at most to pass from one to another of such executions; for when this time is past, men begin to vary in their customs and to transgress the laws. Unless something arises by which punishment is brought back to their memory and fear is renewed in their spirits, soon so many delinquents join together that they can no longer be punished without danger. (III.1.3)

As it happened, Rome did not keep to the decennial schedule which Machiavelli here sets; and so Rome, from time to time, was faced with the prospect of administering mass punishments (III.49).

The dictatorship was one office through which punishments were inflicted and order maintained. Another was the censorship, an office established in 443. The purpose of the censorship was modest enough—as the name would indicate, to take a new census of the population (work long overdue at the time of the office's creation and by then too tedious a burden for consuls busy with war). Despite these trivial origins, and in confirmation of Machiavelli's maxim that "titles do not give luster to men, but men to titles" (III.38.1),[10] the censorship grew into an important magistracy with power to determine membership in Rome's propertied classes, to remove as punishment individuals from the senatorial order and the centuries of knights, to manage some state revenues, and to decide the location of buildings, both public and private (Livy, IV.8). In due course, notes Machiavelli, the censors became "arbiters of the customs of Rome" and "were a very powerful cause why the Romans delayed more in corrupting themselves" (I.49.1). Specifically they guarded the republic, along with the tribunes and certain laws, "against the ambition and insolence of men" (III.1.3), watching to see that individuals did not "do evil under the shadow of good" (I.46.1); and they protected the regime from slow-moving, demographic change (III.49.4). But Machiavelli does not emphasize the role played by the censors, and when he does speak of the office, it is mainly to discuss the problems that it caused. For it was ill-made in the beginning, with an overlong term of office; and efforts nine years later to reduce the term from five years to 18 months, while successful, cost the reforming dictator, Mamercus Aemilius, his seat in the senate, his tribal membership, his eligibility for office, and much of his property (I.49.1; Livy, IV.24); and a century and a third after that, another censor, Appius Claudius Caecus, was still not willing to accept the reduction in tenure (III.46.1).

Social Classes

The first thing to be noted about Roman society of the early republican period is that it was divided by classes, and that these classes viewed each other
with suspicion and hostility. Rome was composed of two cities, in effect—one
consisting of patricians, the other of plebeians.[11] But then Machiavelli takes it as
axiomatic that "two diverse humors," the people and the great, make up the
population of all cities (I.4.1); and so he is accepting of the divisions in Rome
and of the tumults that ensued from a politically active populace. The question
he asks is whether it was necessary for Rome to have a populace which exercised its citizenship. The question he fails to ask—at least with comparable ex-
plicitness—is whether it was necessary to have a great, named patricians and set
apart legally, who exerted influence through the institution of a senate. We detected the question and inferred a reply from the analysis of Rome's "right way"
(*diritta via*) toward perfection as against Athens's hapless meanderings through
the cycle. Even so, Machiavelli does not entertain the possibility that Rome—
say, after the fall of the Tarquins—could have done away with the patrician-
plebeian class distinction. He does not, although his friend and patron, Guicciardini, does. Guicciardini attributes the animosity of Rome's classes to the legal
separation of patricians and plebeians and to the patrician monopolization of
offices. A class-based senate, he suggests, was harmful to Rome as was the senate's slow letting go of authority, for it was these two mistakes which caused the
creation of the tribunate and the steady augmentation of its powers—and it was
the tribunate which disturbed the peace most of all.[12] Since Machiavelli is
mainly silent on this subject, we can only guess—and somewhat as before—that
his uncritical stance toward Rome's divisions is due to the belief that the classes,
as humors, are inevitable; that they mostly are irrational, self-absorbed, and deaf
to the remonstrances of their counterpart;[13] that only with legally established
class identities can the humors defend their interests; and that the alternative to
such defense is the defeat of one humor by the other and the consequent alteration of simple regimes along the cycle. It may also be the case that Machiavelli
wishes to keep the differences between classes clear and distinct because their
unlike characters are alternately useful to the regime;[14] having "diverse citizens
and diverse humors" is an advantage to republics, he argues in III.9.1. On the
other hand, formalized class division was where Rome began, not where Rome
ended; and it may be the case that Machiavelli welcomes the changes in Roman
society as much as he approves of the original plan. The question, to be considered later, is when Rome reached its constitutional perfection and when Rome
began its decline.

A second feature of Roman society, and one seemingly at odds with the
first, was the poverty of its citizens and the rough equality of their wealth. Despite the division into patricians and plebeians, Roman citizens were sufficiently
equal and poor for a civil way of life to exist among them. Thus Rome's patri-

cians were not the equivalent of the titled nobles of medieval and Renaissance Europe, men who "command from a castle and have subjects who obey them" (I.55.4). The gentlemen of Venice make a better comparison, for the title of "gentleman" (*gentiluomo*) was a nominal dignity conferring no special jurisdiction over others. Also, Venetian gentlemen had exclusive control over the offices of state, as did the patricians for many years. But then these gentlemen possessed "great riches . . . founded in trade and movable things," whereas the patricians of Rome were landowners and were at one point barred from trade.[15] On the other hand, Roman patricians may have had "great incomes from possessions" (as said of the Venetians [§6])—for it is hard to know just how poor the Romans actually were.[16] Machiavelli concedes that Rome was not perfectly ordered with respect to the agrarian law and the social equality it intended to impose, that "either it [the law] was not made at the beginning so that it did not have to be treated again every day; or they delayed so much in making it because looking back might be scandalous; or if it was well ordered at first, it had been corrupted later by use" (I.37.1). It seems that agrarian legislation (maximums on personal landholdings and equal distribution of captured territory [§2]) is the preferred way "to keep the public rich and [the] citizens poor" (§1); but other ways are acceptable second-best remedies if "looking back might be scandalous." Rome's other way came from the mores of a timocratic culture which caused Romans to love honor more than wealth. The legendary example is that of Lucius Quintius Cincinnatus who in 458 was called from "plowing his small villa, which did not surpass a limit of four *jugera*" (three and a third acres) and made dictator of Rome in order to save an army which was then under siege. Unable to attribute to agrarian legislation the deference paid to this poor but talented citizen, Machiavelli instead observes that one cannot "believe that any greater order produced this effect other than seeing that the way to any rank whatever and to any honor whatever was not prevented for you because of poverty, and that one went to find virtue in whatever house it inhabited" (III.25.1). Because Rome was timocratic in outlook, no presumption existed equating wealth with virtue. And so, when Cincinnatus completed his job as dictator, he returned to the small property which was barely sufficient to nourish him. But Machiavelli fails to mention a salient detail in the life of Cincinnatus. This noble Roman was impoverished, not because he loved honor only, but because he made bail for his criminal son, Caeso, who then fled Rome rather than appear for trial (Livy, III.13). Rome may have sought out "virtue in whatever house it inhabited," but that does not mean that those dwelling within these humble abodes resided there by choice.[17] Nor was it the case that only in the republic's dotage and as a consequence of its corruption did Roman patricians have citizens privately subject to them; for the patron-client relationship, so called, was a part of Roman society from the days of the kings[18] (even though Machiavelli gives no hint of its long lineage).[19] Rome was not Sparta. Imperialism brought Rome great wealth; and the most that can be said about citizens kept equal and poor is that a timocratic ethos, caused by the city's many wars (III.16.2), prevented the regime from quickly succumbing to oligarchic temptations.

Civil Religion

The five chapters from I.11 to I.15 make up the section on Roman religion.[20] These chapters teach us: (1) that religion is the glue of society and is important to national success; (2) that religion is untrue but politically useful to the extent that the rulers feign belief and manipulate the rites; (3) that the control of the plebeian population is the primary use of religion; and (4) that religion used militarily is helpful but of less certain value.

It was Numa, the second Roman king (715-672 BC), who ordered Rome's religion. Numa thus shared with Romulus the honor of founding by adding to warlike Rome the civilizing "arts of peace" (I.11.1). Or so it seems. The strange thing is that religion, as Machiavelli presents it, is a preparation for war more than a cultivation of peace.[21] Religion's purpose is to tame ferocious spirits, to make them obedient and thus useful for achieving the enterprises of state. "As the observance of the divine cult is the cause of the greatness of republics," says Machiavelli, "so disdain for it is the cause of their ruin" (§4). Religion serves the end of greatness, less so of liberty. Religion disciplines the people by causing them to fear the punishments of God. Livy makes many of the same points about the religion Numa introduced in Rome, that it tamed and disciplined and filled the populace with fear. But he adds a detailed account of the calendar and priestly offices created by Numa and concludes that the task of propitiating the gods became so intricate and complicated that it gave the Romans something besides war with which to occupy themselves (Livy, I.21).[22] Because divine intervention was ultimately determinative of success or failure, the rites and rituals that promised divine favor and averted divine wrath were more important to Rome than military training. Machiavelli accepts that the Romans took their religion seriously, but this complicated, time-consuming system of appeasement he reduces in I.11 to just an oath. And in the examples he supplies, oath-taking is hasty, not deliberate; and it fosters patriotism and advances the cause of war, though not necessarily justice and the rule of law.

Machiavelli, then, diminishes somewhat the stark differences separating warlike Romulus from peaceloving Numa. This alteration helps if we are looking for Numa to reform inside, not outside, the orders of Romulus. What hurts, however, is the imputed rivalry between Rome's first two kings. We have noted before the mutuality of interest binding founders and reformers together, how sharing and mending are helpful to them both. But rather than build upon the theme of continuity and cooperation, Machiavelli sets Romulus against Numa in a contest for glory. (Of course he did the same with Rome and Sparta, emphasizing their rivalry for the title of best-founded republic while only hinting at their similarities and the need for each to be more like the other.) Machiavelli wants to know which prince provided Rome the greater benefaction, Romulus who armed Rome or Numa who civilized it. Machiavelli chooses Numa on grounds that introducing religion where there are arms is more difficult than introducing arms where there is religion.[23] Numa did the former, and Romulus did. . . . Well, he didn't exactly do the latter since there was no organized religion existing when he introduced arms to Rome. Romulus is not placed in exact opposition to Numa, and so Numa's superior ranking is a little uncertain. What Machiavelli argues is that the task facing Numa was the more difficult since Numa had to appeal to divine authority. But later Machiavelli says that the "times were full of religion," that the "men with whom [Numa] had to labor were crude," that their crudeness "made much easier the carrying out of his designs," and that Numa "could easily [*facilmente*] impress any new form whatever on them" (§3). So how difficult was it to give religion to Rome?[24]

It may not have been difficult, given the gullibility of the Roman people, but the job did require that Numa be alone in power. Orderers of religions, unlike orderers of senates, are extraordinary legislators. They have recourse to God because "a prudent individual knows many goods that do not have in themselves evident reasons with which one can persuade others" (§3). But this explanation is identical to the one given by Machiavelli for why a founding prince has to be "one alone," that "many are not capable of ordering a thing because they do not know its good" (I.9.2). How different then is the religious founder if it was Numa's "goodness and prudence," not his conversation with a nymph, which caused the Roman people to yield "to his every decision" (§3)?[25] Machiavelli offers a human explanation for the success of religious orders. He thus plants the suggestion that human authority underwrites divine authority even though it is the very opposite which he asserts.

The founding prince, we have heard it said, is alone through violence—fratricide in the case of Romulus. The religious founder, at least in the case of Numa, is alone without violence. Divine revelation appears to provide a nonviolent avenue to power. But we question how independent of Romulus's violence and of Romulus's arms Numa truly was. Machiavelli uses Friar Girolamo Savonarola as the modern-day counterpart to Numa. Savonarola gave extraordinary laws to sophisticated Florentines, proving thereby that either the Florentines were not so sophisticated after all, or that modern men, whatever the level of sophistication, can imitate ancient simplicity.[26] But Savonarola was a failure, the "unarmed prophet" of *Prince* 6 who came to a bad end because he could not compel when his followers ceased to believe. Machiavelli says that it is more difficult to introduce religion where there are arms than arms where there is religion; but if extraordinary laws require for their institution not only recourse to God, but recourse by a prophet who is armed, then Numa's task was made easier by having the arms of Romulus at his disposal, that is, by being king in a city founded by Romulus.[27] Another reason for doubting Machiavelli's claim (a claim which tries to lift Numa above Romulus) is that it contradicts what Machiavelli says in *Prince* 12, that "there cannot be good laws where there are not good arms, and where there are good arms there must be good laws." What's more, Numa, in chapter 19, is conclusively demoted in rank; for there he is described as little better than a parasite living off the reputation of his virtuous predecessor. Rome was fortunate with Numa, not because he gave it religion (although that benefaction is again said to be necessary), but because Rome rid itself of him before lasting damage was done, and because his successor, Tullus Hostilius, was of a different temperament altogether. Tullus is praised in chapter 21 for restoring "in a stroke" military virtue to Rome after 40 years of indolent rule; and he is used to demonstrate what "is more true than any other truth that if where there are men there are not soldiers, it arises through a defect of the prince and not through any other defect, either of the site or of nature" (§1). By this account Numa was doubly defective since he failed not only to make Romans soldiers but even to keep up the virtue of Romans who had been made soldiers by another. Any prince, it appears, associated with peace, is weak and effeminate; at best he is fortunate if ensconced between warlike princes who alone are called virtuous. Rome did benefit from religion, but because religion made Romans obedient to authority, not because it civilized them through the arts of peace. After all, it is uncivilized mountain men who provide the best material for republican government, not "those who are used to living in cities, where civilization is corrupt"; for "a sculptor," says Machiavelli, "will get a beautiful statue more easily from coarse marble than from one badly blocked out by another" (I.11.3).[28]

Although religion provided Numa and other extraordinary lawgivers with monarchical power, religion itself is not monarchic nor does it serve only to make the city great. Here we return to liberty and republicanism. Religion, understood as the fear of God, produces civil obedience. Without religion it falls to the prince to exact this obedience by inspiring this fear. It is not as if Machiavelli worries that the prince is unequal to the task. The problem rather is that princes die, and if all depends on the prince's virtue, then the death of the prince will mean the death of his state. Human mortality would not present so grave a danger if virtuous princes had only virtuous sons. Hereditary succession would then enable the prince to preserve both his power and his orders. But nature does not provide for a race of virtuous kings; also, God is against it—or so the quotation from Dante implies. For lest human beings come to forget the source of their virtue, God sees to it that probity rarely descends by the branches. God distributes virtue widely in order to keep human beings grateful and submissive, roughly equal to each other but decidedly inferior to himself. God, it seems, is a self-interested republican!

Accordingly, the temptation must be resisted to hold onto power until the very end, trusting that hereditary succession will keep one's orders intact. Princes become wise when made to contemplate their own mortality and the deficiencies of their offspring. They become wiser still when they agree to reduce their own significance and to share authority with other elements of society. It is important then that the prince's virtue be institutionalized and that fear of the prince be supplemented by fear of God. Religion supplies this fear, continuous fear, which causes the population continuously to obey. And insofar as religion's power is internal, with oaths more restraining than laws, the citizens, policing themselves, become somewhat their own masters, and the regime becomes somewhat democratic. Religion is democratic when viewed against the alternative of princely coercion.

Religion also is a hidden cause of obedience. Its punishments are not visible and immediate like the punishments of the law. The hiddenness of religious restraint allows the people to suppose itself freely good and thus virtuous. Religion works that side of republicanism that depends on trust and goodness; religion creates community. It refutes that side of republicanism that depends on suspicion and selfishness and that breeds faction. But the fact that religion hides its punishments and restraints means that religion, like custom, is a corruptible cause of goodness.

We were a bit hasty in supposing that the Roman religion, in the hands of Machiavelli, reduced to oath-taking and the fear of God. For Machiavelli adds in chapter 12 that oracular predictions and hope for the future constituted the foundation and defining principle of Rome's religion. Romans, and pagans generally, believed that the God who could predict the future could also bring it about; thus the purpose of pagan faith was the control of one's future, both personal and communal. Machiavelli also allows that toward this end of controlling the future the Romans constructed temples; developed sacrifices, supplications, and ceremonies; and made sacred the oracles. But never does Machiavelli suggest that through these labors the Roman population shifted its concern from war to peace. On the contrary, the paganism of the ancients caused their cities to be healthy and strong, whereas the Christianity of the moderns causes their cities to be corrupt and weak. Expansion through strength continues to be an objective, but so is unity and self-rule.

One lesson of the chapter is that religious conviction in the populace requires the pretense of belief among the rulers. Before it was the case (although Machiavelli gave us reason to doubt) that the wise needed the authority of religion if their laws were to be obeyed; now it is the case that religion needs the support of the wise if its tenets are to be believed. In particular those who are "more knowing of natural things" are to give credence to miracles and oracular predictions, even to the rank superstitions of the people (§1). Furius Camillus is Machiavelli's example. He was the Roman victor at Veii who promised and then dedicated a temple to Queen Juno, the reigning Veientian deity (396 BC). His actions encouraged piety in his troops who asked the statue of Juno if she wished to be removed to Rome. The statue nodded and spoke her assent—or so thought the credulous troops.

It is noteworthy that division in Rome was not just between the nobles and plebs but also between the wise and the ignorant. In some ways this second division is more unbridgeable and disruptive than the first. For how can those "more knowing of natural things" live as friends and equals with those who believe in speaking statues?[29] To be sure, Machiavelli will explain how (an explanation which reinforces the importance of hiddenness); but the impression continues that Rome—and not just Rome—consisted of two populations radically unlike. The other impression is that all religions are equally false, equally superstitious, and equally silly in their reliance upon miracles; that the revelation to Moses by the God of the Burning Bush is as fictional an event as Numa's commerce with Egeria the nymph. And the connection between pagan and Judeo-Christian belief is hard to miss, for Machiavelli next counsels Christian princes to be as supportive of the orders of Christianity as Camillus was supportive of the popular superstitions of paganism.

How do matters now stand with religion? It has been shown that paganism made the Roman people fearful and obedient, if not exactly peaceloving; that it hid the cause of its fear, in the sense that God is less visible than a prince, and so nurtured the roots of civic virtue and republican self-government; that it helped to accomplish the enterprises of the senate by using oracular predictions to instill confidence in the city's armies; and that it succeeded in its double mission of conquest and unity because the political class, the senate, was too clever to believe in religion but disciplined enough to say that it did.

Clearly, religion was a means for effecting social solidarity and mitigating the antagonism of the classes. Law was another means as were the rhetorical interventions of dignified and reputable individuals. Machiavelli has chosen Rome over Sparta, but he is ever mindful of the difficulty that a democratic mixed regime has in holding itself together. The title of chapter 13 remembers the problem and scandal of tumults in Rome, and it looks to religion for a cure.

And what then was the nature of this cure? Deception was its nature; the people was deceived into believing that it had no interest apart from the common interest which the senate could be trusted to defend. Religion was a tool used effectively by the nobility to make it appear that Rome was one community with a single common good. That appearance, however, depended on the suppression and manipulation of the plebs, who, when suitably duped: (1) elected an all-patrician slate of military tribunes; (2) persisted with a siege and conquered Veii; (3) backed away from a law to codify the consulate and to limit its powers (the Terentillian law of 462-61 [I.39.2]); and (4) put down a slave revolt and obeyed a new consul even though its oath was to his predecessor. In all cases portents, Sybilline books, and oaths were used to move the people to accomplish these "enterprises" of the senate.

Machiavelli observed in chapter 12 that Roman religion lent itself to abuse, that oracles could be induced "to speak in the mode of the powerful" (§1). Chapter 13 gives evidence that Rome's rulers did in fact use religion to promote their class's advantage. Having allowed, reluctantly, the creation of military tribunes with consular power (an office instituted in 445 to replace the consulate and continued until 367 when the consulate was restored), and having watched as a plebeian finally was elected to the post (Publius Licinius Calvus, elected in 400), "the nobles," says Machiavelli, "used the opportunity in the next creation of tribunes to say that the gods were angry because Rome had used the majesty of its empire badly, and there was no other remedy for placating the gods other than to return the election of tribunes to its place"(§1).[30] Machiavelli worried in I.12 that such self-interested use of religion would cause the oracles to be exposed, cause the people to become incredulous, and cause good orders to be disturbed. In I.13 the oracles (or their equivalent) are exposed; for the people's tribunes (not military tribunes) exposed those persons encharged with consulting the Sybilline books. (The books, says Machiavelli, were "made to respond" [§2].) Already, it seems, the religious orders were unraveling—even if, on the occasion, the people ignored the tribunes and fell in line behind the magistrates. And that these orders would unravel is easy to see. For if religion is a fraud, then those in power will use religion to defraud. No more can nobles be trusted to use religion for the common good only than can plebs be counted on to remain forever stupid and inert. We remember the warning that hidden causes of goodness are in fact hidden malignities, which for the sake of the common good are best brought out into the light of day. Is religion though a special case? Machiavelli seems to welcome the duplicity of nobles (fraud is required for the system to work), and he leaves undisturbed the credulity of plebs (unless his revealing the insincerity of rulers is meant to awaken the ruled from its slumber). All that we can say now for sure—and have said already—is that religion is the reverse of tumult in the relations between classes.

Having previously stated that the oracles provided the foundation of Rome's pagan faith, Machiavelli extends this honor in chapter 14 to auguries and auspices.[31] But then these various means of divining the future all served the same one purpose, "to make the soldiers go confidently into the fight, from which confidence victory almost always arose" (§3). The secret of achieving desirable results was for the military authorities to show proper respect for religion without permitting religion ever to be in command. At the Battle of Aquilonia (293 BC) both conditions were met.

Papirius Cursor judged the time right for attacking the Samnites, but he needed a favorable auspice from the chicken-men, the *aruspici*, in order to inspire the troops. Apparently, predictions of victory were not too difficult to secure, since pecking chickens were a good omen and since hungry chickens typically peck. Nevertheless, chickens can be obdurate, and on the occasion they failed to do as Papirius bid. The head chicken-man, however, came to the rescue; he "corrected" the auspice and sent word to Papirius that the gods were on his side. The Roman system, we now understand, relied upon a cooperative clergy as well as upon hypocritical generals—the union of church and state, but also the subordination of church to state. Unfortunately, news of the deception leaked out, first to a few soldiers, who told Papirius's nephew, who then reported to Papirius that the divine go-ahead had never been given. The consul's reply was that the auspice still was good for himself and for the army, and that if the chicken-man lied, the punishment would fall solely upon him. In order to ensure that the chicken-man would incur this punishment and that the army would be purged of all fault, Papirius commanded that the chicken-men be placed in the front ranks where their head, "by chance," was, by a Roman javelin, promptly killed (§2). Machiavelli commends Papirius's judicious use of religion which combined deference to its forms with control of its substance; and he blames the contrasting example of Appius Pulcher, half a century later, who threw his unobliging chickens overboard.

Let's consider now some of the difficulties. The killing of the chicken-man, with the explanation that he was a liar and divinely punished, made it publicly known that the auspice was against the battle. And yet the battle was fought and won. A prediction which affected the whole army (defeat) was allowed to come true with respect to one individual only (death). But would such an outcome be intelligible to the soldiers and supportive of their faith? And even if the soldiers somehow were satisfied, the chicken-men must have been a little unnerved; for if death was to be their reward for subordinating religion to military necessity, they would think twice about cooperating in the future. Finally this: Machiavelli concludes the chapter by noting that foreigners used religion as well. But how long will predictions of victory sustain the confidence of an army when its foe is sustained by predictions of its own? Perhaps we should regard religion then as a cheap form of confidence-building (holy men predicting favorable outcomes), which, because it is available to everyone, is no more than partially effective for anyone.

That armies other than Rome's could have recourse to religion is a point established in chapter 15. The Samnites, often defeated by Rome, tried reviving an ancient oath in order to induce obstinacy in their soldiers. Since it is still the Battle of Aquilonia which provides Machiavelli his example, we have a chance to see how the two sides used religion to prepare for war.

To use religion well, as the chapter calls for, is, apparently, to use it as did the Romans, the victors at Aquilonia. The Romans used religion to inspire confidence; by contrast the Samnites used it to instill fear (although Roman religion had its fearful side, too [I.11.4]). The Romans used religion always; the Samnites used it as an "extreme remedy" (title) and last resort. Nevertheless, the Samnites thought that "no better means than religion" were available to them and that they could have no other refuge; the Romans, on the other hand, placed greater faith in their own virtue. The Romans expected to win because of many past victories, and religion confirmed their confidence; the Samnites expected to lose because of many past defeats, and religion compounded their fear—"of citizens, gods, and enemies at the same time" (§1). The Roman leaders managed

religion, professing belief in portents while acting on the basis of military judgment; the Samnite leaders, determined to defend liberty, substituted religion for
forces of their own or of their allies. At the same time, the Roman consul,
Papirius Cursor, depreciated the value of religion, telling his troops that oaths do
not produce victories; the Samnites made a spectacle of oath-taking and of fancy
uniforms.

Machiavelli returns to the subject of religion as a morale-booster in III.33.
In a treatment highly detailed but dependent on other accounts (I.12, I.14,
III.12-14), he stipulates: first, that the soldiers "be armed and well ordered";
second, that the soldiers be native-born and familiar with one another; and third,
that the captain inspire confidence by showing himself to be ordered, solicitous,
spirited, and dignified. Regarding the last of these qualities, the captain defends
the majesty of his rank by punishing his soldiers when they err, by avoiding
useless exercises which squander his soldiers' strength, by keeping promises
made to them, by taking easy routes to victory (if they are available), and by
concealing difficulties which lie off in the distance. An additional method of
confidence-building, and the one associated with Rome, requires that officials
show punctilious respect for the rites and ceremonies of religion.

Machiavelli makes it seem as if the Romans utilized religion almost to the
exclusion of the other modes listed. Says Machiavelli: "The Romans used to
make their armies pick up this confidence by way of religion"; also, "For in
these little things [of religion] is the force for holding the soldiers united and
confident, which thing is the first cause of every victory" (§1). The "little
things" include consulting the auspices before electing consuls, conscripting an
army, marching forth on campaign, and coming to battle. Favorable auspices
proved to the troops that the gods were on their side and that victory would be
theirs. If a consul failed to heed the auspices, as did Claudius Pulcher in the First
Punic War (I.14.3), the Romans punished him severely, whether he failed or
succeeded. An ancestor of this Claudius, Appius Claudius Crassus, lectured the
people of Rome on the singular importance of respecting the auspices, even
though depending on chickens to reveal the future might seem like a silly superstition or a "little thing." Appius Claudius, as Machiavelli describes him, was a
most pious man; and such piety, Machiavelli declares, was the foundation of all
Roman confidence. But we know from Livy that Appius Claudius was more
partisan than devout, that he invoked religious scruples in order to keep the consulate a patrician preserve (no plebeian should be a consul, he argued, because
only patricians could fulfill the consul's religious duty of taking the auspices
[Livy, VI.41]). We know also from Machiavelli's next example that Roman
commanders were capable of sidestepping the "little things" of religion when
they threatened to undermine the army's confidence. For instance, when the
Praenestians encamped on the river Allia (380 BC), thinking the site a place of
ill omen for the Romans who once suffered there ignominious defeat at the
hands of the French (Gauls) (390 BC), the dictator, Titus Quintius Cincinnatus,

commanded his master of horse to attack the middle of the line, "trusting in arms and spirit." And Machiavelli adds that "true virtue does not fear every least accident" and that "a true virtue, a good order, a security taken from so many victories, cannot be eliminated with the things of little moment" (§1). Apparently, the "little things" of religion, so vital to Roman morale, have become "the things of little moment," ignored when inconvenient—for belief that clucking chickens communicate divine instructions is no less a superstition than the belief that certain places are unlucky. Strauss observes that religion is differently treated depending on the audience being addressed, that Claudius was speaking to a popular assembly and Cincinnatus to a fellow patrician.[32] Certainly the Roman ruling class harbored doubts not fully shared by the populace. (Sebastian de Grazia relates that "Cato the Censor could not see how in Rome two diviners could pass each other on the street without grinning.")[33] Skepticism Machiavelli expects, and professions of piety he advises. But the problem that existed in I.14, of a battle fought and won without an approving auspice, is effectively repeated here in III.33; for it could not have escaped the notice of the soldiers that they were indeed fighting at the river Allia. Livy reports that July 18 commemorated a double disaster for Rome, the death of the Fabii at Cremera (479 BC) and the defeat of the army at Allia, and that the date, named the Day of Allia, was a day of ill omen (Livy, VI.1). Allia belonged among the "little things" of religion and not only among "every least accident." (Machiavelli commends the Praenestians for exploiting Rome's superstitious fears.) Nevertheless, says Livy elsewhere, the army was not unnerved by the battle's location since it was certain that the Latin enemy it had once beaten at Lake Regillus (496 BC) was still its inferior a century later (Livy, VI.28). In other words, the army, too, trusted more in its virtue than in its religion.[34] This same conclusion was drawn from the religion chapters (I.11-15), and it is supported by Machiavelli's next example, that of a Roman army's fighting to victory despite the incompetence of its two captains (Publius and Gaius Manlius [379 BC]). Order, discipline, and the habit of winning sustained the army in this moment of trial; religion was not a factor. The last example, that of Fabius Rullianus in Tuscany (310 BC),[35] reaffirms the captain's contribution (lest it be thought that his troops are more important [III.13]), since it was by Fabius's promise of secret advantages that the army screwed up its courage. In sum, Machiavelli's position on the "little things" of religion is that "virtue must accompany these things; otherwise they have no value" (III.33.1).

Further evidence that religion is merely a supplementary source of courage can be found in II.16. The chapter begins with the announcement that the Battle of Veseris during the Great Latin War was the most important battle Rome ever fought (340 BC). That was so because the Latins were the equal of Rome, and had they prevailed at Veseris (and at Trifanum), they would have become Rome's master just as Rome by prevailing became the master of the Latins. Machiavelli is struck by how similar the two peoples were in language, customs, and military virtue; and he postulates, in accordance with Livy, that the victory went to Rome because of the superiority of its commanders. Manlius Torquatus and Publius Decius, co-consuls for Rome, kept firm the spirits of their troops by performing extraordinary acts of personal sacrifice. The former killed his son for disobeying an order, while the latter killed himself. But it is interesting that Machiavelli would report as a suicide what in Livy is presented as a solemn religious ceremony—the ritual know as "devotion." (Decius put on special robes and chanted special prayers then rushed headlong into the enemy's ranks all in an effort to expiate by his death the anger of the gods [Livy, VIII.9].) Not only is the commander's virtue more important to victory than the virtue of the soldiers, but neither's virtue is ascribed to religious conviction; nor is it said that the Latins shared with the Romans a common faith, for the two peoples were alike, notes Machiavelli, "in language, order, and arms" (§1).

Obstinacy is what causes armies to prevail; and armies are made obstinate by commanders who impose necessities on their own troops while removing like necessities from the troops of the enemy:

> Because of this they [commanders] often opened the way to the enemy that they could have closed to it, and to their own soldiers they closed that which they could have left open. Thus he who desires either that a city be defended obstinately or that an army in the field engage in combat obstinately ought to contrive above every other thing to put such necessity in the breasts of whoever has to engage in combat. (III.12.1)

Obstinacy can also be induced by badgering compatriots into becoming complicit in one's own crimes. Rebel leaders, fearing selective punishment in the event of failure—and fearing abandonment for that very reason—seek safety in numbers by inciting the multitude to commit some new offense (III.32.1). Because people expect to suffer the penalty that appears deserved, and so fear that penalty most of all, crime is a tiger's tail which can never be released. Crime unites, and in unity there is strength. Also in strength is the means to escape penalty. It happens then that collective criminality performs the same political function as religious persuasion—to make people united and strong. Surely this implicit identification of crime and religion is one of Machiavelli's more scandalous suggestions.

Perhaps it is good that we are finding substitutes for religion, because in point of fact the Romans were not all that religious. Machiavelli praises their piety in I.55.1, but in a comparison with present-day Germans, the Roman people come off quite badly. In order to carry out Camillus's vow to dedicate one tenth of the spoils from Veii to Apollo, the senate called upon the citizens, to whom the spoils had already been distributed, to return one tenth of what they had received. Mostly, though, the citizens refused; and had not the women of Rome made up the difference by contributing their jewelry to the public treasury (Livy, V.25), Camillus's vow to Apollo would have gone unfulfilled. Machiavelli, wanting something positive to say nonetheless, contends that the Romans demonstrated their integrity by openly defying the edict rather than by claiming fraudulently that they had given back what was owed, and he is impressed by the fact that the senate thought fit to trust the people's goodness (§1). But how much better the Germans appear, who take an oath and are on their honor to pay in taxes whatever amount they as individuals think is fair. And Machiavelli is assured that this system works, for if less than the true amount were paid, the revenues received would fall short of the expected sum; the fraud would then be detected, and other tax-collecting methods would be devised. It also happens that the Romans compare poorly with their own contemporaries, and with pirates at that! For when the ship carrying this same booty from Veii was captured by Liparians on its way to Apollo's temple at Delphi, the pirate-prince Timasistheus, learning "what gift this was, where it was going, and who was sending it, though born at Lipari . . . bore himself as a Roman man and showed the people how impious it was to seize a gift such as this" (III.29.1). Indeed, he bore himself as something more than a Roman man, for the Romans in time expelled Camillus for keeping faith with his vow (III.23.1), whereas Timasistheus helped Camillus to fulfill his vow by sending the legates on their way.[36]

We asked before, and now ask again, how matters stand with religion. Religion was important to Rome, and none of the foregoing animadversions, nor all of them taken together, contradict this claim.[37] Religion was a cause of national unity, and modern states, lacking this cause, are correspondingly weak. But the title to chapter 12 reads as a question, not as a statement of fact: "Of How Much Importance It Is to Take Account of Religion. . . ." The answer to this question, as Mansfield suggests, is that religion was important, but not incalculably so;[38] and it certainly presented problems for Rome.

To review: The founder of Rome's religion, Numa Pompilius, is said to have contributed more to Rome's good orders than his predecessor Romulus; but Numa is later described as a weak prince who dissipated the military virtue of his subjects and whose reign Rome managed to survive only because a strong prince succeeded him. It is asserted that Numa's religion civilized the early Romans with the arts of peace. Livy mentions that Numa, wanting to soften a savage people by the disuse of arms, built the temple of Janus as an indication of the oscillating rhythm of war and peace. When opened, the temple signified that the country was at war; when closed that the country was at peace. But since Numa's day, as Livy goes on to observe, the temple was only twice closed, once after the First Punic War and once again after the battle of Actium when Augustus Caesar pacified the world (Livy, I.19). Obviously then, the truth of the temple, that war and peace naturally alternate, was never a part of Roman history, a nation always at war. And the use Rome made of religion was not Numa's, the domestication of a savage temperament, but the disciplining and further hardening of this temperament through the fear of God and the sanctity of oaths. The result of religious hardening was that Roman citizens were habitually disposed to obey authority. Religion did help to bring domestic peace to Rome, but not because it made citizens brotherly and sisterly; rather it was a device used by patricians to control plebeians. The danger was that the rulers would betray the public trust and use religion for class advantage. The danger also was that the effects would wear off with time, both because of exposés of abuse and because religious conviction is most vigorous in the beginnings of a society when the citizens are primitive and superstitious. What's more, the decline of faith is an inevitable by-product of societal success—of victory, power, wealth, leisure, and enlightenment.[39] Machiavelli allows that revivals are possible even among sophisticated people; nonetheless, mountain men make better candidates for religious conversion. There was a third danger arising from the unpredictability of pagan ritual, for the auspices could always go against the consul's plans, and casuistic explanations, no matter how clever, would slowly erode the people's belief. Dependence on religion also meant that power was divided, notwithstanding the fact that Roman priests were subordinate to secular authority or even secular themselves. In light of these difficulties, it is not surprising if Rome's rulers had other ways of instilling obstinacy in their troops; nor is it surprising if Rome's military success depended ultimately on the prudence of its leaders.

The chief drawback of Roman religion was that to work its effect of strengthening and unifying the state, it needed the people to be both obstinate and pliable, willing to stand firm and yet ready to turn on a dime; and it needed the rulers to be both manipulative and trustworthy, pious disbelievers who used the cover of hypocrisy to advance the common good, not their personal and partisan interests. Religion is important for utilitarian reasons, but then paganism was only partly useful to Rome's success. Such a conclusion, however, might in fact be welcomed, since the reclamation of Roman virtue would be a most unpromising project if it required of modern Christians that they resume worship of Queen Juno and company.

Senatorial Modes

We have been shown two modes by which the nobles ruled the plebs. When tumult threatened, one of their number would put on the insignia of office and address the plebs in a calm and soothing manner. More commonly, though, the nobles would lie—religion being an elaborate deception for the sake of patrician rule. But to say that the patricians ruled is to overstate their influence and to forget that the Roman republic was a democratic mixed regime. The nobles were the lesser partner and weaker power; rather than rule the state, they managed it from behind the scenes.[40] This they did through the practice of temporizing. Temporizing is how the weak, like trainers of some elephantine beast, manage and control the strong. Temporizing is the deception, the indirection, and the feigned goodness of cooperation and compromise by which the weak "rule" the strong. And it is the weak who temporize, not the strong. For by temporizing the weak hope to prevent the strong from discovering the true extent of their strength, since consciousness of strength is an inducement to war, the result of which is the destruction of the weak.

The senate disguised its weakness when in 508 it relieved the plebs of all taxes. The Tuscan (Etruscan) king Porsenna was then besieging the city on behalf of the Tarquins, and the senate needed the people to stay loyal to the republic, although the lateness of the benefit barely concealed the weakness which inspired it (I.32.1). The senate did better a century or so later when just before commencing siege operations against Veii, it granted a public wage to men serving in the military (previously they contributed their service); also the attendant tax that supplied the revenue for the senate's liberality fell most heavily on the nobles who were the first to come forward and pay their assessment. By these maneuvers the senate accomplished two objectives: it disguised as a free gesture what in fact was a compelled action (no wage, no siege); and it undercut the authority of the tribunes whose responsibility it was to demand benefits for the people (I.51.1).

In foreign policy, too, the senate contrived to keep up appearances, even when muscle-flexing exceeded its means. Devastated by disease in 463, Rome could not come to the aid of the Latins and Ernici (Hernici), peoples who had long been dependent on Roman protection. The senate therefore decided to grant the right of self-defense to its endangered allies. Because dependent states, with or without permission, will defend themselves, it is better, reasons Machiavelli, to agree to their defense when circumstances make it impossible for the hegemonic power any longer to provide this service. The value of such a policy is that it disguises necessity and weakness behind a veil of freedom and strength, and it prevents others, "having disobeyed by necessity," from "disobeying by choice" (I.38.2). Weakness is not a condition which any state wishes to advertise. But there is a right way and a wrong way to conceal unavoidable vulnerabilities. The wrong way is to insist on one's dignity, spurning compromises and overtures of peace (II.27). It is dangerous to run a bluff; for should the bluff be called, the true extent of one's weakness is laid bare. Bluffing though is permissible so long as it is done intelligently. Intelligent bluffing surrenders what necessity in any event is going to take (I.53.1). When hard times fell upon Rome, it was able to lower its sights and take "the less bad policy for the better" (I.38.2). By so doing, Rome temporized, for temporizing, in one of its manifestations, is accepting as good what is merely less bad. Machiavelli previously stated that winning is honorable if the alternative is losing (I.6.4). But when winning is not possible, as it is not for the weak, the "honorable part" belongs to temporizing (I.38.2). Temporizing then falls midway between winning and losing. It forestalls defeat by suggesting that the weak have options and that the concessions they make are freely chosen rather than extracted by force. It also quiets the appetites of the strong who failing to realize the helplessness of their opponents never conceive the notion that all is possible. The strong are most violent when resistance has collapsed and their will is law, for the prospect of unlimited power is a stimulant to appetite. An example is the sack of a captured city.[41] By contrast, temporizing maintains respect for boundaries and is tantamount to an ordinary mode.

In two areas chiefly did the senate exhibit its temporizing skill: agrarian legislation and consulate eligibility. The agrarian law was first proposed by Spurius Cassius in 486 (III.8.1; Livy, II.41); but since Machiavelli gives the law a 300-year career in Rome (I.37.3) ending with the tyranny of Caesar (45 BC), its real beginning is put in the mid-fourth century.[42] The law's main intent, to repeat, was to equalize landholdings by imposing personal maximums and by distributing newly acquired lands among the plebs. The law was offensive to the nobles on both counts, since it would have required most of them to give back some of what they already possessed, and it would have taken from all of them "the way to get rich" in the future (§2). Hence the senate resisted agrarian legislation, but indirectly, by distracting the people with a war (the authority of the tribunes did not extend to armies on campaigns), by enticing one tribune to oppose the others (a divide-and-rule tactic known as cooptation),[43] by conceding a part of what the plebs demanded (usually debt relief), or by establishing colonies in captured territories (also a cheap mode of defense [II.6.1]). By indirect methods such as these, the senate kept the people at bay and itself in charge. And all was well in Rome until the duty of temporizing passed from the nobles to the plebs. For after the Punic Wars, when the authority of the senate was uncontestable, it fell to the people, now the weaker element *de facto*, to temporize with the nobles, and to do this by not reviving the agrarian law, out of fashion since Rome moved "to the farthest parts of Italy or outside Italy" (§2). But the people did not know how to play the part of the weaker partner who by indirection manages the stronger. Instead the people, led by the Gracchi, made its usual but long-forgotten demands, only to confront a nobility confident of its strength and unwilling to compromise. The result was violence, the incapacity of magistrates to arbitrate disputes and enforce the law, and recourse to private armies commanded by aspiring tyrants. Machiavelli blames the plebs and their leaders, not for wanting agrarian legislation, but for failing to assess the situation properly. As stated previously, one of the advantages of the Roman path to a mixed regime was that it required temporizing from the nobles and goodness from the people. When the roles were reversed, the plebeians were unable to be wise like the patricians, and the patricians were unable to be good like the plebeians.[44]

The agrarian law performed a double function in Rome. It forced the patricians to temporize; at the same time it was itself a form of temporizing, since for 300 years it guarded liberty and put off slavery. In the chapter title Machiavelli calls agrarian legislation a scandal, an example of a law that "looks very far back and is against an ancient custom of the city." Machiavelli does not specify what ancient custom was ignored, but presumably it was the custom of private citizens' having exceptional wealth and exceptional power (III.16.2, III.28.1). And presumably what agrarian legislation looked backed to was the republican principle of public wealth and private poverty.[45] Even so, agrarian agitation, like tumult, was for several centuries a scandal which benefited Rome because it held in check the ambition of the great. The people was the stronger party in Roman society, but it too temporized in the sense of putting off the loss of liberty by tumult and agitation. It was an unconscious temporizer,[46] unlike the great who temporized by carefully contrived deceptions and strategies of indirect rule.

The political battle in Rome was over access to the consulate—the patricians had it, and the plebs wanted it. Agitation began in 462 with the Terentillian law (I.13.2, I.39.2) and continued for about a decade (the decade which saw the rise to prominence of Cincinnatus) until constitutional reform and the decemvirate supplanted the legislative initiative altogether; and the struggle came to a compromised conclusion in 445 when the Canuleian law eliminated the consulate, replacing it with the military tribunate with consular powers. This new office had an indefinite number of officeholders, greater than two but no more than six; and it was opened to patrician and plebeian competition alike.[47] Machiavelli calls the compromise a "middle way" (I.47.1). Like Livy, he is interested in the electoral results, the fact that an all-patrician slate of candidates was elected—and not just once, but for 45 years (Livy, V.12). The explanation from Livy is that the people judges differently and impartially when not contending for the liberty and honor of its class (Livy, IV.6). In Machiavelli's rendering, the people is deceived about general things, but about particular things its judgment is honest and correct. These general things are opinions citizens hold about which class deserves to rule, or about distributive justice. The people's opinion was that the plebs was deserving of power, the power of the consulate in particular, because the plebeian class "carried more dangers in war, because it was that which with its arms kept Rome free and made it powerful."[48] So certain was the people of the reasonableness of its position that "it turned to obtaining this authority in any mode" (§1). Accordingly, the nobles had to change the focus of the debate away from the controversies surrounding distributive justice. This they did by conceding the people's point that as a class the plebs was deserving of high office—hence universal eligibility—while contesting the point that individual plebeians were more deserving than individual nobles—hence head-to-head competitions in which honest assessments of individual merit overrode the hardened prejudices of class. Freed of the obligation to reason in generalities—that is, to be a judge in its own case—the people became sharp-eyed reasoners about particular candidates.

But something more was needed than a straight-up election to ensure such satisfying results. Machiavelli explains in I.48 that the senate was careful to present the electorate with candidates of starkly contrasting qualities—either the best of the nobles or the worst of the plebs, vile individuals who, persuaded by the senate to stand for election along with other, more dignified plebs, caused disrepute to fall upon the whole order. Now Machiavelli declares toward the close of I.47 that "a prudent man should never flee the popular judgment in particular things concerning distributions of ranks and dignities, for only in this does the people not deceive itself" (*non s'inganna*). But he also says that in the next chapter he will discuss "the order that the Senate held to so as to deceive the people in its distributions" (*per ingannare il popolo nelle distribuzione sue*). That order, the stacked election, he then offers as proof that "the people . . . does not deceive itself in particulars" (*de' particulari non s'inganna* [I.48.1]). If the plebs did not deceive itself, i.e., choose unwisely, it was only because it was deceived by others. The people was ashamed to choose the very vile or the very wicked and ashamed not to choose the very noble and the very good. So the senate provided the people with clear-cut choices. This election chicanery prejudiced the people against members of its own order who were truly deserving, but it relieved the people of the prejudice that all members of its order were truly deserving. The senate made a concession which in one sense cost it nothing, since patricians continued to be elected. But in another sense the senate served an interest larger than its own. For it taught the plebeians, if not how to reason with strict impartiality, then how to set aside the inveterate biases of class; and it obliged the nobles to put forward their very best candidates.

At issue in the creation of military tribunes with consular powers was the enlargement of governing opportunities for plebeians. The concession granted by the temporizing nobles allowed ambitious plebeians to run for high office but under election circumstances which effectively prevented their success. In time, though, the plebs did break the patrician hammerlock on power; and in time, the plebs came to think that equal access to this non-consular consulate was not enough. At first Machiavelli describes this change of heart as the payoff for a decades-long strategy of senatorial temporizing. For after nearly eight decades of rule by military tribunes, the people recognized its error and "recreated consuls" (I.39.2). Unable to resist the people directly, the senate placated the people with a partial concession, then waited patiently until the people, learning from history, gave back what the senate had conceded. What the people learned, apart from the merits of individual patricians, was that Rome's many wars were caused by the relentless hostility of its neighbors, not by "the ambition of the nobles, who, since they were unable to punish the plebs when defended by the tribunate power inside Rome, wished to lead it outside Rome under the consuls so as to crush it where it did not have any aid" (§2). Machiavelli presents the opinion as false, an example of the people's mistaking the doctor for the disease. But we know that the opinion was true, for Machiavelli stated in I.37.2 that "with patience and industry the nobles temporized with it [the plebs], either by leading an army out [*trarre fuora uno esercito*], or by. . . ." The people, it appears, traded a true opinion for a falsehood. But the people learned from this mistake as well; for when the agitation began anew, in 377, the people's demand was for a restored consulate that reserved one of its offices for plebeian candidates. The people learned not only to value consuls ahead of military tribunes, but also to guard against its own predilection for favoring nobles over plebeians.

The next significant stage in the struggle between the classes was the ten-year effort to pass, or to delay passage of, the Licinian-Sextian laws (377-367), named after their authors, tribunes Gaius Licinius Stolo and Lucius Sextius Lateranus. This package of legislation provided debt relief, limited landholdings to 500 jugera, and abolished the office of military tribune, replacing it with a re-formed consulate, restructured to ensure plebeian success (Livy, VI.35). Once again the senate went into its temporizing mode, recruiting some tribunes to veto the initiative and playing the religion card to scare the plebs away. Appius Claudius reminded the nobles that "they always found someone who was either fearful or corruptible or a lover of the common good so that they disposed him to oppose the will of the others, who wished to press forward some decision against the will of the Senate. That remedy," adds Machiavelli, "was a great tempering of so much authority, and it often helped Rome" (III.11.1). Cooptation was a tried-and-true tactic long associated with the Claudian clan.[49] Machiavelli, though, describes as private advice to fellow nobles what in Livy is a public speech delivered to assembled Romans, a speech in which Appius employs a different form of divide-and-rule tactics; not cooptation, understandably, but the separation of ordinary, economically motivated plebeians from their politically ambitious leaders. For Licinius and Sextius wanted to be consuls themselves; and after nine years of strenuous campaigning on behalf of the legislation, they sadly discovered that the people was prepared to forego the political reforms in order to achieve the economic. The tribunes responded to this perceived ingratitude by threatening to withdraw from the election, leaving the offices they had held throughout the period, unless the people stood firm in demanding that one consular post be a set-aside for plebeians. This split in plebeian ranks was the division which Appius tried exploiting in a speech which went on to explain the religious scruples which forbade plebeians from serving as consuls (III.33.1). But within a year the Licinian-Sextian legislation passed in its entirety, and the patricians' century-old battle to maintain exclusive control of the consulate was lost (Livy VI.36-42). Even so, giving back a part in order to keep for a time the remaining whole is temporizing in a longer view. It is to fight a war of strategic retreat where victory is determined by the time it takes the other side to win.

Except for one thing. People temporize, Machiavelli admits, not only to postpone an evil, but to escape it altogether (I.33.5, I.37.3, I.46.1). The chief hope behind the temporizing mode is that a feared evil will eliminate itself if not confronted directly. In book 1 there are some five perceived evils for which temporizing is the recommended strategy. It is asserted: (1) that an emerging power, such as Rome, is better ignored than challenged, since a confederation of

hostile neighbors will only cause it to find new sources of strength and unity
(I.33); (2) that regal power, the most practical of these new sources, can be controlled and tempered by conversion into ordinary executive power, such as the
lawful order of the dictatorship (I.34); (3) that when an ambitious individual,
already too powerful, aspires to tyranny, the smart thing is to leave him alone
(I.33); (4) that when a whole class is too arrogant, as the nobility always is, the
best remedy is a countervailing institution, a tribunate using faction and tumult
to promote the people's economic interest—e.g., agrarian legislation (I.37); and
(5) that when the other class is the insolent party, its demands for political honors can be deflected and delayed by senatorial modes of indirect rule: religious
superstitions, self-serving largess, needless wars, divide-and-rule tactics, and
partial concessions.

The difficulty is that these appeasement policies are nowhere shown to
have achieved their ultimate objective, that temporizers be delivered from final
harm. Rome did grow slightly in its early history because anxious neighbors
tried preventing its emergence as a regional power; but then Rome grew vastly
in its later history because distant powers equal to Rome stood idly by while
Rome swallowed up weaker and nearer states. Samnium, Carthage, Macedon,
etc., held back and stayed neutral in hopes that others would defeat Rome for
them; as a consequence Rome burgeoned into a world empire (II.1.2). The dictatorship did work to contain and conceal regal power, but it was nonetheless
the office through which Caesar became a tyrant.[50] And while it is true that
every would-be tyrant who was resisted acquired a tyranny (Cosimo de' Medici
and Julius Caesar [I.33.3-4]), it is also true that every would-be tyrant who was
not resisted acquired a tyranny (the house of Medici and Augustus Caesar
[I.52.2-3]); and an ill-conceived attempt to coopt Octavian "was the destruction
of the party of the aristocrats" (§3). Agrarian legislation did temporize with the
ambition of the great, but it also started the civil wars which were the ruin of the
Roman republic. Finally, and as just noted, the consulate was opened to plebeian
participation despite the senate's efforts to keep it a patrician-only office. In
each of these cases temporizing put off an evil but did not prevent it from coming to pass. Is postponement then enough? It is one thing to retard the slide into
ruin and quite another to endure in perpetuity. By the same token, is trusting to
time and fortune a mark of true virtue, or should rulers be taking more decisive
action? The response to both queries will prove to be the same: that decline can
be reversed by periodic renewals, though not permanently arrested; and that
periodic renewals require princes of true virtue, not temporizing senators. But
more on these matters later.

One other point before leaving the subject of senatorial modes. Machiavelli's advice to the great is to hide themselves—they are weak and so must rule
from behind the scenes. But his advice to the people is to expose all that is hidden—concealment is the breeding ground of malignities that issue in oppression. The question therefore arises: Is Machiavelli trying to teach the great how

to manage the people or teach the people how not to be managed by the great? More specifically, in this conflict of the orders, does Machiavelli promote the interest of the great or the interest of the people? What, finally, does Machiavelli want to occur?

The Conflict of the Orders

There is no doubting Machiavelli's sympathies regarding the institution of the tribunate. Romulus placed Rome on the right path by creating an incomplete mixed regime (kingship combined with aristocracy); but it was the addition of the tribunate which brought the mixed regime to its perfection (I.2.7). We are left to wonder then if further democratizing of the constitution was good or bad for Rome. While Machiavelli does applaud the arrival of tribunes, he seems decidedly nervous about the work they performed and the influence they achieved. For example, their initial push for access to the consulate occasioned a wholesale reform of the constitution modeled after the laws of Solon (I.40.2).[51] But Solonic law gave Athens a democracy, a regime which Machiavelli deems inferior to Rome's (I.2.6-7). And when the tribunes tried again, with the Licinian-Sextian legislation, Machiavelli describes the authority they exercised as "insolent" and "harmful to Roman freedom" (III.11.1). What's more, he calls into question the capacity of the plebs for judging affairs of state—only particulars can the people judge rightly (I.47). Thus increases of people-power and of the power of the tribunes were hardly unqualified blessings for Rome. Still, when all is said and done, Machiavelli endorses the opening of the consulate to plebeian participation: "Therefore it was fitting at an early hour that the plebs have hope of gaining the consulate, and it was fed a bit with this hope without having it; then the hope was not enough, and it was fitting that it come to the effect" (I.60.1). On the other hand, the senate is not condemned for having delayed the fulfillment of this hope, and the eventual granting of access, says Machiavelli, was a thing "very much to be disputed." All that Machiavelli concedes is that in a city organized for expansion like Rome, it is a "necessity" of distributive justice that contributions be rewarded. Plebeian consuls, therefore, no less than plebeian tribunes, were a necessary, if not immediate, consequence of Rome's imperial ambitions. It seems then that Rome's constitutional perfection was a delicate equilibrium, or a balance of forces, which the necessity of empire would not allow to endure. Empire pulled Rome away from its perfection by exaggerating the democratic component of its mixed regime. Empire, which is dynamic, destroys the mixed regime, which is static.

But rather than fix on the moment when Rome achieved the perfection of its orders, Machiavelli emphasizes the need for new orders to rectify a ceaseless procession of new problems (I.49.1). In a world characterized by change, no perfection is anything more than a temporary remedy, useful one moment but harmful the next (I.18.2-4). What mattered was that Rome be timely, not that it be perfect—or timeliness is perfection. But then not all times are equally desirable. Some are corrupt and near the end; others are healthy and fresh. Thus, while change was inevitable for Rome, change also was decline. Accordingly, the senate was right to put off change for as long as possible, that is to resist the democratizing of Rome's high offices.[52]

This the nobles did by temporizing, or by hiding. Whenever the contest was in the open and purely partisan, the advantage was with the plebs. Or if the plebs did not prevail, then the state teetered on the brink of tyranny; for a truculent nobility, its partisanship exposed to plain view, created conditions favorable for liberty's usurpation. To paraphrase the adage of Ferdinand, king of Spain: Men are like lesser birds of prey, who, intent upon catching their own prey, do not notice when a greater predator enters the area (I.40.7). Either the nobles yielded to the people's demands, or the people found itself a champion to defend its cause. If the nobles did likewise, potential tyrants had both parties racing to make themselves slaves.[53] Thus in the main the nobles found discretion to be the better part of valor.

But hiding by the nobles came to mean more than the hiding of their motives. It meant as well the hiding of their order, which meant the effective dismantling of their order, or the amalgamation of patricians and plebs. Plebs became eligible for all of the offices of state, including membership in the senate;[54] and the tribunes, we saw, intervened in patrician disputes (I.50.1). Given that plebeians held office alongside patricians and that tribunes not just defended the popular interest but negotiated differences among nobles, the strict demarcation of the social orders was beginning to break down. And the nobles added to the confusion by presenting themselves less as members of a separate class than as representatives of the people. For one of the temporizing devices used by nobles was to anticipate what the tribunes would do and to beat them to it. The senate anticipated the tribunes' populism when it granted the unrequested benefit of pay for military service (I.51.1). Reflecting on this liberal policy which earned the senate the gratitude of the people, Machiavelli offers the remarkable opinion that had the nobility "been maintained in this order, every tumult in that city would have been removed and the credit that the tribunes had with the plebs would have been taken from them and, by consequence, their authority" (I.52.1). The purported effect of a senate quick to please is a city rid of tumult and of the plebeian tribunes who stir it up—a happy result indeed since it would guard the city from the tyranny of ambitious demagogues who court favor with the people by acts of seeming generosity. If smaller birds of prey are united, or reduced to only one (the senate), the larger bird of prey (the tyrant) has not the advantage of surprise. But we hesitate to accept a "good" senate free of tribunate interference since without checks to its power the senate is sure to turn bad. The natural selfishness of men, and of the great in particular, requires a countervailing force in the people if liberty is to be preserved. This by now is familiar reasoning, that no one can be trusted and that efforts to render oneself trustworthy are themselves suspect.

But there is another consequence of senatorial "goodness" not so familiar. It is that the nobility itself might dissolve. Chapter 52 argues that the easiest and least scandalous way of removing the arms of a popular leader is to block his ascent by anticipating his moves. To anticipate a popular leader is to become popular oneself, as when the senate conferred benefits not even demanded. The purpose is to discredit and superannuate a rival, chasing him from the field so as to be alone in power. But having once crossed the class divide to take up the cause of the people, would the nobles reconstitute themselves as a class apart united in opposition to insolent men advertising their populism? If the way to power is through the people, might the nobility fracture and come instead to represent the popular will more than it represents itself? The situation in Capua during the Second Punic War provides a telling account of how an exclusive nobility is transformed into a classless elite. The local magistrate, Pacuvius Calavus (Calavius), concerned that an angry plebs was prepared to revolt and hand the city over to Hannibal, persuaded the nobles to place themselves in his custody so that he could save them all, amazingly, by inviting the people to kill them one-by-one (a dangerous plan to be sure, especially in light of recent talk about birds of prey!).[55] Pacuvius's idea was to offer the people the senators' heads on condition that the people replace the senators with plebeians better qualified for the office. Again, when forced to reason about particulars, the people admitted that whatever its rights collectively, individually its own kind failed to measure up. And assured by Pacuvius that this near-death experience would leave the senators humble and humane, the people concluded that the devils it knew were preferable to the devils it did not know (I.47.2). Pacuvius conceded to the people the right to elect its leaders, while he convinced the nobles that such a right, the equivalent of universal suffrage, would not work to their detriment. The nobles of Capua, "elected" by deferral of punishment and by default, became in effect the people's representatives. And dependence on the people concealed the nobles better than did patronization through occasional acts of liberality. Hidden thus inside of democratic elections, the nobles were safe from public anger. The public also was safe from the nobles' abuse since the nobles were accountable to it. And the city was relieved of tumult in the bargain. To a degree, the mixed regime, which distributes power between officially recognized social classes, was evolving into a representative democracy, in which classless elites compete for the public's approval.[56]

It is Mansfield's contention that party government was successful in Rome because the people provided a non-partisan context within which partisan competition among elites could safely occur. Necessary to this argument is a distinction between the apolitical people and their tribune leaders. Like the nobles, the tribunes were ambitious; but unlike the nobles the tribunes were new, out-of-office, and illegitimate. Politics rightly conducted is a contest for power among society's ambitious few, individuals divided by the convention of class or by the accident of incumbency—i.e., an old guard fighting to retain office and a new guard fighting to seize it. The people is uninvolved except as judges of the contest, bestowing power on the persons or parties who please it most. On the other hand, politics is wrongly conducted when the people becomes a partisan competitor itself, when the whole of the people is pitted against the whole class of the nobles. Killings, banishments, and widespread lawlessness are the consequence of politicizing the people, a mistake committed by Athenians among the ancients and by Florentines among the moderns.[57]

But did not Rome commit this mistake, too? Indeed, is not Rome defined by this mistake? For Rome's politicized populace is what distinguishes it from Sparta, a republic whose populace was politically quiescent. Rome used its people for war and conquest but only slowly and grudgingly rewarded its people with power and wealth. Wanting what was denied it, the people resorted to tumults, three times refusing service and quitting the city for the Sacred Mount;[58] at the same time the nobles, unbeholdened to the people, insisted on their superiority and the privileges of class. But perhaps the people of Rome confined its activism to moments of crisis; otherwise it stayed clear of politics, leaving that business to a plebeian elite authorized to represent its interests?[59] Popular revolts would then be needed to finalize constitutional change which others initiated but could not on their own bring to completion.[60] By this account Rome was ill-formed in the beginning and never perfect thereafter; and that perfection ascribed to the addition of tribunes means only that the resources were then on hand for continuous change. It means also that change brought improvements to the constitution, better and less riotous ways of managing the antagonism of patricians and plebs. The "conflict of the orders" is thus a story of progress, not decline; a story of how an archaic mode of guarding liberty, the mixed regime, was gradually replaced by the newer and more inclusive modes of representative democracy.

But it is hard to say for sure if this is what Machiavelli thinks, for he expresses no firm opinion about the democratizing process underway in Rome, and he greets with far less enthusiasm the opening of the consulate near the end of the process than the institution of the tribunate at its beginning; nor does he chide the senate for acting all along as a brake.

Perhaps though we can find some help in I.53 and I.54, the chapters following Machiavelli's discussion of anticipation. It happens that in the first example of chapter 53 there is resistance to, rather than anticipation of, the people's demands. The Roman plebs wanted half the city's population to migrate to the conquered city of Veii. But the senate said no, and it protected itself from popular indignation by standing behind "some old and esteemed citizens" whom the people revered and trusted (§1). The point is repeated in chapter 54 where a "grave man of authority," decked out in the ensigns of his rank, comes before an angry crowd and quiets its passions. August individuals such as these are an indispensable remedy "for checking an excited multitude." And the multitude needs checking because its opinions are a danger to the republic. The people, says Machiavelli, is a sucker for policies promising easy victories and sudden riches. It has a weakness for gambling and will repeatedly put its fate in the hands of big-talking demagogues. Three instances are cited from the Hannibalic wars in which the people gave authority to junior officers who promised it quick results against the Carthaginian foe. All three engagements were disasters or near-disasters. The people leaps without looking and so is in need of leaders whose temperaments are more cautious. Machiavelli is particularly conservative in these chapters. Caution is the mark of wisdom, and the impetuous public is not wise. Accordingly, the senate resists the people's will, or it makes concessions that it cannot withhold; but it does not anticipate in order to become popular. What indeed would have happened with Veii had the leadership been drawn from the people or had come to resemble the people by careers spent anticipating its wishes? Rome stayed together then and was later saved during its long struggle with Hannibal because it had leaders of a separate order, independent of the people but still respected by it.[61]

In the *Florentine Histories* Machiavelli contrasts the effects of class struggle in Rome and in Florence. In Rome the effects were inspiriting because the nobles did not stoop to conquer but lifted up individual plebeians, instructing them in the ways of rule; in Florence the opposite occurred with opposite, dispiriting, effects:

> In the victories of the people [over the nobles] the city of Rome became more virtuous, for as men of the people could be placed in the administration of the magistracies, the armies, and the posts of empire together with the nobles, they were filled with the same virtue as the nobles, and that city, by growing in virtue, grew in power. But in Florence, when the people conquered, the nobles were left deprived of the magistracies, and if they wanted to regain them, it was necessary for them not only to be but to appear similar to men of the people in their conduct, spirit, and mode of living. From this arose the variations in coats of arms and the changes of family titles that the nobles made so as to appear as the people. So the virtue in arms and the generosity of spirit that were in the nobility were eliminated, and in the people, where they never had been, they could not be rekindled; thus did Florence become ever more humble and abject. (III.1)

It is a question then of who influences whom. By going slow and raising up plebeians one-by-one, the senate managed to share power while passing on patrician values. The senate coopted the best and the brightest of the plebeians and made them its own. But when the senate, or some of its members, instead chose to anticipate the plebs, in the sense of embracing plebeian values, the plebs became a revolutionary force bent on destroying the old nobility (I.37.2, I.52.3). Such was the situation during the civil war years and such was the manner in which Caesar came to power (*Prince*, 16). Regarding then the issue of representative democracy as an improvement on the mixed regime, the answer would seem to depend on whether the "representative" was aristocratic in outlook or popular. Since Machiavelli does not sanction the demise of the nobility,[62] he would not countenance temporizing, or hiding, carried to the point of conversion.[63]

There is though one needed alteration to this description of Machiavelli as an aristocrat in a democrat's clothing. It is not the case that Machiavelli simply criticizes the people for its impetuosity or praises the nobles for their caution. Granted that on the occasion popular impulsiveness did Rome grievous harm; but this same impulsiveness brought final victory to Rome when after many years of fighting with Hannibal the mantle of authority passed to Scipio. The public's habit of favoring "the beginnings of things . . . that have some virtue in them and have been done by youths" (I.33.2) allowed Rome to discard a proven strategy of delay and adopt an untried strategy of attack, while entrusting the same to a relatively young commander. It was the public which made this change possible, for it was to the public that Scipio threatened to take his plan of attacking Africa if the senate refused him. Scipio is described as a demagogue or insolent man, someone "who knew very well how much such decisions please peoples" (I.53.4). But his plan did not lead to the ruin of Rome, and in a later chapter his plan is said to have saved Rome since "Hannibal would still be in Italy if it had been up to him [Fabius]" and since "if Fabius had been king of Rome, he could easily have lost that war" (III.9.1). The Scipio example is a reminder that Machiavelli is better known for his impetuosity than for his caution and that generally he is an advocate for the young as against the old (*Prince*, 25). In fact, the real reason why Machiavelli favors the opening of the consulate to the plebs was that the consulate was opened also to the young.

Machiavelli reports that "after the consulate came to the plebs, the Roman republic conceded it to its citizens without respect to age or to blood" (I.60.1). But then he confusingly changes what he just said, adding that "respect to age was never in Rome" (*il respetto della età mai non fusse in Roma*) because Rome "always went out to find virtue, whether it was in the young or in the old" (*ma sempre si andò a trovare la virtù, o in giovane o in vecchio che la fusse*). The evidence he offers is the consulship of Valerius Corvinus in 348 when Valerius was only 23. But Valerius's election occurred 18 years after the opening of the consulate to the plebs (366 BC). It therefore confirms the first remark that including plebs led to the inclusion of the young, but not the second remark that Rome always preferred virtue irrespective of age. And the statement of Valerius to his soldiers that "the consulate was 'the reward of virtue, not of blood'" (§1), uses plebeian eligibility (blood) to imply his worthiness for office—his youth notwithstanding—because Rome was impartial in its selection of candidates. In other words, the soldiers of Valerius could be assured that their commander was not promoted at such a young age simply because of his patrician heritage.

But what are we to make of the statement that Rome always sought out virtue irrespective of age? The statement could be true but of no practical consequence if the measure of virtue was determined by the old. Yes, the young were always eligible, but only were they favored if they acquitted themselves in the manner of the old, which the young rarely or never did.

There is a second peculiar phrasing in chapter 60; it reads that "in choosing a youth for a rank that has need of the prudence of the old, it must be that some very notable action makes him reach that rank, since the multitude has to choose him for it." The prudence of the old was the standard. How then were the young to measure up? With the multitude as the electorate, it was enough for the young to present some notable action. For example, Manlius Torquatus won notoriety by threatening the life of his father's accuser (I.11.1, III.34.2). This outrageous breach of legal procedure was the first of a series of memorable actions which earned Manlius his reputation with the multitude. It was not, however, an act of elderly prudence. The multitude was always the electorate in Rome (though divided by centuries so as to enhance the voting power of the wealthy). But what the electorate thought worthy depended in some degree on whom the electorate was asked to elect (I.47.1-2). If only prudent patricians experienced by age and past service stood for office, then the multitude would be unlikely ever to favor a youth. But that mold of rectitude and worthiness was broken once the multitude came to look seriously on plebeian candidates because forced by law to choose them as consuls. Thus youth and plebeian birth made common cause against the old order of patrician privilege. While Rome might have in theory always sought out virtue regardless of age, it was not until plebeians broke into the consulate that Rome was prepared to widen its definition of virtue beyond the prudence of the old to the daring of the young.

Machiavelli takes the part of the young against the old, claiming that

> when a youth is of so much virtue that he makes himself known in some no-
> table thing, it would be a very harmful thing for the city not be able to avail
> itself of him then, and for it to have to wait until that vigor of spirit and that
> readiness grow old with him, of which his fatherland could have availed it-
> self of at that age. (I.60.1)

In addition to the natural division of humors, the people and the great, there is a natural division of age, the young and the old. And although no exact correspondence exists between humoral and age differences, still the people in its impetuosity has an affinity with the young, while the great, bearing the burden of responsibility, have an affinity with the old. The young, notes Machiavelli in the preface to the second book, exude energy and force, whereas the old possess judgment and prudence. No matter how different then a noble from a pleb, all of the old have attitudes in common as have all of the young. The old would like to see energy confined to the past, as a safe memory and a compliment to their own, but now exhausted, energetic selves. They react with anxious scorn to signs of energy in the young, telling the young not to presume that the present can ever be a match for the good-old days gone by. The old, on the whole, prefer that the world move at a slower gait. And even though they can claim for themselves the wisdom that comes with age, their exclusive control over the levers of power is nonetheless unwise, since the world moves at its own gait not that of man's. Thus Machiavelli declares that the young have some positive contributions to make, that they are needed at the helm, and that the city would be harmed by their exclusion from office. About the people, on the other hand, he says only that the reward of the consulate was a requirement for an expansionary city needing to use the plebs for soldiers. Also, the title of chapter 60 speaks of age, not of blood. Machiavelli, then, wants the young in high office, and he welcomes the plebeians there as a means to achieving this end.

Chapter Four

Rome's Humors

We have spoken from time to time about the humors in Rome, but no thorough account has been given of their respective natures. Attempting this account will be the first business of the present chapter, with special attention paid to how different the humors actually are; for Machiavelli just as often refers to a uniform humanity as he refers to a humanity divided into classes. His famous advice to lawgivers, for example, is that they "presuppose that all men are bad" (I.3.1). The humors do differ, it will be argued, despite the ubiquity of badness manifested as acquisitiveness, because some men acquire always and on their own initiative, while others acquire intermittently and out of self-defense. The remainder of the chapter will consider the people's virtue—whence is comes, why it corrupts, and how important it finally is to the state's well-being. The conclusion arrived at is that civic virtue (or that part of it respecting religion and law) is *not* vitally important (more important is the reforming prince) and that Machiavelli is careful in the support he gives to it.

The People and the Great

In order to explain why receiving liberty or becoming a free state is a transition difficult to effect, Machiavelli offers this sweeping pronouncement on the nature of the people:

> For that people [used to living under a prince] is nothing other than a brute animal that, although of a ferocious and feral nature, has always been nourished in prison and in servitude. Then, if it is left free in a field to its fate, it becomes the prey of the first one who seeks to rechain it, not being used to feed itself and not knowing places where it may have to take refuge. (I.16.1)

By nature, the people is wild like an animal. To be wild is to be free, and to be free is to do as one likes. By contrast, life in society, and particularly life under

93

princely rule, is the equivalent of captivity; for a creature, made to roam free, is instead confined to a cage (a small cage in the case of a principality, a large cage in the case of a republic). Society, therefore, is a crime against the people's nature. On the other hand, the people's nature is a surprisingly malleable thing, and its reshaping by society might be sought after by the people and in the people's best interest. It all depends on what at bottom this free creature wants and needs. Does it want to govern itself, or does it want to live safely? In the wild this choice can hardly arise, for freedom is a means to preservation before it is an end in itself; the animal is free and self-governing in the wild in order to find nourishment, locate refuge, and elude predators. But other means avail in society, such as the government of princes under the rule of law. In society, then, and only in society, can the full nature of the people be discovered. And what is discovered about a naturalized/socialized people is that it most wants a freedom that is privatively defined. The people, *il popolo*, wants "not to be oppressed" (*non essere oppresso*) (I.5.2; *Prince*, 9; *Florentine Histories*, III.1). The people perceives itself to be not oppressed if it is ruled by a law that is commonly useful and observed by authorities. For examination shows, Machiavelli declares, that the people "desire[s] freedom so as to live secure" (I.16.5). But examination further shows that a small segment of the population, some 40 or 50 persons in any community, "desires to be free so as to command" (§5). These others, called "the great" (*i grandi*)—or, if well-born, patricians, aristocrats, nobles—want a more robust kind of freedom. If they too are wild by nature, then their natural wildness expands in reaction to opportunities provided by society, changing from a desire to be free to a desire to dominate others, which in nature would be no more achievable than a desire to be always safe. In any event, nature's uniform wildness, a consequence of survival necessities, is divided by society into a liberty conceived as security and a liberty conceived as power. Human nature is fulfilled in society, but it also suffers bifurcation.

The people and the great emerge as different humors in society, visibly apart, because they want different and opposite things. The people wants not to be oppressed, and the great want to oppress. But oftentimes Machiavelli's descriptions imply that the humors want the same things. In chapter 37 Machiavelli identifies two passions which he attributes to all men: anxiety and boredom, or fear and desire. "Men are wont to worry in evil and to become bored with good," he claims. But Machiavelli does not try hard to keep these passions separate as he might were his purpose to associate them with the classes or to use them as a basis for moral judgment. He seems rather to view fear and desire as points on a continuum—one followed by and causally connected to the other. He observes in the next sentence that "whenever engaging in combat through necessity is taken from men they engage in combat through ambition, which is so powerful in human breasts that it never abandons them at whatever rank they rise to" (§1). No class distinction is drawn here, except that which corrects the presumption that maybe the great outgrow ambition by satisfying it completely.

They do not; nor is the multitude without ambition either. The continuum conception is utilized again in I.46.1, where Machiavelli says that "when men seek not to fear, they begin to make others fear; and the injury that they dispel from themselves they put upon another, as if it were necessary to offend or to be offended." And the title of chapter 46 indicates that the switch from suffering offense to committing offense is an ascent from "one ambition to another"—not, be it noted, an ascent from necessity to ambition or from fear to desire. It is as if all passion goes by the name of ambition, or as if emotion is not pathos but self-assertion.

Back in chapter 37 Machiavelli offers a fuller account of the human psyche:

> The cause is that nature has created men so that they are able to desire everything and are unable to attain everything. So, since the desire is always greater than the power of acquiring, the result is discontent with what one possesses and a lack of satisfaction with it. From this arises the variability of their fortune; for since some men desire to have more, and some fear to lose what has been acquired, they come to enmities and to war. (§1)

Now it might be thought that the more passive people is the class which fears to lose and the more aggressive great the class which seeks to acquire; that the great start the trouble with their scheming, grasping, and bullying, while the people fights back in self-defense. Even if true ordinarily, the above passages point out that men become ambitious the moment they cease being fearful. Since this is so, one would expect that plebeians, given a respite from patrician pressure, would behave ambitiously themselves and come to resemble ambitious patricians. And indeed, Machiavelli describes plebeians in terms more typical of the great:

> It was not enough for Roman plebs to secure itself against the nobles by the creation of the tribunes, to which desire it was constrained by necessity; for having obtained that, it began at once to engage in combat through ambition, and to wish to share honors and belongings with the nobility as the thing esteemed most by men. (§1)

The usual relationship of the orders is reversed in this quotation, as it is in I.5, for hungry plebeians attack satisfied patricians who want only to maintain what they have. Furthermore, the plebeians are said to have started the civil war, since they were the first to find a champion, Marius, to defend their interest, and their second champion, Caesar, "was the first tyrant in Rome, such that never again was that city free" (§2). By contrast, the nobility's standard-bearer, Sulla, did not destroy liberty; and in naming him the nobles were merely reacting to the "plague" of factional rivalry set loose by the plebeians, whose agrarian legislation is called a "disease." Also the patricians are made to look especially common and ignoble—these proud lovers of glory were more enamored of property than of honor, giving away their power but never their land.

If then, as the foregoing implies, ambition is ubiquitous and the classes alike, why say that the classes are different or that cities are composed of two distinct humors? Part of the answer is that the difference, while real, is situational. Most human beings live their lives limited by the same quotidian necessities—food, clothing, and shelter, acquired and reacquired day after day, generation after generation. The many have not the luxury of being bored and hence the need to contrive new ambitions for the sake of something to do. Necessity stunts the talents and imagination of most people who also would benefit from opportunities provided by wealth. Were they wealthy too, the difference between the classes would seem less stark, less permanent, and less the product of nature.[1]

A second reason is that not all of the great live among their kind. On the assumption that nature has a hand in things and that nurture is not all, naturally ambitious individuals are born to and scattered among the people. Some of them, suffering this and other malignities of fortune, never rise above the obscurity which is their lot. But if they try, and especially if they succeed, they change the perception of the class from which they hail. The people is better than believed because some among it have joined the elite. Conversely, the great are less than supposed since some of their number have nothing but wealth to distinguish them from the vulgar.

There is, as well, a third reason for distinguishing the classes—though more prescriptive is it than descriptive. One consequence of this reversal of types is a confounding of the moral compass. We cannot blame patricians, as we are apt to do, for greedily upsetting the equality of citizens; nor can we sympathize with plebeians, counting them as victims of another's pride. There are no villains if the characters change sides, if ambition is necessitated, and if fear is not an emotion identifying the good. Machiavelli, it seems, defends patricians by extending their qualities to plebeians. This he does because patricians have a role to play in a mixed regime and because successful politics depends more on the counterbalancing of vice than on the empowerment of virtue. For instance, the agrarian law was less a case of public-spirited egalitarianism than of the natural appetitiveness of men ("with this law and with its other appetites" [§3]), or a case of plebeians fighting because of ambition.

If we allow then that ambition is ubiquitous but that the classes do differ, the difference must depend on the intensity of ambition and on its source. The public is the public, we might say, because its desires are less compelling and because it is acquisitive when stimulated from without; otherwise it is subdued, if not at rest. The great, by contrast, have their stimulants supplied from within and, being intensely acquisitive, never are at rest. When Machiavelli first speaks of the people, calling the class a "have-not" acquirer, its counterpart a well-endowed maintainer, he is quick to add that the people's acquisitiveness is a protective reaction to the greed of the nobles (I.5.4). Where the nobles are not greedy, because prevented by law (as in Sparta, for example), the people is not acquisitive or even political (I.6.2). The apoliticism of the people, i.e., the basic "at-restness" of the class, is further attested to in I.16.5. It is oppression which galvanizes the "don't tread on me" people to demand political power and to seek redress for its grievances. Even so, ambition in the people is a purgeable, not persistent, passion (I.4.1), as is the anger the people feels when treated unjustly (I.5.4, I.7.1). Proof that the people is constant and quiet unless pushed from without is provided in the very chapter which purports to establish the universality of unlimited desire. Chapter 37 tells of how the plebs in Rome wanted an agrarian law that would cap property-owning and would distribute conquered lands among the people. Following the capture of Anzio (Antium), the senate agreed to the second of these demands, proposing to send to Anzio a colony of Roman plebs (467 BC). But the plebeians' appetite for land was sated by the mere availability of land; and so only with difficulty could plebs be persuaded to go. Plainly this incident contradicts the proposition it is meant to confirm. For the public's desires are anything but limitless if the possibility of landholding, but not actual possession and use, is sufficient to satisfy them; if, as Machiavelli notes, citing Livy, the plebs was "more willing to desire things in Rome than to possess them in Anzio" (§2). The multitude, it seems, is more envious than acquisitive, and the appearance of equality is concession enough. The same is often true of the franchise—when denied, it is the most important thing in the world; when granted, it goes unexercised. For example, given the right to elect new senators, the Capuan plebs kept the ones that it had; given the right to elect plebeian military tribunes, the Roman plebs chose only patricians (I.47). The people does not so much want equality of property and power, at least not to the point of fighting for them; it does, however, take offense at the imputation of inferiority and wants removed unnecessary affronts to its dignity. When Camillus, victor at Veii, rode in a triumphal chariot pulled by four white horses, the plebs concluded that he presumed himself the equal of the sun, and resenting his pride, they banished him from the city (III.23.1). Were the people as truly ambitious as the nobles, popular participation of any kind would soon result in overcrowding at the top and possibly in a war between the classes. It is of no small consequence, therefore, that the people is different from the great. And it is of no small consequence that this difference be disguised. For the people need to think of itself as equal, and the nobles need to be thought of as blameless.

There is a statement in II.Pr.3 which substantially repeats the lesson of chapter 37, that appetites are insatiable and human beings discontent because desire outpaces the capacity to acquire. Again it seems that plebs and nobles are the same. But the statement should not be taken to mean that all men are equally and ceaselessly acquisitive (for how then explain Machiavelli's concern that frustrated desire will lead to resignation and inactivity—to passive grousing about the present and romanticizing the past? How explain Machiavelli's decision to speak spiritedly so as to arouse to action the spirited young? [II.Pr.3]). The discontent which results from appetites unsatisfied may prevent men from thinking themselves happy, but it does not always stir them to achieve what they desire. Indeed, the difference among humans—and among states—can be determined by how they react to fortune's disappointments. Some accept defeat and settle for less; others fight on unwilling to fail.

The people is on its guard and ready for combat so long as it fears oppression. But once the threatening stimulant is removed, the people reverts to its natural state of disgruntled complacency. And if instead the people goes on the offensive, outside stimulants of another sort are needed. We saw this in I.53, where demagogues won commands by promising the moon. Excited by the prospect of quick riches and easy glory, the people appears for the moment more acquisitive than the nobles; while the nobles appear hesitant and reserved while trying to control plebeian haste. But the people's acquisitiveness requires agitation by tribunes, who—if they are tribunes "by nature" and not "by convention"—belong to the class of the great, and whose own acquisitiveness is self-starting, not reactive. Much of what passes then for popular ambition is but the ambition of the people's leaders. Without Licinius and Sextius there never would have been plebeian consuls.

The people is like the occasional investor, who, seeing fortunes made by others, buys high at the market's peak, and who, late to divest, sells low after the crash. Burned by the experience, this tyro tycoon swears never to buy stocks again; and with his money tucked safely away in a savings account, he avoids risk and protects his principal—until the next market boom, that is. By contrast, the great are like practiced investors, who realize that inflation is always devaluing principal and that growth is needed just to stay even, and who are prepared to incur some risks in the hope of reaping large gains. Machiavelli describes the great as maintainers who also are acquirers because they sense the presence of necessity no matter how secure they might be (I.5.4). The chief difference between the people and the great seems to be then that plebeians see necessity when it is standing before them (when the city is besieged they know it has enemies) but do not see necessity when it is far off in the distance (I.18.4); the great, on the other hand, see necessity everywhere, perhaps even where it is not.

One indication of the difference is the opinion each group holds of necessity as a teacher. The people thinks that necessity reveals little of importance because it reduces human behavior to its lowest common denominator and because its power is intermittent not continuous. When relating the story of the senate's tardy benefaction of tax relief in chapter 32, Machiavelli offered this assessment of popular reasoning: "For the collectivity will judge that it has that good not from you but from your adversaries; and since it ought to fear that when the necessity has passed, you will take back from them what you had been forced to give them, it will not have any obligation to you" (§1). The people figures that actions taken in response to necessity give no true reading of a person's character, that they are common to all and are undeserving of either praise or blame. (The people, after all, is a wild beast when facing nature's necessities but is a domesticated pet when protected by society.) But what a person does when he can do otherwise is illuminating of character and is a better predictor of how that person will behave in the future—because the human future is, or is thought to be, more free than determined.[2] The great instead put little stock in actions freely chosen, thinking them exceptional and eccentric, and they respond to generosity, the freest of all actions, with ingratitude (I.29.1-2; *Prince*, 7). It is the multitude which is generous and grateful and which is most happy when its leaders are magnanimous. The town of Falerii[3] opened its gates to Camillus because its people believed that a general who would freely return hostage schoolchildren would treat benignly a town which had freely surrendered to him (394 BC). From this episode Machiavelli concludes that "one sees too how much this part is desired in great men by peoples, and how much it is praised by writers, and by those who describe the life of princes, and by those who order how they ought to live" (III.20.1). Of course the most magnanimous leader of all is a providential deity who intervenes in human affairs to protect, instruct, and save; and who rewards with redemption those who demonstrate the free character of their virtue. Piety is an attribute of the people, whereas the great are atheists who believe themselves to be alone in the world. And because they feel alone, they are distrusting, fearful, and ever on the lookout for necessity's incursions.

It is amazing how soft sometimes is the necessity which compels the great to act. When the senate initiated payment for military service, the necessity that moved it was not an invasion of Tuscans (I.32.1) or even a plague (I.38.1). The necessity was that the senate "judged that it was necessary" to pay soldiers in order to besiege towns and lead armies far away (I.51.1). But then we know that desire is no different from fear; both are ambitions (I.46.1), and ambition is rated a necessary striving comparable to the necessitated motions of the physical universe. Certainly it is no different for the great, who acquire in order to maintain and who are doubly ungrateful because suspicion and avarice are connected emotions. Machiavelli explains in chapters 29 and 30 the perverse psychology which produces princely ingratitude. A prince is served faithfully and well by his victorious captain, and gratitude is the natural and expected response. But the prince cannot help feeling suspicious of a captain who has accomplished so much. At the same time, a captain cannot help entertaining new ambitions to which his success entitles him. The barest hint of insolence on the captain's part confirms the suspicions of the prince, who, to protect himself, takes precautionary actions which offend and injure the captain. Either the captain suffers this ingratitude or, feeling the same suspicion, protects himself by preemptively usurping the prince's state. Beginning thus as a friend and supporter, the captain becomes a rival and an enemy; while the prince, wanting to show his gratitude, is nevertheless compelled to be ungrateful. Simple self-preservation causes each to commit crimes against the other. The people, on the other hand, is only half as ungrateful, since the people keeps suspicion and avarice apart. But again situational factors apply: The people does not so readily move from fear to desire, maintenance to acquisition, suspicion to avarice because its numbers are too large for the appropriated bounty to be of much use. One reason why "those who are popular" are the designated guardians of liberty is that "since they are not able to seize it, they do not permit others to seize it" (I.5.2). Similarly, one reason why confederations do not expand is that "since there are many communities to participate in dominion, they do not esteem such acquisition as much as one republic alone that hopes to enjoy it entirely" (II.4.2).

Although the people is of a different temperament than the great, by the application of stimulants it comes to appear quite similar. That application can be accidental or deliberate. It is accidental when the domineering nobles cause the people to defend itself—as the Roman plebs resorted to tumults when its interests were overtly threatened. It is deliberate when modes and orders arm plebeians and keep them at war. A martial people has a more noble bearing than has a commercial people; thus plebeians trained for war look like proud aristocrats, just as aristocrats busy with trade look like prosperous plebeians. It is deliberate as well when the people is called upon to sit in judgment of individuals. Passing judgment, whether on candidates running for election or on defendants standing trial, acquaints the people with the heavy burdens and unpleasant realities of governance and is a useful antidote to sentimental naiveté. When a Manlius Capitolinus is condemned for treason (384 BC), the people is taught to put aside its adolescent hero-worship and deal impartially with persons it admires (I.58.2, III.8.1). And when a Capitolinus is hurled from the Tarpeian Rock (I.24.2), the people individually are frightened by the prospect of falling victim themselves to so blind and unforgiving a system of law (I.57.1, III.49.2).[4] The people is "satisfied and stupefied," as Machiavelli remarks in *Prince* 7. Sensational punishments periodically imposed thus remind the people of dangerous powers which the enterprising great encounter routinely (III.1.3).

As suggested above, there is some benefit to minimizing the differences defining the humors, on condition that it is the people which is made to resemble the great. For an "ennobled" populace is better able to defend its liberty when the great go on the attack.[5] It is disposed as well to defend the city's liberty, joining forces with the senate to condemn tyrants who espouse the popular cause. Also, by serving as soldiers in the army, it saves the city from reliance on mercenaries and from defeat by foreign powers, while helping the city to acquire dominion and glory. Perhaps finally there is some expectation that a populace enlightened by experience will prove more amenable to the adjurations of the necessity-obsessed great, who fearing scandal less will have a wider latitude in handling affairs of state. Take for example the case of the Horatii and the Curiatii. Kings Tullus and Mettius gambled the fates of their cities on the outcome of a duel between matching sets of brothers. Machiavelli ridicules the kings for making the wager, if by it they believed that so portentous an agreement would ever be honored by the loser. It would not because kings as a rule are duplicitous, but also because "peoples" would find it intolerable that "three of their citizens had put them in subjection" since "being servile is so important to a city" (I.22.1). The people, it seems, can be as wise as princes in assessing effectual truth.[6] While basically the people is honest and does not think to deceive (I.55.1), at least on one occasion the Roman plebs took instruction in the art of duplicity. After the fall of the decemvirate (449 BC), when the people had gathered on the Sacred Mount demanding, among other things, that the decemvirs be handed over for burning alive, the senators who were dispatched to receive the demands of the plebs had to advise its representatives that "they ought to omit making mention of the Ten and that they should wait until they had retaken their authority and their power; then they would not lack their mode of satisfying themselves" (I.44.1). First addressed in the moral idiom familiar to them, that they were damning cruelty while rushing to commit it, these plebeians gradually were apprised of the amoral reasoning typical of the great; to which Machiavelli adds a particularly notorious maxim of his own: "For it is enough to ask someone for his arms without saying, 'I wish to kill you with them,' since you are able to satisfy your appetite after you have the arms in hand."

But notwithstanding enlightenment efforts such as these, the people's education in realpolitik is strictly limited and hardly equivalent to the wisdom of princes.[7] For the perspective of the people, Machiavelli seems to indicate, remains that of the piazza, not of the palazzo.[8] In Florence after the ouster of the Medici (1494 AD), "popular men" filled with "ambitious license" managed to ascend to the supreme magistracy. Once there they demonstrated their capacity for judging particulars—not persons in this instance, but policies; policies seen close-up, from the palazzo, which when seen from afar, from the piazza, these same men denounced. What they learned was that "the times and not the men caused the disorder" (I.47.3). But the education of "popular men" had no appreciable effect on the education of the populace which believed that these erstwhile firebrands had changed their manner, not from having gained "a truer knowledge of things," but from having been "got around and corrupted by the great." The Florentine people was wont to say of such turncoats that "they have one mind in the piazza and another in the palazzo" (§3), a proverb expressing what we today would say is the public's inveterate "anti-Washington" bias. Accordingly, in the after-years, Piero Soderini could make no concessions to the Medici supporters since exposure of the deal would have ruined his standing with the people (I.52.2).

Civic Virtue

The people's virtue, more generally called goodness (*bontà*), is not the same thing as the people's inertia, which in any event is never so inert as to refute the judgment that all men are presumptively bad. Human nature, including the nature of the people, is selfish. Goodness is defined, however, as selfless devotion to the commonweal. Since goodness is not innate to human beings, it must somehow be implanted in them. As previously discussed, necessity is the agent which makes people good (e.g., II.12.3).[9] Necessity, though, differs by degree, and only one of its degrees is useful to human virtue. Necessity #1, as we shall call it, is a condition of radical isolation brought on by the prospect of widespread destruction and imminent death. It is so forceful that it makes people bad, not good. Irresistible dangers cause people to run and hide, not stand and fight; to hope that the scythe of death misses them and takes another. Necessity, then, when this immediate and extreme, sets people apart in a war of all against all. If people are to survive, to say nothing of prosper, it is imperative that necessity's too-frightening aspect be softened. The solution of course is community. Community pushes back the threat of Necessity #1 because people band together in a common effort; and they band together because cooperation is the only way to turn irresistible force into a manageable opponent. This diminished necessity is Necessity #2, which alone is responsible for human goodness. For as long as necessity is visible outside the city gates, manning the walls is an obligation useful to the individual and the group alike. On the other hand, let the walls be breached, and Necessity #2 quickly reverts to Necessity #1. A third degree of necessity exists when, to continue the metaphor, the defenses have been built so high and so strong that the city seems invulnerable to attack whether or not there are sentries on duty. Necessity #3 is invisible and forgotten, ironically, because Necessity #2 has made people so good that they feel they can afford to be bad. People are bad if there is too little or too much necessity; they are good only when necessity is just right.

The foregoing supposes that necessity exists outside of society and is supplied to it by chance—a harsh environment, an aggressive neighbor, etc. Machiavelli's argument, however, is that necessity should be brought inside of society and under the control of men. Modes and orders, he avows, can do the work of a sterile site (I.1.4). People can be made obedient, dutiful, and patriotic by the laws of their society, in particular by military orders, religion, and restrictions on wealth. In a well-ordered society, law-based necessity keeps the state strong enough to defend against external dangers and disciplined enough to ward off internal corruption.

But as was the case when necessity came from without, the more successful a state is in defeating Necessity #1, the more vulnerable it becomes to Necessity #3. Strength invites decay. Why? First, because strength provides security from outside attack, and security permits the neglect of excellence and of the exacting regimen which is its cause. When Rome had subdued Africa, Asia, and most of Greece, it took to electing mediocrities to high office (I.18.3, III.16, III.30.1). Second, because strength establishes peace, and peace allows factions to emerge (I.6.4, II.19.1, II.25.1). People manufacture enemies within when enemies without are wanting. Third, because strength brings luxury, leisure, and inequality, achievements of civilization but also sources of weakness and division. Goodness is primitive, and so mountain men are better than city-dwellers (I.11.3). Fourth, because strength entails contact with foreign peoples whose foreign ways cause corruption of local customs, most especially the neglect and belittling of religion (I.12.1, I.55.2, II.Pr.2, III.1.2). Rome was nearly ruined by contact with the soft and luxuriant Capuans (II.19.2), and the arrival from Greece of Diogenes and Carneades caused young Romans to admire philosophy, while their arrival caused Cato, in reaction, to bar philosophers from Rome (*Florentine Histories*, V.1). In sum, good people are formed in the crucible of Necessity #2, present by chance or by law; but the goodness of people is endangered by the quick defeats of Necessity #1 or by the slow corrosives of Necessity #3. Goodness is a middle way between too much necessity and too little.

The inverse of too much and too little necessity is too little and too much choice. The proposition that necessity in due measure causes goodness is reformulated to read that choice in undue measure causes defeat or corruption (I.1.4). A city which hasn't the freedom to expand is a likely acquisition of its larger neighbors; and a city which is free of worry becomes soft and self-indulgent. It is though the latter eventuality which captures Machiavelli's attention—the corruption caused by freedom in excess. Too much freedom is the ruin of civic virtue and thus the ruin of states depending on it for unity. It might seem, therefore, that the subjects of a prince, having less freedom, are more virtuous than the citizens of a republic, having more freedom and possibly too much. At least republican citizens are in a position to take extra freedom as it pleases them, whereas princely subjects have their freedom dispensed by another—as when a prince agrees to govern by law. But Machiavelli does not go to principalities in order to find examples of exemplary virtue. On the contrary, he contends that goodness is best achieved in republics (I.58.3, II.2.1). But why is that, if republics are free and if freedom, or choice, causes the corruption of goodness? The answer, presumably, is that goodness entails something more than self-restraint. It is true that in order to be counted good, people must sacrifice and obey, put community first and themselves second, give priority to long-term common needs over short-term personal interests. But the people, *il popolo*, must also assert its rights and defend its liberty. An obedient people, if it is servile, is not good. One problem with princely rule is that it eviscerates the people's capacity for free living. The assumption in I.16.1 is that docility equals corruption and that freedom, far from destroying virtue, practically defines it.[10] A similar lesson is offered in II.2.1 where the love of liberty is taken as proof that Rome and its neighbors were supremely virtuous. A virtuous people will not sell its liberty for bread and peace; indeed it will destroy those who try bribing it with small delights, as did the Roman plebs when it renounced the benefactions of Spurius Cassius and Manlius Capitolinus (III.8.1). Nor does a virtuous people pay tribute in order to lighten the burden of self-defense (II.30) or trade its martial prowess for mechanical occupations (III.5.1). At the same time a virtuous people restrains itself, not allowing its love of liberty to grow into a lust for power (I.46.1) or success to make it insolent and giddy with false hopes (II.27). Civic virtue is twofold then: one part submission to the whole and one part assertion of independence.[11] It is a combination of opposites useful to the city, itself an oxymoronic union of the common and the selfish. For the city of Machiavelli's devising has collective selfishness as its defining characteristic and empire as its overriding objective. Thus the imperial city needs a spirited populace, a people of "moment" (I.53.5) willing to fight in order not to be oppressed. It needs as well a ruling class ever alert to the profits accruing from expansion. We noticed before how the two classes appear similar from time to time—how the great, by acquiring and hoarding property, resemble the money-loving people; and how the people, by asserting its rights and standing on its dignity, resembles the honor-loving great. That being the case, it should come as no surprise if the people's goodness is a mixture of good and bad, of the selfless and the selfish.

Virtue's Value

How important is the people's goodness to freedom and republican self-rule? The question defies easy answering because Machiavelli is inconsistent, or seemingly so. The likely answer is that goodness is vitally important. Machiavelli's most ringing endorsement of civic virtue occurs in I.55.2: "And truly, where there is not this goodness, nothing good can be hoped for. . . ." Goodness means piety, innocence, and equality in I.55. Modern Germans, for example, are bound by their oaths, live apart from the world, and allow no "gentlemen" in their midst. Civic virtue is also important in I.43 where it is defined as soldiers fighting for their own glory. Under the consuls Rome was always victorious, but under the decemvirs Rome was defeated. Thus military success is seemingly dependent on the goodness, or liberty, of the people, military defeat a consequence of the people's corruption. We have seen already what contact with Capuan luxury meant for Rome. The legions sent to garrison the city, seduced by its many comforts and amusements, conspired to seize the town for themselves and to rebel against Rome (343 BC). Machiavelli's assessment of the situation is that Capua would have meant "the ruin of the Roman republic" if Capua had been located at a distance and beyond the close supervision of the senate and if "Rome had been corrupt in some part" (II.19.2). Presumably a corrupt Rome would not have expunged the more advanced corruption of Capua, but would have embraced it instead.

While usually a quality of the people, goodness sometimes was also an attribute of the great. The corruption caused by the prolongation of commands (326 BC), which "in time ruined the republic," would have occurred a century and a third earlier had not Lucius Quintius Cincinnatus, consul at the time (460 BC), resisted the senate's initiative to extend his office in response to extended magistracies given to the tribunes. Cincinnatus rejected the senate's offer, "saying that one should wish to seek to eliminate bad examples, not to increase them with another worse example" (III.24.1). And Camillus could never have disarmed envy and been effectively alone in the office of military tribune had his colleagues not exhibited goodness (III.30.1). Nor could Papirius Cursor have been named dictator had not his former master of horse and bitter rival, Quintus Fabius, been willing to suppress his injured pride (III.47). Similarly, the practice of promoting junior officers to positions of responsibility presupposed goodness on the part of senior officers asked to step aside and to obey (I.36). All in all then, goodness in the hearts of citizens—in the people mainly but in the great to some extent—is what guards republics by beating back corruption, the cause of their demise.

But while goodness guards republics, it does not guard itself; and corruption, we have seen, can occur quite suddenly. Rome was quickly corrupted by the decemvirs who attracted partisan supporters to their cause. The situation was complicated by the extent of decemviral power, but civic virtue, one of the bulwarks against usurpation by dictators, proved of little use here. Machiavelli repeats the lesson of virtue's weakness in chapter 42, the title of which reads, "How Easily Men Can Be Corrupted."

Virtue seems essential to freedom, but virtue is a delicate flower susceptible to disease. What then to do? Chapters 16 through 18 constitute a unit, the subject of which is the coexistence freedom and corruption. Might a corrupt people be free after all, and might virtue, a greenhouse annual, be replaced by some more vigorous plant, a hardy perennial? Judging from the titles of 16 and 17, one would have to conclude that the prospects for freedom in corruption are bleak and declining. For 16 asserts that "with difficulty" can a corrupt people (i.e., one used to living under a prince) maintain liberty, whereas 17 asserts that maintaining liberty by a corrupt people is done "with the greatest difficulty." It should follow, therefore, that virtue is indispensable; for when corruption sets in, freedom dies.

But Machiavelli is not through considering the true worth of virtue. Chapter 18 asks again whether freedom can be maintained in a corrupt state, with it this time suggested that law might serve as virtue's substitute or companion.[12]

Human behavior is held in check by three political and moral constraints: orders (*ordini*), laws (*leggi*), and customs (*costumi*). By orders Machiavelli means the constitutional division of power and the procedures for conducting public affairs: offices of state, modes of election, etc. By laws he means the civil statutes that prescribe and proscribe the conduct of citizens—such as sumptuary laws to control luxuries. And by customs he means the opinions of the citizens themselves, whether they think it ignominious to suffer rejection by the electorate, for example. Customs are the equivalent of virtue and goodness, in that customary controls are internalized, habitual, and seemingly self-willed. These three restraints support each other; their purpose is to protect virtue and fend off corruption, while compensating for corruption as it occurs. For people change. They change in their habits and in their opinions; and mainly they change for the worse. Accordingly, the two other restraints, orders and laws, must change as well in order to keep pace with changing customs. Politics must connect with morals. In the case of Rome, its laws underwent frequent reformation, with new restrictions imposed on sexual morality, the display of wealth, and the ambition of individuals. But the constitution remained mostly the same. The orders by which magistrates were selected and legislation was passed persisted long after the customs which supported them had ceased to be observed. In the early years candidates for office nominated themselves, and legislation originated with the people.[13] These orders were good as long as the citizens were serious and patriotic. But it was insecurity, or necessity, which made them so. Fearing for their survival, the citizens elected only the best candidates to high office; and when they proposed legislation, they spoke only what they believed was in the best interest of the state. But when Rome became a world empire and no single enemy threatened its existence, the citizens could afford to favor the powerful over the meritorious and to pass laws that advantaged certain parties more than others and more than the good of the whole.[14]

Let's restate this argument in light of the previous discussion of the three degrees of necessity. People are good (i.e., obedient, pious, self-effacing, dutiful, deferential, etc.) not because they want to be but because they have to be. The "have to be" is a consequence of external threats. People subordinate their private interests to the common good because survival in a perilous world is possible only with the assistance of others, only within and by means of community. Community is useful and people are most devoted to it when outside dangers are grave and imminent, which typically is the case when a community is young—men are good "in a republic at its birth" (I.18.1).[15] These dangers, in combination with the founder's prudence, generate the customs of self-sacrifice and public service, which the orders and laws depend on and in turn support. Indeed, the support should be such that customs remain healthy even as necessity abates and choice arises. Orders and laws, given by founders and maintained by peoples, are products of choice, which products nonetheless are required to imitate the necessity of nature and chance. Replacing necessity, they defend the customs reflective of goodness. And it is at times when orders, laws, and customs are all in sync that choice is an asset enabling the state to grow strong and expand. Freedom then is useful, not corrupting. This is the condition which describes Necessity #2, with orders and laws the source of the disciplined fear causing citizens to be good.

One correction is needed. The analysis in chapter 18 does not permit us to think in terms of fixed states of being—a perfect alignment of orders, laws, and customs which keep the city balanced and at rest. On the contrary, the city is forever changing. It wants to succeed, to increase and domineer, and it changes because of its success. Success brings safety, plenty, and ease. When the commonweal is cared for and all are secure (Necessity #3), personal sacrifice is less consequential and less required. While this relaxation of effort is a mark of corruption, the antithesis of goodness, in another sense, relaxation is the fulfillment of goodness. For the rationale of community is that through realization of the common good, private goods can best be attained. Personal sacrifice is supposed to be temporary and for the sake of personal enjoyment, goodness being but the means to selfishness the end. Corruption, therefore, is the end of goodness in both senses of the word "end"—its demise and its purpose. But corruption is a false purpose, since corruption destroys community while simultaneously presupposing a world made safe by community.

So it becomes the work of orders and laws to delay redemption of the community's promises by adjusting themselves to the ever-growing corruption of the public. Orders and laws which presuppose selflessness must change as citizens, showing the effects of success, become more selfish and shortsighted. As the state moves from a union made whole and one by the threat of external dangers to a union that is fractured and contentious because the threat is in retreat, it is imperative that orders and laws change from those which promote trust and which honor sacrifice to those which encourage distrust and set loose ambition. If the enemy is not outside the city, then inside the city must the enemy be. If not war against the Tuscans, then vigilance against the nobles. Either way there is necessity causing goodness, although the meaning of goodness changes somewhat. It still means solidarity; but solidarity is with a smaller and more homogeneous group, and its acquisitions are less good because shared with fewer persons. We saw that the people's goodness consists of contrasting qualities: of trust and suspicion, gratitude and ingratitude, deference and defiance, self-sacrifice and self-assertion. Goodness entails the use of one set of qualities with insiders and the use of the other set of qualities against outsiders, however insiders and outsiders are defined.[16] Orders and laws change because the real community to which citizens are loyal is expanding or contracting. When citizens are more loyal to class than to city, orders and laws must reflect the distrusting side of goodness. For example, an evolving Roman constitution added tribunes in order to check the ambition of nobles; and the more articulated became Rome's mixed regime the more distrust superseded trust and the more the people resembled the great. (The community is largest and trust is at its peak in simple regimes which still are good.)[17] At the same time Rome drew upon the trusting side of the people's goodness by maintaining religious traditions and by hiding the government of nobles. Overall, as Rome moved from embattled city to world empire, it was a state corrupting and in decline, for while its borders expanded, its community narrowed—from city to class to indi-vidual. But in the long meantime, Rome kept itself essentially healthy by ad-justing its orders and laws to the changing state of the people's virtue and of its own success. And if it changed not enough, then Machiavelli points out the er-rors which it made.

In fact Rome did err. It changed laws but not orders. It seems that Machia-velli is recommending a constitution that is as malleable as statutory law. If the people are no longer good enough to hold certain offices or make a success of certain practices, change the offices and practices. Machiavelli's focus is on the means of change, of which he says there are two: early and "little by little," and late and "all at a stroke." We remember that Rome fashioned its constitution "little by little," and that Sparta received its constitution "all at a stroke." But apparently the dynamic Roman constitution of earlier periods ossified some-where along the line. For Machiavelli does not point to Rome as an example of a state which reformed its constitution in a regular and timely fashion. Rome instead exemplifies the difficulty of "little by little" reform—that the dangers are at a distance and that human beings see only what is near. If a prescient individ-ual happens to live within the city, he still faces the problem of persuading oth-ers of the dangers which he sees. These others suffer from near-sightedness; and their myopia is aggravated by the conviction that the future will replay the past and that the institutions dear to them and by which they were shaped contain all of the wisdom that there is. Law speaks in universals and pretends to truth. It is revered, and its influence is conservative.[18] Thus ignorance regarding the future as well as prejudice in favor of the past stand in the way of "little by little" re-form, which to work might well require, not the rule of law, but rule by philoso-pher-kings.

"Little by little" reform is a shorthand expression for the continual amending of orders and laws to fit the changing, and declining, customs of the people. Its necessary failure suggests that the plan of maintaining a free state in a corrupt city cannot succeed. If freedom is important, then so too is virtue; and moral corruption is a danger not to be taken lightly.

Even were this gradualism a workable strategy, every adjustment of law to declining morals would leave the citizens a little less free—would remove from them a measure of power which they no longer could exercise responsibly. By this route there must come a point when the citizenry has surrendered its free-dom entirely, when the next and final adjustment is caesarism. If good govern-ment is the end, meaning the best government under the circumstances, then amending the constitution is unobjectionable as the means—for always the con-stitution should match the character of the people, whatever the constitution is.[19] But then the constitution will not always be republican, and the people will not always have liberty. On the other hand, if freedom is the thing, then the citizens' virtue, and not only their constitution, requires attention.

But there is another way, called reform "all at a stroke." Initially such reform seems hardly less utopian than the alternative method, for while problems now are so severe as to be visible to all, their rectification requires use of extraordinary modes, i.e., violence, tyranny, and the usurpation of high office. By contrast, "little by little" reform is ordinary and lawful, but wholly dependent on the unlikely foreseeing of the public. Machiavelli seems to recommend what Caesar in fact did: "become prince of that city and . . . dispose it in one's own mode" (I.18.4). Rome had become exceedingly corrupt, and "all at a stroke" Caesar adjusted the constitution to fit the moral condition and political capacities of the people. But the real challenge lies elsewhere, in using tyrannical power for the purpose of restoring a political way of life. This Caesar did not do. But then the doing almost defies reason—for the means employed suppose a bad man as prince, whereas the end served supposes a good man as prince. Machiavelli would have us believe that violent reform is a psychological impossibility, or nearly that; and that he himself is overwhelmed by the daunting task of persuading a bad man to be good or a good man to be bad. On the other hand, it is a task which suits Machiavelli perfectly. He distrusts attempts to hold to a middle way, such as "little by little" reform implies (modest changes which keep customs, laws, and orders always in balance); and he rather likes—certainly he excuses—the violence that creates orders anew or wrenches them back to their beginnings. Rather than suppose the production of such a prince impossible, Machiavelli arguably makes this task the primary purpose of his *Discourses*. For Machiavelli justifies the actions needed to be alone in power (fratricide), and he identifies the end which solitary power is to serve (the restoration of liberty); furthermore, he explains to the wicked prince the interest he has in doing good (glory). Chapter 9 is addressed to the good prince telling him that he should be wicked in the selection of means, and chapter 10 is addressed to the wicked prince telling him that he should be good in the selection of ends. Thus the distinction among princes is not between good and bad but between farseeing and shortsighted.[20] And the job of persuading one prince that his self-interest coincides with the common good is far easier than the job of persuading unseeing multitudes that distant dangers are for real.

This is not to say that the adviser's job is easy, however, much less that the job of the reformer prince is easy. The lesson of chapter 17 is that freedom may be restored to a corrupt city if "well-ordered laws" are "put in motion by one individual who with an extreme force ensures their observance so that the matter becomes good" (§3). But Machiavelli is uncertain if such a regeneration has ever taken place, or even if one could. For the Theban experiment in republican renewal ended with the death of its author, Epaminodas. From this failure Machiavelli concludes that virtue's restoration requires a reformer who lives a very long time or is succeeded by a person like himself—or, lacking that, a reformer willing to risk danger and shed blood in order to root out the inequality that is causing society's corruption. And the reformer in I.55.5, who would make "a republic from a province suited to be a kingdom" or "a kingdom from one suited to be a republic," must be "rare in brain and authority." Still, Machiavelli does not describe the reformer prince simply to despair of his existence.[21] Reformers are needed, and more of them will appear if they are instructed and have their behavior excused.

Chapter 18 asks if freedom in corruption is a possibility. In a sense it is; not because virtue is unimportant and replaceable by law, but because a virtuous prince can restore civic virtue at a stroke. The citizens can slide, be corrupt and still free, so long as a prince is on hand to pull them back to their beginnings. A prince can take virtue away, as when Appius Claudius, the lead decemvir, corrupted the citizens of Rome; and a prince can bring virtue back. Freedom is less dependent then on civic virtue vigilantly defended, since princely virtue can restore it quickly. Republics depend on principalities, and Rome is like Sparta in having its founding and refoundings "all at a stroke." But then in another sense freedom and corruption cannot coexist; for where there is corruption, freedom—meaning republican self-rule—yields to the government of princes. In a very corrupt state, says Machiavelli, rulers must exercise an "almost kingly power" in order to check the insolence of men who cannot be corrected by law (§5). The reclamation of virtue requires the suspension of republican institutions and a return to regal government. The city, in effect, is starting a new cycle of regimes. The purpose, however, is not the institution of kingship but the quick restoration of republican rule, as if the ship of state were in dry-dock for refurbishing of its hull. And rather like a leaky ship trying to repair itself at sea, a corrupt state, Machiavelli warns, should not attempt repairs to its moral structure within the confines of a republic, for the measures taken would be exceedingly cruel. Cleomenes had only to kill the ephors, and Romulus killed only his brother and Titus Tatius; but in a republic with "universal corruption" (§1), the killings would be countless and reform would be civil war. Safer it is to disarm the factions, suspending the republic for a time until the citizens are up to its challenges again. Accordingly, Caesar was right to make himself prince but wrong not to have used his power to revive the republic.[22]

We return now to Machiavelli's testimonial to the value of civic virtue, that "where there is not this goodness, nothing good can be hoped for" (I.55.2). He follows it with the observation that the states of Italy, France, and Spain lack goodness, or civic virtue, entirely. Nevertheless, some good can be expected from France and Spain because of the virtue and good orders of kings who keep their countries united. (And France is further praised in I.58.2 as "a kingdom that is moderated more by laws than any other kingdom of which knowledge is had in our times" [see also I.16.5 and III.1.5].) Only minimally a free state (it has a titled nobility [I.55.4-5]), France has managed the corruption problem by depoliticizing its public. Thus compared with the province of Germany, next discussed, the French way seems decidedly unattractive. The Germans are free because they are good, and they are good because they are pious, isolated from their neighbors, content to live, eat, and dress simply, and equal one to another. But what is interesting about this explanation is that it does not apply to Rome or account for Rome's virtue. The year was 396. The ten-year siege of Veii had just recently been brought to a conclusion. So splendid was this captured city that the Roman plebs demanded the right to emigrate there. And in anticipation of Veii's fall, the citizens of Rome betook themselves to the front in order to be near at hand for when the plundering began (Livy, V.20). The conquest of Veii represented a new stage in the expansion and enrichment of Rome. Thus one cannot view Rome, certainly not at this juncture, as an isolated and rustic community. Its citizens were greedy for gain, and its ambition was to become great. Nor were the Romans ever much noted for their equality, since from the beginning they divided into classes of rich and poor, and since attempts to equalize property, in the form of agrarian legislation, always met with resistance and were the cause of disturbances. We said this before, but it bears repeating: ancient Romans were not as good (in the more familiar meaning of the word) as modern Germans. In fact, Rome is not even an example of the republicanism lauded in chapter 55. Sparta is the ancient paradigm, not Rome. Roman republicanism was of a different character altogether—factious, acquisitive, expansionist, glory-seeking.[23] Roman goodness, we have seen, was not all self-sacrifice; it had a self-assertive side as well—a quality descriptive of the nobles, encouraged in the plebs, and practiced by the state as a whole against its neighbors. But then self-assertive goodness is more commonly called ambition, the release and use of which led Rome away from ancient, Spartan goodness toward something more recognizably modern. Rome was the prototype of the extended—though not commercial—republic.[24] It follows, therefore, that Machiavelli's final position regarding ancient civic virtue is equivocal. More of it is not necessarily better than less of it, because liberty is not necessarily better than greatness.

Chapter Five

Rome's "Outside" Modes and Orders

At the end of the preface to book II, Machiavelli describes again the structure he has given to the *Discourses*, saying that as the first book covered "decisions made by the Romans pertaining to the inside of the city," this second book will treat "of those [decisions] that the Roman people made pertaining to the increase of its empire" (II.Pr.3). The word "decisions" appears to be equivalent to the expression "public counsel" used in the first description, and "increase of its empire" appears equivalent to "things worked by it . . . outside the city." What Romans did outside of their city was to expand its boundaries through wars of choice waged against their neighbors.[1] Rome's "outside" modes and orders include then: the foreign policy which directed the city's inter-state relations; the military and diplomatic strategy which guided the city's wars; and the training and equipping of the city's armies. The tactics employed by Rome's captains, also a part of "outside" modes and orders, are examined in the following chapter under the heading, the "art of rule." The principal argument herein made is that Machiavelli's espousal of Rome's military modes and orders is on a par with Plato's "noble lie"—a lie, because Roman methods are not invariably successful (and are known not to be), a noble lie, because the virtue behind the methods is the point of Machiavelli's instruction.

Roman Expansionism

Make no mistake about it, Rome was set on an imperial course from the very start. The fertile site chosen by Romulus and lauded by Machiavelli enabled the city to "defend itself from whoever might assault it and crush anyone who might oppose its greatness" (I.1.4). Moreover, succeeding kings kept the city on an expansionary path by absorbing the populations of defeated rivals—"Meanwhile grew Rome on the ruins of Alba," says Machiavelli, quoting Livy, about an annexation accomplished during the reign of Tullus Hostilius (II.3.1). The institutions which Rome added in its republican period, while concerned mainly with perfecting the city's mixed regime, also furthered its expansionist ambition. Rome added the dictatorship in order to provide itself with "a remedy for every accident" (I.34.3), included among which were the ones "that arose at any time against the republic in the increasing of the empire" (I.33.1). And the particular accident which occasioned the creation of the dictatorship was an alliance of neighboring states intended to contain the swelling "reputation, strength, and empire" of Rome (§1). The dictatorship, Machiavelli observes, contributed to "the greatness of so great an empire" (I.34.3). Rome next added the tribunate, which, despite the liabilities incurred from popular tumult and exposure to fortune's malignities, was an invaluable asset providing Rome with the large and loyal fighting force needed for growth (I.4.1, I.6.3, I.60.1) This conflict of the orders made Rome free, says the title of chapter 4, but it also made Rome powerful ("That the Disunion of the Plebs and the Senate Made That Republic Free and Powerful"). Also, Rome's religious practices had an imperialist rationale, since they inspired soldiers with confidence and obstinacy, attributes which helped the army to conquer and the state to expand (I.14-15). Of course military practices made their contribution, too. An abundance of commanders kept Rome safe from the ambition of any one while at the same time supplying the army with an experienced officer corps (I.30.2). These commanders, when unsuccessful, were mildly reprimanded or even honored, lest fear of punishment interfere with the performance of their duties (I.31.1); and their commissions were brief so as to spur them to action (II.6.2). As for the soldiers, the senate adopted the custom of paying them a wage in order to extend the time and distance of wars (I.51.1). And it is noted that Rome was fortunate in being ruled throughout most of its history by republican government, because a well-ordered republic with virtuous successions has acquisitions and increases which are great (I.20 [title]).

Population is the foundation of political greatness: "Those who plan for a city to make a great empire should contrive with all industry to make it full of inhabitants, for without this abundance of men one will never succeed in making a city great" (II.3.1). Two policies did Rome follow which ensured that the city's population would forever increase: Rome opened its doors to immigrants, and Rome assimilated the inhabitants of defeated cities. "By love and by force," as Machiavelli puts it, Rome expanded its population base. Machiavelli likens Roman policy to the practices of a "good cultivator" who prunes the branches of a plant in order to thicken its trunk; in time this thickened plant is able to support larger branches with greener foliage and plumper fruit.[2] Rome tended to the trunk, while Sparta and Athens permitted growth in the branches. Machiavelli now commends these cities for their good laws and their domestic harmony,[3] but he blames them for policies which kept their citizen bodies relatively small. Sparta, for example, discouraged immigration by denying newcomers the rights of marriage and citizenship, and it discouraged trade with foreigners by adopting a form of currency peculiar to itself. The upshot of such measures was that Sparta, and Athens too, "never passed beyond twenty thousand each"; whereas

Rome, as far back as the time of Servius Tullius (578-535 BC), "had eighty thousand men able to bear arms." Nevertheless, with this smaller number, Sparta and Athens tried to rule over cities equal or larger in size. By doing so, they violated the law of nature which ordains that thick branches not spring from thin trunks. For any strong wind will break off such branches, and in a powerful storm, as was the rebellion of Thebes against Sparta, the tree itself will be uprooted. Machiavelli chooses Rome over Sparta because Rome was equipped for expansion, which means that Rome gave itself the population base necessary to acquire and maintain.

The superiority of the Roman way seems perfectly evident; and those Spartan laws designed to keep strangers at a distance seem certain to have been the cause of that city's undoing, insofar as Sparta too aspired to empire.[4] There is this though to be said for Sparta: by such quaint employments as leather money, the Spartans protected their distinct identity; they knew who they were, who belonged to their community, and who benefited from the common good. The Romans, on the other hand, diluted their identity by widening their community and thus the number of people sharing in the profits of expansion. (Maintaining a national identity involves more, it seems, than honoring the founder's memory.) At the same time, the Romans exposed themselves to corruption by foreign and inferior customs. Conquered cities take their revenge by corrupting the habits of the conqueror, argues Machiavelli in II.19. It is difficult to commingle with conquered peoples without succumbing to the agreeable, but enervating, customs which brought about their defeat. Vice causes weakness and weakness leads to defeat; but the vanquished weak undermine the victorious strong by tempting them with pleasures. The Roman legions on guard duty at Capua were infected by the pleasure-loving habits of the place (and the soldiers of Hannibal suffered similar corruption a century and a third later). Proximity and an intact moral core kept Rome from being ruined by its annexation of Campania. But Rome's trunk-thickening objective ensured the absorption of populations at ever greater distances and practicing customs ever stranger and more unroman. One remedy (and we shall speak again of it later) was to dilute the voting power of newcomers by gathering them all in urban tribes (III.49.4). Another was to treat captured peoples differently depending on their level of civilization and the degree of their Roman-like love of liberty. When the Privernates, following a rebellion in 330, were brought to Rome for judgment, one of their number, upon questioning, expressed the dignified sentiments of a liberty-loving republican— and the senate applauded his bravery and extended citizenship to his kin. In the opinion of the wiser members of the senate, "only those who think of nothing except freedom are worthy to become Romans" (II.23.4). Rather than attempt to suppress the patriotic passions of the Privernates, the senate wisely regarded those passions as a qualification for Roman citizenship. Rome could admire the liberty of others because Rome needed freedom-loving peoples to assist with its quest for greatness.

Diplomatic and Military Strategy

Machiavelli chooses Rome as his model for imitation because Rome achieved empire. Rome made profits (*profitti*), he says, the likes of which were never before and have never since been equaled (II.1.1). But Rome is no model if its singular success was mainly the product of fortune. Some have thought that it was, including, it seems, the Romans themselves—or so the very grave Plutarch infers from the number of temples dedicated to Fortuna. Livy is also suspected of crediting Rome's success more to fortune than to virtue. And an unidentified "they" has put forth the argument that Rome was lucky for never having had to fight two wars at once or to face multiple enemies combined and fresh.

By way of rebutting this unnamed "they," Machiavelli reveals the first precept of Rome's diplomatic and military strategy. Rome fought one enemy at a time: the Samnites, then the Latins, then the Samnites again, then the Tuscans—and so on throughout its history until "in all the world there remained neither prince nor republic that by itself or together with all could oppose the Roman forces" (§1). But it was by wise policy, Machiavelli insists, and not by gift of fortune that Rome faced only single enemies, finishing with one before engaging another. Rome traded on its reputation for warlikeness, using fear to keep some neighbors quiet and false promises of friendship to lull others to sleep. At the same time, remote states, thinking Rome's wars none of their affair, stayed neutral and unconcerned; and when finally they did act, they sometimes made the mistake of joining Rome instead of Rome's enemies. Carthage, France, Philip of Macedon, and Antiochus are placed in this category.

It is interesting how states react to power. If immediately threatened, they are compliant; if distantly threatened, they are complacent. Necessities #1 and #3 work to eviscerate their virtue. Most states are predisposed to weakness, which predisposition makes conquest by one who is strong and ambitious almost automatic: "It is a very certain thing," proclaims Machiavelli, and "it always happens" that when facing an aggressive neighbor with a reputation for power, princes and people are afraid to attack it, and when not endangered themselves, they are hesitant to come to the assistance of those who are. Accordingly, Machiavelli promises that "all those princes who [proceed] like the Romans and [are] of the same virtue as they would have the fortune that the Romans had in this aspect" (§2).

Machiavelli is sounding like a monarchist, claiming that the world is ordered for empire because the forces of freedom are lame and disorganized. He most definitely is not sounding like a republican, who here might argue that an expansionist power is held in check by the combined strength of its neighbors, or that such a power compels a targeted state to adopt its own warlike customs and thus to become the aggressor's equal and rival. Thucydides takes this view, for his imperial Athenians, adept at the art of naval warfare, caused frightened

Syracusans to become proficient seamen themselves, allowing them, in time, to halt and reverse the Athenians' advance. On this "republican" view, international relations are like the game of "Risk": No sooner does one player gain an advantage than the others form an alliance against his emerging power. The alliance holds as long as the threat remains; and when it subsides, the former enemy, humbled and weakened, becomes a friend and partner in a new alliance against a new foe. The chief lesson of the game is that relations among states tend toward an equilibrium, that nature ordains equality and enforces it over time, and that achieving empire is a near impossibility (as is winning the game a near impossibility). But Machiavelli has an entirely different interpretation of political behavior. States are lazy, trusting, and fearful, easily victimized by virtuous aggressors. Rome achieved empire, and others, by following Rome's example, can achieve the same.

A second precept of Roman military strategy was to fight wars quickly and on the cheap. As an expansionary power Rome usually chose its enemies and its wars. Since chosen wars can be declined, Machiavelli offers the following observation as to when they are useful: "The intention of whoever makes war through choice—or, in truth, ambition—is to acquire and maintain the acquisition, and to proceed with it so that it enriches and does not impoverish the country and his fatherland" (II.6.1). It occurs to Machiavelli that wars of choice must pay if they are to be sensible and the policy sustainable. Similarly, he expostulates in the second preface on how frustrated appetites cause dissatisfaction with the present and a listless nostalgia for the past; and in II.18-19 he berates his contemporaries for acquiring by modes which are unprofitable and which subtract from rather than add to the state's strength (also Athens and Sparta he criticizes in II.4.1). So it matters how one acquires, and Roman imperialism points the way to success.

The Roman way was this: (1) apply massive force so as to get in and get out quickly; and (2) settle colonists on captured territory so as to reduce the cost of frontier defense. When Rome began to fight wars of longer duration, it nonetheless managed to economize by (3) holding the consul to a term of one year (six months of which were spent in quarters); the consul thus had a private inducement to bring the fighting to a speedy conclusion. And when Rome began paying troops on campaign a wage, after the siege of Veii,[5] it economized by (4) depositing booty in the public treasury. In fact, so successful and routine was this method of enriching the city that a Roman general could not expect a triumph unless along with his victory he filled the state's coffers with loot. As for the citizens, while poor, they found employment in war, and so war for them was a kind of "jobs program." Also, because the state grew wealthy from the plunder of war, war was prosecuted without need of taxes from the citizens (II.6).

In addition to quick victories and colonial defenses, Rome acquired economically by eschewing sieges when attacking walled cities. Siege operations were the most expensive and protracted way of taking enemy towns, and while Romans sometimes laid siege to a city,[6] for the most part they relied on other means. The most direct and muscular form of attack was storming (*espugnazione*) by open violence (*violenza aperta*), of which there were four kinds: (1) a simultaneous assault on all sides, called "crowning"; (2) a breach in the wall made by battering rams and sundry engines of war; (3) a mine or a tunnel dug beneath the wall; and (4) a tower or an embankment built equal to the height of the wall. But counter-measures available to defenders (e.g., sorties, torching of towers, etc.) rendered each of these methods either dangerous or doubtful. Thus an alternate and perhaps more attractive form of storming was by furtive violence (*violenza furtiva*), of which there were two kinds: (1) conspiracies with refugees and dissidents; and (2) diversions and nocturnal attacks. But again, both methods were of uncertain utility, for conspirators might prove unfaithful (II.31.1, III.6.4; *Prince*, 19), and nighttime operations were subject to false imaginings and misadventures. Besides storming a town and seizing it outright, there was the option of inducing its inhabitants to surrender, either willingly or forcibly. The willing surrender (*dedizione volontaria*) occurred when a town faced some extrinsic necessity, such as attack by a third party, or when the desire for good government caused the town to accept the laws and rulers of a large and well-governed state. Forced surrender (*dedizione forzata*) occurred when a besieged town finally submitted to its attackers, or when "continual crushing by raids, depredations, and other ill treatment" caused the same result (II.32.2). This last was Rome's preferred method, used most often and with best effect, and it is the method recommended by Machiavelli.

Forced surrenders by raids gave evidence of the muscle behind Roman arms, particularly when compared with the furtive violence of conspiracies and sneak attacks. But when compared with the open violence of taking a city by storm, these wars of attrition were controlled, patient, and slow to unfold—not unlike a siege but without the expense. They fell somewhere between "the defeat of an enemy army" by which "they acquired a kingdom in a day" and the capture of "an obstinate city by siege" which "consumed many years." For 450 years Rome gained reputation over it neighbors by tiring them out "with defeats and raids" (§2). The Roman method was in fact a combination of direct and indirect warfare, about which more will be said later.

A third precept of Roman diplomatic and military strategy, and the foundation of Rome's expansionism, was the alliance of unequals—Rome supported by subordinate partners. Rome had allies in its march toward greatness, "but not so much that the rank of command, the seat of empire, and the title of the enterprises" did not remain plainly with Rome (II.4.1). This method Machiavelli calls the "true mode" (§2) for any "republic that wishes to expand" (§1). But there are two other modes which Machiavelli chooses to examine, modes deemed second-best and useless respectively. The first is confederation, or a league of equals. Among the ancients, the Tuscans, Achaeans, and Aetolians were confederal powers, while modern confederations are the Swiss and the Swabians. The second is imperium, or dominion over subjects without help from allies. Athens and Sparta built their empires in this way.

While Machiavelli is an ardent booster of the Roman mode, he concedes that there are serious advantages to confederal expansion. What particularly recommends it is that confederations fight fewer wars and keep what they obtain (no small accomplishment given that many states are injured by expansion [II.19; *Florentine Histories*, VI.1]). They stay within bounds because the number of partners and the distance between their capitals interfere with consultation and decision-making. Also their desire for conquest is abated because the spoils of war have to be shared among so many. Thus there is a structural reason for moderation (that the confederates can't coordinate action) and a psychological one (that the confederates have little inducement to expand). The Tuscan alliance, for example, "could not go with their acquisitions beyond Italy" (§1). Of course it is quite possible that Machiavelli appreciates this limitation insofar as he intimates that Italian unification marked the highpoint of Roman expansion (I.20.1). Rome's "ultimate greatness" (*ultima grandezza*), he maintains, came "in as many years as it was under the kings" (*in altrettanti anni che la era stata sotto i re*). Since Rome was under kings for 244 years (753-509 BC), Rome reached its highpoint in 265, or just before the outbreak of the First Punic War (264 BC) when Rome had united Italy but was not yet a transnational empire.[7] Confederations are alliances for mutual security, not continuous acquisition; "they do not seek larger dominion" because "necessity does not constrain them to have more power" (II.4.2). Machiavelli's choice for Rome in I.6.4 was predicated on the belief that necessity does constrain states to have more power; that either a state is rising or it is falling, but never is it just standing still. Now, however, (and if only for now) he all but takes back his belief—confederations of fixed size satisfy nature's necessity to expand. When they have reached this size (12 to 14 cities as a rule), finding no advantage in going further, they do two things: they extend protection in exchange for tribute, and they hire out soldiers to serve as mercenaries under foreign commands. The Swiss are the example as are the Aetolians of old. Aetolian mercenaries were reputed for their avarice and faithlessness. King Philip of Macedon, who spoke with one while negotiating terms of peace with the Roman consul Flaminius, thought it particularly despicable that the Aetolian insignia were often seen flying in opposing camps (197 BC). Among military men, these mercenaries hailing from small confederacies are nothing but moneymakers lacking in honor. Machiavelli has been known to say the same. And if we apply Machiavelli's critique of mercenaries back to his description of confederations, we begin to see that they are not above reproach.[8] How modest are their appetites if their soldiers are profiteers rather than patriots? More importantly, how few are their wars if selling protection to cash-in-hand supplicants is the use they make of their surplus strength? Machiavelli does not specify any particular liability that would cause confederations to rank second in worth; but in a letter to Francesco Vettori in August of 1513, he comments on the distending ambition of the Swiss: that successful against the dukes of Austria, they became esteemed at home; and successful against Duke Charles,[9] they earned a reputation abroad; that having sent their soldiers forth to fight for stipends under the command of others, they acquired knowledge of men and countries and a higher opinion of themselves, so that now they fancy themselves the reincarnation of the ancient Romans.[10] Machiavelli is not prepared to go this far in praise of the Swiss, as he explains in a second Vettori letter of the same month;[11] but a year or so later he is again writing to his friend about the growing Swiss menace, predicting that these ultramontanes will enlarge their ambitions with every success until finally they set their sights on mastering all of Italy; "for the truth is," he pronounces, "that one conquest, one victory, causes thirst for another."[12] It seems then that confederations, no less than single states, find it difficult to contain their appetites. But if they are going to enter the imperial competition, they need a proper organization to equip them for the race. Their lethargic decision-making and the chaos of their command structure are handicaps like those which afflicted the early Roman republic, but which Rome remedied by concentrating executive power in the person of a dictator. On the other hand, if confederations somehow manage to stay small and unthreatening, they risk conquest by a larger aggressor.[13] Although Machiavelli implies that necessity is satisfied by a defensive alliance, we can hardly fail to notice that the Tuscan confederation was first weakened by the French (the Gauls) who took Lombardy from it and then destroyed by the Romans, whose first success, the capture of Veii, was the product of Tuscan disunity (II.2.1). For even when a confederation is the dominant power in a region, its strength is compromised by internal bickering; and when it goes on the offensive, its force is spent after just the first thrust (III.11.2). Furthermore, that passage from I.20 naming the pre-Punic War years as the period of Rome's "ultimate greatness" is followed by the declaration that a republic's capacity for expansion exceeds that even of a principality with successive virtuous princes; for if Philip and Alexander "acquire[d] the world," a republic with "infinite most virtuous princes" "should do so much more." Machiavelli is cold to the modest ambitions of confederations, whatever the final word on necessity (e.g., II.19.2); and the statement that Rome reached its imperial peak with the unification of Italy may be meant as a critique of Rome and not of world empire.[14]

The Athenian-Spartan way is judged useless because it is an example of a thin trunk straining to support heavy limbs. When Athens and Sparta each chose to expand (Athens in the fifth century after the Persian Wars, Sparta in the fourth century after the Peloponnesian War), they did so by conquest and subjugation. But they expanded alone, without substantial help from allies; nor did they enlarge themselves by extending citizenship to conquered opponents. They needed massive strength to defeat by violence peoples used to living freely. But the only way to accumulate such strength is to seek out partners in a common enterprise of aggression—in effect to lessen or better target the violence. It is no judgment against Athens and Sparta that they sought to conquer free peoples, for Rome established its reputation by doing the same. The failure of Athens and Sparta was that they declined to prune the branches and thicken the trunk.

The Roman way, and approved way, is then the Athenian-Spartan way merely executed correctly. Rome amassed great strength through alliances, mainly with the Latins and Ernici. But it was careful always to be in charge; and although Machiavelli does not explain exactly how this preeminence came about, probably a few early victories were sufficient to persuade Rome's neighbors to accept the status of subordinate partner (II.6.1, II.32.2). The situation changed, however, when Rome took its armies outside of Italy (e.g., the Punic and Macedonian Wars of the third and second centuries) to fight against subject peoples. These enemies were defeated more easily, and more easily were they ruled.[15] Used to living under kings, they happily adjusted to living under Roman governors. And they supplied recruits for armies with which to encircle the free Italians,[16] who, discovering the deception too late, conspired, revolted, and when defeated, found their status worsening from ally to subject (probably the Social War of 90 to 88 is intended).[17] By stealth as much as by force, Rome completed the conquest of Italy.

Just like the senate in its dealings with the plebs, Rome proceeded indirectly in its dealings with allies, neighbors, and enemies. In II.9 Machiavelli distinguishes between wars of choice and wars of chance.[18] There he labels as a chance event the outbreak of hostilities between Rome and Samnium in 343. By chance Machiavelli means entangling alliances, the obligations of which can draw a state inadvertently into war. Rome wound up the enemy of Samnium, its recent friend and ally (a treaty of friendship was signed in 354 [Livy, VII.19]), because the Samnites attacked the Sidicini; the Sidicini in turn appealed to the Campanians for support, and the Campanians, after suffering two battlefield defeats, appealed to the Romans. Bound by treaty to Samnium, Rome agreed to Campania's request only when the region surrendered itself to Roman rule. Honor then bound Rome to defend what now was a part of its own state, and when the Samnites refused to respect Rome's new obligations and to give up their siege of Capua, war broke out between these two great powers.

Machiavelli is quite insistent that Samnium stumbled into a war with Rome, but he invites us to think that Roman motives were never so ingenuous. Although Rome claimed to be forced by honor to defend Campania, the force in question was Rome's ambition for "empire and glory" and its recognition that refusing aid to a supplicant "would shut the way to all those who might plan to come under their power" (§1). Rome's involvement was chosen, not inadvertent (and necessary only insofar as ambition is necessary). What looked like chance, particularly to those affected by honorable motives, was in fact shrewd calculation. Chance is sometimes an appearance manipulated by states not wanting to be found in flagrant violation of treaty commitments. Usually the manipulation is on the side of the offense (Hannibal's attacking Saguntum in order to attack Rome [218 BC]), but it can also be practiced by the defense, as when the Latins in 340 took on the defense of the Sidicini against the Samnites so as to provoke a war with Rome (II.13.2). Lest there be any doubt about Roman motives on the occasion of the First Samnite War, Machiavelli informs us in II.1.3 that Rome came to the aid of Campania in order to have a pretense for entering Samnium: "In new provinces they [the Romans] always tried to have some friend who should be a step or a gate to ascend there or enter there, or a means to hold it. So they were seen to enter by means of the Capuans into Samnium." This practice Rome utilized repeatedly, moving into Tuscany, Sicily, Spain, Africa, Greece, Asia, and France.

The Roman mode of alliance was itself a form of indirect warfare since by it Rome expanded without the trouble and expense of subduing its neighbors. Slowly, equal allies became inferiors and subjects because Rome, always in command of the league, shared the reputation from victory with no one. The Latins discovered the change which had occurred when after the defeat of the Samnites, "far-off princes" acknowledged the Roman name but not the confederation whose arms had helped win for Rome its victories (II.13.2). Rome began in weakness and obscurity, but it employed "all the modes necessary to come to greatness" (§2), including deceit. The lesson of chapter 13 is that men of small fortune and republics without power rise to rank and greatness more by fraud than by force.

The focus heretofore has been on how, by means of Capua, Rome entered Samnium and eventually possessed it. It should not go unnoticed, however, that in the process of seizing Samnium Rome also entered and possessed Capua and Campanian lands. Attacked by Samnium in retaliation for its aid to Sidicine, Capua appealed to Rome as its deliverer. Rome obliged by sending an auxiliary force which, once the Samnites were chased from the area, stayed on to defend the city against future Samnite attacks. There is talk about the lure of easy living and the temptation to appropriate the wealth of weak and dependent people, of the corruption which Capua worked on the virtue of Roman legionnaires; and assurance is offered that "the intention of the Romans was not to break the accord and the conventions they had made with the Capuans," that the trouble was due to the ambition of the soldiers left behind as a garrison in the city. But the teaching on auxiliaries is that they present princes and ambitious republics their greatest opportunity "for seizing a city or a province." Now Rome of course was an ambitious republic. And it is from ancient examples that Machiavelli would have moderns learn that "the more liberality is shown toward neighbors and the more aversion to seizing them, the more they fling themselves into one's lap" (II.20.1). Also, that Rome affected indifference toward the territory of its neighbors is information supplied in the very next chapter: "This tameness and liberality made the Capuans run to the Romans to ask for a praetor" (II.21.2).

While Machiavelli stays with Capua in chapter 21, he moves ahead about 25 years to the time when Rome sent out its first praetor. In 317 Capua requested and received a Roman praetor to reorder and reunite the town (and Anzio [Antium] followed suit, asking for a Roman prefect of its own).[19] The chapter's title associates this event with the 400 years during which Rome was making war. Four hundred years earlier, in 717, Rome was in the last year of Romulus's reign; and in that year, or thereabouts, Rome was at war with the Tuscans. (Livy provides a description of the fighting and then follows it with a summary statement of Rome's military and political achievements up to that point [Livy, I.14-16].) Romulus, though, was soon replaced by Numa, who in 716 ushered in a long era of peace, lasting until his death and the succession of Tullus Hostilius. Thus the first extended period of what Machiavelli calls warmaking by Rome was in fact a time of peaceful coexistence with its neighbors. But might Rome have made war, or expanded its jurisdiction, by peaceful means? Chapter 21 suggests an affirmative reply since its main topic is Rome's creation of an invisible empire during the 400 years prior to 317.[20] And we remember the statements of two previous chapters that Rome expanded imperceptibly, converting equal partners into subjects under a hegemon (II.4.1, II.13.2). To be sure, Rome fought plenty of real wars during these same four centuries (II.1.1-2, II.32.2); but the judgment in chapter 21 is that recourse to arms ought to be a "last place" option "where and when other modes are not enough" (§2). Since Rome is again the model, it can be presumed that Rome was the proving ground for this advice.

Rome played a waiting game in the years before praetors were sent out to rule in other cities. What Rome was waiting on was for cities accustomed to political freedom to grow desperate for domestic peace. Eventually cities tire of freedom if freedom is the cause of ruinous divisions. But nothing can unite cities like the appearance of an outside threat. The Romans, for example, back when they were newly republican and fighting against the Tuscan power, allowed their characteristic factiousness to escalate into military insubordination (480 BC). A consular army withdrew from battle because the troops could not be trusted to obey (Livy, II.43). Word spread that Rome was crippled by factional disputes, and so the decision was taken by Veii and other Tuscan towns to "extinguish the Roman name." But to attack Rome (and to insult its soldiers), these towns soon discovered, was all that was required to draw patricians and plebeians together; and a united Rome, helped by good generaling, repelled the invasion (II.25.1).

It seems then that expansion should not be possible if at the first sign of danger opposition coalesces against it. Machiavelli, though, is quick to observe that Rome's enemies were none too bright. Wiser foes would have kept their distance, waiting for "leisure and peace" to corrode the republic's virtue; waiting also to be summoned as the arbiter of the republic's differences. Rome was in this position when Capua called for a praetor to secure the peace. Outsiders are trusted to mediate disputes if they have a reputation for humaneness and show scrupulous respect for the independence of their neighbors. But if solicitousness is excessive, and especially if there is any aggressive move on a stranger's part, then instantly the locals close ranks against outside interference. Machiavelli stipulates that Romans sent a praetor to Capua "not from their ambition but because they were asked by the Capuans, who, since there was discord among them, judged it necessary to have a Roman citizen inside the city who would reorder and reunite them" (II.21.1). But what we learn from II.25 is that the arbiter's purpose is not the peaceful resolution of a quarrel but its prolongation and exacerbation, achieved by maneuvering between the factions and giving "favors slowly to the weaker party" (§1). A strategy of divide-and-conquer fatigues the targeted city until finally it throws itself into the arms of a protector. Florence played this game with Pistoia, and we are invited to suppose that Rome was similarly conniving in its dealings with Capua. Thus by artful indirection can an expanding power escape the dilemma of curing divisions by attempting to exploit them.

In another context Machiavelli explains how this game of divide-and-conquer is played. A captain besieging a city promises pardon to those who lay down their arms. The necessity of self-defense is thus removed, and the citizens surrender without a fight. If the city though is a republic, and not only punishment is feared but the loss of liberty, the captain promises as well to respect the city's freedom while eliminating only the ambitious few responsible for offenses against the attacker. This way the citizens are split from their leaders; this way, too, the presence of an outside threat divides rather than unites the people within. Says Machiavelli: "Although such coloring over as this is easily recognized, and especially by prudent men, nonetheless peoples are often deceived in it who, greedy for present peace, close their eyes to whatever other snare might be laid under the big promises" (III.12.2). With offers of peace, of forgiveness, and of liberty if need be, a good captain can take control of another captain's people. By this method the Spanish became lords of the Florentines (1512 AD), and the Parthians assumed command of Crassus's troops (53 BC). Borders dissolve, states disappear as the conquest of foes gives way to the governing of new citizens. Reduced to its simplest elements, governing is the business of constructing unions, and enemies no less than friends are within reach of a good captain's powers of composition.

Chapters 26 and 27 of book 3 give advice on how a hegemonic power should manage the cities it has acquired. Machiavelli takes us to Ardea, a small town in southern Latium, in the year 443. The city was torn in two, nobles against plebs, because a rich woman, of plebeian stock, wanted her daughter to marry the nobleman asking for her hand, and to marry him in preference to her plebeian suitor. Soon the city's classes took sides, and soon after they took up arms. When the plebeians were beaten and chased from town, they appealed to Volsci to aid them in their battle. Likewise the nobles appealed to Rome. Before long Ardea was besieged by the Volsci, who not long after were besieged by the Romans. The Volsci surrendered ignominiously and quit the area,[21] while the Romans restored peace to Ardea by executing "all the heads of the sedition."

Apart from the insistence that women are the cause of political ruin, the lesson from the Ardean episode is that unity is best restored by harshness: Rome killed "the heads of the tumults." Never recoiling from necessary violence, Rome disposed of these party leaders with the same decisiveness that it punished the sons of Brutus. But we learn from chapter 27 that other, less brutal, remedies are available and are sometimes employed. Short of execution, for example, there is exile, and short of exile there is peacemaking. The last of these modes is useless, Machiavelli declares, since the parties still live together, and with every day come new opportunities for strife. A fourth mode is included, though not identified as such; it is to foment faction as a means of keeping the subject population divided and weak. While the chapter looks for methods of reuniting and reconciling divided cities, the "fourth mode" contends, contrarily, that division is preferable to union.

Chapter 27 is similar to *Prince* 5, where Machiavelli outlines the three modes for administering captured cities accustomed to living under their own laws. The options listed there are to destroy them, to live among them, or to allow them their own laws but under governments composed of native proxies. Again Machiavelli declares that the last and most gentle of the remedies is altogether useless, and again he favors destruction as the safest way to go. *Prince* 5 and *Discourses* III.27 are thus kindred in their topics and in their conclusions. But they seemingly are inconsistent with what Machiavelli proposes in II.21 and II.25. In II.21, Rome practiced what amounted to the third mode of administration, an invisible empire which allowed subjects and allies their own laws "but obliged them to some conditions" (§1) (following the third mode in *Prince* 5, Rome exacted tribute and installed oligarchical governments friendly to it). The reason for concealing its power and administering from a distance was that cities "used to living freely or accustomed to being governed by those of their own province remain content more quietly under a dominion they do not see . . . than under one they see every day which appears to them to reprove them every day for their servitude" (§2). But the teaching of *Prince* 5 is that free people never forget the name of liberty or their ancient orders; accordingly it avails not to remove the signs of imperial rule. Either the city must be destroyed, which Machiavelli recommends, or the prince must go there and live, in which case the locals are confronted with daily reminders of their servitude. So, does the third mode work, as II.21 affirms; or, as *Prince* 5 insists, does it lead to rebellion? It works as a mode of low-cost expansion, the main point of II.21; it was how Rome made war for 400 years ("One sees, therefore, how much this mode made Roman increase easy" [§2]). As a mode of governance, however, the record is mixed as to whether free peoples "remain content more quietly under a dominion they do not see" (§2). Rome tried this with many of the cities subject to its rule, while other cities it destroyed utterly; but always Rome avoided the middle way, declares Machiavelli in II.23. What though is the middle way in this context? Is it the second mode of administration, going there to live? This, in effect, was what Rome did when in 317 it sent its first praetor to Capua. The provincial praetorship pierced the veil of invisible government by which subject cities lived under their own laws. Requested by Capuans to "reorder and reunite them," the Roman praetor gave laws and settled disputes (Livy, IX.20). Presumably, therefore, the praetor incurred the "burden or infamy," the "calumny and hatred" directed against "the judges or magistrates who render civil or criminal justice." Presumably he was an irritant to a free people jealous about its liberty and resentful of the daily reminder of its servitude. But Machiavelli does not describe the praetorship as a "middle way" mistake in the art of governing, comparable to France's trying to administer Genoa with a French governor.[22] Rather he offers the praetorship as convincing proof of how "tameness and liberality" induce lesser states to "fling themselves into your lap" (II.21.2). The praetorship represents a second stage in the strategy of easy, cost-effective expansion, a strategy which depended for its success on the gradual corruption of liberty-loving citizenship. Rome could enter Capua easily by establishing a record of indifference to growth; but Rome could rule Capua by the third (native proxies) and then second (praetors) modes of administration only by persuading Capuans to want contentment more than they wanted liberty. In order then for Rome's method not to qualify as an irresolute "middle way," the maxim of *Prince* 5 would have to be untrue that for free peoples "the memory of their ancient liberty does not and cannot let them rest." In fact, *Prince* 5 does exaggerate; for while it took a long time for Greek cities to lose the memory of their freedom, eventually they came around, as Machiavelli states in *Prince* 4: "But when their memory was eliminated with the power and long duration of the empire, the Romans became secure possessors of them."

There is also an inconsistency regarding III.27 and II.25. The problem with II.25 is that it congratulates Florence for having implemented a strategy of divide-and-conquer with respect to the factions of Pistoia. Maneuvering "between the parties as arbiter until they [came] to arms," Florence then slowly favored "the weaker party, both to keep them at war longer and make them consume themselves." Not "by any other art than this" did Pistoia come under Florentine rule (§1). But in III.27 such machinations are seemingly condemned as exemplifying the false opinion of "the wise of our city . . . that one needed to hold Pistoia with parties and Pisa with fortresses" (§2).[23] The opinion is false because a factious city is never entirely loyal; when a foreign power comes into the region, the beleaguered and dissident party conspires with it and rebels, causing enemies to exist both inside and outside the city (*Prince*, 20). Furthermore, factions in the subject city infect domestic politics in the imperial city (Pistoia infected Florence with its own factional divisions: the Whites and the Blacks and later the Panciatichi and the Cancellieri).[24] Thus it is better to unify a factious city than to try holding it by exacerbating its divisions. But holding is what differentiates III.27 from II.25: in the latter, the subject is how to "assault a disunited city so as to seize it" (title); in the former, how to "unite a divided city" so as to "hold" it (title).

Since inconsistent passages have required some reconciling, and since the reconciliation is less than perfect, we might try offering a general assessment of the problem at hand. The worst result of acquiring a free city, it would appear, is to have it unite and rebel against you, the imperial state. One reason for union and rebellion, as Machiavelli explains, is the aggressiveness of an outside power (II.25). To avoid just such a development, the outsider is advised to lie low and hang back, to allow, in effect, the subject city its own laws and government. But local rule inside another's empire might fail to satisfy the appetite for liberty; and the absence of supervision offers ample opportunity for conspiracies to form. The remedy then is to send forth a provincial governor. But while the governor is well-positioned to keep watch over the locals, his very presence is an incitement to revolution (II.21). In that case, the consequent remedy—and the proposal of *Prince* 5—is to destroy a city that cannot safely be ruled. But this is a desperate solution and a last resort; for what is not said in *Prince* 5 is that a destroyed city is of no use to the empire and adds nothing to its power. Furthermore, a reputation for brutality can only hurt the empire's chances for further expansion. So what's the answer? Besides rebellion resulting from home rule, another possible outcome is factional strife. If the imperial state is distant and non-threatening, the locals, rather than uniting, are apt to fly apart. Left to themselves, they may fall upon each other; "for the cause of the disunion of republics is usually idleness and peace" (II.25.1). Nature is another cause, or another way of saying the same, "for it is given by nature to men to take sides in any divided thing whatever" (III.27.3). A dispute over a marriage contract can set a state to warring with itself (III.26).[25] Self-government loses much of its charm when civil war is the result. On the other hand, if the locals behave themselves and get along, then the imperial power can interfere in a manner calculated to stir up trouble and foment faction (II.25). Plainly, a good way to guard against rebellion in the provinces is to keep the opposition divided—and Machiavelli concedes that "in quiet times" these diplomatic arts sometimes help (III.27.4). But he is not enthusiastic, since, when times are dangerous, divided cities provide an opening to foreign aggressors, and since divided cities export their divisions to the home country. Instead, he recommends healing divisions and restoring unity. Of course a city restored to unity is strong again and able to rebel. But it owes its unity then to the good government of the imperial power. And what is good government? In the case of suppressing factional division, good government requires, not peacemaking among the parties, since the peace will not hold. (In fact, so fruitless is the effort that ulterior motives might be suspected of the arbiter [II.25.1].) It rather requires execution of party leaders or their banishment from the city (III.27.1). Good government solves problems; it does not perpetuate them. And good government—when supplied from without and when contrasted with bad government supplied from within—is much of the answer to the imperial power's dilemma. The objective, throughout the process, is to render subject states increasingly dependent and compliant and to ready them for grafting onto the hegemon's trunk.

Machiavelli's most extensive treatment of the good governing of subject states is provided in II.23. Between the years 340 and 338, Latium, observes Machiavelli, was the "unhappiest" state of all; and he quotes Livy to the effect that the cities of Latium were able to "endure neither war nor peace." They came to so sad a condition because of consistent misunderstandings of the true extent of their forces: They chose cooperation with Rome when confrontation was in their power,[26] and they chose resistance to Rome when temporizing was all that their power would allow.[27] They therefore suffered alike from Roman friendship and Roman enmity. Defeated by Rome in the Great Latin War, the Latins resolved upon a middle course, as Livy calls it, of staying inside their cities so as to reassure Rome of their peaceful intent and of assisting any of their brethren that might fall victim to Roman attack. When Rome laid siege to Pedum in 338, many of the Latins came to its defense. But Pedum fell nevertheless, and Camillus, the Roman commander,[28] went on to assault and capture every city in Latium (Livy, VIII.13).

The question then was what to do with these allies who had rebelled. Machiavelli quotes from Camillus's address to the senate to show how the Romans, in governing their empire or in passing judgments of state, "always fled from the middle way and turned to extremes." While the address is also used to show the Roman mode of expansion, the focus is clearly shifting from acquisition to governance. The Roman praetor sent to Capua was the first indication of this shift; but the point there was to explain how a reputation for gentleness and good government could add to Rome's dominion. Here the point is to show how Rome governed its empire; and to that end Machiavelli offers a definition of government. Governing, he explains, is nothing other than "holding subjects in such a mode that they cannot or ought not offend you" (§2). They cannot if they lack the power because the government has taken from them every means of resisting; they ought not if desiring a change is unreasonable because the government has befriended and benefited them. Thus wise governance, when passing judgments, aims at leaving subjects disarmed or delighted. And this result is accomplished either by eliminating subjects or caressing them. The alternative eschews these extremes and aims for the middle, where subjects receive what they deserve but are neither happy enough to wish the government well nor oppressed enough to do it no harm. It may be that people tend naturally to middle ways because they appreciate the justice of due measure and proportional equality when viewed abstractly; but those on the receiving end of justice, Machiavelli contends, resent its findings and contest its distributions. They expect more than what justice allows because they judge themselves better than they are; and if they concur with the judgment of law, still they are not grateful since the reward they receive is entirely their due (I.16.3).[29] Either way, they must be granted more than is their due (caressed), or they must be granted nothing at all (eliminated).

Given these options, plus the fact that in passing judgments it is the welfare of the judge that matters most, one might suppose that the safer course is always to eliminate; for even though benefited subjects have no reason to rebel, still they have the means; and to rule them by kindness is to depend too much on the reasonableness of their conduct. Since mad passion sometimes prompts people to act in self-destructive ways, a ruler would be well-advised to keep his people dispersed, disordered, and distressed. Such is the logic behind absolute tyranny. But the Roman senate did not act the part of the perfect tyrant, nor was Camillus neutral in his presentation of the choices. He tilted the decision in favor of "forgiving," suggesting that by this choice Rome could increase its empire, having at hand the matter "for growing by means of the greatest glory" (II.23.2). Rome's ambition for greatness was incompatible with the safer course of tyranny or with the narrow selfishness which constrains the frightened tyrant. Because Rome wished to expand, it had a countervailing interest in the well-being of its newly acquired subjects. As noted previously, Rome dealt leniently with the rebellious Privernates, extending citizenship to them, because Rome wished to thicken its trunk with the addition of freedom-loving citizens.

The Roman senate departed from Camillus's recommendation in one crucial respect. Camillus noted that the senate had in its hands the decision "whether Latium is to be or not to be," and he proposed that the senate either "destroy all Latium" or accept "the conquered into citizenship." But the senate did something different; it decided to judge each town separately, benefiting some and eliminating others (Livy, VIII.14). If the senate, as Machiavelli attests, avoided the middle way in the punishments it administered, it nonetheless adhered to a middle way with respect to the parties it punished, judging not all of Latium together but each of its cities separately.[30]

Because Rome was discerning in its rewards and punishments, even making citizens of many conquered peoples, it can be difficult to understand the adage of II.2.4 that "of all hard servitudes, that is hardest that submits you to a republic."[31] Of course there is no mystery with regards to cities whose punishment was demolition. But what of those which were peaceably absorbed by Rome? When Machiavelli is explaining the peculiar severity of a republican empire, he says first that its long duration makes escape from it impractical, and he says second that its purpose is the enervation of surrounding states "so as to increase its own body" (§4). Republican empire is cruel to those states which wish to retain their separate identities and which pine for independence after it is lost. Although Rome was respectful of the rebellious Privernates, it nonetheless required that they express their spiritedness as members of a larger union—that they love Rome more than they love Privernum. If Italy was to become a nation with Rome as its capital, there had to be some lessening of the intense loyalty which Italians felt for their home cities, a taming of the savagery which liberty-loving republicans directed against Rome (II.2); there also had to take hold a preference for good government provided by outsiders over the partisan politics of indigenous elites. From one perspective, this satisfaction with the compensations of empire was a mark of a people's corruption; but from another perspective this satisfaction was a necessary step toward a people's transformation into national citizens.[32]

Training and Weapons

Perhaps nothing so attracts Machiavelli to ancient Rome as that city's reliance upon citizen-soldiers. Rome, it appears, did not follow Plato's advice and create a professional warrior class, nor did it commit the typical modern mistake of entrusting its defense to foreign mercenaries. Rome aimed for the middle, manning its armies with patriotic amateurs. In *The Art of War* the case is made for why an army of amateurs is preferable to an army of professionals. The dialogue's protagonist, Fabrizio Colonna, explains that the professional soldier, whether a commander or an infantryman, faces the problem of having nothing productive to do in times of peace. The skilled professional, he reasons (and of which he is one), can hardly be also a good man (*uomo buono*) since either he will plunder in war so as to support himself in peace, or sabotage the peace so as to stay at war; and when peace does finally come, either he will commit crimes of violence against his fellow citizens, or set out as a soldier of fortune to ravage the lands of neighbors. The solution, Fabrizio advises, is to ensure that all soldiers have peacetime occupations from which to make a living; that way they will return gladly to their homes and not agitate for war. The citizen is a farmer, a shoemaker, or a carpenter by profession; only by avocation is he a warrior. But will the amateur warrior be good enough to defeat the competition? And if forced into service will he not be as averse to war as the professional is averse to peace? The amateur is not a novice, Fabrizio responds; he trains regularly in peace and when conscripted joins forces already in service and able to sharpen his skills still further. And having become proficient in the use of his weapon, he goes gladly to war, wanting to do for real what he has so often done in practice.[33]

Machiavelli is a stickler for military training. If mercenary arms are to be rejected, a well-trained civilian force must be ready to take their place. But not all militias will do. There are three kinds of armies, Machiavelli explains in III.36: those with natural spirit (*animo*) and fury (*furore*), such as the French; those with natural fury and accidental order (*ordine accidentale*), such as the Roman; and those without fury or order, such as the Italian.[34] The last is useless; the first is useful in the beginning of battles but loses energy and confidence if its first thrust is resisted; the second is the best, as proven by the Romans who "conquered the world." The second also is universally applicable since fury can arise from order as well as from nature (§2).[35] Thus any population of men not trained for war is the fault of the prince (I.21.1, III.38.2).[36]

One advantage of peacetime training is stoic-like equanimity in the face of good and bad fortune. An army which is well-ordered with respect to weapons, tactics, and maneuvers has confidence in its own abilities, whether the fortunes of war favor or oppose it. Defeated three times by Hannibal (at Ticino, Trasimene, and Cannae), the Romans maintained their composure and resolve; triumphant over Antiochus, they refrained from exulting in their success. By contrast, the Venetians, at the height of their imperial grandeur, boasted that the king of France was the son of San Marco; but then suffering a half-defeat at Agnadello (Vailà), they fell prostrate before their enemies. This difference in temperament Machiavelli traces to education. A "weak and vain" education leaves people ignorant of military technique; thus victory and defeat are outcomes badly understood by them and so open to interpretations which flatter or excuse.[37] If people were "better knower[s] of the world," trained in good military orders, they would "rejoice less in the good and be less aggrieved with the bad" (III.31.3). We notice that Machiavelli's stoicism is hardly of the conventional sort, since he offers it as a strategy for combating fortune not as a consolation to those ruined by fortune.[38] An even-tempered disposition, caused by training and experience, is the secret to long-term success, Machiavelli advises.

This training, according to Fabrizio, consists of rigorous physical exercise, plus practice in the use of weapons and in marching and fighting in place (*Art of War*, II, 609). The Roman legion was a unit, the effectiveness of which required that each of its parts—its 5,000 to 6,000 soldiers—knew exactly what to do and when to do it. Machiavelli lays great stress on the Roman order of battle, the fact that Rome ordered its armies in three successive battalions (*astati*, *principi*, and *triari*) each trained in the art of withdrawal and regrouping.[39] (Outside the formation were placed the light-armed troops [*velites*] and the cavalry.) When the first line was beaten and forced to retreat, it was absorbed by the second line, which made space for it, and the two together resumed the fighting. If these two were also forced to retreat, they were absorbed by the third, and all three fought together. Machiavelli regards it as simple common sense that three chances at victory are better than one. Even so, no modern commander adopts the ancient modes. Modern armies are ordered in width, shoulder to shoulder, and with one mishap they are driven from the field (*Art of War*, III, 641; IV, 649). Only when forced to by the terrain do they order in depth; but then, because of lack of training, retreating front ranks become entangled with ranks in the rear, and the whole line is quickly broken. Machiavelli, in *Discourses*, II.16.2, can conceive of no explanation for why tactics so "easy to understand, and very easy to do" are not imitated by modern-day captains; and Fabrizio, in *The Art of War*, can only explain why he, a mercenary captain, has been slow to adopt ancient practices.[40] But elsewhere in that text Fabrizio suggests that it is Christian armies in particular which cannot be made to master the art of infantry maneuvers (*Art of War*, V, 669). Surprisingly, the fault of Christianity is to have humanized war to the point where few combatants ever die and conquered cities rarely are destroyed. One might well applaud such a development and call it moral progress. But it has had the ancillary effect, Fabrizio observes, of undermining military virtue. For if violent death, permanent enslavement, or homeless destitution are not the consequences of defeat; if the price instead is but a tax increase and a different ruler, why should any city take the trouble of militarizing its population? Military virtue is irrational and anachronistic in a world made safe by Christianity, or so Christians are wont to believe. But then another explanation closes *Discourses*, II.16: that technological progress, specifically the invention of artillery, has rendered ancient modes useless to the moderns.

Christianity is one impediment to imitating the ancients. Is technology another? Machiavelli's whole project of reclaiming ancient virtue is called into question by the "universal opinion" about artillery—to wit, virtue is an accessory of technology, and ancient virtue is incompatible with modern technology. The consensus opinion holds that if Roman armies had had artillery to face, they never would have acquired on the scale which they did, conquering provinces all over the world and forcing peoples to pay them tribute.[41] The consensus further holds that firearms prevent soldiers from displaying their virtue and that artillery prevents armies from keeping to "the orders of those times, so that war will in time be reduced to artillery" (II.17.1). Is it the case that modern armies wisely forsake the Roman battle order because of the devastation that artillery fire would cause? Machiavelli mentions that cannonballs shot from heavy guns "either go high and [do] not find you or go low and [do] not reach you" (§5). Given artillery's inaccuracy as to range, it might be a sensible tactic to stretch the line wide and thin, because to form up narrow and deep is practically to ensure that inaccurate shelling will always find its mark.

Machiavelli answers these charges in considerable detail. Regarding the first, he distinguishes between the use of artillery for offense or for defense and between the size of the town being defended by artillery and between towns and stockades. In all cases he concludes that artillery advantages the offense. Since Rome fought mostly wars of choice and in an offensive posture,[42] the presence of artillery in the ancient world would have enhanced, not lessened, Rome's power. Nor does artillery interfere with the display of virtue. In point of fact, modern soldiers face dangers unknown to their ancient counterparts, because the moderns fight outside the protection of large formations, in small groups, and because their commanders, even though in the rear and surrounded by bodyguards, are within range of artillery fire. We expect to hear then that modern armies suffer many more casualties, despite Machiavelli's oft-repeated claim to the contrary; but for some reason this higher exposure to harm does not result in higher rates of death among soldiers; and among commanders, fewer have died in the 24 years of Italian wars than died in ten years of wars fought by Rome. These explanations may be unsatisfying, but then the meaning of virtue is not so much braving death as it is fighting effectively;[43] and modern armies, "lacking virtue in the whole . . . cannot show it in the part" (§4). The final charge, that artillery renders obsolete the ancient formation and prevents troops from engaging in hand-to-hand fighting—this charge, which seems the most plausible of the three,[44] is said by Machiavelli to be "altogether false." His reasons are that artillery can impede close combat only briefly, unlike elephants and scythed chariots deployed throughout the fighting in battles past; that soldiers can protect themselves by taking shelter or hugging the ground; that artillery's aim is not precise enough to do much harm;[45] and that artillery, if positioned in the front or on the flanks where it is most effective, can be easily captured by the enemy. Machiavelli does, however, make one concession to modern technology, for he allows that artillery is useful when supplementing, not replacing, ancient virtue.

Chapter 18 joins with chapters 16 and 17 to comprise a section of book 2 the subject of which is the superiority of ancient military practices to those of the moderns. After examining the battle formation employed alike by Rome and its Latin enemy (II.16), Machiavelli moved to a defense of its continued utility in an era of gunpowder (II.17). Since he was forced to imagine how ancient Romans would have fared against modern weaponry, it was not sufficient for him simply to invoke the Roman example. The authority of Rome had to be vindicated. That done (Romans "would have had more advantage, and would have made their acquisitions more quickly, if there had been [artillery] in those times" [II.17.3]), he proceeds to invoke Rome's authority in the title to chapter 18: "How by the Authority of the Romans and by the Example of the Ancient Military Infantry Should Be Esteemed More Than Horse." And when another authority is remembered to have challenged the authority of Rome—Hannibal, who thought that dismounted cavalry were as good as prisoners—Machiavelli asserts that Rome, with its "many very excellent captains," is more authoritative than the "one Hannibal alone" (§2).[46] Machiavelli wants his readers to esteem infantry above cavalry, and he wants them to do so relying mainly on the authority of the Roman example.

The funny thing is that Machiavelli's Roman authorities do not support him.[47] Machiavelli gives five examples of the superiority of Roman infantry to Roman and foreign cavalry. In the last of these a Roman army under the command of Marcus Regulus Attilius is massacred by an undersized Carthaginian force, commanded by a Spartan and assisted by elephants and cavalry (255 BC). The Carthaginians prevailed because the elephants (the ancient equivalent of modern artillery [II.17.5]) crashed through the center of the Roman maniples, while the cavalry surrounded the Romans and destroyed them from the rear. All but 2,500 of the Romans were killed or captured.[48] Against such a disaster Machiavelli defends his thesis by lamely avowing that Regulus had confidence in the virtue of his infantry (§4). And it is immediately following this inapt example that Machiavelli repeats the thesis that ordered infantry can only be overcome by infantry ordered better. In the first example, the battle against the Latins near Lake Regillus in 496, the Roman cavalry was ordered to dismount and to fight as infantry; from this incident Machiavelli concludes that the Romans trusted their horsemen "more when they were on foot than when they were kept on horseback" (§1). But in Livy the point is rather that patrician equestrians were willing to share the same dangers as plebeian foot soldiers, not that unhorsing the cavalry was a wise battle tactic (Livy, II.20). In a similar episode, against the Samnites at Sora in 316, the Roman cavalry dismounted, constraining the Samnite cavalry to do likewise. Machiavelli declares that "no example could be greater than this in demonstrating how much more virtue there is in infantry than in horse," because "doing combat on horseback against horse, they judged that while they could not overcome them on horseback they could more easily defeat them by dismounting" (§3). But again, Livy has a decidedly different opinion. As he tells it, both cavalries dismounted to defend the bodies of their fallen commanders (Livy, IX.22). Machiavelli does mention that the commanders were down and that the soldiers were "without government"; but he says nothing about their fighting to retrieve their commanders' bodies, an effort suggestive of their continued dependence and loyalty. Instead he observes that it was these leaderless Romans who demonstrate the maxim in its purest form, unaffected by ancillary considerations, that infantry is superior to cavalry. In a sense, Machiavelli too is leaderless, since the authorities to whom he appeals have deserted him. Despite invoking the Roman precedent, he is essentially on his own in recommending that reputation be given to the infantry. (This is not to say that Rome valued cavalry ahead of infantry, only that Machiavelli's *chosen* examples fail as authorities[49]—or that Machiavelli chooses to be on his own.)

The final examples, that of Crassus and Antony among the Parthians, are no less surprising. Like Regulus defeated in Africa, Crassus was beaten in Parthia—so another defeat is strangely offered to establish the prowess of Roman infantry. Machiavelli's explanation is that the Parthians deceived and harassed the legions of Crassus but never dared to attack them directly. There was indeed deception and harassment aplenty; but a major battle also was fought, at Carrhae in 53, where Roman infantry suffered a massive drubbing at the hands of Parthian cavalry.[50] Marc Antony fared better some 15 years later when he too was retreating from Parthia. He escaped unhurt by traveling through mountains and avoiding the plains.[51] But Machiavelli does not disclose this fact; he rather implies the opposite: "For being in an extensive country, where mountains are rare . . . Marc Antony nonetheless . . . very virtuously saved himself" (§3). We are invited to picture a Roman legion, in tight formation, marching briskly across a desert, with enemy cavalry swirling about its flanks but never able to do it much harm ("Nor did all the Parthian cavalry ever dare to try the ranks of his army."). And with this picture in mind, we are expected to conclude that ordered infantry can only be overcome by other infantry (not by elephants, not by cavalry). Indeed, Machiavelli's point appears to be that Roman orders have universal applicability (useful to plainsmen as well as to moderns). But one of the reasons that argue in favor of infantry is that "a man on foot can go many places where a horse cannot go" (§2). For instance, a man on foot can climb a mountain. By the same token, however, a man on horse can better traverse a plain. Machiavelli seems aware (and in *The Art of War* Fabrizio most certainly is [II, 602-03; VII, 719]) that if mountains are suited to foot soldiers, an "extensive country" is suited to horse soldiers (§3). One of the principles of Aristotelian political science is that military practices are greatly influenced by geography and terrain (open country requires cavalry, mountains require lightly armed troops); also that military practices influence the determination of the regime (naval power points toward democracy).[52] But Machiavelli says little about the Roman army's suitability to the Italian countryside and even less about the regime implications of the Roman legion. The focus instead is on exposing the "sins" of Italian princes who have made Italy weak by taking reputation away from the infantry.

We come then to this impasse: that Machiavelli underscores the importance of Roman authority only to intimate his independence therefrom; that it is a "leaderless" Machiavelli who discovers the truth of the infantry's superior fighting qualities; and that this superiority is at least exaggerated if not falsified by Machiavelli's insistence that it is everywhere in evidence. Given the fact that contemporary Italians are of the opposite opinion, that cavalry is superior to infantry (and professionals to amateurs, or mercenaries to citizen militia), it stands to reason that Machiavelli would want to appeal to the authority of Rome; and given the intensity of this belief, it might follow that he would judge it useful to overstate the case for fighting on foot.[53] He explains that the condottiere system (which had dominated Italian war-making for a quarter century) is responsible for the reliance on cavalry and the undervaluing of infantry. The condottieri were princes without principalities. Their "states" were well-armed (they had soldiers) but were without territory or citizens. Lacking access to men and money, they found it necessary to devise a low-cost method of warfare. Since a few hundred cavalry were cheaper to keep than thousands of well-trained infantry, the condottieri altered the style of war-making from foot to horse. They also arranged it, as we read in *The Prince* and the *Florentine Histories*, that war would be less burdensome and hazardous for everyone involved (no stockade building or nighttime fighting or winter campaigning).[54] But this "gentlemen's agreement" to fight mock wars with a handful of troops has not served Italy well, now that Italy has become the battleground of foreign armies.[55] It is a system that rests upon the self-interest of a few, of princes and captains who want acquisition without effort; and even though the unhappiness of Italy should be proof of the system's failure and the lessons of history a guide to reform, still the habit holds fast of preferring cavalry to infantry.

Chapter 19 provides further assurance that Roman means are still relevant despite the development of new technologies. Here the new technology is the man-at-arms, the heavily armored knight emblematic of combat in the Renaissance and the late Middle Ages. Conventional wisdom has it that a squadron of men-at-arms can smash through a cliff, to say nothing of a battalion of infantry. It thus would be foolishly retrograde, conventionalists believe, to undertake the revival of Roman orders.[56] In fact, as Machiavelli remembers, Roman infantry once did fight against armored horsemen, so it is not necessary to speculate on the outcome of a contest between ancient and modern arms, as was true in the case of artillery. According to the histories, with only a few infantry, Lucullus defeated 150,000 cavalry of Tigranes, including a contingent equipped like men-at-arms (69 BC). And the recent victory of the Swiss at Novara (1513 AD) demonstrates the continued effectiveness of well-ordered infantry. From these examples Machiavelli concludes that what the histories narrate is all true and that moderns would be better off if they adopted Roman orders in their entirety.

But in the Lucullus example Machiavelli has his facts all wrong: the army of Tigranes, while overwhelming, consisted mainly of heavy infantry.[57] And his armored cavalry, called "cataphracts," were not exactly beaten by Roman infantry, since they broke rank before the battle was even joined. They did even worse—they turned into Tigranes' infantry, causing the entire army to take flight. Though outnumbered twenty to one, the Romans sustained but five dead against 100,000-plus for the enemy, which throughout the battle was in retreat.[58] As for the Swiss victory at Novara, Machiavelli mentions that it is an "example often cited by us" (§1). Does he return to it, we wonder, because there are so few others? After all, these same Swiss were defeated two years later at Marignano.[59] In any event, it seems that Machiavelli is once again straining to make the case that the old is always better than the new.

The Noble Lie

To be virtuous, in the sense of good, is to sacrifice personal satisfaction for the well-being of the group. In a virtuous army there are no individuals performing separate feats of bravery (Manlius Torquatus executed his son for trying the same [II.16.1]); rather there is a disciplined unit keeping its formation intact. In a virtuous army the unglamorous work of the infantry is more highly valued than the spectacular exploits of the cavalry.[60] Virtue is not individualistic; virtue is not easy; virtue is not glorious. And yet virtue is necessary for success. What success means here, and in book 2 especially, is collective acquisition. But collective acquisition is a temptation to individual acquisition, and acquisitive individualism is destructive of civic virtue. Civic virtue needs the equivalent of a noble lie to defend it, an opinion which holds that innovations to the Roman modes of making war spell the ruination of the city. The reason is less that Roman authority is above reproach than that Roman modes are difficult to master and sustain and that the attraction of easy substitutes invites a dangerous relaxation of effort.[61] So far two alternatives have been considered—artillery and cavalry—and Machiavelli rejected them both, conceding only that they might be useful as accompaniments to virtue but not as virtue's replacements.

This pattern is first set in chapter 10, where the subject is the value of money to the prosecution of war. "Money is not the sinew of war," the title reads and the chapter repeats; and the opinion that it is, though ancient in origin and the conventional wisdom of the day, Machiavelli disputes.[62] Now it is true that the lack of money can force an unwanted battle, but then there are other contingencies that may limit a commander's options, such as the imminent arrival of enemy reinforcements or a shortage of supplies. Money helps, provided that it is not by itself and "without faithful arms" (§1). But money also hurts, since having great treasure gives others an inducement to attack. Money hurts as well, and chiefly, when it engenders the false opinion that money is strength and that wars are won by the richest combatant. The Capuans undertook the defense of the Sidicini against the Samnites because they, the Capuans, measured their power by the extent of their wealth and not by the number and virtue of their soldiers. Similarly Athens went to war with Sparta because Pericles believed that Athenian money and industry would overwhelm Spartan arms. Machiavelli is something of a primitivist, betting that well-trained, patriotic soldiers will get the better of well-paid mercenaries even when armed with the latest in military hardware (e.g., men-at arms).[63] Simple virtue, he attests, will win out over sophisticated professionalism and by winning out will have at its disposal what the professionals deem most essential—money. "Money is quite necessary in second place, but it is a necessity that good soldiers win it by themselves; for it is as impossible for money to be lacking to good soldiers as for money by itself to find good soldiers" (§3). Good arms are the sinew of war, the sine qua non of victory; and money, a "second place" aid, can provide no shortcut to military prowess.[64]

The same, however, cannot be said about fraud. When the weak and the lowly attempt to rise, fraud is the recommended means of ascent. Force alone is never "found to be enough, but fraud alone will be found to be quite enough" (II.13.1). It would appear that fraud is the easy way to empire, the way of the wily fox without help from the brawny lion. Individuals rise mainly by fraud (Philip of Macedon, Agathocles of Sicily, Xenophon's Cyrus), and republics, confronting similar necessities, rise by similar means. Rome deceived its allies when it put itself at the head of a coalition bent on increase and expansion. On the other hand, Rome did not subdue the Latins by trickery alone. Eventually the Latins caught on (following the defeat of the Samnites), and when they dared Rome to forbid a Latin war against Samnium, Rome's new ally, Rome attempted to placate the Latins by responding to their provocations with humility and patience. But Rome's conciliation only aggravated the arrogance of the

Latins; thus Machiavelli censures Rome for deceiving itself instead of its enemies (II.14). Even though chapter 13 stipulates that fraud "is less worthy of reproach the more it is covert" (§2), the assumption in chapter 14 is that all frauds
are discovered at some point or another; and the argument made is that feigning
innocence after the truth is known sends a message of weakness when a display
of strength is what most is needed. Fraud is the instrument by which the weak
obtain force; since the weak cannot forever hide the force they have obtained,
they must use force or risk becoming contemptible in the eyes of their opponents. Thus the lion is redeemed, as is the hard virtue that accounts for the lion's
terrifying roar.

But is there no alternative to Roman expansion with its concomitant requirement that the city be always armed for war? Chapter 19 entertains the possibility that there is. Those responsible for "a civil way of life" might choose to
maintain their states without choosing to expand them. Indeed, Machiavelli recommends that if the Roman way of increase is not pleasing, then no increase
should be permitted, since acquisition by other means leads to ruin. Sparta and
Venice were the expansionary alternatives to Rome in I.6; in II.4 it was the Tuscan league, of which the Swiss Confederation was the modern-day representative. We also were introduced in I.55 to the German republics and told about
their antique virtue. Here these republics are brought forward as an instance of
states which have remained small, not wanting to expand at all, and yet have
been able to maintain their liberty. But Machiavelli warns that the German republics are an exception and that other states, choosing "quiet" and "little borders," are molested by their neighbors and become acquisitive in response; or if
no enemy without endangers them, then enemies within rise up to disturb the
peace. Such is the fate of all "great cities," which means that for great cities at
least, maintenance is a false option to expansion (§1).[65]

German exceptionalism is a consequence, partly, of an emperor with more
reputation than power (II.11). The German cities came to independence at a
time when the Holy Roman Empire was too feeble to keep them subject and in
tow. They bought their freedom from the emperor and had no princes about
asserting a substitute authority. They also were part of a larger province that
included the duke of Austria and the Swiss Confederation. Machiavelli claims
that the emperor, while threatening no one, has had reputation enough to arbitrate many of the province's disputes. And those disputes which have exceeded
his powers of persuasion, such as the wars between the Swiss cantons and the
Austrian duke, have been fought to a standstill because of the military virtue of
the Swiss. Nor has the union of the empire and the dukedom (the fact that the
last three Austrian dukes have worn the emperor's crown)[66] upset the balance of
forces in the region, since the German republics have refused to make war on
other republicans and the princes of Germany have been too poor or too envious
to lend the emperor effective aid. Machiavelli concludes that imperial authority
has reduced the aggressiveness of member states by removing fear of molesta-

tion as a cause of desiring more. At the same time this authority has invigorated civic virtue by applying sufficient outside pressure to keep the various communities "united inside their walls" (§2). But because these conditions are in place nowhere else, Machiavelli observes, it is reckless to suppose that one can escape the necessity to expand or that one can expand by means other than Rome's.[67]

In the following chapter, II.20, Machiavelli again cautions his contemporaries not to succumb to the lure of virtueless acquisition. The temptation in question is the employment of auxiliary troops, defined by Machiavelli as "those whom a prince or republic sends, captained and paid by it, for your aid" (§1). Auxiliaries are dangerous because their allegiance is to the power that pays them, and either that power is plotting some ill or "through their own ambition" the auxiliaries accomplish your ruin themselves. Weak states are enjoined to stay clear of auxiliaries, and weak states are especially culpable if they resort to auxiliaries for the sake of unearned acquisitions they cannot defend. Such is an example of acquiring empire without force, the cardinal sin of chapter 19. The predictable consequence is that states with virtue acquire easily by exploiting the ambition of the weak, who mistakenly believe that the easy way to acquire is to employ auxiliaries from the strong.

Machiavelli has been considering the various excuses offered by contemporaries for why a revival of Roman orders need not be counted a high priority: money is the sinew of war, they say, and artillery has rendered the Roman formation obsolete. Machiavelli consistently claims that these opinions are false. In chapter 22 he examines another false opinion: that a victorious army is weakened by battle and is easily beaten by a new foe. The chief example is the decision of Pope Leo X to remain neutral as the Swiss and the French hammered each other at the Battle of Marignano. The thinking was that the pope could lay back, ostensibly protecting his possessions in Lombardy, watch the combatants exhaust themselves, and then pounce on the victor whose ranks had been depleted by the fighting. But the French no sooner won than the papal forces and their allies (the Spanish) retreated from the area. Machiavelli is not surprised by the result, for in his estimation victory produces few losses, and it so enhances the reputation of the victor that even if casualties are high, the morale of a second opponent collapses. Leo hoped for an "easy" (*facile*) win, using forces that were otherwise no match for either the French or the Swiss. His objective was to drive out the foreign powers (Spain excepted) and to return Italy "to its ancient liberty" (*ridurre nell'antica libertà*). Machiavelli wants the same, but he cautions that effortless acquisition is a false expectation. Only to the strong does easy increase belong.

In chapter 24 Machiavelli imagines that contemporary strategists would find fault with Rome's decision to forgive the Privernates and to extend citizenship to them (they rebelled unsuccessfully in 330, and their leaders were brought before the senate to plead Privernum's case [II.23.4]). Not that these thinkers would recommend the opposite extreme of eliminating rebellious cities (III.27).

Rather they believe that a third option was available to Rome, a middle way we might call it, between caressing and eliminating. Rome could have governed Privernum, and rebellious Latin towns, by means of fortresses.

The attraction of a fortress is that it requires fewer soldiers to hold a subject people in line, either one's own people or those captured in war. A ruler can thus avoid the hard work of developing a citizen army and need not gamble his state on the loyalty of others. The impregnable walls of the fortress keep him secure no matter what his subjects think, and the fortress provides a refuge against enemies in times of war. But Machiavelli explains that the ruler's security is itself a danger, since it allows him, even causes him, to be abusive toward the people. Moreover, the ruler is mistaken to believe that the people's hatred can do him no harm. War provides many opportunities for betrayal, and a hated prince is an enticement to war. Thus Machiavelli reasons that a prince is secure to the extent that his subjects support him, that they support him to the extent that he treats them justly, and that he treats them justly to the extent that he needs their help and fears their scorn. Since a fortress imbues a prince with false notions of omnipotence and self-sufficiency, building a fortress is the one action a prince must always avoid. There are ancillary employments to which fortresses are put, such as defending a frontier against surprise attack, but fortresses are useless without armies to relieve them: they are laid siege to, bypassed, or have their walls knocked down by artillery.[68] The strength of the state depends finally on the virtue of its arms, and the need for a citizen army capable of fighting in the field forces the prince to give due attention to the interests of the people. Machiavelli is making the Aristotelian argument that justice is advantageous and that ruler and ruled share a common good.[69]

Justice is especially advantageous in the case of a ruler with high ambitions. He wants much but needs others to assist him in obtaining his goals. Thus an enlightened acquisitiveness leads to forbearance and respect, whereas an unenlightened acquisitiveness leads to tyranny and ruin. The prince is enlightened by having it explained that his fortunes are tied to the people's good will and that limits apply to the pleasures he seeks. The people needs also to have its appetites restrained, for it is goodness the people brings to the acquisitive pursuit. What is expected of the people is honesty, piety, and patriotic devotion. Numerous alternatives to popular virtue have heretofore been offered, but Machiavelli steadfastly denies that any suffice as instruments for gain: not money or artillery or auxiliary troops; not cavalry in place of infantry or the wide, thin line in place of formation in depth; not neutrality, fortresses, or confederations. Only virtue will do, only a well-trained army of citizen-soldiers. On the other hand, Machiavelli stops short of endorsing the virtue of Sparta. Sparta did Rome one better by trusting entirely in the virtue of its troops. Sparta had no walls; whereas Rome, hedging its bet, built walls and continually extended their compass. Rome even had a fortress, and it was the fortress which saved Rome on the one occasion when its virtue failed (390 BC). So it is possible to be an extremist in the matter of virtue or to see that Rome, the city which supposedly avoided the middle and favored extremes, was itself situated midway between the extremes of unwalled Sparta and fortress Milan.

Sometimes middle ways are easy ways, and sometimes easy ways succeed. Fraud, for example, is a middle way between war and peace. Rome was fraudulent in its manner of conquest, and so Rome expanded without great expense. When middle ways are not a consequence of expecting too much (that precise justice is attainable and is appreciated by those it benefits) or an excuse for having too little (neither the prudence to caress nor the courage to eliminate), they are useful means of acquisition; and Machiavelli consistently allows middle ways and easy ways to cities that are otherwise strong—e.g., fortresses save when supported by virtuous arms. There is a danger of corruption here, that having conquered by fraud one will neglect the virtue that permits conquest by force. But to eschew all easy means for fear of corruption is to make increase too difficult and gain too costly; it is to defeat the very project of acquisition and to deny virtue its instrumentalist rationale.

That acquisition should enrich and enlarge is one of Machiavelli's simpler axioms (II.19.2). Acquisition does the opposite, however, if a state buys its empire and buys peace with its neighbors. The lesson of chapter 30 is that a state ought not adopt tribute-paying as a strategy of defense. A strong state like Rome receives tribute from others. Like Rome a strong state depends on its own citizens and those added to its "trunk" (the Latin colonies); it is strong at the core and weak at the periphery, where buffer states, paying tribute, provide a first line of defense. Weak states, by contrast—and Machiavelli names Florence, Venice, and France—buy defense from their neighbors, just as elsewhere weak states seek assistance from auxiliaries and find deliverance in fortresses. They leave their citizens unarmed and so are stronger on their borders than they are at home. Machiavelli is reiterating the truest of all truths that princes should develop their own arms (I.21.1), and he is reaffirming an opinion, offered at length in II.12, that Rome fought better when at home than when abroad.

Another point which Machiavelli repeats is that a well-armed citizenry is a valuable protection against princely misconduct. Needing the people for defense, the prince is obliged to treat the people with kindness and consideration. A citizen army has then the same liberalizing effect as has a fortressless city (II.24). Moreover, a citizen army, along with improving ruler-ruled relations, puts the defense of the city on a firm foundation able to withstand the ups-and-downs of fortune. Poorly ordered cities, on the other hand, experience what seem to be "miraculous losses and miraculous acquisitions" (*miracolose perdite e miracolosi acquisti*). The world is full of miracles to those unarmed against fortune and exposed to its caprice. Such cities, most of them modern, give up on reason and let themselves be carried away by false hopes and false fears. Thus Machiavelli's recommendation to build strength at the core is an attempt to augment the role of reason in politics. He even conjectures that a prince who trains his reason on the orders of antiquity has a fair chance of defeating fortune's power (II.30.5).

Chapter 31 offers another instance of the trouble caused by false hope. The subject is refugees promising easy victory to the prince who takes up their cause. Alexander of Epirus, the brother-in-law and uncle of Alexander the Great, led an army into Italy at the behest of Lucanian exiles (332 BC). But he came to a bad end, betrayed by the exiles he undertook to assist (326 BC). And so Machiavelli advises that a prince not rely on the word of refugees since likely they will betray their benefactor if offered the hope of repatriation by their city. Trusting in refugees is for the sake of "taking towns furtively and through intelligence" (§2), and "furtive violence" was a less Roman mode of attack than "forced surrender" (II.32.1, 2).

Machiavelli calls for imitation of the ancients, and in book 3, chapter 10 he gets what he wants. Unfortunately, the imitation is all bollixed. The lesson taken by modern states from the example of Fabius Maximus Cunctator—Fabius the Delayer—is that by avoiding battle victory can be assured. As is the case in book 2, the moderns are accused of looking for an easy way, for a victory without the risk of battle or the martial virtue needed to prevail. But the true lesson, drawn from a clear understanding of Fabius's actions, is that a captain cannot escape battle if the enemy is set upon it. Fabius did not run from Hannibal any more than Hannibal ran from Fabius. Fabius rather was careful always to have the advantage, and Hannibal refused to engage on Fabius's terms. Delay was mutual, as Fabius kept his army in strongholds near to Hannibal's camps and as Hannibal kept his army away from Fabius's strongholds. By this method Fabius, with a weaker army, managed to stay in the field, and he managed to avoid a pitched battle during a period when Rome could ill-afford defeat (217 BC). But in order for the Fabian method to succeed, two conditions must be met: the virtue of the army must be sufficient to discourage or repel attack, and the material needs of the adversary must be steadily declining. These conditions had been satisfied in Fabius's case, and so it made sense for Fabius to delay combat. But delay for his modern-day imitators means simply that they "do battle to the enemy's purpose and not" their own (§1).

For modern armies, lacking virtue, the consequences are threefold when they imitate Fabian delay: either they keep at a safe distance from the enemy, allowing him therefore to ravage the countryside; or they seek refuge inside a city and suffer a siege; or they take flight when attacked and hope that the terrain will cover their escape. An ancient imitator of Fabius was Philip V of Macedon, and his experience with the Fabian policy is a fair predictor of what modern armies might expect. Philip tried shadowing the Romans while protecting himself behind strongly fortified positions (197 BC). But Philip's army was not as virtuous as Fabius's two decades earlier: The Romans overran Philip's stronghold, and Philip was forced to flee. Not wanting to be dislodged again, nor wanting to retire inside a city, Philip chose to retreat whenever the Romans advanced. But his situation and that of his subjects worsened the longer the war went on, for the maneuvers of both armies and their scorched-earth policies left the territory in ruins. Desperate for an end, Philip tried his luck in a straight-ahead battle and was defeated (Cynoscephae). Thus the moral of the story is that battle eventually comes—and at the enemy's choosing—whether one keeps to the field or takes shelter behind city walls; nor does it help to avoid battle by precipitate flight, since the dishonor incurred causes morale to fall and allies to defect and brings destruction to the army more certain than the action of combat, which has always about it the element of chance (II.10.2, II.27.4, III.31.3). The remedy lies in maintaining an army virtuous enough to defend a strong place even if it is not virtuous enough to fight out in the open.

Machiavelli finds three other occasions to repeat his general point that modern states ruin themselves by relying on an easy, ersatz virtue, but that easy ways do avail for those who first have strength. In III.11 there is consideration of the chances of one state's standing against many. No state is strong if many states confederate against it. But confederations are inherently unstable, and if the target state has strength enough to withstand a first thrust, temporizing diplomacy can dismantle the enemy's alliance. With timely concessions Venice could have divided the League of Cambrai and saved its empire. But "not having virtuous arms," Venice despaired of its courage when only half-beaten at Agnadello (1509 AD), and thereafter it let pass the chance for disingenuous negotiations (III.11.2). The subject in III.14 is deception. On the battlefield deceptions abound: camp followers mounted on mules can be made to look like cavalry, or camels wearing hides can be made to look like elephants; flaming spears and like novelties can be employed to terrify the enemy. By such deceits and inventions do armies often prevail. But these devices are useful depending on whether they "have more of the true than the fictional" about them, "because, having very much of the mighty, one cannot expose their weakness so soon." Real might lends credibility to apparent might and so increases the opportunities for economical acquisitions. But when dissimulations "have more of the fictional than the true . . . they are soon exposed and do harm to you" (III.14.3). Harm also is done to cities (and this is the third occasion) when they deceive themselves into believing that divide-and-rule is the clever way to manage subject states. This false opinion cities are apt to espouse "when they see that they cannot hold states with force and with virtue" (III.27.4). Virtue is foundational, the source of strength and the means to acquisition. Thus Machiavelli accepts no substitutes for virtue and is unequivocal in its defense.

Nowhere is he so adamant than when quoting from Papirius Cursor as he dilates on the importance of discipline in the ranks and continued faith in the old-time religion. The occasion for this speech, reported in III.36.2, was a victory over the Samnites by the master of horse, Quintus Fabius Rullianus, fought against the expressed orders of Papirius, the dictator, who had left the army in order to retake the auspices in Rome (325 BC). Papirius wanted Fabius punished, in the tradition of Brutus and Manlius who executed their own sons for treason and disobedience. But Fabius's father, the tribunes, and the Roman populace all wanted Fabius spared. Even Livy takes the side of Fabius, arguing that the threat of punishment had the same salutary effect as executions had had in the past. But Machiavelli provides none of this context—not the speech the of the father reminding the assembly of Rome's contrary tradition of leniency toward failure (from which the father infers an obligation of gratitude toward success [I.31.2]); not the decision of the dictator, once assured of his authority, to excuse Fabius his crime; and not finally the blessing of Livy conferred upon these proceedings (Livy, VIII.32-35). All that Machiavelli provides is Papirius's stern warning of the consequences that flow from slackened attention to good orders. In light of this truncated presentation, we can only conclude that Machiavelli regards Fabius's youthful initiative as a hazard to the state; also that he regards as wholesome Papirius's by-the-book severity and his religious scrupulosity.[70] Because good orders are everything, not only complementing nature but causing it ("from order arises fury and virtue" [III.36.2]), it follows that the work of maintaining good orders is vital to the welfare of the state—even if that work involves the execution of young Fabius.

Something though is surely amiss. For this same initiative was what took an older Fabius into the Ciminian forest, an action for which he and Rome are lavishly praised by Machiavelli in II.33.[71] Fabius's expedition against the Tuscans in 310 is offered as an example of the free commissions which Rome gave to its captains. It seems that the senate and the people reserved for themselves the right to declare war and ratify peace, but that the conduct of the war, from the selection of a campsite to the decision to wage battle, was left to the discretion of the captain. The reason why captains were given such latitude was to encourage their exploiting every chance for victory and to discourage senators, former captains themselves, from presuming to manage affairs from afar. And the reason why the war-declaring power remained with the government back home was to prevent individual captains, deceived by false hope, from starting new wars. As stated in II.27.1, men often "pass beyond the mark" and losing "the opportunity of having a certain good through hoping to have an uncertain better" ignore the limit "to the harm of their state." The Romans prospered, however, because their authoritative senate knew better than to meddle, while their enterprising commanders knew better than to overreach.

Balance, then, is the seeming remedy—divided power plus a just-right blend of independence and submissiveness. Strangely, though, the example in II.33 fails to communicate this message; for the consul Fabius paid the senate no heed whatsoever. Fabius defeated the Tuscans at Sutri then marched his army farther into Tuscany through the Ciminian forest. This country Machiavelli calls "new" (*paese nuovo*), and he has the senate refer to the incursion as "that war" (*quella guerra*). If, then, Fabius's advance into the Ciminian forest represented a new war for Rome,[72] by rights the decision belonged to the senate and the people. The principle which Machiavelli articulates and for which he gives Rome credit, that captains should have full authority over military operations but not authority to initiate war—this principle is unmistakably violated in the example. Is the example simply inapt and self-referential, a reminder of Machiavelli the writer as the person who chose it?[73] Perhaps. But we notice that not only is the principle violated by the example, but that a party within the example, the senate, expected just such a result. The senate feared that the jurisdictional boundary separating its authority and the consul's would not be respected by Fabius: "It had heard," reports Machiavelli, "of the victory Fabius had had and feared he would take up the policy of passing through said forest into Tuscany. Judging that it would be good not to attempt that war and run into that danger, it sent two legates to Fabius to make him understand he was not to pass into Tuscany." The senate's anxiety was not misplaced given that commanders had risen through the ranks of an agonistic system, were motivated by the desire for personal glory, and had only a short term in office during which to prove their worth. Because ambition would frequently override deference, the principle of sharing authority was itself flawed or prone to unpredictable results. But then what Machiavelli finally commends is not divided power, or the coexistence of free commissions and senatorial authority;[74] he rather commends the senate's gracious acceptance of a victory in defiance of its authority. "Whoever will consider this limit well," says Machiavelli, "will see it was used very prudently." The prudent use of the limit effectively nullified the limit. The senate stood aside as the consul started a new war. No doubt it helped that the consul was successful; but then Rome never seriously punished its failures either (I.31).

The principle attempts to set up jurisdictional boundaries, something like the dual sovereignty of state and federal governments here in America. The principle does not work. It is instead used prudently, which is to say covertly abandoned. In its place, operating as the only restraint, is glory: "Because of this they wished that the consul should act by himself and that the glory should be all his—the love of which, they judged, would be a check and a rule to make him work well." The senate trusted that a commander in the field, limited by little more than his desire for reputation, would conduct affairs in a manner conducive to the state's well-being. The senate was obliged to be so trusting because it wanted greatness for Rome, and restrictions on commanders would have impeded Rome's expansion.[75] The quest for greatness privileges individuals who best can achieve it, including individuals who are young. The Romans trusted that the energy and optimism of youthful captains would do more good to the state than their inexperience and recklessness would do harm (I.60). Of course it was expected that non-captains of all ages would follow the orders of their superiors lest their enterprising heroics jeopardize the chain of command and cause scandal to the troops. Thus Machiavelli can support the senate which yielded authority to Fabius and also support Papirius who wanted punishment for Fabius, because the rules which apply to commanders, that they innovate and take chances, are not the rules which apply to staff officers and mere soldiers, that they obey and hold fast. Rome needed commanders no less than it needed soldiers (its debt to each is a topic explicitly raised [III.13]), and it needed commanders and soldiers whose actions, if not characters, differed somewhat. Accordingly, when Fabius is viewed as a commander, his qualities of dash and decisiveness are lauded; but when he is viewed as a subordinate and soldier, these same qualities are condemned.[76]

Civic virtue is Machiavelli's noble lie, or it is a corruptible creation protected by a noble lie. It stipulates, this noble lie does, that acquisition, if not survival itself, depends essentially on citizens' bearing arms and fighting on foot. It is a lie—or less than fully true—because it discounts the alternate, and more agreeable, means by which acquisition is accomplished (e.g., cavalry, the value of which is surreptitiously recognized in II.18), or it insists—too strenuously, perhaps—that these means (money, fortresses, etc.) are useless unless accompanied by virtue. One would think that Machiavelli would welcome easier means of acquisition, given civic virtue's evident vulnerabilities. But Machiavelli quashes every alternative which common opinion finds attractive and promising. In his resistance to technology and change, Machiavelli seems like a Platonic guard dog barking at an approaching stranger or a Platonic warrior defending his perfect education against reforms and innovations (while at the same time like a Platonic philosopher-king who supplies the education taught to others). The lie also is noble, because, while it is a means to an end, it partakes of the end it serves. If civic virtue is not the only means to acquisition, it is the only means to glorious acquisition, where empire and fame, and not security and wealth, are the desiderata of ambition. Without civic virtue, there could be no conquering heroes, any more than without spirited warriors there could be philosophers who rule as kings. Like spiritedness, which Plato's noble lie elevates to the rank of reason's auxiliary, civic virtue is auxiliary to the city's imperial ambitions and to the glory-seeking of its princely individuals. And like the virtue of Plato's auxiliaries, defended by prejudice rather than philosophy, by beauty rather than truth, Machiavelli's civic virtue is defended by dogmatic assertions of its utility and by a romanticized picture of Rome. Civic virtue does need defending and may in fact be more fragile than Platonic moral virtue, since it has no philosopher to supervise its transmission and since it operates outside the protected confines of small and closed cities. Large and open cities, powerful and acquisitive like Rome, are persistently tempted by luxury, leisure, and license; accordingly, they need persistent, if not always truthful, reminders of why virtue matters. Machiavelli is one such advocate of civic virtue—at least in the case of the trunk-thickening hegemon and at least that part of it dealing with arms. Regarding the other part, that dealing with law and religion, he is equivocal, or so we had reason to believe. But then it is Machiavelli's conviction that where there are good arms there must also be good laws.

Chapter Six

Rome's Captains

It is no mean trick ascertaining the subject of book 3. Based on the outline at the end of I.1 ("the things worked by it [Rome], which . . . ensued either through public or through private counsel, and either inside or outside the city"), we are wont to expect a third book concerned with things done by private counsel inside the city, followed by a fourth book devoted to things done by private counsel outside the city.[1] Only obliquely does Machiavelli return to the description in I.1.6, declaring that actions of particular men affecting the greatness of Rome (outside the city) or producing good effects within Rome (inside the city) would be the third book's subject (III.1.6). In light of this pronouncement—and since no fourth book was ever written[2]—we must suppose that book 3 combines the subject matters of books 1 and 2 regarding the theaters of Roman action. (And the third book, in point of fact, is as much interested in foreign as domestic affairs.) We must also suppose that the actions of particular men replace the counsel of deliberative bodies, and that these actions are public—i.e., redounding to the benefit of Rome—since opposed to them are the private actions of Roman kings; for Machiavelli stipulates that the "great and notable" actions of Rome's kings, because detailed in other histories, will be omitted from his account "except for anything they may have worked pertaining to their private advantage."[3] Private advantage stands in stark contrast with public benefit, especially the benefits of greatness without the city and good effects within.

But it is not the case that book 3 is only about the exploits of republican patriots, since kingly selfishness, as in the Tarquin tyranny, is the cue for a prolonged excursus on the subject of conspiracy. Conspiracies are unmistakably private affairs; and because conspiracies are plotted before they are executed, the theme of private counsel seems to figure in the topics of book 3 after all.

The conspirator is countered by the patriot—in fact by the reformer who uses conspiracies to haul the regime back to its uncorrupt beginnings. One princely type conspires to destroy; the other princely type punishes to preserve. But no matter the direction of a prince's ambition, be it toward destruction or preservation, all such princes employ the same one art of rule. If conspiracy is a form of private counsel, so also is the art of rule to which conspiracy belongs. For the art of rule is practiced behind closed doors, its techniques invisible to the ruled. By contrast, the art of lawmaking, or public counsel, is practiced in the open for all to see. Lawmaking presupposes the authority of the city and the equality of the citizenry (even when public counsel is delivered by a Scipio); but the art of rule underscores the superior virtue of the princely individual and the danger of his ambition. The art of rule is unrepublican: inaccessible, unaccountable, non-ministerial; and yet the art of rule is essential to the growth and longevity of republics and of all regimes. What generally happens in book 3 is that republican modes and orders move to the side so that virtuous individuals—some subverting, some defending—can come to center stage.

Preserving the State

The opening chapter of book 3, which reads like and serves the purpose of a preface, introduces the theme of preservation. Machiavelli contends that both simple bodies formed by nature and mixed bodies formed by men maintain themselves, not eternally, but for as long as heaven allows, by resisting alterations or by changing in a manner conducive to their safety. Machiavelli ignores the first option of alteration-free preservation. Perhaps he is convinced that the world is always in motion, rather than tending toward rest, and that bodies endure the longest which are nimble and quick to adapt. He does, after all, prefer dynamic Rome to static Sparta. But Spartan conservatism is not entirely rejected, since change is safe, asserts Machiavelli, to the extent that it returns a body to its beginnings: "And it is a thing clearer than light that these bodies do not last if they do not renew themselves" (§1). The presumption here is that origins are good, or good enough for the body to have survived its birth,[4] and that "increase" from the beginning (§2), while partly good, includes harmful accretions that must be cured or purged if the body is to regain its health (II.5.2). It is Machiavelli's belief that necessity forces the adoption of good institutions when the mixed body of the state is young and fragile; but that as the state grows and necessity recedes, the goodness caused by necessity is gradually replaced by the corruption caused by freedom (I.1.4, I.3.1, II.12.3, III.12.1). Thus a state is preserved if it reexperiences necessity and reforms itself on the model of its beginning.[5]

There are two means by which a state is brought back to its beginnings: external accident (*accidente estrinseco*) or intrinsic prudence (*prudenza intrinseca*). Rome was delivered by both, but the defining moment in the city's history, marking off a "before" and an "after," was the external accident of its capture by the French in 390. When initially discussed in II.29, the capture of Rome was presented as a providential intervention by the goddess Fortuna, who wanted Rome humbled but not destroyed. Here it is attributed to the Romans themselves, who had strayed from their customary observance of religious rites and the law of nations and who had ceased to esteem the virtue of worthy men. The incident was accidental in the sense that Rome did not intend to be admonished and a force outside of the control of Rome was required to administer the correcting punishment. But however important was this accident to Rome's revival, it put Rome too much at the mercy of chance; and so Machiavelli concludes that rescue by external accident "is not in any way to be desired" (§6).

Far preferable is that rescue which comes from intrinsic prudence, of which, says Machiavelli, there are two kinds: laws and the examples of good men. Machiavelli remembers two laws, or orders, which brought Romans back to their beginnings, the office of tribunes and the office of censors. These orders worked their restorative magic by punishing "the ambition and insolence of men" (§3). To return to beginnings is to be reacquainted with fear and with the awesome power of the state to execute; and the more awesome the execution, or "excessive and notable" (§3), the better the results. It can even be useful for this power to commit injustice, as was the case when the two Scipios suffered the ingratitude of the state (§3; also I.29.3). Fear is what makes people good; thus the state must induce fear in the populace even though, in another sense, the state's function is to deliver people from fear by providing them with security and prosperity (II.2.3).

After listing several notable executions carried out by Rome, Machiavelli declares that not ten years should go by without such a return to beginnings. But in a rare example of modern orders surpassing ancient orders, he observes how the rulers of Florence from 1434 to 1494 (the Medicis) held that every five years the state should be regained (*ripigliare*).[6] Regaining the state meant "putting that terror and that fear in men that had been put there in taking it, since at that time they had beaten down those who, according to that mode of life, had worked for ill." The Medicis "took" the state; their regime had enemies whom they "beat down" initially and whom they kept down by periodic reapplications of revolutionary terror. Just barely is this violence sanctioned by law; certainly it is not the ordinary and regular administration of justice. On the contrary, says Machiavelli, these "orders have need of being brought to life by the virtue of a citizen who rushes spiritedly to execute them" (§3).

Given the prominence of individual virtue in the execution of punishments, the distinction is not so great between law as a manifestation of intrinsic prudence and the examples of good men—even though Machiavelli says of the former that it is "law that stimulates you to any execution" (§3). The more obvious difference is that the examples in question are acts of heroic self-sacrifice which cause good men to imitate them and wicked men to be ashamed to hold to a contrary life. The good examples of outstanding men—and Machiavelli names several heroes from Rome's republican past—are a supplement to judicial terror. Goodness, it seems, is preserved by a combination of legalized violence striking dread into the hearts of citizens and patriotic heroism inspiring citizens with a love of the noble. Machiavelli asserts that if these acts occur together and every ten years, a city need never suffer corruption. But even though he has divined the secret to political immortality, he is, one supposes, none too hopeful of the result; for the two lists of virtuous Romans fail to show that Rome ever adhered to the schedule of decennial renewals.[7] No doubt there were more instances of virtue than those few named; but Machiavelli does not use the lists to demonstrate that Rome practiced this spiritual medicine on itself.

According to the statement in III.1.6, the kings of Rome are cast as selfish villains, preoccupied with private advantage, whereas individual republicans play the role of "particular men" who "made Rome great and caused many good effects in that city." This they did, we presume, by executing the law or by sacrificing their personal well-being for the sake of Rome's revival. The first of these heroes, Junius Brutus, exhibited both brands of heroism at once, for the terribleness he showed toward others he applied also to himself, in that the conspirators he punished were of his own family. When his sons conspired against the republic, he sat on their tribunals, voted for their condemnation, and was present at their execution (III.3.1). "To kill the sons of Brutus" is Machiavelli's catch phrase for the severity needed to secure a new regime, be it a republic or a principality. Soderini lost his state because he failed to move against the Medici conspirators, and the Roman kings Tarquinius Priscus and Servius Tullius were each assassinated because they left alive and at liberty rival heirs to the throne.

It is a little surprising that Machiavelli would present two of Rome's kings as the victims of others' villainy when he had promised to confine his remarks to those actions "pertaining to their private advantages."[8] So far are Priscus and Servius from selfish villainy that they are included in the list of new republicans who make a free state but then fail to kill the "sons of Brutus" in order to maintain its liberty. At the same time, so far is Brutus from patriotic self-sacrifice that he is first celebrated for the self-regarding fraud he perpetrated against the royal family. Brutus simulated craziness (*pazzia*) so as to be near the Tarquins and yet not endangered by them or encompassed by their ruin. Initially Machiavelli is intent on redeeming Brutus's reputation for patriotism against what he supposes is a too cynical account present in Livy—to wit, that Brutus was motivated by private concerns for security and wealth. On the contrary, states Machiavelli, Brutus was plotting a public outcome all along, since he kissed the earth upon his return from Greece (the Delphic oracle had foretold that the first of the emissaries to kiss his mother would be Rome's next ruler;[9] apparently Roman soil was Brutus's mother) and since he, Brutus, was the first to remove the knife from the dead Lucretia's body and to force his companions to swear their opposition to kingship. In fact, Machiavelli's Brutus is almost too patriotic. But when we come to the lesson which Machiavelli draws from Brutus's "eminent work" (III.2.1), about where to position oneself relative to the prince, it is evident that Machiavelli has not forgotten the importance of self-seeking in the gamut of human motives:

> They should enter on all those ways that they judge to be necessary, following his [the prince's] pleasures and taking delight in all those things they see him delighting in. This familiarity, first, makes you live secure, and without carrying any danger it makes you enjoy the good fortune of that prince together with him and affords you every occasion for satisfying your intent. (§1)

In the event that the prince is never removed from power, the disguised fool has the benefit of a safe and pleasure-filled existence. And if the prince is toppled, the fool is positioned to replace him. These happy outcomes assume, of course, that the conspirator is none too proud: Brutus earned a reputation for prudence, but he first had to endure a reputation for stupidity, and throughout it all he ran the risk that his countrymen would never know of his wisdom.[10] Also assumed by these outcomes is that the prince is not overthrown by his declared enemies; for declared enemies are honorable men of quality, and such men usually are averse to associating with fops and lackeys.

The fact is that Brutus, first on the list of noble Romans whose executions restored Rome to its beginnings, was a rebel against the old order. He not only "recovered" a traditional liberty that was usurped by the Tarquin tyranny (*ricuperare* [III.2.1, end]), but he "fathered" a new liberty (*padre della romana libertà* [III.1.6]) when he crushed the kings and liberated his fatherland (*opprimere i Re e di liberare la sua patria* [III.2.1, beginning]). Brutus and the republic mark the beginning of something new, not mainly the restoration of something old (I.25). And the chapters that follow III.1 are about conspiracies against established regimes. It is passing strange that the theme of preservation would serve as an introduction to a book whose early chapters are about subversion. The book is set on this course by Brutus's "eminent work" of simulated stupidity. Though not technically a conspirator himself, Brutus shares with conspirators a craftiness not untouched by selfish regard and private ambition, for even the severity that he showed toward his sons was in defense of "the liberty that *he* had acquired" in Rome (III.3.1, beginning).[11] Book 3 does not in fact recount the biographies of selfless heroes, as might be expected from the close of III.1.[12] Perhaps the reason is that there were no "particular men" who fit this description or that they were too few to matter. On the other hand, if Rome's "particular men" were also private men, conspirators on behalf of their own ambitions, a significant problem of supply and demand would then be ameliorated—namely, that the supply of good men meet the decennial demand for good men. Machiavelli advises that the state "contrive that it be either good orders or good men" that deliver the city every ten years (III.1.6). Good orders are only somewhat reliable (I.18), and they depend on good men to enforce them. But how does the state contrive to have good men come along on a regular basis? Machiavelli does not say; but to the extent that good men are required to be selfless servants of the common good, their appearance is a rare, not a frequent, occurrence; and dependence on them is like dependence on external accident. If, however, deliverance of the city were simultaneously a self-interested act, the appearance of these deliverers, ruthless executioners and inspirational heroes, would be more usual and predictable, and the city would be less a plaything of fortune. Book 3 then would have as its subject the union of private ambition and public benefits in the domestic and foreign affairs of Rome.[13]

Thwarting Tyranny

"I say that a republic without reputed citizens cannot stand, nor can it be governed well in any mode" (III.28.1). Rome depended on its individuals, on their virtue inspired by their ambition. That dependence is nowhere better seen than in the relation Rome had with Camillus. Upon his death in 365 he was accorded the title of Rome's "second founder" (Livy, VII.1), since he had saved Rome from the French and from abandonment by its own people. He also was the conqueror of Veii and the commander of Rome's armies against many of Rome's enemies. He is the subject of a chapter detailing the ways in which a citizen might gain the authority to do a good deed for his republic (III.30). But Camillus was also exiled by Rome when its people suspected him of aspiring to a power incompatible with republican equality. The problem here is that a citizen who has the reputation to save a city has also the reputation to impose upon it a tyranny. The virtue that does a good deed is close to, if not the same as, the virtue that does a bad deed. Sometimes popular resentment of a reputed citizen is nothing more than envy born of quiet times; sometimes though it is vigilance in defense of republican institutions. Accordingly, the virtuous individual might become a conspirator against the regime because he is victimized by ingratitude or because his ambition, excited by the class divisions and personal rivalries of republican politics, demands greater scope and recognition than that afforded by elective office. The problem was especially acute in republican Rome, since ambition had no outlet other than political and military power. Either Cincinnatus, for example, was an imperious dictator over Rome's armies, or he was next to nothing at all, merely the proprietor of a small estate (III.25). When private life is spare and unsatisfying, the desire for public responsibilities is proportionately stronger. Timocracies train their citizens to be more public-minded than private, but one consequence of timocratic education is intense competition for honor and office. While jealousy among competitors helps keep the country safe (I.30), wounded pride can easily turn patriots into traitors (I.29, III.17).

Frankly, Machiavelli is more attentive to the dangers posed by reputed citizens than to the advantages they provide. A cautionary retort follows the above quotation from III.28: "On the other side, the reputation of citizens is the cause of the tyranny of republics." Thwarting tyranny is the main concern once the city's dependence on its individuals is recognized. But in order to close off all avenues to tyranny, it must first be possible to identify a tyrant in the making. Early indications, however, are none too encouraging.

Machiavelli announces, quoting Sallust's Caesar, that "all bad examples have arisen from good beginnings" (I.46.1). The beginning, it appears, supplies no true reading of what is intended and is about to happen.[14] Prominent citizens, for example, are the target of lesser men's envy. In response, they seek protection from harm, and their actions taken to defend themselves seem justifiable to others (Machiavelli is on their side in III.16 and III.30). By acts of liberality and free assistance, prominent citizens make friends and allies and so protect themselves from the malice of their enemies. Since giving and helping are virtuous deeds (in the traditional sense), the person who is generous with his wealth and influence is a good citizen deserving the trust and kindness of his fellows. But this good citizen, if trusted and befriended by many, possesses an authority equal to or surpassing that of elected magistrates. Either he starts to make demands, or the magistrates start to curry his favor and defer to his wishes. Soon enough the reputed citizen comes to think himself above the law, entitled not to be offended by it just as he is entitled not to be offended by his rivals. From here it is but a short step to the informal tyranny of private citizens ruling the state behind the facade of republican government. (The Medicis came to and exercised power in precisely this way.) Even if beginnings are truly good and the actors well-intentioned, "men ascend from one ambition to another," and so the good are made bad by the satisfaction of their rightful desires. Not until it is too late can this conversion from good to bad be discovered, except in those rare cases when "citizens who live ambitiously in a republic" (I.46.1) expose themselves by changing too quickly or by committing some inexplicable mistake. Appius Claudius, the head decemvir, ignored the teaching of history that the way to tyranny in a republic is to embrace the people and denounce the great. He betrayed the popular interest, whose support he had cultivated, without first completing the destruction of the nobles (I.40-41).[15] A second example is Girolamo Savonarola, who remained silent after a law he had promoted was violated by the authorities. The law granted those condemned by the Eight of Ward (*Otto di Guardia e Balìa*) and by the Signoria the right of appeal to the people. But when his own enemies, Medici conspirators, were denied this right, and in his many sermons he offered no word of protest, he revealed his partisanship, and his reputation suffered lasting harm (I.45.2).

One possible sign of incipient tyranny is the program promoted by a reputed citizen. If it caters to the people's weakness for bold initiatives, the proposer likely is a demagogue seeking to circumvent the constitution's checks and balances. Alcibiades excited Athenian passions with a plan to invade Sicily, and Scipio came to power by proposing to attack the African coast (I.53.4).[16] But in the latter case, the time was right for offensive action (III.9.1), and Scipio, rather than a demagogue and tyrant, was Rome's exemplary republican; for as the only perfectly guiltless victim of the people's ingratitude (I.29.3), "he gave place," says Machiavelli in the *Tercets on Ingratitude or Envy*, "to the evil desire of others as soon as he saw that Rome must needs lose either freedom or himself" (ll. 121-22). Confusing matters further is Machiavelli's pronouncement in II.15.1 that a good citizen, "especially in things that cannot wait on time," never resists the crowd but stands aside and lets popular fervor have its way. In fact, if someone is too resistant, it is his motives that warrant looking into not the motives of the rabble-rouser. A proposal's substance, therefore, offers no sure clue of the intentions of its author.

Might then formalities reveal the truth? There was one formality, to be sure, upon which the Roman republic insisted: respect for citizen equality with no tolerance of anyone ambitioning the name of king. For 400 years the Roman people was hostile to the kingly name and visited punishments on persons suspected of aspiring to it (I.58.3). In defense of this republican form, the people executed Spurius Cassius (486 BC), Spurius Maelius (439 BC), and Manlius Capitolinus (384 BC). And yet the power of the king was carried over to the republican constitution, existing in the office of consuls and more obviously in the office of dictator (I.2.7, I.25.1). By way of defending the propriety of this latter office, Machiavelli asserts that the name and rank of dictator did Rome no harm: ". . . if the dictatorial name had been lacking in Rome, they would have taken another; for it is forces that easily acquire names, not names forces" (I.34.1). This same point is made again in a discussion of Valerius Corvinus, that rank must be guarded by virtue, or else it is lost (III.38.1). In any event, it is most unlikely that an author who celebrates new princes and justifies conspirators would attach much significance to the formalized anti-royalism of the Roman people. Abjuring the name of king, then, while it may have helped some, did not by itself save Rome from the ambition of its reputed citizens.

Rousseau believes he has found a way to distinguish the tyrant from the deliverer. It is to notice the time when major reforms are proposed or a founding occurs. If the times are tumultuous and the people disposed to accept measures which in peace and prosperity it would reject, then it is a good bet that the prince is a tyrant notwithstanding the populism of his rhetoric.[17] But this technique is of no use to Machiavelli, who against Rousseau believes that tumult—and certainly advanced corruption visible to all—provides the opportunity for reform at a stroke (I.18).[18] By waiting so long, however, the reformer must resort to extraordinary modes, meaning extra-legal powers usurped from legitimate authorities as well as extreme violence against those most privileged by the old order. Neither popular consent nor the rule of law help here to separate the good from the bad; and the bloodshed and oppression which accompany the reform suggest a tyranny in the making. Camillus was lucky that his colleagues yielded "him the summit of command" (III.30.1), for otherwise he would have had to eliminate his envious rivals in order "to do any good work in his republic" (title). Not so lucky was Moses who, "if he wished his laws and his orders to go forward . . . was forced to kill infinite men" (§1).[19] Savonarola, too, sought to employ this method, but he lacked the authority; and those who had the authority failed to comprehend his message delivered in sermons against "the wise of the world" (§1). Since Machiavelli himself might be counted among the worldly wise and as an opponent of Savonarola,[20] we are reminded that the public good is often a matter of perspective, and that when princes step outside the boundaries of law, the task of separating the patriotic from the ambitious, the excellent from the envious, is very difficult indeed. (Such was the reason Soderini gave for why he would not "strike his opponents vigorously" [III.3.1].) Machiavelli's escape from this dilemma—the ambiguity caused by use of extraordinary modes—is to judge the intention by the end.

Perhaps there can be some knowing of tyrants after all, on grounds that tyrants do not produce results that are verifiably public and good. Romulus rose to power as any tyrant would, by killing off his rivals, even his brother; but Romulus used his solitary power to found a civil way of life, and he shared power thereafter with a senate. Founders are not tyrants if what they found is a mixed regime or republic. Likewise, reformers are not conspirators if they reform inside rather than outside of ancient orders, if they mend rather than destroy (I.9). Machiavelli's postmortem on the Soderini regime makes much the same point, that the public can distinguish good men from bad by the results of their actions. Soderini could have saved the republic by irregular, tyrannical means (by "killing the sons of Brutus"), without worry for the health of the republic, since "his works and his intention" would have been "judged by the end . . . if fortune and life stayed with him"; for everyone would have certified "that what he had done was for the safety of the fatherland and not for his own ambition" (III.3.1). It is after the fact that the good are known and separated from the bad. Thus having victory and success as the finished fact is a matter of first importance.

But what if "fortune and life" had not stayed with Soderini? What if, at the crucial moment, he, like Castruccio Castracani, caught a cold and died?[21] When Machiavelli next invokes the "ends justify the means" rationale, in III.35.2, he is noticeably less sanguine than before, perhaps because the focus is more on the means than on the ends. People can know something of the end because they experience some of the results. But their judgments regarding means are not so astute, especially when the means are the recommendations of an adviser rather than the actions of a prince. Says Machiavelli, "all men are blind in this, in judging good and bad counsel by the end." This widespread prejudice is not without foundation, however, since the plain purpose of counsel is to show the way to successful results. But wise counsel can always be defeated by chance, as by chance foolish counsel can be rescued; so results alone do not prove a counsel's worth. The best laid plans go sometimes awry through no fault of the planner. The public, though, is inattentive to contingencies such as these, impatient with caveats and unforgiving of failure. Accordingly, the maxim, "the end justifies the means," rather than reaffirming a moral order even amid the vagaries of political action, renders that order hostage to the dispensations of fortune.

When Machiavelli applies this maxim in *Prince* 18, there is little hint of a moral order and a common good. The blind men of *Discourses* III.35 now see perfectly well, but then sight is not the sense that they need: "Men in general judge more by their eyes than by their hands, because seeing is given to everyone, touching to few." Vulgar men see outward appearances but do not penetrate to the substance beneath, a hidden reality different from and disguised by surface phenomena. Included among these phenomena are the outcomes of human actions, most particularly the acquisition and retention of a state: "So let a prince win and maintain his state: the means will always be judged honorable, and he will be praised by everyone." What people praise need not be a public good in which they share, like the civil life created by Romulus; it may instead be a private good taken and defended with panache. People are impressed with history's winners, and if their victories are grand enough and no court exists to call them to account, even the crimes they commit are justified and commended.[22] Nothing gives greater encouragement to tyranny than the people's fascination with success and the individual's conviction that beyond good and evil lies a nobility whose measure is magnitude. In any event, the discussion in *Prince* 18 is a cold bath to any hope of identifying the tyrant by his deeds.

Machiavelli does offer one tried-and-true method of differentiating public servants from ambitious adventurers. It is to determine whether an individual's benefactions are delivered in a public or a private mode. A citizen operates publicly when he counsels well and when he performs deeds for the common benefit. He operates privately when by doing favors for private persons he attracts partisan supporters to himself (III.28). But how is it known when an action is public? The example in chapter 28 is of Spurius Maelius, a wealthy corn dealer, who in 439 made good the city's shortages of corn with supplies of his own. Maelius, however, was not guilty of "doing benefit to this and to that other private individual—by lending him money, marrying his daughters for him, defending him from the magistrates, and doing for him similar private favors" (§1). On the contrary, Maelius acted publicly, in that he benefited everyone, not just a favored few. What then was Maelius's failing? Most obviously, he acted without the authority of public office; he was a private citizen.[23] Public care is expected of public officials; when they perform their duties, no special debt is owed to them. But this same care provided by private persons, while in one sense a mark of exceptional patriotism, in another sense is a betrayal of country, since the gratitude it earns is—or might become—an inducement to unpatriotic ambition.[24] On the other hand, an earlier Spurius, Spurius Cassius, who tried returning to the people the money made from the sale of imported corn (486 BC), suffered a similar fate notwithstanding the fact that he was a consul at the time (III.8.1; Livy, II.41). So the holding of office is no sure barometer of actions taken in a public mode. Is it to act in a public or a private mode for a gentleman (and former ship's captain) to quiet a tumult between sailors and citizens which the magistrates are unable to control? The gentleman in question, whose intervention, Machiavelli remarks, one can read about from "among the ancient things of the Venetian republic," seems to have performed a public service of singular importance. But the senators of Venice, suspicious of his evident popularity, either had him imprisoned or had him executed (III.22.6). In *Florentine Histories*, VII.1, where this same discussion is carried on, Machiavelli distinguishes between harmful and harmless divisions in a republic. Harmful divisions are those based on parties and sects. Parties and sects derive their purpose from and owe their allegiance to the private ambitions of charismatic individuals. These individuals rise by doing favors in private, but also by sponsoring public entertainment and bestowing public gifts. They try ingratiating themselves with the populace. But since the scope of their generosity blurs the line between private and public giving (like Maelius's gift of corn), and since republican leaders routinely are kind to the plebs, spotting the tyrant by the character of his liberality is not the litmus test Machiavelli supposes it to be. Even less helpful is this method when applied to counsel spoken in a public forum. Since counsel pertains to future actions, the wisdom of counsel is impossible to establish at the time it is given; and the motive for counseling one course or another can rarely be known with assurance.[25] Moreover, the remedy for private ambition, namely accusation backed up by the "kingly arm" of the dictator, is half dependent on a civic virtue which the aspiring tyrant is working tirelessly to corrupt.[26] The dictator is needed because the people is apt to be "blinded by a species of *false good*" (III.28.1), that is by a Spurius (false) Maelius (good) giving it corn.[27] On the other side, the reward for public benefits is a triumph. But Manlius Torquatus, we are told in III.34.2, earned more reputation "by some extraordinary and notable action, even though private" (e.g., the defense of his father against the accusation of a tribune) than by "any triumph and any other victory" because "in those victories Manlius had very many like him; in these particular actions he had either very few or no one." In other words, triumphs were the way Rome *publicly* honored its heroes, whereas celebrity status for attention-grabbing exploits was the way Rome *privately* honored its heroes. And more fame and reputation accrued to him who was privately honored, even when private action was the cause.

The upshot is that Rome had difficulty discovering which of its reputed citizens were conspirators and which were loyal sons. It managed somewhat to suppress the former by promulgating the rule of law as its public philosophy: all were equal and no man above the law, regardless of the heroics which brought him influence and distinction. (Horatius, the surviving brother of the duel with the Curiatii, was, in the afterglow of his triumph, tried [though not punished] for the murder of his sister [I.22.1, I.24.1].) This republican preaching no doubt did some good, since Rome could boast of numerous self-sacrificing patriots among its governing elite, men who set aside their commissions early (I.30.2), refused enlargement of their powers (III.24.1), abstained from using public office for personal gain (III.25.1), granted authority to their equals (III.15.2, III.30.1), or forgave private injuries for the good of their country (III.47.1). But by and large, Rome handled the problem of ambition as it handled the problem of faction: not by suppressing it but by controlling its effects. Being always at war, Rome maintained a large cadre of capable commanders and encouraged their ambition through a policy of mandatory rotations (I.36.1). These reputed citizens, jealous rivals more than admiring colleagues, competed for the public's attention and performed some of the public's work of supervising others in office.[28] Usually this competition among elites furthered the city's interests, as when Fabius Maximus came forward to criticize the qualifications of Titus Ottacilius, whom Fabius judged a mediocrity unsuited to the job of containing Hannibal (III.34.4).[29] Sometimes though jealousy hampered good orders, as in the Sergius-Virginius episode (I.31.2), and envy was a special problem in quiet times (III.16.2). It was then that Rome placed its faith in constitutional forms, organizing the offices of state so as to protect against the ambition of particular magistrates. Most offices derived their authority from popular consent (free suffrage); most had multiple occupants (e.g., two consuls, ten tribunes) exercising unspecified powers (e.g., tribunes intervening in disputes among patricians), or they had single occupants (e.g., dictators) operating within jurisdictions narrowly defined (e.g., exposing a conspiracy); most were limited in their terms (six months for dictators, one year for consuls and tribunes, eighteen months for censors). Occasionally these offices underwent reodering, as when plebeians were at last admitted to the consulate; but "little by little" reform exceeded Rome's competence, and so the offices of state were not always in sync with the moral health of the people (I.18). In the end, too much depended on the state of civic virtue, especially the vigilance of the plebs as exhibited by the accusations it laid against the great.[30]

The above precautions were the ordinary measures taken by Rome to handle the problem of ambition. When these proved insufficient, Rome had recourse to extraordinary modes. For example, the customary vigilance of the Roman plebs, when agitated by crises, turned to ingratitude. Despite denials issued by Machiavelli, Rome, like other ancient republics, was ungrateful, though perhaps not to the same degree.[31] The threat of ingratitude from a suspicious public protective of its liberty often was enough to keep the great in line, who, by controlling their own ambitions, did little to provoke the people's hostility (I.30, III.22). Hence Rome was less ungrateful because it had less occasion to show ingratitude. Nor was Rome ever as ungrateful as Machiavelli would have had it be, since the wise course for Rome, when once it had offended a citizen, was to continue the offense by banning him permanently from public office. In the case of Claudius Nero, reprimanded for letting Hasdrubal escape defeat in Spain, Rome should never have entrusted him with command again for fear that he would use his office to obtain his revenge. When asked why he had taken so huge a risk in removing his army from the south of Italy where it was watching Hannibal to the north of Italy where it did combat with Hasdrubal (Metaurus River [207 BC]), Nero replied that the risk was Rome's and not his, since he would win fame in the event of success, and he would have vengeance in the event of failure (III.17.1).[32]

What ingratitude is to the patriotic public, so anticipation and temporizing are to the prudent great. The great protect the city and themselves from the ambitions of virtuous individuals by obstructing their ascents to power. If an individual means to purchase the people's favor with kindnesses and benefits, the great do the same and do it faster and so blunt an individual's appeal with an equal popularity of their own. This is anticipation, a species of indirect rule. Although an extraordinary mode, anticipation seems ordinary because it does not produce scandal (I.52). But to do its work, and to do it safely, some rather exacting conditions must be met: (1) the base of support of the individual to be obstructed must lie with the people (because anticipatory overtures to the people are not scandalous to the great, whereas overtures to the great are scandalous to the people [e.g., Soderini and the Medicis]); (2) the people must be corrupt to a degree (i.e., open to bribes and willing to abandon its true defenders); and (3) the target for cooptation, if there is one, must not be an inveterate enemy of one's cause (e.g., Octavius Caesar). If anticipation is impossible, or if the great are slow off the mark, then the fallback option is to temporize (I.33). This the great do with concessions and sundry deceits and manipulations, all in the hope that the danger will disarm itself or that the final surrender will be postponed indefinitely. But temporizing, while an action becoming the fox, is devoid of lion-like virtue and delivers results never more than partly satisfying.

The modes most extraordinary for managing ambitious individuals are political executions and reforms "at a stroke." In the final analysis, they may be the only modes able to do the job. If ambition is undetectable in the beginning when it is weak; if causes espoused may be equally bold or cautious, achieved by methods violent or peaceful, and implemented during times tumultuous or quiet; if common objectives are apparent only after they are achieved (if even then); if titles are unnecessary as a means of advancement and public modes hard to distinguish from private modes; if constitutional forms and the rule of law depend ultimately on the corruptible virtue of the people; and, finally, if indirect rule by the great is but a delaying tactic lacking in vigor—then the ambitious individual is triumphant in the city unless checked and defeated by another like himself. For every Manlius Capitolinus conspiring to be king, there must be a Manlius Torquatus willing to execute his son. However important are legal orders to political well-being, the state can never outgrow its dependence on princes or escape the turmoil caused by their colliding ambitions. Machiavellian politics is a battle among titans. The struggle for power is too elemental, Machiavelli seems to say, ever to be tamed by the well-crafted institutions of "a new science of politics."[33] If Machiavelli opens doors to this new science, say, by the compliment he pays to faction, he does not himself pass through these doors, as might be the case were he, for instance, to throw over Rome's mixed regime for a representative democracy.[34] But expansionary mixed regimes are his preference, since these tumultuous republics aspire to world empire, whereas representative democracies, reflecting the aspirations of the populace, busy themselves with trade. The new science of politics holds sacrosanct the rights of individuals, but in Machiavelli sensational punishments take the place of individual rights. Likewise the new science tries exorcising the conspiracy demon with doctrines of legitimate power, whereas Machiavelli is silent on the subject of legitimacy, wanting to talk instead about new princes (usurpers) who by their own ambition ascend from a private station to public office. Conspirators will always arise, the message is; and perhaps it is useful that they do. For if every ten years the city needs a memorable execution, every ten years it needs a conspirator to execute. The challenge to the city then is not to smother ambition under a blanket of domestic tranquility, but to find a champion in time to defend its interests, someone able and willing to "kill the sons of Brutus" and to wrench the state back to its beginnings.

Finding a champion is mostly a matter of letting free market competition operate among political elites. Still, champions are hard to come by (and the Roman record on this score short of impeccable) because there is a price to be paid for policing the ambitions of others. The policeman is apt to be hated, and by being hated prevented from accomplishing ambitions of his own. The conspirator, on the other hand, is apt to be loved, because often he is a corrupter, and corruption is pleasing to the corrupt. This is not to say that it is easy to conspire; but traveling the conspiratorial path can be quite agreeable, and the opening moves are positively enticing. Machiavelli is enticed, even if by discussing conspiracy he must break faith with the theme of preservation or find subtler ways of investigating it.

Conspirators

Because the chapter on conspiracies, III.6, is by far the longest in the *Discourses*, it will help to start with a synopsis of its argument.

Machiavelli divides his subject by the regimes against which conspiracies are formed. Thus there are conspiracies against republics, called fatherlands, and conspiracies against principalities. He first takes conspiracies against principalities and considers the motives that incite conspirators to action. These are universal hatred for the prince and the encouragement this hatred provides to particular enemies seeking retribution for personal injuries. Three kinds of personal injury are discussed: injury to life (more of a problem when life is menaced than when life is taken), injury to property, and injury to honor, both the conspirator's own honor and the honor of the women near to him. An additional motive is the desire to liberate the fatherland, or to replace a principality with a republic.

Machiavelli then moves from the motives underlying conspiracies to the dangers hampering their success. These he divides into three groups: dangers at the managing stage, dangers at the execution stage, and dangers at the aftermath stage. Before examining the dangers, however, he first identifies three categories of conspirators: lone assassins (who are not truly conspirators and who experience none of the managing dangers), weak men unfamiliar with the prince (who usually content themselves with cursing), and great men benefited by the prince (who are the source of most, if not all, conspiracies, and who have ambition as a new motive to conspire). The dangers at the managing stage include discovery by report, caused by lack of faith, lack of prudence, or levity; and discovery by conjecture. But remedies are available to meet these dangers. The number of conspirators can be held to a minimum in order to guard against exposure; exposure can be forestalled if courage is displayed by arrested conspirators and by those still at large; and exposure can be prevented altogether if execution follows immediately upon disclosure of the plot (this is called "the first and the most true" remedy and "the only one" [§6]). If it is necessary to reveal the plan in advance of its execution, one person alone should be told— this way, a faithless co-conspirator cannot substantiate his accusations. But substantiation is provided if anything is written down; thus an additional point is that nothing should be in writing, especially in one's own handwriting. And a last point, connected to the chief remedy of immediate execution, is the necessity of moving quickly against a prince who has been discovered to be moving against the conspirators—unpremeditated conspiracy, in effect.

At the execution stage of conspiracies there are six dangers to be overcome. They are, first, a change of order (*perturbazione di ordine*) to accommodate a change in circumstances. Men's spirits harden over time and around a set plan of action; thus any last-minute varying of the order runs a risk of unnerving their spirits. Lack of spirit (*poco animo*) is also the second danger; its cause this time is reverence for the person of the prince or vileness in the conspirators. The third danger, similar to the second, is confusion of the brain (*confusione di cervello*); it is called an error, and it results from a lack of prudence or a lack of spirit. One form of error and the fourth danger are multiple targets (*due capi*) for assassination, some of which are left alive. The fifth danger is false imagination (*falsa immaginazione*). Conspirators with a bad conscience imagine that others know what they are about to do and are speaking of it. Finally, every conspiracy, no matter how well planned, can be defeated by accident (*accidente*), the sixth danger.

There are two aftermath dangers, the first of which is a consequence of the fourth execution danger. It is the vengeance of survivors expecting to inherit power. Multiple targets in different locations is the excusable reason for why there are survivors; the inexcusable reason is negligence or lack of prudence. A second danger is the vengeance of the people when a beloved prince is taken from it.

Conspiracies against republics are generally easier. Dangers at the managing stage are fewer since "a citizen can order himself for power" (§19), that is, ingratiate himself with the public without revealing his conspiratorial designs; and since republics are slower to act than princes, less suspicious and less cautious, and more respectful of their great citizens. At the execution stage dangers are the same as for those conspiracies aimed against a prince (e.g., change of plans, lack of spirit, false imagination); but they also are different, for an army is needed to overcome a republic, and either it is one's own army (the conspirator is a commander of troops), or it is acquired by deceit and art, or it is supplied by foreign powers. The aftermath dangers are non-existent, other than those which imperil new principalities.

This finishes the outline supplied at the chapter's beginning; but Machiavelli thinks to add a new category to the analysis, namely the instrument or weapon used in the execution. Swords are the weapon of choice and are featured in most of the examples, but Machiavelli allows that poison is sometimes favored. The trouble with poison, though, is that it is less predictable than steel and often requires consultation with experts; thus the likelihood of betrayal is increased.

Before leaving the subject, Machiavelli advises princes and republics on how to suppress conspiracies once begun. The first step is to determine the strength of the cabal. If it is weak, the ruler should destroy it at once. But if it is strong and widespread, then delay is advised until the regime can gather its forces. And the best way to buy time is to provide conspirators with an ideal but distant opportunity in which to strike. On the other hand, to act impulsively, without first testing the extent of the conspiracy, is to risk defeat in an open confrontation. Other mistakes are to punish informers as a way of showing one's confidence in the goodwill of the people and to sponsor pseudo-conspiracies ("sting" operations) in hopes of drawing real conspirators out of the shadows. The latter is a mistake because it gives the prince's agent an easy path to a conspiracy of his own.

⚜

As a topic of political inquiry, conspiracy implicitly raises the question of who the prince is. Princely authority rests upon power; but that authority is compromised the moment anyone conspires to take power away. Coercion is the prerogative of the prince; but some conspirators act like a prince even before the conspiracy has made them one, for they force unsuspecting associates into becoming accomplices. What further confuses the matter of identifying the prince is the fact that the prince himself is sometimes a conspirator, plotting to entrap suspected enemies rather than taking direct action against them. In a world where power is seized and hierarchies are unstable, the weak are conspiring to take what they lack and the strong conspiring to hold on to what they possess.

But the reason Machiavelli gives for investigating conspiracies is not to conform his thought to a world in flux or to make conspiracies routine. On the contrary, he stresses the dangers incident to conspiracy for princes and private persons alike. His purpose, he insists, is "that princes may learn to guard themselves from these dangers and that private individuals may put themselves into them more timidly" (§1). There is, oddly, a common good binding prince and conspirator together; for princes lose their lives more through conspiracies than through open wars, and conspirators almost always fail in their objectives. Indeed, the common good embraces the whole of society, for whoever conspires, says Machiavelli, "often ruins himself and his fatherland" (§1); he later adds that "one does not do good either to oneself or to the fatherland or to anyone" (§16). It is necessary to issue this warning—despite conspiracy's record of disappointment and unintended consequences—because it "is granted to everyone" to conspire (§1). Conspiracy is a kind of democratic warfare that empowers the lowly to pull down the exalted (§2, 8). It is so threatening to the social structure that Machiavelli invokes what appears like Christian pacifism to combat it. Resigned acceptance of one's political fate is what Machiavelli recommends, and he blesses this acquiescence with a "golden" quotation from Tacitus: "Men have to honor past things and obey present ones; and they should desire good princes and tolerate them, however they may be made" (§1). It seems that strong and worldly-wise Romans, as well as weak and otherworldly Christians, admit the importance of deferring to the powers that be.

At other points in the chapter Machiavelli reiterates the folly of conspiracy, claiming that "the greed for dominating" (§3), which generally is blinding, also blinds conspirators, causing them to mismanage the enterprise; that "great luck" is needed to bring a conspiracy off (§4); that exposure through malice, imprudence, or levity is "impossible" to guard against (§6); that "grave errors" are committed by men little experienced in "the actions of the world," especially when the undertaking is "extraordinary" (§8); that a conspiracy against "one head" cannot be completed, but a conspiracy against "two heads" is "easily" not completed, for it is "almost impossible" and a thing "altogether vain and flighty" (§15); finally, that some conspiracies miscarry because of rare accidents immune to remedy (§17). Nor does Machiavelli much approve of conspirators: some he calls ingrates deserving of punishment (§3); others he calls wicked (§14).

But hardly is Machiavelli consistent in his opposition to conspiracy. He applauds the intention, if not the prudence, of weak conspirators braving futile insurrections (§3). However laudable is bravery ordinarily, to praise bravery when brave assassins are causing everyone harm is indiscreet; and yet this very indiscretion Machiavelli commits. More importantly, he devises remedies for all of the dangers threatening exposure of a conspiracy in its managing stage. Regarding the most important of these remedies, quick execution, Machiavelli guarantees success and escape from danger, declaring that all conspiracies quickly executed have "had a happy end" (§6). And even the Tacitus quotation is not sure proof of Machiavelli's sympathies, since it is a character and not Tacitus who is quoted,[35] and since Rome during the imperial age was like the Christian principality that replaced it—corrupt at the top and servile at the bottom (thus an unworthy model). Machiavelli's other topic in book 3, besides preservation of ancient orders, is private ambition that redounds to the public's benefit. The conspirator is a private man, and ambition is one of the motives causing private men to conspire. Some ambivalence, therefore, is to be expected, some concern for satisfying this ambition, especially if conspiracy can be found to be the source of public good. He has said otherwise—conspiracy hurts everyone. But his opposition was predicated on the belief that conspiracies always fail. If sometimes they succeed, because well-planned and well-executed, then his attitude might change. His attitude might also change depending on the regime that is toppled and the regime that is installed. And it might change if in some regimes—in republics to be precise—not the satisfaction of ambition but the defeat of ambition is how the public good is served.

The subject of regimes arises necessarily because Machiavelli places republics and principalities at the center of his study of conspiracies. The question he asks is which regime is more difficult to conspire against and which regime puts conspirators at greater risk? His answer is that principalities are better protected and that republics provide conspirators a safe and easy target. "Conspiracies that are made against the fatherland," he maintains, "are less dangerous for the ones who make them than are those against princes. For in managing them there are fewer dangers than in the latter; in executing them they are the same; after the execution there is not any" (§19). "Fewer than," "same as," and "none at all" are the dangers of an anti-republican conspiracy as compared with an anti-principate conspiracy. But twice Machiavelli upgrades the level of danger, saying that in executing a conspiracy against a republic "there are more difficulty and greater dangers" (unless the conspirator has his own army, which is "rare"); and that after the execution the dangers are the same as those that trouble any principality (§19). Republics are not quite the patsies they are first made to seem—even less so if one remembers that love of liberty threatens only principalities and is a "humor" against which there is no defense (§2). A new prince, therefore, has more to worry about than "the natural and ordinary dangers that tyranny brings him" (§19). Moreover, the reasons people have for conspiring against a principality are several in number (universal hatred, particular grievances, liberty of the fatherland, and personal ambition), whereas only one motive is the cause of conspiracies against republics—ambition—and even that is not explicitly identified.[36] In any event, republics seem more secure because they give less offense. One weakness though of republican government is the lenient and deferential treatment it accords to conspirators (§19). Not having this weakness causes princely government to be feared and respected. (Also, subjects do not criticize a prince in the same way that citizens criticize a republic—a point made in I.58.4.) But there is a downside to this fear-induced respect, namely, that people malcontent with the prince are forced to become conspirators if ever they open their mouths and speak their minds. Necessity obliges them to kill the prince, since in a principality there is no middle ground between strict obedience and insurrection, between submitting to the authority of the prince and becoming prince oneself. Herein lies an advantage for republics: by being less harsh with those who complain of them, republics do not turn dissidents into rebels.[37]

Both regimes are endangered by individual ambition. The republican solution, as explained in I.30.2, is to multiply the number of citizens deserving of honors; the princely solution is to avoid dependence on any one individual. If that is not possible, perhaps because the prince is sponsoring multiple operations and cannot take personal charge of them all, the advice, given here in III.6.3, is to keep some interval between the authority of his friends and the principate. King Ferdinand of Aragon, who in 1487 benefited Coppola too much, in 1507 was ungrateful to Gonsalvo Ferrante who fought for Ferdinand in Naples (I.29.2). It seems that for princes to maintain this interval they must commit acts of ingratitude, which acts, or the expectation of the same, are one reason why captains conspire against princes (I.30.1). Enterprising republics, then, would seem to have an advantage in the gratitude department over enterprising principalities. And by teaching the equality of citizens (that all are under the law and that no one citizen holds supreme power), republics actively discourage the "desire to dominate," which Machiavelli says is "as great or greater than is that of vengeance" (§3). In a non-corrupt republic even the thought of this ambition "cannot befall one of its citizens " (§19).

Republics are slow to respond to conspiracy at the managing stage but have no difficulty punishing conspirators when the execution has gone awry. The sons of Brutus, who in fact were apprehended while plotting a conspiracy, were severely punished without harm to the republic. Indeed, their punishment was the first of the memorable executions which brought Rome back to its beginnings. Conspiracies are, or can be, a benefit to republics; for since treason is a crime against the body politic (and not just against the prince), the punishment of traitors—in the words of *Prince* 7—is both satisfying and stupefying: it satisfies the people which happily takes vengeance against a public enemy, and it stupefies the people which is frightened itself by the awesome display of life-and-death power.[38] Conspiracies provide this renewal at some risk to the republic's stability; but the same is true of faction, that it strengthens the state but at the risk of discomposing it.

Principalities, however, are not so fortunate. Princes are in a bind; for when they punish, they provoke hatred, not salutary fear. It is as if memorable executions do them no good.[39] Says Machiavelli:

Princes therefore have no greater enemy than conspiracy, for when a conspiracy is made against them, either it kills them or it brings them infamy.
For if it succeeds, they are dead; if it is exposed, and they kill the conspirators, it is always believed that it was the invention of that prince to vent his
avarice and cruelty at the expense of the blood and property of those whom
he has killed.(§20)

Princes cannot escape the ingratitude charge, even when they are the injured
party. Furthermore, princes do not take kindly to assassination attempts. Invariably they become more suspicious, temperamental, and cruel. And a prince
whom the generality hates is a target for every citizen with ambition or a
grudge. This is where the analysis began, with a hated prince conspired against
by men of quality looking to advance their own careers or to settle a score.
While a prince might survive a single assassination attempt, a sustained campaign of conspiratorial attacks is certain to wreck his authority. Republics, on
the other hand, grow stronger with every opportunity to punish their enemies. At
the start of the chapter, Machiavelli asserted that princes and private persons are
threatened by conspiracies; he did not say that republics are.

Republics, then, are tough regimes not easily toppled. But their survival,
and the survival of principalities too, are ultimately matters of distributive justice. For in the aftermath stage of a conspiracy, a regime stands or falls depending on how well it matches the capacities and expectations of the people. Corrupt citizens believe that corrupt rulers are a benefit to them and are deserving
of power. Romans at the time of the civil wars wanted a caesar to protect and
enrich them; accordingly, the conspiracy by Brutus and Cassius to liberate the
fatherland reflected a misunderstanding of the mathematics of distributive justice. Likewise, the attempt to impose a tyranny on a freedom-loving people runs
afoul of the conviction that equal citizens deserve an equal share of power. In
these situations tyrants can guard themselves only "by laying down the tyranny"
(§2).

Princely Types and the Art of Rule

There is then more to conspiracy than an individual's wanting to have
power. The people must want the same, at least to some degree. Thus in chapter
8 Machiavelli reiterates that the people as "subject" (*suggetto*) and "material"
(*materia*) sets limits to the regime as "form" (*forma*). A free people cannot receive a servile form, nor can a free form be imposed upon a servile people (I.16-
18, I.55). If the regime is good, this material limitation is also good, protecting
the regime by inertia.

Although Machiavelli declares that in an uncorrupt republic, no opening
exists for even the thinking of conspiratorial schemes (III.6.19), plainly he is

exaggerating, since not just the thinking but the doing is twice reported in chapter 8: Spurius Cassius in 486 and Manlius Capitolinus in 384 each conspired to set up a tyranny in Rome.[40] Machiavelli condemns their efforts, calling the conspirator a "wicked citizen" and his ambition "an ugly greed to reign." The examples in question show Roman goodness defeating nefarious corrupters (although opposite results occurred when Marius, Sulla, and unnamed "others" [Caesar] tried corrupting a Rome that was no longer good); and so the feeling is that healthy republics are well-guarded against tyrannically-minded individuals. These larger birds of prey are most successful when the lesser birds of prey, the humors of the city, are intent upon partisan advantage, staring at each other and not bothering to look above (I.40.7). But the nobility provided Manlius no succor, even though it was their custom to defend one of their own; nor did the tribunes offer him support, even though their custom was to favor measures benefiting the people and hurting the nobles. The classes united against what was perceived to be a threat to their common liberty.

Good republics are further protected by the ineptitude of conspirators, who are blinded by their ambition, impatient in their mode of proceeding, and deceived by their desires. Even if it were possible to ruin a good republic, apparently there is not the talent needed to complete the job.[41] Republics do, of course, deteriorate over time, but the emphasis here is on keeping the people good, either by reformer princes whose "good examples" and "new laws" pull the state back to its beginnings (§2); or by the citizens themselves, who, permitted to act politically, measure up to the responsibilities of power—in the case of Manlius, the Roman plebs ceased being a defender when it was made a judge. Finally, good republics are greatly assisted by the fact that corruption takes too long to be of any benefit to the corrupter.[42] Why would a person undertake to subvert a republic if the certain result was his own destruction?

This rhetorical question does suppose that the individual has a choice as to whether he supports a republic or conspires against it. The chapter's title also implies the power of choosing in that it addresses the wants of individuals and what they should do ("Whoever Wishes to Alter a Republic Should Consider Its Subject"). "Bad choice" is listed, along with "natural inclination," as an explanation for why an individual might be in discord with the times (§2). And this same individual is advised to "accommodate" himself to the times by selecting glory-seeking modes suitable to a city living politically (§1). The message is to give up an ambition that can do a person no good; and the assumption is that ambition is voluntary and under control.

In chapter 9 Machiavelli stays with the subject of matching the times, but the focus is more emphatically on the fortunes of the individual. How to have consistently good fortune is the question, and the answer is to vary with the times, as if choosing to be one thing or another were within a person's power. The best type of choosing, called "the true way," is to observe the limits suitable to any trait—caution or impetuosity, for example (§1). Machiavelli doesn't say exactly if "suitable limits" represent an Aristotelian-like mean (neither too much caution nor too little). But probably they don't, since impetuosity is a separate trait with limits of its own, not the name for insufficient caution; furthermore, good fortune is the goal, not the happiness provided by a well-formed character. So likely a different mean is intended (more on which later), except that adhering to this mean is also dismissed as humanly impossible. Thus Machiavelli offers his second-best alternative, surrendering to the pull of one's nature while being fortunate enough to have a nature that is in harmony with the times. Half the trick of having good fortune is having the good fortune to be fashionable; the other half is letting go without regard to how far one goes. Extremism replaces moderation as the essence of virtue. Any intimation that people are in charge of themselves and fully responsible for their behavior is now gone, as Machiavelli comes round to the position that personal character is impervious to control. The example of Fabius Maximus bears out the claim that people act by nature and not by choice. Fabius succeeded after Rome's defeats at Ticino and Lake Trasimene because his natural cautiousness suited the perilous times; but a dozen years later, when the times had changed, he failed to appreciate the strategic wisdom of attacking Carthage because his cautiousness recoiled against so audacious a plan. In most cases it is nature, not reasoned choice, that is determinative. Moreover, notes Machiavelli, when nature is confirmed by long experience, the likelihood of a person's doing other than he has always done is practically nil: "When one individual has prospered very much with one mode of proceeding, it is not possible to persuade him that he can do well to proceed otherwise" (§3).

One additional influence forming a person's character is education. Education, as elsewhere discussed, operates at the communal level and inside of families. Communal customs (e.g., French perfidy, Florentine credulity) diversify what is underneath a uniform human nature (men "have and had always the same passions" [III.43.1]), and familial habits (e.g., cruel Manlii, kindly Publicoli, ambitious Appii [III.46.1]) diversify what basically is a uniform communal character (e.g., audacious but disciplined Romans [III.9.1, III.36.2]). Education may in fact be more consequential than nature,[43] since there is no community which cannot be made virtuous by its prince (I.21) and since family traits are enduring despite the dilution of nature through intermarriage (the mixing of "blood lines" [III.46.1]). But however character is formed—by nature, education, experience—once formed it remains forever the same.

Were this Aristotle speaking, no problems would arise from the fact of fixed characters, since virtuous action, Aristotle argues, is a consequence of character solidified by habit—character formation being the very purpose of Aristotelian ethics. But for Machiavelli the point rather is to escape character formation, since a fixed character is a handicap in a person's contest with fortune.[44] The situation is engagingly depicted in the *Tercets on Fortune*. Fortune, as the poem relates, is a queen who dwells in and reigns over a palace. Inside this palace are revolving wheels, as numerous as are the ways of climbing to and attaining the objects of human desire. Many have attempted to ride Fortune's wheels, and the cries and blasphemies which echo off of the palace walls register their failure and disappointment. There are, however, a lucky few, riders who choose a wheel in tune with Fortune's wishes. But even these favorites of Fortune are ruined eventually, when Fortune, in order to demonstrate her presence and unsuppressible power, halts in midcircle a rising wheel of good fortune.[45] Still, this power might be outwitted and continuous success achieved if one were somehow able to leap from wheel to wheel just as the stops and reversals were about to occur. The poem dreams on the possibility of staying always a step ahead of Fortune. In like manner, *Discourses* III.8 and III.9 toy with the notion of simply choosing to be in harmony with the times. But on both occasions the conclusion reached is that human beings are not this nimble or this malleable. The wheel the individual has chosen reflects the content of his character; and, unable to discard his character, he also is unable to jump to a new wheel. Man is heavy-footed, not quick-of-foot, because character is fixed and final. And because Queen Fortune is variable, unchanging man is at her mercy.

Machiavelli's most familiar description of fortune's power occurs in chapter 25 of *The Prince*. After comparing fortune to a flooding river which dikes and dams might otherwise have controlled, Machiavelli turns the discussion from what he calls the general (*in universali*) to the particular (*al particulare*), presumably from the fortune of provinces to the fortune of individuals;[46] at which point the analysis follows the pattern set in the *Tercets* and the *Discourses*: i.e., success is a matter of matching one's character to the times, but matching the times is a chance affair, since character, the product of nature and experience, is inflexible. The example is Pope Julius II, who was compelled by his impetuous nature to act impetuously in all of his dealings (rushing in where wise men feared to tread), but who was consistently successful because he lived in times consistently impetuous. The fact that the times did not change while he was pope was simply his good fortune. For he would have remained the same no matter the change of times; and remaining the same, he would have been undone.

There seems to be some question as to how much virtue virtuous princes actually have. For if a prince controls neither his character nor the character of the times in which he lives, then it is luck, not virtue, which produces the successful match. This derogation from virtue's virtue occurs again in the *Discourses* where Machiavelli concludes, after relating the disaster of the French capture of Rome and fortune's role therein, that "men who live ordinarily in great adversity or prosperity deserve less praise or blame. For most often it will be seen that they have been brought to ruin or to greatness through a great advantage that the heavens have provided them, giving or taking away from them an opportunity to be able to work virtuously" (II.29.1). Success is not praiseworthy and failure not blameworthy because fortune is the great contriver of human events, providing or withholding opportunities for virtuous displays. And whereas in *Prince* 6 the opportunity for virtue is but a small advantage ("one does not see that they had anything else from fortune than the opportunity"), here in the *Discourses* the opportunity is nearly all, for it effectively eliminates desert and culpability. The best Machiavelli can do toward restoring the value of virtue is to assert its power to "second fortune but not oppose it," to "weave its warp but not break it" (§3), in light of which assertion he enjoins his readers always "to have hope" and to persevere. But having warned his readers two chapters earlier of the dangers of false hope (III.27), this pleading at the end of 29 seems more fatalistic than optimistic, almost Christian in its resignation to higher powers. At the start of *Prince* 25, Machiavelli sounds a similarly defeatist note, confessing to partial acceptance of the common opinion that "worldly things are so governed by fortune and by God, that men cannot correct them with their prudence," and the bargain he next strikes with fortune concedes half or more of human affairs to fortune's control.

More was expected, however, when Machiavelli first unveiled the prototype of the Machiavellian prince. Schooled in the ethics of "effectual truth," this prince was to put on and take off qualities as though they were articles of clothing, costumes designed for pleasing or deceiving a multitude. Thus the prince might be liberal, merciful, and faithful; or he might be miserly, cruel, and treacherous. The occasion would determine the attire. As a tuxedo would be inappropriate dress for someone attending a barbecue, so humaneness would be out of place for someone needing to scare off an aggressor. What mattered most was the effect these qualities had on the prince's standing with the people. Better for the prince if he could "wear" only those qualities which the people esteemed. But a prince would find consistent goodness to be the ruin of his state; and so the advice to him was to "avoid the infamy of those vices that would take his state from him" and not to "care about incurring the reputation of those vices without which it [would be] difficult to save one's state" (*Prince*, 15). The model prince was to be elastic and chameleon-like, having none of the qualities for real but appearing to have them when they proved useful. For "by having them and always observing them, they are harmful; and by appearing to have them, they are useful." The prince could *be* "merciful, faithful, humane, honest, and religious" only on condition that he retained "a spirit built so that, if [he] need[ed] not to be those things, [he was] able and [knew] how to change to the contrary" (*Prince*, 18). The prince could *be* virtuous, in the traditional sense, if virtue did not interfere with his being vicious, in the traditional sense. If it did— as likely it would—then the prince could have no character whatsoever other than the astuteness of the fox and the courage of the lion, real virtues essential to all acquisition.[47] Were the prince to have more character than this, then likely he would be slow and clumsy and false when the times required that he put on qualities contrary to his character. Like the fleet-footed rider of the *Tercets*, able to stay atop Fortune's whirling wheels because he had no character to hold him back, the prince needed "to have a spirit disposed to change as the winds of fortune and the variations of things command[ed] him" (*Prince*, 18). In order then that he might be anything in appearance, it was important that he be nothing in truth.

But just a few chapters later, the prince reappears with a character so set by nature and experience that the success of his ventures depends more on his luck than on his virtue—impetuous Julius was fortunate to live in impetuous times. It is as if the previous chapters have been a dream, Machiavelli's own imaginary republic presented in the form of an ideal prince.[48] For the characterless prince of chapters 15 and following is replaced in chapter 25 by princes who are either cautious or impetuous, violent or artful, patient or impatient. Princes are what they are, they do not change, and they succeed or fail depending on the quality of the times. Thus Machiavelli reverses himself, or he is simply unable to decide about the relative power of virtue and fortune.

There is evidence that Machiavelli turned this question over in his mind and that his first reflections were not identical to his later thought.[49] But the charge of incurable ambivalence need not be our final judgment of the matter.[50] It will help though if we begin by gathering together all of Machiavelli's dichotomized categories respecting the character of the prince. First, there is the central division between intelligence and strength, qualities personified by the figures of the fox and the lion. Next is the contrast between changeable qualities and fixed characters (related perhaps to foxes and lions insofar as faithless foxes are changeable and faithful lions constant [*Prince*, 18]). *Prince* 25 sets the young lover alongside the forethinking dam builder. In *Discourses* I.18 the contrast is drawn between princes who reform "at a stroke" and princes who reform "little by little." *Discourses* III.1 gives us the reformer prince who returns the state to its origins, while *Discourses* III.9 is about the opportune prince whose character harmonizes with the times. Finally, there is the opposition of rule by love and rule by fear, treated in *Prince* 17 and *Discourses* III.19-23.

These opposing pairs do not all line up in two neat columns, producing just two contrasting princely types: for instance, an intelligent, foxy prince who changes qualities to suit the times and who is impetuous for being so indeterminate and violent because he is bold. Some connections do exist: the lion is faithful, and the youthful lover is impetuous. But it is not for certain that the "at a stroke" reformer is a lion or that the "little by little" reformer is a fox. A better way to organize these multiple categories is to distinguish those applicable to the accumulation of power from those which apply when power is exercised.[51] Governance is a two-part operation whereby the obedience of followers is secured and a course of action is selected and pursued.[52] The prince is, fundamentally, an equal human being, no more powerful than any of his fellows. He has power because they agree to obey, and they agree because he has persuaded them; or he has persuaded some of them who, obeying his commands, coerce the others. It is said that a prince should have his own arms and not rely on mercenary or auxiliary forces. But unless persuasion has occurred, no arms are his other than—quite literally—*his own arms*, or the sling and the knife David wielded in his fight with Goliath (*Prince*, 13).[53] As the prince moves beyond these literal arms to figurative arms, he puts capital in the bank for later spending on a chosen project. The point is that in this business of capital accumulation, or the care and tending of public opinion, the prince is expected to be all things to all people, a showman who wows the public with feats of self-transforming prestidigitation. On the other hand, in the matter of capital expenditure, or the choice and achievement of policy objectives, the prince is allowed to be (the fact perhaps lamented) a captive of his nature. Fabius was compelled to wage war cautiously, but Scipio was not compelled (or should not have been compelled) to use only love to win the loyalty of his troops.

Acquiring power over men and ruling them by love or by fear are for Machiavelli kindred subjects. He explores these subjects in chapters 15-19 of *The Prince*. The beloved prince shows to the world half or so of the qualities listed in chapter 15: he is liberal, merciful, faithful, humane, chaste, honest, agreeable, and religious. He is basically a man of peace who, if he fights, fights by law after the fashion of human beings (*Prince*, 18). He is praised by the people and the great alike because he is gentle without being effeminate and pusillanimous; but were he to go further in the direction of gentleness, he would incur the contempt of the great and certainly of the military. This same prince, however, is capable of creating an altogether different impression upon his subjects. He can present himself as miserly, cruel, faithless, fierce and spirited, proud, clever, hard, and grave. These are the qualities which make him feared and the qualities of a man of war, which he must sometimes seem to be, fighting by force after the fashion of beasts. These beastly qualities involve evildoing, which goodly men are reluctant to condone; but even goodly men admire the strength which these qualities exude, or at least accept them when they are seen to be useful in defeating enemies and maintaining discipline. Nor do these qualities make a prince hated unless he carries them to excess, confiscating his subjects' property and violating their women (*Prince*, 17, 19). A prince cannot be rapacious and lascivious any more than he can be effeminate and pusillanimous; and before the people especially it is important that he not appear irreligious. Some of the qualities listed in chapter 15 can only bring the prince blame,[54] but most earn him praise whether the effect upon others is love or fear, since by either of these emotions are men moved to obey (*Discourses*, III.21.2). At the extremes, so to speak, are qualities producing too much love and too much fear and so changing love into contempt and fear into hate (*Prince*, 16, 19). These qualities cause the prince to be blamed and his state to be weakened. In between these extremes are qualities producing love and fear in due amounts, with the result that subjects obey and the prince is reputed virtuous. All of these in-between qualities, loosely grouped under the headings of love and fear, should be at the prince's disposal, part of his wardrobe, because the best answer to the query, is it better to be loved than feared or feared than loved, is that "one would want to be both" (*Prince*, 17).

The prince, when traveling this middle way of praise-winning love and praise-winning fear, between the blame-incurring extremes of contempt and hate, behaves quite differently than when he releases his nature to follow its own course. In the one case he is careful about appearances; in the other he does his own thing, "proceed[ing] as nature forces" him (III.9.1) and "second[ing] his fortune but not oppos[ing] it" (II.29.3). The difference is that between convincing others to follow you and deciding where and how to lead them. The first is a public performance, whereas the second is a choice made in private with little account taken of how the choice appears to others. The performing prince, like an actor on stage, does better if he is no one type but is able to play a variety of roles.[55] This variability Machiavelli advises and seems to expect, although he immediately acknowledges that being both loved and feared may overtax the acting skills of any given prince. Appius Claudius, the decemvir, tried alternating his modes, but he proved an inept thespian, leaping "too quickly from one quality to another" (I.41.1). On the other hand, amateurish acting might not have been at the root of Appius's problem; for Appius had the nature of "a cruel persecutor of the plebs" (I.40.2), which nature was fortified by family education (III.46.1). Having a fixed character meant that he had to play against type, though this he tried to do and with some success. In other cases, apparently, the effort was never made, and the prince on stage was indifferent to his audience. The unparalleled ferocity of Caracalla made him "most hateful to all the world," and Commodus was both hated and despised because of his "cruel and bestial spirit" (*Prince*, 19). And while Hannibal became "venerable and terrible" by his much remarked "inhuman cruelty," this "virtue" was not only a pose for the benefit of his motley army, but also an expression of his true self. It was partly the former in that it produced the effect of obedience for which his other virtues did not suffice (*Prince*, 17); but it was partly the latter in that it veered out of control and caused him to be hated as well as feared. We know that Hannibal the actor gave artless performances because he relied on "excessive virtue" (*eccessiva virtù*) to mitigate the hatred in the ranks (III.21.3). Excessive virtue is separate from the skill by which a captain motivates and disciplines the soldiers under his command. Excessive virtue compensates for the failure to walk a middle path between contempt and hate; hence excessive virtue is not the capacity by which a captain charts this middle path. A captain is excessively virtuous because of the greatness of his character and the record of his achievements (achievements being taken as proof of greatness and greatness being thought the cause of achievements),[56] and the reputation for virtue saves the captain when, in the distribution of rewards and punishments, he misses the "true way" of ruling by love and by fear. Invariably the captain errs because human nature does not consent to his holding precisely to the true or middle way (III.9.1); but his troops remain loyal out of respect for his virtue.[57]

This distinction between virtue and showmanship, or character and technique, might better be understood if we compare a captain's motivational methods with a teacher's dispensing of grades. Some teachers give grades not as an honest assessment of the quality of student work but as an inducement to better work in the future. A harsh grade might serve the purpose of jolting a complacent, cocky student who is neglecting the course (rule by fear); conversely, a generous grade might be given to encourage a struggling student who is trying his or her best (rule by love). For the teacher using grades in this way, it is difficult, if not impossible, always to hit the mark and produce the desired result, to know when to frighten and when to encourage and by how much (Will a C get the student's attention, or will it take a D?). What then happens when the teacher misses the mark and gives a high grade for a paper of little value and the product of little effort, or a low grade for a paper much labored on and representing a student's best work? In the first case, the student might very well feel contempt for the teacher, describing the teacher as an "easy grader" and the course as a "gut." In the second case, the student might feel hatred for the teacher and express this hatred by means of a low evaluation of the teacher and the course. Is there any chance though that the student might forgive the teacher his or her mistake? The student might if the teacher exhibits what Machiavelli is calling "excessive virtue," in this case mastery of the material and command of the classroom—accomplishments which incline the student to respect the teacher despite receiving grades that are either too high or too low.

We saw that Appius was inept but also character-bound. If ineptitude is what prevents the prince from appearing both lovable and fearsome, and if as a consequence the prince can convincingly only be one or the other, the advice is to be feared rather than loved on grounds that "love is held by a chain of obligation which . . . is broken at every opportunity . . . but fear is held by a dread of punishment that never forsakes you" (*Prince*, 17). On the other hand, if it is the burden of character which so limits the prince, then lucky is the prince whose nature predisposes him toward the fearsome qualities. Every prince in his decision-making, executive mode is thought to be burdened by some character trait or another, by caution or impetuosity, violence or art, patience or impatience.[58] There is no chance, Machiavelli concludes, of a prince's being character-free in choosing his course of action and his manner of proceeding. Julius could not be cautious, and Fabius could not be bold. This being so, it is better to be impetuous, Machiavelli reasons, for more often than not the times are impetuous themselves; or, as Machiavelli likes to say, fortune is a woman whose favors she reserves for violent young lovers.[59] Thus once again, when flexibility is beyond reach, one princely type has an edge over the other—luckier to be fearsome by nature than lovable, and luckier to be impetuous by nature than cautious.

We have assumed that character is always a handicap, whether the prince is attending to his popularity or trying to vanquish his foes. That assumption, however, may not be altogether right. For what if having character is tantamount to being a lion? Certainly deceiving the public is behavior becoming the fox. The prince is a fox who puts on qualities in order to rule his people by love or by fear. So is not the prince a lion whose character is firmly this or that? More likely he is bold by nature rather than cautious, but even the cautious Fabius is a lion compared with the variable showman (and poll-reading politician), or compared with the light-footed player in Fortune's palace who leaps adroitly from wheel to wheel. Although the imagery of the *Tercets* does not go this far, it is a fair surmise that if weightlessness is useful at the moment of leaping, then gravity is useful when riding the wheels. Without gravity, or character, the player would fly off the wheel he was on. And since only occasionally does the player need to jump or the prince need to change, constant character is arguably more important than removable qualities. Machiavelli's opinion in III.31 is that republics and men who "retain the same spirit and their same dignity in every fortune" (title) do better overall in their struggle with fortune than those who are hopeful in good times and dejected in bad. Rome did not despair following triple defeats delivered by Hannibal (218-216 BC), nor did it grow giddy in consequence of its victory over Antiochus (190 BC). The same was true of Scipio, who prevented his fellow officers from fleeing to Sicily in the aftermath of Cannae (I.11.1) and who, after beating Antiochus at Magnesia, offered his opponent the same terms of peace as had been negotiated before the battle. In any event, not just the fox, but also the lion is an essential part of the prince's make-up, because without a foundational character trait the prince would lack the confidence he needs to be in command. This character trait, when exceptional and accompanied by successes, is called excessive virtue. But the single prince who is both fox and lion is a rarity: Severus was both but not Caracalla, Commodus, or Maximinus, Severus's imitators (*Prince*, 19). It is for this reason that Machiavelli prefers republics to principalities, since republics can play the mercurial fox, changing leaders to fit the times, while their princes play the steadfast lion, having from nature and experience a character that is solidly one quality or another (III.9.2).

The prince, when using power as opposed to acquiring it from the people, appears in Machiavelli's text as either a lawgiver or a captain. The lawgiver is generally a reformer who adjusts for the people's corruption with "little by little" reforms or who returns the state to its beginnings with reform "at a stroke" (I.18.4). In the first case especially, the lawgiver is like the dam builder of *Prince* 25, for as the one sees that dangers await just over the horizon, the other sees that a flood might occur even though the sky is clear and the times are quiet. Distant dangers and quiet times encourage the false belief that reforms are unneeded and flood control a waste of effort. In quiet times no one wants to take precautions because the hard work of reform and dam construction, always disagreeable, is doubly off-putting for seeming needless as well. Quiet times cause corruption (III.16), but then the slide into corruption is what the reformer tries to reverse or contain. This he does by replenishing depleted stores of civic virtue, just as the prudent builder, by constructing dams, dikes, and canals, accumulates resources against the day when the river floods. One way to combat fortune is to plan and prepare in advance of trouble, for fortune "shows her power where virtue has not been put in order to resist her and therefore turns her impetus where she knows that dams and dikes have not been made to contain her" (*Prince*, 25). A similar warning is issued in II.30.5, though with special attention to the kind of prince needed to organize the flood control effort: "For where men have little virtue, fortune shows its power very much . . . and republics and states often vary and will always vary until someone emerges who is so much a lover of antiquity that he regulates it in such a mode that it does not have cause to show at every turning of the sun how much it can do." This lover of antiquity is a conservative reformer who looks to history for guidance and who lays foundations that endure—in a timely fashion if he can, but in a violent fashion if he must.

There is, though, a second way of combating fortune, one which relies more on impulse than on foresight and which is practiced more by the captain than by the lawgiver. The impetuous lover does not stop to think and does not map out his seduction before ever feeling his passion. And yet, since fortune is a woman, the impetuous lover is more successful than is the decorous suitor. Machiavelli is amazed by the career of Julius II. This pontiff accomplished by his chronic impetuosity what no prudent leader could have hoped to achieve. In Julius's case, prudence would have hobbled his progress and diminished his greatness. Thus for the Julian lover, prudence is a cautiousness bordering on indifference and timidity. Prudence can sometimes seem like caution, a character trait opposite impetuosity, or it can seem like foxy intelligence which chooses between qualities.[60] When the latter, it is a faculty utilized by various character types, not only the cautious (e.g., the violent reformer is also prudent). But never, it seems, is prudence prescient enough to alert the individual to the need of changing his ways, or strong enough to prevail in a contest with character; for no man is "found so prudent as to know how to accommodate himself to this [matching his mode of proceeding to the changing times]" (*Prince*, 25). The prince who needs to change his ways, from cautious to impetuous, and so forth, is usually a captain commissioned to defend the state against enemies external and internal. The times which change refer to opportunities and necessities that affect military and domestic policy. These are the times that caused Fabius and Soderini to be first useful and then harmful to their respective states. Not the moral health of the people, but outside and inside emergencies determined their fitness for office. When the times are so understood, the remedy is a captain in sync with the times—e.g., a Scipio, not a Fabius, when the time is right for taking the war to Carthage. But the times can also refer to the changing character of the people, in which case the remedy is a lawgiver trying to arrest the decline into slackness and corruption by "varying the orders of republics with the times" (III.9.3)—i.e., with the people. While this lawgiver may be in sync with what the people needs, he is likely out of sync with what the people wants (though sometimes the people tires of princes who play to its moods and wants instead a leader who goes against the times). He is severe and judgmental when others are soft and forgiving. He is a taskmaster who "kills the sons of Brutus" or who seizes power in order to refound the city. He looks back to an original goodness, hoping to revitalize it in the present. Rather than jumping to an adjacent wheel in Fortune's palace, he keeps to the wheel he is on, though struggling to return to an earlier and ascending point on its arc (like someone attempting to climb the stairs of a down escalator). By contrast, the captain is chosen because his character matches that of a wheel whose arc is rising. Here it is nimbleness which saves (not the individual's but the republic's), whereas in the case of the lawgiver it is fixity. Fixity is what the leader requires when changing times refer to the people's declining character.[61]

Some lawgivers are less harsh than others—some reform "little by little," some reform "at a stroke"; likewise, captains are variously exacting—some are severe, some are kind. It is not necessary, in order to be in sync with the times, to rule with a gentle touch. Hard times call for hard princes, and so a hard prince like Manlius Torquatus, who killed his son in order to discipline his army, can be appreciated and utilized no less than a soft prince like Valerius Corvinus, who fraternized with his troops (III.22.1, 4). Hard times though are not for their own sake but for the peace and prosperity of easy times. Consequently, the hard prince is unwelcome, and even though he is utilized when dangers threaten, he is probably not admired and is certainly not liked. It is the soft prince who is liked, the prince who rules by love. While both princely types can be in harmony with the times, the soft prince is the popular one in that his qualities are attractive and his practices gratifying to the people. What the people ultimately wants, as suggested by the exploits of Camillus in III.20, is to be ruled by a protective patriarch, someone who is as attentive to its well-being as doting parents are to their young. Benevolent monarchy is where rule by love is heading; Valerius and Scipio are way-stations on the road to good prince Cyrus. Thus in rendering judgment on the two styles of ruling, it becomes Machiavelli's purpose to defend the style that is instinctively disliked, to make the case for cruelty over against kindness.

⚜

Chapters 19 through 23 of book 3 have the question of governing styles as their common theme—whether it is better to rule by love or to rule by fear. Strauss calls the five chapters the "Tacitean subsection" since the discussion centers around an invented opinion attributed to Tacitus which Machiavelli first disputes then proceeds to save. Tacitus is (mis)cited as an authority recommending severity in the ruling of multitudes; thus the five chapters present the spectacle of Machiavelli's own conversion to Tacitean harshness.[62]

In fact, there is a discernible movement from leniency to cruelty in the chapters in question. The initial example from chapter 19 produces a clear victory for mercy over severity (the kindly Quintius was successful, whereas the proud and coarse Appius was not); but in order to accommodate the contrary opinion of Tacitus, Machiavelli allows that indulgence is best shown toward republican multitudes, "men who are ordinarily partners," and that subject peoples are best controlled by punishments. Thus the issue of ruling by love or by fear is settled by reference to the regime. Also in chapter 20, "one example of humanity" (Camillus's return of the kidnapped schoolchildren) was sufficient to bring the Falisci to surrender; then two more instances are added, each with the same effect (Fabricius and Pyrrhus; Scipio and the young bride), and the chapter ends with a testimonial to the "humane and affable" Cyrus. But in chapter 21 diverse modes are discovered to be equally effective in dealing with enemies, so long as "excessive virtue" is present in the ruler (Scipio and Hannibal). It is possible then to achieve one's objectives through cruelty as well as through mercy. Soon though the balance shifts toward cruelty and fear, since ambition, Machiavelli concedes, causes men to "forget every love." The comparison of diverse modes continues in chapter 22 (the hardness of Manlius Torquatus versus the softness of Valerius Corvinus) with each mode shown to have a proven record of success. But in the case of republics, harshness is now recommended (opposite the conclusion of chapter 19) since a hated commander poses no threat to republican equality; likewise kindness is recommended for a prince whose security depends on his people's love. In the last chapter, 23, Marcus Furius Camillus is described as belonging to the Manlian-type of severe ruler. This is the same Camillus who in III.20 is a humane savior of schoolchildren. By and large, cruelty seems to have displaced mercy—in republics, the better regime, and in the hearts of humane leaders.

A second change is in the type of multitude governed by fear or by love. In chapter 19 three multitudes are implied: those consisting of citizens, of citizen-soldiers, and of subjects. The lesson is that one must treat citizen-soldiers gently because they are "ordinarily partners" or fellow citizens. Subjects, on the other hand, should be treated harshly to prevent their turning insolent. Nevertheless, notes Machiavelli, citizen-soldiers can be ruled imperiously if the commander possesses "excessive virtue"; and nevertheless, he continues, princes should moderate their harshness lest by shedding blood and stealing property they incur the hatred of their subjects. Already the door to republican severity is opening, while the door to princely severity is closing. In chapter 20 the multitude changes from friends (citizens and subjects) to enemies, and all examples show enemies ruled by acts of kindness (i.e., persuaded to cooperate with their antagonists' wishes). Cyrus is the model for republican conquerors, and so regime-based distinctions seem no longer to apply. But then the point might be that to vanquished enemies all conquerors rule like princes. And how do princes rule? First told to be harsh, then told to be just, now princes (republican conquerors) are told to be humane. In chapter 21 the multitude is again composed of enemies, of Italians for Hannibal and of Spaniards for Scipio. The Italians were treated cruelly by Hannibal who was mostly successful, while the Spaniards were treated with kindness by Scipio who was entirely successful (§1).[63] Kindness seems to be the better means of winning over enemies. But multitudes of friends also appear in the chapter, the armies of Hannibal and Scipio respectively. Ruling by a "terror that arose from his person," Hannibal suffered no "dissension in his army neither among themselves nor against him although it was composed of various kinds of men."[64] Ruling by humanity, Scipio suffered a mutiny of his soldiers. Cruelty, therefore, seems to be the better means of managing friends. The probability of this result is contested though in the next chapter where the kindly rule of Valerius Corvinus led to no disobedience in the ranks. Even so, Manlius Torquatus was equally successful ruling by opposite modes, and his cruelty had the added advantage of quieting the suspicions of jealous republicans nervous about their liberty. The teaching seems then to be that just as subjects are better treated than citizen-soldiers, so enemies are better treated than friends. Machiavelli's initial pronouncement that equals should be ruled by love and unequals by fear has thus been turned on its head. And yet this opinion is partly redeemed when a new multitude appears in chapter 23, or rather an old one forgotten—namely republican citizens who are "ordinarily partners." Camillus was severe with citizens and soldiers alike; but he soon discovered that the people would not be ruled harshly, for they were rulers themselves apt to be ungrateful toward virtuous individuals whose ambitions they suspected.

Let's return now to chapter 20 and consider the one act of humanity that was "able to do more . . . than any Roman force" (title). The Falerian schoolmaster, upon delivering the children to Camillus, said that "through them the town would give itself into his hands." This statement proved to be true, though not as the schoolmaster intended it. The town did give itself into the hands of Camillus, not out of fear for the safety of its children but out of love for a humane enemy and out of confidence in the continued benevolence of his rule. Camillus, in effect, removed the necessity the Falisci had for defending themselves (III.12). He achieved his own ambition without it seeming that the Falisci had sacrificed theirs. Indeed, his one act of humanity created the appearance of a common interest, specifically a common devotion to morality that superseded attachment to separate and private interests. Camillus and the Falisci were one in their recognition of a single, unifying good higher than the exclusive good of victory that set them apart. Losers in a contest will always appeal to a common good;[65] but when the winner does the same, he shows that he is not an enemy. Thus by his one act of humanity Camillus changed himself from a conquering enemy to a fatherly governor. Machiavelli mentions that the public wants its great men to perform magnanimous deeds and that writers encourage princes to live morally. It is not too much to say that what the public desires and what writers encourage is princely rule as benign and loving as that of a father for his children. Paternal rule is natural and best, and monarchy, if the prince is kind, is the nearest political equivalent to patriarchy. A good prince cares for his people, sparing the people the trouble of caring for itself. Machiavelli has suggested before that the people would rather be secure than free (I.16.5). Its longing for humaneness, morality, and common goods betrays its frustration with republican equality and the competition among partisan interests.[66] Men are equal because they are needy and selfish. They struggle to acquire against opponents needy and selfish like themselves. The struggle is bearable but rarely is it inspiring, and so equal men praise those few who attain to a higher moral excellence. And should ever the balance be upset and inequality prevail, the weak dream about a strongman who is benevolent and wise, and they happily surrender themselves to a protector brandishing his humanity. Cyrus appears as the prototype for this kind of ruler, and Xenophon, in his fictional rendering, "toils very much to demonstrate how many honors, how many victories, how much good fame being humane and affable brought to Cyrus" (III.20.1). But Cyrus is among those princes who in II.13 rose by fraud. We are left to suspect, therefore, that Camillus's humanity was also a fraud and that humanity is but the easy way in which the strong prey upon the weak. If so, then the transition from humanity to cruelty is not indicative of moral decline.

Humanity may be the easy way to conquest, but it is not the only way; and the example of Hannibal requires Machiavelli to consider how diverse modes can be equally effective for the captains who use them. The answer to chapter 21's "whence it arises" question (title) is that moral qualities such as cruelty or kindness do not much matter. Novelty is the main thing, for "those who are well off desire newness as much as those who are badly off" (§2).[67] Merely to be "head of an innovation in a province," Machiavelli declares, is to attract sufficient allies that "in whatever mode he [the captain] proceeds he succeeds in making great progress in those places" (§2; also *Prince*, 3). The other piece of the victory puzzle lies in the fact that people can be motivated by love or by fear. Captains, therefore, employ diverse modes successfully because the human psyche responds to diverse motivations. But rarely do captains hit the mark exactly, and so their motivational techniques, to reiterate, need supplementing by excessive virtue (§3). One reason for thinking the middle unnavigable is that the ruler cannot divine the dispositions of the ruled, whether love or fear is the mode that will move them. A second reason is that the ruler's character, rather than the needs of the ruled, might predetermine the choice of the mode.

Chapter 22 repeats the teaching of chapter 21 but uses a different cast of characters. Again it is noticed that diverse modes produce similar effects. But in place of Scipio ruling by love, we have kindly Valerius Corvinus; and in place of Hannibal's exceeding cruelty, we have the "Manlian commands" of Manlius Torquatus. Scipio and Hannibal were more virtuous than their respective predecessors; but then Scipio and Hannibal needed to be, since they were less expert than Valerius and Manlius at governing armies and mollifying enemies. Valerian kindness never invited rebellion in the ranks, and Manlian severity never incited a hatred that did injury to Manlius. A further compliment is paid to the lesser generals when Machiavelli describes their diverse modes as "praiseworthy," but describes as "detestable" the modes of one of their two successors (III.21.4).

The discourse in chapter 22 is organized around four questions: (1) why Manlius was so rigid; (2) why Valerius could be so humane; (3) why different modes produced the same results; (4) why one mode was better and should be the model for imitation. Manlius "was constrained to proceed so rigidly" because his nature and upbringing made him severe and unforgiving. His three most striking qualities were strength, piety toward his father and fatherland, and reverence toward his superiors. He displayed these qualities when he defeated the Frenchman in single combat, when he defended his father against the tribune, and when he secured permission from the consul before fighting the duel. Hard on himself, he was equally hard on others; and when he issued harsh commands, he harshly had them enforced; for "it is a very true rule," notes Machiavelli, that mild enforcement invites deception (§1). Thus Manlius was constrained by his nature, his "natural appetite" (§3), to choose severity; and once having chosen, he was constrained by the desire to have his orders obeyed to punish severely any neglect of duty. When his son ignored orders and accepted an enemy's challenge (as Manlius himself had done, though not on his own authority), Manlius commanded that his son be bound to the stake and beheaded (340 BC). The execution was carried out forthwith, as the soldiers watched in horrified disbelief; but discipline was restored, and the war with the Latins was subsequently won (Livy, VIII.8).

Machiavelli interjects a brief lecture of his own on the art of rule: ". . . if one wishes to be obeyed, it is necessary to know how to command; and those know how to command who make a comparison between their qualities and those of whoever has to obey, and when they see proportion there, then they may command; when disproportion, they abstain from it" (§1). "Proportion" could mean a correspondence between the captain's character and the character of his troops; in which case successful rule would require the fortuitous matching of a severe captain with severe troops ("he desires to find all men similar to himself" [§1]), or it would require a captain who took the measure of his troops before deciding on his mode of command, on whether to rule by love or to rule by fear. In the latter case the captain is not constrained by his nature; he has no compelling nature and so is free to aim for the middle way. But Machiavelli adds to this digression the advice of "a prudent man" whose use and understanding of proportion is altogether different from the conjectural rendering above. The prudent man contends that in order "to hold a republic with violence, there must [be] proportion from whoever is forcing to that which is forced" (§2). Proportion, then, is not conformity in character between the ruler and the ruled; it rather is preponderant strength in support of coercive command, which command lasts as long as does strength. Here the ruler or captain is a tyrant imposing his reign on a free city. He incapacitates his people more than he secures their cooperation; he conquers more than he governs. His excessive virtue shows itself not in victories over enemies but in the oppression of citizens, whose reactions to his modes he simply ignores; for he is rendered immune by his virtue and his power.

What's interesting is that when Machiavelli returns from this digression on the tyrant's "proportion," he applies its lesson to the republican captain who commands "strong things" and then enforces them with the "strength of his spirit" (§3). The Manlius who saved Rome was a tyrant in his means; he was different from the Manlius who subverted Rome (Capitolinus), who was a tyrant in his ends. Machiavelli commends such strong things, "extraordinary commands," claiming, as he did before, that they return republics to their beginnings and their ancient virtue (III.1). And he announces, as he has before, that a republic would be perpetual if periodic renewals not only restrained it from running to ruin but pulled it back toward its origins. The long-term health of a republic depends essentially on the presence of non-republican practices, on coercion as opposed to consent.

We know why Manlius acted so rigidly: it was his nature to do so. Manlius had a character he could neither ignore nor control. Nevertheless, he succeeded as a captain because he was stronger than the soldiers who feared his wrath. But it was not nature that constrained Valerius to practice humanity (at least nature is not stressed). Valerius "could proceed humanely" (*potette procedere umanamente*) because Roman customs were sound (§3), and it was enough for disciplinary purposes that transgressions be punished by ordinary means with the reputation for cruelty attaching to law. Valerius, therefore, was allowed to be humane rather than constrained by his nature. And what provided Valerius this allowance were the good customs prevalent at the time, which customs were maintained in their goodness by the extraordinary commands of Manlius and Manlian-type princes. Valerius represents the vigorous life that healthy bodies enjoy, while Manlius represents the diet and exercise from which health arises. Manlius exists for the sake of Valerius (cruelty for the sake of humanity). Ordinarily the end would rank higher than the means. But given Machiavelli's anxiety over corruption, the end is more feared than appreciated; and so it ranks lower than the means, which are morally closer to the purity of beginnings.[68] Valerius was less valuable to Rome than was Manlius—Valerius was allowed, whereas Manlius was needed.

Both commanders, however, were obeyed; and because they were obeyed, "they could produce the same effect while working diversely" (§3). The answer then to the third question is obedience—caused by fear and tyranny, or caused by love and the rule of law.

The fourth question, which mode was better, changes to which mode was more praiseworthy in the estimation of those who write advice-books, often called "mirrors of princes." Since both modes were proven equally effective, it stands to reason that writers would prefer humanity to cruelty. Xenophon is plainly on the side of the humane prince, and Livy seems so too when he praises the easygoing habits of Valerius. But Livy's honorable speech on behalf of Manlian severity implies even greater appreciation for Manlius, the general who is twice said to have been the sole cause of Rome's victory over the Latins in a war which, we remember, was the most momentous in Rome's history (II.16.1). Valerius, on the other hand, while many times victorious, was never fully responsible for the obedience that produced his victories; for Valerius was dependent on good customs and could be humane because Manlius (and others like him) had been severe.

Machiavelli agrees with Livy's implied preference for Manlius, but for a different reason.[69] Returning to the regime criterion used in III.19 and forgotten mostly since, Machiavelli states that Manlian severity, once the province of princely government, is particularly appropriate to republics since a harsh but patriotic commander acquires no partisans with which to endanger the common good. Republics are associations of free and equal citizens; they are endangered when one man, standing above the mean, is surrounded by supporters more loyal to his ambition than to the commonweal. But a harsh commander, especially one who goes too far and incurs the hatred of his troops,[70] does his city a favor, since he presents no threat to the city's liberty and equality; and inadvertently he does himself a favor, too, since he is not suspected by his fellow citizens and so the target of their ingratitude. Conversely, in principalities, the Cyrus-like prince is more desirable, since observing the laws and being reputed virtuous are sufficient to cause him to be obeyed, and since being affable, humane, and merciful are sufficient to cause him to be loved. It is appropriate for a prince to be loved because the prince, being synonymous with the state, has partisans who are synonymous with patriots.

Valerius, then, was ill-suited to republican Rome. And yet Valerius was not suspected of ambition and victimized by popular ingratitude. Why? Because Valerius was again the beneficiary of good orders, this one being the prohibition against extended military commands (III.24). He was never consul long enough to turn the soldiers who loved him into a partisan force. Nor was his forebear and namesake, Publius Valerius Publicola (Friend of the People), ever a threat to the liberty of the republic; for "the spirits of the Romans," says Machiavelli, "were not yet corrupt, and he [Publicola] had not been in their government for long and continually" (§5). Manlius, on the other hand, did suit republican Rome, but only because he accepted the restraints upon ambition that came with being hated; nor was severity his chosen mode, but he was compelled to it by nature.

It seems though that even hatred is no surety against public jealousy and suspicion. If virtue is excessive enough (and apparently it was not in Manlius's case), then the people are wont to suspect the captain of anti-republican ambition, even though his severity should cause him to be hated and even though hatred should preclude his reaching for ultimate greatness. Superlative virtue commands respect and obeisance no matter the animosity toward the person who has it. Perhaps we are confronting the Aristotelian problem of what to do with the superior individual too large for republican equality: either the citizens must surrender power to him and institute a monarchy, says Aristotle, or the citizens must ostracize him for a time (which was what the Romans did to Camillus).[71] Machiavelli tries finessing the issue, treating Camillus—whom elsewhere he calls "the most prudent of all the Roman captains" (III.12.3) but whom in III.23.1 he calls "hardly prudent"—as responsible for provoking a crisis that could easily have been avoided. The hatred that caused Camillus's exile was brought on by Camillus himself; furthermore, it was "without profit" to him. After the capture of Veii, Camillus entered Rome in triumph riding in a chariot pulled by four white horses. To his fellow Romans these white steeds signified that Camillus regarded himself the equal of the sun and no longer the equal of other men. Apparently, what Camillus wanted as payment for his superlative virtue was an equality-denying honor, and for this honor he was cashing in all the gratitude the public owed to him. But the honor was without profit because he did not intend by it a claim to kingly office; and it was without profit because it cost him the freedom from suspicion that public hatred ordinarily supplies. Camillus was also hated because he was "more severe in punishing them than liberal in rewarding them." Such hatred arose because Camillus, like Manlius, was a defender of the public good. He kept the people poor while making the city rich, placing in public coffers, rather than distributing as booty, the proceeds from the sale of Veientian goods; and he upheld the people's piety by fulfilling his vow to give one tenth of the booty to Apollo, even though he had to try commandeering the same from the soldiers already paid. The Romans resented the goodness they were forced to practice, and they hated the man who denied them their pleasures. But while they hated Camillus because he deprived them of "something useful," they exiled him because his greatness derogated from their equality. And while affronts to equality cause the people "no disadvantage" (just as they provide the captain no benefit), nevertheless, Machiavelli observes, nothing can be "more hateful to peoples, and especially to free ones," than a captain's "appearing proud and swollen." Accordingly, the captain must conceal his virtue, or he must do something about it. Thus Machiavelli advises the captain (called prince) to be modest, unpretentious, and retiring; or he advises, if only by implication, regal power for the captain as the attainment of "something useful."[72]

Excessive virtue saved Hannibal when, erring on the side of rule by fear, he went too far and incited hatred among his troops. It did not save him though with respect to a second multitude, his enemy, the Romans, who because of their hatred were determined to complete his destruction; and whether it saved him or ruined him with respect to yet a third multitude, the people back home, is uncertain since Machiavelli provides little information on Carthaginian domestic politics aside from indicating the opposition of Hanno, the leader of the aristocratic, anti-Barca party (II.27.1, II.30.4, III.31.2; Livy, XXI.3). Camillus also erred in the governing of men, causing the Roman citizens and citizen-soldiers to hate him on account of his illiberality; but in his case excessive virtue only exacerbated his troubles since it exposed him to suspicions which ordinarily would have lain dormant. Manlius's virtue was not excessive, and his errors in governing, insofar as he too was hated, did him no harm because his ambition was not larger than the republic he served. Had he aspired to tyranny, however, the hatred he had incurred from his harsh mode of governing would have prevented his ascent. Manlian cruelty along with Manlian patriotism are largely accounted for by reference to nature—nature made him cruel, and nature limited his ambition. Manlius did not choose his character or his role. Nor are there many who would choose to be hated by their peers. So lucky it is for republics that nature supplies what free choice does not.

Camillus was the exception. He chose to be severe having on other occasions proven that he could be humane. With enemies he was humane because he wanted them to love and obey; with fellow citizens he was severe because he wanted to preserve their fitness for liberty. But why the latter? Not for his own protection, since superlative virtue would cost him that protection anyway; and not because the citizens were vigilant republicans, since at the time of the fall of Veii they were not that virtuous. If it seems irrational to choose to be hated, it seems doubly irrational when hatred brings punishment, and triply so when lovable modes coupled with superlative virtue could catapult the individual to the summit of power. A possible explanation, though it falls outside the range of Machiavelli's psychology, is that Camillus was magnanimous, i.e., indifferent to power and above caring about the honors of his community.[73] In Aristotle's analysis, the magnanimous man prefers beautiful objects and profitless honors. But honors "without profit" are to Machiavelli a mere vanity, which no "prudent" man would ever pay to possess. Aristotle adds equanimity to the magnanimous man's portfolio of virtues, an even-temperedness regarding the allotments of fortune. The magnanimous man is serene and unperturbed because nothing, including honors, are of great moment to him.[74] Machiavelli also discusses equanimity, and he even uses Camillus to illustrate its character (III.31.1). But Machiavelli's Camillus is even-tempered because he, like the Romans generally, is an experienced combatant, a "knower of the world" (§3), and because equanimity is the means to long-term, political success (his reputation is later redeemed)—not because he undervalues worldly glory and can gladly live without it. Thus when Camillus suffers for his greatness, Machiavelli must find an error in his proceedings and propose a means of his escape. Machiavelli reckons on ambition and expects the struggle for power to encompass the personal motives of political men. His Camillus then does not transcend politics, as the magnanimous man of Aristotle's description is wont to do. Accordingly, the chariot incident is explained as a failure of the fox, and the prince who elsewhere is both a fox and a lion (III.20) comes to be seen as a lion only— a too-proud beast who falls into a snare.

Manlius, for sure, was a lion—fierce, direct, and honorable, with a character fixed by nature. He ruled by fear and served his country's interests at cost to himself.[75] He was a patriot who did battle with corruption, the breeding ground of conspiracy. His opposite, the prince who rules by love, if not a conspirator, is nonetheless in a position to conspire. He is beloved by the people and by writers alike, because he gratifies and does not offend. But for these same reasons he endangers the republic. Thus to protect the republic Machiavelli defends Manlian cruelty against popular and literary reproach; for whether a republic lives long or dies soon is often a matter of whether the charismatic conspirator meets up with and is blocked by the scowling martinet. Manlius Capitolinus subverts by love; Manlius Torquatus saves by fear. There can be no foolproof protection from the former; but then his ambition provides the latter the occasion he needs to restore the people's virtue. And herein lies one advantage (already noted) that republics have over principalities—that conspirators against republics are traitors whose punishments serve as memorable executions both satisfying and stupefying, whereas conspirators against principalities are viewed as victims of princely paranoia and lust. Both the conspirator and his punisher are useful to a republic wanting to run the full course of its life. Their dynamic helps to keep the state near the beginning of its life cycle or helps to retard the downward progression toward its end.

Republican Glory

In the closing chapter of book 3, Machiavelli is as explicit about the need for decennial punishments as he is in the book's opening chapter. Indeed, the two chapters, working like book ends, hold the unruly middle chapters together, giving the third book some measure of coherence and integrity. The state is a declining institution, and only heroic efforts to reclaim its original purity can stave off its demise. Rome was exemplary in managing the accidents which invariably arise in cities, purging the body politic of its many infections. The purge was administered as punishments for private and public wrongdoing; and to Rome's credit, the city did not temporize when wrongdoing was widespread or when the disease had overtaken the entire body. Three examples are provided to indicate Rome's willingness to practice this invasive medicine: the prosecution of Roman matrons—what seemed like all the women of Rome—for conspiring to poison their husbands (331 BC);[76] the execution of thousands of Bacchic worshippers for lewd and criminal acts (186 BC); and the banishment to Sicily of the legion defeated at Cannae (216 BC). Rome displayed its "greatness," says an admiring Machiavelli, by the scope and severity of its punishments (III.49.1).

But the punishment thought most terrible was decimation, where one in ten was chosen by lot to suffer execution. This was how Rome punished a multitude when "all cannot be punished because they are too many." The rationale was that to punish a part and

> leave a part of them unpunished would do wrong to those who are punished, and the unpunished would have spirit to err another time. But if the tenth part of them is killed by lot when all deserve it, whoever is punished grieves for his lot and whoever is not punished fears lest another time it touch him, and guards himself against erring. (§2)

It is a little unclear what these alternatives represent. In both cases one part suffers punishment and another part escapes it. But in the first case, "the author is not certain," whereas in the second case the author is known to be everyone, since "all deserve" to be punished. In the first case the result of discriminatory punishment is injustice toward the punished and emboldenment of the unpunished to commit further crimes. In the second case, that of decimation of the ranks, discriminatory punishment is salutary in its effects, deterring the unpunished and grieving, but not wronging, the punished. Presumably, the alternative to decimation by lot is judicial verdict, where the authorities claim to be rendering justice and an attempt is made to identify the guilty. But punishing a part without knowing it to be the author of the crime breeds contempt, not fear, of the proceedings. (The teacher does not know who spoke the obscenity or threw the spitball; the class as a whole is not responsible, but then no one is telling; so the teacher singles out the class cut-up for detention; meanwhile among themselves the students mumble, "Not fair!") By comparison, the lot method is rather casual about guilt and innocence, holding all responsible more or less ("all deserve it") and not caring to inquire into degrees of culpability (yes, the Cannae survivors ran for their lives, but not before all was lost; or yes, the maniple threw down its weapons, but some of its fighters started the rout while others struggled bravely to prevent it). In fact, decimation is quite emphatic that particular punishments are not by just determination but by chance selection. Psychologically, the effect is universal terror and a scrupulous regard for personal conduct. Why this is so is a bit of a puzzle, since chance punishment should be more of an inducement than a deterrent to wrongdoing, especially when the malefactor has a nine in ten chance of being excused and set free; and since guarding against future error affords no protection in cases where a person's fate is not determined by a person's guilt. Nonetheless, decimation works[77]—as demonstrated by the Romans, attested to by their historians, and now vouched for by Machiavelli. But what is most surprising is that Rome, which destroyed "an entire legion at once, and a city" (§1), would think that multitudes could be too numerous to punish in their totality. Is it not the point of the chapter to prove that Rome applied maximum punishment no matter the number punished? Compared with a whole legion destroyed (of which no example is given), the decimation of an erring legion is a kinder and gentler form of punishment—or rather a wiser and more economical form of punishment, if by killing a tenth the same effect can be achieved as by killing all. The chapter appears to celebrate judicial severity; but the title calls for daily acts of foresight by a prudent physician rather than, as elsewhere (III.1.3), decennial acts of ruthlessness by reformer princes. And the very last example of the *Discourses* is a modest constitutional reform that diluted the voting power of "new men" (§4).[78]

The foregoing analysis has emphasized the personal over the institutional, the fact that good orders need vigorous execution by virtuous princes. It has stressed as well that these princes, depending on circumstance and the mystery of their ambition, divide between saviors and conspirators, menders and destroyers. From this contest of titans the conclusion has been drawn that Machiavelli is not properly regarded as the architect of a "new science of politics" understood as a structure of powers designed to suppress ambition.[79] While this conclusion stands, some acknowledgment is nonetheless called for of the role played by ordinary modes. The rule of law, even if subservient to the abuse of law (as in judicial terror and political trials), factors significantly in the health and endurance of regimes.[80] It is a large and glaring fact that Machiavelli decides to close his *Discourses* with homage to the lawful incrementalism of the "little by little" reformer, not with excuses for the violent usurpations of the "at a stroke" reformer. The "at a stroke" reformer satisfies and stupefies the public with his spectacular punishments, displays of power which make him feared by all and hated by some. Conversely, the "little by little" reformer operates by ordinary modes and so escapes the public's loathing. He is like the beloved prince, except that as a reformer he is swimming against the current of public opinion, and as a reformer his fame is always greater. Fabius Rullianus earned the surname Maximus not for having executed disobedient underlings (he was once himself in this position), but for having accomplished a "little by little" reform which did not cost him greatly his standing with the people. Machiavelli, it seems, is hesitant to ask of princes that they forego their present ambitions, much less that they sacrifice themselves for the common good. After all, he affords some excuse to princes who, wanting to retain their principates, refuse to reform the orders of their cities. Only that prince is fully culpable, who, like Romulus, is able both to reform and to rule, and who, like Caesar, chooses to destroy rather than to mend (I.10.6).[81]

So Fabius helped his city—and in the bargain helped himself, receiving the surname Maximus—by enacting one "little by little" reform to the Roman constitution. In Fabius's case—and no doubt in the case of Camillus too—patriotic service was less a function of implacable nature (loyalty to the republic because a severe nature caused hatred and hatred constrained ambition) than of a desire to win his city's highest honors. The Roman senate operated on the assumption that a virtuous commander could be trusted to exercise his own judgment and take the initiative, even at the expense of the senate's rightful authority, because credit for victory would then be his alone, and the love of glory "would be a check and a rule to make him work well" (II.33.1). The commander about whom this is said is the same Fabius. He was instructed to subdue old enemies but to refrain from starting new wars, since the power of declaring war belonged to the senate and the people. But when he prevailed in a new war, the emissaries sent to impede the action "turned into ambassadors of the acquisition and the glory that was gained" (§1). Fabius shared the conqueror's glory with no one, and yet part of his glory came from adding to the glory of Rome. It is well understood that glory is the private ambition most in harmony with public goods; for the commander who wants glory is beholden to the people who can bestow it—he serves them, they honor him. But it matters—or it might—who it is that does the honoring. A republican people, because it is more nearly equal to its commander, bestows higher honor than do the subjects of a prince. Thus a commander, who otherwise would be tempted by tyranny, stays loyal to the republic in order to enjoy its special accolades. And if it is true that a republic expands farther and endures longer than does a principality, then the republic's greatness enhances the commander's glory—Scipio would hardly be remembered if posterity did not first have cause to remember Rome. Rome took a chance when it encouraged the ambition of its citizens while providing ambition no outlet save that of public service. It gambled that competitive individuals would find satisfying the respect of equals and would not lust after the tyrant's supremacy.[82] It finally lost that gamble when Caesar put an end to the republic.

PART TWO

MACHIAVELLI

Chapter Seven

Machiavelli's Modes and Orders

"Modes and orders" (*modi ed ordini*) is Machiavelli's preferred phrase for describing the principles and operations of government. Unfortunately, the phrase is ill-defined and its terms not clearly differentiated. Perhaps the closest Machiavelli comes to explaining the phrase is in I.18 where modes and orders—but orders especially—are distinguished from laws and customs: "The order of the state was the authority of the people, of the Senate, of the tribunes, of the consuls; the mode of soliciting and creating the magistrates; the mode of making laws" (§2). The laws of the state, which were reinforced by its customs, included "the law on adulteries, the sumptuary [law], and that on ambition, and many others." Apparently modes and orders refer to constitutional divisions of power, whereas laws designate the formal restraints upon citizen behavior, and customs describe the opinions and habits by which citizens restrain themselves. Sometimes "modes" and "orders" are used interchangeably as when Machiavelli says of self-nomination for the consulate, "this order was good in the beginning" and "this mode later became very pernicious" (§3). But just as often a difference is detectable, with "orders" used for offices and institutions and "modes" for the manner of their administration. Generally the manner of administration is ordinary or extraordinary—that is, in compliance with law or outside the boundaries of law. The ordinary exercise of power, it would seem, is not much different from the power itself: the officeholder is a minister of the will of others as that will is reflected in the office's structure. Thus a mode is most like an order when the mode is ordinary. It is least like an order when it operates extraordinarily. Extraordinary modes require that magistrates be alone in power, and not infrequently extraordinary modes are the means by which magistrates come to be alone in power. Ordinary modes, on the other hand, are compatible with shared power. Machiavellian orders tend in the direction of mixed government and divided powers, whereas Machiavellian modes (especially when extraordinary) tend toward princely magistrates who have solitary power and are *uno solo*. Machiavelli disperses power through his orders, and he concentrates power through his modes.

But does Machiavelli even have modes and orders of his own? We noticed a certain backhandedness in Machiavelli's announcement respecting the new modes and orders he supposedly was bestowing on mankind. We understood he had them not because he said that he did, but because he said that the finding of new modes and orders has always excited the envious nature of men. Only because he professed himself a philanthropist willing to brave the envy of others did we have cause to believe that he too is a finder of modes and orders. In any event (and since we do not wish to make too much of this doubt), Machiavelli has said absolutely nothing about the substance of his own discovery. Instead, he has written two prefaces and 142 discourses all about the workings of Roman modes and orders and about their superiority to modern alternatives.

Before turning then to Machiavelli, to his purportedly new modes and orders and to the question of his originality, it might prove useful to review the Roman model recommended for imitation.

Rome Reviewed

The Roman republic was a democratic mixed regime. It was democratic, as opposed to aristocratic, because the plebeian population was granted a share of power through the office of the tribunate. It was democratic as well because the people, and not its class rival or a king, functioned as guardian of liberty—meaning that it protected its own liberty by veto powers over policies and elections and that it protected the liberty of patricians by the natural modesty of its ambitions. As a democratic mixed regime, Rome submitted its affairs to the rule of law; it thus was quick to develop a judicial power with which to defend the rights of citizens—a power which it lodged in the tribunate and in popular assemblies converted into courts. But if lawfulness was a consequence of the people's involvement in politics, of its need for security and regularity, so too was faction and tumult. Rome experienced a turbulent domestic life because plebeians demanded and were granted a voice in political affairs. In Machiavelli's judgment the democratizing of Rome's mixed regime was the cause of antagonistic class relations—when Rome decided to include the plebs, it decided to sacrifice its domestic harmony. On the other hand, Romans never thought that domestic harmony could be restored by excluding the patricians. Nor does Machiavelli propose such a plan, because he assumes the naturalness and ubiquity of the humoral division of humanity, and because (in light of what otherwise is a highly malleable human nature) he judges the great to be invaluable to society's well-being. Initiative and ambition were the special contributions of Rome's aristocratic element, as lawfulness was the special contribution of its democratic element. The patrician order supplied the state with its magistrates, the most visible and commanding of which was the dictator. Executive power was then the purview and responsibility of the great (though not without regular challenges from below), just as judicial power was the province of the people. Strangely, though, no class of the city was identified by special alliance with the legislative power, that power which in both classical and liberal theory is supreme above all others, is exercised by the sovereign, and is definitive of the regime. But in a mixed government, where the objective is to check action rather than to facilitate it, the legislative power is rightly demoted and disguised. A mixed regime is deliberately unclear about this central question of distributive justice—who should rule—and as a pale substitute for sovereignty denominates some party the guardian of liberty, or its institutional equivalent. Machiavelli, then, pays so little attention to legislative power because Rome had no sovereign body which legislated authoritatively but had instead antagonistic classes which fought each other over the privilege of rule.[1]

The other reason for Machiavelli's indifference to legislative power was the unstable character of Rome's founding, the fact that Rome was not founded by a single individual at a stroke but by a continuous succession of founders and reformers responding to the accidents of their times. Rome had a second-best founding compared with Sparta which issued whole and complete from the mind of Lycurgus. But then second-best foundings are discovered to be best after all, since the secret of success is adaptability to accidents, and not a once-and-for-ever perfection resistant to change. Thus the orders of an original lawgiver are not particularly important because they are not particularly lasting, and subsequent lawgiving is similarly subject to reform. The one exception is the order which renders a people flexible. This order is apparently traceable to the site on which a city is constructed; for a fertile site makes possible expansion, which excites in people acquisitive appetites, which in turn cause people to imagine better futures and to develop enterprising habits. The Roman character was bent on increase and novelty. But it also, like the Spartan character, reverenced its past, for the populace was pious toward ancestors and gods, and the rulers were respectful of political traditions, reforming inside, not outside, of ancient orders. Rome changed—from kingship to republic to empire—but it never began anew and it never gave back its growth.

Religion was the chief cause of the people's goodness, of that willingness even on the part of selfish individuals to sacrifice personal happiness for the commonweal. Religion inspired the hope that a future foreseen by the gods could be achieved or averted if the proper sacrifices were performed. Hope turned to confidence, and confidence supported by training produced virtue. From virtue came victories which validated and further fortified confidence. At the same time, religion instilled fear, fear of the gods which carried over to a fear of authority. Fear caused obedience, and obedience, coupled with hope, brought about victories.

Obedience to authority had the additional benefit of meliorating class animosities. The separate communities of patricians and plebs were knitted together by a common religious faith and a common destiny under the care and supervision of civic gods. Except that plebeians believed in the truth of auspices and their leaders did not. More than wealth, more than privilege, more than power—more than any of these divisions, knowledge of the world, so called, divided patricians from the true-believing, superstitious plebs. Thus it was imperative for the rulers to feign belief, though doing so in such a way as always to accomplish the enterprises of the senate. Along with a pious populace Rome had an astute ruling class, which maintained itself in power by religious hypocrisy, indirect government, and the tactics of temporizing. These management skills were needed since the nobility's supremacy was unofficial and its numbers too few to survive a test of strength with the plebs. Nor could it survive without conceding a slow but inexorable change in the composition of its order. Plebeians gradually won admittance to all of the higher offices of state. In this ideological battle known as the "conflict of the orders," Machiavelli is mostly a neutral; or if he tilts to one side, it is to favor slightly the patricians, the class which supplied the state with its perspicacious leaders. To the extent though that coopted plebeians remade themselves as patricians, their admittance to the governing class was all to the good. And what was even better about the success of their agitation was that democratizing the regime cleared the way for the energetic young. Rome combined the caution of age with the boldness of youth.

It was important that Roman character be risk-taking and ambitious because it was necessary that Roman policy toward neighboring states be aggressive and imperialistic. The way of the world, professes Machiavelli, is growth and decay, and Rome was the republic which knew best how to grow. The typical city-state of the ancient world was small, homogeneous, and isolationist. This was the formula also prescribed by Greek political philosophy which conceived of the polis as an educational laboratory unaffected by the slings and arrows of marauding invaders. Domestic life was what counted and the moral worth of the individual citizen. But for Rome what counted was conquest, and moral worth gave place to acquisitive ability. Rome expanded by absorbing the populations of its defeated enemies and by opening its gates to immigrants in need. With an ever-thickening trunk Rome was sturdy enough to withstand the storms of warfare; and with a shrewd grasp of human psychology, Rome was able to choose its enemies and to fight them one at a time. Some opponents stayed quiet out of fear of Roman arms; others avoided the fray on the promise that Roman ambition was directed elsewhere, or in the vain hope that Rome would exhaust itself before presenting a threat. Rome managed these hopes and fears to its own advantage; thus it was by sound planning and not by good fortune that Rome fought always against single enemies. Machiavelli is in awe of the achievement and of the grand strategy that produced it.

There were two other distinctive features to Roman foreign policy. The first was a determination to extract profit from conquest. This Rome accomplished by fighting wars quickly and cheaply. The application of massive force brought about quick results, and a short term of office put the spur to the consul's ambition. Wars were economically waged because booty was deposited in public coffers, because costly sieges were generally avoided, and because colonists did the work of a garrison force. Rome also joined with allies whose manpower doubled its own numbers; but always—and this was the second distinctive feature—Rome retained command, and so the reputation for victory (and an increasing share of the spoils) went to Rome. Rome therefore grew with the aid of partners who were not quite equals and who over time were reduced to inferiors. While waging direct warfare against its enemies, Rome simultaneously was waging indirect warfare against its friends. Machiavelli is almost as admiring of the strategy by which Rome deceived its allies as he is of the strategy by which it intimidated competitor states.

The final point to note about Roman modes and orders is the latitude that was extended to commanders in the field. Just as Rome chose to capitalize on the energy of youth, so it saw profit in allowing its glory-hungry commanders to do as they thought fit. On the one hand, Rome divided power in order to keep it safe. To this end it created senators, consuls, tribunes, and censors; it also maintained a large officer corps and multiplied the number of magistrates in the belief that envy would supply a check to ambition. On the other hand, Rome concentrated power in a single chain of command. While every consul suffered the scrutiny and second-guessing of jealous rivals, every consul, within his jurisdiction, had total authority and was not held accountable for his actions until the close of his term. It even happened that a consul might exceed the limits of his jurisdiction, start a war as well as prosecute one; and yet the senate was forgiving of the transgression because the ambition of the prince alone in power was the driving force behind Rome's unprecedented and unparalleled expansion.

These in brief were the modes and orders of Rome and the modes and orders which Machiavelli lovingly describes for the benefit of his contemporaries. Modern men, and especially the Florentines, know nothing of war, and so they suffer the ravages of foreign invasion; and their domestic institutions are ill-made, both with respect to the protections they afford to liberty and to their use in achieving national greatness. (For example, the law courts of Florence were unable to punish the powerful and the well-heeled [I.7-8, I.49], and reliance on mercenary captains and their men-at-arms was stifling the development of indigenous talent and civic spirit.) The root causes of these failures are a Christian education which despises worldly glory and a renaissance which ignores the lessons of history (I.Pr.). Correcting these deficiencies so as to prepare the ground for a revival of Roman modes and orders is the stated purpose of the *Discourses*. As to the purported newness of Machiavelli's teaching and his authorship of the modes and orders he champions, Strauss observes that "the restoration of something which has been disestablished for a long time is no less revolutionary or shocking than the introduction of something wholly new."[2] Machiavelli is an original in his capacity as moral and political archeologist.

Rome's Imperfections and Machiavelli's Reforms

Strauss has something additional to say on the subject of Machiavelli's originality. The Roman polity, Strauss believes, was "a work of chance," its institutions discovered "absent-mindedly" and maintained obdurately "out of reverence for the ancestral." But Machiavelli's analysis of Rome, being deliberate and clear-sighted, effectively transforms a happy accident into a "goal of rational desire and action." Strauss concludes that because Machiavelli understands the Roman republic better than did its makers, "the modes and orders recommended by Machiavelli, even those which he took over bodily from ancient Rome, are rightly described by him as new modes and orders."[3]

Were there then modes and orders not taken over bodily from ancient Rome, but revised, amended, and improved for modern consumption? Strauss is not one to think that Machiavelli adheres slavishly to the Roman model or that he is swept away with fawning admiration. Machiavelli, he argues, is critical of the Roman paradigm and critical as well of Livy's less than faithful rendition. Machiavelli's criticisms, says Strauss, can be inferred from the numerous mistakes which Machiavelli makes in recounting events from Roman history—such as the statement that two legates were dispatched to Fabius, rather than five envoys and two tribunes, as Livy tells it (II.33.1; Livy, IX.36). This is a controversial proposition, that Machiavelli's true opinions lie hidden inside of factual errors, or that other techniques of esoteric writing are employed by him.[4] (I too have had occasion to question parts of this proposition, while other parts I have freely assumed.) Somewhat less controversial is the contention of several scholars that Machiavelli misrepresents Roman practices and the Roman ruling class, that he "Machiavellianizes" each by making Rome more aggressive and fraudulent than in fact it was and by making its rulers more skeptical and hypocritical than in fact they were.[5] Less controversial still—in fact beyond dispute—are Machiavelli's explicit criticisms of Rome. For agreement's sake, these only will we look at, since they minimize the problems which arise when comparing texts and observing differences or when imputing to Machiavelli a clear understanding and deliberate rejection of some stipulated truth about Rome.[6]

The more important of Rome's mistakes fall roughly into two categories, categories which conform to the distinction between orders and modes. The first mistake—and by far the most enduring—was the controversy over agrarian legislation. The trouble began shortly after the founding of the republic. Its cause, in Machiavelli's judgment, was an error made respecting property rights. Machiavelli subscribes to that maxim of ancient republicanism which states that cities should be wealthy and citizens should be poor (III.25).[7] While classless communism is not required by this principle, equality and austerity most certainly are. But Rome permitted unequal and unfrugal ownership of property. Given this original misstep, it was not wrong of the plebs to agitate for an agrarian law, for redistribution of lands and upper limits on private holdings, since that agitation maintained liberty in Rome; but it was wrong, after many generations of quiet, for it to resume the struggle at the time of the Gracchi, since that resumption looked very far back and was the cause of scandal (I.37). Although credited with safeguarding liberty, the agrarian law was also responsible for destroying the republic (III. 24.1).

The most blameable of Rome's faulty orders was the decemvirate created in 451. What was intended as a "blue-ribbon" commission for the study of the constitution became a tyranny terminating the republic. The cause was overheated competition between the classes with each wanting to use the decemvirs for its own advantage (I.40). But the decemvirate lasted for only two years; thus no matter how damaging and dangerous its tenure, the decemvirate was less a new regime than a temporary suspension of the old.

In the aftermath of the decemvir debacle, Rome committed its second constitutional blunder. It replaced the consulate with the military tribunate (445 BC). This mistake persisted for nearly 80 years (I.39.2), and even though patrician duplicity mitigated the damage, still the tribunate was an unwise reform because it violated, with its multiple commanders, the principle of *uno solo* execution (III.15). So did the consulate, of course, but never to the same degree and rarely with the same results. The nut of the tribunate problem was this, that unifying the command in order to make it effective depended on the self-abnegation of self-regarding magistrates, equals in authority who were called upon to acknowledge their inferiority in talent (III.30.1). Again, the consulate suffered from a similar disability, since the appointment of a dictator required the consent and practical resignation of each of the consuls. But two consuls were still few enough that each could be held responsible for political and military failures; thus they each had a motive, during moments of great trial, for passing the buck to a dictator whose more expansive powers were better suited for the handling of emergencies. By contrast, the military tribunes could escape blame by hiding inside a wholly fractured command.

The mid-fifth century was apparently a bad time for Rome, since its third constitutional mistake was committed in this period. This was the censorship, established in 443. Its particular failing was that the term of office was originally too long (five years). When the error was rectified nine years later, another defect was detected, that individuals were allowed to be judges in their own case; for the then current censors punished the dictator who shortened their terms.

The last of Rome's orders which fell short of perfection was the law of 326 establishing the office of proconsul. This was the law which prolonged commands, as Machiavelli puts it. Prior to this time Rome had managed to hold on to the tiger's tale of individual ambition. Rome encouraged its princes to dream dreams of grandeur; and Rome then saved itself from their grandiose schemes of usurpation and tyranny by rotating them among commands. Thus did Rome prevent charismatic consuls from turning the city's legions into private armies. But when, for the sake of speedy victories, it allowed consuls to stay in place, changing only their title, a Rubicon was crossed which set Rome on a course toward caesarism.[8]

It was less any order—i.e., law or institution—which kept ambition directed toward public purposes than it was a style of execution, or mode. We saw before that Rome fared best in the war against conspirators when it called upon unpopular magistrates to punish extraordinarily. Not the law as such, but the severity and spectacle of its execution was what did the trick. But if there was one failing to which Machiavelli returns again and again, it was the Roman practice of treating miscreants leniently. His criticism can perhaps go unnoticed given that he just as emphatically praises Rome for the unblinking severity of its punishments. Even so, Machiavelli judges that Rome let its magistrates off easy. Varro supplies the best example. This incompetent blunderbuss was responsible for the worst defeat in Roman history, the catastrophe at Cannae—which would have finished Rome had Hannibal not erred in delaying his assault on the city; and yet instead of suffering execution, he was welcomed home by the senate and honored for not despairing of Roman affairs (I.31.2) (while at the same time the legion which survived the debacle was exiled to Sicily). Likewise, the punishment of Sergius and Virginius, the squabbling tribunes at the siege of Veii, was excessively forgiving (§2). Then too, there was the excusing of Horatius, who should have been executed for the murder of his sister (I.24), and Fabius, who should have been punished for his insubordination to the dictator (III.36); finally, there was the election of Claudius Nero (207 BC), who, once offended, should not have been entrusted with high command (III.17). While Machiavelli praises Rome for having behaved ungratefully less often than any other ancient republic (I.28), he follows his praise with a blunt explanation of the political value of ingratitude, that fear of its bite causes ambitious men to police themselves (I.29). Hence grateful Rome was at fault for being too kind and just. And while he contends that accusation, an ordinary mode, accomplishes legitimate political and legal objectives (e.g., the venting of plebeian hostility, the righting of personal wrongs), whereas calumny, an extraordinary mode, turns the city topsy-turvy; the difference between these modes, as Mansfield shows, is difficult to pin down, since accusation derives its effectiveness from a vigorous execution reflecting the virtue of the magistrate.[9]

The Roman constitution moved in contrary directions: It tried dispersing power for the protection of liberty, and it tried concentrating power for the effectiveness of execution. Founders and reformers, for example, were alone in power in order that they might create and renew institutions which divided and distributed power. The foregoing review of Machiavelli's most salient criticisms of Rome suggests that Machiavelli appreciated the tensile strength of the Roman constitution but thought it improvable by reforms that would augment the pull of its opposing forces—more safeguards against ambition, more energy in the executive. To the degree then that Roman modes and orders become Machiavelli's modes and orders by the repairs he makes to them, Machiavelli is an original for wanting a mixed regime with an executive more tightly circumscribed in ordinary times but with greater freedom of operation in extraordinary times. As to the determination of the character of the times, that power lies officially with no one, but is fought over on a case by case basis; and in those instances when the executive loses, he suffers what appears to him the public's ingratitude.

We promised to look only at Machiavelli's explicit criticisms of Rome as a way of delineating the novelty of his teaching. But not far from explicit criticism is explicit praise, so we might be excused expanding the search if consideration is given to those practices of Rome which Machiavelli commends but others disparage. Three come to mind. Machiavelli reckons it advantageous for a city to be imperfectly founded; imperfection is a form of necessity which summons from succeeding generations their best rectificatory labors. By contrast, the classical tradition tends to favor Sparta's perfect founding to Athens's continuous founding (Athens serving as a foil to Sparta for Plato and Aristotle); and even though Cicero (speaking through Scipio, speaking through Cato) defends the continuous founding of Rome against the foundings of all other regimes, his reason is not that of Machiavelli. Realizing that the wisdom of one person and of one period is incomplete, Cicero hopes to achieve perfection through adjustments and refinements implemented over time.[10] Machiavelli, on the other hand, welcomes imperfection because it offers equal opportunity to princes with ambition kindred to the founder's. Machiavelli also welcomes the uncertainty and risk attending continuous foundings because he has, most evidence suggests, the temperament of a gambler. A second feature of the Roman experience lauded by Machiavelli was the turbulence of its domestic politics. The cause of faction in Rome was the inclusion of the plebs or the democratizing of the mixed regime. Machiavelli finds great value in participation carried this far—liberty is defended and expansion is facilitated; Livy, though, embarrassed by the sight of plebs boycotting the army and abandoning the city, condemns the factious disquiet to which the humors were prone (IV.9). Finally, and related to the above, Machiavelli wants credit for disputing the opinion, espoused by Livy and by all other historians, that the multitude is unfit to share in the responsibilities of rule (I.58.1). When shackled by law, the multitude is constant and wise and equal to any prince. Although Machiavelli will retreat somewhat from this unprecedented endorsement, the impression takes hold that he staunchly advocates the popular interest. The larger impression is that a raucous and agonistic politics is entirely to his liking.

Of course a raucous and agonistic politics was the politics of republican Rome. Machiavelli learns from the Roman example what republicanism is all about. Which means that as a constitutional thinker, Machiavelli is more Roman than modern, more old than new. Whatever the improvements Machiavelli may envision and recommend, at this point his political modes and orders remain chiefly an imitation of Rome's.

Machiavelli's Originality

A convincing case, then, has yet to be made for the originality of Machiavelli. Strauss has commented that Machiavelli's newness can be found in his revival of modes and orders long since dead, or that it can be found in Machiavelli's criticism of the same, whether overt or covert. He says finally, and most significantly, that Machiavelli copied those who copied no one but were themselves originals. The Romans discovered their own modes and orders without benefit of authoritative example; thus to imitate the Romans is to go one's own way not following Roman authority.[11] Strauss does not explain how Machiavelli was a complete original in the matter of modes and orders, at least not when modes and orders are taken to mean constitutional practices and the exercise of political power. But then Strauss's student, Harvey Mansfield, does attempt to fill this gap with his argument that Machiavelli was the originator of the impartial regime.

The impartial regime is Machiavelli's alternative to the mixed regime of the ancients. Among classical political philosophers—and Aristotle is Mansfield's primary source—the mixed regime is seen as a remedy for the partiality of simple regimes. In simple regimes—aristocracy, oligarchy, democracy—a single social class, on the strength of the claim it advances for the justice of its rule, monopolizes the offices of state. This claim, being perforce partial and unjust, provokes a rebellion on the part of excluded classes (usually either oligarchs or democrats); which rebellion, if successful, brings to power a new regime reflective of the victors' own partial view of justice. Revolution, in an ever-revolving pattern known as the cycle of regimes, is the consequence of unresolved quarrels over distributive justice. The mixed regime, then, is an attempt to work through this problem to a resolution. Viewed ideally, the mixed regime combines the wisdom of the few with the goodness of the many; viewed practically, it is the most that partisans will agree to, since experience teaches that participation by all parties is the precondition for universal agreement.[12] Hence the mixed regime is not regarded by philosophers as true and best by nature but is offered instead as an acceptable second-best alternative. Its success depends on the persuasion of democrats as to the merits of virtue-claims made by aristocrats and property-claims made by oligarchs, as well as the persuasion of aristocrats and oligarchs as to the merits of egalitarian arguments made by democrats. But whether mixed or simple, the classical regime rests on the conviction that those in office deserve their power and can make the best use of it for common objectives. Because those out of office tend to hold to different convictions, the simple regime in particular is vulnerable to attack; and to a lesser degree the mixed regime is vulnerable too, because education is a weak reed against the tide of partiality and the lure of total power. But for better or worse, classical politics is about the large questions of justice, and while it aspires to harmony, the usual results are class strife, revolution, and the cycle of regimes.

Machiavelli's impartial regime offers two improvements to the classical mixed regime. It redirects the business of politics from debates about justice to debates about acquisition. It thereby manages the problems of partisanship and faction by removing from politics that grand question about which the humors disagree, namely the equality or the inequality of human beings. It affirms that all humans are equal by virtue of their common need to acquire; and it affirms that no humans are equal by virtue of their varying capacities for acquisition; or—better said to allow for the humoral bifurcation of humanity—it affirms that the one true distinction between the great and the people is that the great want to oppress and the people wants not to be oppressed. Once it is realized that the classes cannot agree about distributive justice, the prescription for domestic tranquility is a change of subject—not who should rule, but who gets what. Ordinarily acquisition would pit individuals against each other in a competition for scarce resources, since one person's gain is commonly another person's loss. But acquisition is harmony-producing if the pie is expanding and if some acquirers are less hungry than others. It matters then that the state is expansionist and that the people is satisfied with liberty and is willing to leave power and fame to others. Thus we come to the second improvement wrought by the impartial regime: the removal of the people from politics except as an electorate and judge of ambitious elites. Party politics, as previously explained,[13] is ruinous to a state to the degree that the parties represent the humors, for then the issue is sovereignty and opponents are mortal enemies promoting partial ideas of justice. But party politics is healthy if competition is confined to the elite, some of whom are old guard calling themselves nobles, others of whom are new men bearing the stigma of illegitimacy. In place of warring camps caught in an ideological struggle, what one has instead are contestants for office willing to present their credentials before a neutral arbiter. Politics is a game governed by rules enforced by an umpire. As with other sporting events, the mayhem is contained inside of boundaries and the violence is largely simulated. Consequently, the tumult resulting from electoral politics is not the sort that leads to civil war. In sum, the impartial regime is what's original in Machiavelli, his new modes and orders (politically understood), because it affords a solution to the faction problem consistent with energy and expansion. Indeed, so successful is the impartial regime that it replaces the cycle of regimes with a perpetual republic.[14]

The explanation by Mansfield of the mechanics of the impartial regime is clear and convincing. But some of its clarity may derive from his looking backwards to Machiavelli across several centuries of liberal theorizing. For frankly Mansfield is better at differentiating healthy and hurtful faction than usually is

Machiavelli, who sometimes stops short of identifying first causes (as when he tries accounting for the dissimilar effects of humoral faction in Rome and in Florence [*Florentine Histories*, III.1]).[15] Mansfield would credit Machiavelli with the "de-Aristotelianizing" of politics, owing to the stress Machiavelli lays on acquisition; but it is Hobbes, more than Machiavelli, who rules out of court the controversies arising from distributive justice.[16] And Montesquieu, cited by Publius, is a better source for the exclusion of the people from an active role in public affairs.[17] Mansfield is not unaware that he is sometimes viewing Machiavelli through the lens of latter-day liberalism, admitting that "today's liberal democracy is, of course, very different from Machiavelli's harsh preferences for martial republics and Borgia-like principalities."[18] For that matter, Mansfield's hindsight would hardly be objectionable if Machiavelli is himself anticipating the contributions of his followers.[19] As such, the impartial regime might be one way of describing that "destined place" (*loco destinato*) to which those who come after Machiavelli will have but a "short road" to travel (I.Pr.2). This in fact is where Mansfield appears to be, claiming that Machiavelli is laying a foundation upon which others will build the impartial regime of liberalism.

The question though is how closely the edifice fits the foundation or how short is the road ahead. We observed before that Machiavelli opens a few doors to modernity (his acceptance of faction especially), but we also wondered whether he passes through these doors himself or whether he walks off in other directions.[20] For instance, does he (or would he—allowances being made for the work of future disciples) welcome the reduction of the people to electorate status? The question is pertinent since according to Machiavelli the inclusion of the people in the Roman regime was what brought that constitution to its so-called perfection. Mansfield distinguishes, quite rightly, between the people and its leaders, arguing that only the latter have the ambition and the talent to make their way in politics. Plebeian elites, in other words, are the natural kin of patricians and only the conventional kin of plebs; they are new princes demanding a place at the table. But Machiavelli warns the people not to trust generous patricians and not to trust coopted tribunes (I.3.2; III.11.1). The people's liberty, he cautions, requires hands-on defending by the people itself—i.e., tumults in the streets and strikes against the military, not just the casting of ballots in rigged elections.[21] The problem with treating plebeians as non-partisan judges is that either they are too weak, and so fail to guard liberty, or they are too strong, causing the elite to become like themselves. Machiavelli is fully cognizant of the people's propensity to acquire without virtue if given the chance (book 2), and that captains, as a consequence, will imitate the people and turn into merchants. But if the state intends to conquer and expand, a spirited people led by virtuous captains are the instruments necessary for achieving this greatness. It will not do, therefore, for the two humors to become interest groups in a pluralist society.[22] Nor does it seem to be Machiavelli's idea of healthy politics for parties to represent the selfish ambitions of rival elites as opposed to the permanent interests of humors or classes.[23] After all, the chief difference between the domestic politics of Rome and Florence was that in Rome the classes fought each other whereas in Florence the *ottimati* fought among themselves.[24] While depoliticizing the populace may well be the formula for peace adopted by modern republics, it is questionable whether these republics are in fact the brainchildren of Machiavelli. It is also doubtful that a depoliticized populace is even a very modern idea, since Aristotle proposes it as part of his mixed regime.[25]

If we discount as Machiavelli's innovation the impartial regime (because of its tendency to amalgamate the humors), what else have we that represents Machiavellian modes and orders? When last we heard from Strauss, he was intimating that Machiavelli's admiration for Rome extended to the point of foreswearing Roman authority in toto, on grounds that since Rome was an original, any true imitator of Rome must be an original himself. We did not mention it at the time, but on this reading so new are the modes and orders of Machiavelli, that the very theme of imitation all but vanishes from his thought.

Another scholar answers the question of what's new about Machiavelli, not by minimizing the imitation theme, but by magnifying it. This is Herbert Butterfield, who maintains that Machiavelli's novelty lies less in the modes and orders of a mixed regime than in a methodology of rule. Machiavelli, Butterfield argues, is the originator of the science of statecraft.[26] Essential to this science are three suppositions: that history is repetitive, that human nature is unchanging, and that the past is superior to the present.[27] Consequently, the science of statecraft is constructed on a science of history—practice follows from theory. Machiavelli devises his new modes and orders and walks his "path as yet untrodden" by compiling "true knowledge of histories" and by exhorting his contemporaries to imitate past examples of political and military success (I.Pr.). Most significantly, the imitation is to be direct, exact in every detail, for statecraft must be carried on with the same concern for faithful reproduction as that practiced by Renaissance artists, jurists, and physicians, all of whom aimed at replicating classical works and techniques. Butterfield can quote Machiavelli on the need for what seems like mechanical imitation (artists "strive with all industry to represent it [ancient statuary] in all their works"; "for the civil laws are nothing other than verdicts given by ancient jurists"; "nor is medicine other than the experiments performed by ancient physicians" [I.Pr.2]); thus Butterfield is confident that a literalist reading of Machiavelli's new science is the correct one. "It is wrong," says Butterfield,

> to imagine that he was merely pleading for the growth of wisdom, the widening of experience which may come to any man from historical study; or to think that he would have been satisfied to see his contemporaries vaguely inspired with the ideal of conducting themselves like Romans. . . . His doctrine of imitation does in fact mean the imitation of definite specimens of success-

ful policy, with a particular stress on the action of great men and on the examples of antiquity. . . . [T]he position he takes up rests on the view that if a
certain expedient has proved successful in some conjuncture in the past, the
trick ought not to be forgotten in a world in which historical situations are
being constantly repeated.[28]

What Butterfield is calling the science of statecraft, Leslie Walker denominates the inductive method. Machiavelli, and not Francis Bacon, was the originator of the inductive method, Walker claims. Walker identifies six distinguishing features of Machiavelli's method, which method also is Machiavelli's
untrodden path: First, Machiavelli looks to history for recurring patterns of political and military behavior. Second, he confirms their lessons with like results
from comparable examples, ancient and modern. Third, he infers causal generalizations from historical data. Fourth, he tests these generalizations against conflicting evidence. Fifth, he examines the desirability of outcomes from a variety
of perspectives. And sixth, he applies utilitarian standards to moral precepts.[29]
Walker notes that Butterfield once excludes Machiavelli from the company of
inductive reasoners; but Butterfield's reservation, Walker is assured, proves not
that induction is absent from Machiavelli's method but that it is compromised
on those occasions when Machiavelli preaches to his contemporaries about the
glories of Roman modes and orders. (In other words, a good empiricist ought
not dabble in "oughts.")[30] But aside from the occasional lapse or misapplication,
Machiavelli's new science is the inductive method.[31]
    While Walker seconds Butterfield in believing that Machiavelli originates
a new science of history and statecraft, Butterfield seconds Guicciardini in believing that this science is bunk.[32] In his collection of political maxims, the Italian title of which is *Ricordi*, Guicciardini states time and again that human affairs are too complicated and human beings too unpredictable for there ever to
be a political science rooted in historical study. Even the smallest of differences
can negate the applicability of past models, and the law of unintended consequences—as we would call it today—sabotages all large attempts to manage the
future.[33] Another voice added to the chorus of skeptics is that of Mark Hulliung,
who accepts the Butterfield analysis that Machiavelli's originality lies in his
purported founding of "a scientific unity of theory and practice," and who accepts the Guicciardini critique of this union, a critique which drives "a wedge
between 'experience' and 'reading'" and which denies, "in the name of the former, the relevance of the latter as a guide to perplexed political actors."[34]
    We wonder though whether Machiavelli understood his novelty in this
way. In the first place we ought not assume, as some of the above scholars do,
that Machiavelli's modes and orders and his untrodden path are one and the
same.[35] The long, first sentence of the *Discourses* does allow for their identification,[36] in that the finding of new modes and orders is described as perilous and
the traveling of an untrodden path is expected to bring "trouble and difficulty."
But discovery is perilous owing to the envious nature of men, whereas owing to

the humanity of those who consider the end (*il fine*) of Machiavelli's labors, the untrodden path holds out the possibility of rewards. So humanity, in place of envy, is one difference; and reward, in place of injury, is another. Also, Machiavelli declares that he will walk a path never before traversed by man; but many discoverers before him have suffered the envy of persons "more ready to blame than to praise." Even though the content of Machiavelli's modes and orders may be new, it is their finding, not their content, that is emphasized in the book's first sentence—and the finding is an act with many precedents. Thus it appears that there is more originality in Machiavelli's path than in his discovery. This may seem like an innocuous distinction, but it is the basis for, or is congruent with, Strauss's claim that Machiavelli is original less for what he says than for the audience to whom he says it.[37]

What then is the path? It is hardly new ground for a Renaissance historian to turn his attention to the ancients or even to derive general lessons from the past.[38] But all previous studies are apparently lacking in one crucial respect: they fail to convince their readers that imitation of the ancients is a realistic objective. They please their readers with tales of virtuous deeds, just as unearthed fragments of ancient statuary honor the houses of their new owners. But ancient statuary is lent out for copying by local artists, whereas ancient history generates no equivalent imitative effort. The chief reason why imitation of ancient political and military practices does not follow from the reading of histories is that "true knowledge of histories" is not thereby acquired. So what is this true knowledge? The simplest answer—and the one which Butterfield seems to give—is knowledge of cause and effect: general maxims induced from the record of the past used as a road map for actions taken in the present. These maxims—collected, collated, cross-referenced, and double-checked—constitute the systematized knowledge of a science of statecraft, the underlying assumptions of which are that history is cyclical and that human passions are constant. Machiavelli expresses these beliefs and his confidence in "scientific" statecraft on numerous occasions:

> No one, therefore, should be terrified that he cannot carry out what has been carried out by others, for as was said in our preface, men are born, live, and die always in one and the same order. (I.11.5)

> Whoever considers present and ancient things easily knows that in all cities and in all peoples there are the same desires and the same humors, and there always have been. So it is an easy thing for whoever examines past things diligently to foresee future things in every republic and to take the remedies for them that were used by the ancients, or, if they do not find any that were used, to think up new ones through the similarity of accidents. But because these considerations are neglected or not understood by whoever reads, or, if they are understood, they are not known to whoever governs, it follows that there are always the same scandals in every time. (I.39.1)

But the weakness of men at present, caused by their weak education and their slight knowledge of things, makes them judge ancient judgments in part inhuman, in part impossible. (III.27.2)

And truly, not without cause do good historians, as is ours, put certain cases particularly and distinctly so that posterity may learn how they have to defend themselves in such accidents. (III.30.2)

Prudent men are accustomed to say, and not by chance or without merit, that whoever wishes to see what has to be considers what has been; for all worldly things in every time have their own counterpart in ancient times. That arises because these are the work of men, who have and always had the same passions, and they must of necessity result in the same effect. (III.43.1)

There is, however, one problem with the contention that Machiavelli is knowingly creating this science and means it to represent his innovation and his untrodden path. The maxims are only as good as the information on which they are based. Accuracy as to detail is therefore of the utmost importance—how, when, by whom, and to whom something was done. But if getting the facts straight is the starting point of true knowledge, why does Machiavelli choose those books of Livy which most resemble historical fiction, in which knowing for certain who did what to whom, when and how, is all but impossible?[39] (Did Romulus really kill Remus? Was Lucretia really raped? Did the plebs vacate the city and assemble on the Sacred Mount? Was Manlius Capitolinus thrown from the Tarpeian Rock?) It is beyond reckoning how Machiavelli could think himself inventing a science of history when even Livy complains of the untrustworthy character of the early sources (Livy, II.21).[40] But if the historian is merely guessing, or sometimes falsely reporting the facts, how is a political actor supposed to imitate history's heroes? Plainly put—he isn't. We conclude then that in commenting on Livy's *First Decade*, Machiavelli is more poet than historian, a user of history for his own creative purposes rather than a student of history seeking to found a new historical science.[41] Nor is Machiavelli the only historian to take such liberties, for in his opinion

most writers obey the fortune of the victors, so that to make their victories glorious, they not only increase what has been virtuously worked by them but also render illustrious the actions of their enemies. They do it so that whoever is born later in whichever of the two provinces, the victorious or the defeated, has cause to marvel at those men and those times and is forced to praise and love them most highly. (II.Pr.1)

Most writers embellish; most writers tell lies. Hence "direct imitation"—Butterfield's understanding—seems not to be what Machiavelli has in mind.[42]

Still, there are these statements about recurring patterns and constant passions causing historical knowledge to be useful. These statements are not dismissible, and in fact they have some truth in them. In all essential respects, human beings remain the same—needy, mortal, rational.[43] Thus there is much to be learned from history regarding the behavior of human beings—who do indeed find themselves facing similar problems because human nature is indeed constant in its broad outlines. But while these statements are not dismissible, neither are they Archimedian fulcrums upon which to leverage an interpretation; for there are better places in Machiavelli to establish one's footing.[44] Plus it is the case that each statement comes with qualifications lessening its import.

In the first quotation, Machiavelli is concluding, in light of the career of Savonarola, that human beings always are suckers for religious charlatans. But he also admits that what can be done with civilized men is not quite the same as what can be done with coarse and ignorant men. At the very least, belief in a repetitive cycle requires that imitation be of those actions belonging to a comparable period. The second quotation occurs in a chapter which reports the causes and results of a Roman mistake, namely the creation of tribunes with consular power. But the chapter's lesson is not that the present can learn from the past, in this case avoiding mistakes of the past, but that the same accidents occur among diverse peoples. The Florentines do learn, but not from the study of history; they learn from their own experience that the Ten of War are not the cause of war, just as the Romans learned from their own experience that executive power, by whatever name, is vital to the safety of the state. The third quotation from III.27.2 is to be compared with it counterpart in I.Pr.2. It is noteworthy that the preface's "true knowledge of histories" has been demoted from the whole cause of why moderns fail to imitate ancients to only half the cause, and that Christianity, pushed to the side in the preface, is in III.27 given equal billing. For both "weak education" (Christianity) and "slight knowledge of things" (insufficient true knowledge) explain why ancient practices are judged "inhuman" and "impossible." In the fourth quotation, about the techniques and objectives of historiography, Livy is credited with putting a case "particularly and distinctly" in order to teach valuable lessons to posterity. Presumably, descriptive and explanatory accounts better serve the object of teaching through history. But Livy merely reports that a third army was recruited by Camillus for the internal defense of Rome, not the manner of its enrolling or the reasons making its recruitment necessary (Livy, VI.6), which some unnamed many are expected to judge superfluous given the ordinarily warlike character of the Romans. In point of fact, posterity is indebted to Machiavelli, the historical poet, for putting the case "particularly and distinctly" so as to teach the lesson of how to avoid tumult while arming the people.

The fifth quotation is the most important because in context it is the most dogmatic. It would have us believe that state policy can be made on the basis of ancient history. Does Machiavelli mean to be taken seriously when he says to contemporary Florentines: Don't trust the French because 18 centuries ago they cheated your ancestors (which ancestors, if they were Roman colonists [I.1.3], were not even Tuscans!)? There are two reasons for skepticism: one is that historical knowledge cannot be useful without undermining the knowability of its subject; another is that the subjects of history—national characteristics—are insufficiently differentiated to be of much use.

Machiavelli begins his disquisition on the value of history by declaring that the future is discoverable in the past. Although human nature is constant, and human beings acting on the same passions produce invariably the same results, a uniform and unchanging human nature is only the substratum; above it is education working to diversify and solidify nature. If nature makes us all one and the same, education divides us by custom and habit. One province is virtuous, another is not. At any rate, uniform nature is not so determinative that accurate predictions of particular behavior can arise from it: "To see a nation keep the same customs for a long time, being either continually avaricious or continually fraudulent or having some other such vice or virtue, also makes it easy to know future things by past" (III.43.1). Custom, which is local, determines conduct more than does nature. And national character traits, produced by long-standing customs, are what history uncovers and teaches to those who will learn.

The odd thing is that those who do learn change their customs. Machiavelli wants the Florentines to learn that the French and the Germans are chronic liars and cheats. The Florentines, by contrast, are chronic naifs and dependents. Not nature—but law, custom, tradition have made them that way. Custom gave a special character to the Florentines, that of the desperate dupe. But their character can be changed by historical learning. If the Florentines had known that their forebears, the Tuscans (Etruscans), had allied with the French (Gauls) in order to defend against the Romans (300 BC), and that the French deceived them, taking their money but supplying no aid; the Florentines of the Quattrocento would not have allied with the German emperor in their war with the Visconti dukes (1401 AD)—again paying money and receiving no aid; nor in more recent times would they have bargained with the French king for the return of Pisa (1494 AD). Were the Florentines to learn from history, they would change their ways; and changing their ways, they would defeat the stereotypical pigeonholing which others count on in their dealings with Florence.

As to the second caveat, the cultural distinctiveness of nations is certainly compromised when Machiavelli allows the Germans to be stand-ins for the French. Perhaps from the Italian perspective all ultramontanes appear as Gallic barbarians. But they were not so described in I.55.2-3; and by calling ancient Gauls by their modern name, Machiavelli obscures whatever common beginnings these two nations might have had, making it difficult to connect the German emperor who betrayed the Florentines with the ancient French who betrayed the Tuscans. What also is obscured is the "one province" (title) from which these two peoples come. How can the Germans and the French be counted a single people when Machiavelli identifies the French as those "who inhabited Italy on this side of the Alps"?[45] It seems as if Machiavelli does not want us to define too precisely who the French and the Germans are; and if we cannot know who they are, we cannot say exactly what their characters are like. Machiavelli attests that they are greedy and unfaithful. But he has just finished explaining in the previous chapter that all princes are unfaithful (III.42). Why should faithlessness then be looked upon as a national trait? Or if it once was, does not competition make it universal? But do the Florentines even compete? If there is any people in this chapter with a character which is certain and constant, it is the gullible Florentines. They do not learn from the example of their antagonist; they do not think to become deceitful themselves. Chapter 43 is thus an exhortation to the Florentines to become more like the world, which seems to reflect not so much the diversifying power of custom (since the French and the Germans are one) as the unifying power of nature (since all princes are faithless). But then philosophy would be the better foundation for a scientific statecraft since philosophy is a better discipline than history for the study of nature.

We are still investigating the meaning of Machiavelli's untrodden path and the meaning of true historical knowledge. Machiavelli explains that his purpose in writing a commentary on Livy is that "those who read these statements of mine can more easily draw from them the utility for which one should seek knowledge of histories" (I.Pr. 2). This knowledge is not for its own sake but for the sake of some higher utility, not, that is, for the idle edification of contemporary readers but for the active imitation of ancient virtue. Ancient virtue is the prerequisite for improvements in the arts of politics and war, and political and military improvements are the means for bringing an end to "the weakness into which the present religion has led the world" and an end to "the evil that an ambitious idleness has done to many Christian provinces and cities." Such is the goal of historical knowledge. We might say then, as was said before, that Machiavelli's path is a style of writing able to move its readers from admiration to imitation, *or that Machiavelli's path, as opposed to his modes and orders, is ideology, the subordination of thought to action.*[46] (Machiavelli is an ideologist long before Marx gives to intellectuals their history-making function.) We might further say, in contradistinction to the explanation attributed to Butterfield, that this movement depends on a knowledge that is both easy and useful. In one important respect, "true knowledge of histories" is neither true nor scientific but consists of little more than wanting for one's country the glory of ancient Rome. Perhaps this is the respect in which historical knowledge is easy. Modern readers need persuading that Rome is a worthy model and that its achievements are repeatable in the modern world. For some readers then, true knowledge is true opinion, the firm belief in the desirability and the feasibility of resurrecting ancient Rome. Perhaps we have here an explanation for why Machiavelli describes in mechanical terms the imitative practices of Renaissance artists, jurists, and physicians—namely, to convince his contemporaries that devotion to the original, not exceptional talent, is all that is needed to accomplish great things.[47] The *Discourses* is a rhetorical book written to inspire its readers with visions of empire and glory (II.Pr.3). To this end it paints Rome in the brightest colors possible. Hulliung, who spurns the scientific pretensions of the book, acknowledges its mythologizing objective, classifying it as a type of history which Nietzsche calls monumental.[48] But Hulliung goes on to conclude that "Machiavelli was himself a believer in the myth of antiquity and remained convinced that a science of 'general rules,' distilled from examples of ancient virtue, was his greatest discovery."[49]

It might though be better to say that Machiavelli has a second readership in mind, one for whom true knowledge is something more than ardent desire and something less than scientific knowledge. While the *Discourses*, we believe, does not spell out a science of statecraft derivable from history (for how square then Machiavelli's comments on the *faithless* French in III.43 with his analysis in *Prince* 3 of Louis XII's failed invasion of Italy, a failure attributed to Louis's *faithful* observance of a promise made to Pope Alexander VI; or that the purportedly faithless French are there judged to be deficient in statecraft, the central principle of which is faithlessness?)—while the *Discourses* aspires not to science, it does try to teach an art of prudence to those with the brain to understand. For Machiavelli there are three orders of brains: "one that understands by itself, another that discerns what others understand, the third that understands neither by itself nor through others" (*Prince*, 22). There also are varying levels of originality and imitation. The imitator who understands how to replicate the achievements of another has a higher order of brain than the imitator who mechanically applies maxims. The former has prudence; if faced with difficulties, the prudent brain is capable of devising novel solutions.

The prudent brain first needs training, however, which it receives through confrontations with difficulties artfully arranged. The *Discourses* supplies this artful arrangement (*The Prince* too) by presenting readers with mental exercises not unlike the exercises in tactics provided to captains by the typography of the land (III.39).[50] In some cases these exercises are worked on by Machiavelli himself, in plain view, as when he considers the pros and cons of fighting at home or abroad (II.12), the advantages of artillery as an offensive or a defensive weapon (II.17), and the consequences of ruling by love or by fear (III.19-23); or when he weighs the relative importance of captains and their soldiers (III.13), or calculates the likely success-rates of impetuous and cautious modes (III.45). In many cases, though, Machiavelli simply asks his readers to consider prudently and well, as when he says in III.39.2, "whoever considers all this text will see how useful and necessary it is for a captain to know the nature of countries."

Machiavelli is teaching the art of prudence, or statecraft as an art, in the only way which this art can be taught, through maxims derived from experience and applied prudentially. What this art entails is best explained in III.39, the chapter from which the above quotation is taken. Statecraft has military command as one of its branches, and military command has hunting, "an image of a war," as its starting point and training ground. Hunting provides the captain-in-training with particular knowledge of sites. From particular knowledge his mind ascends easily to general knowledge; and with general knowledge his mind reasons usefully about new sites. The expert captain is a master of inductive and deductive reasoning, a practitioner of the "firm science" of topography. "Firm science" combines the general and the particular, the theoretical and the practical. But "firm science" is not a rigid methodology, and it certainly is not book-learning ungrounded in and unrefreshed by experience. The chapter's lead example bears out the importance of adjusting theory to practice, and it does so in a manner complementary to its lesson—by defeating firm science when its promises balloon into rodomontade.[51]

Publius Decius was a military tribune under the consul Alus Cornelius. When Cornelius fell into an ambush in the woods outside of Saticulum (343 BC), it was Decius who saved the army by seizing an unoccupied hill; but he had next to save himself, stuck on top of that hill and surrounded by Samnites at the base. In both actions Decius succeeded, as Machiavelli attests, owing to his knowledge of terrain. But only in the first action (determining from afar the utility and accessibility of the hill) did firm science assist Decius. For the claim that by "knowledge perfected" was Decius able to get past the guard posts and back to the consul (since "he would not have been able *from afar* to take sight of the ways to get away and the places guarded by enemies" [emphasis added])— this claim is flatly contradicted by the preceding statement that Decius, in disguise and with some companions, reconnoitered the enemy camp before making his escape ("'Go with me so that while some light remains we may find out the places where the enemy have posted their guards and where the way out from here lies open.'" [§2]). In other words, not by the prior study of sites was Decius able to ascertain the location of the enemy guard posts and so pass by them; rather, by first-hand observation of this particular site did he learn the way to elude his foe. Machiavelli is not repudiating firm science or perfected knowledge, but he is, it seems, insisting upon its flexible application, insisting that theory "from afar" not dictate to practice.

On other occasions Machiavelli leaves it to the reader to work out the implications of his discourses. For example, chapters 40 to 42 of book 3 present a single and evolving argument about the role of fraud in military affairs. In chapter 40, Machiavelli contends that in war glory is compatible with fraud but that there are rules to be respected and observed (break no faith; deceive avowed enemies only). In chapter 41 he allows that necessity permits suspension of these rules (the fatherland is well-defended in whatever mode), but that actions justified by necessity may be ignominious. Finally, in chapter 42 he concedes that fraud is glorious irrespective of rules (neither forced nor unforced promises bind, nor even unuseful promises), also that fraud is glorious irrespective of necessity (glory can be acquired in any action whatsoever; princes are always perfidious, and, if successful, are always praised). The transition from morality to immorality is complete, but it also is artfully disguised. The reader must be alert to small changes in the argument, able to reason with Machiavelli as well as be lectured to by him.[52]

Hulliung denies that any such instruction is going on, and he even accuses Machiavelli of cheating fortune and cheating the game of politics:[53]

> It may be added that even if Machiavelli's rules of political conduct were true, they would hold only for the opening moves of a protracted conflict. Renaissance diplomacy has been likened to a 'game of chess,' with moves and responses, strategies and counterstrategies, and one can find something of this attitude in the many letters in which Machiavelli calculates the interests of various European states. But when Machiavelli writes his political treatises he forgets politics is give-and-take, and assumes that the opening move, if clever and crafty, will win the game. He goes further: in effect he eliminates competition from the game by assuming the opponent is a poor player, easily duped.[54]

But we find in *The Prince*, one of Machiavelli's political treatises, the following discussion of fortified cities: A prince, the argument goes, who holds up inside a strong city and is not hated by his people cannot successfully be attacked by a larger force since protracted sieges are expensive and unpredictable. To this the objection is raised that the people's support will wane once the invading army burns fields and farms outside the city walls. Not so, comes the reply, not if the prince is virtuous and adopts measures to shore up the people's morale and guards himself against the chance of treachery within. What's more, most attackers will burn and pillage upon arrival, at a time when citizens' spirits are still hot for combat. But once their property is gone and they have nothing more to lose, citizens will feel a special bond with the prince who is now obligated to them and they strangely to him, since "the nature of men is to be obligated as much by benefits they give as by benefits they receive" (*Prince*, 10).

At this point Hulliung's complaint seems entirely justified, that Machiavellian opponents are poor players and easy dupes. But Machiavelli closes with the cautionary reminder that "if one considers all this well, it should not be difficult for a prudent prince to keep the spirits of his citizens firm in the siege, at first and later, provided he does not lack the wherewithal for life and defense." What does it mean to consider all this well? Is it the mark of prudence, for instance, to count on the enemy's making a mistake? Machiavelli warns about the same in *Discourses*, III.48. If, on the contrary, the prudent prince demonstrates his prudence by presupposing prudence on the part of his opponent, then the prudent prince does not rely on his opponent's committing a mistake so vital to the prince's own survival. He expects instead that the enemy will camp outside the walls leaving fields and farms undisturbed for a time. What effect then will such prudent restraint have upon the prince's subjects? Will they stand by him when the threatened punishment for their loyalty is the loss of their homes and the promised reward for their betrayal is the return of their property? This question the prince must ask himself, considering that "men forget the death of a father more quickly than the loss of a patrimony" (*Prince*, 17). This question, too, the prince must speedily decide, in advance of the enemy's arrival and before the countryside falls under enemy control. What then must the prudent prince do who has "the wherewithal for life and defense"? Machiavelli does not say, because to say would be to spoil this carefully contrived exercise in the art of prudence and so to cheat his readers of the opportunity to consider all this well.[55]

Machiavelli is an artful writer, and the presence of esotericism in his works is well documented by Strauss. One cannot read III.48 and still believe that Machiavelli is honest and straightforward with his prose, saying all that he means and meaning all that he says[56]—since after warning that fraud underlies all obvious errors committed by enemies, Machiavelli proceeds to commit an obvious error himself[57] (from which Strauss concludes that Machiavelli's errors are not lapses, but deceptions, and that Machiavelli is not a friend, but an enemy—an enemy of Christian modes and orders and of their adherents).[58] But is it necessary to suppose that Machiavelli's many deceptions add up to a hidden teaching, that they are like pieces of a puzzle which when assembled construct a picture otherwise not visible? Or is it enough to say that Machiavelli's esotericism, at least in part, serves the more modest purpose of teaching prudence to that portion of his readership with the brain to understand?[59] To this we might add that some mistakes are perhaps just that—mistakes—and that not every oddity need portend deep meaning.[60]

That mistakes are sometimes mistakes is what III.48 after all shows, contradicting in the process its own chapter title: "When One Sees a Great Error Made by an Enemy, One Ought to Believe That There Is a Deception Underneath." In the example above, the obvious mistake of leaving open the city gates was not a fraud. Now the fact that there was no fraud can be seen as a mistake by Machiavelli and in turn as a fraud by Machiavelli; or the mistake can go toward disproving the lesson of the chapter, that all obvious mistakes are frauds; for what the example itself shows is that men sometimes are foolish and cowardly (the Romans lost their nerve) and that it is itself a mistake, bordering on paranoia, always to impute fraud and conspiracy to their errant actions. (And so why not include Machiavelli's errant actions in this advice?)

The chapter's first example of a fraudulent error is also problematic, though not because it is double-edged like the second, but because of information supplied in other places. This is the shepherd's disguise used by Tuscan troops trying to lure the Romans into a trap (302 BC). The Roman legate left in charge was not fooled by this ruse, and so the Tuscans failed in their plan.[61] But then Machiavelli absolutizes the maxim delivered in the title, saying that "fraud will always be underneath" an error of the enemy (not even a "great error"), "as it is not reasonable that men be so incautious." The difficulty is that Machiavelli has recently explained, four chapters earlier (III.44), that reckless behavior is entirely reasonable, or can be, in that it imposes useful necessities upon reluctant allies and would-be opponents: The Samnites, their armies beaten by the Romans and their ambassadors refused by the Tuscans, marched into Tuscany and induced the Tuscans to take up the fight (297 BC). Likewise, Pope Julius extracted support from the French and neutrality from the Venetians by moving forcefully against Bologna (1506 AD). And Monsieur de Foix rescued Brescia by demanding safe passage through the dominion of a startled and frightened Marquis of Mantua (1512 AD). Even more troublesome is Machiavelli's argument in III.9 that audacity is the by-product of an inflexible nature. How then is one to know that a mistake is a trick and not the consequence of a character naturally impetuous? Extreme incaution may not be reasonable; on the other hand, it may be, and it may be that men are unreasonable in their behavior. In light of these examples, the conclusion seems inescapable that there can be no consistent counsel on how to respond to enemy mistakes; certainly there can be no scientific statecraft based on direct imitation of the ancients. Nor is it likely that Machiavelli supposes otherwise.[62]

⁕

While we are inclined to believe that Machiavelli's modes and orders are more imitative than innovative, prescribing in effect body-building for an already muscular politics (more terrifying punishments, more decisive execution, more combativeness from the plebs, etc.), others, as we have seen, are of the opinion that Machiavelli is a complete original—either that he invents a wholly new republic, called the impartial regime, or that he converts the art of statecraft into a history-based science. One of the attempts at explaining the originality of Machiavelli focused on the political content of his modes and orders. The other, setting politics aside, looked at Machiavelli as a first-of-a-kind researcher—the Galileo of political science, in the words of Ernest Cassirer.[63] A third attempt continues this movement from practice to theory; it regards Machiavelli as a moralist, and it construes new modes and orders to mean a new understanding of ethics. While this school of thought has many exponents, many indeed who are deserving of notice, our primary attention will go to Isaiah Berlin and his seminal essay, "The Originality of Machiavelli."[64]

Machiavelli effects a rupture with the past and is an original thinker, Berlin contends, because of what he discards, ignores, or does not countenance. Much is missing from Machiavelli that is foundational to classical and Christian thought: natural law, teleology, revelation, piety, conscience, sin, grace, redemption, absolute values.[65] Machiavelli is new because he counsels liberation from all such concerns, from hierarchies of every kind and from the great chain of being.[66] But scholars disagree as to how far and to whom this liberation extends. Berlin defines himself in opposition to Benedetto Croce, who separates the political from the ethical and who is the source of the phrase, "the autonomy of politics."[67] Croce and his followers carve out an exemption from classical-biblical morality for those political actors, few in number, who trade their souls' salvation for the good of the state—since the injunctions of the Ten Commandments and the valuations of the Sermon on the Mount are disabling encumbrances in the world of realpolitik. In effect, there is but one moral truth, Croce advises; but tragically it is a truth unacknowledged in the political arena. One consequence of the divorce of politics from ethics, where politics supplies the means and ethics supplies the ends, is that Machiavelli, the political reasoner, becomes a mere technician of power without values, passions, and purposes of his own; and his books become "how-to" manuals.[68] Wanting then to give Machiavelli a moral grounding, Berlin postulates—and this is his central insight—the existence of two moralities, one pagan and affirmed by Machiavelli, the other Christian and rejected by Machiavelli—though not rejected because it is untrue. Both moralities are true in the sense that both are ultimate ends, ways of life defensible for humans to lead. Machiavelli simply prefers and chooses the pagan values of "courage, vigour, fortitude in adversity, public achievement," etc.; while the Christian values of "charity, mercy, sacrifice, love of God, forgiveness of enemies," etc., he simply disfavors and ignores.[69] His advice, therefore, is that others must choose as well; but his fear is that men will "effect compromises, vacillate, and fall between two stools,"[70] only to leave themselves ineffective on the one hand and unsanctified on the other. Of course Machiavelli is not indifferent about the choice. The pagan end of the strong and glorious state is Machiavelli's end, too. Nevertheless, Machiavelli does not attempt to transpose values or "correct the Christian conception of a good man."[71] It is sufficient for Machiavelli, Berlin seems to say, that Christianity, as the reigning ethical doctrine, recognize the legitimacy of its pagan challenger. That done, what follows is the sorting out of means and ends, for it is imperative that the means appropriate to one ethic not be employed to achieve the ends of the other. Specifically, Christian meekness must be kept apart from politics and never permitted to pass judgment on the actions of government[72]—an example of which is the commonplace demand that elected officials be held to a higher ethical standard.[73] The significant point though is that Berlin, by ascribing moral value to political ambition, extends the range of that liberation wrought by Machiavelli; for politics, with its freedoms, is a good in its own right and not just a necessary means to a moral end.[74]

This liberation would extend further if it could be shown that Machiavelli is not so respectful of Christian morality as to hold it immune from attack and available for choosing by those who are disposed to it. Berlin says insistently that Machiavelli directs no fire against Christianity; its values he leaves untouched and unharmed. Proof of this accommodating spirit is that when Machiavelli uses the Christian vernacular, "he means by good works what any man brought up to live by Christian values means by good."[75] But the fact that Machiavelli uses moral language in its common sense does not mean that he endorses that common sense or that it survives intact his employment of it. As

Hulliung observes, "'good' . . . is frequently only a way station on the road to *virtù*."[76] What Berlin fails to appreciate is that a glorious state needs more than a few Machiavellian leaders who have made their choice for pagan morality; it needs also a great many Machiavellian followers, i.e., spirited citizens who love their fatherland and happily fight on its behalf. Actually, Berlin concedes as much ("The subjects or citizens must be Romans too. . . ."),[77] but the significance of his remark never quite registers with him, for he later expresses indifference regarding the choice which citizens make. What matters finally is that those choosing the Christian way—because they find pagan modes detestable or frightening—not assume responsibility "for the lives of others or expect good fortune."[78] In other words, what matters is that the Crocean separation of politics and ethics be respected.[79] But surely Machiavelli cannot afford this indifference. He needs soldiers, not monks. He must therefore rid society of Christians, which he can only do by attacking Christian values; for those who believe in the soul's salvation will either not want a glorious state or will try to achieve it through Christian means.[80] Hulliung delivers the knock-out blow to Berlin's two moralities:

> A much more provocative and violent thing than Berlin realizes, Machiavelli's paganism was designed to destroy part of the pagan tradition (Stoicism) and all of Christianity. Not the mutual coexistence of alternative moralities but the birth (or rebirth) of one world-view and the death of another was Machiavelli's intent—an intention quite incompatible with modern liberalism, the ideology of tolerance, pluralism, and compromise.[81]

As the quotation implies, the conviction driving Berlin's analysis is the sensibleness and desirability of liberal pluralism (a hobbyhorse ridden by Berlin in many of his writings). Automatically Machiavelli is on the side of the angels if it can be demonstrated that he helped to deliver the West from the tyranny of absolute truth.

Hulliung's alternative formulation to Croce's "autonomy of politics" (adopted partially by Berlin, his animadversions notwithstanding) is the "ubiquity of politics."[82] Liberation takes a great leap forward because gratifying appetites and pursuing the main chance is the dominant ethic in fact, though not in theory. Far from tolerating Christian and stoic morality, Machiavelli makes it his business to destroy them,[83] by redrafting the image of Rome admired and lauded by Renaissance humanists. That image has stoicism at its core, particularly a conception of virtue which subordinates expediency to nobility or aims at proving that the honorable is also useful. At the extreme, stoicism assigns all of virtue to good intentions, leaving nothing for good results; or, more radical still, it requires that results be injurious to the agent, losses instead of gains, since by self-injury alone can the agent know for certain that advantage is not his motive. (Christianity continues in this vein, making purity of heart the touchstone of virtue and the innocent child the exemplar of saintliness.) Cicero is chiefly responsible for supplying the stoic overlay to Roman history, but also Virgil, Livy, and assorted others who write as apologists for Roman imperialism. It is Cicero, for example, who warns his readers to stay clear of behaviors typical of the lion and the fox, since force and fraud are the twin seeds of human wrongdoing.[84] Cicero is eager for glory, as are the Latin humanists who precede Machiavelli, but Cicero believes that greatness can be achieved in this world without releasing the beast within man and that fame is genuine only when based on a record of good deeds. By contrast, Machiavelli relishes the force of the lion and the fraud of the fox, delights in the prospect of human beings behaving as beasts, and promises a glorious name for those accomplishing great things through evil means. "Machiavelli's innovation," states Hulliung, is "that he underscore[s] how a name can be gained by committing evil acts as well as good ones."[85] To this Hulliung adds that Machiavelli's discovery is "that humanism [is] itself incipiently Machiavellian."[86] An example is the preference of Renaissance humanism for republican politics; Machiavelli endorses this preference while turning it in an imperial direction, explaining that republics are superior regimes owing to their matchless potential for acquisition. Machiavelli is "the great subversive of the humanist tradition," Hulliung concludes, the man who "transform[s] humanism into power politics."[87]

Mansfield agrees that Machiavelli's (philosophical) newness can be found in his dispute with humanists and in the transformations he effects to their ideals.[88] Humanism is tainted by its attachment to classical philosophy and the greater value which classical philosophy places on the contemplative over the active life. What to Aristotle is leisure (*scholê*) is to Machiavelli idleness (*ozio*).[89] Likewise, classical philosophy is tainted by its attachment to Christianity, in that the classical pursuit of excellence invariably invites a divinization of its ideal. The best man of Aristotle, whose virtue is all but unattainable, becomes the providential God of Christianity before whom mere mortals humble themselves. "Any ideal elevated above human beings," says Mansfield, "is bound to be personified by them and made responsible for their good. . . ."[90] Even Roman manliness is, or can be, an ineffectual ideal, because the proud lion is often too honorable to take counsel from the wily fox and so is unfit for the dirty work of acquisition.[91] Thus the entire tradition—from Plato and Aristotle, to Cicero and Livy, to Petrarch and the humanists—being otherworldly in its orientation, is ripe for capture by Christianity. As the enemy of Christian modes and orders, Machiavelli, therefore, is simultaneously the enemy of the classics and of their humanist imitators.[92] Machiavelli, Mansfield argues, is engaged in a top-to-bottom overhaul of moral and political thought, one determined to ferret out idealism of every kind, leaving an earthbound and friendless humanity with nowhere to go, no one to help it, and nothing but acquiring to do.[93] Machiavelli is an original, a wholly new phenomenon, because he is the first committed secularist in the Western world. He also is the first modern, less for any particular innovation than for esteeming the principle of innovation and for his receptivity to change.[94]

While Mansfield and Hulliung locate the novelty of Machiavelli in the content of his modes and orders, they hesitate counting all of humanity as the intended audience of Machiavelli's teaching. According to Mansfield,

> Machiavelli enlightens princes and those who want to become princes but leaves good people in the dark they want and make for themselves. The latter are shown the seamy side of moral virtue and offered instruction in scheming evil, but Machiavelli knows his teaching will not take, for it is the good, not the evil, who are incorrigible.[95]

Hulliung seems to agree, comparing Machiavellian with Kantian ethics:

> "What if everyone did it?" is the question that Kant insists we ask ourselves. Promises must be kept and lies avoided, for if everyone broke promises and no one told the truth, life would be impossible. "Everyone will not do it," would likely be Machiavelli's reply; therefore those of us who desire to be immoralists have a license to do so.[96]

Even though Machiavelli wages war against Christian values, he does not anticipate, or for that matter desire, the complete rout of the opposition, since the success of princes and potential princes depends on their strict separation from the people.[97] While it is not quite the case that Machiavelli is a latter-day Thrasymachus, teaching an art of rhetoric to selected students in order that they might pass off as justice what in fact is their private advantage, still there is much about Machiavellian rulers which remains in the dark, if only because the ruled want it that way.

Strauss is the scholar who gives the liberation initiated by Machiavelli its widest scope. Strauss never specifies in any detail the content of Machiavelli's modes and orders,[98] perhaps because, in the end, Strauss denies that these modes and orders have any claim to originality. Nothing discovered and taught by Machiavelli, especially about the beast within man, escapes the notice and understanding of the ancients, argues Strauss. The difference is that the ancients are careful to conceal the dark side of humanity through use of poetic images and esoteric discourses, whereas Machiavelli discards such reticences and declares loudly that man is half human and half animal;[99] further, that the human half is an outer form or appearance, while the animal half, a composite of lion, fox, and wolf, is the inner reality and the seat of reason in man (*Prince*, 18).[100] What this boldness implies, says Strauss, is "a wholly new estimate of what can be publicly proposed, hence a wholly new estimate of the public and hence a wholly new estimate of man."[101] The new estimate of the public is that it can be the audience for a liberationist teaching, the liberation of appetite from moral constraint,[102] and the new estimate of man is that he is a needy, acquisitive creature without the potential for transcendence. Strauss is dismissive of Machiavelli's new estimate of man, calling it a "stupendous contraction of the horizon,"[103] but Strauss cannot fail to credit the accomplishment involved in Machiavelli's new style of teaching. Machiavelli's rhetoric, Strauss believes, is propaganda for the modern project of relieving the estate of man:

> Machiavelli is the first philosopher who believes that the coincidence of philosophy and political power can be brought about by propaganda which wins over ever larger multitudes to the new modes and orders and thus transforms the thought of one or a few into the opinion of the public and therewith into public power. Machiavelli breaks with the Great Tradition and initiates the Enlightenment.[104]

Having twice advertised the novelty of his ideas, in *Prince* 15 and in *Discourses*, I.Pr.1, Machiavelli stands just over the dividing line demarcating ancient and modern thought.

There is an enlightenment project underway in Machiavelli, and it may warrant designating Machiavelli an originator. Enlightenment is Machiavelli's untrodden path, his use of history for practical purposes, or his reduction of history to propaganda. Machiavelli takes his message to the public and so breaches the barrier dividing the few and the many. But the breach, I think, is more like a gate (loosely guarded) than a total demolition of the wall. I lean toward the Mansfield-Hulliung view that Machiavelli speaks boldly because he presumes the many to be mostly deaf to his pronouncements rather than toward the Straussian view that Machiavelli's outspokenness reflects a wholly new estimate of man. Machiavelli offers no new estimate if that estimate entails radical egalitarianism. Machiavelli is not one to combine the humors or delegitimize the elite. He respects the division between the few and the many, for he counts on having a ruling class that is astute and a public that is good. His enlightenment, therefore, is partial and attenuated, aimed at reclaiming for Christian princes the freedom of their pagan counterparts.

Next we will consider what teachings this enlightenment reveals, or how much of princely (mis)conduct the people is expected to countenance. We also will notice and ponder the fact that the liberation which enlightenment implies is sometimes tightly circumscribed, or that middle ways, ostentatiously denounced by Machiavelli, are commonly employed.

Chapter Eight

Machiavelli's Middle Ways

Scholarly opinion is by and large agreed that Machiavelli's ethical teaching is new and consequential, that it is what separates him from the past, more clearly than do his political modes and orders—an adaptation of Rome's—and that it is meant for general propagation, if not for universal adoption. So far, that teaching has been described as pagan, secular, and animalistic. The purpose of the present chapter is to examine Machiavelli's ethics using the category of the middle way (*il modo mezzo*). Very emphatically, Machiavelli rejects the middle way of classical and Christian thought, the middle way of moderation, choosing instead the extreme way of uninhibited acquisitiveness. Rome is the model for Machiavelli's ethical extremism, because Rome set its sights on world domination. But then many of Rome's practices and institutions seem situated between opposing extremes, exhibiting middle-way characteristics of their own. As it happens, the *Discourses* is replete with middle ways even as it scorns the use of them. So is Machiavelli's ethical teaching—what scholars take as the mark of his modernity—extremist or moderate? And is it new or old? We will explore some byways of this labyrinthine mystery before attempting in the final chapter to find the thread that will lead us through.

Still it will help to offer here a brief (if cryptic) mapping of our passage through the maze. Machiavelli's ethical extremism is an acquisitive strategy, which has the look of modern egoism by reason of its aggressive, impetuous, and selfish manner, but which is better compared with the glory-seeking of ancient princes. Machiavelli's ethical moderation, his attraction to the middle way, is likewise an acquisitive strategy, which resembles modern utilitarianism by virtue of its cautious and compromising temper, but which is better compared with the love of independence of ancient republicans. Machiavelli *seems* new for being so single-mindedly acquisitive; but the objects of his desire are decidedly old—greatness and liberty. He pursues them both, but at different times and with different strategies. Machiavelli also *is* new for politicizing ethical reasoning (the end justifies the means), but the change he effects is less than radical (except to his Christian contemporaries) and is limited in its range, with rulers and ruled still differentiated by the extent of their enlightenment.

Imperfect Nature

Put in the simplest of terms, Machiavelli's new morality rests on the belief that some problems are intractable and that imperfection is the way of the world. The *Discourses* bears fourfold witness to nature's deficiencies: (1) Virtue, it is maintained, is shadowed by vice causing simple regimes, trusting in the virtue of their rulers, to degenerate into corrupted versions of themselves; hence kingship becomes tyranny, aristocracy oligarchy, and democracy ochlocracy. "[N]o remedy can be applied there to prevent it [the simple regime] from slipping into the contrary because of the likeness that the virtue and the vice have in this case" (I.2.2). (2) Domestic tranquility is said to be incompatible with national greatness because the latter ambition requires an armed and politicized populace whereas the former requires that the people be disarmed and disenfranchised. Thus "one inconvenience can never be suppressed without another's cropping up" (I.6.3). (3) The tribunate is thought to have saved Rome from corruption by posing a check to patrician insolence, and yet over time the tribunate itself became corrupt and a hazard to the state. Consequently, "new orders" were needed "because in everything some evil is concealed that makes new accidents emerge" (III.11.1). (4) It is deemed wise, in the case of making war against a new enemy, to rid one's army of irrational fears by testing the enemy in advance of battle; but small fights, meant to supply morale-boosting victories, can end instead in morale-deflating defeats. Accordingly, "in the actions of men . . . besides the other difficulties in wishing to bring a thing to its perfection, one finds that close to the good there is always some evil that arises with that good" (III.37.1).[1]

As is implied by the last quotation, an imperfect nature is contested by men who expect and demand perfection. So men devise remedies in the hope of fixing nature, including remedies for many of above mentioned problems. For example, the mixed regime impedes the corruption characteristic of simple regimes; cooptation neutralizes demagogic tribunes; and observation of the enemy from the safety of well-positioned fortresses eliminates the need for risky skirmishes. Still, there are limits to reason's remedial powers, and optimism about the future is mostly out of place. We skipped over the second problem, of combining harmony with greatness, because it admits of no remedy but requires a choice instead. Those who choose greatness also choose tumult, and those who choose harmony also choose weakness. In addition, the quotation from III.37.1 concludes with the dispiriting reminder that good without evil is difficult to acquire unless assistance is given by fortune.

Imperfection abounds. Rome had a better founding than Sparta, and yet Sparta was happy and Rome was not. Happiness, apparently, is a concomitant of domestic tranquility. Sparta opted for concord and was the happiest of regimes; Rome opted for glory and suffered "some degree of unhappiness" (I.2.1). Likewise, the prince who is ambitious for glory will want to rule over a thoroughly corrupt state, since correcting corruption is supremely glorious, whereas maintaining goodness is forgettably ordinary. And yet this same prince, "if he is born of man . . . will be terrified away from every imitation of wicked times and will be inflamed with an immense desire to follow the good" (I.10.6). Wanting the good and wanting glory are incompatible desires; and the prince who achieves glory through employment of extraordinary means is not happy. He is not happy if, for instance, he has many enemies and must secure himself with many scandals; whereas he is happy if without scandal he secures himself because his enemies are few and the public supports his rule (I.16.4). The most beloved and happiest of princes is the hereditary prince who governs justly and looks after the common good; but security makes him unambitious, and lacking ambition he adds little to his state. Conversely, the new prince hungry for glory—although unloved, unhappy, and insecure—expands his state. And when this new prince is a captain in a republic, he runs the risk of being treated ungratefully by a people jealous of its liberty. A free city has two ends, not one—acquisition and liberty; and so "it must be that in one thing or the other it errs through too much love" (I.29.3).

As acquisition suffers when liberty is too much loved (ingratitude toward the city's most able acquirers), so liberty suffers when avarice is without limit. Rome's "ultimate greatness" came at a point well short of its ambition, when it had conquered and unified Italy but had yet to subdue the world (I.20.1). Apparently, once Rome expanded beyond Italy, each addition of new territory cost Rome a portion of its old liberty.[2] Part of the cause was that conquered peoples took their vengeance by corrupting Roman mores (I.19.2). Another part came from within Rome itself, from the fact that imperial success eliminated all opponents able to threaten the city. With too much security Rome relaxed its defenses, electing to high office demagogic and free-spending individuals, while neglecting to honor its more capable captains (I.18.3, III.16.2). External danger (nature's necessity for cities with fertile sites) helped to make Rome virtuous, so with danger's abatement Rome slid into corruption. On the other hand, when still facing this danger, and for the better management of the same, Rome prolonged commands; but extended commands were what caused the demise of Rome. To anyone who studies closely the Roman experience, the world exhibits all of the perfection of a sardonic Catch-22.[3]

Middle Ways Rejected

Machiavelli is shrill in his opposition to the middle way because it identifies a morality confident that perfection inheres in nature or emanates from God, a morality associated with untainted goods and formal ends.[4] While the middle way can be variously conceived—and in Machiavelli there are as many as five different understandings—when first it appears, in I.6.4, it describes the perfect politics of the aristocratic mixed regime, the "true political way of life and the true quiet of a city." This is the regime to which reason would bring you if necessity did not intervene. It is a regime modeled after the Spartan and Venetian governments, that is, a mixed regime without substantial popular involvement—and so without tumult—but also a regime settled in a strong place with no empire on its borders and with no imperial ambitions of its own. This middle-way republic represents a perfect balance of forces, an equilibrium and place of rest which might endure forever were it not for the fact that necessity does intervene.

For the truth about nature is that it is penurious, not bountiful; accidental in its superintendence, not purposeful; friendly toward man only—and ironically—by the necessities it imposes. Nature is motion; so balanced states depending on rest are idealized perfections unsustainable in practice. Nature is acquisition; or acquisitiveness, a form of motion, is by nature. Nature punishes moderation since moderate ambition is weakness when measured against the unrestrained appetites of others. In order for moderation to be good, everyone else would have to be moderate, too. But everyone is not moderate (I.1.4); nor is everyone faithful (*Prince*, 18). Thus even if a person were content to hold on to what he had already, he still would need to accumulate more just to protect against those who would leave him with less. Maintainers become acquirers (I.5.4), and princes whose ingratitude arises from suspicion become princes ungrateful because they are avaricious (I.29-30). One appetite blends into another; when fear is allayed, desire is aroused (I.37.1, I.46.1); when defense is successful, offense takes over (II.27). The human soul has no right order, no means and no cause to keep appetites in tow.[5] No due measure exists, so only relative measurement obtains, meaning that more is always better than less. In sum, virtue is not for its own sake, and the rule of reason is either a tyranny or a mirage.

The morality of unattainable perfection is thus one of the manifestations of the middle way. A second, and related, manifestation is the "neutral way" of exact justice. The two are related but not identical since justice is an imaginary good both because humans cannot provide it and because humans do not want it. We covered this before: Justice is the giving and receiving of what is deserved. Because justice is an entitlement, a benefit owed, it is taken for granted and under-appreciated except in those case where, injustice being feared, justice comes as a relief and a surprise (I.16.3). People are more grateful when not suffering the injuries they dread than when given the rewards they have due. The advice then to the prince is that he hold justice in reserve, dispensing it sparingly and when least expected; that way justice is seen as a free gift and not as an earned wage. Justice should be partisan, not neutral, used to caress friends and eliminate enemies. Rome dealt with rebellious subjects in just this manner, governing them so that they could not offend (having no means) or would not offend (having no cause). Never did Rome "use the neutral way" of giving to subjects their just deserts (II.23.2). Rewards and punishments in Rome rather served the political purpose of deterring offenses or of encouraging loyalty.

The middle way is not only some moral perfection, more talked about than real; it is also a compromise, unwelcome but acceded to nonetheless. The tribunate with consular authority is called a middle way (I.47.1). It was a compromise with the plebs who for years had demanded the abolition of the consulate or its opening to plebeian candidates. Neither party got all that it wanted; each settled for half-a-loaf. In the short run, the patricians came out the better since plebeian deference and patrician trickery cooperated to keep the magistracy a patrician preserve. In the long run, however, the plebs was the victor, since a restored consulate included the provision that one office go always to a plebeian. For his part Machiavelli is disapproving, noting that this middle-way compromise compromised executive authority (I.39.2, II.33, III.15). He also is disapproving of the middle way in III.2.1, where the man of quality renounces ambition, claiming to be satisfied with peace and quiet. The middle way here is a compromise, a mean between advancement and loss, which the man of quality believes can be his if he adheres strictly to another middle way, that between befriending the prince and opposing his rule. But, says Machiavelli, "men who have quality [cannot] choose to abstain even when they choose it truly and without ambition, because it is not believed of them."

A fourth meaning of the middle way also involves the element of choice (and will occasion a second look at the Croce-Berlin thesis). This is the middle way between complete goodness and inhuman cruelty. The new prince of I.26 is advised to avoid this middle way, just as the man of quality of III.2 is advised to avoid the middle way of political neutrality. The new prince with weak foundations can only preserve his state by making everything new and dependent on himself. Philip of Macedon, father of Alexander, is the exemplar. He moved populations around as if they were sheep and he were their shepherd; by this and like modes "from a small king [he] became prince of Greece." But so heartless are these modes, "the enemy to every way of life, not only Christian but human," that "any man whatever" should prefer a private life of goodness to a public life of crime. Perhaps it is the case that a man of quality cannot choose to be other than he is; but a man in a private station can choose not to become a new prince, and Machiavelli beseeches him "to live in private rather than as king with so much ruin to men." On the other hand, a private man is free to choose princely power if he "does not wish to take this first way of the good." There is a choice to be made, and in making this choice personal preference is allowed to override moral absolutes. What the new prince cannot do—at least not with Machiavelli's blessing—is choose the rigors of new power and then behave as if he never has left the sheltered confines of private life; since worse than the total wickedness of new power is the middle way between the "altogether wicked" (*tutti cattivi*) and the "altogether good" (*tutti buoni*). This middle way tries combining the ends of wicked politics—the getting and keeping of state—with the means of private goodness. But politics is governed by its own rules; it exists in its own world; it is autonomous. So Croce is right! (Chapter 26 is, after all, the locus classicus for the autonomy of politics thesis.) Berlin too is right in calling politics a second morality, if only because politics rises above mere technique by the evil it prevents and by the good it can do. Politics is a morality in that, when done right, common goods are its product. But doing politics right, particularly in those extremities brought on by new power, requires a complete disavowal of classical and Christian morality, the objectives of which are individual happiness and the soul's salvation.[6] The trouble is that political men are timid, diffident, and vacillating, unconvinced that all is permitted in defense of the state. So they backslide, try having it both ways, combine realpolitik with paternosters. Weakened by their scruples, they gravitate toward a middle way of moral cowardice, with worse results than if they had opted for the altogether evil.

However much of traditional morality can be tolerated in private life, little of it can be tolerated in public life and none of it at all (except for mere pretense) in the public life of new states. Thus the Berlin-like choice which Machiavelli describes in I.26 (wholly good, partly good, wholly evil) applies chiefly to individuals and not to the communities they inhabit. Communities have public lives and public men to manage the commonweal. Berlin supposes that communities choose whether to be large or small, powerful or weak, prosperous or poor;[7] and that in making this choice, no "correct, objectively valid solution to the question of how men should live can in principle be discovered."[8] Or Berlin supposes that the classical-Christian tradition has failed to satisfy modern-day liberals as to the reality of the summum bonum; that free choice, unsupported by God or nature, is therefore the truth about the human condition; and that the discovery of this truth by Machiavelli was the "dynamite" which blew apart the rock upon which Western civilization had been founded.[9] Berlin, though, is better at explaining liberal relativism than he is at explaining Machiavelli; for while Machiavelli may have doubted the reality of revelation and of natural law, the summum bonum of the tradition, he did not doubt, anymore than did Hobbes after him, the reality of necessity, the summum malum of nature. Nature's great evil is necessity, or death. States then have no real choice about how to constitute themselves, a choice which they are free to make but unable to justify. Either they choose growth, power, and prosperity, or they die. Necessity settles the issue and justifies the choice. Although Berlin maintains that buried within Machiavelli's thought is a time-bomb of disorienting doubt, Berlin also admits that necessity is what orients Machiavelli and that his convictions are firm regarding the one right course of action: Machiavelli, says Berlin, "is convinced that states which have lost the appetite for power are doomed to decadence and are likely to be destroyed by their more vigorous and better armed neighbours."[10]

We might add that Machiavelli is oriented not only by the summum malum of eventual death but also by the summum bonum of endless life, or by glory.[11] If the necessities of new power justify evil-doing in I.26, the ambition for greatness justifies it in I.27. Giovampagolo Baglioni of Perugia is the example in I.27 of the wickedness of the insufficiently wicked. Baglioni failed to kill Pope Julius II when the pope, as part of his campaign against the tyrants of the Romagna, entered Perugia unarmed and removed Baglioni from office. Machiavelli happened to be among the "prudent men who were with the pope" and who were dumbfounded by the pope's recklessness and by Baglioni's cowardice. Baglioni was a coward, in the estimation of these prudent men, because he did not assassinate a pope and enrich himself on the booty of his cardinals. The explanation agreed upon was not that Baglioni had scruples and a conscience and so could not bring himself to employ unholy means against the servants of God; for Baglioni was "a villainous man, who was taking his sister for himself, who had killed his cousins and nephews so as to reign," and into whose breast "no pious respect could descend" (§1). In the chapter above, I.26, the explanation for taking half measures and steering a middle course was that conscience doth make cowards of us all (so to speak). But the prudent men of chapter 27 bent their analysis in another direction, claiming that Baglioni "did not know how" or "did not dare . . . to engage in an enterprise in which everyone would have admired his spirit." Baglioni's hesitation originated not in conscience but in smallness of mind. He was perfectly prepared to commit heinous crimes on behalf of small ends, of "being incestuous or a public parricide" for the sake of personal pleasure and the princedom of Perugia. But when it came to an enterprise "that would have left an eternal memory of himself," his courage failed him (§2). The world, it seems, is full of petty criminals; but big criminals are a rarity. The story is told in Augustine's *The City of God* of a captured pirate who, when reproached by Alexander the Great for infesting the seas, accused the emperor in turn of infesting the world.[12] What the pirate had done with a single craft and at risk of punishment—so went the retort—Alexander was doing with a mighty fleet and with impunity. Augustine uses the story to reveal the unprettified truth about politics, that it is brigandage and that cities are criminal gangs too powerful to punish. But rather than suppose, with Augustine, that an emperor is the moral equivalent of a pirate—only worse, because of the multitude of the emperor's crimes—Machiavelli supposes that acquisition on the scale of empire-building changes criminality into history and self-gratification into public responsibility. Machiavelli speaks of an evil that "has greatness in itself or is generous in some part." His lament is that most men—the Baglioni's of the world—"do not know how to enter into it" (§1).

In chapter 26 Machiavelli opposed the "altogether good" of private life with the "altogether wicked" of political life. Here in chapter 27 he puts opposite the "perfectly good" a new category called the "honorably wicked" (*onorevolmente cattivi*) (§1). Apparently, the killing of Pope Julius would have been "honorably wicked," not "altogether wicked." Apparently, too, the honorably wicked is a mean between the altogether wicked and the altogether good. Strauss points out that Machiavelli's condemnation of middle ways is in fact a condemnation of "certain middle ways" (*certe vie del mezzo* [I.26.1]).[13] Honorable wickedness is an approved middle way because it is unlike the middle ways we have examined thus far: it is not a state of moral and political perfection midway between vices and defective regimes; it is not a distribution of rewards and punishments in exact accordance with what is owed; it is not a compromise begrudged by all; nor is it an instance of moral weakness. Instead, it represents one half of those praiseworthy qualities useful to a prince in governing his subjects. A prince rules by love or by fear, and preferably by both—alternating between these modes as required by the times. The lovable qualities—such as liberality, mercy, faithfulness—are called good by the generality and earn the prince praise. The fearsome qualities—such as rapacity, cruelty, faithlessness—are called wicked by the generality and earn the prince blame. Condemned for their wickedness but condoned for their usefulness, they are the source of much moral confusion. These are the qualities which Machiavelli calls "honorably wicked"—wicked, ordinarily, but praiseworthy nonetheless because they take "the more honorable part" (I.6.4), the part of strength,[14] in responding to necessity. The good and the honorably wicked qualities occupy a middle ground whose territory is liberally defined—not that one point of equilibrium which represents the just-right middle of Aristotelian virtue. Machiavelli's middle is comparatively spacious, with room enough for princely maneuvering. But still it is bracketed by extremes which if entered bring the prince blame. At the one extreme is the altogether wicked; an altogether wicked prince is hated, especially by the populace. At the other extreme is the altogether good; an altogether good prince—a do-gooder and a goody-goody—is despised, especially by the great. The do-gooder, though, is not necessarily despised by the public, which supposes the perfectly good prince to be the ideal (but which, as part of its moral confusion, prizes toughness in the bargain). Machiavelli warns against this popular tendency to praise the altogether good, and he comes to the defense of the honorably wicked. *In fact, we might say that the substitution of the honorably wicked for the altogether good within that category of praiseworthy qualities constitutes the essence of Machiavelli's new ethical teaching, his new modes and orders.*[15] At the same time Machiavelli adopts wholesale from conventional morality its valuations of the good and the altogether wicked.[16] Machiavelli has no misgivings about those lovable qualities which people praise and call good. They lie in the virtuous lane of the middle way of praiseworthy conduct. But because the other lane, consisting of fearsome and honorably wicked qualities, is equally useful for travel (even more useful), Machiavelli advises the prince to drive in them both, skirting around "traffic" so as to maximize his speed. (The "left lane" of honorably wicked qualites usually is better for speed, but sometimes it backs up causing the "right lane" of good qualities actually to be faster.) Likewise, Machiavelli accepts from conventional morality its condemnation of the altogether wicked. Such conduct is indeed unchristian and inhuman, and the hatred it provokes is entirely justified. Such is true even of the new prince in a new state—he is a tyrant and is understandably hated for his tyranny; Machiavelli does not say otherwise (at least not directly). What he does say, however—and this should be added to his defense of the honorably wicked—is that the altogether wicked is sometimes necessary and in any event does less political harm than the partly good.[17]

Presumably, if the altogether wicked is outside the parameters of praiseworthy behavior, it also is disqualified from receiving glory. Machiavelli's primary example of a prince who forfeited glory because of his wickedness is Agathocles of Syracuse, the subject of *Prince* 8. Agathocles is labeled a criminal prince because crime was his means to power, as was virtue the means to power for the founder princes of *Prince* 6, fortune for the vassal princes of *Prince* 7, and election for the civil princes of *Prince* 9. Even though Agathocles' accomplishments were sufficient to rate him a "most excellent captain," nevertheless, "his savage cruelty and inhumanity, together with his infinite crimes" have kept him forever outside the company of the "most excellent men." Thus Machiavelli is not forcing his readers to countenance the conduct of an altogether wicked prince. Agathocles he condemns using conventional standards of praise and blame.

But while Machiavelli accepts these standards, he also plays with them some, pushing the boundaries of the middle way in Agathocles' direction. In the cavalcade of princes presented above, Agathocles is positioned next to Cesare Borgia, the fortunate prince of chapter 7. Cesare was fortunate because power was given to him by his father, Pope Alexander VI, and by the king of France, Louis XII. But Cesare took all the right steps to solidify that power and to make it his own, and he is twice recommended as someone to emulate; thus he is a model for imitation not unlike the virtuous princes of chapter 6. Among Cesare's more spectacular deeds was the betrayal and execution of his allies at Sinigaglia. We mention this because Agathocles did much the same thing—he summoned the citizens of Syracuse to assembly and then ordered his soldiers to execute the nobility. So we wonder what difference there is between Cesare's virtue and Agathocles' crimes and why the actions of Agathocles deprived him of glory.[18]

Machiavelli says that Agathocles lacked virtue: "Yet one cannot call it virtue to kill one's citizens, betray one's friends, to be without faith, without mercy, without religion; these modes can enable one to acquire empire but not glory." What Agathocles lacked were those qualities of goodness which make a prince loved. Goodness is needed for glory, it seems, but not for empire. We are not talking about genuine attributes of character but only about the face of character which the prince reveals to the public. Agathocles wore always the face of a cruel prince; he was too cruel, perhaps because "savage cruelty and inhumanity" bespoke his true nature and caused his "infinite crimes"; or, alternately, because he "became king of Syracuse not only from private fortune but from a mean and abject one." Machiavelli seems to prefer the latter explanation: "Born of a potter, he [Agathocles] always kept to a life of crime at every stage of his career. . . ." Agathocles belongs to a category of princes that is neither virtuous nor fortunate. Perhaps then his problem was that in being so independent of fortune, no veneer of legitimacy could cover his rise to power, and he had always to use criminal means to accomplish his ascent. By this argument, fortune, while it may detract from virtue, is the necessary precondition of glory. Machiavelli says of the emperor Maximinus in *Prince* 19 that he lost his state in part because, having "herded sheep in Thrace . . . the whole world was excited by indignation at the baseness of his blood."[19] And in the *Discourses* Machiavelli notes that good fortune can save a prince from scandal: ". . . when fortune is so propitious to the virtuous man that they [his envious rivals] die ordinarily, he becomes glorious without scandal, when without obstacle and without offense he is able to show his virtue" (III.30.1). Fortune's role is to clear the way, and the way is clearest of all for an hereditary prince, since he is free to take from the example of Marcus Aurelius those parts "which are fitting and glorious to conserve a state that is already established and firm" (*Prince*, 19). Most glorious of all would be the hereditary prince with so clear a road that he could afford to *be*—and not just *appear to be*—"all mercy, all faith, all honesty, all humanity, all religion" (*Prince*, 18), or the prince who is altogether good.

This line of inquiry leads to the conclusion that glory belongs to the safest of princes because they have the least cause to give offense. One element of glory is that the prince show respect for the moral opinions of the generality. But another element of glory requires that something difficult and consequential be achieved; and hereditary princes, observing ancient orders (III.5; *Prince*, 2), achieve little of consequence. We remember also that Machiavelli reserved the highest glory for princes who take on the rough job of reforming corrupt cities. Although Machiavelli on the occasion invited the juvenile belief that glory is a pursuit without danger or disadvantage,[20] his description of the reformer in I.18.4 established conclusively that reforming corruption is a hazardous and bloody affair. And yet still the reformer is glorious, or Machiavelli would have it that glory is his prize. Being cruel, it seems, does not preclude being glorious—at least it should not. Hannibal, after all, was inhumanly cruel, but Hannibal is counted glorious all the same (III.21.4; *Prince*, 17). And Julius Caesar acquired glory by crime (I.52.3). Sometimes political achievements are so enormous that glory cannot be withheld from their authors. In these cases historians are wont to praise the achievement but condemn the cruelty that was its cause (*Prince*, 17). They are wrong to do so, Machiavelli implies, because one cannot approve the end without approving the means. If fortune, therefore, is the precondition of glory, what fortune supplies is less a scandal-free, give-no-offense path into the hearts and minds of the public than an opportunity for greatness, scandalous and offensive to the degree that the opportunity is great. A prince's glory comes from his virtue which needs opportunity from fortune to show what it can do.

Agathocles lacked virtue, it is said. But then thrice it is said that Agathocles possessed virtue. The common view of virtue is that it is goodness. Machiavelli would have it mean honorable wickedness as well, another term for which is "cruelty well-used" (*crudeltà bene usate*). Machiavelli finds in the career of Agathocles all of the elements of cruelty well-used; indeed, it is by way of Agathocles that Machiavelli introduces this most important concept. To use cruelty well is to commit crimes early and all at once and then to turn these crimes to the benefit of the people—a sign of which is the people's loyalty even in times of war. So Agathocles was not persistently and naturally cruel; he used cruelty when it served his and, increasingly, the public's interest. That interest culminated with the expulsion of the Carthaginians from Sicily, a feat accomplished by attacking Syracuse's besiegers in their own land. More than a century before Scipio invaded Africa and won a war against Carthage, Agathocles did the same and showed the way. And yet Scipio is glorious, the hero of the Second Punic War, and Agathocles is a villain. Why? The fault lies less with Agathocles than with historians responsible for his fame, those same historians who approve the end but condemn the means. Polybius denounces one such historian, Timaeus, for what Polybius regards as a slanderous and one-sided account.[21] Machiavelli, though, prefers a more circuitous route, endorsing the indictment and making a hash of the evidence.[22] Thus Agathocles is classified a criminal prince, and criminal princes are treated as separate from virtuous, fortunate, and civil princes. But when Machiavelli gets down to particulars, these categories of new princes lose much of their distinctiveness: The civil prince of chapter 9 is elective in theory and a usurper in fact, playing the class warfare card in a bid to become absolute despot. At the same time the criminal prince of chapter 8 is elected to office, or can be; Agathocles was chosen for the praetorship and promoted to all lesser ranks and could have had the principate "conceded to him by agreement." The fortunate prince of chapter 7 employs modes, as noted, that are at once virtuous and criminal; Cesare converted the arms of others into arms of his own, and he betrayed his associates and had them all murdered. Conversely, the virtuous prince of chapter 6 is also fortunate, not only by the opportunity which fortune provides him, but also by the fact—in the cases of Moses, Cyrus, Romulus, and Theseus—that he is "to the manor born," a member of a royal household. Plus Moses killed "infinite men" (III.30.1), Romulus killed his brother (I.9.1), and Cyrus rose by fraud (II.13.1); so the virtuous prince is a criminal. And since Moses was elected by God, this virtuous prince was something of a civil prince to boot. By rendering these classifications practically indistinguishable, Machiavelli—quietly, discreetly—redeems Agathocles and nominates him for glory. All new princes need virtue, are fortunate, use crime, and rule for the sake of, if not with the consent of, the people.

One other point. Machiavelli's reputation is kindred to Agathocles'—that is, too cruel for glory. Machiavelli is ostentatiously cruel, condoning fratricide and calling on princes to assassinate popes. He gives offense and risks the condemnation of history. But then, like Agathocles, Machiavelli uses cruelty well, for his purpose is to harden people, contemporary Christians, to the necessities of political life. Glory motivates princes; but glory will not be awarded if princes stray too far from what the generality believes and if princes offend too much.[23] Thus princes must conceal; but also the generality must be taught to regard cruelty well-used as an honorable evil and honorable evil as a cause of fame.

The topic of enlightenment has come up before, i.e., the propagation of erstwhile secret truths to the masses. Strauss contends that Machiavelli is the architect of *the* Enlightenment and on the modern side of the ancient-modern divide for the reason that he tells the truth about the bestiality of man, exposing in the process the moral pretensions of the ruling class. One consequence of this view, of a low but equal humanity, is the return of democratic government and the leveling of social barriers. Some distinctions may nevertheless persist, as between teachers and students, and leaders and led; but since all that is known is widely disseminated and since those in office serve at the sufferance of the public, the tendency of history is toward the homogenization of groups and types. A fair inference from Strauss's argument is that Machiavelli believes in the natural identity of the people and the great and that he devotes his work to bringing about the union of the two. But it seems hardly necessary to carry Machiavelli's enlightenment project this far.[24] However bestial is the human race, the people and the great are different (in their acquiring capacities), and all that Machiavelli intends by instructing the public is to furnish his princes with the latitude they require to function and prosper in a world structured by necessity. Moreover, the knowledge Machiavelli imparts is old, not new; it is the knowledge of how Rome acquired.

In our survey of Machiavellian middle ways, four have been discussed already. There is a fifth, although it too has been considered under the heading of the "honorably wicked" (I.27). The fifth middle way is that of maximum acquisition. The prince is one manifestation of this middle way—the prince who acquires and maintains state by avoiding the extremes of the altogether good and the altogether wicked. Machiavelli calls it the "true way" and contends that Rome followed it closely. Rome followed the true way when it acquired with profit: by enfranchising new peoples, allying with unequal partners, dispatching colonists, placing booty in state coffers, attacking by raids and by battles instead of by sieges, enriching the public while impoverishing the private, and enforcing strict military discipline (II.19.1).[25] Rome veered from the true way when in quiet times it disesteemed its reputed citizens or allowed them and others to use private favors to ascend to public power. But institutional remedies, plus the consequent disorder, soon returned Rome to the true way (III.16.2, III.28.1).

Mainly, though, the true way is occupied by individuals whose attachment to it proves impossible to sustain, by princes who desire too much to be loved or who delight too much in being feared (III.21.3), by captains who breech the suitable limits of impetuosity or caution because their actions are determined by nature and by habit (III.9.1), or by men of quality who try in vain to position themselves between open hostility and genuine friendship toward their rulers (III.2.1). No more then is this middle way consistently open to travel than are all other middle ways; the difference between them is that this middle way, called true because its object is acquisition, should be traversed, whereas the other middle ways interfere with acquisition and should be avoided.[26] Thus we are brought back to Machiavelli's much reiterated advice, best stated in III.9.1, that "since one cannot observe the true way . . . he comes to err less and to have prosperous fortune who matches the time with his mode . . . and always proceeds as nature forces you." Walking the true way, because it is a corridor bounded on its sides, broader than a point but narrow nonetheless, a *via stretta*, we might say—walking the true way involves continuous looking to the right and to the left to check where you are—am I too loved, am I too feared? It involves a certain cautiousness even among those whose mode and nature are impetuous. Likewise, leaving the true way involves a certain heedlessness even among those whose mode and nature are cautious. Machiavelli counsels leaving the true way, letting go, applying no brakes.[27] Translated into today's lingo, Machiavelli's advice is to "let it all hang out" and to "just do it!" But then Machiavelli has a parable of his own which captures the devil-may-care spirit of his advice: A young Florentine was once afflicted by a mysterious running disease. Wherever he went the urge to run overtook him, and he broke into a gallop. A doctor applied a cure, which for a time worked. The young man assumed a decorous and sensible air, full of respect and regard. Then one day, as he approached the *Via Larga*,

> his hair began to stand on end. Nor could this youth restrain himself, when he saw this street so straight and wide, from turning again to his old pleasure; and everything else abandoned, there came back to him the fancy for running, which goes on working and never is quiet; so when he came to the head of the street, he dropped his cloak on the ground and said: "Christ can't keep me here," and off he ran.[28]

Middle Ways Adopted

Machiavelli is notorious for his rejection of the middle way and the morality of self-control it entails, for his embrace of boundless acquisition in its stead, even to the point of propagating a counter-morality of self-interest and self-indulgence (if not of self-discovery and self-expression). The middle way is out; the extreme way is in. And yet the opposite is just as often true, probably more often true—that Machiavelli proposes following the middle way. This middle way, no less than the extreme way of the "runner," has acquisition as its objective; but since the way is middling, the means are moderate. There is in Machiavelli a recommendation for acquisition by moderate means. Like its counterpart, the middle way of the deceiving prince, this moderate middle way is a difficult path to negotiate, Machiavelli concedes. But rather than foreswear the effort with his usual disclaimer, that staying on course is impossible because human nature will not permit it, Machiavelli fixes his sights on adhering to the mean and holding the center together. The thesis propounded here, and developed in the last chapter, is that the middle way bespeaks Machiavelli's genuine regard for liberty, as the extreme way bespeaks his regard for greatness.

First among the middle ways which Machiavelli is determined to secure is the mixed regime. The mixed regime combines elements from all of the simple regimes. If one supposes that it combines the best elements of kingship, aristocracy, and democracy, then the impression is created that the mixed regime is a political ideal where energy, wisdom, and patriotism cohabit and endure. But Machiavelli does not conceive of the mixed regime this way.[29] It is not an ideal intended by nature and accomplished by art. In the first place, the mixed regime rests on the conviction that human beings are bad and in need of watching. Power is divided to prevent its abuse, not to increase participation and to utilize talent. Unchecked power is oppression and tyranny; checked power is liberty, the pay-off for vigilance. Liberty, not moral virtue, is the first object of the mixed regime, while justice is an inadvertency—what happens when princes, without fortresses for safety or friendships purchased by tribute, are forced to deal fairly with their own people (II.24.2, II.30.2). The mixed regime is thus consonant with "the effectual truth of things"; by contrast, simple regimes, because of the confidence they place in the rulers and the goodness they expect of the ruled, resemble imaginary republics. Simple regimes are short-lived, whereas the mixed regime is stable and long-lasting. While not a perfect remedy for factious tumult or a permanent escape from the cycle of regimes, the well-ordered mixed regime experiences the full life which nature has ordained for it. This it does by keeping all of its elements in balance and by returning periodically to its origins.

The mixed regime is also a government under law. Now the rule of law is another middle way, for it is a mean between necessity and choice. Nature's necessity forces people to be hard-working, self-sacrificing, and public-spirited.

If the site is sterile, for example, there can be no relaxation of effort. At the other extreme choice proliferates; but what people choose is corruption, as when, on a fertile site, labor is neglected. In between there is law, a substitute for necessity compatible with choice. Law is chosen when it is made and chosen ever after as it is maintained; but law also imposes limitations. Law is freely chosen restraint, or self-mastery and self-control. It is a middle way that is at once fragile, because open to corruption, and powerful, because an instrument of acquisition: the lawful republic on a fertile site is the regime best constituted and situated to acquire and expand. As for the citizens who abide by law, they occupy a mean between humble servitude and proud domination. Without law they are an excitable mob, careening from passion to passion. But when law has them shackled, they are constant, steady, and reliable (I.58.2).

Citizens divide into plebs and patricians. The plebs is of a middling sort, positioned in a middle between too much suspicion and too much deference. In order to protect itself from misrule, the plebs must expose the hidden malignities lying beneath the benefactions of its rulers (I.3.2). The tribunes, especially, perform this task, serving as prosecutors, ombudsmen, and investigative reporters all in one. But these tribunes need to serve a people able to hear bad news, a cynical people bruised by collisions with the great and selfish in its own right. Otherwise the accusations of tribunes will fall on deaf ears (as when their exposing the fraud of the Sybilline books had no effect [I.13.2]). So there is badness in the people; but not so much that it is ungrateful or so ungrateful that it directs its vengeance against the whole order of the nobility. Class warfare is one extreme which at all costs must be avoided. The other extreme is patriarchy. The people wants security more than it wants liberty. It wants to be cared for, loved, and protected. It wants a benevolent prince, a father-figure, to hold its hand and feel its pain. The people comes to this state of childlike dependency because the other side of its character is goodness. The good people sacrifices for the commonweal, prays to the gods, and respects the dignity of august individuals. There could be no community without a people willing to obey; but the people's trust can easily turn to obsequiousness, especially when there is a prince who knows how to beguile and deceive. So liberty requires that the people hoe to a middle way between the extremes of goodness and badness.

Liberty also requires a guardian, someone with quasi-sovereign power to safeguard the constitution. The people is nominated because it is less ambitious than the great and so a trustworthy defender of the liberty of others. But the under-ambitious people is nominated for an over-ambitious state, that is for an expansionary state with empire on its mind. Ironically, the state which is out to get more needs as the guardian of its liberty the class which is satisfied to keep what it has. But then the guardian of liberty is not so much the captain at the helm as the ballast in the hold. The guardian of liberty stabilizes the ship of state as it sails the seas of acquisition. The imperial enterprise is itself a balancing act, with equal attention paid to war on the frontiers and to unity back home.

Of course the masters of the midway are the nobles. They lack the power to oppress the people, so lions they are not; but nor are they foxes exactly, since their social position is exalted. They are in the middle, needing to temporize in order to stay in charge. Temporizing is a mean between resistance and capitulation. One of their favorite tactics is to pretend to religious belief, a simulation comparable to Brutus's feigned stupidity, except that in the eyes of the public they sacrifice none of their dignity by being so credulous. Piety makes them approachable and trustworthy. By seeming like the people, they hide their distinctiveness, their radical skepticism tending toward atheism. Hiding is what the nobles do, and for malignant reasons. Religion is a fraud, but if the nobles use it to defraud—to march the people off to needless wars, to dissuade it from electing its own kind—they risk exposing themselves and bringing religion into disrepute. So the nobles must use religion for public purposes only. In this instance it is not the people's vigilance which holds them in line; it rather is their own self-discipline. To some degree, the nobles internalize restraint and achieve what looks like true moral virtue.[30] The middle way they walk is thus tighter than the balancing of powers in a constitutional system. But the nobles are the smart ones and should be able to maintain their footing and find their way.

Even princes know something of the middle way. The founder prince enjoys great latitude in his rise to power. Of course there is nothing of middle-way restraint in the killing of one's brother, and the endorsement of *uno solo* execution is the ultimate expression of power-politics extremism. But the founder prince is enjoined to share power with others, to arm the people and create a senate. More importantly—for the long-term health of his state—he is advised not to imitate Lycurgus in outlawing constitutional change. Part of the reason is that no order is so perfect as to be perfect always—people change who live under it; the order itself changes as these changed people interpret and administer it; the world around changes, too. Motion, not rest, is the effectual truth of things. The other part of the reason is that a perfect founding—deemed such by law and tradition—draws all glory to the founding prince. Subsequent generations have the maintenance of this perfection as their sole responsibility (such as occurs when citizens submit their legislation to constitutional review).[31] It might seem the crowning achievement of personal ambition to shine so brightly as to blot out the lights which shine from all others. But the founder cannot monopolize glory without jeopardizing it at the same time, since his descendants are apt to grow indifferent and sluggish if burnishing his image is all that they do; or, what's worse, they are apt to grow resentful and restless and undertake reforms outside of ancient orders. In other words, they overthrow the ancient regime—some of them do—simply to become founders themselves (usurpation and revolution having been the founder's own modes). Perhaps Machiavelli reveals the truth about foundings to quash the hope that a mythologized past will permit the founder to keep all of the glory for himself. In any event, the founder who is told to be alone in power is also told to create incomplete and open-ended modes and orders; or told that foundings are continuous affairs, that reformers are the equal of founders, even that reformers, facing greater dangers, earn the greater glory. Sharing is the order of the day, and a community of equals, each dedicated to a common enterprise larger than himself, replaces the vandalizing individual determined to be first.

The founder-reformer prince experiences a second sort of middle way, besides that of sharing his glory with others. He is a psychological oddity, a person who employs evil means for the attainment of good ends (unlike the moral cowards, so called, who do exactly the reverse). He is a combination of opposites—the quintessential middle way. He transgresses constitutional barriers or usurps power altogether, not to install himself as prince, per se, but to restore the republic to a condition of health. He is a republican in his ends and a tyrant in his means. To be sure, he is a rarity, but Machiavelli does not despair of him for that—no hand-wringing here over the untenableness of middle ways. On the contrary, one might say that Machiavelli's reclamation project depends precisely on the appearance of just such a man. Or better put, the project depends on the regular occurrence through education of just such *men*. Nature does not produce these men who are both good and bad, but good men can learn to be bad and bad men can learn to be good. The good can learn that cruelty is needed in the means, and the bad can learn that generosity is needed in the ends.

There was much of middle ways as well in how Rome composed itself and in how it related to others. In the first place, Rome was an amalgam of new and old. It was old like Sparta in that it utilized and depended on certain elements of ancient republicanism: a frugal, timocratic way of life with the focus more on public than on private affairs; a patriotic and pious populace willing to make sacrifices for the common good; a citizen army which (to continue the search for middle ways) was a mean between professional mercenaries and untrained farmers. Rome also was new: acquisitive, imperial, cosmopolitan—a brash young republic always on the make; but a martial republic, not a commercial one. Thus Rome stood midway between the small, closed, homogeneous city-states of the past and the large, open, heterogeneous nation-states of the future. Likewise, Rome stood midway between unwalled Sparta and fortress Milan. This we noted previously. What also we noted was that Rome kept to a middle way when punishing its subjects—not that Rome punished precisely, proportionately, justly, for its judgments were always extreme; but that it decided on a case by case basis whom to eliminate and whom to caress.

Rome followed a middle course in its foreign relations and in its mode of expansion, increasing its trunk with new arrivals but resisting the demands of its Latin allies for total unification. Rome was the hegemon, the Latins were it partners, but unequal and for a long time politically distinct. While Rome fought many wars of choice against formal enemies identified as such, indirect warfare was for 400 years the principal mode by which Rome expanded. The indirect approach of forming alliances, defending subjects, arbitrating disputes was a mean between declared enmity and genuine friendship. Another mean was the raid, Rome's preferred mode of attack, which fell between open violence and furtive violence in the amount of force expended and which compelled the enemy's surrender in less time than the "many years" consumed by a siege and in more time that the "one day" required by storming (II.32.2). Rome also preferred defensive over offensive wars. Close analysis of these two strategies reveals that by fighting at home rather than abroad Rome sacrificed the chance for quick and serendipitous acquisitions (II.12.1). Through the Second Punic War at least, Roman strategy was somewhat middle-way. And Rome was decidedly middle-way in its reaction to fortune's allocations, neither exulting in good fortune nor despairing in bad but keeping an even temper through every vicissitude.

What then should one make of the fact that the middle way is rejected and the middle way is adopted?[32] While it is true that Machiavelli's extremism receives most of the attention—and not infrequently a favorable press (the autonomy of politics)—one must not be misled by the seeming enthusiasm with which Machiavelli abandons the middle and seizes the extreme. Abandoning the middle is tantamount to an admission of failure, for it is in the middle where reason devises its remedies and virtue's war with fortune is under maximum control. To leave the middle is to surrender to fortune's power, to forget about plans and to cease preparations in the desperate hope that womanly fortune will smile upon an impetuous lover. Machiavelli acknowledges the role of luck in worldly affairs, as well as the strange fact that impetuous lovers seem to have more of it; but depending on luck is an unvirtuous action unless desperation is accompanied by courage.[33] In any event, better is it to be in control, to stay the course for as long as fortune allows. And since holding to the mean entails thinking ahead, being on guard, managing passions, inevitably the habits of a cautious disposition are passed on to those who navigate the middle.

Common Goods

This particular middle way, which obliges its travelers to be calculating, watchful, and disciplined, has the effect of transforming selfish individuals into responsible members of a community. It is a morality, albeit a utilitarian one, and it is one road from Machiavelli to the moderns,[34] the other and shorter road being the egoism of the new prince.[35] It does not say that the city is natural, like the glove which fits the hand; that man is a political animal, unfulfilled outside of his polis; or that virtue brings happiness and is for its own sake.[36] There is little or no inclination supporting this morality, though it comes to depend on emotional attachments and on mores, beliefs, and the ways of the fathers.[37] But it depends also—and perhaps chiefly—on instruction, since it claims to be useful and so tries to show how. Machiavelli takes a turn at explaining the utility of the middle way, or explaining the good which different actors have in common. For instance, he reminds founders, who wish to play God, creating *ex nihilo* a world in their own image, that they are mortal and in need of disciples; that sons are unvirtuous and dynasties unstable; that strangers are needed to maintain the old orders. These maintainers come first from the many, bedrock conservatives, who carry on as always unless disturbed in their habits (I.9.2., I.58.3). They come second from the few, new princes ambitious for glory, who effect this disturbing and work to subvert unless the orders are progressive and there is room at the top. At the same time, new princes are reminded that if they are altogether new, they risk destruction at the hands of the old guard. Caesar is an object lesson for impatient usurpers. So a common good obtains binding founders to reformers and reformers to founders and binding them each to the people. Personal interest is where this good originates, but in time the selfishness is suffused with feelings of respect.[38]

Similar to founders and reformers are princes and conspirators. The latter pair have also a common good since conspiracies usually end in the ruin of both parties. Practically all conspiracies are found out in the plotting stage or foiled in the management stage. So woe is the cabal. But the apprehending and punishing of conspirators actually damages the reputation of the prince, whose motives are distrusted and actions reviled; and a hated prince, like a wounded deer, excites the appetites of other predators. So woe is the prince. On the other hand, a beloved prince is safe against conspiracy, since fear of the people's rage in the aftermath stage is what mainly prevents conspiracies from forming. A prince is loved by his people if he respects their property and their women and if he rules them in accordance with law. Justice is in the prince's interest; his survival needs are in concert with the moral aspirations of the public. Justice can also put the prince in good stead with the few, who hold the prince accountable if crimes committed against them by private persons are allowed to go unpunished. King Philip of Macedon, father of Alexander, was assassinated (336 BC) because he delayed avenging an injury done to a subject (Pausanias) and then insulted him further by rewarding the malefactor (Attalus) with an office of state (II.28.2).

Patricians and plebs share in a common good. They are class antagonists, but they have a mutual interest in keeping tyrants at bay. They are the little birds of prey who are alike destroyed when the larger bird of prey swoops down from above. The plebs does its part by loving liberty and fighting (nobles) to defend it; also by obeying (nobles) and showing proper regard. The patricians do their part by hiding their authority and providing benefits to the plebs. Indirect rule by patricians is a species of fraud, since selfishness, not goodness, is what inspires the largess. The senate gave tax relief to the people because the people's support was needed in the war against Porsenna and the Tarquins (I.32.1); or the senate paid soldiers a wage because public assistance allowed larger, longer, and more distant wars to be fought (I.51.1). Had the senate persisted in these modes, the tribunes would have lost their authority with the people (I.52.1), while the people, fully convinced of the senate's good will, would have thrown itself in the senate's lap. A perfectly fraudulent senate, its malignities completely hidden, would have ruled a people pleased to be deceived and oblivious to its oppression. In a perfect fraud, the "mark" never catches on. But then the mark is off its guard because new benefits confirm its trust. The Roman senate at its shrewdest not only acceded to the people's demands but anticipated its needs. So deceitful could the senate be that its selfishness was indistinguishable from true liberality—so deceitful, that is, that it virtually deceived itself. (For instance, it let plebeians run for high office and so required patricians, in competing for plebeian votes, to represent plebeian interests.)[39] Ironically, fraud can become the basis of a community in which all the parties benefit, where government is by the few and for the many. It hardly matters then what the real motives are, since the intelligent pursuit of interest requires that others be given a share.

Rome deceived its neighbors no less than the senate deceived the plebs. First the Latins, then the Italians were pulled into Rome's orbit. They may not have computed correctly the price to be paid—in autonomy and equality—for allying with Rome or asking for Rome's assistance, but what they received in exchange for their freedom was better government than sometimes their own leaders could supply (II.32.2), protection from outsiders, and association with greatness or a chance to take part in history. In addition then to the issue of self-interest and the common good, there is the question of how common the common ought to be. Many free cities were created at the expense of free villages, as were free villages created at the expense of free families. Freedom is always greater the smaller and more local the association; in fact, freedom is at its maximum where there is no association at all, in a state of nature. But people need and want to associate, and it is not always a mistake for them to associate at levels higher than the city-state. The "unhappiest" state is "a prince or a republic brought to the point where it cannot accept peace or sustain war." States are unhappiest which cannot get over the idea of freedom or defend freedom by their own arms; instead they "must either throw themselves forth as prey for whoever aids them or be left as prey for the enemy" (II.23.2). Freedom at any cost is not then Machiavelli's intention, nor is it a good idea. There are communities which would be well-served trading their freedom for the protection of a stronger state. And some territories are simply better ordered for peaceful prosperity if larger populations are united. Independence may be a good ordinarily, but the price of independence can be staggering; and since the desire of most citizens is for peace, not glory, and since only a handful of citizens fully exercise their freedom by seeking to rule (I.16.5), the loss of political freedom, it might be thought, is no great sacrifice, particularly when there are compensations to be had. In order for this supposition to be true, however, the conquering state cannot behave in the manner ascribed to barbarian princes and imperial republics (though not so clearly to Rome),[40] destroying countries and wasting civilizations (II.2.4). It would need to set its sights on nation-building, overcoming the temptation to exploit the helpless. But there is good reason for making the adjustment, since in ancient days the brutality of victors was what compelled the weak to resist so tenaciously, and tenacious resistance by the weak, or the obstinate love of liberty, was what drove up the cost of conquest. To the intelligent observer, therefore, a common good is detectable.

This common good is actively promoted by Machiavelli with dire warnings against immoderate appetites and false hopes. Worried about the fragility of virtue, Machiavelli advises "legislators of republics and kingdoms . . . to check human appetites and to take away from them all hope of being able to err with impunity" (I.42.1). It seems that even well-bred youths and men of quality, tempted only by little benefits and the bad example of Appius Claudius, came in a very short time to support the tyranny of the decemvirate.[41] Likewise, Machiavelli cautions that the false hope of victory, entering the breasts of men, pushes them "beyond the mark" (II.27.1). Four examples prove the wisdom of knowing when to say when: Carthage, after its victory at Cannae, should have followed Hanno's advice and negotiated a settlement (216 BC). Tyre, after fighting Alexander to a standstill, should have been satisfied that Alexander was willing to accept its original offer (332 BC). Florence, strengthened when a general uprising failed to materialize after Spain's victory at Prato, should have been conciliatory when the Spanish agreed to let slide one of three of their initial demands (1512 AD). In these latter two cases the weak state did as Machiavelli elsewhere bids; it made its own destruction costly to the aggressor and thereby extracted more favorable terms of peace (II.14.1). But mesmerized by the false hope of total victory, each state pressed on, even though at stake was its own survival. Here we are given a maxim prescribing the conduct appropriate to small states: Never risk what is most dear or gamble what one cannot afford to lose. Hannibal, in the fourth example and the second to deal with Carthage, provides the model, for he sued for peace rather than risk his army, which at that stage in the contest was his country's one remaining hope (202 BC). And in the first Carthaginian example a maxim is also discernible, this one pertaining to the conduct of the strong: Use victory to return to peace.

So there are limits which states should respect; acquisition is not without bounds.[42] If these limits are observed and acquisition held in check, something like an international order begins to take shape. Not all nations are equal, but all—and certainly most—can coexist. Rome and Carthage can live as rivals; Tyre can find its place within Alexander's empire; Florence can maintain its independence amid the comings and goings of foreign powers. If the parties are intelligent about their interests and take accurate readings of the extent of their forces, if they are not tempted by false hopes and fooled by false opinions but are "better knower[s] of the world" (III.31.3), they can avoid the moment when states are destroyed. Most differences are negotiable and most enemies can be partners to agreements which are acceptable to each: "For one [accord]," Machiavelli confidently asserts, "will never be offered so base that there is not inside it in some part the well-being of him who accepts it, and there will be a part of victory for him" (II.27.4). It is when the parties pass beyond the mark that states meet their ruin and the order is disrupted. Chapter 27 delivers then a cautious, conservative message: Don't overreach, don't tempt fate, don't trade a "certain good" for an "uncertain better" (§1). Perhaps more than any other chapter, II.27 is an admonition to stand down, a Greek-like warning against excess and a premonition of the tragedy awaiting hubristic ambition.

We have now a Machiavelli who is interested in common goods, who hunts them out, explains their merits, urges their adoption, who even contemplates their expansion beyond national borders—who gives us, for example, Timasitheus, the Liparian pirate. Out of respect for the property and religious rites of Rome, Timasitheus released a gold-laden ship bound for Delphi (III.29.1); he thereby extended the boundaries of community and in gratitude for the universality of his mind was granted the status of "honorary guest" of the Roman people (Livy, V.28). He followed in the footsteps of Camillus who by returning the Falisci schoolchildren obeyed a higher law than collective selfishness, or who, at any rate, increased the size of the collective (III.20.1). While it is the main lesson of III.29 that princes are responsible for the virtue of their people, that Timasitheus, as a case in point, set a good example which filtered down to affect the character of his piratical followers; it is also noted that Timasitheus ruled "with the consent of the collectivity"—i.e., that his modes were republican and moderate. Likewise Camillus, whose objective was the conquest of Falerii, chose the in-between mode of indirect warfare. When attention is paid to the moderate means of the middle way, moderate ends—common goods— emerge as a consequence. Not only does the end justify the means, but the means transform the end.

The end of a utilitarian morality is the efficient satisfaction of desire—the greatest happiness of the greatest number, as is said. Efficient satisfaction comes often from use of moderate means, such practices and attributes as cooperation, compromise, trust, dependability, discipline, frugality, order; and these moderate means back up upon acquisitive ends, moderating them in turn—in place of everything for me, something for all. Machiavelli claims in the first preface to be bringing "common benefit to everyone." One way of explaining how is by attributing to him a proto-utilitarian ethics.

His ethics is actually reminiscent of the account of justice tendered by Glaucon in Plato's *Republic*: What's best, states Glaucon, is to live as a tyrant, satisfying desires the moment they are felt. What's worst is to suffer the tyranny of another. What's in between and an acceptable compromise is freedom, the agreement to foreswear tyranny on condition that others do the same.[43] Freedom is the result of a social compact among the weak, the foxes of the world, to band together so as to defeat the superlative virtue of the lions of the world.[44] These foxes, who begin as selfish, conniving egoists, are turned into dutiful citizens through the cultivation of a careful, sober, sensible disposition. And just as Machiavelli's middle-way ethics resembles Glaucon's social compact (the paradigm for the contractarian thought of modern liberals), so Machiavelli's rhetorical method resembles the pedagogy of Socrates,[45] who takes an acquisitive Glaucon, wanting fine food and comfortable furniture, and tricks him into accepting an austere republic dedicated to justice and to the moral improvement of its citizens.

Machiavelli's Antinomies

But have Machiavelli's lions really been tamed, or are they about to bare their teeth, reminding foxes of nature's true hierarchy? We have brought the argument of moderate means and common goods to the point where Machiavelli is practically envisioning a new world order of peaceful coexistence among states. Book 2, chapter 27 makes the case for compromise and restraint. But how is this chapter consistent with book 2, chapter 1, where common goods are out of the question because the entire world is the imperial state's target and victim? How could any state coexist with Rome, a republic whose single ambition was for world conquest? Perhaps some small states—endangered, exhausted, or corrupt—might find advantage in being absorbed by a hegemon—Capua, for instance—but not states of near-equal reputation and power, not Carthage. Whatever might be said in exoneration of Rome—e.g., that wars are better fought soon rather than late (*Prince*, 3)—the fact remains that Roman policy was as much the cause as the consequence of warfare in the ancient world, that Rome's wars were wars of choice, and that Rome planned from the outset not only to expand and become great but to reject any limitations on its growth and to destroy all of its competitors, one by one. If it were Machiavelli's intention to moderate desire, to defend liberty and the common good, or just to avert disaster, he would object to acquisitiveness on such a scale as this; likely he would seize upon the confederation option practiced with success in both ancient and modern times.[46] But there is no word of remonstrance when introducing the Roman mode of conquest (II.1), no warning to go with the advice in II.27 not to overreach.[47] Does Machiavelli then want relentless expansion aiming for world domination, or does he want a community of republics able to contain the imperial aggressor, an international mixed regime, as it were, whose lesser states, working like tribunes, check the ambition of greater states, scheming like nobles? Machiavelli faults Rome for destroying the free republics of the ancient world (II.2.2), and his Fabrizio maintains that virtue is at its peak when distributed across many states, or that multiple republics augment the opportunities for virtue and thus the sum total of virtuous men (*Art of War*, II, 623). But however true and attractive this sentiment may be, the fact remains that Machiavelli prefers imperial Rome.

The confusion only increases when we remember all of the antinomies present in Machiavelli's thought.[48] We have been discussing middle ways as a strategy of acquisition. The extreme way is another such strategy. The latter is an instance of impetuosity, the former of caution. Both ways work, and results depend upon the times. Machiavelli does seem partial to impetuosity, but then he writes many chapters advising caution.[49] Resoluteness and neutrality represent a similar dichotomy. Mainly Machiavelli is for decisive action, but neutrality is sometimes smart policy for the weak.[50] The weak employ fraud and are foxes; the lion-like strong resort to force. Better to be strong than weak, except that the strong Romans are also praised when they conquer by indirection, or use fraud like the weak. Perhaps it is the economizing which Machiavelli admires, or perhaps it is intelligence, which the weak need more than the strong. But where precisely does Machiavelli stand amid all this? As to modes of rule, there is rule by love and rule by fear. Again, either will do, and again Machiavelli prefers the shocking and the ostentatious. But no Manlian leader equals the beloved Scipio; plus princes are advised to appear good whenever they can.[51] Then, too, there is the opposition of ordinary and extraordinary modes. Nothing so distinguishes Machiavelli as his gleeful embrace of illicit measures in domestic affairs—usurpation, tyranny, violence, scandal. And yet it is an ordinary mode, a law regulating citizenship, which concludes the *Discourses*. States are best preserved by periodic returns to their beginnings, to an original goodness born of fear and necessity; and it is the tyrant-prince who "at a stroke" effects the return. But an alternate strategy is to accept the corruption and change the laws; and a different sort of prince is needed for this "little by little" reform. In any event, Machiavelli's gaze is turned backward to a young and healthy past, and it is turned forward to the greatness which comes with new acquisitions. Nor is it entirely clear, in this matter of corruption, whether virtue or law is a society's primary support. And who are the rulers? Machiavelli does not quite say. No one is sovereign, and rival cases are made for the vigilant and stout-hearted plebs, the guardians of liberty, and for the crafty and patient nobles, who manage the state from behind the scenes and by indirection. Probably the nod goes to the nobles, graybeards in the main, but there is equal interest in empowering the young. Finally this—what is Machiavelli's ultimate commitment? Is it to a community of citizens, to their virtue, their achievements, their history; or is it to the ambition of the individual, which so often is the republican community's worst enemy? Coming to grips with Machiavelli's dual allegiance to acquisitive communitarianism and acquisitive individualism is perhaps the most difficult task of all. Appetite is released to gorge itself, even as spiritedness tightens its enforcement of the protocols of honor; lasciviousness alternates with severity, playfulness alternates with gravity. Machiavelli begins the *Discourses* alluding to his "end," his "intention," and his "destined place." But what could be more uncertain now than the object of Machiavelli's ambition?

Chapter Nine

What Machiavelli Wants

Scholars have for generations wrestled with the question of what Machiavelli stands for and what he intends. I will consider briefly some of the reigning explanations before venturing an answer of my own.

The Machiavelli Question

Perhaps it fits with the Elizabethan view of an evil "Machiavel" and diabolical "Old Nick," that by one interpretation Machiavelli is accounted the chief advocate of the acquisitive self.[1] This is a Machiavelli deeply affected by the power of ambition. As raw energy and untamed willfulness, ambition is a volcanic force inside the human soul—one which Plato calls eros and tries to suppress but which Machiavelli is happy to have roam free. The Machiavellian man is an innovator, a new prince, whose ambition is unbound. He is no respecter of hierarchical orderings, of ancient customs, or of hereditary bequests. Without place, property, or prospects, he is an outlaw and a predator. He says what he thinks, goes where he likes, takes what he wants, does as he pleases—and all the world is aghast. He is the rebellious adolescent who delights in scandalizing the grown-ups. And he is simpatico to Machiavelli, who applauds his independence, his cunning, his ferocity of spirit. Quite simply, the new prince is Machiavelli's hero (including a knave like Cesare), because the new prince is vital and his ambition is grand.[2]

It is *The Prince* especially which comes to mind when the new prince's immoral *virtù* is cried up for imitation. But does the protagonist of *The Prince* exhaust the universe of possibilities? Not at all—for the new prince, whose appetites are voracious, is the antithesis of the republican prince, the hero of the *Discourses*, who shares the offices of state and stays within the confines of law. These two are opposites, as are the advisers in each of Machiavelli's books. The adviser in *The Prince*, fresh from the discovery that fortune befriends the impetuous lover, counsels his lord to go for the gold of a united Italy (*Prince*, 25-

26); whereas the adviser in the *Discourses*, a cautious courtier playing it safe, foregoes the glory of being "head in counseling" (III.35 [title]) and "alone against many" (§2); instead, he stays to a middle course of speaking honestly but "moderately" (*moderatamente*), and he allows other counselors to contradict and the prince to feel that he accepts or rejects advice freely.[3] How do these advisers relate? How do they or the princes they advise fit inside of Machiavelli's thought?

Remembering *The Prince* causes forgetfulness of other topics recently discussed. What, for instance, has become of moderate means and common goods? What also has happened to mixed regimes evolving over time? Slow growth and continuity are their hallmarks. How are they compatible with new principalities, tyrannies, whose hallmarks are sudden change and innovation? And whither has gone the constitutionalist Machiavelli, that political philosopher of checks and balances who strains to equipoise the several parts of his mixed regime; whose job is all the harder since nature is not his partner (men being more wicked than good, more anomic than political), since effectual truths are not ignored (like the saliency of foreign affairs), and since liberty is no one's first love (the nobles wanting power and the plebs wanting safety); who, acting as his own guardian of liberty, defends the tribunate when under attack by nobles and decemvirs (I.40, I.50) and defends the patriciate when marked for destruction by Antony and Octavian (I.52.3); who also steps forward to defend the Florentine republic, even if that means sacrificing Soderini to the envy of his opponents (I.52.2)?

Yes, Machiavelli so loves his fatherland, and maybe his job, that he will sacrifice his boss to save either or both! He also will advise the French regarding the proper strategy for conquering and annexing Italy. What is so remarkable about Machiavelli is that he passes no judgment on the ambitions harbored by men. His seeming indifference to the ends of human striving leads numerous scholars to proffer the interpretation that Machiavelli is a technician of power, the prototype of the value-free social scientist.[4] There is much to support their thesis. We might note that whenever Machiavelli undertakes to talk about creating republics, he permits himself to talk also about destroying republics, or about creating principalities and tyrannies instead (I.16, I.25, III.3; *Prince*, 9). Moreover, he appears to be neutral regarding the kind of regime which finally is instituted, giving advice to republics and tyrannies alike (I.40). He even speaks as if the choice of regime depends solely on the wish of the founding prince. He frequently uses the "if a prince wants" or the "he who desires" formulation: "Therefore, if a prince wishes to win over a people that has been an enemy to him" (I.16.5); "If someone who desires or who wishes to reform a state in a city" (I.25.2).[5] The end is a given; it is never looked into, contested, or reproved. Tyrannies are as valid as republics. Consequently, Machiavelli causes his readers to question his republican bona fides, to wonder whether he is in fact a guardian of liberty or merely an adviser to any party who will pay his fee.

Everyone knows of Machiavelli's persistent attempts to curry favor with the Medicis,[6] so it is an easy thing to combine this biographical information with the textual evidence above and conclude that Machiavelli was an unprincipled schemer with no larger purpose in life than devotion to his craft. But other ways avail of discovering the true Machiavelli—of handling what has been called the Machiavelli Question.[7] One explanation is that *The Prince*, the main cause of these confusions, is not what it seems to be. It seems to be a handbook for tyrants, but in fact it is a satire, an exposé, a comedy, a trap, or a plot. This interpretation has a long and estimable pedigree, beginning with near contemporaries of Machiavelli,[8] carried on by liberal writers of the seventeenth and eighteenth centuries,[9] and kept alive by various critics of today.[10] What drives this interpretation is the conviction that the true Machiavelli is the Florentine patriot who served as chancellor of the Second Chancery and as secretary to the Ten of War and who labored tirelessly to equip his city with a militia; the Roman-pagan-republican Machiavelli who later authored the *Discourses* and *The Art of War*. Such a person could also have written *The Prince* only if that treatise has some secret meaning and hidden agenda. It is an interpretation, however, which is frequently embarrassed by the many "Machiavellianisms" discernible in the *Discourses*.[11] For the *Discourses*, dedicated to noble youngsters who *ought* to have power,[12] is thought to be the "good book" and the voice of the authentic Machiavelli.

A second explanation is that *The Prince* and the *Discourses* are incompatible in their teachings. Machiavelli wrote two political books which differ diametrically, an autocratic and a republican book. He wrote two and they differ because he changed his mind. It is at this juncture that entire interpretations of the man and his works hinge on the narrow point of when *The Prince* and the *Discourses* were respectively composed, with each scrap of period information being highly treasured (e.g., the moment when a Latin translation of Polybius VI first became available to Machiavelli).[13] Did Machiavelli, while at the Second Chancery and still brimming with republican confidence, begin drafting the *Discourses*, write its first book (or perhaps only it first 18 chapters),[14] but then set the project aside following the republic's collapse and his ouster from office; did he next, transferring his hopes from the humors of Rome to the potentates of the day, write quickly *The Prince* to impress the new powers that be; and did he finally, rebuffed and disappointed in his effort to find employment with the Medicis, return to the *Discourses*; and as a hardened and cynical man, convinced now that republics were a thing of the past, that absolute monarchies ruling over centralized states were the wave of the future—did he pen the remaining books of the *Discourses* which celebrate empire and the exploits of virtuous individuals? Such is the interpretation of Frederico Chabod, who reads Machiavelli as an author on the cusp of a new age, reconciling himself to, anticipating by a little, this next turn in European political history.[15] On the other hand, did he begin with *The Prince*, writing it in the months after his fall from

grace and expressing in it his first-hand experiences of realpolitik; did his service to the republic, in other words, turn him into a realist, a Machiavellian; and
did his forced retirement, his time spent reading the ancients and conversing
with friends at the Orti Oricellari, turn him into an idealist, a Renaissance humanist? Such is the interpretation of Hans Baron who regards Machiavelli, the
true and the final Machiavelli of the *Discourses*, that is, as an heir to and col-
laborator in the Quattrocentro resistance movement waged against absolutism.[16]
Baron's central argument—and that of most scholars applying the "genetic"
method—is that the two books relate as stages in the author's development
(whether to or from idealism).[17] Accordingly, ascertaining the composition dates
of *The Prince* and the *Discourses* is scholarship's top priority.

Or not. According to John Geerken, subsequent scholarship simply by-
passes the problem by postulating that the two books "were in fact interdepend-
ent aspects of an organically unified outlook."[18] What that outlook is Geerken
does not say; Hulliung, though, supposes it to be Baron's republicanism ("Today almost no one doubts Baron's contention that Machiavelli was fundamentally republican in his political outlook").[19] But if both books arise from the
same republican inspiration, how then explain the decidedly unrepublican
Prince? Sheldon Wolin's explanation is that the agent of political reform is the
heroic individual in *The Prince*, whereas in the *Discourses* the agent is the people: ". . . the difference between *The Prince* and the *Discourses* consists in a
greater appreciation on Machiavelli's part of the political capabilities of the
masses and correspondingly greater doubts about the utility of political heroes."[20] We still have here a change of mind characteristic of the genetic
method, but the change no longer concerns the end of politics but the means of
its attainment.[21] There are republican themes in *The Prince*, like the efficacy of
the citizen militia and the need to build foundations on the people; and the
common good is arguably the ruler's ultimate intention. Nevertheless, in *The
Prince* the people is treated as matter to be pounded and shaped by the artist-
hero;[22] whereas in the *Discourses* the people emerges as a political force able to
maintain the constitution and expand the state without supervision from the
founder. In fact, like Moses outside the Promised Land, the founder in the *Discourses* is an anachronism, if not an embarrassment, who shows his virtue by
speedily departing the scene.[23] So either Machiavelli reevaluated the public's
capacity for self-rule, or *The Prince* and the *Discourses* describe consecutive
stages of a community's development.[24]

Something wonderful happens once the founding prince is spirited away:
Machiavelli's republic begins looking like Aristotle's polis. At least it does to
civic humanist scholars.[25] J. G. A. Pocock sees a connecting thread running from
citizens under arms, to personal independence, to care for the common good
over private interests; likewise a connecting thread running from an unarmed
citizenry, to dependence and inequality, to corruption of virtue.[26] Thus Machiavelli's preoccupation with good arms is harnessed to Aristotle's concern for

good laws and good character. Pocock defines civic humanism as "a style of thought . . . in which it is contended that the development of the individual towards self-fulfillment is possible only when the individual acts as a citizen, that is as a conscious and autonomous participant in an autonomous decision-taking community, the polis or republic."[27] Although Machiavelli's relationship to the tradition of civic humanism is a complicated and controversial matter,[28] Pocock is satisfied that its "language and its theoretical refinements . . . reach a peak in the works of Machiavelli and Guicciardini."[29] Nor does it stop there, since Pocock postulates the existence of a continuous political tradition—an Atlantic republican tradition—rooted in Aristotle, flowering in the Italian Renaissance and in Machiavelli, branching out toward classical republican England and revolutionary America, and coming to full maturity in the communism of Marx and Lenin.[30] The connection, it seems, is to Aristotle's second-best regime. When Aristotle tires of discoursing on "imaginary republics" and gets down to the serious business of considering what's practical, he describes a state composed of two humors, rich and poor, ruled by law, and capable of guarding liberty and maintaining stability;[31] a polity where citizens participate in rule, not as a reward for their merit, or as a test of their skill, or even as an opportunity to grow in virtue, but simply as a protection of their interests against the abuses of power.[32] This much of Aristotle civic humanist scholars find preserved in Machiavelli. But invariably they find more. S. M. Shumer, for instance, after allowing that participation begins in self-defense, supposes that over time and with success it transmutes itself into love of the city and devotion to the commonweal.[33] She further supposes that "citizens who know that they are an effective part of the polity, and who are willing to resist its decisions, are also the citizens who can 'be used in important affairs,' and can be expected to make sacrifices, which involve devoting care and attention to their city."[34] Politics is the resolution of necessary conflicts arising from the collision of public goods and private interests. Accordingly,

> a political people is one that accepts as theirs the complicated business of working out a meaningful collective life that does not destroy the conditions for individual integrity. Such a people recognizes that the quality of their individual and their collective lives is defined by how they manage those tensions and balance those values. . . . A mistake in either direction, can destroy the conditions for fully human living. . . . This is not very different from Aristotle's idea that man fulfills himself only within politics where he can define and exercise "acting well."[35]

Of course there is one point on which Machiavelli departs from Aristotle: Machiavelli's republic is large and imperial, whereas Aristotle's polis is small and stationary. But Machiavelli's choice of Rome, says Maurizio Viroli (who ties the humanists to Aristotle and Machiavelli to the humanists), represents no repudiation of Aristotle, but is merely a repositioning of Aristotle inside the crucible of effectual truth. For the effectual truth is that stationary cities are absorbed by expansionary cities. Thus the advice which Machiavelli tenders respecting war without and discord within should not be taken as an argument for giving "priority to the pursuit of greatness over the preservation of the *vivere politico*. Expansion and war . . . can have no priority over liberty and the good order of the city." Machiavelli speaks as a realist in the service of political idealism, explaining bluntly that a city must "fight to protect its liberty and that both citizens and rulers must go to war in order to have peace but should not disturb peace in order to have war." Machiavelli, says Viroli, does "not change the goal of politics, which remains for him the *vivere politico*."[36]

Liberty and Greatness

There can be no doubting that Machiavelli favors liberty, that he favors republican government as liberty's proper home, and that he favors the people as liberty's surest guardian. Four qualities exhibited by the people earn it this place of honor in Machiavelli's political thought: gratitude, constancy, prudence, and trustworthiness. The first of these we have considered already: the people is more grateful than a prince since suspicion is the people's only cause for ingratitude, whereas a prince has avarice as a second cause and indolence as a third (I.29.3, I.30.1). The people also is more constant, as proven by the long duration of the Roman plebs's hostility toward the name of king. This is stated in I.58, the chapter where Machiavelli most conspicuously champions the people's cause, advertising his break with the college of historians and with Livy his mentor. The people is constant, Machiavelli avers, and it is wise; indeed, in most respects the two qualities combine into one ("I say that a people is more prudent, more stable, and of better judgment than a prince" [§3]). In various ways does the people demonstrate its wisdom. It has a mysterious ability to foresee ill and good fortune; its voice is comparable to the voice of God, Machiavelli is not embarrassed to say. When presented with conflicting counsels, it is adept at selecting the right course. When serving as an electorate, it invariably chooses the better candidate.[37] Finally, the people proves its wisdom by returning to the good way when spoken to by a good man; princes, by contrast, are deaf to reason—only steel can cure them. In the following chapter, I.59, Machiavelli adds trustworthiness to the people's qualities. The people is trustworthy in that treaties made with a republic are more likely to be honored than treaties made with a principality. Neither regime will ruin itself because of treaty obligations, but princes break faith for small advantages, whereas republics keep faith even at the cost of large advantages. The net effect on politics of the people's several qualities is greater attention to the common good. It is claimed, for instance, that the people is cruel against those who would betray the common good, but that princes are cruel against enemies of their own good (I.58.4). Because the common good "is not observed if not in republics," as said later in II.2.1, said here in I.58.3 is that "governments of peoples are better than those of princes."

Popular governments are better because under them states grow in wealth and in size. This contention is first made in I.58; in II.2 the proof is supplied. The question Machiavelli asks here is why the love of liberty was so wide and deep among the ancients. His answer is that liberty demonstrates its own value; it is the secret to increased dominion and riches. Thus where republics exist, people are taught to love liberty by the advantages they experience. Republics expand rapidly and prosper because the common good is their object and benefits are shared in by all. Conversely, tyrannies are small and poor because the tyrant's private good is the end for which subjects labor. Republics also provide security for their citizens and opportunities for governing. There is energy in republics, but laziness in tyrannies, since people who feel secure and hopeful work hard and raise families, confident that what they acquire they can enjoy and hand on to their children.[38] It is easy to see then why ancient Italy was awash in republics (for no cities south of Lombardy were ever ruled by kings, except Rome in its formative years and Tuscany under Porsenna [II.2.1]) and why Rome's neighbors were so obstinate in defense of their liberty.

This in brief is Machiavelli's case for liberty, for republics, and for the people. It is a strong case, giving rise to the opinion that Machiavelli is a democrat; but in several respects it is not sincerely argued. To begin with, in chapter 58 Machiavelli presents himself as a brave, first-of-a-kind defender of the people's wisdom and constancy against the common opinion, professed even by Livy, that the people is foolish and fickle. But in chapter 57, the prelude to 58, Machiavelli expresses contempt for the people's behavior. Without a head, says Machiavelli, an unshackled multitude is at first a most formidable thing, but without a head it soon becomes "cowardly and weak." Machiavelli is elaborating on a statement by Livy, that "from ferocious together, when isolated, each with his own fear, they [the people] became obedient" (§1). In chapter 58, however, Machiavelli denounces Livy for having stated that the nature of the multitude is either to serve humbly or to domineer proudly. Are these sentiments so different that Machiavelli can embrace the one (formidable and cowardly) and repudiate the other (domineering and humble)? If they are not, then Machiavelli is neither so far from Livy nor so close to the people as he is trying to be.[39]

Livy is ostensibly called to task for implying that the Roman plebs was inconstant when it wanted back Manlius Capitolinus after just having executed him (384 BC); and Livy is further called to task for charging the same inconstancy against the Syracusan plebs following the death of Hieronymus (215 BC). But Machiavelli proceeds to explain away the inconstant longings of the Roman plebs as admiration for the virtues but not the vices of Manlius. Even princes, Machiavelli avows, are capable of such impartial admiration, and "it is the verdict of all the writers that virtue is praised and admired also in one's enemies" (§2). "All the writers" is a category which includes Livy; thus Livy understood and respected the change of heart he reported in the Roman plebs. More telling of Livy's innocence, however, is the assertion by Machiavelli that "what our historian says of the nature of the multitude he does not say of that which is regulated by laws, as was the Roman" (§2). There was then no criticism of the Roman plebs by Livy, and so on this score there can be no criticism of Livy by Machiavelli. As for the condemnation of the Syracusans, Machiavelli supports it, because the Syracusans were a multitude unshackled by law.

Still, Machiavelli makes a great show of quarreling with Livy, of rejecting authority, and of marching courageously to wherever his reason leads him. And where it leads him is to the discovery that "governments of peoples are better than those of princes" (§3). Machiavelli, it seems, is a democrat and the first intellectual to defend the people's capacity for self-rule. But his defense is carefully couched in the republican language of limited power, in particular those limits that are imposed by law (the limits that come from divided government are not in evidence). The argument is less a brief for democracy than an encomium to the rule of law, for any regime is improved by having its rulers "shackled" by law. Plus the comparison of people and princes obscures the fact that in a republic the people is joined and guided by the great.

At first Machiavelli wants merely to attain a fair hearing for the people, contending that the universal prejudice against it stems from the practice of falsely comparing a good king bound by law to an unruly multitude sinning one day and repenting the next. But his own fair comparisons allow him to conclude that even though "all err equally when all can err without respect" (§2), the people in fact errs much less; and when obliged to show respect (when subject to law) the people is more grateful, prudent, and stable, is of better judgment, and is more prosperous than are princes also subject to law.

The proof of these assertions, however, is less than compelling. What is first said about the Roman people is that it demonstrated its stability by detesting the name of king for 400 years. It is true that the Romans were persistent in their opposition to the regal title, for even Caesar had to join in denouncing it; but their intolerance for a name did not ensure their guardianship of liberty or their immunity to demagogic appeals. Next said is that the Romans were not ungrateful despite the fact that they were ungrateful to Scipio. After volunteering this piece of noncorroborating evidence, Machiavelli reminds the reader of his previous explanation—suspicion of superlative virtue (I.29.3)—an explanation which found in multiple commanders a remedy for republican ingratitude, but which also found in energetic princes a remedy for princely ingratitude (I.30). The people's prudence is then likened to the voice of God, by which is meant that the people possesses some "hidden virtue" enabling it to forecast its future. It is not uncommon for democratic theorists to credit the people with an uncanny wisdom respecting the large issues of its national existence. But Machiavelli has himself just said, two chapters earlier, that forecasting the future is the business of airy intelligences—that is, of some ill-defined part of the spiritual hierarchy of popular religion (I.56). We wonder, therefore, whether the notion that God's voice is heard through the people is not some political superstition equivalent to the religious superstitions which knowing leaders disparage but profess nonetheless (I.14). In two ways is the superior judgment of the people now shown, by its ability to decide between orators recommending different policies, and by its ability to choose candidates for office. Regarding the first of these presumed talents, it is flatly denied that the people possesses it, since the people reasons well only about particulars, individuals for office, and never about generalities, public policies and constitutional disputes (I.47).[40] That leaves the judging of candidates. This the people can do well, and so well did the Roman people perform as an electorate that not four choices of consuls or tribunes did the people have cause to repent (I.58.3). But we also know that the nominations were often manipulated by the senate so that the people had little choice but to elect a patrician too noble to refuse and to refuse a plebeian too vile to elect (I.48). After comparing the progress enjoyed by republics and principalities respectively,[41] noting the complementary functions of princes and people (ordering and maintaining), and reiterating the salutary effects of law on all regimes; Machiavelli observes that a licentious and tumultuous people can be brought back to its senses by the soothing words of a good man,[42] whereas assassination is the only cure for a wicked prince since words alone do not move him. The fact that the people, however enraged, is amenable to persuasion does testify to its moral worth; but in light of the many chapters so far devoted to the theme of popular corruption, one is tempted to conclude that killing an evil prince is an easier task than preventing corruption or restoring virtue once it is lost. Machiavelli next suggests that a wicked prince represents the summum malum of politics and that the craziness of the people is a political evil not for what it is as such, but only for what it portends, namely the rise of a tyrant. But insofar as Machiavelli has us looking forward, we see past the present evil of tyranny to the anticipated good of liberty ("men persuade themselves that his wicked life can make freedom emerge" [§4]); likewise we see past the present craziness of the people, which causes no fear, to the anticipated evil of tyranny, which causes great fear. Those who experience the anarchy of popular rule live in terror of the future, while those who suffer the oppression of tyranny live in hope of the future. Thus Machiavelli takes what could have been a definitive, albeit negative, argument in favor of government by the people—that anarchy is preferable to tyranny—and dissipates its force by focusing attention on what comes next in the cycle of regimes. Machiavelli then states that the people is protective of the common good and is cruel toward its enemies; and that princes, on the other hand, are protective of a private good and are cruel toward those who would seize it. This charge may be true, but it also suggests that the atrocities committed by a frightened populace will be indiscriminate and widespread, whereas those committed by a suspicious prince will be few and targeted against his political opponents only.

If the claim is suspect that the people is more stable and wise than are princes, what of the final claim that it is more trustworthy? Republics are honest and good, it is said, whereas principalities are duplicitous and greedy. But how do republics appear when seen from within, by someone depending on their prudence and strength, rather than from without, by someone needing to put trust in their word? Is it an accomplishment or a deficiency of republican rule that the government is slow to change course despite the presence of "urgent danger" (I.59.1)? It is doubtful that Machiavelli intends a compliment here since the republic is risking its own survival. Even more risky is the nobility of republican leaders and the people who elect them. In one example from chapter 59, Aristides reports to the Athenian people that Themistocles' plan for making Athens the master of all Greece (480 BC), told to Aristides alone, is very useful and very dishonest; and so the people reject it, choosing honesty over utility. Clearly the people felt that in matters of mere advantage, humans are free to be noble or base; but that in matters of preservation, necessity compels and fear excuses. But Machiavelli has repeatedly denied that ethical distinctions can be drawn between fear and avarice (I.5.4, I.37.1, I.46.1). The people believe in such distinctions, and such distinctions define their goodness. But the people's goodness is harmful to a state if it is unmediated by virtuous leaders. Philip of Macedon would never have done, says Machiavelli, what Aristides and the Athenians did. Philip was previously associated with the principle that in politics being wholly good is unwise, if not impossible, and that being wholly bad is better than being partly bad (I.26). Philip, of course, was a new prince in a new state; and what was required of him was not required of Athens, an established democracy. Still it is hard to believe that the wholly good behavior of the Athenians and their leaders is something which Machiavelli means to condone. He says in conclusion that "the people make lesser errors than the prince," but the errors are again in relation to outsiders who depend on the people's word.

In book 2, chapter 2, where the defense of republics is continued, Machiavelli's main concern is to marvel at the ferocity with which the ancient republics fought to preserve their liberty and to lament the passing of this spirit from the modern world. But there are indications even here that all is not right with this liberty-loving obstinance. Virtue is the union of the lion's spiritedness and the fox's craftiness, as Machiavelli explains in *Prince* 18. We notice, however, that some of Rome's obstinate neighbors were a bit too obstinate and that it was the love of liberty which made them that way—i.e., stubborn to the point of stupid. The Tuscans refused help to Veii (one of the twelve cities of Tuscany [Etruria]) when it elected a king to organize its defense against Rome (403 BC). Now the previous chapter informs us that Rome acquired an empire by defeating its enemies one at a time. In the case of Veii, Rome was allowed this luxury because Tuscans, seeing the world through ideological lenses, "enjoyed [their] freedom so much and hated the name of prince so much that . . . they decided after many consultations not to give aid to the Veientes so long as they lived under the king" (§1). And what was the Veientian offense? Except for the name, the Veientes did what the Romans a century before had done when they created a dictator to deal with the Latin alliance (I.33.1). Responding to an emergency, the Veientes, like the Romans, upgraded executive authority. It also is Machiavelli who gives the affair a political spin, for the explanation in Livy is primarily religious: that the man made king was unacceptable to the Tuscan nation because he had outraged religious feelings by peremptorily removing his dependents from a sacred festival already in progress (Livy, V.1). Thus Machiavelli forces us to think that loving liberty compromised the self-interest of the Tuscans.

What is best about free republics is their devotion to the common good. Compared with principalities, which sacrifice the common benefit for the private advantage of the prince, republics seem like temples of justice. But the good of the collective is not synonymous with the good of its members, considered individually; furthermore, a collective body intent on its own interest is an awesome force unfazed by the objections of a dissident few. It proceeds toward its end, says Machiavelli, "against the disposition of the few crushed by it" (§1). While such ruthlessness can hardly count for much with the ruthless Machiavelli—whose project, after all, has little to do with the rights of individuals[43]— nevertheless, the crushing of the few suggests that republics are another of those half-goods and blemishes of an imperfect nature.

It is a mark against successful principalities that the profits from expansion go to the prince, called a "virtuous tyrant," as opposed to the state, called a "republic" (§1). He can neither honor particular citizens nor oblige conquered territories to pay tribute to the home city, for he does not want to suspect the former or strengthen the latter. Whatever the losses incurred from sharing honors with no one, the prince is wise not to become indebted to his captains and his subjects, as Machiavelli has elsewhere explained (I.29-30, III.6.3). For confirmation of his thesis that principalities are inimical to the common good, Machiavelli refers the reader to Xenophon's *Of Tyranny*, a fictitious dialogue between Hiero, the fifth-century Syracusan tyrant, and Simonides, the lyric poet from Ceos and Athens. Hiero makes all the points for which Machiavelli references him, but in a tone of lament for the private pleasures lost and the public dangers run. Tyranny is hard on subjects and tyrants alike—hence no one should want to be a tyrant. But then Simonides explains, with arguments foreshadowing chapters 19 and 21 of *The Prince*, that an intelligent tyranny can easily combine admiration and security for the tyrant with prosperity and greatness for the city.[44] So the Xenophon reference does more harm than good to the thesis Machiavelli is propounding. But even if it is stipulated that the tyrant's interests are perforce incompatible with the people's, the hostility of the tyrant toward the common good gives him reason to build a larger common good between his own city and the provinces he has conquered, treating all peoples equally. Republics, by contrast, exaggerate and codify the differences between themselves and the people under their rule. The dark side of republican rule is the barbarity it practices against defeated opponents. Republics enervate and weaken their foes so as to direct all increase to themselves. And republics last much longer, so there is little hope of escape (§4). Seen from the perspective of weak and soon-to-be-absorbed states, nothing could be worse than to have an expansionary republic in the neighborhood. Athens and Sparta fit this description of unenlightened republics (II.4.1), but in its better moments Rome was an exception, making partners, not subjects, of Italians and being "less punitive to [its] enemies" by allowing them to keep their lands (I.37.2).

Hieronymus of Syracuse is the next example used for touting the marvels of republican liberty. The moment he died the city was swept up in a whirlwind of republican enthusiasm, and even the soldiers under his command soon responded to the shouts of liberty. We would be wise, however, not to get too carried away ourselves. Machiavelli has spelled out in some detail the difficulties and dangers of receiving liberty (I.16-18); a corrupt people, such as were the Syracusans, has little chance of making a success of it. There is also the warning not to attempt converting to the cause inveterate enemies of the name of liberty, as Cicero tried with Octavian (I.52.3). Finally, the speed and eagerness with which Syracusans became republicans was offered as evidence, just a few chapters back, of the fickleness of a multitude unshackled by law. The example spoke against the people, not in favor of liberty.

In order to explain the depth of feeling which animates the partisans of liberty, Machiavelli takes us to Corcyra during that city's civil war (427 BC). The humors of Corcyra were badly divided, and each sought assistance from without, the people allying with Athens and the nobles allying with Sparta. Often the balance of power shifted depending on which of the empires had more ships in the area. But eventually the demos gained the upper hand. It imprisoned the nobles, executing them surreptitiously in groups of eight or ten. After a while the prisoners realized their fate and undertook to defend the building in which they were housed. But the demos was not to be denied its vengeance; so it removed portions of the roof, and hurling tiles and firing arrows, it slaughtered all of the people within. True enough, the Corcyrean demos loved its liberty and visited unspeakable cruelties on those who would seize it. But the revenges it took upon its class enemy eliminated any possibility of Corcyra's developing a mixed regime (I.28, III.7). What's more, by waging war upon the nobles, the demos weakened the city and left it prey to foreign powers (I.2.4). Thus the love of liberty led to disunion and defeat as opposed to a united resistance against foreign aggression as the chapter promises. The chapter tells the story of how liberty, experienced and enjoyed by Rome's neighbors, complicated the business of defeating them; for "nothing made it more laborious for the Romans to overcome the peoples nearby and parts of the distant provinces than the love that many peoples in those times had for freedom" (II.2.1). But the suspicion is growing that Rome's neighbors were easy to conquer for the reason that they were too stubborn about their liberty. Liberty means localism, and localism means hostility toward combinations needed to combat imperial expansion—be these combinations of nobles and plebs or of cities within a national confederation. After all, the secret of Rome's remarkable success was that Rome never had to face more than one enemy at a time. Rome never did because it was virtuous and its enemies were ardent (III.36).

⚜

We are moving to the conclusion (albeit a provisional one) that Machiavelli values liberty not for its own sake but as a means to an end. That end could be survival, for he has mentioned often enough that necessity obliges states to expand. But more likely the end is empire, greatness, and glory.[45] We say this, in part, because Machiavelli's choice of expansionary Rome over sedentary Sparta was poorly explained when survival was offered as its justification. Sparta, for instance, was said to have suffered destruction because, when it needed to expand, it lacked the requisite institutions (I.6.4). As it happened, though, Machiavelli delineated the precautions by which a state like Sparta could protect itself: a defensible location, a martial people, and a record of non-aggression. Originally—in deference to Machiavelli's pronouncements on necessity—we dismissed these precautions as utopian fancies. But they deserve more serious attention, if only because the case for Rome and against Sparta was never that convincing. We note that Sparta did protect itself for an impressive stretch of time; that if the theoretical possibility and eventual fact of defeat are taken as decisive, then Rome too was exposed to this possibility and Rome too was defeated—sooner than was Sparta; that Machiavelli omitted mention of the necessity which forced expansion on Sparta;[46] that he exaggerated the harm done to Sparta, for the loss of her empire did not mean the loss of her freedom, much less that the "republic was altogether ruined" (§4); finally, that the enervation caused by peace can be successfully counteracted by the good orders of a prudent lawgiver—so Machiavelli declared when rejecting the necessities provided by a sterile site (I.1.4) and so he implied when describing the state of Venice (I.1.2, 4).[47]

Survival then is not the end, but survival in style, or greatness, is the end. Liberty contributes to this end by toughening the plebs and so requiring of ambitious nobles that they direct their energies outward, toward conquest; also by exciting within the plebs—otherwise a sleepy and complacent lot—an appetite for imperial expansion. Aristotle recognizes the connection between liberty and empire, noting that spiritedness, the seat of the liberty-loving desire, seeks also to exercise mastery over others; he further remarks that some persons even argue the rectitude of conquering foreign populations just for the chance of ruling over them. The problem with spiritedness then is its lust for power. With Plato this lust shows itself inside the city, as warriors become tyrants oppressing the workers; with Aristotle this lust goes outside the city, having war and conquest as its objectives. So Aristotle endeavors to domesticate spiritedness, claiming that war is for peace, that peace is for leisure, and that leisure is for contemplation, or that philosophy is an activity higher than politics, particularly the apolitical governance of captives and slaves.[48] Machiavelli, by contrast, leaves spiritedness free to pursue its own business—first liberty, then power, then empire. We can see that liberty is not an end in its own right by the use to which it is put in II.2. However much liberty is admired in the chapter, its function is to demonstrate the caliber of Rome's opponents in order that their destruction might intensify the brilliance of Rome's glory. Machiavelli wants mainly to establish the scope of the Roman achievement, to which end he adopts the historian's practice of enhancing the glory of victors by "render[ing] illustrious the actions of their enemies" (II.Pr.1). Thus Machiavelli celebrates the liberty-loving obstinacy of the peoples around Rome so as to illuminate the "excessive virtue" by which Rome brought these peoples to heel (II.2.1). Not liberty as such, but the strength required to destroy liberty is what Machiavelli seems to value.

Liberty is different from greatness. Liberty is an equilibrium resting on a balance of power, and it is a stubbornness resistant to the abuse of power. But greatness violates balance and is practically synonymous with abuse. Greatness is limitless magnitude—more and more; liberty is sufficiency and middle ways. Liberty describes the relations among equals, where compromise, restraint, and settling for one's due are the prescribed modes of behavior. Greatness belongs with necessity and war, where winners take from losers and the vanquished pay homage to the victor. Of the two, greatness is the more attractive (supposing victory the result of competitive struggle), for it gratifies vanity and nourishes desire. Liberty, by comparison, is a shabby sort of making do. Greatness is the stuff of everyone's dreams (though only a few have the courage to pursue it), and its attainment by one destroys the liberty of all others. Greatness is the sum of all liberties gathered together and put at the disposal of just one. Greatness is unsurpassing power. It is to liberty what excellence is to equality. For as there cannot be excellence if all are equal, so there cannot be omnipotence if all are free.

It follows then that in choosing Rome for its greatness, Machiavelli simultaneously chooses the extirpation of liberty. To his credit he does not try hiding this fact from himself or from his readers. In what is perhaps the most astonishing admission in all of the *Discourses*, Machiavelli concedes that "the Roman Empire, with its arms and its greatness, eliminated all republics and all civil ways of life" (II.2.2). Roman greatness destroyed the liberty of the ancient world. But it did more; for it destroyed as well its own virtue. Standing alone at the apex of success, Rome turned soft and lazy; mingling its customs with the customs of conquered peoples, Rome fell to corruption. It is no small paradox that Rome destroyed the very thing which Machiavelli would have moderns resuscitate by imitating Rome. He chooses Rome for its expansionary capacities, but he confesses that successful expansion is self-consuming—that Rome's time on the stage was strictly limited, its remedy for the cycle of regimes a hoax.[49] Machiavelli's intentions are thus a little murky, as he causes us to question the worth of what he seemingly holds most dear—virtue productive of greatness. If he supports Rome nonetheless, it is because Rome was strong enough long enough that its increase brought it glory. With a mixed regime, it conserved its strength, avoiding the rapid rise and fall of simple regimes. Is glory then the goal?

Yes, likely it is, though there is trouble ahead for this answer in II.5, the chapter on the collapse of civilizations. Machiavelli reasons that the world might be eternal,[50] despite the fact that we know so little of it, because the memory of things is extinguished in two ways: by the actions of men and by the actions of heaven. Human beings deliberately destroy the record of the past when as sectarians they institute new religions. And heaven destroys civilizations when it visits floods, plagues, and famines upon the earth. Other names for "heaven" are "accident" and "necessity"; for two of the three actions of heaven (floods and plague) are attributed to accident in the chapter's title, and the "three modes" of purging humanity come about by necessity (§2). It appears then that this power that destroys memory of the past can be interpreted in various ways: first, as heavenly interventions expressing divine will (mention of a universal inundation destroying all lowland people save one is an allusion to Noah and the Ark); second, as accidental or chance occurrences beyond the ken and control of human beings; third, as necessary events ordained by natural law. Necessity is nature writ large, for necessity purges the mixed body of the human race of its excess population just like nature purges simple bodies of single organisms of their surplus material. This nature, or necessity, is thought to be eternal by the philosophers. It moves in cycles, renewing itself through periodic destructions. Its floods and plagues and famines restore the mixed body to health by removing excesses that are both material and moral—too many people, too much "astuteness and malignity." Humans "may live more advantageously and become better" for having endured the cataclysm, but it is the species which is improved by being made young. Individuals and their achievements are sacrificed for the good of the whole, or for the good of nature itself.[51] Such a nature, because it operates according to laws of growth and decay, can be comprehended by the human mind, and Machiavelli says that "it seems reasonable that it [purgings by inundations, plagues, and famines] should be so" (§2). But while the laws of nature can be known, the particular history of nature cannot, except for references in written records to some past catastrophe and for the effects of the devastation still visible in the present.

It is nature's way to thin out the human race on a regular basis, to make its numbers few and its condition beaten. It is, however, the way of states, especially the Roman state, to grow large and prosperous, to thicken the trunk by assimilating foreign and defeated populations. What humans want is at variance with what nature wants. And even when humans destroy, they do so for purposes of reputation—a new sect extinguishes the old "to give itself reputation" (§1). States seek greatness through expansion, whereas nature seeks health through reductions. Nature's preservation comes at the expense of its creatures, simple bodies, all of whom are mortal. In fact, the state represents man's attempt to defeat nature's destructiveness; it is a mixed body meant to live eternally or at least to achieve a fame too great to be obliterated. Thus man's relation to nature is necessarily antagonistic. And both the state with its tendency toward empire and Christianity with it promise of immortality reflect this antagonism.

How then should humans live given the fact that nature is at war with their deepest aspirations? Machiavelli rejects Christian other-worldliness.[52] Quite plainly Machiavelli does not believe in Christianity's promise of total victory, for Christianity is treated as just another sect with an expected life span of between 1,666 and 3,000 years.[53] But neither is empire-building especially attractive when seen against the backdrop of nature's eternal cycle. Nothing of man endures because nature denies immortality to any modes and orders other than its own. Machiavelli is in a position similar to Cicero's Scipio Aemilianus, whose spirit, carried aloft by the ghost of his adoptive grandfather, Scipio Africanus, surveys the Roman empire and declares it a paltry and shameful thing. It covers no more than a patch of the earth's surface; it is cut off by deserts from other peoples; and its fame, he is told, reaches the hearing of no one from the past (who living before Rome knew nothing of it) and of not many in the future, since fires and floods, occurring at fixed periods and destroying all records, preclude the winning of everlasting fame. So disheartened is the younger Scipio by the earth's transitoriness and so enamored is he of the majesty of the heavens that death seems preferable to life; and he must be told by Africanus that the gods favor patriots and that the security of one's country is the noblest occupation of the soul.[54] This claim, of course, is egregiously contradictory, but it is untroubling to Aemilianus because the reality of willful gods and immortal souls is attested to by his ancestor. But Machiavelli makes the ascent unaccompanied by celestial spirits, and he discovers this same truth about empire and glory without reassurances to the contrary that the fatherland is nevertheless important. At this point Machiavelli might want to reassess the stock he has placed in acquisition and the choice he has made for imperial Rome. But in fact he has nowhere else to put his faith since he is not willing to fly from this world in search of immortality beyond.[55]

Unable to transcend the false immortality of fame, Machiavelli returns to the cyclical process by which greatness is nurtured. That process, however, can itself temper the enthusiasm for greatness. The tempering comes about like this: Human beings, mostly equal, have a deep need to witness displays of excellence. In daily life the search for heroes is constant—anything that rises above the mean and is memorable. In sports, people applaud winners and want competitors to be better and better. There is uneasiness among sports fans when quality players are dispersed and the level of play declines. Concentrated quality is what produces true champions; and quality that endures produces dynasties. How eager are fans in their anticipation of the next dynasty, of a team whose accomplishments are record-making and glorious. Ardent fans want a team— preferably their own team—to win and to win always, to win easily by delivering crushing blows to the opponent. Ardent fans want to force from the lips of disbelievers acknowledgment of their team's preeminence. More than this, ardent fans want applied to their team every conceivable superlative. Even more, they want its praises continuously sung, for how else is glory achieved than by having spectators speak always of the exploits of *the team*. In sum, ardent fans want a Super Bowl victory of 52 to 17! But smashing victories carry their own liability: even though they testify to the invincibility of the victor, they are rather tedious to observe. After a quarter of one-sided play, interest wanes and by half-time the channel is changed. More interesting is a game in which the teams are evenly matched and the contest is close. Although in such a game the victor does not wear the patina of invincibility, such a game is remembered as the "Game of the Century," and to have played and prevailed in such a game is to be talked about forevermore.

The desire to see quality concentrated, to see champions, dynasties, and the greatest ever, runs headlong into the need to have this quality challenged, put to the test, and brought to life; for otherwise it is a museum piece, an imaginary "dream team" composed of the very best but with no competitors against whom to prove its mettle. The aesthetic appeal of greatness, therefore, is not one-dimensional, not a case in which more is always better. There are built-in limits even to a quest which seems limitless. Glory is limiting since glory is conferred on active greatness, and active greatness exists where there is comparable greatness in others. Glory is the meeting point of excellence and equality. For the highest praise is given by those near enough to excellence to appreciate its rarity. Plus glory, as noted, is an imperfect good; viewed from eternity's perspective, this summit of human striving is but a protuberance on the horizon.

We have reached the heart of a most important question, the relationship of liberty to greatness. Mark Hulliung supposes that the former is simply a means to the latter (and we have entertained this interpretation ourselves). He argues against the civic humanists who, he contends, are oblivious to Machiavelli's imperial theme.[56] Hulliung is mostly right. But he is himself too dismissive of Machiavelli's liberty theme. For it is not that liberty and greatness are opposites demanding a commitment to one or the other.[57] Differing by degree rather than by kind, they represent separate stages in the history of that human excellence called *virtù*. The love of glory is a manifestation of *virtù*, but so is the love of liberty. *Virtù* is not the same for everyone: those who have it in small measure fight to be free; those who have it in larger portions fight to domineer; those who have it to "excess" fight to be remembered. Such persons are plebs, nobles, and princes respectively. Machiavelli admires them all and encourages alike their ambitions even though their ambitions are in conflict. As a connoisseur of *virtù* he is pleased by the prospect of *virtù* spread all around, just as he is pleased by the prospect of *virtù* concentrated in one spot. He is ambivalent, as are we all; for one cannot help, when seeing equality, to long for the sight of excellence, to wonder how grand it could be if one alone were to occupy the pinnacle of success. At the same time it is clear that below the pinnacle is a wasteland of mediocrity saddening to behold; that without real competitors to keep life interesting, possessing the pinnacle is a dead testimonial, as moribund as the monument-city which Alexander's architect proposed building on Mount Athos (I.1.5); and that no sooner is the height scaled than the virtue which sustained the ascent begins to decline. Machiavelli, then, is not consistently republican because his imagination runs to heroes; but neither is he consistently monarchic because heroes without rivals become weaklings and villains. In any event, *virtù* is appreciated for its own sake, in whatever concentration it is found.

That Machiavelli welcomes the dispersion of *virtù* is attested to by the fact that he takes for his subject early, republican Rome. That he also welcomes the convergence of *virtù* is attested to by the fact that the Rome he admires expanded and became great: "Those who read what the beginning was of the city of Rome . . . will not marvel that so much virtue was maintained for many centuries in that city, and that afterward the empire that the republic attained arose there" (I.1.1). Civic virtue is most vigorous when necessity threatens destruction—a time at or near the beginning of a city's existence (and by returning to the spirit of the beginning does a city restore the vitality of young life). Greatness, though, resides near the end; the Rome of the late republic and of the caesars bestrided the world, whereas the Rome of Camillus lorded it over Latium. Machiavelli values equally the beginning and the end, and all stages in between. He is like the proud parents of a toddler, who anticipate the time when their child is full-grown; and like the proud parents of a college graduate, who remember the time when their child was just born. Looking down from his historian's perch, Machiavelli watches as states rise and fall, and he pronounces the movement good. Goodness is present in all stages of the cycle, for liberty and justice are the benefits when many states share equally in virtue, and greatness and glory are the benefits when one state is supreme. There is no tragedy in this transformation of virtue, thus no desperate attempt to make virtue, in any of its modes, last forever. Machiavelli is at peace with his choice of Rome, because Roman virtue, though self-destructive, is most in harmony with nature's motions.[58]

That being the case, Machiavelli can contemplate the demise of Rome with perfect equanimity: Rome reached for the brass ring of superlative virtue, fell off its horse, and other riders, following close by, took Rome's place. Virtue rebounded, because the sum of virtue like that of energy is constant and indestructible: "I judge the world always to have been in the same mode and there to have been as much good as wicked in it. But the wicked and the good vary from province to province" (II.Pr.2). Virtue then rebounded, and it moved on; not this time to gather in one locale, but to be possessed by numerous equals:

> And if no empire followed after the Roman Empire that might have endured and in which the world might have kept its virtue together, it is seen none-theless to be scattered in many nations where they lived virtuously, such as was the kingdom of the Franks, the kingdom of the Turks, that of the sultan, and the peoples of Germany today—and that Saracen sect earlier, which did so many great things and seized so much of the world after it destroyed the eastern Roman Empire. The virtue that is desired and is praised with true praise has thus been in all these provinces after the Romans were ruined, and in all these sects, and still is in some part of them. (§2)

Machiavelli is largely indifferent as to where virtue should locate, in multiple republics or in one great empire, because virtue has two faces: virtue in the many, called liberty, and virtue in the one, called greatness. Each is a facet of the same phenomenon, or each is a point on the arc of the same circle; and they relate reciprocally as cause and effect: liberty causes greatness, and greatness, inadvertently, causes liberty; for by destroying liberty, greatness soon destroys itself; and when greatness is brought low, the circle spins round again to liberty. Life is process, and as long as the process renews itself, Machiavelli is satisfied. Machiavelli's thought, therefore, is neither tragic nor comic—neither does it rebel against nature's annihilative cycles nor does it seek to impose upon nature a human remedy and a happy ending.[59]

We noted before the manifold antinomies present in Machiavelli's thought, many of them circling about the opposition of middle and extreme ways. Might we now say that when guarding the middle way, counseling balance, restraint, and common goods, Machiavelli is taking the side of liberty and of republics. It is a side which looks plausibly modern in that it preaches the utilitarian morality of enlightened self-interest. But Machiavelli's concern is not the greatest happiness of the greatest number; rather what he values is the virtue, the face of virtue, manifested in the defense of liberty. Similarly, when Machiavelli flies from the middle way toward the extreme, advising the impetuosity of youthful suitors, he is taking the side of greatness and of principalities (imperial republics end as principalities and are principalities to their subjects). The new prince acquires state, after which he acquires more state. Greatness is ceaseless acquisition culminating in ruin. This emancipated appetite is another of modernity's telltale signs, the raw egoism of unenlightened self-interest—or deemed unenlightened by liberalism's careful acquirers.[60] On the other hand, middle-way virtue is unsustainable; and were it capable of permanence, still it would be unfulfilling since a part of virtue would always escape its notice—that part at work in greatness, a face of virtue more exalted than the love of liberty. Machiavelli wants them both, and because the cycle is permanent, he can have them both: Liberty yields to greatness, and greatness yields to liberty. Virtue endures.

Even if Machiavelli cannot complain about the death of virtue, he can lament its long absence from most of Europe. Like air in a balloon, virtue, since the fall of Rome, has been squeezed into other quarters of the world. But why has there been no significant revival in Rome's former dominions? Rome did destroy virtue in the ancient world—its own greatness and the liberty of others; but that destruction was inevitable since "worldly things," as Machiavelli explains in the *Florentine Histories*, "are not allowed by nature to stand still. As soon as they reach their ultimate perfection, having no further to rise, they must descend." It is given that worldly things decline; but it is also expected that "once they have descended and through their disorders arrived at the ultimate depth, since they cannot descend further, of necessity they must rise" (V.1). Cities must and do rise, but on condition that no "extraordinary force" blocks their way. This force, which Machiavelli fails to name in the *Florentine Histories*, in the *Discourses* he pointedly identifies as the Christian religion.

Christianity

The fact that Machiavelli discusses Christianity as a man-made sect subject to the life cycles of mixed bodies is enough to convince most readers that Machiavelli is no Christian.[61] Some would have it that he is simply anti-church;[62] but his deepest aversion is to the principles of the Christian faith, blaming them for the weakness of the modern world (I.Pr.2). Although said to be "the truth and the true way" (II.2.2), Christianity, by inculcating weakness, runs afoul of what Machiavelli calls "more true than any other truth," namely "that if where there are men there are not soldiers, it arises through a defect of the prince" (I.21.1). Christianity prevents Christian princes from making soldiers of their citizens.[63] This it does by teaching humility in place of worldly glory; by commemorating contemplative men, such as monks and saints, over active men, such as captains and lawgivers; and by admiring strength in suffering, not strength in bold enterprises and vengeance for injuries.[64] Christian sacrifices are delicate, unlike pagan sacrifices which were magnificent. The foremost Christian sacrifice is the celebration of the Mass, honoring the death of Christ on the cross. Pity is the appropriate response to the scene of crucifixion; and pity, as in *pietà*, is the Christianization of Roman duty, or *pietas*. Christians are made compassionate by the vision of their suffering Lord, who by his death and resurrection delivered men from their sins. Pagans, by contrast, were made ferocious by the terrible slaughter of their sacrifices, which foretold the outcomes of worldly enterprises. Inspired by such ferocity, ancient pagans could ambition conquering the world. Not modern Christians, however, whose sinews have atrophied under the influence of Christian modes and orders, the source, says Machiavelli, of "our education" (II.2.2).

Christianity, then, destroys the appetite for greatness; it also destroys the love of liberty. One consequence of Christian compassion is that modern men have not "the harms that peoples and cities receive through servitude" as a reason for loving liberty (II.2.1). The ancients had this negative reason along with a positive reason in prosperity. Machiavelli does not specify what he means by harms, but elaboration can be found in *The Art of War*. There Fabrizio explains that

> our way of living today, as a result of the Christian religion, does not impose the same necessity for defending ourselves as antiquity did. Then men overcome in war either were killed or kept in perpetual slavery, so that they passed their lives wretchedly; conquered cities were either laid waste or the inhabitants driven out, their goods taken from them and they themselves sent wandering through the world. Hence those conquered in war suffered the utmost of every misery. Terrorized by this dread, men kept military training alive and honored those who were excellent in it. Today this fear has for the most part disappeared; of the conquered, few are killed; no one is long held a prisoner because captives are easily freed. Cities, even though they have rebelled many times, are not destroyed; men are allowed to keep their property, so that the greatest evil they fear is a tax. Hence men do not wish to submit to military regulations and to endure steady hardships under them in order to escape dangers they fear little. (II, 623)[65]

Men are weak because the necessities that make them strong exist no longer. And being weak, they are not free.

It is charged against Christianity that in rendering the world weak, it has "given it in prey to criminal men, who can manage it securely, seeing that the collectivity of men, so as to go to paradise, think more of enduring their beatings than of avenging them" (II.2.2). Oppression is now the problem, to which the solution is not teaching the criminal to be good, but enabling the weak to defend themselves. The plebeians of Rome defended themselves by means of tribunes, and balanced power between the classes meant that Romans lived free. Liberty requires a proud and energetic populace unwilling to take abuse. Machiavelli's complaint then is that Christianity emasculates citizens with its doctrines of charity, humility, forgiveness, and submission; that princes become tyrants when they encounter no resistance to their rule; and that needless suffering is the result of weak peoples governed by omnipotent masters.

Such was the result of the reform movements of the Duecento. Saints Francis and Dominic reestablished Christianity on the basis of its first principles, poverty and imitation of the life of Christ; and so much authority did they have with Christians that the religion did not lose credibility despite the scandalous misbehavior of its leaders. The Christian religion managed to endure this corruption at the top, as the followers were taught that "it is evil to say evil of

evil" (*egli è male dir male del male*), that obedience is laudable, and that punishment of wrongdoers is best left to God. Machiavelli sounds generally approving of the good example of the Christian reformers—after all, they saved
Christianity from ruin. But then he draws this conclusion: "So they [the Church
hierarchy] do the worst they can because they do not fear the punishment that
they do not see and do not believe" (III.1.4). Christian faith, patience, and docility have all led to the tyranny of arrogant non-believers. The Roman patricians were also characterized as non-believers in the pagan faith; and they used
religion to extract obedience from the plebs (I.14). But the patricians had the
good sense to disguise their disbelief, and the very effort to maintain the fraud
required that they be in league with the people rather than opposed to the people
as alien oppressors. The patricians could hardly do otherwise, since the people
was armed and accustomed to rebelling. Where citizens are free and able to look
after themselves, they are treated justly by their leaders. Here Machiavelli's objection to Christianity is on behalf of liberty and justice—that the sanctity of the
pope makes checking his power practically impossible; rather than on behalf of
greatness and glory—that Christianity's tyrants are prelates inexperienced in the
art of war.

But that they are inexperienced at war—or that prelates make lousy captains—is another of Machiavelli's objections. This one he registers in I.12,
where the charge laid against the Church of Rome is that it has kept Italy divided. He notes that the temporal might of the Church (the Papal States) has
been insufficient—and its ministers too lacking in virtue—to unite the province
of Italy; but that the Church's might has been equal to the task of preventing
unification by any other power. The recent history of Italy, therefore, has not
tracked that of France and Spain, where strong kings created nations by crushing
the nobility and the free states within their realms. Machiavelli gives voice to
the discontents of Italian nationalists. What he wants is for Italy to become a
single country free of outside interference,[66] and he blames the Church both for
failing "to seize the tyranny of Italy" itself and for inviting in foreigners, barbarians, who blocked others from doing the same.[67] His reason for wanting nationhood is that "no province has ever been united or happy unless it has all
come under obedience to one republic or to one prince" (§2). Apparently national unity is more important to Machiavelli than the form of government under
which Italy is ruled, and more important as well than the freedom of Italy's several republics, including the republic of Florence. It and all other cities would
become part of a single, Italian entity. But then growth is nature's order, and
Machiavelli is accepting of all stages of the cycle of growth and decay. Similarly, if the time is not yet right for Italy's unification,[68] then a Tuscan empire—
costing the free cities of Tuscany their independence—is the growth which Machiavelli endorses (I.55.4).

There are, it seems, three counts to the indictment of Christianity: that it
dissuades men from undertaking great enterprises; that it robs men of their lib-

erty, delivering them into the hands tyrannical masters; and that it divides the Italian peninsula, keeping that province weak and insignificant. What then is to be done? On a practical level, one course of action is to capture or destroy the papacy. Machiavelli has already stated that popes and all lesser clergy are fair game, that "whoever lives and reigns as they do" is to be removed from office, killed if necessary, and that the papacide's prize is the promise of "eternal memory" (I.27.2). But since popes are readily replaced, the assassination of Julius would alone accomplish little. With this in mind, Mansfield conjectures that the Baglioni episode is a veiled invitation to murder all popes, or to abolish the papacy itself.[69] John Scott and Vickie Sullivan build on this insight by reading *The Prince* as a plot against the papacy and its court, the College of Cardinals. Cesare's failing, they contend, was that he allowed "anyone" to become pope, for Cesare, with his effective veto power, could have brought the institution to an end by blocking every election attempt.[70]

There certainly is reason to believe that Machiavelli is out to disarm Christianity and to defeat the power which priests exercise over the laity. The clergy is an intimidating confraternity because it possesses the authority to threaten eternal perdition, if not exactly to consign the faithful to hell. So Machiavelli writes a fable, *Belfagor*, in which Pluto's domain is agreeably portrayed. It is, as Theodore Sumberg notes, a kingdom well-governed, a limited monarchy in fact, where finding the truth and doing justice are pressing concerns, where human frailties are understood and human complaints sympathetically heard, and where—to underscore the blasphemy—a devil made flesh ascends to earth in order to save men from those of their sins caused by the marriage state.[71] This is a Christianity without the fires of hell, without the power, therefore, to direct man's thoughts to the afterlife and away from worldly pursuits; it thus is a Christianity attractive to Enlightenment liberals, who seek not the abolition of religion as such, but its systematic devaluing through doctrinal simplification and the privatization of belief. Machiavelli could be mapping the way to the latitudinarianism these liberals finally do reach, and he could be suggesting a separation of church and state as the surest means of neutralizing religion's power. He could be. But his works are conspicuously lacking in the biblical revisionism so characteristic of liberal philosophizing. There is nothing equivalent in Machiavelli's corpus to Hobbes' *Leviathan*, Parts 3 and 4, to Spinoza's *Theologico-Political Treatise*, or to Locke's *First Treatise of Government*. Nor is a privatized Christianity, tolerant of dissent, consistent with Machiavelli's professed regard for civil religion.[72]

It is as a champion of civil religion that Machiavelli demands from Christian princes public displays of reverence for the Christian faith. This is false reverence, to be sure, modeled after the pretended piety of pagan princes. But the closer these princes are to the Roman Church, Machiavelli observes, the less do they fulfill their obligation. Thus he deduces that the Church itself is the source of this corruption, and he conjectures that were the pope and his court sent into Switzerland, even this most virtuous of modern states would in short order be ruined. Corruption and ruin are the consequences, says Machiavelli, of having departed from the principles upon which the religion was founded (I.12.2). Christianity's founding principles are charity (as stated in *An Exhortation to Penitence* [173]) and poverty and Christlikeness (as stated in *Discourses* III.1.4). But Christian principles do not lend themselves to political use of the sort which Machiavelli admires—the achievement of liberty and greatness. For what rather has resulted from their revival in the thirteenth century is, in the sixteenth century, the tyranny of prelates and the devastation of Italy.

Machiavelli thus suggests taking an alternate route. He declares that "our religion" has been falsely interpreted by cowardly and lazy men; that Christianity is not averse to virtue, or need not be; and that in fact "it permits us the exaltation and defense of the fatherland" (II.2.2). A fighting Christianity is thus what Machiavelli wants. But where does he go to find it? One possible answer is that he goes to the Old Testament rather than the New. The God of Moses fights for the survival and greatness of his chosen people; whereas the God of the Apostles surrenders his life, explaining that his kingdom is not of this world. When read "judiciously" (*sensatamente*), the Old Testament shows a hardy race led by princes willing and able to take matters into their own hands—a Moses, for instance, who because "he wished his laws and his orders to go forward . . . was forced to kill infinite men" (III.30.1); or a David, who as a new prince made "new governments with new names, new authorities, new men." To read judiciously is to read the New Testament in light of the Old, to take, in this case, what Luke says of God, that he "filled the hungry with good things and sent the rich away empty,"[73] and apply it to King David, saying that he made "the rich poor, the poor rich" (I.26.1).[74] A judicious hermeneutics would also allow comparison with outside sources, as when a pagan text is used to reveal the effectual truth of the biblical narrative—for example, that entry into the Promised Land was a necessary war, not a covenant fulfilled, in which a migrant and homeless people, the Israelites, displaced an indigenous people, the Maurusians, who migrated west and in turn displaced another indigenous people, the Africans (II.8.2).[75]

There are indications as well that New Testament Christianity is not altogether alien to Machiavelli's purposes. Machiavelli has made frequent use of the dignified individual, the man in uniform whose status, demeanor, and good sense are sufficient to pacify an angry crowd. It seems that this function can be performed as easily by a bishop of the Church as by a senator of Rome. Francesco Soderini, bishop of Volterra, managed to quiet a mob of Arrabbiati (opponents of Savonarola) which had gathered to sack the home of Pagolantonio Soderini, the bishop's brother (I.54.1). Christian princes have then the authority to command. Likewise Christian peoples have the disposition to obey. German citizens have a conscience (presumably developed by Christian doctrine) which obliges them to keep their promises. This it does more surely than paganism caused Romans to abide by their oaths. For Roman legionnaires, unwilling to respect their oath to Camillus, jeopardized Camillus's oath to Apollo; by contrast, the Christian Germans always pay in full their assessed taxes even though they pay only the amount which they swear is fitting and rightly owed (I.55.2). One of Christianity's first principles, the goodness of poverty, was also a building block of Roman civic virtue. Romans individually were poor in order that Romans collectively might be rich (III.25). Similarly, Christians preach that poverty is sanctifying and yet allow their Church in Rome to wallow in wealth; as such, Christians are accustomed to the odd combination of republican austerity and imperial greatness. It was just said that Machiavelli's *Belfagor* tries lessening the terrors of hell and abridging the power of priests. True enough—but that does not mean that there is no political capital to be had from Christianity's afterlife. Christianity is a religion which puts little store by justice. Its distributions, like the wages paid to vineyard workers,[76] are mystifying at best, if not out-and-out unjust. Paradise is more reward than any sinner earns, and eternal damnation is more punishment than any temporal wrongdoing deserves. Rather like Rome, Christianity caresses or it eliminates (though it does have a middle way in purgatory). It sacrifices precise justice for the behavioral benefits of rule by love and rule by fear. Christians, therefore, are acquainted with the political uses of justice.[77] Christians also are usefully superstitious, believing in angels, in miracles, in signs from on high. Already sensitive to divine presences, they may be prepared to acknowledge the existence of airy intelligences compassionate toward men, demi-deities forewarning of grave accidents just in time for men to arm and protect themselves (I.56.1). The interventions of these spirits have Machiavelli's approval, for they are not part of a single, providential plan denying human freedom or diminishing the significance of the city. On the contrary, they imply an activist humanity divided politically and bound strictly to the earth. Here then is one instance of how Christianity might be reinterpreted so as to aid in the defense of the fatherland.[78]

And in some places Christians literally do defend the fatherland. Hungarians and Poles (Magyars and Slavs) are warlike Christians able to hold back the migrations of Tartars (none for 500 years) and responsible for saving Italy and the Church from Tartar rule (II.8.4). While necessity is likely what keeps these borderland Christians virtuous, their obstinacy still proves that Christianity is not totally destructive of good arms. On the other hand, good arms at the periphery are no substitute for good arms at the core (II.30).

The question before us is Machiavelli's intentions regarding Christianity—whether to turn it into a state religion along pagan lines or to relegate it to private spaces far removed from politics. In several of the chapters considered above, Machiavelli seems inclined to select from Christianity those elements that are politically useful: (1) hierarchy as a cause of reverential deference; (2) conscience and poverty as causes of civic virtue; (3) extremism in the administration of justice as a cause of gratitude and obedience. His ambition thus

seems to be the transformation of Christian doctrines into politically useful superstitions defended by secular authorities who do not believe in their truth; also
the union of church and state, with the papacy captured, eliminated, democra-
tized, or brought under the control of an all-Italian republic.[79] The Church of
Rome, catholic in both precepts and mission, would become the Church of Italy,
supporting Italian war aims against France, Spain, or England, each in turn supported by a national church of its own.[80] Christianity would thus fracture along
national lines. From here one can easily project the Protestant Reformation, the
Counter-Reformation, and the two or more centuries of religious warfare which
their disagreements produced. Europe did indeed experience the consequences
of an armed Christianity. But then the fighting was a case of the religious tail
wagging the political dog, of kingdoms and republics captured by sects fighting
for the glory of God, not the glory of man.[81] Surely Machiavelli would have
wished for a different future and a different resolution of the theologico-political
problem—at least a resolution like the state religion suggested by Hobbes.[82] But
whether Hobbes' state religion or Machiavelli's civil religion were ever achievable goals in the Christian era is a doubtful proposition. Commenting on the
catastrophe of sectarian Christianity, Rousseau observes:

> Of all Christian authors, the philosopher Hobbes is the only one who cor-
> rectly saw the evil and the remedy, who dared to propose the reunification of
> the two heads of the eagle, and the complete return to political unity, without
> which no State or government will ever be well constituted. But he ought to
> have seen that the dominating spirit of Christianity was incompatible with his
> system, and that the interest of the priest would always be stronger than that
> of the State.[83]

An added problem is this. While there are a few hints that Machiavelli's
plan is to paganize Christianity, hardly is there enough material here to support
his claim that he has left for his followers "a short road" to travel (I.Pr.2).
Clearly Machiavelli is displeased with Christianity and from time to time targets
its teachings and its practices. But the *Discourses* presents no sustained assault
on Christian principles and is not itself seriously engaged with Christian doctrine; it offers, as alluded to above, no revisionist retelling of the Sermon on the
Mount, where "Turn the other cheek" is discovered to mean "Bloody thine enemy's cheek."[84] This or its equivalent we would expect from a book ostensibly
locked throughout in a spiritual war with Christianity.[85] We conclude, therefore,
that the religion issue is unresolved and that Machiavelli never finally decides
what to do about Christian modes and orders.[86]

Reclaiming Ancient Virtue

There is nothing tentative, however, about his admiration for the ancients. Machiavelli wants his contemporaries to imitate the virtue of Rome. He wants modern men to be strong like the Romans. But why? What is the good of strength? The question may seem an impertinence given that Machiavelli has assumed all along that strength is good and that weakness is a condition more despicable than pitiable. We ask this question, impertinent though it may be, because the probable effect of Machiavelli's teaching is to increase the quantity of violence, not to reduce it as is often said—more strong men trained in the arts of acquisition; hence more war, more destruction, more bloodshed and dying.[87] When prideful pagans, steeled to the hazards of combat, replace compassionate Christians, sensitive to everyone's pain, the world is likely to become a more dangerous and frightening place. And yet Machiavelli can take the side of Christian compassion and speak quite movingly about the ravages caused by ambition and avarice: survivors weeping for their dead relations; fathers killed while clutching their children to their breasts; mothers stabbed still carrying their young in their wombs; the dispossessed left to wander the countryside; daughters raped and sons butchered (*Tercets on Ambition*, ll.133-52). Are these not heartrending tragedies, wrongs to be condemned and redressed? But how will reviving Roman modes and orders set matters right or even lessen the carnage? On the contrary, will not the body count increase if Roman legions are once again loose upon the land? They make for exciting history, these Romans do, but they also make for impossible neighbors. They remind us of the dinosaurs of Jurassic Park—fantastic giants from a bygone age, now miraculously alive and moving about; but also absolute terrors when fences are breached and humans are their prey. Living dinosaurs truly are a wonder to behold, but would any sane person wish to share the planet with them? If not, why bring them back to life?

Apart from the misery caused by war and warmongering, there is the obvious fact that strength is a relative quality. One is strong in relation to others who are weak. Who then would Machiavelli have modern men be strong against? Against each other, surely, since they cannot test their strength against ancients long dead. But how can moderns fighting moderns all be strong? Or if they can, what's the point of universal strength? He castigates Christian armies for their desultory order of battle—lines drawn up thin and wide (II.16). What though is the difference if one badly ordered Christian army fights another like itself, or if two well-ordered Christian armies fight each other? What is accomplished if weak Christians all become strong Christians? The number of dead may increase when battles are fought, but otherwise the results should be the same. Why complain then if mercenary armies want to fight mock battles in which no one dies? Would it be better to have many die, to involve whole populations in the struggle, to have cannonballs rain down upon cities?

An answer, of course, comes readily to mind. Not all modern armies are equally ill- or well-ordered. In particular, Italian armies are Europe's punching bag. In the same *Tercets* noted above, Machiavelli excuses the ambitious city its aggression on grounds that a "hidden power" implanted ambition in its breast; and he advises that in place of exorcising this demon, the city should combine it with virtue so as to be on the winning side of a contest which nature ordains and which no state or person can escape (ll.25, 82-108, 160-65). Italy then should become strong; it should construct dikes and dams in order to protect its banks from floods. But if cities up river do as Machiavelli instructs, save themselves with flood walls built in quiet times, cities down river suffer far greater devastation as rising waters sweep across the plains. In order for some to win, others must lose. Switzerland is currently doing quite well—a small, confederal nation which manages nonetheless to intimidate the great powers of Europe, and which Machiavelli forecasts will one day shortly be a great power itself. Switzerland is one of two Christian states which imitate Roman modes and orders (the German republics being the other); and much advantaged is Switzerland in facing so little competition. Machiavelli's call to arms in the *Discourses* cannot, therefore, do Switzerland any good. Nor will France or Spain be much helped if Italy undertakes a serious Roman revival. But Italy will be helped, and helping Italy is what Machiavelli wants. Machiavelli is an Italian patriot, or a Tuscan patriot, or a Florentine patriot—depending on which unit of government is ready for greatness.

Except for one thing. Machiavelli's advice, written down and soon to be published, respects no national boundaries. The French can read and learn about the art of acquisition as easily as can the Italians—better even, since the French are not as corrupt and since specific instruction is provided them on how to conquer Italy. So Machiavelli is not a patriot after all, but is, as many in fact think, a technician of statecraft, an adviser without loyalties, happy to offer his knowledge to any who understand ("But since my intent is to write something useful to whoever understands it" [*Prince*, 15]). Of course many readers object to classifying Machiavelli as an adviser-for-hire; but whether he is or is not, the technician interpretation takes on fresh credibility when thought is given to the relativity of strength.

Machiavelli claims to be bringing "common benefit to everyone" and to be fulfilling the duties of a good man (I.Pr.1, II.Pr.3). But he fails to show how he can commonly benefit the Italians and the French, and the good that comes from the competition between them is at this point difficult to perceive. If French territory, defended by better arms, escapes "flooding," Italian lands, defended by weaker arms, are "inundated." The most that can be done is to fashion a common good within the borders of one state, a common good between nobles and plebs which lasts as long as there are enemies without to threaten them harm. On the other hand, since there is not a fixed understanding of what constitutes a state, and since states endeavor to expand, defeated enemies sometimes are assimilated and have the common good extended to them. Even so, this state-based, zero-sum system of acquisition has not the capacity to benefit all. Thus another of nature's imperfections is the division of the human race into warring communities.[88]

It is the view of some scholars that the only way to make good on the common benefit claim and to remedy this last of nature's imperfections is to base acquisition on commerce rather than on war. In war there are victors and vanquished; in trade there are buyers and sellers mutually advantaged by economic transactions. People can acquire by producing new wealth as well as by appropriating old wealth long in the possession of others. New wealth, enough to liberate appetite and relieve the estate of man, requires science and technology—of which there is precious little in Machiavelli's day. But after Machiavelli comes the scientific and industrial revolutions; after Machiavelli comes capitalism. While modern science and capitalistic economics do not eliminate the humoral division among men, they do for the first time create a middle class larger than the classes of rich and poor. These middle class populations, consuming the produce of industry and trade, are the ultimate beneficiaries of an enterprise which begins with the observation that acquisition is "a very natural and ordinary thing" (*Prince*, 3).[89] Machiavelli initiates the modern project of appetitive gratification, but others are needed to prove its worth and feasibility. Accordingly, Machiavelli is a transitional figure who must wait on Bacon, Hobbes, Smith, and the like to redeem his promise to bring benefit to each.[90] Without them, standing alone among the Romans, Machiavelli is simply too blood-stained to pass for a philanthropist—or, as he himself says, a good man who teaches others the good that malignant fortune has put beyond his reach.

Machiavelli's Heritage

We are back to seeing Machiavelli as a proto-modern, as a writer and an activist whose gaze is fixed upon the future. The two objections to resuscitating the Romans, that war is cruel and the results uneven, are based on modern assumptions that people should be pacific and distributions should be equal. But again we ask if this vision of the future, in which all are benefited by peace and prosperity, is in any way Machiavelli's own. It might be his own, or acceptable to him, if strength were appreciated solely as a means to acquisition (the strong prevail and the weak submit, so be strong and acquire). In that case, while Machiavelli would advise imitation of Roman valor, he also would be open to improvements in organization and technology which make acquisition easier and more universal, to free markets and assembly lines, and to unions in place of citizen militias. Any instrument of acquisition more efficient and less partisan than martial strength ought to be welcomed, as should the conquest of nature in place of the conquest of men. To support this expectation there is Machiavelli's chastisement of his contemporaries whose acquisitions cost more than they are worth, who lose strength even as they acquire dominion. War-making must be cost-effective, Machiavelli argues in II.6 and II.19, and in the *Florentine Histories* he explains why:

> It has always been the end of those who start a war—and it is reasonable that it should be so—to enrich themselves and impoverish the enemy. For no other cause is victory sought, nor for anyone else are acquisitions desired than to make oneself powerful and the adversary weak. Hence, it follows that whenever your victory impoverishes you or acquisition weakens you, you must forgo it or you will not arrive at the result for which wars are made. (VI.1)

It seems clear that acquisition is the purpose of war. But then it seems no less clear that power is the purpose of acquisition ("nor for anyone else are acquisitions desired than to make oneself powerful"). Moreover, the further purpose of acquisition, as Machiavelli next implies, is the cooperation of the public, its support paid for with lower taxes and bread and circuses: "Ancient and well-ordered republics were accustomed to fill their treasuries with gold and silver from their victories, to distribute gifts among the people, to forgive the payment of tribute by their subjects, and to entertain them with games and solemn festivals." The expansionary state pays attention to balance sheets, not to maximize its wealth as such, but, by using its wealth, to sustain the public's appetite for acquisitions of a higher order. The many's desire for booty is satisfied in order that the few are free to chase after glory. Machiavelli advises princes to be parsimonious with their own resources but liberal with the spoils of victory: "For the prince who goes out with his armies, who feeds on booty, pillage, and ransom and manages on what belongs to someone else, this liberality is necessary; otherwise he would not be followed by his soldiers." By "spending what is someone else's," princes have "done great things with their armies"—Cyrus, Caesar, and Alexander in particular (*Prince*, 16). Doing great things is the objective, and acquisition, while in one sense a measure of greatness, is mainly but a means. We saw in book 2 that Machiavelli was unwilling to countenance virtueless acquisitions, that he stood foursquare against innovations in war-making if they threatened to undermine the discipline of the army. Machiavelli is a warrior, we thus conclude, not a humanitarian. His intent is not the modern project of relieving man's estate but the ancients' ambition of achieving world empire.[91] He means to reclaim a lost glory, not chart a course for progress in the future.[92]

Mansfield maintains, to the contrary, that Machiavelli is a modern and a progressive: "He began a project, later picked up and developed by other modern philosophers, for a permanent, irreversible improvement in human affairs establishing a new political regime. The project is often called 'modernity.'"[93] Standing in the way of this project, Mansfield explains, were two ideas which had to be displaced: the classical idea of the cycle and the Christian idea of redemption history. For a cycle denies that progress is possible, and redemption history denies that improvement to the human condition is the responsibility of man. We do not dispute that Machiavelli has his differences with Christianity, profound and irreconcilable, but the claim that Machiavelli rejects the ancients' cyclical understanding of history seems a hard one to substantiate. Mansfield makes the effort by examining the two chapters of the *Discourses* most troublesome for his progressivist thesis, I.2 and III.1. The Polybian cycle of regimes, in which goodness suffers corruption and corruption invites the return of goodness, is interrupted by exogenous forces, by conquering neighbors or by nature's cataclysms. Consequently, the mixed regime, that half-remedy devised by the classics (half because it retards the cycle rather than providing an escape) is superseded, Mansfield argues, by the "perfect republic," the "perpetual republic." But the realization that regimes live in a crowded world affected by foreign affairs might only bring to full clarity why simple regimes are an unaffordable luxury (since their rapid demise and easy turnover leaves a city vulnerable to outside attack), not force the conclusion that mixed regimes, the corrective, need replacing. The mixed regime should rise in importance the more it is understood that managing relations between the humors is the secret to longevity. We discovered that Machiavelli was a frequent visitor of the middle way, eager to hold in balance its opposing forces, because the mixed regime, itself a middle way, was his remedy for oppression and political instability, and because the democratic mixed regime was his means of expansion. Machiavelli, we believe, approves of mixed regimes. As regards that other cycle, the cycle of civilizations (II.5), Machiavelli adopts the view that a return to primitiveness is a necessary part of nature's renewal. Civilization-wrecking calamities—floods, famines, plagues—are an ineluctable fact of nature, and never is it Machiavelli's objective to escape these calamities or deny this fact. The existence of the civilizational cycle, therefore, should in no way count as testimony against the efficacy of the mixed regime.

Mansfield reminds us that returning to beginnings, called for in III.1, is not intended as a restoration of original institutions, long out of date and inapplicable to current conditions, but as a re-experiencing of the fear that causes goodness and a reacquaintance with "the condition of being new and exciting."[94] Mansfield is right to observe that the maintenance of past acquisitions accompanies periodic renewals, that Rome did not each century (to say nothing of each decade) give back its empire and start over again as a village along the Tiber. Rome instead tried combining increased power with refreshed goodness, the purpose being to keep the engine of acquisition forever running. But eventually, and inevitably, the fuel supply was used up. Machiavelli understands that the pursuit of greatness—to switch metaphors now—is a self-immolating ambition, like Icarus being drawn into the flame of the sun.[95] Ascent is not endless. At some point a summit is reached, and further movement is decline, even though new acquisitions continue to be added (in Rome's case conquest outside of Italy). Or—to change metaphors again—the imperial state, like the horse-boy on the *Via Larga*, sprints the final leg of its race in order to see how far and how fast it can go.

But there is something else working against the idea of progress besides the fact of eventual exhaustion. The beginning has a special appeal once it is realized that time and achievement bring corruption and decline. Youth is preferred over maturity since youth is further from decay and has longer to last.[96] There is a parallel between the state which returns to its origins and the individual who changes his character to suit the times. Each is attempting to postpone the finality of a developed form, hoping to pass through life without ever becoming some one thing. Perhaps this explains why Machiavelli lays such stress on history and imitation and warns of entrapment in the prison of one's own experience (III.9.2). History is the record of someone else's experiences. Thus the study of history allows for critical distance and the liberty to choose. Similarly, imitation is nicely artificial in that the imitator is not really the person he imitates and so remains free to follow the example of a different model. Why then this fear of maturation? Because maturation terminates in ruin. It is death, the great evil, which elevates youth above maturity. Aristotle supposes, contrarily, that youthful potential is properly replaced by mature actualization, that the virtuous man, having struggled to reach a plateau, lives the balance of his life performing virtuous deeds and experiencing true happiness. But then Aristotle, through contemplating the eternal, as well as Christianity, through the promise of salvation, achieve an indifference toward death which Machiavellian secularism finds impossible to comprehend. To Machiavelli, all bodies, including all mixed bodies, are merely mortal; hence the growth of states, from a longer view, is simultaneously the death of states; and death is not progress.

But Mansfield, it seems, does not disagree. His perpetual republic is no better equipped for unending progress than is the classical mixed regime it supposedly replaces. If thought of as a particular state, it suffers the life cycle that afflicts all states: it grows, decays, and dies; it is temporal, limited, and exclusive. It coexists with other states like itself, no one of which is predestined for greatness or favored by Machiavelli.[97] But then the perpetual republic can be differently conceived, as the idea or movement called modernity. Even so, Machiavelli's conception of modernity is a peculiar one, according to Mansfield. It is not the conquest of nature by science and technology, a collective enterprise to which all contribute and under which all are united.[98] This it may be for Machiavelli's successors, liberal philosophers who promise common benefits for all mankind. Mansfield, though, takes Machiavelli at his word when he promises to bring common benefits to "everyone," or to "each" (*comune benefizio a ciascuno*).[99] Common benefit is individuated for Machiavelli, meaning that division and conflict persist, or that the human community, in the era of the perpetual republic, continues to be divided into separate states contending among themselves for preeminence and glory.[100] Machiavelli's ambition is not to have peace and prosperity extended worldwide, but to have virtue shine in state after state. Such rotating brilliance requires that virtue be tested and challenged, made to overcome necessities and hardships;[101] that it proudly compete and risk suffering defeat; that there be winners and losers. Benefit is common, despite the fact that some contestants stumble and fall, because the competition itself, and not the spoils of victory, represents the benefit. "Spirited selfishness" is the common benefit, the chance given to every body politic to defend its life and fight for its glory.[102] The thought that humanity is benefited by the rout of fortune, by perpetual peace and inexhaustible wealth, is alien to Machiavelli. Without fortune there can be no virtue, and "any supposed betterment of mankind at the cost of virtue is no bargain."[103] So virtue is the thing, the object of Machiavelli's ambition. And the perpetual republic, rather than any particular constitutional ordering, is basically but a locution describing the agonistic condition which perpetuates virtue.[104]

Fair enough. But how then is that condition different from the cycle of regimes and the cycle of civilizations, each of which also uses the decay of virtue to renourish the growth of virtue? How also is Machiavelli's defense of virtue, of the soul's longing for spirited exertion, to be reconciled with the modern project of appetitive gratification? Even Mansfield confesses that "in attempting other, more regular and scientific modes of overcoming fortune, Machiavelli's successors formalized and emasculated his notion of virtue."[105]

Machiavelli is an ancient, not a modern, in at least this one respect, that he tries ennobling the ambitions of men, lifting their sights from security and wealth to liberty and greatness. There can of course be no pretense to ennobling unless it is thought that the soul has a right order.[106] Does Machiavelli, then, subscribe to this Platonic concept of right order or natural right? Yes he does,[107] though admittedly in attenuated form: spiritedness ranks higher than appetite and should dominate the soul. The acquisitive enterprise is the spirit's assertion of itself, an exercise in command over others and over the environment. To acquire state is to proclaim one's identity and to give notice of one's arrival, to make a statement about who one is and where one belongs. Life is combat. Those who welcome combat are fully alive; those who excel at it acquire. But the acquiring is not for the sake of consuming the commodities acquired, for that would be corruption. Acquisition is for its own sake. Put otherwise, the what and the how of acquisition determine its worth. Liberty and greatness constitute the what, and the how is by fighting. Both are more important than the extent and duration of the acquisition, and more important than the numbers who participate in the benefit. Consequently, glory surpasses safety; power surpasses wealth. Easy acquisitions, if they come at the expense of martial virtue, are to be discouraged, and technological innovations are rightly given short shrift. Artillery, Machiavelli argued, is useless on defense and of only marginal value to an attacking force ordered like Rome's. But in point of fact (and it is a fact which Machiavelli most likely recognizes), artillery radically democratizes war, since any state of modest means can buy a cannon, and since any cannon-ball can land inside a maniple, blowing it to bits and all of the hard work which went into making it virtuous.[108] How useful is this virtue if it is so easily destroyed? But then utility is not the point, for virtue is the end rather than the means.[109] Machiavelli's position is merely reactionary (and practically unintelligible in a person so determined to acquire) unless it is supposed that virtue is honored in its own right irrespective of its instrumentality; furthermore, that of the two qualities composing virtue, the lion's strength and the fox's astuteness, the former is the more noble of the two and the reason for the latter.[110] For if one starts out weak and small, the purpose is to grow strong and big, not the other way around. The fox admires the lion and, so to speak, hopes to become one when it grows up; certainly states long for the day when they can set scheming aside and simply command. Thus the point of it all is for spiritedness to flourish and rule.[111]

As mentioned, liberty and greatness are the proper objects of acquisition. They are for Machiavelli what justice and magnanimity are for Aristotle—the two faces of virtue and the twin peaks of moral excellence respectively. Security and wealth are permissible substitutes in cases where the emasculation of some contributes to the greatness of another; where one state breaks free of the equilibrium of forces and rushes toward the goal line of empire. Latium, Tuscany, Campania, and numerous other provinces surrendered their freedom so that Rome could become great. Their loss of virtue was regrettable; but then a competition among equals inevitably produces a single champion, whose crowning is at once the culmination and the termination of the game. It is not a sad fact that Rome destroyed all of the republics of the ancient world, since the survival of them all would have meant the obscurity of them all. But neither is it a sad fact that imperial Rome declined and fell, since only by the toppling of the champion can the contest of equals begin anew.

We noted before that nothing much changes if the virtue of armies is increased across the board: train moderns in the modes and orders of the ancients, and the result is that moderns fight at higher proficiency levels. Prudence is one explanation of why this improvement might nonetheless matter. It is not sensible to suppose that others will always keep to the bargain of mutual weakness or that an interloper will never enter the area and bust up the game. But prudence alone cannot explain why Machiavelli is so adamant about reviving ancient virtue. There is then the partisan explanation, that Machiavelli is a fan of the home team, giving it advice on how to beat the opposition. But the partisan explanation, while it accounts for the passion, fails to notice that Machiavelli, like Aetolian mercenaries, flies his colors in opposing camps (II.4.2); and frankly it is demeaning to Machiavelli to label him a patriot. Lastly, there is the technician explanation; but while it accounts for Machiavelli's neutrality, it does not account for his idealism. Why then is Machiavelli so distressed by the sight of Christian armies lined up thin and wide? The only remaining explanation is an aesthetic one. Machiavelli lives in a time of "third-stringers" whose accomplishments pale in comparison with the "hall of famers" of the past. Machiavelli desires to upgrade the skills of all contestants in order that he, the historian, might have a spectacle worthy of recording and memorializing. If weaklings like Italy would cease being such chumps, conquered by Charles using chalk for a sword (*Prince*, 12), potentates like France would start behaving like champs. Or others would take their place, including Italy someday. Competition is what causes all to improve; through competition the world might again see the likes of a Rome. And lest it be thought that Machiavelli favors too much the single victor over the field of also-rans, he demonstrates his evenhandedness by counseling the weak on the fine points of conspiracy, on rising by fraud to bring low the great. The common benefit then comes sequentially to each, as each takes its turn at striving for glory. Glory spread round is the common benefit, plus liberty in the interim. What Machiavelli wants is simply this—a first-rate performance by champions and challengers alike. In any event, Machiavelli's paganism shows in his aesthetics: accomplishment, excellence, magnificence count as beautiful, not innocence, humility, simplicity.[112]

Far from seeming a modern, Machiavelli is reminiscent of Plato's timocrat. The timocrat is a warrior set free from the superintendence of philosopher-kings.[113] He is a lover of victory and a lover of honor. He is stubborn, sometimes cruel, and careless about justice. Educated in gymnastics and the hunt, he is unmusical.[114] His claim to rule is based on his martial prowess and not on his powers of speech.[115] His life he devotes to the fatherland,[116] and he lives by the opinions of others.[117] The timocrat loves what is noble, but he cannot explain why it is good. Thus he is vulnerable to the temptations of appetite. For the timocrat is also a lover of money; his spiritedness is intermixed with eros. He is embarrassed, however, by his appetitive and erotic desires, and so he hides his wealth and his women in private homes protected by walls. In fact, the timocrat is no pure type; he is called a timocrat for as long as the love of honor is ascendant. But he is part oligarch, and the tug of avarice is always strong and is eventually triumphant. The change occurs when the timocrat is penalized for his nobility.[118] Humiliated, he (or his son) begins to doubt the worth of honor, to suspect that wealth is the real good and that honor is but an illusion.[119]

Machiavelli, it appears, is in a strikingly similar position. He affirms the nobility of spiritedness, its moral superiority to mere appetite. The warrior is admirable, the merchant is not.[120] Likewise he liberates spiritedness from dependence on reason. Rather than serving as reason's loyal adjutant, policing the conduct of appetite, spiritedness uses reason (as the lion uses the fox) to help it achieve its own ambition, victory in war; to help it also in the governance of appetite. And yet spiritedness is tainted by appetite, if not itself a form of appetite, in that it too is an acquisitive desire. Publicly it seeks to acquire glory, while privately it seeks to acquire wealth. The nobles of Rome found sharing their honors more palatable than sharing their land and their gold. Behind the veneer of aristocratic respectability hid the vulgarity of grasping oligarchs. Indeed, there was always an interior life separate from exterior appearances, multiple frauds perpetrated by crafty foxes. The crafty fox, keenly attuned to effectual truths, is inclined to regard the lion's pride as silly posturing. The fox represents reason, which in the Machiavellian soul can align with spiritedness, the lion, or align with appetite, the wolf (*Prince*, 18). But given the fox's talent for debunking and conspiring, given its cynicism and resentment, chances are it will throw in with appetite, thinking it the part of the soul more in step with nature's way—acquisition being "a very natural and ordinary thing," and the acquisition of commodities being the more ordinary form of acquiring. So it is with Machiavelli: he tries ennobling desire, but fearing the fox's charge of naiveté, he loses confidence in the effort. His idealism is put to shame by his realism.[121]

The strong timocrat is Machiavelli's ideal, whether he is fighting in defense of freedom or fighting in pursuit of greatness. Machiavelli is himself a Platonic timocrat lacking the philosopher's vision of the Good. As such he is never quite sure that nobility is a genuine good and is never quite clear as to how spiritedness can rule in the interest of everyone. And so always the calculating oligarch can be heard in the background sneering his "get-real" contempt, a contempt which puts the soul on an appetitive path heading toward democracy and ending in tyranny. Machiavelli the ancient changes looks and becomes Machiavelli the modern. Back and forth he goes. Although essentially retrospective in outlook, an ancient and not a modern, Machiavelli, it seems correct to say, unleashes ideas which exceed his power to control and which in time prove the undoing of his reclamation project.

Notes

Chapter One: Introduction: Reading the *Discourses*

1.   H. Butterfield, *The Statecraft of Machiavelli* (London: G. Bell and Sons Ltd., 1940); Isaiah Berlin, "The Originality of Machiavelli," in *Studies on Machiavelli, ed.* Myron Gilmore (Firenze: G. C. Sansoni Editore, 1972), 149-206; Harvey C. Mansfield, Jr. *Machiavelli's New Modes and Orders: A Study of the* Discourses on Livy (Ithaca: Cornell University Press, 1979); Bruce James Smith, *Politics and Remembrance: Republican Themes in Machiavelli, Burke, and Tocqueville* (Princeton: Princeton University Press, 1985), 29-38, 93-101; A. J. Parel, "The Question of Machiavelli's Modernity," *Review of Politics* 53 (1991): 320-39; Vickie B. Sullivan, *Machiavelli's Three Romes: Religion, Human Liberty, and Politics Reformed* (Dekalb: Northern Illinois University Press, 1996).

2.   Gennaro Sasso, *Niccolò Machiavelli: Storio del suo pensiero politico* (Napoli: Nella Sede dell'Istituto, 1958); Sydney Anglo, *Machiavelli: A Dissection* (New York: Harcourt, Brace and World, 1969); Silvia Ruffo-Fiore, *Niccolò Machiavelli* (Boston: Twayne, 1982); Mark Hulliung, *Citizen Machiavelli* (Princeton: Princeton University Press, 1983).

3.   Felix Gilbert, *Machiavelli and Guicciardini: Politics and History in Sixteenth Century Florence* (Princeton: Princeton University Press, 1965); Nicolai Rubinstein, "Machiavelli and the World of Florentine Politics," in *Studies on Machiavelli*, 5-28; J. G. A. Pocock, *The Machiavellian Moment: Florentine Political Thought and the Atlantic Republican Tradition* (Princeton: Princeton University Press, 1975); Quentin Skinner, *The Foundations of Modern Political Thought*, vol. 1 (Cambridge: Cambridge University Press, 1978); eds. Gisela Bock, Quentin Skinner, and Maurizio Viroli, *Machiavelli and Republicanism* (Cambridge: University of Cambridge Press, 1990).

4.   Pasquale Villari, *The Life and Times of Niccolò Machiavelli*, vol. 1 (London: T. Fisher Unwin, 4th impression); J. R. Hale, *Machiavelli and Renaissance Italy* (London: English Universities Press, 1961); Roberto Ridolfi, *The Life of Niccolò Machiavelli* (Chicago: University of Chicago Press, 1963).

5.   In the dedications to both the *Discourses* and *The Prince*, Machiavelli attributes his political understanding to practical experience as well as to historical-theoretical reading.

6.   Why this preference? Because the statement, "I have a secret plan," is more arresting than the statement, "I draw upon my experience."

7.   *The Political Philosophy of Hobbes: Its Basis and Its Genesis* (Chicago: University of Chicago Press, 1963), xvi.

8. *Thoughts on Machiavelli* (Seattle: University of Washington Press, 1958), 55, 62, 79.

9. *Thoughts*, 61.

10. *Thoughts*, 79.

11. Letter to Francesco Vettori, 16 April 1527 (#225). The numbering of the letters (unless otherwise stated) is that given by Allan Gilbert, *Machiavelli: The Chief Works and Others* (Duke University Press, 1989). Quotations from the letters, the minor works, and *The Art of War* are from the Gilbert translation, vols. 1-3. Quotations from the *Discourses* are from the Harvey C. Mansfield and Nathan Tarcov translation (Chicago: University of Chicago Press, 1996). Also used are the Mansfield translation of *The Prince* (Chicago: University of Chicago Press, 1985) and the Mansfield and Laura F. Banfield translation of the *Florentine Histories* (Princeton: Princeton University Press, 1988). Citations of the Italian are from *Opere di Niccolò Machiavelli*, ed. Ezio Raimondi (Milan: Ugo Mursia editore, 1966).

12. *Thoughts*, 10, 80, 97.

13. *Thoughts*, 19.

14. *Thoughts*, 175.

15. *Thoughts*, 202-03.

16. *Thoughts*, 223-25. For more on Machiavelli's indebtedness to Aristippus and Diogenes, see Strauss, "Machiavelli and Classical Literature," *Review of National Literatures* 1 (1970): 8-10.

17. *Thoughts*, 130-31.

18. *Thoughts*, 155.

19. Dante Germino remarks that "Strauss's Machiavelli . . . resembles a reclusive philosopher or perhaps a gnostic sage who pores over ancient texts" ("Blasphemy and Leo Strauss's Machiavelli," in *Leo Strauss: Political Philosopher and Jewish Thinker*, eds. Kenneth L. Deutsch and Walter Nicgorski [Lanham, Md.: Rowman & Littlefield, 1994], 304).

20. *Thoughts*, 285, 290, 294-95.

21. *Thoughts*, 244, 288.

22. *Thoughts*, 137, 148.

23. *Thoughts*, 121; see also 47, 104.

24. *Thoughts*, 78, 83, 139.

25. *Thoughts*, 121; letter to Francesco Vettori, 10 December 1513 (#137).

26. Letter #137. See Wayne A. Rebhorn, *Foxes and Lions: Machiavelli's Confidence Men* (Ithaca: Cornell University Press, 1988), 152; Hulliung, *Citizen*, 133-34.

27. Letter to Francesco Vettori, 9 April 1513 (#120). Of course Machiavelli reasons about government (*ragionare dello stato*) when he writes tracts and treatises, such as *The Prince* and the *Discourses* (the contrast in the 9 April letter is between politics and business, not theory and practice). But Machiavelli is responding to Vettori who in his letter of 30 March expresses discouragement over his inability to predict the course of political events (e.g., the election of the Medici pope). Thus what Machiavelli appears to mean by reasoning about government is discourse concerning to the events of the day. Later in the month, and again in response to Vettori, Machiavelli agrees to break the vow he never did take and answer Vettori's questions about Spain's truce with France (29 April 1513 [#128]). (The Vettori letter of 30 March is printed in *Machiavelli and His Friends: Their Personal Correspondence*, trans. and eds. James B. Atkinson and David

Sices [Dekalb: Northern Illinois University Press, 1996], 223-25. The Italian text of Machiavelli's 9 April reply is found in *Opere*, 15; it also is printed in John M. Najemy, *Between Friends: Discourses of Power and Desire in the Machiavelli-Vettori Letters of 1513-1515* [Princeton: Princeton University Press, 1993], 108.) Hale agrees that the politics about which Machiavelli must speak is "present politics" (*Renaissance Italy*, 141).

Two years later, when Machiavelli is fully at work on the *Discourses*, he tries hiring on as adviser to Paolo Vettori (Francesco's brother) who is then being talked about as a lieutenant to Guiliano de' Medici, should he, Guiliano, be named prince of a new state consisting of Parma, Piacenza, Modena, and Reggio (letter to Francesco Vettori, 31 January 1515 [#159]). While Machiavelli is careful not to ask for Francesco's help in securing this position, a letter nixing the idea from the papal secretary, Piero Ardinghelli, to Paolo Vettori is a clear indication that Machiavelli's name has come up and that he is a serious contender for the job. Even if Machiavelli did nothing to put his name forward, the letter of 31 January shows him curious about politics and eager to get back into the game; and it ends with a cryptic plea not to forget "Macone" (a European name for Muhammad or Mahomet). (The Ardinghelli letter is printed in Ridolfi, *Life*, 162.) For discussion of the "Macone" reference, see Najemy, who reads the whole letter as ironic (*Between Friends*, 321, 330-34). However inviting may be Najemy's ironic interpretation (e.g., the comparison of Paolo with Ramiro de Lorqua [Remirro de Orco], Cesare Borgia's agent in Cesena), it does not square with the fact that Machiavelli seems to have encouraged Paolo to pursue the post of Guiliano's lieutenant: "I spoke of it with him; it pleased him and he will consider making use of it." If Machiavelli is nonetheless hinting at the dangers of Paolo's playing Ramiro to Guiliano's Cesare, then perhaps he is also hinting at the need for Paolo to have an astute counselor at his side should the appointment come his way.

28.   Neal Wood maintains that Machiavelli is an "impassioned theorist of action" ("Machiavelli's Humanism of Action," in *The Political Calculus: Essays on Machiavelli's Philosophy*, ed. Anthony Parel [Toronto: University of Toronto Press, 1972], 35). Wood's argument is that Machiavelli is a humanist on three counts: a cultural humanist who participates in the recovery of classical texts; a secular humanist who separates politics from theology; and a humanist of action who encourages men to take charge of their lives (56). See also John Plamenatz, *Man and Society: Politics and Social Theories from Machiavelli to Marx*, vol. 1, 2nd ed., rev. M. E. Plamenatz and Robert Wokler (London: Longman, 1992), 47. For an opposite opinion, see Butterfield, *Statecraft*, 129. "In spite of himself," writes Butterfield, Machiavelli "was a thinker rather than a man of action."

29.   *Thoughts*, 175-76.

30.   The Spartan king Cleomenes was inspired to restore the laws of Lycurgus "because of the records and writings he had found of Agis," his predecessor. When Cleomenes succeeded to the throne (237 BC), he married Agis's widow, Agiatis. According to Plutarch, it was the queen who first instructed Cleomenes as to the life and plans of Agis, and this instruction continued under the influence of Cleomenes' male lover, Xenares (*Cleomenes*, 1, 3, in *Lives* [London: William Heinemann]). But where Plutarch says queen and lover, Machiavelli says "records and writings." This conspicuous alteration calls attention to Machiavelli the author. It thus suggests the following parallel: that what Agis was to Cleomenes, Machiavelli is to his disciples—by reading the records and

writings of Agis (a republican reformer suspected of tyranny and killed by the tyranni-cally-minded ephors), Cleomenes was able to put Agis's plan into action; likewise, by reading the books of Machiavelli (a republican of suspicious reputation and removed from office by the Medicis), his disciples are able to accomplish his ambition. See Strauss, *Thoughts*, 172; Mansfield, *New Modes and Orders*, 66.

31.   *Thoughts*, 154.

32.   *Thoughts*, 26.

33.   See Dante Germino, "Second Thoughts on Leo Strauss's Machiavelli," *Journal of Politics* 28 (1966): 815, n. 48. Says Germino: "One is tempted to conclude that if Ma-chiavelli's true meaning requires as much ingenuity as Strauss demonstrates to uncover, then he hid it much too well for the posthumous revolutionary disciples to make much use of it." Harvey Mansfield provides an answer to this objection with his doctrine of the invisible founder: to wit, disciples are faithful to the founder to the extent that they think themselves free of his influence; thus better is it if they do not suspect that they are his ministers executing his knowledge (*Machiavelli's Virtue* [Chicago: University of Chi-cago Press, 1996], xvi, 313-14). The answer is part of a larger argument about Machia-velli's patience as a founder. It is an intriguing answer and one which I will use myself in another context; but it does not explain the practical problem of how hidden instructions can have an effect.

34.   *Thoughts*, 133; also 86, 176.

35.   *Thoughts*, 35, 102, 138, 171-72.

36.   *Thoughts*, 50.

37.   *Thoughts*, 132.

38.   *Thoughts*, 144.

39.   *Thoughts*, 34.

40.   *Thoughts*, 120.

41.   *Thoughts*, 176-80.

42.   *Thoughts*, 207.

43.   Claude Lefort, *Le travail de l'oeuvre Machiavel* (Paris: Gallimard, 1972), 302; Shadia B. Drury, *The Political Ideas of Leo Strauss* (New York: St. Martin's, 1988), 115.

44.   Toward the end of explaining how Machiavelli's conspiracy might hope to succeed, Strauss identifies the groups which constitute the Machiavellian faction. They are "Ghibellines," secularists, "lukewarm Christians," and "people 'of little faith.'" But while courageous in their opposition to ecclesiastical corruption, they "become afraid," Strauss admits, "once they realize the ultimate consequence of their actions" (*Thoughts*, 172). If so, how reliable and how numerous are they likely to be? See also Berlin, "Originality," 172.

45.   *Thoughts*, 9.

46.   Drury suggests that Machiavelli hides, not his anti-Christian sentiments, but the extent of his opposition to classical philosophy (*Political Ideas*, 118). Mansfield suggests that Machiavelli hides, not his criticism of Christianity, but his appropriation of Christian modes and orders (*Virtue*, 230).

47.   *Thoughts*, 182.

48.   *Thoughts*, 163.

49.   *Thoughts*, 114.

50.   *Thoughts*, 143.

51. *Thoughts*, 157, 167. See also Leo Strauss, *What Is Political Philosophy?* (Westport: Conn.: Greenwood Press), 44.

52. *Thoughts*, 49; see also 111, 157, 188.

53. *Thoughts*, 185.

54. The betrayal of the Samnites by pious Romans is what occasions this critique of religious hypocrisy (*Thoughts*, 140); but the same critique is later directed against Christianity (157).

55. *Thoughts*, 180.

56. *Thoughts*, 190.

57. *Thoughts*, 192.

58. *Thoughts*, 188.

59. *Thoughts*, 173.

60. *Thoughts*, 231.

61. *Florentine Histories*, Pr.

62. Ferdinand wished to despoil the Marranos (Jews forcibly converted to Christianity [Moslems suffering the same fate were called Moriscos]) in order to "undertake greater enterprises" (*Prince*, 21); Machiavelli implies, therefore, that Ferdinand used the cover of religion (that the Marranos were not true Christians) to conceal his confiscatory policy. Is this not just the sort of "wretchedness" which Machiavelli would commend? See Maurice Rowdon, *The Spanish Terror: Spanish Imperialism in the Sixteenth Century* (New York: St. Martin's Press, 1974), 43-52; cf. William H. Prescott, *History of the Reign of Ferdinand and Isabella the Catholic*, vol. 2 (Philadelphia: J. B. Lippincott Company, 1872), 148-49.

63. *Thoughts*, 127, 265-74, 283.

64. *Thoughts*, 192.

65. Machiavellian hypocrisy, because it is self-conscious, may have some integrity in it, more than is evidenced by disingenuous moralism; but utility, not integrity, is what recommends this hypocrisy of the "fox." To find integrity one looks to the "lion." For an extensive treatment of the subject, see Ruth W. Grant, *Hypocrisy and Integrity: Machiavelli, Rousseau, and the Ethics of Politics* (Chicago: University of Chicago Press, 1997), especially 55, 67-71.

66. *Thoughts*, 120. In fairness to Strauss, it should be noted that he elsewhere differentiates the esotericism practiced by early moderns from the esotericism practiced by ancients. The ancients concealed their true meaning from a public judged to be naturally and permanently incapable of philosophic instruction; the moderns, wanting to end the persecution of heterodox opinion, enlighten a wider public than the philosophic few but still write with some reserve for reasons of self-defense (*Persecution and the Art of Writing* [Glencoe, Ill.: Free Press, 1952], 34). Strauss specifies that in making this distinction, he is thinking principally of Hobbes; but Strauss may wish to have the distinction applied also to Machiavelli, since Strauss subsequently attributes to Machiavelli the beginnings of modernity.

67. *Thoughts*, 10, 59, 78, 173, 232, 296-98.

68. *Prince* 15, 18; *Discourses*, I. Pr.1, 2.

69. Describing as "immanent" rather than as "transcendent" Machiavelli's concept of fortune, Thomas Flanagan explains one sense in which Machiavelli is a prephilosophic ancient: "In the immanent conception, the human contest with Fortuna is a closed field of action. It is assumed without question that each man would like to possess

the *bona fortunae*, the 'goods of fortune,' however variously they may be imagined. . . . But it never occurs to the contestant to ask why he should compete for Fortune's favours in the first place. As soon as this question is asked, the spell is broken, and a new conception of Fortune arises. For there is no compelling reason why one has to strive for the prizes which Fortune can distribute. There are other goods, goods of the mind and soul, which do not lie within the power of Fortune to confer or to remove. This insight is at the core of the Socratic teaching that it is better to suffer injustice than to commit it" ("The Concept of *Fortuna* in Machiavelli," in *Political Calculus*, 143).

70.   *What Is Political Philosophy?*, 41.

71.   *Political Ideas*, 126-27.

72.   See Anthony J. Parel, *The Machiavellian Cosmos* (New Haven: Yale University Press, 1992), 153-58. Parel nicely observes that Machiavelli's princes do not fail simply because their moral standards are too high or succeed because their moral standards are appropriately low (158). In Parel's opinion—which is not my own—Machiavelli is pre-modern in his cosmological and anthropological thought.

73.   Hannah Arendt, who divides the *vita activa* into labor, work, and action (i.e., politics), says of the Romans that they were "perhaps the most political people we have known" (*The Human Condition* [Chicago: University of Chicago Press, 1958], 7, 9).

Chapter Two: Why Rome ?

1.   For discussion of Machiavelli's choice of Livy, see J. H. Whitfield, *Machiavelli* (New York: Russell and Russell, 1965), 110-21; Whitfield, "Machiavelli's Use of Livy," in *Livy*, ed. T. A. Dorey (London: Routledge and Kegan Paul, 1971), 73-96; Hulliung, *Citizen*, 189-98.

2.   *Ab Urbe Condita* (London: William Heinemann, 1967), or *From the Founding of the City*, consisted of 142 books, 35 of which survived from antiquity. The first ten volumes, recording events from Rome's founding by Romulus to its final victory over the Samnites (753-293 BC), are called the *First Decade*. Another extant account is the history by Dionysius of Halicarnassus (*The Roman Antiquities of Dionysius of Halicarnassus*, vols. 1-7 [Cambridge: Harvard University Press]).

3.   That it is Livy who comes first is an essential part of Strauss's analysis. Better put, it is Strauss's contention that the authority of Rome first replaces that of the Bible, that the authority of Livy next replaces that of Rome, and that the authority of Machiavelli finally replaces that of Livy (*Thoughts*, 30, 37, 92-93, 96, 109, 115, 122-23, 141, 144, 165).

4.   Here and throughout the word "title" in parentheses refers to the title of the chapter currently under discussion (in this case I.1). The reference indicates that the preceding quotation is from the chapter title.

5.   Polybius, *The Histories*, VI.3-10, vol. 3 (London: William Heinemann, 1922). For antecedents and discussion of the cycle theory, see Kurt von Fritz, *The Theory of the Mixed Constitution in Antiquity: A Critical Analysis of Polybius' Political Ideas* (New York: Columbia University Press, 1954), 60-75.

6. Strauss interprets the substitution to mean that Machiavelli "abandoned the teleological understanding of nature and natural necessity" (*Thoughts*, 222, 280).

7. Polybius stipulates that every governing form has a corrupting vice peculiar to it. For analogical confirmation he points to rust which corrodes iron and to worms which eat at timber (VI.10). Thus no notice is taken of the fact that monarchy actually comes in three forms, not two: strongman, king, and tyrant.

8. There is a cycle also in Cicero. It resembles, not a roller coaster, but a ski slope, one which plateaus periodically before resuming the descent. The plateaus are mixed regimes—assorted mixtures of the elements of simple regimes. Mixed regimes are not the best regime (kingship is best because it resides at the "mountain's" top); they rather are like brakes applied to the descending motion of the cycle. And the statesman is like the ski lift which permits the skier additional runs (*De Re Publica*, II, V [Cambridge: Harvard University Press, 1913]).

9. See J.G.A. Pocock, *Politics, Language and Time: Essays on Political Thought and History* (New York: Atheneum, 1971), 88. Pocock says of politics in a Polybian mixed regime that its aim is "to escape from time; that time is the dimension of imperfection and that change must necessarily be degenerative."

10. See Edmund Burke, *Reflections on the Revolution in France* (London: Penguin Books, 1968), 229-30; also Montesquieu, *The Spirit of the Laws* (Cambridge: Cambridge University Press, 1989). Like Machiavelli, Montesquieu speaks of kingships, ill-formed in the beginning but capable of improvement, which by accident perfected themselves as mixed regimes. These were the German monarchies at the time of the fall of the Roman empire. Begun as mixtures of monarchies and aristocracies, these regimes eventually extended liberty to the people, bringing the three estates, plus the clergy, into a perfect balance. And because their monarchs ruled not in towns but over dispersed tribal peoples and during the conquest period were often far from home fighting against Rome, the public business was conducted by deputies; accordingly, representation became the salient feature of Gothic government (XI.8). Rome's perfection occurred inside a single city, and it made little or no use of representation.

11. *Virtue*, 29, 241-44, 246, 253-54. Livy's nobles need correcting in one particular: While allowing that the senators sacrificed Coriolanus, Livy also notes that they carried their remonstrances on his behalf to the point of exposing to accusation the senate itself. This they should not have done, for it was to turn an individual's trial into a partisan contest. The special advantage of accusation over calumny (the subjects of *Discourses*, I.7 and I.8 respectively) is that the public naming of an accused separates him at once from the party to which he belongs (*Virtue*, 246, 253).

12. Aristotle explains that when Athens became an empire in the fifth century and went to war often, its strength depended on the navy, manned by democrats, not on the hoplite army, manned by aristocrats: "For because the people were the cause of [Athenian] naval superiority during the Persian wars, they began to have high thoughts and to obtain mean persons as popular leaders when they were opposed politically by the respectable" (*Politics*, II.12.5; also V.4.8 [Chicago: University of Chicago Press, 1968]). Kurt Raaflaub states that "in Athens and elsewhere in Greece, the ruling aristocracies lacked cohesion and discipline. Largely due to the absence of external pressure, factionalism and rivalries abounded and in many cases led to the establishment of tyrannies. At Rome, on the contrary, the deadly combination of external (enemy) and internal (plebeian) pressure forced the patricians to close their ranks, to limit and formalize their com-

petition and to develop an extraordinary collective ethos and discipline, cohesion, and community-oriented value system" ("From Protection and Defense to Offense and Participation: Stages in the Conflict of the Orders," in *Social Struggles in Archaic Rome*, ed. Kurt Rauflaub [Berkeley: University of California Press, 1986], 226-27.) Von Fritz conjectures that uniform economic interests (agriculture untainted by commerce) was what held the Roman aristocracy together (*Mixed Constitutions*, 197).

13. See James Burnham, *The Machiavellians: Defenders of Freedom* (Washington, D. C.: Gateway Editions, 1943), 79-80.

14. Here is the first intimation in the *Discourses* of the ethical maxim, "the end justifies the means." Other statements—more explicit, though never quite using the quoted words—can be found in I.9.2, III.3.1, III.35.1, and in *Prince*, 18.

15. Rousseau is of the same opinion, but then he gets the opinion from Machiavelli (*On the Social Contract*, III.10, note [New York: St. Martin's Press, 1978]). So too is Thomas Jefferson who says famously, "a little rebellion, now and then, is a good thing" (letter to James Madison, 30 January 1787, in *The Life and Selected Writings of Thomas Jefferson* [New York: Modern Library, 1944], 413). See Paul A. Rahe, *Republics Ancient and Modern: Classical Republicanism and the American Revolution* (Chapel Hill: University of North Carolina Press, 1992), 698-701.

16. Those who do "no other than read" of tumults most likely do their reading in Livy, the chief source of early Roman history. Machiavelli implies, therefore, that Livy did not understand the value of faction (Livy in fact cursed it [IV.9]) and that Rome was better ordered than Livy's account would suggest.

17. Plato, *Republic*, 421d-423c, 2nd ed. (New York: Basic Books, 1991); *Laws*, 704b-705b (New York: Basic Books, 1980). By contrast, Cicero, who discovers the best republic in historical Rome, prefers fertile sites with access to the sea (*De Re Publica*, II.3-5). Aristotle is somewhere in between (*Politics*, VII.6.1-5).

18. Human law not only can substitute for nature's necessities but surpass them as well; for Machiavelli finds in the kingdom of Egypt an example of how law countered "the agreeableness of the country" by imposing "a necessity to exercise on those who had to be soldiers," making "better soldiers there than in countries which have naturally been harsh and sterile" (I.1.4). And the fact that modern Egypt (under the sultans) repeated the feat of ancient Egypt (under the pharaohs) is a happy confirmation of the thesis that reclamation by imitation is possible.

19. Von Fritz, *Mixed Constitution*, 209.

20. See *Tercets on Ambition*, ll. 91-100.

21. Another accident was the confederation in 501 of 40 hostile neighbors to contain Roman expansion (I.33.1, 5). It is of secondary concern, for the refinement it provided to executive power, namely the office of the dictatorship, did not involve the humors of the city, the senate and the plebs, whose competition, says Machiavelli, set Rome on the right path toward perfection (I.2.7). Also of secondary concern is the rape of Lucretia by Sextus Tarquinius, which triggered the republican revolution of 509 but whose causal importance Machiavelli subordinates to the tyranny of Superbus Tarquinius (III.5.1). The tumult caused by Coriolanus's assault on the tribunate in 491 is called an *accidente* by Machiavelli (though Mansfield and Tarcov translate it as "incident" [I.7.1]). It was discussed above as an instance of senatorial prudence.

22. *Democracy in America*, vol. 1 (New York: Vintage Classics, 1972), 13, 176, 256; vol. 2, 299. See also Louis Hartz, *The Liberal Tradition in America* (New York: Harcourt Brace Jovanovich, 1955), 35-66.

I am assuming that the government in question was the one instituted by Romulus; if so, then two and a half centuries separated Rome's founding as a kingship from its refounding as a republic. Given this immense span of time, is it plausible to claim that the numbers killed during the first event would determine the numbers seeking vengeance during the second? Who would remember or any longer care? Maybe then the government that fell bloodlessly because it also was made bloodlessly was the tyranny of Tarquinius Superbus, which was seized with the assassination of Servius Tullius but which required no additional killings after that (III.5). Princes like Servius, Ancus Martius, and Piero Soderini among the moderns, who have heirs to kill but who appease and placate them instead, live in constant danger of conspiracies against their persons (III.3). On the other hand, if they act to root out and crush the conspirators, they run the just as certain risk of multiplying enemies and alienating the populace (III.6.20)—that is, of resting their governments on widespread violence; which violence, argues III.7, is then repaid when the governments fall. But Superbus was fortunate; there were no heirs whom he needed to kill, and so Superbus was free to regard himself as heir (title) and to rule in compliance with ancient orders after the fashion of hereditary princes. He had every opportunity to win the public's support; but foolishly he broke the laws, governed tyrannically, disempowered the senate, burdened the people, and despoiled Rome of its liberty.

Perhaps it is difficult to know which of these regimes Machiavelli has in mind, for while the Tarquin tyranny obviates the problem of time and memory, it does not fit so well the description of a state "caused by common consent of a collectivity that has made it great." On the other hand, the Romulus kingship was indeed made great by the approval and participation of the Roman people (I.1.1, 5; I.4.1; I.9.4).

23.   As with III.7, there is some uncertainty as to whether the baneful influence posited of monarchical rule is meant to apply to the whole period of kingship in Rome or only to the tyranny of the last of the Roman kings.

24.   Pocock observes that "the Roman *plebs* displayed *virtù* in demanding their right, virtue in being satisfied when their demands were granted" (*Moment*, 203).

25.   *Politics*, III.11, 13.

26.   *Considerations on the 'Discourses' of Machiavelli*. In *Selected Writings*, ed. Cecil Grayson (London: Oxford University Press, 1965), 70-71.

27.   When attempting to argue the case for the rule of law as against the rule of men, Aristotle suggests that in circumstances where some citizens must exercise rule they "be established as law-guardians [*nomophulakas*] and as servants of the law" (*Politics*, III.16.4).

28.   Machiavelli is critical of plebeian ambition in I.37.2 and III.11.1.

29.   For example, Roman moderation, rather than placing the brakes on expansion, was itself caused by expansion (I.37.2); and Rome became more ambitious to the degree that the people participated in public affairs (I.53) and to the degree that high magisterial offices were opened to plebeians (I.60).

30.   John Stuart Mill makes a similar argument in defense of the emancipation of women (*The Subjection of Women*, in *On Liberty and Other Writings* [Cambridge: Cambridge University Press, 1989], 204-07).

31.   In Aristotelian parlance, the former is a polity and the latter is an aristocracy (*Politics*, IV.3-4).

32.   In I.37.1 it is said that the agrarian law "was the cause of the destruction of the republic"; likewise in III.24.1: "If these things [the hazards of agrarian legislation and prolonged commands] had been known well from the beginning, and proper remedies produced for them, a free way of life would have been longer and perhaps quieter."

33.   Mansfield, *New Modes and Orders*, 48-49.

34.   At least in the holding of office, possession is a cause of moderation.

35.   Since the rebellion in Thebes (379 BC) signaled the beginning of the end of the Spartan empire, the capture of the Theban citadel in 382 might be taken as the empire's high-water mark.

36.   This battle is cited frequently in the *Discourses* and *The Prince*: in I.6.4, where Venetian strength was more in money and diplomacy than in arms, hence when put to the test, Venice lost; in I.12.2, where Italy is divided and weak because the papacy is in the habit of calling in foreigners, as it called in the French against the Venetians; in I.53.1, where the Venetians could have prevented the formation of the League of Cambrai and so have avoided defeat at Agnadello if they had given back some of what they had taken; in II.10.1, where Venice is an example of how money is not the sinew of war (Venice was unable to use its wealth in its own defense); in III.11.2, where Venice was insufficiently strong to temporize and so use the divide-and-conquer strategy against the League of Cambrai; in *Prince* 12, where Venice lost in one day what it had spent eight centuries acquiring because of its reliance on mercenary captains; in *Prince* 20, where the Venetians suffered rebellion following their defeat at Vailà because they ruled their subject cities by faction, thus there was in place an organized, hostile party ready to take over the moment Venice was weakened in war; and in *Prince* 26, where Vailà, listed as one of seven defeats occurring over the past 20 years, helps prove the weakness of Italian arms. Also *Florentine Histories*, I.29 provides a listing of the subject cities which made up the fifteenth-century Venetian empire, as well as statements respecting its reputation, its quick destruction, and its current status.

37.   *Politics*, I.2.11.

38.   See Abraham Lincoln's *Address to the Young Men's Lyceum of Springfield, Illinois* (in *Lincoln: Selected Speeches and Writings* [New York: Vintage Books, 1992], 13-21); also Harry Jaffa's commentary on the same (in *Crisis of the House Divided* [Chicago: University of Chicago Press, 1982], 183-232).

39.   See John McCormick, "Addressing the Political Exception: Machiavelli's 'Accidents' and the Mixed Regime," *American Political Science Review* 87 (1993). Arguing that a regime "built by *accidenti* will be more adept at managing *accidenti* (893), McCormick contends that "Sparta is not as stable as Rome" (895).

40.   Strauss speaks of continuous foundings (*Thoughts*, 44, 287-88). See also Hanna Fenichel Pitkin, *Fortune Is a Woman: Gender and Politics in the Thought of Niccolò Machiavelli* (Berkeley: University of California Press, 1984), 277-79.

41.   Strauss, *Thoughts*, 44; *What Is Political Philosophy?*, 42-43. See also David E. Ingersoll, "The Constant Prince: Private Interests and Public Goals in Machiavelli," *Western Political Quarterly* 21 (1968): 588-89, 594-96; Dan Eldar, "Glory and the Boundaries of Public Morality in Machiavelli's Thought," *History of Political Thought* 7 (1986): 426.

42.   Plutarch, *Lycurgus*, 29.

43.   For Moses' recourse to violence, see III.30.1. In Plutarch's account of the life of Lycurgus, the Spartan lawgiver went into voluntary exile following the birth of his nephew, Charilaus. Upon returning many years later and finding Sparta in disorder, he planned a total reformation of its laws; he then journeyed to Delphi to receive the sanction of the god. That done, he searched about for allies and at the decisive moment armed a small party of men to help him subdue his opponents. Plutarch says nothing else of violence except that the institution of the common meal provoked a short-lived uprising that resulted in injury to Lycurgus, the loss of one eye. But Lycurgus befriended his attacker, bringing the young man into his home and converting him to the cause (*Lycurgus*, 3-5, 11). Cleomenes, however, cited Lycurgus's armed ascension to power to justify the use of violence against his own enemies (*Cleomenes*, 10). And Plutarch, when recounting the life of Solon, compares Solon's powerlessness as a private citizen with Lycurgus's well-established authority; for Lycurgus ruled as king for many years (*bebasileukôs etê polla*) and employed force more than persuasion (*bia mallon ê peithoi*) (*Solon*, 16). Of the three figures named by Machiavelli as alone in power, Solon used force least of all (the factions agreed to have Solon rewrite the constitution), but then his laws were the least successful; for no sooner were they delivered than the demand for amendments began, and by the time he returned from ten years of traveling, the factions had resumed their quarreling and the city was close to civil war (*Solon*, 16, 25, 29). See also, Aristotle, *Constitution of Athens*, 5, 11, 13 [New York: Hafner Publishing Company, 1950]). In *Discourses* I.11.3, Lycurgus and Solon, but not Moses, are said to have used religion to establish their orders.

44.   *Agis*, 5.
45.   *Agis*, 7.
46.   *Agis*, 6.
47.   *Lycurgus*, 13.
48.   *Lycurgus*, 31.
49.   *Cleomenes*, 7.
50.   *Cleomenes*, 5.
51.   *Cleomenes*, 15-16.
52.   *Cleomenes*, 18.

53.   Polybius's judgment is far more sweeping, that Cleomenes overturned the ancient polity completely (II.47). This judgment Leslie Walker attributes to the admission of the *perioci* to citizenship and to the imperial ambitions entertained by Cleomenes (*The Discourses of Niccolò Machiavelli*, vol. 2 [London: Routledge and Kegan Paul, 1950], 26). Machiavelli lists Cleomenes, along with Caesar and Agathocles, as princes of armies who "seized their fatherland[s] at a stroke and with their forces" (III.6.19).

54.   *Cleomenes*, 27. This was the battle of Sellasia fought in 222 against Antigonus of Macedon. Antigonus came into the Peloponnesus at the invitation of Aratus, who never quite reconciled to Cleomenes' leadership. With greater forces and revenues at his command, Antigonus was gradually wearing Cleomenes down; so Cleomenes decided to risk what remained of his army in a single, great battle. He lost. Cleomenes was unaware, as was Antigonus, that Macedon was at that time under attack by Illyria. Two days after the battle of Sellasia, a messenger arrived bringing news of the invasion and a summons for Antigonus's return. Plutarch concludes that if Cleomenes had continued retreating for but two days, the Macedonians would have withdrawn and Cleomenes could have dictated what terms he liked to the Achaeans. (Machiavelli does not report this battle or the

lesson drawn by Plutarch, that money is the sinew of war, perhaps because Machiavelli argues in II.10 that money is not the sinew of war.)

55.   *Lycurgus*, 7. Plutarch reaffirms the lateness of the ephorate in his *Life of Cleomenes* (10): Having assumed the office of ephor for himself alone, Cleomenes justified his actions by saying that Lycurgus created the council of elders, the *gerousia*, to assist the kings but that only later, during the Messenian War when the kings were too long away from home to administer justice, did they, the kings, appoint some of their friends to do this work of judging for them. At first these friends, called ephors, were duly submissive; but afterwards they acted independently of the kings and elevated themselves into a distinct magistracy. It was for this reason, coupled with their then violent obstruction of Cleomenes' reforms, that the ephors were punished and the office remade. Aristotle also attributes the ephorate to Theopompus (*Politics* V.11.2). He describes the office as democratic, and its increasing influence he credits with changing the regime from an aristocracy into a democracy (II.9.19-22).

Not all ancient authors agree, however, about the origin and character of the ephorate. Herodotus traces it to Lycurgus (*The Histories*, VI.56-58 [Baltimore: Penguin Books, 1972]). Plato does the same (*Eighth Letter*, 354b, in *Letters* [London: William Heinemann, 1927]), while still describing the institution as a democratic addition (*Laws* 692a). And even Plutarch remarks, at the end of his *Life of Lycurgus* (29), that the ephorate, though thought to be a democratic innovation, in fact heightened the aristocratic character of the regime. Plato says that it added a tyrannical element to the regime (perhaps because of the strict control it exercised over the lives of citizens [*Laws* 712d]), having previously judged it democratic owing to the fact that election to it was by lottery (692a). See von Fritz, *Mixed Constitution*, 103-11.

56.   W. G. Forrest, in *A History of Sparta, 950-192 B.C.* (New York: W. W. Norton, 1968), 76, makes a similar comparison: Elected annually by the assembly, the ephorate, he says, "drew its authority from a non-aristocratic source, and if there were at any time coherent opposition to a king or to the aristocracy, the ephorate would be its weapon."

57.   *History of Sparta*, 18, 40, 50, 53; J. M. Moore, *Aristotle and Xenophon on Democracy and Oligarchy* (Berkeley: University of California Press, 1975), 68-69.

58.   There is a story, told in Cicero's *De Re Publica*, that Romulus was assassinated by the senate. But the account preferred by Scipio, the dialogue's lead character, is that Romulus was transported to the heavens under cover of a solar eclipse (II.10; see also I.16; II.2, 30; III.28). Thus was Romulus's name revered by a wise posterity. See also, Livy, I.16.

59.   H. H. Scullard, *From the Gracchi to Nero* (New York: Frederick A. Praeger, 1959), 154.

60.   Strauss, *Thoughts*, 33.

61.   See *Prince*, 2 where hereditary princes are likened to the dentations of a wall.

62.   "Imperial Rome" is hardly enough since the republic was already an empire.

63.   Shakespeare, *Julius Caesar*, I, ii 199; II, i 167-70; II, ii 44-48; V, iii 94-96 (New York: New American Library, 1963). See Allan Bloom, *Shakespeare's Politics* (New York: Basic Books, 1964), 91.

64.   Throughout the Middle Ages, caesarian Rome, not republican Rome, was remembered and celebrated. During the Renaissance, opinion went back and forth. See

Hans Baron, *The Crisis of the Early Italian Renaissance* (Princeton: Princeton University Press, 1964), 54-61, 66-67, 149-50, 161.

65.   Machiavelli disputes Caesar's opinion about the relative worth of good captains and good armies in III.13.2.

66.   Baron, *Crisis*, 70-71; Plamenatz, *Man and Society*, 75-76; Alfredo Bonadeo, *Corruption, Conflict, and Power in the Works and Times of Niccolò Machiavelli* (Berkeley: University of California Press, 1973), 17, 29.

67.   Machiavelli never says that it was revivable, much less does he supply details as to how the revival might have been accomplished. He leaves his position unproved because his true purpose, presumably, is not to convict Caesar on the charge of unwarranted usurpation, but to persuade would-be princes that reforming inside of ancient orders offers the surer path to glory.

Chapter Three: Rome's "Inside" Modes and Orders

1.   For remarks on the structure of the *Discourses*, see Felix Gilbert, "The Composition and Structure of Machiavelli's *Discorsi*," *Journal of the History of Ideas*, 14 (1953): 139-40; Strauss, *Thoughts*, 99-107, 160, 313, n. 24, 314, n. 36.

2.   *Politics*, III.9.1-4; V.1.2-7, 12-14; *Nicomachean Ethics*, V.3 (Cambridge: Harvard University Press, 1968).

3.   Rome had three assemblies and one council: the *comitia curiata*, the *comitia centuriata*, the *comitia tributa*, and the *concilium plebis*. The first of these, dating from the kingship period, organized the people by curies, subdivisions of the original ethnic tribes. Its function was to bear witness to royal decrees and to give official approval to decisions taken by others; for example, it was in the *curiata* that elected magistrates were formally invested with the power of command. The *comitia centuriata* also dated from the kingship period. It divided the people into five economic classes, each of which consisted of varying numbers of military centuries, for it was from this assembly that the army was recruited. Of the 193 centuries in all, 80 belonged to the first class, with another 18 reserved for a separate order of cavalry. Together, these two comprised a voting majority. Since this was the assembly where most of Rome's laws were passed, sovereign power resided here if it resided anywhere. In addition, the centuriate assembly was the electorate for all higher magistracies and the court for trying most capital cases. The *comitia tributa* originated in 471 as an assembly for the election of lesser magistrates and tribunes of the plebs. In it the populace was organized by tribes, of which there eventually came to be 35. But previous to and coexistent with this tribal assembly was a council of the plebs, the *concilium plebis*, which did much of the same work. Its membership though was restricted to plebs, and its legislative initiatives (*plebiscita*) applied only to plebs. This changed in 287 when with passage of the *Lex Hortensius* plebiscites were made binding on the whole state (accordingly, effective sovereignty shifted from the centuriate assembly to the plebeian council, or perhaps to the tribal assembly). By the end of the republic the tribal assembly and the plebeian council were distinguishable only by the magistrates which presided over them, if even by that. (While conceding this last point, von Fritz speculates that the *comitia tributa* was but the *concilium plebis* re-

named after its plebiscites had attained the force of law. Being now subject to the council's decisions, patricians were admitted as voting members; and having now a membership which included patricians, the council of plebs needed of a new name. As for the many tribes known to have pre-existed this nominal change, they were used, von Fritz contends, for organizing the *concilium plebis* [*Mixed Constitution*, 238; nn. 50 and 51, 451-52].) See, Claude Nicolet, *The World of the Citizen in Republican Rome* (Berkeley: University of California Press, 1980), 217-26.

    4.   Chapters are given to the contributions of Romulus, Numa, and Tullus; but Servius is mentioned only in a listing of Rome's orderers (I.49.1). Later he is the unnamed king reigning at a time when Rome had 80,000 men able to bear arms (II.3.1), and later still he is discussed in light of the conspiracy that brought him down (III.4.1, III.5.1).

    5.   The consuls were elected by the *comitia centuriata*. Upon finishing their one-year terms, they automatically were admitted to the senate and held their seats for life. See von Fritz, *Mixed Constitution*, 196.

    6.   A contrary assessment is offered below.

    7.   Mansfield, *New Modes and Orders*, 118.

    8.   The rule of law might seem like an exception to the utilitarian ethic of "the end justifies the means." But in light of these political considerations, it is not.

    9.   Harvey Mansfield, Jr., *Taming the Prince* (New York: Free Press, 1989), 2-4, 131-35, 144.

    10.   See also I.2.7 and I.34.1.

    11.   There are competing explanations—political, racial, chronological, economic, military—for the patrician-plebeian distinction. Livy states that Romulus created 100 senators to advise him, that he named them "fathers," *paters*, and their descendants "patricians." By inference then, all others not so privileged were plebeians (Livy, I.8). Some scholars contend that the plebeians were a conquered people, racially distinct from its conqueror; but whether the original inhabitants were subdued by invaders or they themselves subdued surrounding tribes and brought them back to Rome is a matter much disputed. Others believe that Rome was first composed of patrician clans living on the Palantine Hill and that plebeians were the newcomers assigned quarters on the Capitoline and Aventine Hills. Judged inferiors for having no family-based religion and thus for having no lineage, hearth, or consecrated property, they were in the early days without political rights or even the protection of the law; instead they depended for their security on the favor of the king. It is sometimes thought that "plebeian" is equivalent to "proletarian," a class outside the military structure and sharply differentiated from the dependents of the clans, who along with the patricians fought in the army's legions. Sometimes, though, "plebeian" is a designation applied to all of the poor, including clan dependents. Still other scholars believe that the patrician-plebeian distinction was a function of economic success and failure, with the successful forming themselves into a closed caste. On the other hand, martial prowess may have been the first measure of success; accordingly, the first senators/patricians may have been warlords and clan leaders. See B. H. Niebuhr, *Lectures on the History of Rome*, vol. 1 (London: Walton and Maberly, 1853), 48, 76; Fustel de Coulanges, *The Ancient City* (Garden City: Doubleday Anchor Books), 229-34; Theodor Mommsen, *The History of Rome*, vol. 1 (New York: Charles Scribner's Sons, 1883), 126-32; W. E. Heitland, *The Roman Republic*, vol. 1 (Cambridge: Cambridge University Press, 1909), 42; Howard H. Scullard, *A History of the Roman World*, 753-

146 B.C. (London: Methuen, 1935), 42-47; von Fritz, *Mixed Constitution*, 194-95; Fritz M. Heichelheim, Cedric A. Yeo, and Allen M. Ward, *A History of the Roman People*, 2nd ed. (Englewood Cliffs: Prentice-Hall 1984), 39-40; and Arnoldo Momigliano, "The Rise of the *plebs* in the Archaic Age of Rome," in Raaflaub, *Social Struggles*, 175-97.

12.   *Considerations*, 68-69. See also Montesquieu, *Spirit of the Laws*, XI.13.

13.   Mansfield, *Virtues*, 24. But Mansfield goes too far, I think, when he says that the humors, "not being rational in nature . . . cannot be reconciled by speech or argument"; for there is evidence in the *Discourses* of one class persuading the other (e.g., I.39, I.47).

14.   See Kent Brudney, "Machiavelli on Social Class and Class Conflict," *Political Theory* 12 (1984): 513.

15.   Cicero, *De Re Publica*, IV.7; Montesquieu, *Spirit of the Laws*, XX.4. The *Lex Claudio* of 218 prohibited senators from engaging in oversees trade (Livy, XXI.63). See F. E. Adcock, *Roman Political Ideas and Practice* (Ann Arbor: University of Michigan Press, 1959), 48-49.

16.   Machiavelli refers to "one Spurius Maelius, who was very rich for those times" (III.28.1).

17.   The chapter's two other examples of Roman poverty are similarly tainted: Marcus Regulus wanted to be relieved of duty in order that he might attend to his villa. Machiavelli puts a positive spin on his request, noting that Roman commanders would not have worried about their property back home if war-making were an alternate, and more lucrative, means to personal wealth. That's true—Rome was not so corrupt in 256 that its generals became rich while in office. But how timocratic was Rome if even a general was more concerned for his farm than for his glory? In the last example goes to Paulus Emilius who made Rome rich but "kept himself poor." But then Paulus Emilius was already wealthy, and while his in-laws he kept poor (such that the reward of a silver cup was the first silver in his son-in-law's home), his own sons (including Scipio Africanus Minor) he enriched with a king's library. See Plutarch, *Paulus Aemilius*, 28; Walker, *Discourses*, vol. 2, 191; Mansfield, *New Modes and Orders*, 389-90.

18.   Cicero, *De Re Publica*, II.9. Livy, II.16.

19.   Machiavelli alludes to the existence in Rome of patrons and clients, but always the system is seen as a mark of Rome's, and/or other republics', corruption: I.18.3, I.34.2, I.35.1, I.37.2, I.46.1, I.55.4, III.16.2, III.28.1; *Prince*, 16.

20.   The *Discourses* turn to religion because Machiavelli is still answering his critics who in I.9.1 wanted to hear about the founder, about religious orders, and about the military.

21.   Mansfield, *New Modes and Orders*, 70-71.

22.   See also Cicero, *De Re Publica*, II.14; Plutarch, *Numa*, 8-9, 12-14.

23.   Christianity's conversion of the barbarians might be taken as an instance of introducing religion where there are arms, while Machiavelli's self-given task of restoring virtue to an unarmed Christianity might be taken as an instance of introducing arms where there is religion. Will Machiavelli really want it thought that Christianity had the harder job of the two?

24.   Guicciardini is skeptical of Numa's superior ranking for the same reason (*Considerations*, 80).

25.   Rousseau also stresses the importance of the religious lawgiver's character: "But it is not every man who can make the Gods speak or be believed when he declares

himself their interpreter. The legislator's great soul is the true miracle that should prove his mission. Any man can engrave stone tablets, buy an oracle, pretend to have a secret relationship with some divinity, train a bird to talk in his ear, or find other crude ways to impress the people. One who knows only that much might even assemble, by chance, a crowd of madmen, but he will never found an empire, and his extravagant work will soon die along with him. False tricks can form a fleeting bond; wisdom alone can make it durable" (*On the Social Contract*, II.7 [New York: St. Martin's Press, 1978]). See Joseph Masciulli, "The Armed Founder versus the Catonic Hero: Machiavelli and Rousseau on Popular Leadership," *Interpretation* 14 (1986): 265-80.

    26.   Strauss, *Thoughts*, 109.

    27.   Because he was king, Numa did not run afoul of the admonition of *Prince* 14, that "it is not reasonable that whoever is armed obey willingly whoever is unarmed, and that someone unarmed be secure among armed servants."

    28.   Ezio Raimondi, "The Politician and the Centaur," in *Machiavelli and the Discourse of Literature*, eds. Albert Russel Ascoli and Victoria Kahn (Ithaca: Cornell University Press, 1993), 159.

    29.   See Pitkin, *Fortune*, 89

    30.   This was in 398. In 399 five plebeians and one patrician were elected military tribunes (Livy, V.13).

    31.   The distinction between the two is that auguries are signs sent by the gods while auspices are procedures for ascertaining the divine will. The augur is "talked to" by birds in their flight (au - av - *avis*; gur - gar- *garrire*); the auspex is a "watcher of birds" (avi-spex). The auspex takes the auspices, but the augur interprets their meaning, as well as the meaning of other signs, such as rain, thunder, and lightning, and sundry celestial phenomena. See, Heitland, *Roman Republic*, 23. "Other forms of divination," says Heitland, "were later importations. The *haruspices*, whose chief function was to find signs in the entrails of victims, were Etruscan. Sibylline [sic] books and oracles were borrowed from the Greeks."

    32.   *Thoughts*, 150-51.

    33.   *Machiavelli in Hell* (Princeton: Princeton University Press, 1989), 327.

    34.   Sullivan, *Three Romes*, 109-10.

    35.   See II.33 for more on Fabius in Tuscany.

    36.   In Livy, he even provides safe escort (V.28).

    37.   Reviewing much the same evidence, Sullivan comes to the more radical conclusion that the "new Rome" of Machiavelli's devising will do without religion altogether. Paganism, she argues, left Rome prey to the extravagant promises of demagogues and readied the population for Christianity's even more alluring promise of eternal salvation (*Three Romes*, 6-8, 66-72, 102-21, 188-89). My objection to the purported plan for an irreligious politics as a defense against tyranny is, in the first instance, Machiavelli's emphatic assertion that states need civil religion to teach deference and so dispose men to obey authority (I.11). A second objection is that states need religion to mollify the disappointment of men when their unbounded appetites run up against scarcity and their strictly limited capacities for acquisition. States need religion as well for the hope religion supplies, especially in desperate times when the citizenry feels itself alone in the world. Rome faced no harder times in its years as a republic than when the city was captured by the Gauls in 390. Although Machiavelli believes this event to have had purely human causes (III.1.1), still he is happy to present the Livian account whereby disap-

proving gods taught corrupt Romans the value of virtue (II.29). Finally, religion's higher truth, while sometimes a tool for use by tyrants, can also be an aid in helping people resist the threats and temptations of tyranny. (See Strauss, *Thoughts*, 226-31; Drury, *Political Ideas*, 122; Grant, *Hypocrisy*, 49; Edward Bryan Portis, *Reconstructing the Classics: Political Theory from Plato to Marx*, 2nd ed. [Chatham, New Jersey: Chatham House, 1998], 89-90.)

38.　*New Modes and Orders*, 73.

39.　*Florentine Histories*, V.1. See also, Rousseau, *First Discourse* (in *The First and Second Discourses* [New York: St. Martin's Press, 1964], 39-47). Roman paganism was as corrupt in Livy's day as Christianity was in Machiavelli's (III.13.2; Livy, III.20).

40.　The senate was an advisory body created by Romulus. In the republican era its members, usually 300 strong, were patrician ex-magistrates, appointed by consuls and serving for life. The senate did not legislate, although until 339 it ratified laws passed in the assemblies. Its power lay in the opinions it gave when advice was sought by magistrates. A decree of the senate was a *senatus consultum*, which the presiding magistrate helped to formulate, was needed to enforce, and could at any time revoke; or a plebeian tribune could intervene and veto it, in which case a decree became instead an authoritative opinion (*senatus auctoritas*). The senate's other chief power was its control over state finances—most appropriations came from the senate. See Heichelheim, et al., *Roman People*, 51-52. According to von Fritz, there are indications of senatorial weakness in Polybius's account as well as indications that much of the senate's power was informal or extra-constitutional: e.g., mediating incompatible demands for funding between consuls, each on campaign and each with the full legal right to withdraw moneys from the treasury (*Mixed Constitution*, 159-64). On the senate's indirect manner of rule, see Mansfield, *Virtue*, 247.

41.　William V. Harris, *War and Imperialism in Republican Rome, 327-70 B.C.* (Oxford: Clarendon Press, 1979). Harris observes that indiscriminate slaughter "was the normal Roman practice" and that "captured cities were very often thoroughly destroyed" (52).

42.　The most significant legislative event of the period was the passage of the Licinian-Sextian laws in 367, which, in addition to restoring the consulate, restricted landholdings and provided debt relief to the plebs (Livy, VI.35, 42). Later in this period laws were passed limiting interest rates (357 BC [Livy, VII.15]) and prohibiting usury (342 BC [Livy, VII.42]).

43.　The full powers of the tribunate resided in each of its ten members (there were two tribunes initially, in 494, then five in 471, and ten in 457). Thus any one tribune could veto the decision of the other nine. See Heitland, *Roman Republic*, 62-63.

44.　Scholars criticize the senate for its refusal to accept needed reforms (e.g., landless peasants were not subject to conscription in the military) and criticize the Gracchi for their impatient and provocative manner (e.g., Tiberius's appointment of himself and members of his family to the commission which redistributed land). See Scullard, *Gracchi*, 23-40; von Fritz, *Mixed Constitution*, 255-72, 343-44; R. E. Smith, *The Failure of the Roman Republic* (Cambridge: Cambridge University Press, 1955), 75-85. Smith observes that clientship was the solution to the mid-second century problem of the *latifundia*, i.e., large landholdings, the property of absentee owners, who used slave labor to farm the estates. The dislocated peasant became a rich man's client, voting the rich man's wishes, and living as a pampered proletarian in the city. But lacking property, this erstwhile peasant could not do service in the army; so schemes were put forward (by Scipio and Laelius in the decade before the troubles began) to resettle these proletarians on new allotments. Smith disparages these plans as examples of Greek theorizing unsuited to the temperament of practical-minded Romans. For they failed, he claims, to address the economic factors which drove the peasants off the land in the first place, namely the presence of vast new wealth looking for land as an investment, the influx of slaves from the provinces, and the inefficiency and disrepair of family farms caused in part by lengthy military service far from home. The purpose of agrarian legislation, from the state's perspective, was to increase the population eligible to serve in the army, but army service was one of the chief reasons why peasant-soldiers would lose their farms. See also Michael Crawford, *The Roman Republic* (Atlantic Highlands, NJ: Humanities Press, 1978), 103-06.

45.   Also revived in this period was the tribunate as an institution defending the interests of the people. It had been absorbed by the senate over the past century and a half because the plebeian elite had become a part of the ruling class and because cooptation had rendered its powers ineffective. But Tiberius Gracchus, himself a tribune, removed the colleague who was obstructing his plans. See Smith, *Failure*, 83: "By using the tribunate as an independent means of initiating legislation they [the Gracchi] revived latent powers which had in the process of evolution long remained dormant, and which in the increased complexity of imperial administration should have continued dormant."

46.   The opposite of unconscious temporizing by the people was unconscious guarding of liberty by the great (see above, 38).

47.   Heitland, *Roman Republic*, 86.

48.   Machiavelli repeats, in effect, the argument of the democrats in Aristotle's *Politics* (III.9.6). In Livy there can be found as well the argument of Aristotle's oligarchs. It is a speech by Titus Quinctius Capitolinus, consul in the year 446. He reminds the plebeians, whose cause has been ascendant for many years, that the nobility supplies the military leadership needed for plunder and for protection against the plundering of others (Livy, III.17-18). His rhetorical prowess carries the day, and for an additional year the consulate remains exclusively patrician.

49.   The clan patriarch, the Sabine Attius Clausus, who changed his name to Appius Claudius upon moving to Rome (Livy, II.16), was the first to propose coopting tribunes in 480 (II.44). His great-great-grandson revived the practice in 416, calling it an old family custom and explaining to the senators that new men tasting power for the first time can easily be manipulated by the great political families (IV.18, V.2). Apparently, there was legislation aimed at preventing cooptation in the strict sense of the term, namely the selection of additional tribunes by those already elected. For when, in the wake of the decemvir debacle, tribune Marcus Duillius, supervising the elections of 448, allowed some tribune seats to go vacant rather than permit sitting tribunes to stand for reelection, and when these seats were subsequently filled by successful candidates choosing, or coopting, others—in fact patricians—to be their colleagues, another tribune, Lucius Trebonius, had passed into law the requirement that the election of tribunes continue until all seats were filled (III.64-65). This Trebonian law, irregularly observed, was later defended by a descendant of its author, one Gnaeus Trebonius, who in 401 vociferously complained that patricians or their lackeys were again being coopted into the tribunate (V.11).

50. Plutarch, *Caesar*, 57: "However, the Romans gave way before the good fortune of the man and accepted the bit, and regarding the monarchy as a respite from the evils of the civil wars, they appointed him dictator for life. This was confessedly a tyranny, since the monarchy, besides the element of irresponsibility, now took on that of permanence."

51. Rome dispatched to Athens a party of three citizens to examine "the laws that Solon gave to that city so that they could found the Roman laws on them" (I.40.2). Upon the embassy's return, ten citizens, decemvirs, were chosen to do the work of legislative reform. The product of their labors was the Twelve Tables. Momigliano claims that "the Twelve Tables were compiled in response to plebeian pressure" and that "plebeians were included in the second Decemvirate" ("Rise of the *plebs*," 192). He thinks also that "the Roman *plebs* was oriented toward the Greek world, whereas the patriciate was tradition-ally linked with Etruria" (191). See Heichelheim, et al., *Roman People*, 58. The authors describe the Twelve Tables, one third of the text of which is preserved in the works of later writers, as "neither a constitution nor a comprehensive code of laws" but as a codi-fication of pre-existing custom which "established in principle some equality in law be-tween patrician and plebeian and, more or less, the equality of all free citizens before the law," but which did not "get at the roots of plebeian discontent." The content of the Ta-bles was both civil law and public law, addressing such subjects as burglary, road repair, and family relations.

52. Hulliung is of a different opinion, detecting "enthusiasm for the coming of democracy" in Machiavelli's "treatise on Roman politics" (*Citizen*, 86). See also Skinner, *Foundations*, 159.

53. Whenever Machiavelli describes a competition that is dangerously overheated, his attention turns invariably to the ambitious individual waiting in the wings (I.16.5, I.40.5-6, I.46.1).

54. The consuls filled vacancies in the senate, choosing usually from among ex-magistrates. Thus when the plebeians became eligible for magisterial offices, they also became eligible for election to the senate. "After the fifth century," says Scullard, "it [the senate] was opened to plebeians" (*Roman World*, 112). According to Robert Develin, however, the exact moment of entry is unknown ("The Integration of Plebeians into the Political Order after 366 B.C.," in *Social Struggles*, 341).

55. In point of fact, Pacuvius Calavius does fit the description of a "bird of prey." Livy portrays him as a patrician who supported the popular party and who wished to make the senate subservient to himself and the commons. But Pacuvius did not wish to destroy the senate entirely because he feared disintegration of the state in the absence of a deliberative council—and he feared Hannibal (XXIII.2).

56. A mixed regime might be thought of as a primitive form of representative gov-ernment. A mixed regime exists where there is a divided population, or rather where there are separate populations inhabiting the same territory (separate because of race, class, conquest, etc.). Until the population can come to regard itself as one people, it is necessary that there be group representation. But once a single people has emerged, the mixed regime can yield to a system which represents equal individuals or ever changing majorities. Domestic politics then becomes more peaceful because impermanent majori-ties replace permanent groups.

It is understood in the *Federalist Papers* that representative democracy—albeit in an extended republic—has superseded the mixed regime of old. *Federalist* 51, for exam-ple, offers "hereditary or self-appointed authority," described as "a will in the community independent of the majority," as the old-fashioned way of guarding one part of the society from the injustice of another (Alexander Hamilton, James Madison, and John Jay, *The Federalist Papers* [New York: New American Library, 1961], 323, 324).

57. Mansfield, *Virtue*, 94-97, 115-16, 253-54.

58. This occurred in 494 when the tribunate was first created, in 449 when the decemvirs were overthrown, and in 287 (just outside of Livy's *First Decade*) when plebiscites passed by the tribal assembly became law for all of Rome.

59. Says Madison in *Federalist* 63: "It is clear that the principle of representation was neither unknown to the ancients nor wholly overlooked in their political constitutions. The true distinction between these and the American governments, lies *in the total exclusion of the people, in their collective capacity*, from any share in the *latter*, and not in the *total exclusion of the representatives of the people* from the administration of the *former*" (387). See also, Montesquieu, *Spirit of the Laws*, XI.6, XIX.27.

60. Von Fritz would seem to agree: Neither the people nor its tribune representatives could initiate legislation; thus the secessions were attempts to extract much wanted reforms from the curule magistrates who alone had this power. The secessions stopped when with the passage of the Hortensian law (287 BC) the people was empowered to propose and pass legislation binding on the whole community (*Mixed Constitution*, 214).

61. Polybius, VI.51.

62. For a contrary opinion, see Alfredo Bonadeo, "The Role of the People in the Works and Times of Machiavelli," *Bibliothèque d'Humanisme et Renaissance* 32 (1970): 369. Citing *A Discourse on Remodeling the Government of Florence*, Bonadeo contends that Machiavelli supports elimination of the nobility as a first step toward achieving republican equality. For proof, Bonadeo quotes a passage describing the measures necessary for instituting a free state in Milan: "In order to form a republic in Milan, where inequality among the citizens is great, necessarily all the nobility must be destroyed and brought to an equality with the others, because among them are men so above all rules that the laws are not enough to hold them down, but there must be a living voice and a kingly power to hold them down" (*Discourse*, 106-07). It is doubtful, however, that what is said of Milan can be applied to Florence; and even more doubtful is it that Machiavelli intends a leveling of the classes, since what comes next is his assertion that in all cities three qualities of men exist, "the most important, those in the middle, and the lowest" (*primi, mezzani e ultimi*), and that it is the responsibility of government to satisfy each group—with high offices of state going to the first (107-08). Bonadeo believes that Machiavelli criticizes the people only when it follows "the behavior pattern of the 'grandi'," and that he envisages "the creation of a condition which would suppress both the need for conflicts and the people's opponents." I dispute that Machiavelli is trying to suppress either; but then my disagreement with Bonadeo may be less than it seems, since the patricians of Rome were not the *grandi* of Florence, to say nothing of the titled nobility of Renaissance Europe. Plamenatz maintains that Machiavelli accepts all social classes except the feudal noblility (*Man and Society*, 58-59, 78).

63. See Strauss, *Thoughts*, 113, 127, 129, 265, 271. Strauss credits the Roman ruling class with undeceiving the people as to the intentions (necessarily selfish) of its champions and leaders. Consequently, the plebs joined with the patricians in punishing demagogues. Without such restraining counsel, which required that the patricians remain a class apart, the plebs would have deified its defenders—as it almost deified Manlius Capitolinus (Livy, VI.17) and as the Athenians deified Demetrius (205-07 [Plutarch,

Demetrius, 10, 13; *Discourses* I.59.1]). From this popular appetite for religious saviors, observed by Strauss (206-07), comes the Sullivan thesis, not supported by Strauss (230-31), that religious tyranny resting on promises to the people can only be prevented by the elimination of religion (*Three Romes*, 8). An answer closer to Machiavelli, it seems to me, is that tyranny (religious and otherwise) can best be prevented by preserving a Roman-like patriciate.

Chapter Four: Rome's Humors

1.   Wood, "Humanism of Action," 45.
2.   Mansfield, *New Modes and Orders*, 151.
3.   The residents of this Etruscan town were called Falisci (Livy V.26-27).
4.   In American politics the stupefaction of the public comes through encounters with the Internal Revenue Service.
5.   See Dante Germino, "Machiavelli's Thoughts on the Psyche and Society," in *Political Calculus*, 60, 75-77. From the people's need to be on guard against the great, Germino extrapolates a democratic Machiavelli: "Machiavelli's critical study of politics, then, far from shoring up the position of the political elite and providing them with esoteric 'secrets of rule,' has the effect, if seriously pursued, of democratizing politics through the spread of political knowledge to elites and non-elites alike" (76). Even so, Machiavelli is no democrat.
6.   In fact, it was the plebeians of Alba who made Mettius go back on his word (Livy, I.27).
7.   The natures of princes and peoples are mostly distinct in the dedication to *The Prince*. Their differences are laid out by Rebhorn, *Foxes and Lions*, 101-16.
8.   For a similar view, see Roger Masters, *Machiavelli, Leonardo, and the Science of Power* (Notre Dame: University of Notre Dame Press, 1996), 221-23.
9.   As liberalism develops it changes its opinion about the causes of human goodness. Locke, for example, supposes that civil society civilizes; accordingly, the conduct expected of nations at war is far more altruistic than the conduct expected of individuals in a state of nature (*Second Treatise*, §180, 9, in *Two Treatises of Government* [Cambridge: Cambridge University Press, 1988]). Montesquieu takes it as the responsibility of society to govern by more humane means than cruel and unusual punishments (*Spirit of the Laws*, VI). Hume imagines a moral improvement in human beings, even to the point of their no longer requiring justice, as their wants are supplied and as they more and more are safeguarded from necessity (*A Treatise of Human Nature*, III.2.2 [New York: Penguin Books, 1967], 536-54; also *An Inquiry Concerning the Principles of Morals*, III.1 [Indianapolis: Bobbs-Merrill, 1957], 14-23).
10.   Freedom, treated as a synonym for Platonic appetite, is a cause of corruption; whereas freedom, treated as a synonym for Platonic spiritedness, is a cause of virtue.
11.   See Pitkin's discussion of the fraternal Citizen as one of the images of Machiavellian manhood: "The Citizen . . . image is neither selfish nor self-sacrificing, but a way to 'give thought to public *and* private advantages' *together*" (*Fortune*, 94-95; more generally, 80-83, 90-97).

12.   See Pocock, *Politics, Language and Time*, 101-03, for a discussion of liberalism's efforts to replace virtue with law and soldiers with merchants.

13.   Presumably, Machiavelli is referring to plebiscites when he says, "A tribune, or any other citizen whatever, could propose a law to the people, on which every citizen was able to speak, either in favor or against, before it was decided" (I.18.3). In the centuriate assemblies, whose laws were binding on the whole community, "only a higher magistrate," says Nicolet, "with the right of *agere cum populo*, could propose legislation to them" (*World of the Citizen*, 223). See above, 304n60.

14.   On the subject of corruption, see Pocock, *Moment*, 204-11.

15.   Montesquieu, *Spirit of the Laws*, V.7.

16.   Helping friends and hurting enemies is Polemarchus's definition of justice in book 1 of the *Republic* (332d). In book 2 of the *Republic*, Socrates incorporates this definition into his city in speech, for gentleness toward friends and cruelty toward enemies are required behaviors of the warrior class (375c). Rousseau observes that "all political societies are composed of other, smaller societies of different types, each of which has its interests and maxims. . . . The will of these particular societies," he continues, "always has two relations: for the members of the association, it is a general will; for the large society, it is a private will, which is very often found to be upright in the first respect and vicious in the latter. A given man can be a pious priest, or a brave soldier, or a zealous lawyer, and a bad citizen." Rousseau maintains that while the general will ought to take precedence over the corporate will and the corporate over the private, "unfortunately personal interest is always found in inverse ration to duty, and it increases in proportion as the association becomes narrower and the engagement less sacred . . ." (*Discourse on Political Economy* [New York: St. Martin's Press, 1978], 212-13; see also *Social Contract*, III.2).

17.   Socrates argues that the small city of the Republic, because it is unified, is in fact larger than the more populous, but class divided, cities which are its neighbors and against which it might have to fight (*Republic*, 422e-423b).

18.   Von Fritz's explanation for why the "naturally grown constitution" is no more adaptable than the "written constitution," and perhaps even less, is that "its principles are to an even higher degree the product of fortuitous circumstances" (*Mixed Constitution*, 262). Cf. McCormick, "Political Exception," 893.

19.   Aristotle, *Politics*, 4.1.3. One of Aristotle's criteria of a good regime is the suitability of the regime to the character of the people.

20.   Strauss, *Thoughts*, 44, 269, 273.

21.   Bonadeo also sets aside the despair of I.18 (*Corruption*, 82).

22.   The real blame, however, would appear to fall on Caesar Augustus (Octavian), except that as a descendant and namesake of Julius Caesar, he is judged to have been unsuitable to defend the cause of liberty (I.52.3). But here we can see the projected value of the *Discourses*—to teach a future Octavian the interest he has in restoring a republic. See Strauss, *Thoughts*, 177.

23.   Anglo, *Dissection*, 110.

24.   Hulliung, *Citizen*, 65, 89, 128-29.

Chapter Five: Rome's "Outside" Modes and Orders

1.   Strauss believes that the second book is about a great deal more than Roman modes outside the city. It is also, he claims, a critique of Christian modernity. He further suggests that the two subjects are related in that each is about war (Rome's wars with its neighbors and Machiavelli's war with Christianity), each is about militias (a citizen army contrasted with auxiliary troops and a citizen priesthood contrasted with a clergy under a pope), and each is about indirect rule (Rome's governance of its empire and the papacy's governance of Christendom). Strauss's main thesis, to repeat, is that Machiavelli is conspiring to overturn Christian modes and orders (*Thoughts*, 102; also 35, 52, 138, 171-72). I do not dispute the thesis, but I hesitate applying it everywhere. Strauss, for instance, is set on this course by a seemingly innocuous phrase found in II.4.2: "at the end of this matter." From this phrase he concludes that the second book has a "matter" larger than the subjects of its several sections and that the "matter" in question is the "contrast between the armed ancient states and the unarmed modern states" (101-02). It is certainly true that the *Discourses* panegyrizes ancient strength and laments modern weakness; and it may even be true, as Strauss contends, that the second book dwells on the contrast more than do the other two. But need it follow that remarks made about the ancient-modern divide are in fact metaphors for the spiritual war Machiavelli is waging against Christianity? This I doubt, especially when the remarks are casual and referents unspecified.

2.   Machiavelli provides a description of the thickened Roman trunk in II.30.4.

3.   Sparta, at least, had tranquility in its favor, which Machiavelli was unable to combine with Roman liberty and Roman greatness.

4.   It will be remembered, however, that the Spartan case was not simply one of xenophobic isolationism, that under Cleomenes, for example, Sparta sought to expand its population of arms-bearing citizens.

5.   Livy says during the siege (IV.59), and I.51 of the *Discourses* implies the same.

6.   Veii (406-396 BC), Capua (212 BC), Carthage (146 BC), and Jerusalem (63 BC) are the four named by Machiavelli in II.32.1.

7.   Walker (*Discourses*, vol. 2, 48) is doubtful that Machiavelli places Rome's highpoint in the year 265 (or 266, since Walker uses 510 as the year of the Tarquins's fall), because "as yet Rome had made no foreign conquests." Accordingly, the phrase *altrettanti anni* ("as many years as," or "as many years again") Walker takes to mean "twice as many years as"; that is, Rome came to its ultimate greatness in twice as many years as it lived under the kings. But Walker is himself uncomfortable with this interpretation since it puts the greatness of Rome in the year 22 when Rome was no longer a republic but under the dominion of caesars. And in context the interpretation makes little sense. For Machiavelli is trying to compliment the republic; but it is no particular compliment to say that Rome reached its ultimate greatness in *twice* as many years (not *as* many years) as it was ruled by kings. See Strauss, *Thoughts*, 89.

8.   Strauss, *Thoughts*, 261-62; Mansfield, *Virtue*, 92.

9.   This was Charles the Bold, Duke of Burgundy, who attacked and was defeated by the Swiss at Morat in 1476 (III.10) and at Nancy a year later. He is named in II.10 as a prince who believed falsely that money is the sinew of war.

10.   Letter to Francesco Vettori, 10 August 1513 (#131).

11.   Letter to Francesco Vettori, 25 August 1513 (#134).

12.   Letter to Francesco Vettori, 20 December 1514 (#154).

13.   Sullivan, *Three Romes*, 174.

14.   Or it may simply be a recognition of irrevocable limitations.

15.   Sicily, Sardinia, Corsica, and Spain became Roman provinces as a result of the First and Second Punic Wars (between 241 and 200); and Macedon and Carthage were added as provinces a half a century later. See H. H. Scullard, *From the Gracchi to Nero* (New York: Frederick A. Praeger, 1959), 4-5.

16.   M. Rostovtzeff, *A History of the Ancient World*, vol. 2 (Oxford: Clarendon Press, 1927), 88. Says Rostovtzeff: "The formation of the provinces as part of the Roman state was of capital importance in the political development of Rome and Italy. Rome became less dependent upon the Italian allies in military and financial affairs. She had now a great revenue and a full treasury of her own; and she could fill the ranks of her armies from her new possessions. It was therefore natural that she should begin to treat her Italian allies like her allies overseas, interfering in their local affairs and demanding implicit obedience to her edicts. Nor was it less natural that the Italian allies should claim a share in the advantages reaped from foreign dominions which they had helped to conquer. But the citizens were not inclined to share their possessions and revenues with the allies, and their unwillingness to grant an extension of the franchise became more marked. A collision between citizens and allies was plainly inevitable."

17.   See Scullard, *Gracchi*, 66-70. The Italian allies wanted Roman citizenship, which Rome granted once the rebellion was underway in order to contain its scope and hasten its end. Rebels who refused the offer became "*dediticii* when finally they did submit," i.e., subjects who surrendered unconditionally and who had no rights (70). But even these had citizenship extended to them a year later.

18.   Wars of necessity represent a third form of combat (II.8). Such a war is caused by migratory peoples escaping famine, war, or oppression and seeking a new place to settle in territory occupied by others. Since there is not land enough to accommodate both immigrants and natives, this war of necessity is the cruelest and most desperate of all, resulting in the extermination or expulsion of the ancient inhabitants should they fail in their defense.

19.   Livy says that "patrons" (influential citizens who took on a subject city as their client) were sent to Antium and that "prefects" (circuit judges) were sent to Capua after the praetor, Lucius Furius, had given Capua laws (IX.20). The praetorship was created as part of the Licinian-Sextian legislation of 367 that produced plebeian consuls (Livy, VI.42). The praetor took over the judicial functions of the consul. The prefect was the praetor's deputy. See Heichelheim, et al., *Roman People*, 62; Scullard, *Roman World*, 139.

20.   Because Numa brought religion to Rome, Mansfield reasons that the reference to 400 years indicates that religion is the subject of the chapter (*New Modes and Orders*, 254). Religion though was part of Numa's "arts of peace" (I.11.1); and the "arts of peace," in II.25.1, are part of the art of war.

21.   They were made to pass "under the yoke" (Livy, III.10)—a not uncommon Roman practice (e.g., Livy, III.28; IX.15, IX.42), which when done to Romans by Samnites at the Caudine Forks is denounced by Machiavelli as a foolhardy and altogether unroman attempt to hit the middle way (II.23.4).

22. Machiavelli offers that the French managed Genoa properly when they refrained from installing a French governor, as had been their custom, and allowed a Genoese governor to rule on their behalf (II.21.2).

23. The Florentines of an earlier generation (1320s), by their policy of "favoring now one party and now the other," so exhausted the city of Pistoia that, "tired of its tumultuous way of life, it came spontaneously to throw itself into the arms of Florence" (II.25.1). But the Florentines of Machiavelli's day, by using always the third mode with the Pistoiese—and always with "greater tumults and greater scandals" arising from it— became "so worn out" that "they came to the second mode of removing the heads of the parties" (III.27.2).

24. *Florentine Histories*, II.16-24; *Discourses*, III.27; *Prince*, 20.

25. See David Hume, "Idea of a Perfect Commonwealth, in *Essays: Moral, Political, and Literary* (Indianapolis: Liberty Classics, 1985): "Where difference of interest is removed, whimsical and unaccountable factions often arise, from personal favour or enmity" (529); also James Madison, *Federalist* 10: "So strong is this propensity of mankind to fall into mutual animosities, that where no substantial occasion presents itself, the most frivolous and fanciful distinctions have been sufficient to kindle their unfriendly passions and excite their most violent conflicts" (79).

26. In 358 the Latins renewed their treaty with Rome, originally made in 493 (*foedus Cassianum*) but allowed to lapse in recent years. At that time Rome was bracing for war with the Gauls, and so Latin support was heartily welcomed (Livy, VII.12). Walker (who puts the year at 357) notes the pressure applied against Rome by many of its neighbors (Gauls, Etruscans, Hernici) and the shrinkage of Rome's dominion at this time (*Discourses*, vol. 2, 129.)

27. Machiavelli would seem to be referring to the Great Latin War of 340, and especially to that war's second great battle, at Trifanum—since the lesson of II.22-23 is that the Latins miscalculated their strength by supposing that the first battle, at Veseris, weakened Rome more than the Latins; and since Manlius Torquatus, credited with conquering and afflicting the Latins, was the lone victor at Trifanum, his co-consul, Publius Decius, having died at Veseris.

28. This was Lucius Furius Camillus, the grandson and namesake of the great Camillus who captured Veii and rescued Rome from the Gauls.

29. Mansfield, *Virtue*, 16-17, 239-47.

30. Strauss, *Thoughts*, 340, n. 152.

31. Machiavelli's dictum is seconded by Hume: "It may easily be observed, that, though free governments have been commonly the most happy for those who partake of their freedom; yet are they the most ruinous and oppressive to their provinces. . . . When a monarch extends his dominions by conquest, he soon learns to consider his old and his new subjects as on the same footing. . . . But a free state necessarily makes a great distinction . . . [since the] conquerors, in such a government, are all legislators, and will be sure to contrive matters, by restrictions on trade, and by taxes, so as to draw some private, as well as public, advantage from their conquests" ("That Politics May Be Reduced to a Science," in *Essays*, 18-19).

32. The process of nationalization received major legislative attention following the break up of the Latin League in 338. At that time Rome reorganized its population according to four classifications: some were full citizens, some were half-citizens; some were Latin allies, some were Italian allies. Full citizens were residents of Rome or recipi-

ents of individual allotments of public lands (*viritim*); they exercised their political rights as members of one of Rome's 35 tribes. Also counted as full citizens were Roman colonists (300 strong) serving as garrisons in seacoast towns; while they kept their political rights, they had to be in Rome to use them. Finally, Rome incorporated numerous cities (*municipia*) whose populations stayed where they were (Alba Longa being an early exception [Livy, I.29-30]) and who, if they were Latins, enjoyed all the rights of Romans. Non-Latin *municipia* had half-citizenship granted to them; they enjoyed private rights, sometimes called Latin rights (the right of marriage with people from different cities [*conubium*], the right of trade with other cities [*commercium*], the right of appeal of a magistrate's decision [*provocatio*], and the right of migration to Rome with full Roman citizenship [*migratio*]), but they possessed no political rights in the Roman republic; they had *civitas sine suffragio*. Locally they governed themselves, with magistrates, councils, and assemblies of their own making; or, depending on the times and Rome's generosity, they were administered by Roman praetors and prefects and lived under Roman law. They did though assume the burdens (*munia*) of citizenship (mainly taxes and military service), for which reason they were called "burden-bearers" (*municipia*). Half-citizenship was a probationary status, a means of introducing non-Latin peoples to the civic customs of Rome. Cities worked their way up the acculturation ladder until full citizenship was awarded to them. But in the period between 150 and 133 the half-citizenship classification largely disappeared.

In addition to citizens, full and half, there were allies (*socii*), Latin and Italian. Some allies were former members of the Latin League; others were early colonies founded jointly by Rome and Latium; others still were new colonies consisting mostly of ex-Romans who foreswore their citizenship in exchange for land. These peoples enjoyed some of the aforementioned private rights, including the right to resettle in Rome, but only on condition that a son was left behind. This right of migration, restricted in 268, was replaced in the next century with the right of Roman citizenship for all local office-holders, who, when in Rome, were randomly assigned membership in a tribe for purposes of voting. In matters of foreign policy these allies and colonies were wholly subject to Rome, supplying soldiers for the legions though not required to pay taxes; but in domestic matters they had their own governments and even coined their own money. Rome's other allies, many in Etruria and south Italy, were bound to it by separate treaties, the terms of which were favorable or punishing (*aequa* of *iniqua*) depending upon the circumstances of their surrender. Mostly these allies were sovereign states free of Roman supervision, except that Rome arbitrated disputes between them; and again there were conscription quotas which they were obliged to meet, although their units were kept distinct from Rome's. (See Scullard, *Roman World*, 137-43; also Scullard, *Gracchi*, 16-19; and Heitland, *Roman Republic*, 165-74.)

Scullard offers this concluding comment on Rome's strategy of nation-building: "Rome ever followed the policy of 'divide and rule,' and when she had made her divisions she tended to treat each section according to its degree of civilisation. Etruria, which was alien alike in language and religion, was not assimilated till after the Social War, while the more cognate Sabines were soon welcomed into Roman citizenship. But 'divide and rule' is only a half-truth. By this policy Rome had won the hegemony of Italy; she retained her position only because she welded the divisions into a higher unity" (*Roman World*, 140-41).

33.   *Art of War*, II, 573-80, 583-85, 589, 591, 607, 611. How persuasive though is Fabrizio's response? If partly trained patriots are better than untrained conscripts, fully trained professionals are that much better. Such was the reasoning which led Marius to create a professional army of proletarians (107 BC) and which before that led the senate to pay soldiers on duty and to extend the command of consuls. See Adam Smith, *An Inquiry into the Nature and Causes of the Wealth of Nations*, V.i.a.14-28 (Indianapolis: Liberty Classics, 1981). Pocock tries to help out, claiming "that only a part-time soldier can be trusted to possess a full-time commitment to the war and its purposes," because a citizen, "with a home and an occupation (*arte*) of his own, will wish to end the war and go home"; and having "his own place in the body politic, he will understand that the war is being fought to preserve it" (*Moment*, 200-01).

34.   See also *Art of War*, VI, 694.

35.   Sounding a little like Aristotle who chooses Greeks to populate the city of his prayers because Greeks ostensibly combine the spirit of northern tribesmen and the thoughtfulness of eastern subjects (*Politics*, VII.7.2-3), Fabrizio concedes that some peoples are more naturally spirited and some more naturally submissive and that in temperate climates people combine the two qualities or else they lack them both. But it hardly matters what nature supplies since training and discipline are better sources of martial valor, and, in any event, princes have not the whole world from which to recruit their armies (*Art of War*, II, 581; VI, 694). See also Plato, *Republic* 435e and *Laws* 791d; Montesquieu, *Spirit of the Laws*, XIV.2-3, XXI.3 and *The Persian Letters*, #131 (Cleveland: Meridian Books, 1961); Rousseau, *Social Contract*, III.8.

36.   Strauss, *Thoughts*, 253.

37.   Machiavelli does not identify the education he has in mind, but Christian education is the likely culprit: a virtueless Christian is rarely humble in success, and in failure he is generally abject and self-pitying, holding not himself but fortune, or divine providence, accountable (*Prince* 25). Savonarola blamed the invasion of Charles VIII on the sins of Florentines; Machiavelli blamed the invasion on the incompetence of Italian princes (*Prince*, 12).

38.   Mansfield, *Modes and* Orders, 401; *Virtue*, 52; Hulliung, *Citizen*, 194-95; Pitkin, *Fortune*, 144; Flanagan, "Concept of *Fortuna*," 145-46.

39.   These three combat units were differentiated principally by age, with the young in the *astati*, the mature in the *principi*, and the most veteran in the *triari* (Livy, VIII.8). Their equipment was basically the same (helmet, breastplate, and greaves; shield, sword, and javelin), although according to Polybius the *triari* (and not the *astati*) carried a thrusting-spear, or pike (*hasta*), in place of a javelin (*pilum*) (VI.23). Fabrizio expresses disbelief that any Roman infantryman was armed with a spear, notwithstanding the testimony of some ancient historians (*Art of War*, II, 595-96).

40.   Fabrizio, who is accused by Cosimo Rucellai of failing to apply ancient modes to his own profession of war, answers back that a prince or a republic must take the lead since imitating Roman battle tactics presupposes the existence of a citizen army; this army takes time to establish, and no captain-for-hire can do it on his own (*Art of War*, I, 572-80; VII, 721-23).

41.   The obvious implication is that modern Italians ought not to be reprimanded for failing to match the martial feats of Rome. The not so obvious implication is that modern technology favors the cause of liberty, just as ancient virtue favored the cause of empire. In this regard see II.24.1.

42.   Even when Rome was under attack, it fought out in the open rather than from behind walls.

43.   Consider the speech to recruits by General George Patton in the opening scene of the movie *Patton*: "Now I want you to remember that no bastard ever won a war by dying for his country. He won it by making the other poor, dumb bastard die for his country."

44.   It does to Luigi Alamanni, who makes it to Fabrizio (*Art of War*, III, 636). In addition to the explanations Machiavelli is set to offer, Fabrizio cites the Swiss example in support of his (and Machiavelli's) thesis that artillery has brought no significant change to the modern battlefield. Were artillery at all effective, he argues, its fury would rain the most destruction on close formations. But the fact that the Swiss phalanx is the best of modern-day infantry, and imitated by others, is proof that men crowded together are safe against artillery no less than against cavalry and other infantry. For good measure Fabrizio adds that he personally is unafraid of enemy fire (III, 638-39).

45.   Machiavelli risks sounding foolish by pegging his analysis to the current state of technology. See Strauss, *Thoughts*, 181; Butterfield, *Statecraft*, 122.

46.   Machiavelli's usual practice is to revere and defer to the authority of "one alone" (*uno solo*) (e.g., I.9, II.33, III.15, III.30.1).

47.   Says Strauss, "The examples which he adduces in order to establish the superiority of infantry to cavalry are less 'true' than 'beautiful'" (*Thoughts*, 159).

48.   Polybius, I.33-34.

49.   There is at least one example in Livy which supports Machiavelli's point, and Machiavelli refers to it in III.18.2 but for other purposes. It is the heroics of the cavalry decurion Sextus Tempanius, who, in the battle with the Volsci in 423, saved the day when he commanded his horsemen to dismount and fight as foot soldiers (Livy, IV.39).

50.   Plutarch, *Crassus*, 21-31.

51.   Plutarch, *Antony*, 41-49.

52.   *Politics*, VI.7.1-2; II.12.5; V.4.8.

53.   See Frederico Chabod who also believes that Machiavelli exaggerates the case for infantry: "The truth is that Machiavelli advocates the use of infantry above all because he believes that that is the way to get rid of 'mercenarism'" (*Machiavelli and the Renaissance*, [Cambridge: Harvard University Press, 1960], 87, n. 2).

This rhetorical explanation, that Machiavelli exaggerates to persuade, is not nearly so fascinating as the metaphorical explanation offered by Mansfield that "'dismounting' means laying aside authority and putting one's feet on the ground" and that the sin of Italian princes is "the reliance on the otherworldly support that princes erroneously believe will substitute for the only worldly reliance, one's own armies or an armed people" (*New Modes and Orders*, 243, 245). Cavalry, it appears, becomes a metaphor for religion and infantry a metaphor for earthly glory. This interpretation does account for Machiavelli's separation from his Roman authorities, since these authorities, when they talk about cavalry, mean horses, not paternosters. But what does Machiavelli mean? How likely is it that Machiavelli would have written *The Art of War* if military matters interested him only as metaphor?

54.   *Prince*, 12; *Florentine Histories*, IV.6; V.1, 33; VII.20; VIII.16.

55.   Macaulay, "Machiavelli," in *Critical and Historical Essays*, vol. 1 (Boston: Houghton and Mifflin, 1900). Macaulay draws a distinction between the make-believe

warfare of the Quattrocentro and the life-and-death struggles of the Cinquecentro. What may have suited Italy well in one era was causing its ruin in another (154-56).

56. Machiavelli does acknowledge the usefulness of armored cavalry in II.18.4, but only on condition that they dismount and fight as infantry. See *Art of War*, II, 599.

57. Tigranes commanded a force of 20,000 bowmen, 55,000 horse—17,000 of which were clad in mail—and 150,000 heavy infantry (Plutarch, *Lucullus*, 26). Fabrizio repeats the false number of 150,000 horse while adding several details not in Plutarch (*Art of War*, II, 602).

58. Plutarch, *Lucullus*, 28.

59. This battle is often discussed: I.23.4, II.18.4, II.22.1, III.18.1.

60. Hulliung, *Citizen*, 20-21, 39. Note that "cavalier" derives from "cavalry."

61. This formulation is partly question begging: a noble lie in defense of Roman modes and orders is worth the trouble of telling only if Roman modes and orders are truly useful; but if they are useful, why must there be lies? There must be lies because of the tension between private and public goods, as has been noted, and because of the people's incapacity to judge rightly, as will be noted. But there must also be lies because Roman modes and orders are not that useful. Why then have them? I will consider briefly this begged question at the end of the chapter and investigate it more thoroughly in the last section of the last chapter.

62. According to F. Gilbert, this opinion was not all that conventional in the Renaissance; or if it was, Machiavelli was not the only one to dispute it (*Machiavelli and Guicciardini*, 130).

63. There is a touch of primitivism in Polybius, too, who judges Roman martial valor more valuable than Carthaginian naval skill (VI.52). For a general treatment of the theme, see Daniel Waley, "The Primitivist Element in Machiavelli's Thought," *Journal of the History of Ideas* 31 (1970): 91-98.

64. On the value of martial virtue, see Quentin Skinner, *Machiavelli* (New York: Hill and Wang, 1981), 76.

65. If Machiavelli means to confine incurable factionalism to great cities not at war, then he may be conceding a domestic success to the politics of Plato and Aristotle— admitting that the polis, while vulnerable to external destruction, is nonetheless internally sound.

66. These were: Albert III (1438-1440), Frederick III (1440-1486), and Maximilian I (1486-1519).

67. The expansionist league is, however, remembered and allowed.

68. The moderns who commend artillery in II.16 think that it would have made Roman imperialism impossible and that it is therefore, at least by implication, an agent of liberty. Machiavelli proves them wrong, explaining that artillery favors the offense and that Roman power was mostly offensive. But now it happens that artillery is an agent of liberty since it is cited as one of several reasons why princes should not contemplate becoming tyrants. In chapter 16 the threat to liberty was from without (an imperial power using artillery to destroy the walled cities of independent republics), whereas in chapter 24 the threat to liberty is from within (a prince becoming a tyrant because he has a fortress to keep him safe).

69. See, for example, *Politics*, V.11.11-33. Guicciardini accuses Machiavelli of being, shall we say, unmachiavellian, of trusting too much in the goodness of people; for the people, argues Guicciardini, is not so faithful as always to obey a prince who treats it

well; plus the memory of a former prince or of a lost freedom haunts it and makes it unruly; lastly, the prince, from time to time, will have need to give offense (*Considerations*, 117-19). These are all familiar objections since Machiavelli raises them himself in other places and in other writings (e.g., his warning to unarmed prophets in *Prince*, 6). But Machiavelli is not proposing that kindness be a substitute for force; he is rather saying that only the strong can afford to be kind and so acquire and maintain by peaceful and easy means.

70.   Certainly Papirius was not someone who judged by results—a universal blindness lamented in the previous chapter (III.35.1, 2).

71.   Similarly in I.15, the son of this same Papirius is praised by Machiavelli, not for the fervor of his faith, but for the cleverness with which he subordinated piety to military needs.

72.   Machiavelli indicates the newness of the war by stating three times that Fabius passed "into Tuscany" when he entered the Ciminian forest. Machiavelli refers again to this event in III.33.2, saying that Fabius "led it [his army] into a new country against a new enemy."

73.   Mansfield moves from the inaptness of the example to a reflection on Machiavelli its source. Thus it is Machiavelli who is given a free commission and who goes beyond what the authority of the Roman model would warrant. This metaphorical reading allows Mansfield, among other things, to explain why Machiavelli changes the number and composition of the delegation sent to Fabius from Rome (there are seven delegates in Livy, two of whom are tribunes [IX.36]). Presumably, a deliberate error in reporting frees up the detail to represent something else; and in this case—and according to Mansfield—Machiavelli's two legates represent "credulous men" (*New Modes and Orders*, 295). See also Strauss, *Thoughts*, 106.

74.   The lesson of II.33, that captains perform better when granted free commissions, is supplemented by the lesson of III.15, that divided commands are a recipe for disaster.

75.   For much the same reason and about the same time, the senate extended consular terms, creating the office of proconsul for consuls who could not conveniently leave their posts. The first of these was Publius Philo, who in 326 had his command extended in order to hasten the capture of Paleopolis (III.24.1).

76.   Plamenatz distinguishes between the *virtù* of the commander and the *virtù*, or goodness, of the citizen-soldier. For the first, *virtù* is "energy and courage both for good and evil," whereas for the second it is energy and courage "for good alone—that is to say, displayed in honest and just causes for the public good" (*Man and Society*, 66). Although Fabius was no less energetic and courageous in challenging the enemy cavalry than he was in penetrating the Ciminian forest, in the first case, as a subordinate required to follow orders, his daring did damage to the public good and so was not an instance of citizen-soldier *virtù*.

Chapter Six: Rome's Captains

1. Book 1 explored the "things occurring inside and by public counsel," while book 2 investigated the things done outside and by public counsel, or, as the preface states, decisions "the Roman people made pertaining to the increase of its empire" (§3).

2. Although the dedication promises a sequel covering the remaining books of Livy's history, a statement in III.1.6 makes plain that the commentary on the *First Decade* is complete with book 3: "Within these limits this third book and last part of this first decade will conclude."

3. Strauss, *Thoughts*, 103-04. Strauss supposes book 3 to have as its subject private benefits achieved through private deliberations, a theme first raised in book 1.

4. In I.2.1 Machiavelli is less optimistic about the worth of all foundings, supposing that some are so badly constructed that they can never provide the basis of reform. Athens is an example as is Florence in I.49.2. But the emphasis in these chapters is on the regime's capacity for evolution from a simple to a mixed regime. The emphasis in III.1 is on the willingness of individuals to sacrifice for the common good.

5. The model to which a state returns, as Strauss explains, is not the modes and orders of the founding, but the terror felt when facing cruel necessity (*Thoughts*, 167).

6. The Medicis were twice as vigilant as the Romans—unless of course five-year renewals are not a mark of greater vigilance but of a regime so poorly made and ill-suited to its people that conspiracies against it are a commonplace. In *A Discourse on Remodeling the Government of Florence*, Machiavelli advises the Medicis against continuing princely government in Florence, following the death of Lorenzo in 1519, on grounds that Florentines were now republicans and would resist a Medici prince more strenuously than they did in the previous century when "every ten years the Medici were in danger of losing control." The implication is not that the Medici did well to "beat down" their enemies at ten-year (not five-year) intervals, but that the need for these beatings was evidence that the regime was insecure and that its continuation in the 1520s was impossible (*Chief Works*, vol. 2, 105).

7. The intervals range from one year separating Junius Brutus from Horatius Coclus and Mucius Scaevola (509-508 BC) to 103 years separating the two Catos (149-46 BC). Sixty-one years separate Marcus Regulus from Scipio Africanus (250-189 BC). Only one other renewal occurs within ten years (the four years between accusations against the Scipio brothers [189-185 BC]), and the average lapsed time is 36 years.

8. What was privately advantageous in the careers of Priscus and Servius? They were not tyrants, as was Superbus, who removed the public business to the palace (III.5.1); and their rights to the throne were publicly confirmed, notwithstanding the presence of heirs. Strangely, though, Machiavelli takes the side of the disinherited sons, thrice describing them as despoiled and saying of Priscus and Servius that they "usurped" the kingdom (III.4.1). There is more to the story than Machiavelli reveals: Priscus, a foreign national (a Tuscan, his father a Greek), arranged to have the young sons of Ancus Martius out of town when the election was held (Livy, I.35); and Servius, in collusion with Tanaquil, Priscus's queen, concealed the fact of the king's death until he, Servius, could strengthen his own hold upon power (Livy, I.41-42). Priscus and Servius connived to become king, actively promoting themselves at the expense of their predecessor's sons. They were privately advantaged by their assents to power and pri-

vately disadvantaged by their falls from power (they alone suffered assassination). One might conjecture then that in Machiavelli's estimation succession struggles are always for private gain and that contenders delude themselves if they think that the public is involved or that the public can legitimize the results. Ruling may be a public affair, and performance may legitimize the holding of office. But getting to rule is a private affair, a zero-sum game with winners and losers.

9.   Frightened by a snake slithering out of a palace pillar, Tarquin sent two of his sons, Titus and Arruns, and his nephew, Junius Brutus, to consult the priestess at Delphi (Livy, I.56).

10.   Pitkin uses the psychology of the underling to account for Brutus's lack of pride: "The underling may become habituated to the safety and security of his status, captive to his own skills, and permanently resentful" (*Fortune*, 43). Strauss attributes the same to levity (*Thoughts*, 244, 289).

11.   Emphasis added. See Mansfield, *New Modes and Orders*, 309.

12.   There are heroes in book 3: Junius Brutus (III.2-3), Fabius Maximus Cunctator (III.10), Gaius Sulpitius (III.10, III.14), Scipio Africanus (III.21), Manlius Torquatus (III.22, III.34), Valerius Corvinus (III.22, III.38), Marcus Furius Camillus (III.20, III.23, III.30), Lucius Quintius Cincinnatus (III.24-25), Lucretia and Virginia (III.26), Fabius Maximus Rullianus (III.33, III.45, III.47, III.49). In many cases, however, it is questionable whether they are valued as heroic individuals responsible for Rome's greatness or as useful illustrations of Machiavellian maxims.

13.   Strauss, *Thoughts*, 276.

14.   See also I.33.2 and I.33.5.

15.   The senate survived the dismantling of the constitution and was the platform from which a counterattack was launched.

16.   The parallel between these two captains is astonishingly exact. On the eve of the Carthaginian expedition, Scipio was nearly recalled to Rome because of the crimes and impieties committed by his subordinate, Pleminius, at Locri (whom Scipio acquitted and restored to office when charges were first brought against him [*Prince*, 17]). Alcibiades was recalled to Athens because of his suspected involvement in the profanation of the mysteries, a suspicion easy to harbor because of Alcibiades' unconventional style of living. The investigation of Scipio was also motivated by resentments aroused by his unroman dress and bearing (Livy, XXIX.19-20; Thucydides, VI.12, 15, 53, 61, *The Peloponnesian War*, vol. 2 [Ann Arbor: University of Michigan Press, 1959]).

17.   *Social Contract*, II.10.

18.   For other differences between Machiavelli and Rousseau, see Maurizio Viroli, "Republic and Politics in Machiavelli and Rousseau," *History of Political Thought* 10 (1989): 405-20; and Lionel A. McKenzie, "Rousseau's Debate with Machiavelli in the *Social Contract*," *Journal of the History of Ideas* 43 (1982): 209-28.

19.   In *Prince*, 6 Machiavelli calls Moses "a mere executor of things that had been ordered for him by God." If so, then God is responsible for the killing of "infinite men"; if not, then Moses is no different from secular founders like Romulus, Cyrus, and Theseus. Either God, by the inscrutability of his plan, has the look of a tyrant, or there is no God who is interested in political affairs. See Strauss, *Thoughts*, 49, 111, 157, 185, 188.

20.   Letter to Ricciardo Bechi, 9 March 1498 (#3); letter to Francesco Guicciardini, 17 May 1521 (#179). See Sasso, *Machiavelli*, 9-18; Donald Weinstein, "Machiavelli and Savonarola," in *Studies on Machiavelli*, 253-64; Strauss, *Thoughts*, 175. Cf. Whitfield,

Machiavelli, 83-91; and Whitfield, "Savonarola and the Purpose of the *Prince*," *Modern Language Review* 44 (1949): 45-59; also Ridolfi, *Life*, 9-10;

21. *Castruccio Castracani*, 552.

22. Noting that religion is the quality said to be most useful to a prince, Mansfield supposes that the people's forgiving gullibility arises from the belief that divine providence is responsible for the success of men (*Virtue*, 185, 27). See also *Mandragola*, V.iv; Montesquieu, *Spirit of the Laws*, V.14.

23. See *A Discourse on Remodeling the Government of Florence*, 102.

24. As it happened, Maelius did win for himself supporters among the populace, for which reason a dictator was needed to bring him to justice. But because Machiavelli provides few details of the case against Maelius, his popularity seems kindred to that of a war hero. In Livy, Maelius's treasonous intent is clear: he stockpiled arms in his home and held there clandestine assemblies of the plebs (IV.13-14). When summoned to stand trial by the dictator Lucius Cincinnatus, then in his eighties, Maelius resisted and was struck down by the master of horse.

25. The people is satisfied that its interests are being attended to if those offering advice have no competing interests of their own. In fact, the absence of private motives is probably not surety enough: better is it if the adviser gives counsel injurious to himself. Nicias is the model, for he advised Athenians not to undertake the invasion of Sicily even though a new war would have advanced his standing in the city (III.16.1). On the other hand, it was hardly in Nicias's interest to be put in charge of an expedition he expected to fail. Thus divining intentions in order to learn whose advice to trust will always be problematic for the people. See Strauss, *Thoughts*, 264.

26. It would appear, as of the fall of 1998, that the "kingly arm" of Independent Counsel Kenneth Starr is no match for the charisma of President Bill Clinton, who is supported by a public indifferent to his alleged misdeeds.

27. Emphasis added. See Mansfield, *New Modes and Orders*, 397.

28. Mansfield, *Virtue*, 23.

29. What Machiavelli does not report is that Fabius, who as consul was supervising the election for his replacement, was reelected consul in Ottacilius's place (Livy, XXIV.7-9). Private interest is a subtheme of book 3. Despite his silence about Fabius's ulterior motives, Machiavelli alludes to this subtheme when he notes that the act of exposing the defects of candidates is a good order if denunciation contributes to the glory of the denouncer.

30. Pitkin has a higher opinion of the effectiveness of Rome's ordinary modes (*Fortune*, 321-22. See also Gilbert, *Machiavelli and Guicciardini*, 190).

31. *Tercets on Ingratitude or Envy*, ll. 130-32.

32. The detail is all wrong: It was the other consul, Marcus Livius Salinator, who said to Fabius that he would seek a quick engagement either to reclaim his glory (condemned for embezzlement in 219 [Livy, XXII.35]) or to avenge himself on his fellow citizens (Livy, XXVII.40). More striking though is Machiavelli's attempt to dismiss as a psychological mistake (new favors do not erase old wrongs in the minds of the great [*Prince*, 7]) what in fact was a momentous victory for Rome comparable to its defeat at Cannae. Guicciardini is beside himself (*Considerations*, 120-21)!

33. The phrase is from Tocqueville (*Democracy in America*, vol. 1, 7). Alexander Hamilton, who in *Federalist* 9 almost uses the "new science" phrase ("the science of politics . . . has received great improvements"), means by it separation of powers, bicam-

eralism, judicial independence, representation, and—as Publius's own contribution—an enlargement of the sphere within which republican government operates (72-73). So understood, the "new science" contrasts with what Quentin Skinner calls "the strenuous view of citizenship" of the classical republican theorists ("The Republican Ideal of Political Liberty," in *Machiavelli and Republicanism*, 304-06).

Skinner observes in *Foundations* that two answers have been given to the question of how to harmonize the city's interests with the interests of its individuals: "One stresses that government is effective whenever its institutions are strong, and corrupt whenever its machinery fails to function adequately. . . . The other approach suggests by contrast that if the men who control the institutions of government are corrupt, the best possible institutions cannot be expected to shape or constrain them, whereas if the men are virtuous, the health of the institutions will be a matter of secondary importance" (44-45). Skinner considers Machiavelli and Montesquieu to be the leading exponents of this latter tradition and Hume the leading exponent of the former. Strauss is of the opposite opinion; he puts Machiavelli on the side of institutions over against character and thus on the side of a "new science of politics" (*What Is Political Philosophy?*, 41, 43, 47).

Wolin has his own meaning of "new science," which he too attributes to Machiavelli: a secular examination of political phenomena unaffected by religious categories and symbols; a rejection of natural law; a pragmatic analysis of power; a contempt for hereditary rule; a bias against the nobility and a bias favoring the plebs (coupled with a scientist's neutrality respecting the interests of the humors); an unmasking and exploitation of illusions; an economizing approach to violence; and a divorce of statecraft from soulcraft (*Politics and Vision*, 198-203, 213, 221, 230, 237).

34.   See Mansfield, *Virtue*, 28: "Machiavelli may have prepared bourgeois morality, but he stops definitely short of it." Mainly though, Mansfield argues the opposite, that Machiavelli is the first modern and that those philosophers who build the liberal state are reading from Machiavelli's script. See below, 204-07 and 278-81.

35.   The line, spoken by Marcellus Epirus, excused his work as an informer during the reign of Nero (Tacitus, *History*, in *The Complete Works of Tacitus* [New York: Modern Library, 1942], IV.8).

36.   The words, "Thus citizens can aspire to the principality" (§19), is as close as Machiavelli comes to naming ambition as a cause of anti-republican conspiracies.

37.   The United States has a tradition of civil disobedience. It is in effect a tacit agreement between the citizens and the government that the citizens will only pretend to conspire and the government will only pretend to punish.

38.   See Rebhorn, *Foxes and Lions*, 86-89, 116-23; Clifford Orwin, "Machiavelli's Unchristian Charity," *American Political Science Review* 72 (1978): 1225.

39.   For a prince, cruelties well-used are "done at a stroke, out of the necessity to secure oneself, and then not persisted in but are turned to as much utility for the subjects as one can. Those cruelties are badly used which, though few in the beginning, rather grow with time than are eliminated" (*Prince*, 8). Renewal through punishments is recommended to kingdoms in III.5.1; but in France, whose good orders serve as the model, parlements do the punishing, and the king is sometimes the accused.

40.   In 486 Rome was still close to its refounding as a republic (509), and in 384 Rome had just passed through the purifying fires of the Gallic invasion (390). See Strauss, *Thoughts*, 169.

41.   Consider the failings of decemvir Appius Claudius in I.40-41.

42. The same was argued in I.17 about restoring to health a corrupt republic, that the time required would exceed the life of the prince. Regarding the pace of corruption, however, the opposite was argued in I.42.

43. See *Tercets on Ambition*, ll. 113-14: *"può supplire l'educazion dove natura manca."*

44. Donald McIntosh, "The Modernity of Machiavelli," *Political Theory* 12 (1984): 190.

45. *Castruccio Castracani*, 533-34.

46. The distinction between the "universal" and the "particular," found in the astrological writings of Claudius Ptolemy, is taken by Parel as evidence that Machiavelli follows a pre-modern cosmology (*Machiavellian Cosmos*, 67-68). Parel usefully distinguishes between the fortune of a country and the fortune of an individual (the former combated by dikes and dams, the latter by impetuous wooing [pp. 67-85]). But the wall Parel constructs between country and individual is excessively high. He contends, for instance, that "the metaphor of a struggle against woman has no application in international politics" (83). But when Pope Julius marched impetuously into the Romagna, he was engaged in international politics as much as he was engaged in testing his personal fortune. Any principality is at once a "universal" and a "particular," because any principality is at once a state and a person.

47. Strauss, *Thoughts*, 242, 269. Elsewhere Strauss observes that Plato was the first to identify wisdom and courage as ruling class virtues and that Cicero followed suit by separating wisdom and courage from modesty, temperance, justice, and faithfulness ("Niccolo Machiavelli," in *History of Political Philosophy*, 3rd edition, eds. Leo Strauss and Joseph Cropsey [Chicago: University of Chicago Press, 1987], 301).

The literature on the meaning of *virtù* is quite extensive. See, for example: Whitfield, *Machiavelli*, 92-105; Neal Wood, "Machiavelli's Concept of *Virtù* Reconsidered," *Political Studies* 15 (1967): 159-72; I. Hannaford, "Machiavelli's Concept of Virtù in *The Prince* and *The Discourses* Reconsidered," *Political Studies* 20 (1972): 185-89; John Plamenatz, "In Search of Machiavellian *Virtù*," in *Political Calculus*, 157-78; Russell Price, "The Senses of *Virtù* in Machiavelli," *European Studies Review* 3 (1973):315-45; Parel, *Machiavellian Cosmos*, 86-100.

48. See J. G. A. Pocock, "Custom and Grace, Form and Matter: An Approach to Machiavelli's Concept of Innovation," in *Machiavelli and the Nature of Political Thought*, ed. Martin Fleisher (New York: Atheneum, 1972), 174. Pocock concludes that *The Prince's* legislator is an ideal type. See also Plamenatz, *Man and Society*, 51.

49. Letter to Piero Soderini, January 1513 (#116), written just before Machiavelli's arrest in February and known as *I Ghiribizzi* ("The Fantasies"); or—as is now generally thought—letter to Giovan Battista Soderini, 1506. See Roberto Ridolfi and Ghiglieri, *"I 'Ghiribizzi' al Soderini," La Bibliofilia* 72 (1970): 53-74; and Mario Martelli, *"I 'Ghiribizzi' a Giovan Battista Soderini," Rinascimento* 9 (1969): 147-80, and *"Ancora sui 'Ghiribizzi' a Giovan Battista Soderini," Rinascimento* 10 (1970): 3-27. This is letter #121 in *Machiavelli and His Friends*, which the editors, Atkinson and Sices, address to Giovan, Piero's nephew, and date as 13-21 September 1506 (134-36).

50. Pitkin's thesis is that Machiavelli's inconsistencies arise from a deep-seated ambivalence regarding manly autonomy (*Fortune*, 5). Three images of manhood does Pitkin identify: the fox, the Founder, and the Citizen (25-105). The first was derived

from Machiavelli's experience in Florentine politics, Pitkin conjectures, the latter two from his reading of ancient writers (45, 54, 95).

51.   The distinction between accumulation and use of power was also used to sort through discrepant accounts of how Rome managed its affairs with subject states (see above, 125-28). A related distinction is present in Pitkin who separates imitation of technique from imitation of character. The former, part of the repertoire of the fox and associated in Machiavelli's mind with the hope of "overcoming fortune's power by being a chameleon," leaves the agent's character untouched, whereas the latter, representing Machiavelli's hope for renewal in the modern world, is entirely transformative (*Fortune*, 268-70). See also Mansfield's discussion of impressive virtue and of the using and showing of virtue (*Virtue*, 16-19, 41). Mansfield calls *duro* and *facile* (hard and easy), the ninth of eleven pairs of virtues given in *Prince* 15, the "qualities of qualities," meaning by that that "every quality is 'hard' so as to contrast with its opposite, and 'easy' so as to accommodate the use of its opposite" (*Virtue*, 21, also 38). It will be true of the prince that his character is *facile* and *duro*: on the one hand, flexible and accommodating; on the other, solid and unyielding.

52.   De Grazia distinguishes between the "rhetoric of imposture" and the "business of ruling" (*Hell*, 296).

53.   Machiavelli's David is in fact better armed than the Bible's since Machiavelli gives David a knife of his own whereas the Bible has David using Goliath's sword to cut off Goliath's head (1 Samuel 17: 38-51). The lessons, too, are discordant (opposite even), with Machiavelli teaching self-reliance and the Bible teaching reliance on God.

54.   Lightness, opposite gravity in chapter 15, is listed in chapter 19 as a quality which brings the prince into contempt (along with effeminacy and pusillanimity, also in 15, and variability and irresoluteness, new in 19). But when the public is not looking, lightness and lasciviousness are perfectly acceptable qualities because they are part of nature's diversity (letter to Francesco Vettori, 20 December 1514 [#156]).

55.   See Norman Jacobson, *Pride and Solace: The Functions and Limits of Political Theory* (Berkeley: University of California Press, 1978), 35-38.

56.   *Art of War*, IV (662).

57.   Thomas Hobbes, *Leviathan*, XXX.28 (Indianapolis: Hackett, 1994).

58.   Machiavelli is often imprecise in these matters, and so the distinction between the variable public personae and the unchanging private character is not one which he clearly draws himself. Nor does he say whether some qualities are always for show and others always for real. Must impetuosity-caution be for real, as in the cases of Julius and Fabius, or might they in some cases be for their effect (they are treated more as military tactics in III.44-45 than as character traits)? Perhaps the answer is that all qualities are in general alike and equal, but that for particular persons some are genuine and others are fake. Thus one person might be neutral with respect to liberality and parsimony—and thus free to use either—but not neutral with respect to impetuosity and caution. In another case a person might be incurably cheap but cautious or impetuous as it suits him. That one quality or constellation of qualities about which a person is not neutral but is strongly and ineluctably disposed is what defines the character of that person, be he honest, lascivious, or proud.

59.   *Prince*, 25; *Tercets on Fortune*, ll. 164-65; *Clizia*, IV.1; Letter to Piero Soderini, January 1513 (#116) (or to Giovan Battista Soderini, 13-21 September 1506).

60.   Noticing a connection between the prudent dam builder and caution as a character trait, Pitkin suggests additional connections between caution and the guileful fox and impetuosity and the manly lion (*Fortune*, 150-51). But, as noted above, these connections are slippery since the fox might just as easily be associated with characterless flexibility.

61.   See Robert Orr, "The Time Motif in Machiavelli," in *Machiavelli and the Nature of Political Thought*, 200-05. Orr organizes sequentially the various and sometimes conflicting behaviors of the prince/republic: conduct in anticipation of Fortune; conduct in response to Fortune's arrival; and conduct after Fortune's departure. "Dam-building," so called, is action appropriate to the first phase, including the construction of a mixed constitution. In the second phase, three actions are identified: lying low (or temporizing), adjusting to Fortune's mood (i.e., choosing a ruler whose character fits the times), and attacking Fortune directly (i.e., the rough wooing of the impetuous lover). In the third phase, equanimity is in order, and fixed character is its cause. While Orr's schematization does not fit exactly the above analysis (e.g., the characterless prince who puts on qualities to deceive the multitude is missing, and the lawgiver and captain are assigned to different phases of resistance rather than taken to represent alternate strategies of combating Fortune [caution vs. audacity] or as having alternate fortunes to combat [moral decline vs. outside necessities]), it brings much clarity to Machiavelli's diffuse observations, and something like it will be used in the last chapter to resolve what I deem to be an even more pressing discontinuity in Machiavelli's thought.

62.   Strauss, *Thoughts*, 160-65. Walker (*Discourses*, vol. 2, 183) can find no passage in Tacitus corresponding to Machiavelli's Latin quotation; and the only passage that compares *obsequium* (indulgence) and *poena* (punishment) states the reverse of what Machiavelli contends (*Annals*, III.55.5, in *The Complete Works of Tacitus* [New York: Modern Library, 1942]).

63.   The exaggeration that "all the cities of Italy rebelled to Hannibal" is corrected with reference to Neapolitan resistance (§4; also II.30.4). But the exaggeration that Scipio "at once" made Spain "friendly to him" (he at once took New Carthage by siege) is nowhere corrected. See Mansfield, *New Modes and Orders*, 376.

64.   Letter to Francesco Vettori, 26 August 1513 (#134).

65.   Consider, for example, the Melians who tried convincing the Athenians that sparing Melos was in Athens's best interest (Thucydides, V.98).

66.   The American public is currently tired of partisan wrangling and wants its representatives to get along.

67.   See also I.37.1; letter to Piero Soderini, January 1513 (#116) (or to Giovan Battista Soderini, 13-21 September 1506).

68.   At the close of III.24 Machiavelli worries about reaching imperial greatness too soon and so beginning too soon the slide into slavery.

69.   Livy's reason is the good of Rome; Machiavelli's reason is the good of Manlius.

70.   Livy reports that following the victory at Trifanum, Manlius was greeted by the elders of Rome but not by younger men who hated him for the rest of his life (VIII.12).

71.   *Politics*, III.13.13-15.

72.   The same alternatives are presented in I.30.1.

73. Strauss would seem to disagree about the parameters of Machiavellian psychology: "I believe that this rather shocking act of *superbia* was in Machiavelli's eyes a sign of Camillus' magnanimity" ("Niccolo Machiavelli," 315). On the other hand, Strauss states that in defense of earthly glory Machiavelli replaces magnanimity (and humility) with humanity: "But humanity as he [Machiavelli] understands it implies the desire to prevent man from transcending humanity or to lower man's goal" (*Thoughts*, 207-08; see also 78, 167, 244).

74. *Nicomachean Ethics*, IV.17-18, 34.

75. That said, it is important as well that there be some benefit for Manlius in the public hatred he incurred, otherwise the city's deliverance would depend too much on the generosity of self-sacrificing patriots, which, for Machiavelli, is tantamount to depending on chance. Manlius's benefit was that he escaped the people's ingratitude, reserved for those thought to be conspiring against the people's liberty. His other benefit though was his fame, greater even than that earned by Valerius, his kindly contemporary. Manlius developed a hard-bitten character which thereafter determined his actions; but apparently he realized that hatred was no bar to glory, for he is an example in III.34.1-2 of a savvy prince who plots a career comprised of self-promotional stunts aimed at capturing the popular imagination.

76. Actually only twenty of an eventual 170 women were killed. These twenty were summoned to the Forum and required to prove the wholesomeness they claimed for their brew by drinking it themselves. They did, and they died. The others had their crimes attributed to divine madness for which propitiation, not summary execution, was the chosen remedy (Livy, VIII.18).

77. A classroom example affords some confirmation: Essay questions are given out in advance, and the students are told that one or more questions taken from the list will constitute the exam. On exam day the instructor, instead of announcing which questions the students will answer, takes out a pair of dice, rolls them across a desk, and lets the upcoming numbers decide the issue. The students' reaction is always the same—universal stupefaction. There seems to be something especially terrifying about having one's fate determined by chance and something reassuring about being subject to human judgment. If the instructor chooses the questions, the students, believing that they can reason like the instructor, believe also that they can figure out which questions to concentrate on. But when chance does the choosing, they have no control.

78. Fabius's reform in the year 304 undid an earlier reform by Appius Claudius, the blind censor, who in 312, or thereabouts, enhanced the voting power of the urban poor, the *humiles*, by distributing them across all 31 tribes. One effect was the election of Gnaeus Flavius, the son of a freedman, to a curule magistracy. By re-collecting the *humiles* in the four urban tribes, Fabius prevented a democratic take-over of the *comitia tributa*. See Livy, IX.29, 46; Scullard, *Roman World*, 105-06; Jacques Heurgon, *The Rise of Rome to 264 B.C.* (Berkeley: University of California Press, 1973), 195-98.

79. Bonadeo says that Machiavelli was more concerned with "the control and elimination of subversive power" than with delineating "an elaborate political program" because "no law, institution, or public action," in his opinion, "could possibly check those autonomous nuclei of power" (*Corruption*, 123). See also Hanna H. Gray, "Machiavelli: The Art of Politics and the Paradox of Power," in *The Responsibility of Power: Historical Essays in Honor of Hajo Holborn*, eds. Leonard Krieger and Fritz Stern (Garden City, N. Y.: Doubleday, 1967), 49.

80. McCormick ("Political Exception") reverses the relation, giving pride of place to the rule of law: Machiavelli "resisted the temptation to confront the unpredictable nature of politics with a wholly executive-oriented response, instead advocating the mixed regime precisely because he thought it could best withstand the *accidenti* that inevitably arise from time to time" (889). "As a consequence," McCormick concludes, "he [Machiavelli] strongly emphasize[d] the legal over the extra- or supralegal means of defending a regime" (898).

81. The constitution which Machiavelli devises in *A Discourse on Remodeling the Government of Florence* is a monarchy, for as long as the Medici princes are alive; but it is a monarchy lacking nothing needed to become a republic once the Medicis have gone (113).

82. See Strauss, *Thoughts*, 256, 269, 270, 281-82; Skinner, *Foundations*, 179; B. Smith, *Politics and Remembrance*, 52.

Chapter Seven: Machiavelli's Modes and Orders

1. The contrast with Rousseau is instructive. Determined to establish the people's sovereignty, Rousseau closely studies the operations of Rome's assemblies (*Social Contract*, IV.4).

2. *Thoughts*, 317, n. 52; also 86.

3. *Thoughts*, 116.

4. These are, as explained by Strauss: pregnant silences, obvious blunders, innocuous or misleading chapter titles, parodies, changing statements, inappropriate or untrue examples, and exclusions and digressions (*Thoughts*, 29-46).

5. *Thoughts*, 134-36; Strauss, "Classical Literature," 24; Hulliung, *Citizen*, 162-64; McIntosh, "Modernity," 185-87. Hannah Arendt contends that Machiavelli misrepresents Roman respect for authority, portraying it as a celebration of violence (*On Revolution* [New York: Penguin Books, 1965], 37; and *Between Past and Future: Eight Exercises in Political Thought* [New York: Viking Press, 1968], 124). Rebhorn adds that Machiavelli falsifies Roman attitudes toward leisure (*Foxes and Lions*, 150).

6. After discovering a mistake, and after determining it to be intentional on Machiavelli's part (perhaps because the correct fact is reported elsewhere), it still remains to establish the meaning of the mistake. Similar problems attach to charges of revisionism. Is Machiavelli creating an inaccurate picture of Rome, telling it like it ought to have been, or is his account of a hyper-aggressive and deceitful republic the secret truth about Rome, a truth he learned from having deciphered Livy's own esoteric writing? The fact that Machiavelli will not allow Grecophiles of the late republic and early empire period to stand as authentic representatives of Rome (or that his portrait of Rome differs from Cicero's) need not then mean that the Romans described in the *Discourses* are free creations and so proof of Machiavelli's originality.

7. See Xenophon, *Constitution of the Lacedaemonians*, 7, in *Scripta Minora* (Cambridge: Harvard University Press, 1921); Aristotle, *Politics*, 2.9.36-37; Demosthenes, *On Organization*, 28-31 (London: William Heinemann, 1930); Sallust, *The War with Cataline*, 52.22 (London: William Heinemann, 1921); Plutarch, *Lycurgus*, 9-10,

13.3-5; also Alfred Zimmern, *The Greek Commonwealth* (New York: Oxford University Press, 1961), 291-92.

8. Once Rome fell under the rule of caesars, two additional mistakes were committed ensuring Rome's conquest by northern barbarians: the paying of tribute and the hiring of mercenaries (II.30.2; *Prince*, 13).

9. *Virtue*, 242-45. According to Mansfield, Machiavelli conceives of ordinary-extraordinary modes as points on a continuum not as either/or opposites like legal/illegal. See also 305.

10. *De Re Publica*, II.1. Rebhorn notes that Machiavelli's "version of the ideal state of Rome . . . involves a situation of perpetual internecine strife," whereas Cicero can "imagine an ideal republic at peace" (*Foxes and Lions*, 152).

11. *Thoughts*, 119; see also 83.

12. Experience, therefore, is very much against Plato's *Republic*, where the excluded workers, practicing their moderation, agree that warriors and philosophers ought to rule (432a).

13. See above, 86-87.

14. *Virtue*, 92-97, 115-16, 282-86; "Introduction," in *Discourses on Livy* (Chicago: University of Chicago Press, 1996), xli-xlii. Mansfield, however, does not actually mean that the impartial regime is perfect and perpetual (117-22, 280). I will return to this issue in chapter 9.

15. The explanation is all Mansfield's for why the Florentine people was unwilling to share power with the nobles: The people was ungenerous because the spoils of victory were too few for sharing; the spoils were too few because of Florence's reliance on mercenary arms; Florence relied on mercenary arms because the Christian faith disesteemed worldly honor (*Virtue*, 151-58). See also Marcia L. Colish, "The Idea of Liberty in Machiavelli," *Journal of the History of Ideas* 32 (1971), 340-41.

Ronald Terchek contends that healthy conflict is that which returns the parties to the status quo ante, reestablishing their prior relationship and reaffirming the principles of the founding; and that factious conflict is that which ignores long-held opinions of distributive justice and tries imposing a new settlement on the parties, one satisfying the ambitions of the winner but threatening the vital interests of the loser (*Republican Paradoxes and Liberal Anxieties: Retrieving Neglected Fragments of Political Theory* [Lanham, Md.: Rowman & Littlefield, 1997], 104-07). While sensible enough as an explanation of good and bad conflict, Terchek's analysis, it seems to me, applies poorly to Machiavelli, since it makes him out to be a conservative opposed to innovation.

16. *Leviathan*, X.53-54, XV.14.

17. *Spirit of the Laws*, XI.6; *Federalist Papers*, 63, 387.

18. *Virtue*, 115.

19. Quentin Skinner might well object, on grounds that the interpretation is an instance of the "mythology of prolepsis." See "Meaning and Understanding in the History of Ideas," *History and Theory* 8 (1969): 22-24.

20. Machiavelli, for instance, seems not to appreciate the ameliorative effects of multiplied factions. He comments in the *Florentine Histories* that "most other republics about which we have any information have been content with one division by which, depending on accidents, they have sometimes expanded and sometimes ruined their city; but Florence, not content with one, made many" (Pr.). Also, Machiavelli's rationale for preferring expansionist Rome over sedentary Sparta is nothing like Madison's rationale

for preferring the extensive republic: Machiavelli wants size because size means foreign wars and because foreign wars unify the factions; Madison wants size because size prevents concerted action by a majority faction (*Federalist* 10, 81, 83-84).

21.   See S. M. Shumer, "Machiavelli: Republican Politics and Its Corruption," *Political Theory* 7 (1979): 16-18, 30-31. "Citizens," notes Shumer, "are not relegated to the passive role of selecting others to rule them or even to rule for them" (17). See also Brudney, "Social Class," 514-17.

A political life, Machiavelli implies, can exist only among equals. Aristotle says the same, but for Aristotle equality is established by demonstrations of worth and contribution (e.g., the demos deserves a voice because it mans the ships which save the state [*Politics*, II.12.5; V.4.8]). For Machiavelli, equality is established by combat, by fighting opponents to a standstill. The burden of establishing and defending equality falls chiefly on the plebs, since by temperament the plebs wants not to be oppressed. The pacification of the plebs is therefore a danger to politics.

22.   It will do for Wolin, however, who credits Machiavelli with setting the stage for interest group pluralism (*Politics and Vision*, 232-33, 235-36).

23.   One reason why Machiavelli prefers class-based discord—as suggested above—is that it allows honest plebeians to check corrupt patricians and wise patricians to check foolish plebeians. (See Bonadeo, *Corruption*, 65-66; Pitkin, *Fortune*, 85-86.) Another reason is that it requires people—and *the* people especially—to engage in a public life, for with a permanent interest to defend neither class can afford to be wholly private. Perhaps it is not too much of a stretch to say that Machiavelli would find congenial the "identity politics" of the present.

24.   Crick distinguishes faction from class strife, defining the first as division among the *ottimati* ("Introduction," in *The Discourses*, ed. Bernard Crick, trans. Leslie J. Walker [Harmondsworth, Middlesex, England: Penguin Books, 1970], 44). See F. Gilbert, *Machiavelli and Guicciardini*, 187; Germino, "Psyche," 69-70; Gisela Bock, "Civil Discord in Machiavelli's *Istorie Fiorentine*," in *Machiavelli and Republicanism*, 196-97; David Wooton, "Introduction," in *Machiavelli: Selected Political Writings*, ed. and trans. David Wooton (Indianapolis: Hackett, 1994), xxxii-xxxiii.

25.   *Politics*, V.8.15-19, VI.7.5.

26.   *Statecraft*, 33-34, 52.

27.   *Statecraft*, 28.

28.   *Statecraft*, 37-38.

29.   *Discourses*, vol. 1, 82-83.

30.   *Discourses*, vol. 1, 92-93. Butterfield regards Machiavelli as a transitional figure and the Renaissance as a preparatory period laying the ground work for the scientific revolution of modernity (*Statecraft*, 59-61).

31.   See also Burnham, *Machiavellians*, 45-55.

32.   *Statecraft*, 22-25, 71-72, 114-15.

33.   *Maxims and Reflection of a Renaissance Statesman*, Series C: 35, 110, 114, 117, 182; Series B: 35 (Gloucester, Mass.: Peter Smith, 1970).

34.   *Citizen*, 160, 162.

35.   See Martin Fleisher, who provides a valuable study of Machiavelli's new modes and orders and untrodden path in "The Ways of Machiavelli and the Ways of Politics," *Political Theory* 16: 330-55. According to Fleisher, "true knowledge of histories" is the untrodden path; it consists of bringing to full consciousness and correcting

what the ancients did accidentally, instinctively, unconsciously (331). The untrodden path has much the same meaning for Janet Coleman who argues, however, that the path is not new, being but a Renaissance continuation of a medieval practice ("Machiavelli's *Via Moderna*: Medieval and Renaissance Attitudes to History," in *Niccolò Machiavelli's The Prince: New Interdisciplinary Essays*, ed. Martin Coyle [Manchester: Manchester University Press, 1995], 41). For Chabod the untrodden path is a national milita or, alternately, the discovery that politics is separate from morality (*Machiavelli and the Renaissance*, 16, 141). Similarly for Hale, the new route is the assumption that politics should be based on expediency or, like Butterfield, based on history, not philosophy (*Renaissance Italy*, 159, 176-77). Villari anticipates Butterfield in saying that the path untrodden is "a new science of statecraft based on the experience of human events and history" (*Life and Times*, vol. 2, 98; also 220). Germino contends that exposing the role of fraud in politics is Machiavelli's path ("Psyche," 60, 77-78). Strauss implies that the untrodden path is Machiavelli's esoteric style of composition and that the "short road" is traveled by the reader who discerns the intention of Machiavelli which he himself does not state (*Thoughts*, 34-35). In Master's view Machiavelli's new path is a new approach to theory and practice, one in which science, distinguishing fact from value and overriding the protected spaces of opinion and faith, takes the lead in shaping public policy (*Machiavelli, Leonardo*, 165-67). Elsewhere Masters suggests that sexual liberation (the rejection of Christian chastity as part of the rejection of Christian morality) is Machiavelli's new route ("Machiavelli's Sexuality: 'Love, be my guide, my leader'" [paper presented to the Annual Meeting of the American Political Science Association (Boston, September 1998), 28]).

36. It reads: "Although the envious nature of men has always made it no less dangerous to find new modes and orders than to seek unknown waters and lands, because men are more ready to blame than to praise the actions of others, nonetheless, driven by that natural desire that has always been in me to work, without any respect, for those things I believe will bring common benefit to everyone, I have decided to take a path as yet untrodden by anyone, and if it brings me trouble and difficulty, it could also bring me reward through those who consider humanely the end of these labors of mine."

37. *Thoughts*, 232. Later I will consider whether by these terms Machiavelli is in fact an original, the first of the moderns, or a throwback to the pre-philosophic ancients.

38. See F. Gilbert on the humanist concept of "true history" (*Machiavelli and Guicciardini*, 206-218). Gilbert seems generally to agree with Butterfield that Machiavelli's claim to novelty refers to a new science of history ("Composition," 154-55). But then Gilbert takes this new science as evidence of Machiavelli's conversion to "orthodox humanism" (156): "In the *Discorsi*, Machiavelli followed a method which he believed to be the recognized scholarly procedure of his time" (155).

39. All that Machiavelli says by way of explanation is that he will concentrate on "all those books of Titus Livy that have not been intercepted by the malignity of the times" (I.Pr.2). These are the first ten books. After these ten, ten others are missing, after which there are 25, but then nothing of the remaining 97 (the original project ran to 142 books).

40. As it happens, Butterfield arrives at his interpretation without checking any of Machiavelli's examples; many are inappropriate to the point, playful, or simply wrong. See Strauss, *Thoughts*, 36-48; Mansfield, *Virtue*, 227.

41.   See Eric Cochrane, "Machiavelli: 1940-1960," *Journal of Modern History* 32-33 (1960-61): 121-22; F. Gilbert, *Machiavelli and Guicciardini*, 168-70, 215-17, 224-25, 238; McIntosh, "Modernity," 184-85; Anthony Parel, "Introduction: Machiavelli's Method and His Interpreters," in *Political Calculus*. While agreeing that Machiavelli uses history creatively (10), Parel nevertheless stresses the scientific side of Machiavelli's method (5-14).

42.   Skinner expresses a similar opinion (*Foundations*, 169-70). See also Plamenatz, *Man and Society*, 38-42; Coleman, "*Via Moderna*," 57.

43.   Coleman provides a fuller account using maxims from *The Prince* ("*Via Moderna*," 50-52).

44.   One better place, I believe, is with the "noble lie" propagating the infantry's usefulness.

45.   Mansfield, *New Modes and Orders*, 429.

46.   See B. Smith, *Politics and Remembrance*, 29-38. Writes Smith, "In teaching what men had done, Machiavellian history sought to teach men what they might do. This history was less a science of correct action than the origin of action itself" (38). Smith later observes that "Machiavelli's 'new way' involved an investigation into the linking of theory and power" (97). See also Maurizio Viroli, *Machiavelli* (Oxford: Oxford University Press, 1998), 3, 73, 112.

47.   The phrase from I.Pr.2 that "those who delight in that art . . . then strive with all industry to represent it in all their works" suggests the diligence of a faithful copyist not the creativity of an original genius, a Michelangelo, for instance, drawing inspiration from the *Belvedere Torso* or the *Laocoön* group.

48.   *The Use and Abuse of History* (Indianapolis: Bobbs-Merrill, 1957), 12-17.

49.   *Citizen*, 165.

50.   Eugene Garver, *Machiavelli and the History of Prudence* (Madison: University of Wisconsin Press, 1987), 132. Victoria Kahn, "*Virtù* and the Example of Agathocles in Machiavelli's *Prince*," in *Discourse of Literature*, 197, 212.

51.   As suggested above, the most extravagant promise is that made to Florentines in III.43, that their foreign policy can succeed by applying directly the lessons of ancient history.

52.   Cf. Hulliung, who attributes the withholding of glory from fraud in III.40-41 to momentary forgetfulness on Machaivelli's part (*Citizen*, 286, n. 21); also Hans Baron, *In Search of Florentine Civic Humanism*, vol. 2 (Princeton: Princeton University Press, 1988), 109-110. Baron believes that the discussion of promise-keeping in the republican *Discourses* is entirely different from the discussion of the same in the autocratic *Prince*: "Nothing could be more different in the two works than the motivation for breaking promises" (110). The motivation in III.41 is the safety of the fatherland, he says, whereas the motivation in *Prince* 18 is the winning and maintaining of a state. But notice what happens in III.42: First it is said that "forced promises *that regard the public* will always be broken and it will be without shame for whoever breaks them" (emphasis added). Next it is said that "forced promises are not observed among princes, when the force is lacking, but all other promises are also not observed when the causes that made them promise are lacking." What the second statement deletes is the public reason for breaking promises; and what it adds is the consideration of utility. Baron misses this subtlety. He misses as well the fact that *The Prince* is summoned to settle the glory issue, whether promise-breaking is praiseworthy. Impressed, it seems, by the self-sacrificing nobility of

the consul Spurius Postumius (who assumed responsibility for repudiating the treaty and insisted that he and his officers be sent back in chains to the enemy), Baron misses the question which Machiavelli is pondering, how to achieve personal fame even in defeat. Finally he misses the Machiavellian genius of Spurius's surrender, the fact that the Samnites could not accept the consul as prisoner without also accepting the Roman interpretation of the treaty—hence Spurius and his men were returned safely to Rome.

53. *Citizen*, 160.

54. *Citizen*, 159. Hulliung's example of an easily duped opponent is the Latin people who were deceived by Rome during the years of its expansion inside of Italy. But the Latins uncovered Rome's deceit long before Rome had completed the conquest of Italy and at a time when the Latins were the equal of Rome in power (340). Furthermore, these easily duped Latins caused Rome to delay the start of the Great Latin War, to its own disadvantage and discredit, by practicing this same deceit against Rome (II.14, II.16.1, II. 21).

55. Kahn reads chapters 7 and 8 of *The Prince* as "a test of *virtù*" ("Agathocles," 208-210).

56. "For a long time I have not said what I believed, nor do I ever believe what I say, and if indeed sometimes I do happen to tell the truth, I hide it among so many lies that it is hard to find" (letter to Francesco Guicciardini, 17 May 1521 [#179]). Cf. Villari, *Life and Times*, vol. 2, 139; Burnham, *Machiavellians*, 55; Whitfield, *Machiavelli*, 109.

57. Machiavelli notes that the French, victorious at Allia, stopped before the walls of Rome, certain that a mistake so obvious as open gates must be a trap (390 BC). But there was no trap. The gates were left open because, as Machiavelli alternately explains, fortune wanted to chastise Rome (II.29), or the Romans simply had lost their virtue (III.1.2).

58. *Thoughts*, 35-36.

59. Self-protection and particular concealments would be additional purposes.

60. See J. G. A. Pocock, "Prophet and Inquisitor, or, a Church Built upon Bayonets Cannot Stand: A Comment on Mansfield's 'Strauss's Machiavelli,'" *Political Theory* 3 (1975): 392. Mansfield issues this challenge to all doubters of Strauss's interpretation of Machiavelli: "Anyone who thinks it possible to exercise his ingenuity with a consistent interpretation of an inconsistent text, and not be caught, should demonstrate that he can do it" (*Virtue*, 229). This certainly would be impossible if it were required that every jot and tittle of a text be accounted for by the interpretation. But if some details are explained and others let go, the interpreter, by limiting the field, provides himself with room to maneuver. Say there are a million details in Machiavelli and Livy, and say that Strauss constructs his interpretation using one thousand of them. These one thousand pieces might be made to compose a picture different from or clearer than the million-piece puzzle, whose pieces, left in their original places, might show no design at all.

61. Livy reports that the legate had soldiers who were familiar with the language identify the dialect as that of country or city folk; it being city, the legate knew that his prisoners were not real shepherds (X.4). A similar plan though, used by the Samnites at the Caudine Forks (321 BC), was successful (III.40.2).

62. Consider, for example, the statement in I.32.1: "Because like causes happen rarely, it will also occur rarely that like remedies help" See Chabod, *Machiavelli and the Renaissance*, 144; Wooton, "Introduction," xxxv.

63.   *The Myth of the State* (Garden City, N. Y.: Doubleday Anchor Books, 1955), 162-63.

64.   In *Studies on Machiavelli*, 149-206.

65.   "Originality," 159-62.

66.   "Originality," 160. See also Cassirer, *Myth*, 159-73; Jacques Maritain, "The End of Machiavellianism," in *The Social and Political Thought of Jacques Maritain: Selected Readings*, eds. Joseph W. Evans and Leo R. Ward (Garden City, N. Y.: Image Books, 1965), 291-92.

67.   *Politics and Morals* (New York: Philosophical Library, 1945), 59. Translation of *Etica e politica*, trans. Salvatore J. Castiglione (Bari: Laterza, 1931). See also Chabod, *Machiavelli and the Renaissance*, 116, 138-40; Sasso, *Machiavelli*, 300-01.

68.   That this conclusion is at the heart of Berlin's resistance to the Croce thesis is implied on several occasions: "Originality," 164, 177, 179, 180. Cf. 181, 184.

69.   "Originality," 169. Berlin's listing of pagan virtues goes on to include: "order, discipline, happiness, strength, justice, above all assertion of one's proper claims and the knowledge and power needed to secure their satisfaction." These pagan virtues sound suspiciously Aristotelian. They become more so as Berlin proceeds; for even though Berlin has Machiavelli dismissing classical natural right, when trying to give substance to a pagan ethics that is rival to Christianity, Berlin relies heavily on Aristotle (e.g., 174, 178, 180-81). But how can Machiavelli reject teleology and then accept the naturalness of political life? How can the advocate of empire be ally with one who calls the polis the most natural association? If he can, and does, it is because there are deep fissures in his thought—a matter I will explore below.

70.   "Originality," 171.

71.   "Originality," 173.

72.   This is an area of overlap of the Berlin and the Croce theses. See, for instance, "Originality," 174, 182, 185.

73.   Berlin puts it this way: "One of the chief illusions caused by ignoring this [separation of moralities] is the Platonic-Hebraic-Christian view that virtuous rulers create virtuous men" ("Originality," 184-85).

74.   "Originality," 180. Viroli moves in the opposite direction, objecting to the "autonomy of politics" thesis on grounds that it extends the range of liberation too much. Ciceronian virtue is the rule, says Viroli, and departures from its requirements are permitted to political actors only in times of dire emergency (*Machiavelli*, 54, 93-94).

75.   "Originality," 174-75.

76.   *Citizen*, 252; see also 204-18.

77.   "Originality," 180.

78.   "Originality," 182.

79.   Try as he may, Berlin cannot consistently represent politics as an alternative ethic. Berlin thinks that politics is ethical if the end that it serves is "ultimate," a summum bonum, and is not just necessity, expediency, or the avoidance of death as the summum malum. But ethics is about means as well as about ends, and a complete ethics is defensible on both fronts. (When describing ethics, Berlin looks chiefly to the end that is pursued, even though the core of virtue lies chiefly in the means that are employed— i.e., a person is virtuous who first and foremost follows the rules of a prescribed moral code.) Sometimes Berlin speaks as if the means of politics, "pagan" means, are morally worthy, in that the decisions taken and actions performed pursuant to political greatness

are themselves manifestations of virtue; that pagan citizens are courageous, disciplined, loyal, and obedient—in a word, that they are strong (169, 190, 192). Sometimes, though, Berlin speaks as if pagan means are amoral techniques ("the qualities of the lion and the fox are not in themselves morally admirable" [175]) or even immoral acts ("crimes" and "evil things" [189] which require a suppression of "private qualms" [184] because the "values may be erroneous, dangerous, odious" [187]). Once both accounts appear together: "the qualities he admires," namely, "energy, boldness, practical skill," etc., are the source of "his more shocking maxims" (186). On these occasions, when the political ethic is the truncated ethic of "the end justifies the means" (e.g., 188), Berlin slides into Croce's camp, accepting, in effect, that politics has its own ethically neutral rules dictated by necessity (186; cf. 193).

80.   While denying the first half of this sentence, Berlin affirms again the second: "If men practise Christian humility, they cannot also be inspired by the burning ambitions of the great classical founders of cultures and religions; if their gaze is centred upon the world beyond—if their ideas are infected by even lip-service to such an outlook—they will not be likely to give all that they have to an attempt to build a perfect city" ("Originality," 195). See below, 230-36 and 332n17 for a discussion of Machiavelli's attitude toward, employment of, and alterations to good qualities, Christian and human.

81.   *Citizen*, 251.

82.   *Citizen*, 103, 188. For what follows, see mainly 189-218.

83.   Martin Fleisher provides an example, noting that on one occasion in the *The Prince* the usual conjunction of fraud and force is replaced by industry and force: "This startling employment of the good old sober Roman moral virtue of *industria* as a synonym for *fraude, inganno, and ingegno* may stand as a measure of Machiavelli's departure from the moralizing propensities of Cicero and of the Roman Stoicism of Seneca and Epictetus" ("A Passion for Politics: The Vital Core of the World of Machiavelli," in *Machiavelli and the Nature of Political Thought*, 138).

84.   *De Officiis*, I.41 (London: William Heinemann, 1913).

85.   *Citizen*, 208-09. For further discussion of Machiavelli's transformation of Cicero, see J. H. Hexter, *The Vision of Politics on the Eve of the Reformation: More, Machiavelli, and Seyssel* (New York: Basic Books, 1973), 208-10; Marcia Colish, "Cicero's *De Officiis* and Machiavelli's *Prince*," *Sixteenth Century Journal* 9 (1978): 81-93; J. N. Stephens, "Ciceronian Rhetoric and the Immorality of Machiavelli's *Prince*," *Renaissance Studies* 2 (1988): 263-67; Raimondi, "Politician and Centaur," 146-48.

86.   *Citizen*, 235.

87.   *Citizen*, 236, 237.

88.   *Virtue*, 8-11; "Introduction," xvii-xx. See also Wooton, "Introduction," xxxiv.

89.   On Machiavelli's antipathy to *ozio*, see Rebhorn, *Foxes and Lions*, 148-58.

90.   *Virtue*, 279. See also 36, 41, 261; and "Introduction," xxxvi.

91.   *Virtue*, 31-38.

92.   Mansfield says in summation: "Machiavelli wants to give Renaissance humanism a hard face: to deflate its esteem for classical rhetoric, to attack its adherence to philosophical tradition, to unsettle its accommodation with Christianity, to refute its belief in the virtues of the classical gentleman, and to remind it of the value and glory of the military" (*Virtue*, 11).

93.   *Virtue*, 47-48.

94.   *Virtue*, 10, 260; also "Introduction," xix.

95. *Virtue*, 28-29.

96. *Citizen*, 106.

97. The ethical barrier separating the few and the many seems higher and firmer for Mansfield than the political barrier, which is low and porous enough to permit commingling of the groups in a representative democracy.

98. Only rarely—and perhaps only thrice—does Strauss imply—and then only imply—that Machiavelli's new modes and orders are the ethical-political teaching of *Prince* 15-23 (see *Thoughts*, 61, 83, 232). On the other occasions when Strauss refers to Machiavelli's modes and orders, the point usually is to affirm their existence, to explain the sense in which they are new, or to consider their relation to old modes and orders or to Machiavelli their author. See 34-36, 37, 67, 78, 86, 105, 116, 119, 131, 136, 153-54, 169-70, 171, 253, 283, 288, 290, 291, 295, 297. Strauss is more straightforward in *What Is Political Philosophy?* There he states that the new prince and the immoral foundations of society constitute "the substance of [Machiavelli's] political teaching" (44).

99. *Thoughts*, 78.

100. For Plato, too, man's humanity is an appearance, since the form and look of man is that of a human being. But in addition to an outer appearance that is wholly human, one third of man's inner nature is also human: man is one part human being, one part lion, and one part hydra, or multi-headed monster. See *Republic*, 588b-e.

101. *Thoughts*, 232; see also 10, 59, 79.

102. Machiavelli's new estimate of the public, which takes the form of a defense of the multitude against "all the writers" (*Discourses*, I.58.1), is, Strauss maintains, the consequence "of a comprehensive argument meant to lay bare the essential dependence of morality on society: the unmasking of the alleged aristocracy of the classics as oligarchy leads necessarily to a somewhat more favorable judgment on the common people, and the unmasking of the rule of men of moral worth is part of the destructive analysis of moral virtue. The result of that analysis can be stated as follows. Moral virtue, wished for by society and required by it, is dependent on society and therefore subject to the primary needs of society. It does not consist in the proper order of the soul. It has no other source than the needs of society; it has no second and higher source in the needs of the mind" (*Thoughts*, 294).

103. *Thoughts*, 295.

104. *Thoughts*, 173.

Chapter Eight: Machiavelli's Middle Ways

1. See also *Prince*, 20: "Nor should any state ever believe that it can always adopt safe courses; on the contrary, it should think that it has to take them all as doubtful. For in the order of things it is found that one never seeks to avoid one inconvenience without running into another; but prudence consists in knowing how to recognize the qualities of inconveniences, and in picking the less bad as good."

2. The assumption here is that "ultimate greatness" refers to the optimal combination of strength and freedom.

3. Other imperfections of nature are that men cannot acquire all that they desire (I.37.1, II.Pr.3) and that necessary wars are at once the most just and the most cruel (II.8.1). See Strauss, *Thoughts*, 248-50. Wood observes that "if human morality rests upon the security and stability in human relations produced by the violence of the state, then we are confronted with the paradox that historically, morality is wedded to immorality" ("Humanism of Action," 51).

4. Strauss, *Thoughts*, 243-44.

5. Fleisher, "Passion," 119, 130.

6. For interesting remarks on Christian morality, so often juxtaposed against pagan morality and so little discussed, see John H. Geerken, "Machiavelli Studies since 1969," *Journal of the History of Ideas*, 37 (1976): 366-68.

7. "Originality," 185.

8. "Originality," 192-93.

9. "Originality," 193-94.

10. "Originality," 186.

11. Strauss, *Thoughts*, 243.

12. *The City of God*, IV.4 (New York: Penguin Classics, 1984); see also Cicero, *De Re Publica*, III.14; Locke *Second Treatise*, §176.

13. *Thoughts*, 240. See also Alkis Kontos, "Success and Knowledge in Machiavelli," in *Political Calculus*, 90. Kontos distinguishes between decisive action, middle course action, and precise middle course action.

14. See also I.38.2, II.10.2, II.27.4, III.10.2, III.31.3.

15. While moving public opinion just this much may not constitute a revolution in moral reasoning, against the backdrop of Christian quietism, it is an alteration worthy of the designation "new modes and orders." Consider the response of Villari, a generally sympathetic reader: "Words commonly used in praise of the noblest actions of private life are frequently devoted by him to the eulogy of actions that would be deemed iniquitous in private life, whenever, according to his creed, they might be useful or necessary in public life. . . . But no explanation can ever reconcile our ears to the sound of *honourable frauds, generous cruelties*, and *glorious wickednesses*" (*Life and Times*, vol. 2, 143).

16. Strauss, *Thoughts*, 242; Skinner, *Foundations*, 136; Chabod, *Machiavelli and the Renaissance*, 142.

17. The following diagram shows Machiavelli's middle-way ethics (the "left lane" of praiseworthy conduct being slightly wider than the "right" to indicate Machiavelli's preference for rule by fear):

Blame	Praise		Blame
Hate	Fear	Love	Contempt
Altogether	*Honorably*	*Good*	*Altogether*
Wicked	*Wicked*		*Good*

The altogether wicked and the honorably wicked differ in this respect: The altogether wicked is cruelty badly used (see below), or it is cruelty that incites hatred, whether well-used or not. Some feelings of hatred may yield to arguments about necessity and common purposes (and Machiavelli, I will suggest, is hard at work delivering just this propaedeutics); but other feelings are intractable, either because the crimes committed are too heinous to excuse (though inexcusable evil is itself a moving and alterable standard since even the murder of a pope can win a prince praise), or because the interest they serve is the prince's alone (in which case Machiavelli counsels the prince to suffer the public's hatred rather than jeopardize his state—trusting perhaps that "excessive virtue" and future benefits will redeem him in the end).

18.   Wooton has a ready answer: Agathocles (and Oliverotto of Fermo) destroyed republics, whereas Cesare brought order to the Romagna—the preservation of republics being the moral rock upon which Machiavelli stands ("Introduction," xxii). But Cesare also had designs on Florence, and the unforgivable crime of destroying republics is not condemned in *Discourses*, I.55.5; in fact, it is almost recommended as a thing of greatness.

19.   Adolph Hitler, the Austrian-born house painter and corporal, could never win the respect of Germany's aristocratic officer corps.

20.   "In sum, those to whom the heavens give such an opportunity [possession of a corrupt city] may consider that two ways have been placed before them: one that makes them live secure and after death renders them glorious; the other that makes them live in continual anxieties and after death leaves them a sempiternal infamy" (I.10.6).

21.   Polybius, XII.15.

22.   See de Grazia, *Hell*, 305-06, 311, 313-17; Kahn, "Agathocles," 206.

23.   Eldar mostly agrees, though he places the instructional burden not on Machiavelli but on the prince. Eldar's explanation for why Machiavelli endorses the judgment of posterity is that Agathocles overstepped the boundaries of morally acceptable conduct. In order to achieve glory, Eldar argues, a prince must (1) wait on necessity, (2) serve a common objective, and (3) tailor his actions to local standards of propriety; but, failing to abide by #3, a prince must then (4) massage those standards till they accommodate his transgressions, or (5) commit a crime of such grandeur as to stupefy the public ("Glory," 427-37). Agathocles is faulted on most counts, but especially on #4: A prince can manipulate "the perceptions of men as to his ends, motives and means"; he can "stretch the flexible boundaries of what is expected of him if he deceives by using pretexts and by preaching modes of behaviour contrary to those he actually adopts" (Ferdinand of Aragon is the model) (435). But Agathocles, who rose by force rather than by fraud, failed to give the proper coloration to his deeds (428, 430). As good as this explanation is, the description in *Prince* 8 is insufficiently detailed to confirm it, and it is not compatible with the accolade Machiavelli bestows on Agathocles, that he used cruelty well. Thus I think it better to say that Machiavelli disputes the judgment of posterity, his professions to the contrary notwithstanding.

24.   Commenting on Strauss's "Enlightenment" thesis, Drury explains that modernity does battle with the "Kingdom of Darkness" on the conviction that "mass enlightenment is the solution to man's political dilemmas" and that philosophy is "salutary or that no one is harmed by hearing the truth" (*Political Ideas*, 131). But Drury herself supplies the reason for doubting Machiavelli's involvement with the modern project, so described—namely, the abiding need of the mass of people for religious faith and their differentiation from a class of "super-citizens" whose need is for "greatness and worldly immortality" (122, 129). Thus Machiavelli maintains the distinction between the altogether wicked and the honorably wicked because to justify all acts of evildoing (even all instances of cruelty well-used) would be to deprive the people of its goodness. The fact

that most readers of *The Prince* think that Agathocles is condemned by Machiavelli for being too cruel and altogether wicked is an indication, I believe, of Machiavelli's morality-defending reticence.

25. See also II.4.2 where Roman expansionism is called the "true mode."

26. One exception to the linkage of the "true way" with acquisition is the statement in II.2.2 that "our religion [has] shown the truth and the true way." The statement paraphrases John 14:6.

27. Hulliung remarks that for Machiavelli "it was all or nothing" (*Citizen*, 26).

28. *The [Golden] Ass*, I.74-84. For another invitation to reckless abandon, see letter to Francesco Vettori, 4 February 1514 (#142).

29. See Adam D. Danél, *A Case for Freedom: Machiavellian Humanism* (Lanham, Md.: University Press of America, 1997), 152-68.

30. The nobility's self-discipline is an exception to the rule that order is the by-product of opposite and clashing forces. Fleisher sees no exceptions: "The limits are all external to the individual" ("Passion," 128).

31. The American Constitution is Lycurgean for being written "at a stroke"; it is Romulean for having an amendment provision and for allowing loose constructionism practiced under judicial review.

32. Eventually this oscillation will be tied to Machiavelli's reflections on greatness and liberty.

33. The previous distinction between the showman (ruling by love and by fear) and the commander (pursuing enterprises of his own choosing) allowed as to how the possession of character could be useful for the leadership of men (above, 176-77). Character is admirable if character causes courage; and yielding to character, especially to an impetuous character, often will produce favorable results. Nevertheless, character-driven actions, because they occur outside the middle way, expose the actor to the caprice of fortune and are evidence of weakness and of the failure of reason. Rebhorn describes impetuosity as "a form of madness, not totally unlike the madness of ancient heroes, the rage of Achilles and the furor of Ajax." He adds that for Machiavelli impetuosity means "a bold and decisive abandonment of reason at the point where reason reveals its insufficiency" (*Foxes and Lions*, 182).

34. McIntosh, "Modernity," 189-93. Using Weberian categories, McIntosh contends that modern ethics, of which Machiavelli is an important source, is more instrumental (results) than it is either ritualistic (rules) or expressive (intentions). Utilitarianism is one variant of—or perhaps another term for—this instrumentalism. On Machiavelli's consequentialist ethics, see Maureen Ramsay, "Machiavelli's Political Philosophy in *The Prince*," in *Niccolò Machiavelli's* The Prince, 188-90.

35. On the distinction between utilitarianism and egoism, see John Plamenatz, *The English Utilitarians* (Oxford: Basil Blackwell, 1958), 7-10. In *Man and Society*, Plamenatz describes Hobbes as a thoroughgoing egoist (law is the only standard of justice, and self-regarding man is just in society because it is in his interest to be so) and Machiavelli as an undecided ("All that can be said of him is that he believes that honesty and justice, and their opposites, are qualities acquired by men in society, and that he always speaks of these qualities . . . in ways which do not imply that they are refined forms of egoism or that justice is merely obedience to positive law" [66].). It seems that Machiavelli, in Plamenatz's judgment, accepts or is open to the transformative effects of society on human nature: "To hold that morality is an effect of law and social discipline

is not to be committed to hold that man, by necessity of his nature, is always selfish" (65).

Robert Faulkner suggests that Machiavellian selfishness is both destructive (of old hierarchies) and constructive (of managed liberation). Speaking of Machiavelli's comedies, Faulkner observes that "they subvert the apparently natural or divine hierarchies of the household. They then construct artificial associations for private satisfaction" ("Introduction: Clizia and the Enlightenment of Private Life," in *Clizia*, trans. Daniel T. Gallagher [Prospects Heights, Ill.: Waveland Press, 1996], xxiv). These destructive and constructive moments bear comparison, I think, to unenlightened egoism and enlightened utilitarianism.

36.   Plamenatz, *Man and Society*, 56, 61; Gray, "Machiavelli," 43; de Grazia, *Hell*, 267-70.

37.   Emotional attachments are equivalent to the "good" side of civic virtue, that predilection on the part of citizens to trust, sacrifice, and obey. See Grant, *Hypocrisy*, 49.

38.   Honesty, goodness, compassion, and gratitude are thought to have developed in this way (I.2.3). See Germino, "Psyche," 64.

39.   Mansfield's "impartial regime" might come to mind here, that Machiavellian novelty in which a self-identified elite competes for the suffrage of the people. But since we are considering the ways in which Machiavelli is a modern (e.g., his contribution to utilitarian morality), recurrence to the impartial regime is to be expected.

40.   Rome was responsible for the weakness which befell the Samnite people, such that in the time of Hannibal they could not defend themselves against one small legion. Nor could they "grow like the free." But then neither were they "ruined like the slaves," and Rome left them, as it did most subject peoples, "their arts and almost all of their ancient orders." So Rome's management of its empire does not entirely prove the maxim that "of all hard servitudes, that is hardest that submits you to a republic" (II.2.4). Much depends on the value which is placed on liberty as opposed to safety. Villari implies that medieval republics were the guilty parties, not Rome (*Life and Times*, vol. 2, 116-17). See Wolin, *Politics and Vision*, 222.

41   See Gordon S. Wood, *The Creation of the American Republic, 1776-1787*, 2nd ed. (Chapel Hill: University of North Carolina Press, 1998), 147.

42.   *Castruccio Castracani*, 553-54.

43.   *Republic*, 358e-359b.

44.   Plato, *Gorgias*, 482e-484c (London: William Heinemann, 1967).

45.   Strauss argues that Machiavelli's trumpeting of extremes is for the benefit of the young, that they might be drawn to Machiavelli and then captured in his web (*Thoughts*, 81, 243). Strauss doesn't suggest though what is here *provisionally* implied, that Machiavelli is practicing "bait and switch," advertising his extremism in order to sell his customers moderation.

46.   This is Rousseau's solution, though he leaves it undeveloped (*Social Contract*, III.15).

47.   There is this problem with the supposition that II.27 is trying to moderate the ambition of states. The chapter's final example of Hannibal's peace offer does not include a critique of Rome, which rejected the offer, preferring instead to continue the struggle until final victory had been won. Carthage is criticized for a similar hubris when it missed the opportunity to negotiate a peace from a position of strength.

48.   See Wooton, "Introduction," xxxi, xxxvi.

49.   For example, III.30, III.33, III.35, III.36, III.37, III.45.

50.   The Lavinians, who joined the Latin rebellion too late to be of help but just in time to irritate the Romans (340 BC), would have been better served by a policy of neutrality (II.15.2). (See Guicciardini, *Considerations*, 115.) *Prince* 21 contains an emphatic denunciation of neutrality; but there is backpedaling even here: A prince is advised always to "disclose [him]self and wage open war"; but we know this advice to be unsuitable for the weak (cf. *Discourses*, III.2.1). We know as well not to trust the stated rationale for boldly taking sides, that in the event of victory betrayal is not to be feared, since "men are never so indecent as to crush you with so great an example of ingratitude" (cf. *Prince*, 7; see also Strauss, *Thoughts*, 60-61). More generally, the warning not to remain neutral is incompatible with the warning not to ally with a stronger power (cf. *Prince*, 13; *Discourses*, II.20); thus Machiavelli is left to conclude that "all is doubtful" (*Prince*, 21).

51.   Wood states that "Machiavelli's preference always is for a prince who combines *virtù* with goodness" ("Humanism of Action," 52).

Chapter Nine: What Machiavelli Wants

1.   See Parel, "Machiavelli's Method," 20-24; Robert M. Adams, "The Rise, Proliferation, and Degradation of Machiavellism: An Outline," in *The Prince*, trans. and ed. Robert M. Adams, 2nd ed. (New York: W. W. Norton, 1992), 240-42.

2.   Strauss, *Thoughts*, 9-14; Maritain, "End of Machiavellianism," 283-314; Wolin, *Politics and Vision*, 201; Gray, "Machiavelli," 51; Conor Cruise O'Brien, *The Suspecting Glance* (London: Faber and Faber, 1972), 15-31; Grant B. Mindle, "Machiavelli's Realism," *Review of Politics* 47 (1985): 213-19.

3.   Strauss denies the difference, claiming that the advice tendered at the end of *The Prince* is moderate, not radical, "because it is silent concerning the extreme measures required for the liberation of Italy and because it cannot but be very popular with very many Italians" (*Thoughts*, 77). How moderate though would it be if Machiavelli were hired by Lorenzo on the strength of his promise to guide the house of Medici to an overlordship of the whole of Italy? It is hard not to see *Prince* 26 as an instance of taking the lead in counseling extraordinary enterprises.

4.   See Leonardo Olschki, *Machiavelli the Scientist* (Berkeley: Gillick Press, 1945); Meinecke, *Machiavellism*, 25-44; Butterfield, *Statecraft*, 59-86; Cassirer, *Myth*, 190-94; Burnham, *Machiavellians*, 45-55. Wolin gives partial support to this view: "In Machiavelli's conception political theory could furnish a set of techniques useful to any group, but . . . not every group was considered equally useful to the new science" (*Politics and Vision*, 203).

5.   See also I.6.4, I.26.1, I.30.1, I.41.1, II.4.1, II.13.2, II.19.2, III.1 (title), III.8 (title), III.9 (title).

6.   For example, letter to Francesco Vettori, 13 March 1513 (#117).

7.   Villari, *Life and Times*, vol. 2, 197, 207.

8.   Alberico Gentili, *De legationibus libri tres*, III.9 (New York: Oxford University Press, 1924); Traiano Boccalini, *Ragguagli di Parnaso*, I.89 (Bari: G. Laterza e figli, 1912). Boccalini tells how Machiavelli, when on trial for his teachings before Apollo's

court, pled the excuse of being but a copyist of actions performed by originals esteemed sacred by men; that the subject of history, also thought valuable, would alone make Machiavellians of all who but studied it. This defense was about to carry the day when the prosecutor (*l'avvocato fiscale*) intervened, informing the judges that Machiavelli had been apprehended in the night trying to install dog's teeth into the mouths of sheep. How high the price of wool and cheese would rise, the prosecutor worried, and how dangerous the shepherd's trade would become if ever sheep were fierce and able to bite. For it was not the products of sheep but their great simplicity and infinite docility (*la molta semplicità e l'infinita mansuetudine*) which made them useful to men; nor would large flocks any longer be governable by single shepherds unless sheep were completely disarmed of horn, teeth, and intelligence (*il quale non era possibile che in numero grande da un solo pastore venisse governato, quando affato non fosse stato disarmato di corna, di denti e d'ingegno*). Thus Machiavelli was condemned, and a fundamental law was published declaring anyone a rebel against mankind (*ribello del genere umano*) who would dare teach the world such scandalous things.

    9.   Spinoza, *Political Treatise*, V.7, in *Works of Spinoza: Theologico-Political Treatise, Political Treatise* (New York: Dover, 1951); Diderot, "*Machiavélisme,*" in *Encyclopédie* (Saint Amand: L'Imprimerie Bussière, 1963); Rousseau, *Social Contract*, III.6; *Political Economy*, 214; Vittorio Alfieri, *Del principe e delle lettere*, II.9 (Firenze: Felice le Monnier, 1943). On Machiavelli and the philosophers, see Prezzolini, *Machiavelli*, 227-305.

    10.   Garrett Mattingly, "Machiavelli's *Prince*: Political Science or Political Satire? *American Scholar* 27 (1958): 482-91. Germino, "Psyche," 75-77. Terence Ball, "The Picaresque Prince: Reflections on Machiavelli and Moral Change," *Political Theory* 12 (1984): 535, n. 28. Mary Dietz "Trapping the Prince: Machiavelli and the Politics of Deception," *American Political Science Review* 80 (1986): 777-99. John T. Scott and Vickie B. Sullivan, "Patricide and the Plot of *The Prince*: Cesare Borgia and Machiavelli's Italy," *American Political Science Review* 88 (1994): 887-900.

    11.   Macaulay, "Machiavelli," 177; Villari, *Life and Times*, vol. 2, 89-90, 101-02; Butterfield, *Statecraft*, 102.

    12.   Machiavelli dedicates the *Discourses* to two young friends, Zanobi Buondelmonti and Cosimo Rucellai, whose company and conversation he shared at the Orti Oricellari, the fabulous gardens laid out by Cosimo's grandfather, Bernardo Rucellai.

    13.   J. H. Hexter, "Seyssel, Machiavelli, and Polybius VI: The Mystery of the Missing Translation," *Studies in the Renaissance* 3 (1956): 75-96.

    14.   The chief impetus for postulating an early composition date for some part of the *Discourses* is the remark in *Prince* 2: "I shall leave out reasoning on republics because I have reasoned on them at length another time." This remark is widely taken as a reference to the *Discourses*. The chief objection to such a postulate is the argument, advanced by Hexter (above note), that Machiavelli was unlikely to have read a Latin translation of Polybius VI, upon which *Discourses*, I.2 is based, before 1515.

    15.   *Machiavelli and the Renaissance*, 11-17, 30-41, 116, 118, 121, n. 1. Chabod sees Machiavelli as an imaginative, intuitive author subject to radical changes of mood owing to his close involvement with the events of the day (117, n. 1). *The Art of War*, *The Life of Castruccio Castracani*, and the *Florentine Histories*, written after his hopes for an Italian revival had been dashed, reflect the author's change, says Chabod, from an activist with an agenda to a critic dispensing judgments (27-29, 119).

16. *Civic Humanism*, 101-51. The troubling reference to a treatise on republics in *Prince* 2 is explained by Baron as an interpolation added at the time of the Laurentian dedication (120-21, 132-34). Wooton, who supports Baron generally, disputes that any treatise is referred to; he takes the statement to be a private joke, a wry comment on Machiavelli's "conversation" with his interrogators and torturers about the depth of his republican sympathies ("Introduction," xxiv-xxv; also xiv-xvi). See also F. Gilbert, "Composition," 155-56; and "Machiavelli in Modern Historical Scholarship," *Italian Quarterly* 13-14 (Summer 1969-Spring 1970): 19-20. For a helpful summary of the Chabod-Baron debate, see Hulliung, *Citizen*, 232-37. For criticisms of some of the participants, see J. H. Whitfield, "Discourses on Machiavelli VII, Gilbert, Hexter and Baron," *Italian Studies* 13 (1958): 21-46.

17. *Civic Humanism*, 143; Chabod, *Machiavelli and the Renaissance*, 41, n.2.

18. "Machiavelli Studies," 357.

19. *Citizen*, 234. But if Baron wins the substance debate, the chronology debate, Geerken implies, goes to Chabod and Gilbert ("Machiavelli Studies, 357): first came the *Discourses* (up through I.18), then *The Prince* ("'in one spontaneous germination'"), then the *Discourses* again (this time paying close attention to Livy [Gilbert's thesis in "Composition"]). Wooton disagrees ("Introduction," xix-xxv).

20. *Politics and Vision*, 229.

21. In Dietz's helpful classification, Wolin represents the third variant of the "strong republican" view, to wit, "*The Prince* is 'phase one' of a series of events that will lead to liberty and republican government in 'phase two'"—the *Discourses* ("Trapping," 780). (The "weak republican" view holds that *The Prince* is a momentary aberration brought on by the fall of the Florentine republic—Baron is named as a leading proponent [779].) Dietz herself creates a fourth "strong republican" variant—that *The Prince* is "an act of deception" intending through bad advice to sabotage the Medici regime (781). This, to be sure, is an ingenious interpretation; but it relies on historical information, and one small biographical detail stands in its way: Machiavelli is confessedly anxious that the papal secretary, Piero Ardinghelli, will claim the manuscript as his own or purloin its ideas if Machiavelli sends it to Guiliano de'Medici (via Vettori or by traveling to Rome and presenting it himself) and the young prince does not read it (letter to Francesco Vettori, 10 December 1513 [#137]). In light of Machiavelli's advice to courtiers not to stand too close to the prince (III.2) and his advice to advisers not to take the lead in counseling dangerous adventures (III.35), and in light of the undeniably dangerous adventure counseled in *Prince* 26, having Ardinghelli take credit for *The Prince* ought to have been for Machiavelli the perfect way—an exquisitely devilish way—of trapping the Medicis without simultaneously trapping himself.

22. This distinction between heroic and civic virtue is also drawn by Plamenatz ("Machiavellian *Virtù*," 157-78).

23. Wolin, *Politics and Vision*, 229-31. See also Ruffo-Fiore, *Niccolò Machiavelli*, 57-59; Pitkin, *Fortune*, 97-98; Jacobson, *Pride and Solace*, 44-45.

24. I incline to the latter view, that the community evolves, and more importantly, that the prince evolves. *The Prince* and the *Discourses*, I believe, relate as beginning and advanced courses in the education of a Machiavellian ruler.

25. Civic humanism denominates the ideology by which the free cities of northern Italy, of the *Regnum Italicum*, explained and justified their exceptional existence—to

themselves, the emperor, and the Church. It is a fascinating story well-told by Baron (*Crisis*), Pocock (*Moment*), and Skinner (*Foundations*)—and by various others.

26. *Moment*, 194-211.

27. *Politics, Language and Time*, 85.

28. See, for example, F. Gilbert, "The Humanist Concept of the Prince and *The Prince* of Machiavelli," *Journal of Modern History* 9 (1939): 449-83; Skinner, *Foundations*, 113-38, 152-86.

29. *Politics, Language and Time*, 86.

30. *Moment*, vii-ix; *Politics, Language and Time*, 103. For critiques of the civic humanist, or classical republican, school of thought, see Hulliung, *Citizen*, 3-30; Thomas Pangle, *The Spirit of Modern Republicanism: The Moral Vision of the American Founders and the Philosophy of Locke* (Chicago: University of Chicago Press, 1988), 28-39, especially 35; Vickie B. Sullivan, "Machiavelli's Momentary 'Machiavellian Moment': A Reconsideration of Pocock's Treatment of the *Discourses*," *Political Theory* 20 (1992): 309-18; Mansfield, *Virtue*, 319, n. 30; Robert K. Faulkner, *Francis Bacon and the Project of Progress* (Lanham, Md.: Rowman & Littlefield, 1993), 80, n. 1. Rahe's *Republics*, which covers much of the same ground as gone over by Pocock, uses the ancient-modern paradigm.

31. *Politics*, IV.8-9, 11-12.

32. See Patrick Coby, "Aristotle's Four Conceptions of Politics," *Western Political Quarterly* 39 (1986): 480-503.

33. "Republican Politics," 16.

34. "Republican Politics," 18.

35. "Republican Politics," 13. Echoing Pocock, Shumer goes on to state that "the Western tradition that perceives human fulfillment to be in political action stretches from Thucydides to such diverse contemporaries as Merleau-Ponty, Arendt, and Habermas" (14).

36. "Machiavelli and the Republican Idea of Politics," in *Machiavelli and Republicanism*, 159-60; see also Viroli, *Machiavelli*, 47-49, 54, 92, 115-16, 121-43.

37. More information is provided in III.34 regarding the people's electoral abilities: The people does reasonably well when taking the measure of new and youthful candidates (their parentage, associates, and notable deeds being the basis of public opinion), but the people is "almost never deceived"—either by false opinion or by corruption—when making decisions about seasoned individuals (§4). The one requirement is that the people, like princes with counselors, have access to all relevant information, which can happen if by the orders of the state citizens are encouraged to tell what they know about a candidate's qualifications.

38. See Tocqueville, *Democracy in America*, vol. 1, 362.

39. Strauss, *Thoughts*, 131.

40. Even Machiavelli admits that the people "errs in mighty things or those that appear useful" (I.58.3), since he reminds readers that he has said as much before (e.g., I.53.1-3).

41. While this is the central argument in the case for republics, Machiavelli diminishes its cogency by once locating Athens's "most flourishing time" in the period before Pisistratus and before the creation of its popular government (I.28.1). And while Rome expanded rapidly after losing its kings (I.20.1), it continued its expansion under the caesars, and it was under the caesars that Rome enjoyed its golden age (I.10.5).

42.   See also I.4.1, I.13.2, I. 53.1, I.54. 1, III.6.14, III.22.6.

43.   Some notice is taken of individual rights, such as property rights and the dignity of women; but always these rights are secondary to the necessity of acquiring and maintaining power (*Prince*, 19).

44.   *Hiero or Tyrannicus*; in *On Tyranny*, Leo Strauss (Ithaca: Cornell University Press, 1968).

45.   Russell Price, "The Theme of *Gloria* in Machiavelli," *Renaissance Quarterly* 30 (1977): 628.

46.   Sparta expanded following its victory in the Peloponnesian War, when it captured the Theban citadel in a surprise attack (382 BC). But so voluntary and unwarranted was this action that the Spartans fired the commander who did it. On the other hand, so agreeable was this serendipitous acquisition that the Spartans kept a garrison in the citadel, much to the amazement of all of Greece (Plutarch, *Pelopidas*, 5-6). If Sparta was compelled to expand, in the sense that avarice is as compulsive a passion as is fear; nevertheless, Sparta managed for many a century to keep such compulsive temptations under control.

47.   Machiavelli also explains how Venice could have survived its expansion: by a divide-and-conquer strategy backed up by just enough military virtue to repel a first thrust (III.11.2).

48.   *Politics*, VII.2, 3, 14.

49.   *Florentine Histories*, V.1; *The [Golden] Ass*, V.94-105.

50.   Having noted in the previous chapter, II.4, that so little record of the Tuscan empire has survived, Machiavelli undertakes to explain "this oblivion of things" (II.4.2) in chapter 5. Of course there would be little to explain if the world were created and young, as affirmed by the Bible, because then there would be little of the world's history for which to account. Machiavelli raises this objection against "those philosophers who would have it that the world is eternal" (II.5.1). But since Machiavelli proceeds to provide alternative explanations for the oblivion of the past, its foreshortening to about 5,000 years, he in effect defends those philosophers who proclaim the eternality of the world, and likely he embraces this doctrine himself.

51.   States are thus imitating nature when they return to their origins by means of exemplary punishments. The conspirator is a dangerous excess usefully eliminated; he is to the state what the state is to nature.

52.   On the difference between Christianity, which Machiavelli rejects, and paganism, which he admires, see Strauss, *Thoughts*, 207.

53.   Machiavelli asserts that religions change two or three times in 5,000 or 6,000 years. At the near end, a religion would last 1,666 years (three in 5,000), and at the far end it would last 3,000 (two in 6,000). It could also last 2,500 years (two in 5,000) or 2,000 years (three in 6,000). By these calculations it was possible for Machiavelli to imagine that Christianity, a 1,500 year old religion, was nearing the end of its life—and the corruption of the Renaissance popes was certainly one reason for thinking so. Another reason, not mentioned by Machiavelli, was the Protestant Reformation, begun in 1517 just as Machiavelli was finishing the *Discourses*.

54.   *De Re Publica*, VI.9-26.

55.   See Fleisher, "Ways of Machiavelli," 354; Danél, *Case for Freedom*, 207-08.

56.   *Citizen*, 5, and throughout.

57.   Plamenatz seems to treat them this way: "Though he [Machiavelli] loved free-dom . . . he also loved Italy, and wanted her to be great. . . . He never succeeded in rec-onciling his two strongest passions: for political freedom and for the independence of Italy" (*Man and Society*, 82).

58.   See J. E. Seigel, "Violence and Order in Machiavelli," in *Violence and Aggression in the History of Ideas*, eds. Philip Wiener and John Fisher (New Brunswick: Rutgers University Press, 1974). Seigel defines *virtù* as "willing and unhesitating participation in the order of natural necessity" (61). His thesis is that Roman history taught Machiavelli the inescapable character of aggression and violence; and that it taught him further that man and state, by accepting the animal side of human nature, can dominate violence rather than be dominated by it. Seigel remarks: "Men who preserved their ties with the world of natural necessity would find violence an organic part of their lives, but their ability to act effectively would bring them to stability and the domination of vio-lence at the same time. Violence would never be fully banished from their lives, but when it came it would be quickly and cleanly done. . . . In between those moments of violence, human life would possess that dignity and stability which nature and the Ro-mans both achieved, but which contemporary Italian life so sadly lacked" (62). The in-between moments to some degree align with liberty, and to some degree the violent mo-ments align with greatness. On condition that both moments are equally valued, and one is not for the sake of the other (violence for the sake of stability), Seigel's interpretation, I should think, is exactly right.

59.   Cf. Strauss, *Thoughts*, 207, 289, 292.

60.   Rahe defines Cartesian *générosité* as "the hard, unrelenting, willful, aristocratic self-assertion at the heart of modernity's soft, democratic *humanity*: it is the savage *virtù* of Machiavelli redirected from the conquest of fortune through the attainment of empire over men to the conquest of fortune through the establishment of man's dominion over nature" (*Republics*, 290).

61.   In III.1.4 Christianity is again a sect, and it is "our religion" rather than the true religion. If it had not been reformed in the thirteenth century, it "would be altogether eliminated," says Machiavelli, who can contemplate the disappearance of Christianity because he counts it among "worldly things" ("It is a very true thing that all worldly things have a limit to their life . . ." [§1]). See Strauss, *Thoughts*, 51, 204-05, 225-26; Prezzolini, *Machiavelli*, 26-28; Plamenatz, *Man and* Society, 44, 67, 74; Masters, *Machiavelli, Leonardo*, 81, n. 75. There are of course many readers who do think that Ma-chiavelli is a Christian, albeit an irreverent one. See Germino, "Second Thoughts," 796-803; Rebhorn, *Foxes and Lions*, 128, n. 48; de Grazia, *Hell*, 58-70, 89.

62.   Anti-clericalism, says de Grazia, was a commonplace of the Renaissance and of all the prior centuries of Church ascendancy; but, de Grazia continues, Machiavelli was not an anti-cleric exactly; he rather was a "reform clerical." De Grazia's conclusion rests on the supposition that Machiavelli was a genuine admirer of the reform movements of St. Francis and St. Dominic (*Hell*, 90). Wood is of the same opinion ("Humanism of Action," 38).

63.   The Church bears primary responsibility for Italy's reliance on mercenary arms (*Prince*, 12).

64.   B. Smith, *Politics and Remembrance*, 45.

65.   That contemporary warriors engage in mock battles with few casualties is a point which Machiavelli frequently makes in the *Florentine Histories* (IV.6; V.1; VI.28;

VII.20). His primary example is the Battle of Anghiari, fought between the Florentines and the army of Niccolò Piccinino. Says Machiavelli: "In such a defeat and in so long a battle that lasted from twenty to twenty-four hours, only one man died, and he not from wounds or any other virtuous blow, but, falling off his horse, he was trampled on and expired" (V.33).

66.   See also II.18.3; *Prince,* 12, 26; *The [Golden] Ass,* V.106-27.

67.   *Florentine Histories,* I.9, 23; II.10.

68.   Machiavelli does not delude himself into thinking that Italy is ready for nationhood—*Prince* 26 notwithstanding. In a letter to Francesco Vettori, dated 13 August 1513, he is scathingly dismissive of the whole idea: "As to the union of the Italians, you make me laugh" (#131).

69.   *New Modes and Orders,* 12.

70.   "Patricide," 894. See also Masters, *Machiavelli, Leonardo,* 72.

71.   *"Belfagor*: Machiavelli's Short Story," *Interpretation* 19 (1992): 244-45.

72.   Says Machiavelli in *The [Golden] Ass*: "Altogether mad is he who forbids people their ceremonies and their devotions" (V.118-19).

73.   Luke 1:53.

74.   Strauss, *Thoughts,* 49.

75.   Strauss, *Thoughts,* 144.

76.   Matthew 20:1-16. Those who started working late in the day are paid the same wage as those who began working at sunrise.

77.   See Mansfield, *Virtue,* 167, 240-41, 301. Mansfield supposes that Machiavelli first learns the art of punishing and rewarding from Christianity. But it seems truer to say that he learns it from the Romans and then finds that Christians practice it also. Mansfield's larger point is that Machiavelli replaces some Roman modes with better modes in use among Christians.

78.   Machiavelli seems determined to treat Christianity as a continuation of paganism. For as Romans of old were forewarned of the coming of the French (Gauls) by voices in the air, so contemporary Italians were forewarned of the coming of the French (Charles VIII) by the prophesies of Savonarola and by the sound of fighting men heard in the air (I.56). It matters not to Machiavelli that Jupiter and Juno have been replaced by Yahweh and Jesus Christ. The commerce between the human and the divine remains the same.

79.   See Hulliung, *Citizen,* 204-08. On Machiavelli and the conciliar movement, see de Grazia, *Hell,* 118-19.

80.   J. W. Allen, estimating Machiavelli's powers of prognostication, reads the sixteenth century this way, as attempting (in Lutheran Germany, Sweden, and England especially) to institute a secular state by making religion a tool of government. See *Political Thought in the Sixteenth Century* (London: Methuen, 1941), 483.

81.   Strauss, *Thoughts,* 189.

82.   Since the Hobbesian sovereign determines the truth of religious doctrine, the laity, probably, will not be too fervent in its belief; and since religious truth is whatever the sovereign judges to be conducive to peace, the purpose of religion, plainly, is not to prepare the population for war (*Leviathan,* XVIII.9, XXIX.15, XXXVIII.1).

83.   *Social Contract,* IV.8.

84.   That Machiavelli disputes the wisdom of the Sermon on the Mount and tries replacing its beatitudes with maxims of his own is an argument put forward by John

Geerken, who investigates Machiavelli's use and abuse of the Golden Rule ("Machiavelli and the Golden Rule," *Machiavelli Studies* 2 [1988]: 28-32). Machiavelli does contest some parts of the Christian teaching; but what he does not do is advance a revisionist interpretation purporting to render that teaching consonant with his own.

85.   Strauss's reply is that Machiavelli is patient, that he waits on his disciples to bring down the Christian regime—and leaves to them the glory (*Thoughts*, 83, 105, 154, 165, 169, 297).

86.   Rebhorn would appear to agree: "Hence what Machiavelli really wants for the modern world is a full-scale restoration of ancient religion. He never specifies, however, how such a restoration is to be accomplished—or even if it could be" (*Foxes and Lions*, 133). Plamenatz discounts any such hope: Machiavelli "was too much of a realist to suppose that Christianity could be replaced by the undogmatic national cults of antiquity" (*Man and Society*, 73). After speculating on Machiavelli's likely response to Martin Luther ("he probably would have blamed him . . . for helping to create an atmosphere in which it was difficult for men to have different religious beliefs without coming to blows" [72]), Plamenatz concludes that Machiavelli "never troubled to put forward any theory about the proper relations between Church and State" (73).

87.   See Walker, *Discourses*, vol. 1, 158. Hulliung observes, in answer to Wolin's "economy of violence" thesis, that "where unlimited conquest, growth, and aggrandizement is the objective, the economical use of violence at each given moment is canceled out by the endlessness of violent moments" (*Citizen*, 223).

88.   Strauss, *Thoughts*, 284.

89.   See Gregory B. Smith, "Machiavelli's *The Prince* and the Abolition of the Political: A Preliminary Reflection," *Machiavelli Studies* 2 (1988): 49-72. Says Smith, "Machiavelli has built the foundation for the eventual rule of 'advisors' (intellectuals) over the fundamentally economic competition of prosperous citizens" (66). Strauss remarks that "economism is Machiavellianism come of age" (*What Is Political Philosophy?*, 49). Cf. Grant, *Hypocrisy*, 42-53.

90.   Kontos, "Success," 99. Not all of the moderns, of course, focus on gratifying appetites to the exclusion of developing spiritedness. See, for example, A. Smith, *Wealth of Nations*, V.i.f.60.

91.   Pocock's explanation of why Machiavelli chose empire over coexistence—or Achilles over Odysseus—is the same, Pocock contends, as that offered by Hume and the Enlightenment: that Machiavelli "understood nothing except the little furious republics of antiquity, and the little republics of Renaissance Italy that tried to imitate them." Pocock implies that had Machiavelli known of commerce, he would not have "taken the option for conquest and made the Achillean commitment" ("Machiavelli in the Liberal Cosmos," *Political Theory* 13 (1985): 572). I argue, to the contrary, that Machiavelli's choice is not chiefly a function of his having lived in advance of capitalism.

92.   Terence Ball agrees, comparing Machiavelli's prince to a Homeric hero. Ball though believes that the project of reclaiming a bygone ethics is quixotic and dangerous ("Picaresque Prince," 522-27, 532-33). For more on the Homer-Machiavelli connection, see John H. Geerken, "Homer's Image of the Hero in Machiavelli: A Comparison of *Areté and* Virtù," *Italian Quarterly* 13-14 (Summer 1969-Spring 1970): 45-89. For other opinions contesting Machiavelli's modern credentials, see Hulliung, *Citizen*, 240; Cary Nederman, "Machiavelli and Moral Character: Principality, Republic and the Psychology of Virtue," paper presented to the Annual Meeting of the American Political Science

Association (Chicago, September 1992), 23-24; Masters, *Machiavelli, Leonardo*, 190-95, 209-10, 218-19; Grant, *Hypocrisy*, 12-14, 54, 139, 159-60, 176-77.

93. *Virtue*, 109.
94. *Virtue*, 118.
95. *The [Golden] Ass*, V.75; Hulliung, *Citizen*, 57.
96. There is a strain of "Peter Pan" idealism in Machiavelli. It shows up again in Rousseau (*Second Discourse*, 103-04).
97. *Virtue*, 293.
98. *Virtue*, 110.
99. *Virtue*, 280.
100. *Virtue*, xiii.
101. *Virtue*, 118.
102. *Virtue*, 279-80.
103. *Virtue*, 122.
104. *Virtue*, 280.
105. *Virtue*, 280. See also 28: "Whatever legacy he may have left to bourgeois liberalism—and it is considerable—he may also be said to have anticipated the critiques of the bourgeois that were to come from Rousseau, Nietzsche, and their followers on the left and the right. If modern man were defined as Machiavellian, he could not so easily be accused of a dull life, a flat soul, and a lack of patriotism."
106. Strauss observes that Machiavelli never uses the word "soul" (*anima*) in either *The Prince* or the *Discourses*: "he is silent about the soul because he has forgotten the soul, just as he has forgotten tragedy and Socrates" (*Thoughts*, 294, 295; also 31). But *animo* (spirit) is a part of the soul and is a word commonly used. On the preeminence of spirit in the soul, see *Thoughts*, 243, 298. See also Parel, *Machiavellian Cosmos*, 88.
107. The opposite was previously expressed and taken as true (see above, 218, 228).
108. See Masters, *Machiavelli, Leonardo*, 194.
109. Plamenatz remarks: "He [Machiavelli] admires the Romans for being the sort of men they were, and not only because Rome was powerful. Because he is at pains to show how their virtues made Rome formidable, it does not follow that he cares for the virtues only on account of their political effects . . ." (*Man and Society*, 68).
110. See Rebhorn, *Foxes and Lions*: "The word he [Machiavelli] has chosen [*virtù*, from the Latin *vir*] . . . suggests that however important the cleverness and prudence of the confidence man may be, the toughness, resolution, and daring of the hero are more basic" (148).
111. Along these same lines, Fleisher observes that Machiavelli's "hostility to mercenaries lies deeper than the fact that they are unreliable" and "his championing of a militia rests on more than their dependability." Machiavelli is looking for a curriculum with which to educate future citizens; and the best education, he believes, is one which has "military training at its basis since it is the discipline that properly conditions the *animo*" ("Passion," 123). The cultivation of *animo* (the equivalent of *thumos* in the Greek) is Machiavelli's ultimate commitment. See Mansfield, *Virtue*, 40, 44, 45, 50, 51; Wolin, *Politics and Vision*, 236-37.
112. Hulliung observes that Machiavelli economizes on violence because the efficient application of force is more aesthetically pleasing than victory by overkill; elegance, he remarks, is a feature of the heroic code (*Citizen*, 223).
113. Hulliung, *Citizen*, 136.

114.   Although a poet and playwright himself, Machiavelli is indifferent to the artistic renaissance taking place in his day; and he is always critical of the effects which *ozio* has on *virtù*.

115.   Hulliung, *Citizen*, 21-23.

116.   "I love my native city more than my own soul" (letter to Francesco Vettori, 16 April 1527 [#225]).

117.   While Machiavelli exhibits much independence of thought, he also seeks the good opinion of antique Romans.

118.   Consider Machiavelli's concern for Mamercus Aemilius in I.49.1. Mamercus was the patriotic dictator who safeguarded Roman republicanism by reducing the tenure of censors (434 BC). He suffered for his patriotism, and Machiavelli criticizes the orders of Rome which permitted his punishment—or he criticizes Livy for getting the story wrong.

119.   *Republic*, 547c-549a, 553b-d.

120.   *Florentine Histories*, I.39, II.42, III.1; Hulliung, *Citizen*, 65-66, 89, 175; Wood, "Humanism of Action," 48-49.

121.   See Pitkin, *Fortune*, 105. The fox, too, might be guilty of idealism, should the fox come to believe that cleverness is sufficient to rule on its own. The fox is sometimes associated with the idealism of the middle way. See Strauss, "Niccolo Machiavelli," 316-17; Rebhorn, *Foxes and Lions*, 181-82.

Bibliography

Adams, Robert M. "The Rise, Proliferation, and Degradation of Machiavellism." In *The Prince*, translated and edited by Robert M. Adams, 2nd ed. New York: W. W. Norton, 1992.

Adcock, F. E. *Roman Political Ideas and Practice*. Ann Arbor: University of Michigan Press, 1959.

Alfieri, Vittorio. *Del principe e delle lettere*. Firenze: Felice le Monnier, 1943.

Allen, J. W. *Political Thought in the Sixteenth Century*. London: Methuen, 1941.

Anglo, Sydney. *Machiavelli: A Dissection*. New York: Harcourt, Brace and World, 1969.

Arendt, Hannah. *Between Past and Future*. New York: Viking Press, 1968.

———. *The Human Condition*. Chicago: University of Chicago Press, 1958.

———. *On Revolution*. New York: Penguin Books, 1965.

Aristotle. *Constitution of Athens*. New York: Hafner, 1950.

———. *Nicomachean Ethics*. Cambridge: Harvard University Press, 1968.

———. *Politics*. Chicago: University of Chicago Press, 1984.

Augustine. *The City of God*. New York: Penguin Classics, 1984.

Ball, Terence. "The Picaresque Prince: Reflections on Machiavelli and Moral Change." *Political Theory* 12 (1984): 521-36.

Baron, Hans. *The Crisis of the Early Italian Renaissance*. Princeton: Princeton University Press, 1966.

———. *In Search of Florentine Civic Humanism*. Vol. 2. Princeton: Princeton University Press, 1988.

Berlin, Isaiah. "The Originality of Machiavelli." In *Studies on Machiavelli*, edited by Myron P. Gilmore. Firenze: G. C. Sansoni Editore, 1972.

Bloom, Allan. *Shakespeare's Politics*. New York: Basic Books, 1964.

Boccalini, Traiano. *Ragguagli di Parnaso*. Bari: G. Laterza e figli, 1912.

Bock, Gisela. "Civil Discord in Machiavelli's *Istorie Fiorentine*." In *Machiavelli and Republicanism*, edited by Gisela Bock, Quentin Skinner, and Maurizio Viroli. Cambridge: Cambridge University Press, 1990.

Bonadeo, Alfredo. *Corruption, Conflict, and Power in the Works and Times of Niccolò Machiavelli*. Berkeley: University of California Press, 1973.

———. "The Role of the People in the Works and Times of Machiavelli." *Bibliothèque d'Humanisme et Renaissance* 32 (1970): 351-77.

Brudney, Kent. "Machiavelli on Social Class and Class Conflict." *Political Theory* 12 (1984): 507-19.

Burke, Edmund. *Reflections on the Revolution in France.* London: Penguin Books, 1968.

Burnham, James. *The Machiavellians: Defenders of Freedom.* Washington, D. C.: Gateway Editions, 1943.

Butterfield, H. *The Statecraft of Machiavelli.* London: G. Bell and Sons, 1940.

Cassirer, Ernest. *The Myth of the State.* Garden City, N. Y.: Doubleday Anchor Books, 1955.

Chabod, Frederico. *Machiavelli and the Renaissance.* Cambridge: Harvard University Press, 1960.

Cicero. *De Officiis.* London: William Heinemann, 1913.

———. *De Re Publica, De Legibus.* Cambridge: Harvard University Press, 1977.

Coby, Patrick. "Aristotle's Four Conceptions of Politics." *Western Political Quarterly* 39 (1986): 480-503.

Cochrane, Eric. "Machiavelli: 1940-1960." *Journal of Modern History* 32-33 (1960-61): 113-36.

Coleman, Janet. "Machiavelli's *Via Moderna*: Medieval and Renaissance Attitudes to History." In *Niccolò Machiavelli's* The Prince*: New Interdisciplinary Essays*, edited by Martin Coyle. Manchester: Manchester University Press, 1995.

Colish, Marcia. "*De Officiis* and Machiavelli's *Prince*." *Sixteenth Century Journal* 9 (1978): 81-93.

———. "The Idea of Liberty in Machiavelli." *Journal of the History of Ideas* 32 (1971): 323-50.

Coulanges, Fustel de. *The Ancient City.* Garden City, N. Y.: Doubleday Anchor Books.

Crawford, Michael. *The Roman Republic.* Atlantic Highlands, N. J.: Humanities Press, 1978.

Crick, Bernard. "Introduction." In *The Discourses*, edited by Bernard Crick, translated by Leslie J. Walker. Hammondsworth, Middlesex, England: Penguin Books, 1970.

Croce, Benedetto. *Politics and Morals.* New York: Philosophical Library, 1945.

Danél, Adam, D. *A Case for Freedom: Machiavellian Humanism.* Lanham, Md.: University Press of America, 1997.

De Grazia, Sebastian. *Machiavelli in Hell.* Princeton: Princeton University Press, 1989.

Demosthenes. *On Organization.* London: William Heinemann, 1930.

Develin, Robert. "The Integration of Plebeians into the Political Order after 366 B.C." In *Social Struggles in Archaic Rome*, edited by Kurt Raaflaub. Berkeley: University of California Press, 1986.

Diderot, Denis. "*Machiavélisme*." In *Encyclopédie.* Saint Amand: L'Imprimerie Bussière, 1963.

Dietz, Mary. "Trapping the Prince: Machiavelli and the Politics of Deception." *American Political Science Review* 80 (1986): 777-99.

Dionysius of Halicarnassus. *The Roman Antiquities of Dionysius of Halicarnassus*. Vols. 1-7. Cambridge: Harvard University Press.

Drury, Shadia B. *The Political Ideas of Leo Strauss*. New York: St. Martin's Press, 1988.

Eldar, Dan. "Glory and the Boundaries of Public Morality in Machiavelli's Thought." *History of Political Thought* 7 (1986): 419-38.

Faulkner, Robert K. *Francis Bacon and the Modern Project*. Lanham, Md.: Rowman & Littlefield, 1993.

———. "Introduction: Clizia and the Enlightenment of Private Life." In *Clizia*, translated by Daniel T. Gallagher. Prospects Heights, Ill.: Waveland Press, 1996.

Flanagan, Thomas. "The Concept of *Fortuna* in Machiavelli." In *The Political Calculus: Essays on Machiavelli's Philosophy*, edited by Anthony Parel. Toronto: University of Toronto Press, 1972.

Fleisher, Martin. "A Passion for Politics: The Vital Core of the World of Machiavelli." In *Machiavelli and the Nature of Political Thought*, edited by Martin Fleisher. New York: Atheneum, 1972.

———. "The Ways of Machiavelli and the Ways of Politics." *Political Theory* 16 (1995): 330-55.

Forrest, W. G. A. *History of Sparta, 950-192 B.C.* New York: W. W. Norton, 1968.

Garver, Eugene. *Machiavelli and the History of Prudence*. Madison: University of Wisconsin Press, 1987.

Geerken, John H. "Homer's Image of the Hero in Machiavelli: A Comparison of *Areté* and *Virtù*." *Italian Quarterly* 13-14 (Summer 1969-Spring 1970): 45-89.

———. "Machiavelli and the Golden Rule." *Machiavelli Studies* 2 (1988): 26-48.

———. "Machiavelli Studies since 1969." *Journal of the History of Ideas* 37 (1976): 351-68.

Gentili, Alberico. *De legationibus libri tres*. New York: Oxford University Press, 1924.

Germino, Dante. "Blasphemy and Leo Strauss's Machiavelli." In *Leo Strauss: Political Philosopher and Jewish Thinker*, edited by Kenneth L. Deutsch and Walter Nicgorski. Lanham, Md.: Rowman & Littlefield, 1994.

———. "Machiavelli's Thoughts on the Psyche and Society." In *The Political Calculus: Essays on Machiavelli's Philosophy*, edited by Anthony Parel. Toronto: University of Toronto Press, 1972.

———. "Second Thoughts on Leo Strauss's Machiavelli." *Journal of Politics* 28 (1966): 794-817.

Gilbert, Felix. "The Composition and Structure of Machiavelli's *Discorsi*." *Journal of the History of Ideas* 14 (1953): 136-56.

———. "The Humanist Concept of the Prince and *The Prince* of Machiavelli." *Journal of Modern History* 9 (1939): 49-83.

———. *Machiavelli and Guicciardini: Politics and History in Sixteenth Century Florence.* Princeton: Princeton University Press, 1965.

———. "Machiavelli in Modern Historical Scholarship." *Italian Quarterly* 13-14 (Summer 1969-Spring 1970): 9-26.

Grant, Ruth W. *Hypocrisy and Integrity: Machiavelli, Rousseau, and the Ethics of Politics.* Chicago: University of Chicago Press, 1997.

Gray, Hanna H. "Machiavelli: The Art of Politics and the Paradox of Power." In *The Responsibility of Power: Historical Essays in Honor of Hajo Holborn,* edited by Leonard Krieger and Fritz Stern. Garden City, N. Y.: Doubleday, 1967.

Guicciardini, Francesco. *Considerations on the 'Discourses' of Machiavelli.* In *Francesco Guicciardini: Selected Writings,* edited by Cecil Grayson. London: Oxford University Press, 1965.

———. *Maxims and Reflections of a Renaissance Statesman.* Gloucester, Mass.: Peter Smith, 1970.

Hale, J. R. *Machiavelli and Renaissance Italy.* London: English Universities Press, 1961.

Hamilton, Alexander, James Madison, and John Jay. *The Federalist Papers.* New York: New American Library, 1961.

Hannaford, I. "Machiavelli's Concept of Virtù in *The Prince* and *The Discourses* Reconsidered." *Political Studies* 20 (1972): 185-89.

Harris, William V. *War and Imperialism in Republican Rome, 327-70 B.C.* Oxford: Clarendon Press, 1979.

Hartz, Louis. *The Liberal Tradition in America.* New York: Harcourt Brace Jovanovich, 1955.

Heichelheim, Fritz M., Cedric A. Yeo, and Allen M. Ward. *A History of the Roman People.* 2nd ed. Englewood Cliffs, N. J.: Prentice-Hall, 1984.

Heitland, W. E. *The Roman Republic.* Vol. 1. Cambridge: Cambridge University Press, 1909.

Herodotus. *The Histories.* Baltimore: Penguin Books, 1972.

Heurgon, Jacques. *The Rise of Rome to 264 B.C.* Berkeley: University of California Press, 1973.

Hexter, J. H. "Seyssel, Machiavelli, and Polybius VI: The Mystery of the Missing Translation." *Studies in the Renaissance* 3 (1956): 75-96.

———. *The Vision of Politics on the Eve of the Reformation.* New York: Basic Books, 1973.

Hobbes, Thomas. *Leviathan.* Indianapolis: Hackett, 1994.

Hulliung, Mark. *Citizen Machiavelli.* Princeton: Princeton University Press, 1983.

Hume, David. *Essays: Moral, Political, and Literary.* Indianapolis: Liberty Classics, 1985.

———. *An Inquiry Concerning the Principles of Morals.* Indianapolis: Bobbs-Merrill, 1957.

————. *A Treatise of Human Nature*. New York: Penguin Books, 1969.

Ingersoll, David E. "The Constant Prince: Private Interests and Public Goals in Machiavelli." *Western Political Quarterly* 21 (1968): 588-96.

Jacobson, Norman. *Pride and Solace: The Functions and Limits of Political Theory*. Berkeley: University of California Press, 1978.

Jaffa, Harry. *Crisis of the House Divided*. Chicago: University of Chicago Press, 1982.

Jefferson, Thomas. *The Life and Selected Writings of Thomas Jefferson*. New York: Modern Library, 1944.

Kahn, Victoria. "Virtù and the Example of Agathocles in Machiavelli's *Prince*." In *Machiavelli and the Discourse of Literature*, edited by Albert Russell Ascoli and Victoria Kahn. Ithaca: Cornell University Press, 1993.

Kontos, Alkis. "Success and Knowledge in Machiavelli." In *The Political Calculus: Essays on Machiavelli's Philosophy*, edited by Anthony Parel. Toronto: University of Toronto Press, 1972.

Lefort, Claude. *Le travail de l'oeuvre Machiavel*. Paris: Gallimard, 1972.

Lincoln, Abraham. *Selected Speeches and Writings*. New York: Vintage Books, 1992.

Livy, Titus. *Ab Urbe Condita*. Vols. 1-14. London: William Heinemann.

Locke, John. *Two Treatises of Government*. Cambridge: Cambridge University Press, 1988.

Macaulay. "Machiavelli." In *Critical and Historical Essays*. Vol. 1. Boston: Houghton and Mifflin, 1900.

Machiavelli, Niccolò. *Discourses on Livy*. Translated by Harvey C. Mansfield and Nathon Tarcov. Chicago: University of Chicago Press, 1996.

————. *Florentine Histories*. Translated by Laura F. Banfield and Harvey C. Mansfield, Jr. Princeton: Princeton University Press, 1988.

————. *Machiavelli, The Chief Works and Others*. Vols. 1-3. Translated by Allan Gilbert. Durham: Duke University Press, 1989.

————. *Machiavelli and His Friends: Their Personal Correspondence*. Translated and edited by James B. Atkinson and David Sices. DeKalb: Northern Illinois University Press, 1996.

————. *Opere di Niccolò Machiavelli*. Edited by Ezio Raimondi. Milan: Ugo Mursia editore, 1966.

————. *The Prince*. Translated by Harvey C. Mansfield, Jr. Chicago: University of Chicago Press, 1985.

Mansfield, Harvey, Jr. "Introduction." In *Discourses on Livy*, translated by Harvey C. Mansfield and Nathon Tarcov. Chicago: University of Chicago Press, 1996.

————. *Machiavelli's New Modes and Orders: A Study of the Discourses on Livy*. Ithaca: Cornell University Press, 1979.

————. *Machiavelli's Virtue*. Chicago: University of Chicago Press, 1996.

————. *Taming the Prince*. New York: Free Press, 1989.

Maritain, Jacques. "The End of Machiavellianism." In *The Social and Political Thought of Jacques Maritain: Selected Readings*, edited by Joseph W. Evans and Leo R. Ward. Garden City, N.Y.: Image Books, 1965.

Martelli, Mario. "*Ancora sui 'Ghiribizzi' a Giovan Battista Soderini*." *Rinascimento* 10 (1970): 3-27.

———. "*I 'Ghiribizzi' a Giovan Battista Soderini*." *Rinascimento* 9 (1969): 147-80.

Masciulli, Joseph. "The Armed Founder versus the Catonic Hero: Machiavelli and Rousseau on Popular Leadership." *Interpretation* 14 (1986): 265-80.

Masters, Roger. *Machiavelli, Leonardo, and the Science of Power*. Notre Dame: University of Notre Dame Press, 1996.

———. "Machiavelli's Sexuality: 'Love, be my guide, my leader'." Paper presented to the Annual Meeting of the American Political Science Association. Boston, September 1998.

Mattingly, Garret. "Machiavelli's *Prince*: Political Science or Political Satire?" *American Scholar* 27 (1958): 482-91.

McCormick, John P. "Addressing the Political Exception: Machiavelli's 'Accidents' and the Mixed Regime." *American Political Science Review* 87 (1993): 888-900.

McIntosh, Donald. "The Modernity of Machiavelli." *Political Theory* 12 (1984): 184-203.

McKenzie, Lionel A. "Rousseau's Debate with Machiavelli in the *Social Contract*." *Journal of the History of Ideas* 43 (1982): 209-28.

Meinecke, Friedrich. *Machiavellism: The Doctrine of Raison d'Etat and Its Place in Modern History*. New Haven: Yale University Press, 1957.

Mill, John Stuart. *On Liberty and Other Writings*. Cambridge: Cambridge University Press, 1989.

Mindle, Grant B. "Machiavelli's Realism." *Review of Politics* 47 (1985): 212-30.

Momigliano, Arnoldo. "The Rise of the *plebs* in the Archaic Age of Rome." In *Social Struggles in Archaic Rome: New Perspectives on the Conflict of the Orders*, edited by Kurt Raaflaub. Berkeley: University of California Press, 1986.

Mommsen, Theodor. *The History of Rome*. Vol. 1. New York: Charles Scribner's Sons, 1883.

Montesquieu. *The Persian Letters*. Cleveland: Meridian Books, 1961.

———. *The Spirit of the Laws*. Cambridge: Cambridge University Press, 1989.

Moore, J. M. *Aristotle and Xenophon on Democracy and Oligarchy*. Berkeley: University of California Press, 1975.

Najemy, John M. *Between Friends: Discourses of Power and Desire in the Machiavelli-Vettori Letters of 1513-1515*. Princeton: Princeton University Press, 1993.

Nederman, Cary. "Machiavelli and Moral Character: Principality, Republic and the Psychology of Virtue." Paper presented to the Annual Meeting of the American Political Science Association. Chicago, September 1992.

Nicolet, Claude. *The World of the Citizen in Republican Rome.* Berkeley: University of California Press, 1980.

Niebuhr, B. H. *Lectures on the History of Rome.* Vol. 1. London: Walton and Maberly, 1883.

Nietzsche, Friedrich. *The Use and Abuse of History.* Indianapolis: Bobbs-Merrill, 1957.

O'Brien, Conor Cruise. *The Suspecting Glance.* London: Faber and Faber, 1972.

Olschki, Leonardo. *Machiavelli the Scientist.* Berkeley: Gillick Press, 1945.

Orr, Robert. "The Time Motif in Machiavelli." In *Machiavelli and the Nature of Political Thought,* edited by Martin Fleisher. New York: Atheneum, 1972.

Orwin, Clifford. "Machiavelli's Unchristian Charity." *American Political Science Review* 72 (1978): 1217-28.

Pangle, Thomas L. *The Spirit of Modern Republicanism: The Moral Vision of the American Founders and the Philosophy of Locke.* Chicago: University of Chicago Press, 1988.

Parel, Anthony. "Introduction: Machiavelli's Method and His Interpreters." In *The Political Calculus: Essays on Machiavelli's Philosophy,* edited by Anthony Parel. Toronto: University of Toronto Press, 1972.

———. *The Machiavellian Cosmos.* New Haven: Yale University Press, 1992.

———. "The Question of Machiavelli's Modernity." *Review of Politics* 53 (1991): 320-39.

Pitkin, Hanna Fenichel. *Fortune Is a Woman: Gender and Politics in the Thought of Machiavelli.* Berkeley: University of California Press, 1984.

Plamenatz, John. *The English Utilitarians.* Oxford: Basil Blackwell, 1958.

———. *Man and Society: Politics and Social Theories from Machiavelli to Marx.* Vol. 1. 2nd ed. Revised by M. E. Plamenatz and Robert Wokler. London: Longman, 1992.

———. "In Search of Machiavellian *Virtù.*" In *The Political Calculus: Essays on Machiavelli's Philosophy,* edited by Anthony Parel. Toronto: University of Toronto Press, 1972.

Plato. *Gorgias.* London: William Heinemann, 1967.

———. *Laws.* New York: Basic Books, 1980.

———. *Letters.* London: William Heinemann, 1927.

———. *Republic.* 2nd ed. New York: Basic Books, 1991.

Plutarch. *Lives.* Vols. 1-11. London: William Heinemann.

Pocock, J. G. A. "Custom and Grace, Form and Matter: An Approach to Machiavelli's Concept of Innovation." In *Machiavelli and the Nature of Political Thought,* edited by Martin Fleisher. New York: Atheneum, 1972.

———. "Machiavelli in the Liberal Cosmos." *Political Theory* 13 (1985): 559-74.

———. *The Machiavellian Moment: Florentine Political Thought and the Atlantic Republican Tradition.* Princeton: Princeton University Press, 1975.

———. *Politics, Language and Time: Essays on Political Thought and History.* New York: Atheneum, 1971.

————."Prophet and Inquisitor, or, a Church Built upon Bayonets Cannot Stand: A Comment on Mansfield's 'Strauss's Machiavelli,'" *Political Theory* 3 (1975): 385-401.

Polybius. *The Histories.* Vol. 3. London: William Heinemann, 1922.

Portis, Edward Bryan. *Reconstructing the Classics: Political Theory from Plato to Marx.* 2nd edited by Chatham, N. J.: Chatham House, 1998.

Prescott, William H. *History of the Reign of Ferdinand and Isabella the Catholic.* Vol. 2. Philadelphia: J. B. Lippincott, 1872.

Prezzolini, Giusseppe. *Machiavelli.* New York: Farrar, Straus and Giroux, 1967.

Price, Russell. "The Senses of *Virtù* in Machiavelli." *European Studies Review* 3 (1973): 315-45.

————. "The Theme of *Gloria* in Machiavelli." *Renaissance Quarterly* 30 (1977): 588-631.

Raaflaub, Kurt. "The Conflict of the Orders in Archaic Rome: A Comprehensive and Comparative Approach." In *Social Struggles in Archaic Rome: New Perspectives on the Conflict of the Orders,* edited by Kurt Raaflaub. Berkeley: University of California Press, 1986.

————. "From Protection and Defense to Offense and Participation: Stages in the Conflict of the Orders." In *Social Struggles in Archaic Rome: New Perspectives on the Conflict of the Orders,* edited by Kurt Raaflaub. Berkeley: University of California Press, 1986.

Rahe, Paul A. *Republics Ancient and Modern: Classical Republicanism and the American Revolution.* Chapel Hill: University of North Carolina Press, 1992.

Raimondi, Ezio. "The Politician and the Centaur." In *Machiavelli and the Discourse of Literature,* edited by Albert Russell Ascoli and Victoria Kahn. Ithaca: Cornell University Press, 1993.

Ramsay, Maureen. "Machiavelli's Political Philosophy in *The Prince.*" In *Niccolò Machiavelli's* The Prince*: New Interdisciplinary Essays,* edited by Martin Coyle. Manchester: Manchester University Press, 1995.

Rebhorn, Wayne A. *Foxes and Lions: Machiavelli's Confidence Men.* Ithaca: Cornell University Press, 1988.

Ridolfi, Roberto. *The Life of Niccolò Machiavelli.* Chicago: University of Chicago Press, 1963.

Ridolfi, Roberto, and P. Ghiglieri, *"I 'Ghiribizzi' al Soderini."* *La Bibliofilia* 72 (1970): 53-74.

Rostovtzeff, M. *A History of the Ancient World.* Vol. 2. Oxford: Clarendon Press, 1927.

Rousseau, Jean Jacques. *The First and Second Discourses.* New York: St. Martin's Press, 1964.

————. *On the Social Contract, with Geneva Manuscript and Political Economy.* New York: St. Martin's Press, 1978.

Rowdon, Maurice. *The Spanish Terror: Spanish Imperialism in the Sixteenth Century.* New York: St. Martin's Press, 1974.

Rubinstein, Nicolai. "Machiavelli and the World of Florentine Politics." In *Studies on Machiavelli*, edited by Myron P. Gilmore. Firenze: G. C. Sansoni Editore, 1972.

Ruffo-Fiore, Silvia. *Niccolò Machiavelli*. Boston: Twayne, 1982.

Sallust. *The War with Catiline*. London: William Heinemann, 1921.

Sasso, Gennaro. *Niccolò Machiavelli: Storia del suo pensiero politico*. Napoli: Nella Sede dell'Istituto, 1958.

Scott, John T. and Vickie B. Sullivan. "Patricide and the Plot of *The Prince*: Cesare Borgia and Machiavelli's Italy." *American Political Science Review* 88 (1994): 887-900.

Scullard, Howard, H. *From the Gracchi to Nero*. New York: Frederick A. Praeger, 1959.

———. *A History of the Roman World, 753-146 B.C.* London: Methuen, 1935.

———. *Roman Politics, 220-150 B.C.* Oxford: Clarendon Press, 1951.

Shakespeare. *Julius Caesar*. New York: New American Library, 1963.

Shumer, S. M. "Machiavelli: Republican Politics and Its Corruption." *Political Theory* 7 (1979): 5-34.

Seigel, J. E. "Violence and Order in Machiavelli." In *Violence and Aggression in the History of Ideas*, edited by Philip P. Wiener and John Fisher. New Brunswick: Rutgers University Press, 1974.

Smith, Adam. *An Inquiry into the Nature and Causes of the Wealth of Nations*. Vol. 2 (Indianapolis: Liberty Classics, 1981).

Smith, Bruce James. *Politics and Remembrance: Republican Themes in Machiavelli, Burke, and Tocqueville*. Princeton: Princeton University Press, 1985.

Smith, Gregory B. "Machiavelli's *The Prince* and the Abolition of the Political: A Preliminary Reflection." *Machiavelli Studies* 2 (1988): 49-72.

Smith, R. E. *The Failure of the Roman Republic*. Cambridge: Cambridge University Press, 1955.

Skinner, Quentin. *The Foundations of Modern Political Thought*. Vol. 1. Cambridge: Cambridge University Press, 1978.

———. *Machiavelli*. New York: Hill and Wang, 1981.

———. "Meaning and Understanding in the History of Ideas." *History and Theory* 8 (1969): 3-53.

———. "The Republican Ideal of Political Liberty." In *Machiavelli and Republicanism*, edited by Gisela Bock, Quentin Skinner, and Maurizio Viroli. Cambridge: Cambridge University Press, 1990.

Spinoza, Benedict de. *Works of Spinoza: Theologico-Political Treatise, Political Treatise*. New York: Dover Publications, 1951.

Stephens, J. N. "Ciceronian Rhetoric and the Immorality of Machiavelli's *Prince*." *Renaissance Studies* 2 (1988): 258-67.

Strauss, Leo. "Machiavelli and Classical Literature." *Review of National Literatures* 1 (1970): 7-25.

————."Niccolo Machiavelli." In *History of Political Philosophy*, edited by Leo Strauss and Joseph Cropsey. 3rd ed. Chicago: University of Chicago Press, 1987.

————. *Persecution and the Art of Writing*. Glencoe, Ill.: Free Press, 1952.

————. *The Political Philosophy of Hobbes*. Chicago: University of Chicago Press, 1963.

————. *Thoughts on Machiavelli*. Seattle: University of Washington Press, 1958.

————. *What Is Political Philosophy?* Westport, Conn.: Greenwood Press, 1973.

Sullivan, Vickie B. "Machiavelli's Momentary 'Machavellian Moment.'" *Political Theory* 20 (1992): 309-18.

————. *Machiavelli's Three Romes: Religion, Human Liberty, and Politics Reformed*. DeKalb: University of Northern Illinois Press, 1996.

Sumberg, Theodore. "*Belfagor*: Machiavelli's Short Story." *Interpretation* 19 (1992): 243-50.

Tacitus. *The Complete Works of Tacitus*. New York: Modern Library, 1942.

Terchek, Ronald J. *Republican Paradoxes and Liberal Anxieties: Retrieving Neglected Fragments of Political Theory*. Lanham, Md.: Rowman & Littlefield, 1997.

Thucydides. *The Peloponnesian War*. Vol. 2. Ann Arbor: University of Michigan Press, 1959.

Tocqueville, Alexis de. *Democracy in America*. Vols. 1-2. New York: Vintage Classics, 1972.

Villari, Pasquale. *The Life and Times of Niccolò Machiavelli*. London: T. Fisher Unwin, 4th impression.

Viroli, Maurizio. *Machiavelli*. Oxford: Oxford University Press, 1998.

————. "Machiavelli and the Republican Idea of Politics." In *Machiavelli and Republicanism*, edited by Gisela Bock, Quentin Skinner, and Maurizio Viroli. Cambridge: Cambridge University Press, 1990.

————. "Republic and Politics in Machiavelli and Rousseau." *History of Political Thought* 10 (1989): 405-20.

Von Fritz, Kurt. *The Theory of the Mixed Constitution in Antiquity*. New York: Columbia University Press, 1954.

Waley, Daniel. "The Primitivist Element in Machiavelli's Thought." *Journal of the History of Ideas* 31 (1970): 91-98.

Walker, Leslie J. *The Discourses of Niccolò Machiavelli*. Vols. 1-2. London: Routledge and Kegan Paul, 1950.

Weinstein, Donald. "Machiavelli and Savonarola." In *Studies on Machiavelli*, edited by Myron Gilmore. Firenze: G. C. Sansoni Editore, 1972.

Whitfield, J. H. "Discourses on Machiavelli VII, Gilbert, Hexter and Baron." *Italian Studies* 13 (1958): 21-46.

————. *Machiavelli*. New York: Russell and Russell, 1965.

————. "Machiavelli's Use of Livy." In *Livy*, edited by T. A. Dorey. London: Routledge and Kegan Paul, 1971.

————."Savonarola and the Purpose of the *Prince*." *Modern Language Review* 44 (1949): 45-59.

Wolin, Sheldon. *Politics and Vision*. Boston: Little, Brown, 1960.

Wood, Gordon S. *The Creation of the American Republic, 1776-1787*, 2nd ed. Chapel Hill: University of North Carolina Press, 1998.

Wood, Neal. "Machiavelli's Concept of *Virtù* Reconsidered." *Political Studies* 15 (1967): 159-72.

————. "Machiavelli's Humanism of Action." In *The Political Calculus: Essays on Machiavelli's Philosophy*, edited by Anthony Parel. Toronto: University of Toronto Press, 1972.

Wooton, David. "Introduction." In *Machiavelli: Selected Political Writings*, edited by and translated by David Wooton. Indianapolis: Hackett, 1994.

Xenophon. *Constitution of the Lacedaemonians*. In *Scripta Minora*. Cambridge: Harvard University Press, 1921.

————. *Hiero or Tyrannicus*. In *On Tyranny*, by Leo Strauss. Ithaca: Cornell University Press, 1968.

Zimmern, Alfred. *The Greek Commonwealth: Politics and Economics in Fifth-Century Athens*. New York: Oxford University Press, 1961.

Index

accidents, 12, 24, 27–35, 150–51, 188, 292n21
accusation, 26, 60, 62, 159–60, 202
Acquilonia, battle of, 71–72
advisers, 249–50
Aeneas, 22
Agathocles, 233-36, 333n23
Agis, 5, 44–47, 49
Agnadello, battle of, 40, 131, 143, 294n34
agrarian law, 65, 79–80, 83, 96–97, 200–201
Agrippa, Menenius, 29
Alcibiades, 155, 316n16
Alexander VI (pope), 214, 233
Alexander of Epirus, 142
Alexander the Great, 44, 231, 245, 266, 278
Allen, J. W., 342n80
Allia, river and battle of, 73–74
Anghiari, battle of, 342n65
anticipation, 161. See also temporizing
Antigonus, 295n54
Antiochus, 131, 177
Antony, Mark, 53, 134, 250
Appius Claudius (decemvir), 32, 155, 175, 245
Appius Claudius Caecus (censor), 63, 322n78
Appius Claudius Crassus (grandson of decemvir), 73, 82
Appius Pulcher, 72–73
Ardea, 124–25
Ardinghelli, Piero, 287n27, 338n21
Arendt, Hannah, 290n73, 323n5
Aristides, 258

Aristippus, 3
Aristotle: on aristocratic polis, 41; on character, 170; on distributive justice, 56, 291n12; on excellence, twin peaks of, 282; on geography, its political effects, 135; on law-guardians, 293n27; on leisure, 221; on magnanimity, 187–88; on maturity and youth, 280; on mixed regimes, 204, 207, 253; on moderation, 35; on ostracism, 186; on Sparta and Athens, 203; on spiritedness, 261–62
Arrabbiati, 272
artillery, 132–33, 281–82, 312n44, 313n68
assemblies, 297n3. See also legislative power
Athens, 22–27, 32–33; imperial policy of, 114–15, 120–21, 260
Attilius, Marcus Regulus, 133
auguries. See auspices
Augustine, Saint, 231
Aurelius, Marcus, 234
auspices, 57, 71–74, 77, 300n31
auxiliaries, 139
Averroism, 2, 10

Bacon, Francis, 9, 208, 277
Baglioni, Giovampagolo, 231
Ball, Terence, 343n92
Baron, Hans, 252, 327n52, 338n16
battle, delay of 142–43
beginnings: imperfect, 16, 24, 203, 227; as indicator of intentions, 155; return to 16, 150–52, 162, 184

359

About the Author

Patrick Coby is professor of government at Smith College. He is author of *Socrates and the Sophistic Enlightenment: A Commentary on Plato's* Protagoras, and of numerous writings in political theory, including articles on Thucydides, Plato, Aristotle, Machiavelli, Shakespeare, Hobbes, Locke, and Marx.